The INTERVIEW ARCHITECT®
Professional Handbook

The INTERVIEW ARCHITECT® Professional Handbook

IMPORTANT NOTICE FOR USERS OF THE INTERVIEW ARCHITECT®

The INTERVIEW ARCHITECT® is a human resources tool designed to assist employers with the interviewing process. The INTERVIEW ARCHITECT® is not intended to constitute legal advice. If legal advice is desired, users of the materials should seek the services of competent legal counsel.

The INTERVIEW ARCHITECT® assists employers in the selection of the best-qualified internal or external candidates. Employment laws in the country, state, province or locality in which the materials are used may contain prohibitions with regard to certain inquiries during the pre-employment interview process. Lominger International cannot be responsible for implementation and use of the materials that deviates from these legal requirements. Users of the materials should become familiar with applicable laws restricting the types of inquiries which can be made in pre-employment interviews and use the materials accordingly.

© COPYRIGHT 1995, 2002, 2007

LOMINGER INTERNATIONAL: A KORN/FERRY COMPANY

WRITTEN BY: MICHAEL M. LOMBARDO, ROBERT W. EICHINGER AND CARA CAPRETTA RAYMOND.

ALL RIGHTS RESERVED.

No part of this work may be copied or transferred to any other expression or form without a license from Lominger. Send requests to:
Lominger International: A Korn/Ferry Company
5051 Highway 7
Suite 100
Minneapolis, MN 55416-2291

INTERVIEW ARCHITECT® is the exclusive trademark of
Lominger International: A Korn/Ferry Company.

To get more information about the LEADERSHIP ARCHITECT® Suite of Integrated Tools, contact the person within your company in charge of these products or contact Lominger at 952-345-3610
or
www.lominger.com

THE INTERVIEW ARCHITECT® GUIDELINES ON FAIR AND LICENSABLE USE

Fair and Intended Uses

Fair Use–Single Job, Single Interviewer:
You can use the material in an unlimited way to construct aids for a single interview. You can copy portions of or paraphrase any material for that interview and apply it to multiple candidates.

Fair Use–Single Job, Multiple Interviewers:
You can use the material to construct interview aids for a single job with multiple interviewers. You can copy portions of or paraphrase any material for those interviews. Once constructed, you can make as many copies as you need for the multiple interviewers interviewing for that single job for any number of candidates.

Fair Use–Training Interviewers and Demonstrating the Material:
You can copy, display, and distribute sufficient material to demonstrate the processes and methods contained in the INTERVIEW ARCHITECT® materials or to train interviewers in the use of the INTERVIEW ARCHITECT® material as long as the derivative materials are used for training only.

Some Uses Requiring a Copyright Release from Lominger International.

Licensable Use–Creating Standard Interview Protocols for a Success Profile:
You can interview aids for each of a number of competencies of an organizational success profile, then construct specific interviews by mixing and matching the new material for interviews across a number of jobs.

Licensable Use–Creating Custom and Tailored Protocols:
You create a customized or tailored version of the Interview Architect® material to better fit your personal and/or organization preferences and situation and then use that revised material to construct multiple interviews. This creates a derivative "mini-Interview Architect® " and requires a license.

Licensable Use–Creating Hybrid Material:
You combine the Interview Architect® material with other proprietary or your own material to produce new interview aids for multiple jobs. This creates a substitute Interview Architect® and requires a license.

Licensable Use–Use of a Subsection of the Material for Another Purpose:
You take a section or portion of the Interview Architect® such as the Learning Evaluation Scales or the Learning Agility® scales and copy and distribute those for some other application. This is a use other than the intended use and requires a license.

NOTE: Lominger supports customized and tailored use of our material and has a number of types of licenses available to aid those uses. Please call for details or ask your Lominger Associate for information.

The INTERVIEW ARCHITECT® Professional Handbook requires certification.

You must attend a Lominger Certification Workshop or Associate training session. We have found that users can comprehend the products without being certified but have difficulty in fully understanding and implementing all of the possible uses and capabilities.

Visit www.lominger.com for a complete listing of Lominger Associates and certification workshops. Contact Lominger to place an order (952) 345-3610.

INTRODUCTION

Using *The INTERVIEW ARCHITECT® Professional Handbook*

The Interview Architect Professional Handbook is as complex or as simple as you need it to be. For those who need it, we've included eight to ten pages of suggestions and numbers per competency. Others may simply want to ask some questions and evaluate the responses about one competency.

(We compare it to designing a travel atlas. One that contains only a few rivers, main roads, and major cities in a country would be fine for weekend travelers but woefully inadequate for others navigating a cross country expedition.)

The depth of use of *The Interview Architect Professional Handbook* will vary by the importance of the use and the criticalness of the decision you are making. Filling key jobs that will have an important impact on the goals of the organization probably will require a fuller use of the Handbook. Simpler uses might be preliminary screening, filling lots of the same kind of job at lower levels, picking summer interns, or being just one of many interviewers evaluating the same candidate.

In many applications, all you will need to do is:

- Select a few competencies you want to find out about
- Select a few arenas or domains to explore
- Select two questions per competency (one for backup)
- Select some generic probes (how, why, impact on others, and how did you apply it type probes are recommended)
- Select three things to look for, specific to the job and the work context of your organization

TABLE OF CONTENTS

How to Use *The INTERVIEW ARCHITECT® Professional* Book I
    The Goal of the Interview I
    The Role of Learning from Experience I
    Lominger's Four Dimension Interviewing™ (4DI™) Model and Methodology III
    Using The Interview Architect Professional Handbook VII
    Quick/Simple/Light Use VII
    Fuller Use VIII
    A. Definition VIII
    B. Arenas/Domains to Explore VIII
    C. Sample Questions VIII
    D. Follow-up Probes IX
    E. Themes/Things to look for IX
    F. Most Likely Resume X
    G. Learning Agility Evaluation XI
    H. Leadership Architect® Connections XII
    I. Learning Architect® Connections XIII
    J. Choices Architect® Connections XIV
    K. Difficulty to Develop XV
    How to Build a Job Profile XVIII
    Consulting/Counseling/Educating/Problem Solving XXII
    Handbook Layout XXVII

1	Action Orientation	1-1
2	*Dealing with* Ambiguity	2-1
3	Approachability	3-1
4	Boss Relationships	4-1
5	Business Acumen	5-1
6	Career Ambition	6-1
7	Caring About Direct Reports	7-1
8	Comfort Around Top Management	8-1
9	Command Skills	9-1
10	Compassion	10-1
11	Composure	11-1
12	Conflict Management	12-1
13	Confronting Direct Reports	13-1
14	Creativity	14-1
15	Customer Focus	15-1
16	*Timely* Decision Making	16-1
17	Decision Quality	17-1
18	Delegation	18-1
19	Developing Direct Reports and Others	19-1
20	Directing Others	20-1
21	*Managing* Diversity	21-1
22	Ethics and Values	22-1
23	Fairness to Direct Reports	23-1
24	Functional/Technical Skills	24-1
25	Hiring and Staffing	25-1
26	Humor	26-1
27	Informing	27-1
28	Innovation Management	28-1
29	Integrity and Trust	29-1

Note: Italicized words are not alphabetized.

30	Intellectual Horsepower	30-1
31	Interpersonal Savvy	31-1
32	Learning on the Fly	32-1
33	Listening	33-1
34	Managerial Courage	34-1
35	Managing and Measuring Work	35-1
36	Motivating Others	36-1
37	Negotiating	37-1
38	Organizational Agility	38-1
39	Organizing	39-1
40	*Dealing with* Paradox	40-1
41	Patience	41-1
42	Relationships with Peers	42-1
43	Perseverance	43-1
44	Personal Disclosure	44-1
45	Personal Learning	45-1
46	Perspective	46-1
47	Planning	47-1
48	Political Savvy	48-1
49	Presentation Skills	49-1
50	Priority Setting	50-1
51	Problem Solving	51-1
52	Process Management	52-1
53	*Drive for* Results	53-1
54	Self-Development	54-1
55	Self-Knowledge	55-1
56	Sizing Up People	56-1
57	Standing Alone	57-1
58	Strategic Agility	58-1
59	*Managing through* Systems	59-1
60	*Building Effective* Teams	60-1
61	Technical Learning	61-1
62	Time Management	62-1
63	Total Work Systems	63-1
64	Understanding Others	64-1
65	*Managing* Vision and Purpose	65-1
66	Work/Life Balance	66-1
67	Written Communications	67-1
68	*Learning From Experience*	68-1

There are no competencies 69-80. Those numbers are reserved for future additions.

PERFORMANCE DIMENSIONS

81	Quantity of Work Output	81-1
82	Timeliness of Delivery of Output	82-1
83	Quality of Work Output	83-1
84	Use of Resources	84-1
85	Customer Impact/Value Added	85-1
86	Freedom from Unplanned Support	86-1
87	Team/Unit Contribution	87-1
88	Productive Work Habits	88-1
89	Adding Skills and Capabilities	89-1
90	Alignment and Compliance: Walking the Talk	90-1

APPENDIX A. Generic questions that can be used with any competency A-1

APPENDIX B. Generic probes that can be used with any competency B-1

APPENDIX C. Quick reference guide C-1

HOW TO USE *THE INTERVIEW ARCHITECT® PROFESSIONAL HANDBOOK*

The Goal of the Interview

When interviewing or assessing internal or external candidates for jobs and/or for organizations or internal candidates for assignments, the goal is to be able to predict or estimate what people will do in a given set of circumstances. What skills and attributes will they be able to bring to bear to complete the job or assignment effectively or how well will they fit into the organization?

Many times, interviewers are equipped with a predetermined set of competencies, skills or attributes they are looking for. The success profile skills they are seeking can be anything from the wishes of senior officers of the organization or of the manager with the open job that's being filled, to a carefully crafted or possibly well validated set of job requirements.

The interviewers are also equipped with a set of circumstances against which to judge a potential candidate. They know the history of the organization, its current challenges and performance, its strategic outlook, the kind of people who do well there, and the kind of leaders they will need in the future. They also have an idea about how the organization develops its people and therefore the probability the candidate could finish building the required skills after filling the position.

So interviewers are looking for a set of skills, current and/or probable, to be applied in a job or assignment in a somewhat known culture or environment.

The task in the interview is to collect enough information to be able to predict how the candidate would fare in that environment and whether the candidate could apply those required skills effectively in the assignment under consideration.

The Role of Learning from Experience in Success

The research on how successful and effective leaders get to be and stay that way shows that perhaps the key skill is being able to perform well under first time and tough conditions. It's not so much what they have accomplished in the past as it is what they would be able to do when faced with a new business challenge or changing strategic proposition requiring new behavior and attitudes. That variable, which we call learning from experience, helps predict future performance in less known assignments and changing environments.

It's possible to find a person, usually through direct techniques like behavioral event interviewing, who has successfully demonstrated in the near past the exact abilities and skills needed for the job or assignment under consideration. While that most likely assures short term performance in the assignment, it does not alone predict how the candidate might perform under changing conditions and requirements. The ability to perform today is a useful piece of information but it isn't all you need to know to predict into an uncertain future.

The larger backdrop for this proposition for selecting successful people is a rapidly changing world. Nothing is staying stable or constant for very long. People's jobs are changing rapidly as most larger companies are going after the global market under increased competition from foreign firms. It's getting harder to squeeze profit out of the bottom line.

Another point is that the information the interviewer is looking for doesn't "occur" in the interview. While it is certainly useful to get an impression of people face to face and draw some conclusions about them, the majority of the information the interviewer needs lies outside the boundaries of the actual interview.

The information he or she is looking for is more a series of learnings and performing patterns over many years than a single event or story. The traditional face to face interview is the most common format to collect all of that information.

The follow-up reference checks also add data, either verifying what the interviewer had already concluded or might generate new information, good or bad, that did not surface in the interview. Impressions within the actual interview of behavior the candidate shows is useful but not sufficient to be able to predict success with any accuracy.

The changing world, the changing nature of jobs, and the changing shape of organizations requires a more broad band interviewing process.

Research on Interviewing Success

Most of the research on interviewing success and accuracy has found that structured or formal interviews outperform unstructured or informal interviewing. Being prepared for the interview increases the chances of a successful outcome. Knowing ahead of time what you are going to ask and why and what good answers are likely to be will increase the accuracy of the predictions.

Knowing exactly what competencies you're looking for before the interview increases the chances of an accurate impression. Knowing as much as possible about the competencies you're looking for better prepares you to evaluate the information.

Lominger's Four Dimension Interviewing™ (4DI™) Model and Methodology

To organize and evaluate the information received in the interview, Lominger suggests a four-dimension information model, the Four Dimension Interview™ (4DI), to follow when doing interviews with candidates or for jobs that are significant to the organization.

The four dimensions (and questions in each dimension) are:

Dimension 1: Has the candidate had direct personal experience involving the competency where he/she was the prime player?

Dimension 2: Has the candidate witnessed the skill both being done well and being done badly, and learned from others about self?

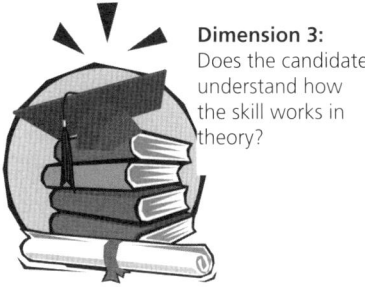

Dimension 3: Does the candidate understand how the skill works in theory?

Dimension 4: Has the candidate made sense of his/her learning? Has he/she learned the competency in one place and applied it in another? Improve from situation to situation? Compare and contrast experiences? Explain personal development related to the competency?

In Dimension 1 interviewing, we try to help you answer the question; "Has this person demonstrated this skill or competency in one or more situations?" While this is crucial, we don't know how cemented or versatile the skill set is, or if the person totally understands why it worked or didn't work. He/she could be a natural.

To search in depth for the real skill, we have added three other types of questions – "Can the person spot and interpret good and bad examples of this skill or competency in others? (Dimension II); "Can your person give you an understandable theory of what works and why?" (Dimension III); and "Can the person learn this skill or competency regardless of their present proficiency?" Or,"If he or she already has this competency, can it be repeated in different circumstances?" (Dimension IV)

Essentially, in Dimension I, you probe in depth about what the person has done; in Dimension II you broaden the search to see if the person can explain what others have done, providing a rough model of the skill or competency; in Dimension III you explore understanding the skill or the academic definition of the competency, and in Dimension IV, understanding the skill or competency from a learning point of view. The 4DI model goes from personal and specific to seeing it in others, then from abstract understanding to personal understanding. It begins with eliciting specific responses about whats, and ends with general rules of thumb about whys and hows.

Dimension 1 of the model relates to collecting information about **whether the candidate has demonstrated in the near past the required competency or behavior in the situation or the job or assignment under consideration.**

This type of interviewing is fairly straightforward. It is sometimes referred to as BEI or Behavioral Event Interviewing. The interviewer explores the past of the candidate for assignments or situations similar to the one under consideration and determines what level of performance the candidate has rendered in the past and extrapolates that to the job or assignment under consideration.

It's important in Dimension 1 interviewing that both successes and failures, good times and bad are examined because people can learn and build skills from both sources.

Dimension 2 of the model relates to **watching and learning from role models.** Some portion of the effective skills and attributes managers and executives build comes from watching others try to do the same behaviors.

One aspect of this dimension has to do with learning as much if not more from watching people do the skill badly as watching successful applications of the skill. It's possible that watching how not to do it imprints more strongly on the learner. It may be a more emotional experience watching someone else struggle than it is to watch someone triumph. It might also require that observers think about what they would have done differently to achieve a better outcome.

In Dimension 2 interviewing, the interviewer explores whether or not the candidate has witnessed both good and bad examples or applications of the skill or behavior under consideration, regardless of the results of Dimension 1 interviewing. A positive finding in Dimension 1 does not negate the need for information across the other three dimensions.

Dimension 3 relates to **knowing how the skill or competency works in people.** It's finding out whether the candidate knows the "theory of the case." In Dimension 3 interviewing, the interviewer explores whether the candidate can articulate a model or theory about the competency in question. Does he/she know where it comes from? How is it learned? What does it look like when done well? When done badly? How does it play in effective performance? How does it interact with other skills? Could the candidate coach and train others?

Many people can do things "naturally" with little understanding about why they can do it. Knowing how a competency functions should increase the chances the person could repeat it again in the future. It also might mean they could pass on the knowledge to others. Many times "naturals" have trouble explaining to a student why they do what they do. Again, regardless of the findings in Dimensions 1 & 2, Dimension 3 is an important piece of independent information.

Dimension 4 relates to two areas: **1) If the skill has been integrated or if not, 2) how readily the person could learn it.** In the first area, Dimension 4 interviewing delves (largely using the probes) into the learning the person has demonstrated as it relates to exercising the skill. Does the person know when he/she has been effective and ineffective using this competency? Is there depth in understanding how he or she applies these principles to dissimilar situations? Are there repeatables in this person's behavior?

This area is different from Dimension 3 above where a person may understand cognitively or theoretically how a skill works; in Dimension 4, the skill becomes integrated with a person's learning style.

Dimension 4 relates to whether the candidate has the learning style and skills that match the behavior in question. In **The INTERVIEW ARCHITECT® Professional Handbook**, each competency is matched with the specific learning skills and attitudes necessary to build that skill and to keep it current. These connections do not mean those are the only learning skills that could be used to learn any specific skill. Rather, they are the most likely.

Dimension 4 interviewing is about how people learn and how they extract meaning from life's experiences. Dimension 4 interviewing can be used to test the probability someone could learn the competency under question if given the opportunity. Even if there are negative findings in the other three dimensions, a positive finding in Dimension 4 might mean they could easily learn the skill in question if given the opportunity. Assuming the candidate had other positive skills, you could take a chance and predict he/she would learn the remaining skill.

If you get a positive D1 finding, they have demonstrated the skill in question, then D4 questioning asks whether they can repeat the skill and build on it.

The following table shows ten (A-J) combinations of interview findings across the four dimensions and what they might mean:

Code: + means a positive finding, they do have the skill; – means a negative finding, they do not have the skill.

The INTERVIEW ARCHITECT® Professional Handbook contains material for examining all four dimensions of the 4DI™ model.

	Dimension 1 Been there, done that	**Dimension 2** Seen that	**Dimension 3** Know that	**Dimension 4** Has integrated that or could learn that	**Conclusions/Implications**
A	+	+	+	+	A complete hit, can do it now and in the future even if it changes; will hit the ground running
B	+	+	+	-	Might be safe but should work on learning skills so he/she can repeat it in dissimilar situations; is there a program for developing learning skills available?
C	+	+/-	-	-	A natural, may not be able to repeat it in situations that are different; question ability to coach others
D	-	+	+	-	Overestimates what he/she can do; would need firm coaching and feedback
E	-	+	+	+	Could learn it quickly with the right opportunity; is there a job like this available?
F	-	+	-	+	Needs classroom/cognitive information and real opportunity; is there an available program?
G	-	-	+	+	Needs a lot of exposure to learn it; understanding is devoid of experience
H	-	-	+	-	Has no idea what it really is but may think he/she does
I	-	-	-	+	With big effort, could learn it; should make sure resources are in place to do it
J	-	-	-	-	Not much to work with

Using *The INTERVIEW ARCHITECT® Professional Handbook*

A common reaction to *The INTERVIEW ARCHITECT® Professional Handbook* is to wonder why all the complexity (8 to 10 pages of questions and tips per competency) just to ask some questions and evaluate the responses about one competency. The answer is that *The INTERVIEW ARCHITECT® Professional Handbook* is just as complex or just as simple as you need it to be.

Our view is that a travel atlas which only contains a few rivers, main roads, and major cities in a country might be plenty for some weekend vacationers but woefully inadequate for others navigating a cross country expedition. We decided to create a complete atlas that contains everything relevant to the competency, then let you decide which pieces you need. You can make it as easy or complex as your need dictates.

Depth of Use

The depth of use of *The INTERVIEW ARCHITECT® Professional Handbook* will vary by the importance of the use and the criticalness of the decision you are making.

- Filling key jobs that will have an important impact on the goals of the organization probably will require a fuller use of the Handbook.

- Making tough decisions where other information gathering methods have not differentiated between two final candidates might require a fuller use of the Handbook.

- Helping someone make a significant career decision probably deserves a fuller use of the tool.

- Simpler uses might be preliminary screening, filling lots of the same kind of job at lower levels, picking summer interns, or being just one of many interviewers evaluating the same candidate.

Quick/Simple/Light Use of *THE INTERVIEW ARCHITECT® Professional Handbook*

In many applications, all you will need to do is:

- Select a few competencies you want to find out about

- Select a few arenas or domains to explore

- Select two questions per competency (one for backup)

- Select some generic probes (how, why, impact on others, and how did you apply it type probes are recommended).

- Select three things to look for, specific to the job and the work context of your organization.

Doing this should take no more than a few minutes per competency.

Record what you have selected on the various interview protocol forms provided in Appendix II at the end of this manual, select some evaluation scales, and then conduct the interview.

Fuller Use of *THE INTERVIEW ARCHITECT® Professional Handbook*

Any fuller use of *The Interview Architect Professional Handbook* begins with profiling a position or group of positions within your organization. For recommendations on doing this, see page XVIII (How to Build a Job Profile) immediately following.

The sections of *The INTERVIEW ARCHITECT® Professional Handbook*:

A. Definition

What behaviors define this competency?

Each LEADERSHIP ARCHITECT® Sort Card (competency) is behaviorally defined. Familiarize yourself with the definition, because all following sections of the Handbook relate specifically to it. Sometimes the definition covers only an aspect of a commonly used but complex concept like **Vision**.

For example, part of the common meaning of **Vision** is communicating and implementing the vision. That aspect of Vision is covered on the Managing Vision and Purpose competency (#65). Creating the vision is either covered by the Creativity (#14) or Strategic Agility (#58) competencies. We wrote the 67 competency definitions to help you make finer distinctions in many cases rather than the usual 15-25 general concepts of other models. Therefore, read and understand the definitions well before interviewing. Don't just use the titles.

B. Arenas/Domains to Explore

Where in the candidate's experience would I find examples of this competency to talk about?

The **Arenas/Domains section** explains **where** this competency is likely to play out —what arenas or activities might be litmus tests for this competency. You can use the arena section to customize your inquiry to match the background and life stage of the candidate. Also use this section to tailor questions or to modify questions for those with limited backgrounds, such as would typically happen in campus interviewing or someone returning to the workplace after a prolonged absence.

For example, the basic question ..."Tell me about a time when you went from a harmonious to a conflict ridden situation..." might be put in the domain of a sports team, negotiations, professional association, community work, PTA, boss/direct report, or work group context, depending on the job and the candidate.

This section can also be used to test the consistency of the competency across domains. Is the candidate always like this or is he/she only that way in some domains and not others?

C. Sample Questions

What questions could I ask that would elicit information about this competency?

There are approximately 100 questions per competency. There are several standard or generic questions that appear with minor modifications for all competencies.

An * appears at the end of questions considered the most suitable for campus interviewing or interviewing candidates returning to the workforce after a prolonged absence. Many of the standard questions might apply as well. Refer to section **B. Domains** to further tailor the standard questions.

There are questions covering the four dimensions of the 4DI™ Model.

Examples:

>Dimension 1 (…demonstrated the skill under consideration?) Chapter 51–1, question 6. Have you ever solved a problem others around you couldn't?
>
>Dimension 2 (…witnessed the skill done well and done badly?) Chapter 51–2, question 43. Which boss was the worst at problem solving?
>
>Dimension 3 (…knows how the skill works?) Chapter 51–3, question 67.
>Have you ever taught a course on Problem Solving?
>
>Dimension 4 (…have the learning skill to learn and integrate the skill) Chapter 51–4, question 100. What do you do when a problem stops you in your tracks?

D. Follow-up Probes

What follow-up probes can I use that would provide more in-depth information about this competency?

There are 25-35 probes for each competency. Some of the probes match the questions you select. Some probes are standard or generic and are listed with slight modifications in each competency. The various probes can be used to explore the four-phase model of predicting behavior in the introduction.

You can probe:

- what he/she did (Dimension 1)
- whether the behavior came from any role models (Dimension 2)
- whether he/she understands the behavior (Dimension 3)
- issues of learning (Dimension 4)
- the context in which the behavior occurred

Choose the probes against the question(s) asked to check for in depth understanding or application of the competency.

In general, you want to probe around issues of why the person did something, how he/she did it, what impact it had on others, and what the person learned that could be applied in the future.

There are probes listed that cover the four dimensions of the 4DI™ Model.

Examples:

>Dimension 1 (…demonstrated the skill under consideration?) Page 33–4,
>probe 1. Are there times when you listen and times when you don't?
>
>Dimension 2 (…witnessed the skill done well and done badly?) Page 33–4, probe 13. How do others you have known approach that?
>
>Dimension 3 (…knows how the skill works?) Page 33–4, probe 6.
>Do you think that's teachable?
>
>Dimension 4 (…have the learning skill to learn, repeat, improve?) Page 33–4, probe 11. How did you come up with that approach to listening in the first place?

E. Themes/Things to Look For

What would this behavior look like on a day to day basis?

There are a number of evaluation sections in *The INTERVIEW ARCHITECT® Professional Handbook*. The Themes/Things to Look For section lists 20-40 indicators of what having or **not** having the competency might look like. Each theme is a small piece of behavior related to the competency.

For example, people who are action oriented often exhibit high tolerance for mistakes and plow on even when their actions aren't well received. On the other hand, people who are not as good at this may prefer to work on something a long time without interruption and be comfortable in only a few areas. Choose the few indicators you are interested in, in response to your questions and probes.

Before the interview, you might want to scan the themes section to find the ones you are particularly interested in. You can then interview against those themes. You can select questions and probes which match the themes you have selected. You can jot the themes down on the interview protocol form (available at www.lominger.com/pdf/IAPSF.pdf) and check them off as you progress through the interview.

Another way to think about the themes section is that there are various ways this competency is expressed. After completing the interview, you can use this section as a rough checklist to gauge whether you think this candidate has this theme at a high level or not. The more themes you think describe the candidate, the more likely it is the candidate has the competency. Theme count can be used as one measure of whether the person has the competency or not at a high level.

The themes section can also be used to write a narrative of your impressions of the candidate. As we said above, each theme is a small piece of behavior related to the competency. If you have determined the candidate has this competency in general, it's likely he or she also has some or most of the themes. You can use the themes you think you have verified to construct your narrative.

The Theme section mainly tests Dimension 1—have they done this in the past?

F. Most Likely Résumé

What would someone's résumé look like if he/she had this competency?

We know from several research studies, that competencies are primarily learned from tough job experiences or on the job training. Building on those findings, this section indicates a likely experience history for someone who is proficient in this competency—major job challenges they may have faced, specific tasks they might have done, and the sources most likely to know their skill level in this competency.

Best for interviewing experienced people, uses are:

- To see if the interviewee mentions challenges from F.1 (Jobs) and F.2 (Assignments) in his/her responses. Are these jobs and tasks mentioned as a source of the competencies?
- To check out a person's résumé to see what competencies should have been learned.
- To tailor questions by setting a specific job or task context—Conflict Management in a fix-it situation or Peer Relationships on a task force.

These are tests of Dimension 1—do they have the competency under consideration?

If the interview is to be followed by some reference checks, F.3 (Best References) indicates which of 15 sources might know the most about this competency. During the interview, these sources can also be used by asking the question, What did your _(source)_ think about you in this area, inserting the specific source F.3 indicates.

F.3 (Best References to Ask About) is also a way to get at Dimension 2 interviewing, looking for role models the person may have used.

A quick reference guide can be found in Appendix C of this handbook. For more extensive definitions, see The CAREER ARCHITECT® User's Manual.

G. Learning Agility Evaluation

Does this person have the Learning Agility to have learned this skill deeply? Can the person adapt the competency to dissimilar situations? And/or, what's the probability he/she could learn it given the opportunity?

There are 22 bipolar (two-sided) scales which describe various ways people learn. A complete listing of the 22 scales can be found in Appendix C.

In Section G, each competency is matched with a few of the scales which relate best to learning and maintaining that competency.

Examples are: Is the person passive in the situation or intrigued and curious, matched with #1 Action Orientation (Scale 7, page 1-5)? Is the person comfortable facing his/her weaknesses in the situation, or was this not mentioned or even avoided matched with # 55 Self-Knowledge (Scale 17, page 55-6)?

This section (G) can be used in three ways:

1. The basic logic is: In order to learn and maintain this competency at a high level, some or all of these learning orientations would have had to be used. If the person has the competency in question, it's very likely he/she has most of the learning orientations listed for that competency.

   During or after the interview, you can check or score your impressions of the candidate's Learning Agility to see if it verifies the competency. Remember, these are all probabilities. It's always possible to learn a competency in an unusual or unique way. This check is another way to increase the probability of correctly estimating whether the candidate has the competency.

2. Another way to use these 22 Learning Agility scales is to project how the candidate might do in future situations requiring this competency. Even though you have evidence the candidate has exhibited this competency once or twice, what's the probability they can repeat the behavior, especially across situations? This is particularly important for people who have limited or narrow backgrounds. A person might be unable to answer many of the negotiation questions for example because of lack of experience, yet show openness to learning new skills across a range of questions in the interview.

   Additionally, the person might rate high on the learning skills we noted under the negotiation competency. The more Learning Agility scales you think are true for this candidate, the more likely it is the candidate will be able to repeat the behavior in the future or learn new related behavior.

3. The last way to use the scales occurs when you have decided the candidate does not now have the competency in question. While this finding may contribute to a negative decision about the candidate, it can also raise the question about whether the candidate could learn the competency. If the candidate has other desirable competencies, is developing this one on the job an option? Since the learning orientations are necessary to learn the skill, you can use this section to make that estimate.

The more Learning Agility scales you can check yes to (yes, they do seem to have that Learning Agility), the more probable it is the candidate could add the skill given the proper learning opportunities. This will, of course, be modified by how difficult the competency is to develop. That information is found in Section K of the handbook.

The Learning Agility section can be used to assess Dimension 4—whether they have the learning style necessary to have learned the competency in the first place and/or can they adapt the competency to adjust to future conditions?

The 22 Learning Agility scales and definitions can be found in Appendix C of this Manual.

H. LEADERSHIP ARCHITECT® Sort Card Connections

How does this competency relate to others?

Seldom, if ever, do single competencies act alone in real life. Any competency coupled with others might become even more of an asset or flip over and become a liability. Would you rather have a Results Driven (#53) person who was low in Interpersonal Savvy (#31) and Ethics and Values (#22), or would you rather have a Results Driven (#53) person who was also high in Caring for Direct Reports (#7) and Fairness to Direct Reports (#23)? Probably you would want the latter.

This section was constructed by looking at the most common "if-thens". That is, IF a person is high in Results Orientation (#53) and low in Caring about Direct Reports (#7), THEN it's very likely they might push direct reports too hard. Each competency has five to 20 if-then combinations listed.

Using this section can help you in six ways:

1. **H1 (Would be good (positive) if this competency is combined with other competencies that are high (positive)) and H2 (Would be bad (negative) if this competency is combined with either high or low competencies)**

   To add texture and detail to what you are looking for (or not looking for) in the competency in question. In H.1. and H.2., we list some possible combinations of competencies and what they might indicate. You should scan these to see if you need to interview for any of the listed combinations. For example, if you are interviewing for Dealing with Ambiguity (#2) but are concerned about fragmented efforts, you might add a Planning (#47) or Priority Setting (#50) question to your list, and/or add "Well organized manager" or "Doesn't fragment; knows what is going on" to your list of things to look for (Section E) or issues to probe (Section D).

2. **H3 (Too much of this competency can contribute to the following Stallers and Stoppers)**

   To help decide whether the competency is becoming a stone around the person's neck. Quite often, people get in trouble not because they are weak in a competency, but because their strengths go into overdrive. The skill becomes so overdone that the strength becomes a weakness—confidence becomes arrogance, having many ideas leads to disorganization or never finishing anything, concern for others becomes paralysis when decisions must be made. If an interviewee shows repeated evidence of overdone tendencies, you can use H.3. to look for patterns across competencies (e.g. the person comes across as defensive in a number of areas), or to look for specific concerns around a single competency (e.g. devalues the opinions of others).

3. **H4 (Too little of this competency can contribute to the following Stallers and Stoppers)**

   To think about the possible consequences of too little of a competency (H.4.). Looking across competencies the person does not have might suggest the person overmanages (Staller number 117—Too little Dealing with Paradox, page 40-7) or might arouse a concern like lack of team building (Staller number 110—Too little Process Management, page 52-8) that you might want to probe further.

4. **H1-H4**

   To make mid-course corrections during the interview. If, for example, you hear statements that cause concern, using this section can help you zero in on probes or additional questions that deal with the area. If used in a multiple interviewing context, you can add some questions for the next interviewer or suggest he/she inquire about certain specifics.

5. H1-H4

To form some summary statements after the interview. For example, you and other interviewers may agree that a person is high in Dealing with Ambiguity but low in Problem Solving or Process Management. This might indicate someone who doesn't think things through as well as he or she could. You might decide, even if you hired the person, that a development plan in this area was in order. This section can aid you in putting together impressions from across interviewers and across competencies to come to some basic statements or questions about the person.

The Connections section (I) is mainly a test of Dimension 1, have they learned this competency in the past? A quick reference guide to the competencies can be found in Appendix C of this handbook.

6. *How could this person compensate for either too much or too little of this competency?*

Any person interviewed will be a bundle of things done well and not so well. Effective people often understand this about themselves and compensate. There are two lists of compensators in this section:

- **H3.C.**—Those that help us compensate when we overdo a competency. A commonly overdone strength is Ethics and Values (#22). The person may become rigid, go to battle too often, and be closed to other views. If an interviewee is given to ethical pronouncements or frequent values statements, you might check for compensators such as Composure (#11), Listening (#33), Conflict Management (#12) or Managing Diversity (#21) to see if the person has reasonable checks and balances on the overdone strength. The key issue is whether the overuse has negative consequences or not. The more compensators you think the person has, the less likely it is that the overuse will have negative consequences.

- **H4.C.**—Those that substitute when we are not strong in a competency. A person who lacks Perseverance (#43) might compensate by at least being Action Oriented (#1) and getting things started, and encouraging others to carry on from there. The key issue here is whether the person could get the same thing done some other way. Could he/she do what this competency does without having it! The more substitutes the person has, the more likely it is that he/she can do what this competency does.

Using this section can help in looking at people as inevitably less than perfect, but who can compensate in various ways for their overdone skills or lack of skill. We particularly recommend this section if you pick up impressions of an overdone strength or a troublesome combination of competencies in H above. In a multiple interview format, you could add questions for the next interviewer or suggest that he/she inquire about certain specifics.

A reference list of competencies can be found in Appendix C of this manual.

I. LEARNING ARCHITECT® Connections

What learning styles and methods are related to learning this competency?
(Mostly for users familiar with The LEARNING ARCHITECT® scales)

This section suggests connections between the competency in question and the learning modes the person may use to build and maintain the skill. As in G. (Learning Agility Evaluation Scales), this section is used to look across competencies to see what learning tendencies a person might have and to project how willing and able he/she might be to learn this competency. The connections are used in the same ways as the Learning Agility connections in G. The more the candidate looks like the listed learning modes or scales, the more likely it is that he/she will be able to repeat this competency across situations or if he/she does not yet have this competency, the connections predict the likelihood it could be added.

The LEARNING ARCHITECT® Connections section is mainly a test of Dimension 4—do they have the learning skills and techniques necessary to have learned this competency in the past and/or can they maintain and expand this competency under different conditions in the future?

A quick reference list can be found in Appendix C of this handbook. More extensive definitions can be found in The CAREER ARCHITECT® User's Manual.

J. CHOICES ARCHITECT® Connections

What learning skills are related to this competency?

(For those who use the CHOICES ARCHITECT® 1st or 2nd Edition cards, paper questionnaires or eCHOICES.)

This section addresses the same two issues as in G & I, looking across competencies to see what learning tendencies a person might have and to project how willing and able he/she might be to learn the competency in question. The connections are used in the same ways as the Learning Agility connections in G. The more the candidate looks like the listed learning modes or scales, the more likely it is he/she will be able to repeat this competency across situations. If he/she does not yet have this competency, the connections predict the likelihood it could be added.

Learning and Maintaining the Competency

The basic logic is: In order to learn and maintain this competency at a high level, some or all of these learning components would have had to be used. If the person has the competency in question, it's very likely he/she has most of the components listed for that competency. During or after the interview, you can check or score your impressions of the candidate's learning skill to see if it verifies the competency. Remember, these are all probabilities. It's always possible to learn a competency in an unusual or unique way. This check is another way to increase the probability of correctly estimating whether the candidate has the competency.

Using the CHOICES ARCHITECT® to project future situations

Another way to use the CHOICES ARCHITECT® Dimensions is to project how the candidate might do in future situations requiring this competency. Even though you have evidence the candidate has exhibited this competency once or twice, what's the probability he or she can repeat the behavior, especially across situations? This is particularly important for people who have limited or narrow backgrounds. A person might be unable to answer many of the negotiation questions for example because of lack of experience, yet show openness to learning new skills across a range of questions in the interview. Additionally, the person might rate high on the learning skills we noted under the negotiation competency. The more CHOICES ARCHITECT® connections you think are true for this candidate, the more likely it is the candidate will be able to repeat the behavior in the future or learn new related behavior.

Using the scales when a candidate doesn't have the competency

The last way to use the scales occurs when you have decided the candidate does not now have the competency in question. While this finding may contribute to a negative decision about the candidate, it can also raise the question about whether the candidate could learn the competency. If the candidate has other desirable competencies, is developing this one on the job an option? Since the CHOICES ARCHITECT® Dimensions are helpful in learning this skill, you can use this section to make that estimate. The more you can check yes to (yes, they do seem to have that Dimension), the more probable it is the candidate could add the skill given the proper learning opportunities. This will, of course, be modified by how difficult the competency is to develop. That information is found in section K of the Handbook.

The CHOICES ARCHITECT® Dimension section is mainly a test of Dimension 4—Does the person have the learning skills and techniques necessary to have learned this competency in the past and/or add it in the future. A quick reference list can be found in Appendix C of this Manual. For more complete definitions, look in CHOICES ARCHITECT® User's Manual.

K. Difficulty to Develop
How difficult would it be to develop and maintain this competency?

This section indicates how difficult a competency is likely to be to develop.

Uses of this section are:

- To rate the difficulty of a job by averaging the difficulty scores of the competencies together. In a job that averages 28, you might want someone who rates high on the competencies and the various learning scales as this job requires continuous improvement (Dimension 4 interviewing). Even someone who had done well previously might not continue to learn in new situations. Additionally, you might decide that anyone in this job would need a development plan due to its tough, changing nature. If the rating were low, 18 or so, you could be safer with a hire now, develop later, decision.

- To look at the internal staffing of task forces, teams and work units in terms of the difficulty of the competencies required. The higher the difficulty, the higher the competency and the learning appraisal of the members should be.

- To look at people who had low competency ratings in the interview, yet high related learning ratings. If this is the case, you might want to consider a hire and develop plan for all but the highest rated difficulty jobs.

- In skills based pay, you would pay more for the higher point competencies than the lower point ones.

- In determining whether it is worth the organization's time and effort to help a struggling person survive, the higher the point total of the needs, the less likely the efforts will pay off and be successful.

- In succession planning, more attention should be paid to the higher point competencies in assigning future leaders to developmental tasks. These needs will be more long-term in nature and development should begin earlier (particularly if the person has a problem in this area).

- In development planning, special attention should be paid to the profile of the person's needs to custom tailor the plan to the situation and the person.

All Competencies are not Created Equal, Some are Harder for People to Develop than Others

We have developed the attached index of the difficulty to develop each of the LEADERSHIP ARCHITECT® 67 competencies and characteristics. The index is made up of three components.

Component #1—The underlying nature of the competency

The first component comes from the nature of the competencies themselves. The difficulty of developing any competency is affected by at least six building block factors:

1. Complexity of the Skills

How complex are the skills that are needed to execute the competency well? The harder the skills involved, and the sheer number of rules and processes there are, the harder the competency would be to develop.

So Business Acumen (#5) is more involved and is harder to get proficient at than Patience (#41). The number of things you have to know and have to know how to do is significantly different.

2. Experience

How much experience is needed before the competency could be executed well? Experience adds context and rules of successes and failures and the lessons of history. Competencies that need lots of experience before you can do it well will be harder (less likely or fewer people have had those experiences) and take longer to develop than those that require little or no experience.

So Perspective (#46) takes more experience to be good at than Perseverance (#43).

3. Beliefs

To what extent does the competency depend on the attitudes, values, opinions and beliefs of the person? There are times when the difficulty in building and performing is not the skill itself but not wanting to do something. The more beliefs are involved in learning and performing, the harder the competency would be to execute.

So Managing Diversity (#21) is more dependent upon enhancing and lubricating beliefs than Functional Skills (#24).

4. Emotions

To what extent does doing the competency involve, engage or trigger the person's emotions. The more emotions a competency involves, the harder it would be to execute for most.

So Conflict Management (#12) involves more emotions than Technical Learning (#61) and would therefore be harder to develop and perform well, all other factors held equal.

5. Cognitive Complexity

To what extent does doing the competency draw upon raw intellectual abilities and the ability to do complex parallel processing of incomplete information? The more the competency draws upon intellectual horsepower and cognitive complexity, the harder it will be to execute the competency.

So Strategic Agility (#58) draws on more native intellectual ability than being Action Oriented (#1) and would be harder to develop.

6. Human Make-up

To what extent does the competency derive from a person's make-up like body chemistry, native skills, predispositions, natural tendencies, brain structure and the like? The more a competency is involved with native make-up, the harder it would be to develop any differently than originally designed.

So Composure (#11) is more dependent upon who a person is underneath than Customer Focus (#15), so changing a person's normal level and tone of Composure would be harder than teaching someone to be more Customer Oriented.

Each of these six components are scored from 1-easy, to 5-difficult. The ratings come from research where available and experience of the authors.

Component #2—Real world skills

The second component come from the norms that Lominger has developed using its VOICES® database. Based upon that norm base, we know how 5,000 learners are rated by 50,000 raters in terms of the 67 skills from highest to lowest. This should be a rough indicator of how difficult it is for people to develop or have gained proficiency in these 67 competencies in the real world.

The theory of the case is that the lower the rated competency, the harder it must be in the real work to develop that competency because fewer people do well at it. Therefore the lower it's rated, the higher the weight on difficulty. Our norms indicate that most people are pretty good at Functional/Technical Skills (#24) which would therefore have a low difficulty weight and most people are much less skilled at Developing Others (#19), resulting in a higher weight on the difficulty index.

Component #3—Perceived importance

The third component also comes from the VOICES® norm base. It is the perceived importance to performing well and succeeding of the 67 competencies from highest to lowest. The theory of the case is that the lower the perceived importance of the competency, the lower the motivation to develop the competency. Our norms say that Customer Focus (#15) is among the most important and therefore would receive a lower difficulty rating since people would be highly motivated to develop this skill because 50,000 raters said it's important. On the other hand, people believe that Personal Disclosure (#44) is much less important and therefore it receives a higher difficulty weight because it would be harder to convince someone that they ought to work on such an unimportant need.

The Grand Difficulty Index

The resulting grand index is made up of these three components added together. Component 1 scores range from 34 (Understanding Others #64), one of the hardest to develop based upon the underlying nature of the competency to 13 (Functional/Technical Skills #24), one of the easiest to develop. Component 2 and 3 are both based upon a 1—easiest to develop to 5—hardest to develop scale.

The difficulty index is under constant review and will from time to time be adjusted to reflect the latest research, norms and experience working with people on their development.

Use of the Index

The index is used to gauge how difficult it would be for a normal person to develop any of the 67 competencies. The higher the index, the harder the task and/or the more time it would take and/or the more resources it would require.

In a sense, each person also has a profile on most of the factors. For instance, a person's emotional system might be enhancing, enabling and a positive factor, that is they seldom get flustered and tend to perform better under pressure and stress.

On the other hand, someone else may have emotions that tend to restrain and get in the way of performance; they may get upset easily, take things personally that weren't meant to be and perform less well under pressure. Their emotions are a restraining factor. For the first person, building a skill that had a high rating on Emotions would be less of a problem than the second person. The same would hold true for enabling or restraining beliefs, broad versus narrow experience, high or low capacity for complexity and more or less gifted naturally.

Many times people ask how many needs they can work on at one time. Part of the answer is in the index. Take the multiple needs the person wants to work on and add up the points. The higher the resulting number, the harder the task.

Generally speaking, 75 points is about all that should be attempted under normal conditions.

How to Build a Job Profile

Profiling the Key Competencies

Some users will need to profile the key competencies of a job or assignment before using *The INTERVIEW ARCHITECT® Handbook.* There are three methods of doing this:

1. By matching a pre-existing competency profile to LEADERSHIP ARCHITECT® Sort categories. This is accomplished by a logical matching of your categories, for example, **Initiative** on your profile, becomes **Action Oriented** (#1) in The LEADERSHIP ARCHITECT® Competencies.

2. By convening a panel of experts (usually a combination of current job incumbents, past incumbents, bosses of the jobs and experts on the job) to select a number of LEADERSHIP ARCHITECT® Competencies. Usually 10-20 competencies are selected, with more chosen as the complexity and the level of the job increases.

3. We recommend the procedure below if you are unsure of the accuracy of the job profile you currently have, the job demands have changed significantly, you don't have much performance data on this job, or you have significant disagreement about which competencies are most important for success in this job.

Building a Job Profile

There are several steps to building a job profile:

Convene a panel of experts

Convene a panel of experts (6-10)—current job incumbents, past incumbents, bosses and job experts (two levels up from the job, job designers, senior human resources professionals).

Record the major challenges on the flipchart

Have them spend at least 30 minutes recording on a flip chart the major challenges this job faces now and in the foreseeable future (one to three years is most common). Why? Because skills have more meaning if they're tied to work objectives and demands. Simply stating what skills are required to do a job often introduces a couple of biases: a) the experts' pet theories of leadership/management skills; b) socially desirable skills like **Motivating Others**; c) skills that are difficult to tell exactly how they relate to job demands.

The outcome of this step should be a series of critical challenges/demands. You should not include any skills at this point. Example: You shouldn't say anyone in this job has to manage conflict well; instead you should list the major conflict situations (negotiations with customers, etc.).

Determine the skills needed to meet job demands

What skills are most important to meet these job demands?

Shuffle the **LEADERSHIP ARCHITECT® Sort Cards** three times to randomize the 67 skills and competencies.

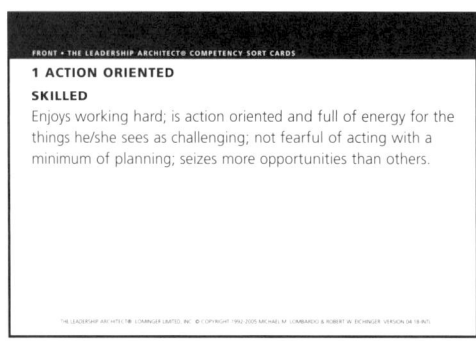

Sort the 67 **Sort Cards** into three piles—the 22 relatively most critical to job success (those one must excel in to respond to the most likely challenges), the 23 of moderate importance, and the 22 relatively least essential for success. This forced choice method is to prevent declaring most or all as equally important. Organizations often put too many skills into their competency profiles and fail to differentiate the critical few from the many other skills that support the most essential ones.

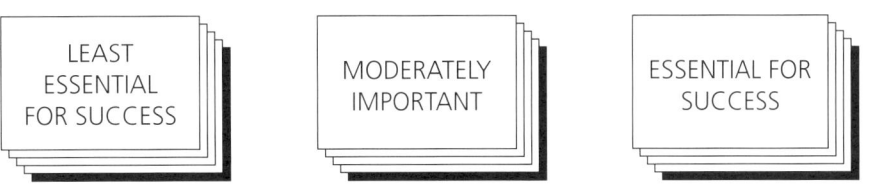

Record individual selections on the Tally Sheet

Have everyone record their individual selections in Column A on the **Tally Sheet.** Record a **1** beside those 22 least critical for business success, a **2** for those 23 moderately important, and a **3** for those 22 most critical.

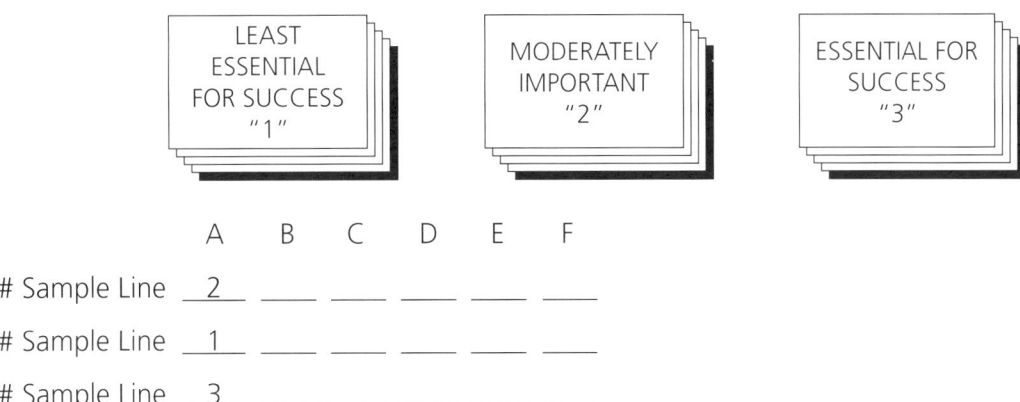

To generate a profile for discussion, use the **Tally Sheet** to record individual sorts and then use one of several ways to summarize and display the results to the group.

One way that has worked well is to have the **Tally Sheet** blown up to poster size and hang it on a wall. Give each person two colors of stick-on dots, available at any business supply store, and have them put the dots on the posters for their 22 best (in one color like green or blue) and their 22 least (in another color like red or yellow).

There will be competencies that have multiple and only green or blue dots (consensus on important for success), those with multiple and only red or yellow dots (consensus on being not necessary or least important for success), those with no dots (truly in the middle, picked by no one as most or least important), and those with equal or unequal amounts of both colors. The last group, those with both high and low colors, should be debated to see if any in the group are willing to change their votes after further debate. If yes, those skills can be added to the 22 highest or lowest. If not, they are candidates for the 23 in the middle.

	A	B	C	D	E	F	
# Sample Line	Green	Green	___	Green	___	Green	(a candidate for one of the 22 most important)
# Sample Line	___	___	___	___	___	___	(a candidate for one of the 23 in the middle)
# Sample Line	Red	Red	Red	___	Red	___	(a candidate for one of the 22 least important)
# Sample Line	Green	Red	___	Red	___	Green	(a candidate for discussion and debate)

The second way to accomplish the same result is to collect the individual **Tally Sheets,** call a break in the session, and have two or more people transfer the votes in two colors onto a transparency of the **Tally Sheet** for display when the group reassembles. Then follow the same discussion process as above.

A third way to decide what's most important and least important is running a simple average plus a frequency count of high and low votes. Record the individual results on a paper or log into a computer spread sheet program and run straight averages. Then count off 22 from the top and 22 from the bottom of the averages for the final results. This method also allows differentiation within the top 22 and the bottom 22. The disadvantage of the pure average method is the skills with both high and low votes automatically go to the middle without debate. Having the frequency counts as well as the averages allows you to pay special attention to the split vote (both high and low vote) skills. These skills need discussion and debate before automatically putting them in the middle. Just putting split votes in the middle can lead to some inaccurate results.

Sample Line 3 2 3 2 1 2 3 2 3 2 3 3 = 29 ÷ 12 = 2.42

Sample Line 1 2 2 2 1 2 3 2 2 1 2 1 = 21 ÷ 12 = 1.75

Sample Line 1 3 1 2 1 1 3 1 3 1 1 3 = 21 ÷ 12 = 1.75

Sample Line 1 1 1 2 1 1 1 2 1 1 1 2 = 15 ÷ 12 = 1.25

- Once the profile is displayed, look for those competencies that are consensus important. A typical rule of thumb is if two-thirds of the group voted something most important and no one voted it least important, the skill is initially accepted as critical. Fifteen skills with two-thirds support is a common result.
- Have each member suggest a skill that is not among the top skills he/she believes is critical, yet received few or split votes. He or she may have been the only one who voted for it. Discuss these nominations and allow the group to add accordingly.
- Look at the split votes—those with many most important and least important votes. Why did this occur? a) Are there major subtypes of this job, meaning that job x in one unit is a somewhat different job than in another unit? (If so, break out the differences while maintaining the core list above.) b) Does the organization not walk its talk? Sometimes a reason for a split vote is, "We say it's important and it ought to be, but name one person who's ever gotten in trouble for not having this skill?" In this case, the skill is critical, but there may be an issue with performance assessment and rewards. c) Occasionally, even experts will think of different challenges when selecting skills; they'll focus on some and ignore others. Upon seeing the split votes, they'll change their votes.
- After discussion, add or subtract to/from the list accordingly.

At this point, the list may be acceptable, but it may also have grown too long for interviewing. To accommodate the time limitations of an interview, the competencies may: a) be grouped into themes and the most representative competency selected (e.g. a number of interpersonal competencies might be summarized as **Interpersonal Savvy**; or b) the list may be pared back. This often happens when the list of critical skills reaches 25 or so, and usually results in cutting back the list to 10-15. To pare back the list, ask the following questions of the group:

- Which of these competencies spell the difference between superior and average performance in this job? All competencies rarely meet this test; there are usually a few that anyone considered for the job can already do. These price of admission skills (for example, most middle managers have demonstrated **Functional/Technical** and **Planning** skills or they wouldn't be job candidates) can be used to set the pool of candidates for interviewing.
- Could we name people who have failed in this job because they didn't have this competency at a high level? Again, the competency may be critical, but anyone chosen for the job had enough of it so it was not a cause of failure.
- Is this competency likely to be seen for the first time in this job or could we have seen it in much the same way at a lower level? Most useful for looking at internal job candidates, the questions help distinguish skills that are new (e.g. below a certain level people aren't asked to participate in **Strategy** in most organizations) or a quantum leap forward in demand (e.g. all jobs require some Composure, but a job with heavy negotiations, customer service, or team building requirements demands much more) from skills that are critical to the job, but could be seen in much the same way at lower levels (e.g. **Organizing** or **Time Management** might be typical candidates).

This step results in two lists: price of admission skills to help form the candidate pool, and the most critical skills that this job demands.

As a final step, some organizations benchmark the results with target organizations, have an outside expert review them or consult any available research on this type of job.

NOTE: Job profiles using The LEADERSHIP ARCHITECT® Competencies can also be quickly built electronically using Lominger's Success Profile Architect™ (SPA).

Consulting/Counseling/Educating/Problem Solving

Use of *The INTERVIEW ARCHITECT® Professional Handbook*

This use of *The INTERVIEW ARCHITECT® Professional Handbook* is not so obvious at first. The material in the Handbook is all about competencies. Five hundred pages of detail. This tool could have been entitled *The COMPETENCY ANALYSIS™ Handbook* or the *PEOPLE Handbook.* It's an Encyclopedia of competencies.

As such, it can be used anytime competencies are involved. Some examples might be:

- Writing a performance review narrative.
- Trying to figure out an opponent in a negotiation.
- Diagnosing why people gave you the feedback they did.
- Preparing a succession planning presentation on a high potential.
- Preparing for a career discussion.
- Trying to make peace with an enemy.
- Figuring out why someone did what he/she did.
- Analyzing what drives someone you need to motivate.
- Doing an in depth self analysis.
- Explaining one person to another.
- Helping someone in trouble.
- Unpack the reasons for a failure or a mistake.
- Determining if two people would work well together.
- Helping two people who are not getting along with each other.
- Aiding someone under stress and understanding why he/she is upset.
- Getting specific on a development plan.
- Fine tuning a success profile.
- Unpack the reasons for success or failure at a task/project/assignment.
- Setting the requirements for a task or assignment.
- Explaining why someone performed badly or well.
- Getting a handle on why someone failed.
- Detailing why a team is performing well or not well.
- Examining an organization's culture (what are its core competencies?).
- Designing competency courses.
- Matching people to assignments.
- Looking for lateral skills in people.
- Examining a role model in detail.
- Selecting the right course to attend for yourself or for others.

These and other tasks can be aided by the Handbook. Each competency chapter has:
- A behavior based definition
- A list of areas in one's life or work where each plays out
- A list of penetrating questions and probes you can ask yourself and others about each competency

- Behaviors (themes) within each competency
- How each competency combines with the other 67 competencies
- What too much of each competency looks like
- How people compensate for too much or too little of each competency
- How each competency relates to learning skills and habits
- How each competency plays out in jobs and assignments

Anytime you would benefit by going below the surface of someone's behavior, the Handbook can be a manual or guide to deeper understanding and adding value to what you are trying to do.

The following is one example of using the Handbook as a problem solving tool.

For use in performance or career counseling

An employee seeking help says, "My boss continues to question my problem solving skills, but when I press for specifics, she gets vague."

Or

"I just got some questionnaire feedback that says I need to work on my problem solving skills and I don't know what to do."

Or

"According to my last performance appraisal..."

Or

"I really need to get better at..."

Or

"I overdo..."

A Variety of Uses

We have identified several uses for the Interview Architect Professional Handbook.

- Find out if the need is general or situation specific (Section B—Arenas)
- Put some meat into the understanding of the need (Section C—Questions and Section D—Probes)
- Provide tips for short term improvement (Section E—Themes)
- Construct more sophisticated developmental strategies such as tasks and multiple feedback sources (Section F—Résumé)
- Look at ways to improve long term learning and development (Sections G, I & J—Learning)
- Look at problematic combinations (Section H—Connections)
- Look at compensation strategies (Section H—Compensators)

Seven Counseling Steps

There are seven steps we've identified for use in counseling.

Step 1. Use the 32 domains in Section B to help the person detect which problem solving situations are most problematic.

Example: The person has the most trouble with first time tasks and helping others solve problems.

Step 2. Use the questions in Section C and the probes in Section D to understand the need:

- Tough problems (e.g. Tailor questions 3, 4, 6, 11, 14, 15, 24)   D I
- Helping others (e.g. Tailor questions 5, 12, 18)   D I
- Learning from models (e.g. Questions 27-53)   D II
- Check for conceptual understanding (e.g. Questions 55, 72-74, 79)   D III
- Check for personal learning alignment (e.g. Questions 82-108)   D IV

Step 3. Use Section E to look for positive and negative themes and potential developmental tips.

Example: The person enjoys the hunt, but becomes bored with first time problems once they begin to look solvable. Needs to finish or ensure that finishing occurs.

Or

The person wants personal credit; tends to reject others' solutions, has trouble unless he/she can define the problem for the person. Needs to learn to focus on others' view of the problem, help them formulate and solve it; not define it and solve it personally for credit.

Step 4. Use Section G, I, & J to look at long-term learning fixes.

Example: In the person's responses, she comes across as a "what happened" person, unable to explain whys and hows.

Or

Tends toward oversimplifying complex situations with comments like "They'd already decided to do it that way and couldn't be shaken from it." No recognition of the political or deadline pressures that may cause the above. Needs to understand the demands and context the problem stakeholders are working within.

Step 5. Use Section F to recommend:

- Developmental tasks

Example: Integrate diverse systems across units might be good for someone who likes to solve problems alone; Handle a tough negotiation might be good for someone who doesn't finish. Research indicates that development doesn't happen unless we have compelling work tasks that require us to develop in an area or fail at the task.

- Feedback sources

Step 6. Use Section H to find problematic combinations, either through the person's responses or through self assessment. This analysis can suggest allied needs that the person might also work on.

Example: While the person creates motion, she doesn't go deep enough and needs too much data. In this case, she might also work on #32, Learning on the Fly.

Or

If the need is an overdone strength, use Section G to help the person understand the consequences of overdoing the skill.

Example: The person analyzes everything to death; prefers to solve problems alone or at least control the solution.

Step 7. Use Section H to look at compensation strategies, other skills the person could work on.

Example: A compensator for the example above might be to work on #1– Action Orientation and/or #60 – Building Effective Teams

Or

Use Section H to look at substitute for lack of the competency.

Example: For a person who doesn't go deep enough, #32 Learning on the Fly, #46 Perspective or #58 Strategic Agility might be recommended as substitutes (or in addition to) Problem Solving.

Example: If the person's boss is not a good source for problem solving feedback, suggest alternative sources such as HR Professionals, past associates, or boss' boss. Research suggests that multiple sources are best, and if the most obvious source (usually boss) isn't particularly good at giving feedback, that other sources are as good or better. Once the person becomes clearer about the need, a conversation, even with an inarticulate or not particularly insightful boss, can be much more helpful.

- Long term challenges

Example: if three years from now, the person has a choice between job assignments and has been actively pursuing problem solving skill development, research indicates that jumps in scope (e.g. single to multiple functions) or jobs with heavy strategic demands will best continue to develop and stretch problem solving skills.

While risky for the person, job changes are the number one source of skills improvement. The greater the problem solving challenge, the greater the potential skill gain, if the person is actively trying to improve in this area.

So, anytime a deeper analysis of a person's behavior would help the solution of a problem, *The Interview Architect® Professional Handbook* can be used to dig into the issue in whatever depth is necessary.

HANDBOOK LAYOUT

A. DEFINITION:
What behaviors define this competency?

B. ARENAS/DOMAINS TO EXPLORE:
Where in the candidate's life would I find examples of this competency to talk about?

C. SAMPLE QUESTIONS:
What questions may I ask that will lead to assessing whether this candidate has this competency or not? (Also see Appendix A for generic questions that fit most competencies.)

D. FOLLOW-UP PROBES:
What probes can I use to follow-up on the questions I ask (from C)? (Also see Appendix B for generic probes that fit most competencies.)

E. THEMES/THINGS TO LOOK FOR:
What would this behavior look like on a day-to-day basis? And/or… How would I gauge whether the person has this competency?

F. MOST LIKELY RÉSUMÉ:
What would someone's résumé look like if they had this competency? And/or…
Where does this competency usually develop?

G. LEARNING AGILITY EVALUATION:
How can I measure whether this person has this competency or not? What's the probability they could learn if given the opportunity? Does this person have the learning agility necessary to have learned this competency in the past or to learn it in the future?

H. THE LEADERSHIP ARCHITECT® SORT CARD CONNECTIONS:
How does this competency relate to other competencies?

I. LEARNING ARCHITECT® CONNECTIONS:
What learning styles and methods are related to learning this competency?

J. CHOICES ARCHITECT® CONNECTIONS FIRST EDITION AND SECOND EDITION:
What learning skills are related to this competency?

K. DIFFICULTY TO DEVELOP:
How difficult would it be to develop and maintain this competency?

1. ACTION ORIENTATION

A. Definition:
Enjoys working hard; is action-oriented and full of energy for the things he/she sees as challenging; not fearful of acting with a minimum of planning; seizes more opportunities than others.

B. Arenas/Domains to Explore:
1. Community involvement
2. Family activities
3. Hobbies
4. Physical activity
5. Social activity
6. Thinking speed/style
7. Time management/delay tolerance
8. Challenges in multiple areas (work and off-work)
9. Looking for opportunities
10. Start-ups/first-time tasks

C. Sample Questions:

Dimension 1: Been there, done that–has had direct personal experience(s) involving the competency–candidate was the prime player   Note: * means OK for campus

1. Do you tend to energize others or be energized by others?*
2. Do you tend to take work home?
3. Has anyone accused you of being a workaholic?
4. Have you ever started something up from scratch?*
5. How do you breathe some life into a group?*
6. How do your work hours compare to others?
7. How much planning do you do before you decide to act?*
8. Tell me about a time when you were not the first person to act in a tough situation.*
9. Tell me about a time when you were the first person to take action on something.*
10. Tell me about a time when your lack of taking action got you into trouble.
11. Tell me about a time when your willingness to take quick action worked really well for you.
12. Tell me about times when you seized opportunities, grabbed something, and ran with it yourself.*
13. What are your hobbies?*
14. What are your typical work habits?
15. What are your typical work hours?
16. What do you do when you have time on your hands, when you really have nothing else to do?*
17. What do you do when you have to do things that do not challenge you?*
18. What do you find challenging, exciting, or fun?*
19. What kinds of vacations do you take?*
20. What motivates you to get up in the morning and go to work?
21. What off-work (extracurricular) activities are you involved in?*
22. What's a typical weekend like for you?*
23. When faced with a difficult problem, what do you tend to do?*
24. When listening to an argument among people you know well, do you tend to jump in or stay out?*
25. Would you or others describe you as a perfectionist or a detail person?*

ACTION ORIENTATION

Dimension 2: Seen/been around others who were involved with the competency–good and bad; learns from others about self

26. Contrast the most and least action-oriented people you know.*
27. Has action orientation ever been in any 360° survey done on you? Was your score among your highest, middle, or lowest?
28. Has not taking action on someone else's part ever created an obstacle for you or got in the way of something you were trying to accomplish?*
29. Have you ever talked about your action orientation with a coach or mentor?
30. Have you ever watched someone fail/get fired due to their lack of action?*
31. Have you ever watched someone overdo taking action to the point that it backfired?
32. Have you ever watched someone succeed because they were action-oriented?*
33. Have you ever worked with a person who excelled at being action-oriented?
34. Have you ever worked with a skills coach on being more action-oriented?*
35. How do you get feedback about yourself on taking more action?
36. How often do you check with multiple sources when you get a piece of critical feedback on your action orientation?
37. Is there a historical figure you consider a model of being action-oriented?
38. What do others who are not your fans say about your action orientation?
39. What do others who like you say about your action orientation?
40. Which boss was the best at taking action?
41. Which boss was the worst at taking action?
42. Which direct report was the best at taking action?
43. Which direct report was the worst at taking action?
44. Which peer was the best at taking action?
45. Which peer was the worst at taking action?
46. Who in your field or business deals the best with taking action?
47. Who do you consider a role model of being action-oriented?*
48. Who do you go to for advice on being more action-oriented?
49. Who have you learned the most from about taking action?*
50. Who is a higher-management role model for you on taking action?
51. Who is a role model of action orientation outside of work?

Dimension 3: Knows how the competency works in theory; shows understanding

52. Are there situations or settings where someone should demonstrate different levels of action orientation?
53. Do you think action orientation skills can be learned? If so, how do you think people develop action orientation skills?
54. Do you think there is a way to compensate or work around low action-orientation skills?
55. Has anyone asked you for your opinions/advice on taking action?*
56. Have you ever attended a course on taking quicker action?
57. Have you ever been in a situation where you and others put action orientation on a success profile?
58. Have you ever been part of an effort to create a policy or a mission statement containing reference to the importance of being action-oriented?
59. Have you ever been someone's coach or mentor who had problems with taking action?
60. Have you ever created a development plan for someone on action orientation?
61. Have you ever criticized someone for not being action-oriented?

ACTION ORIENTATION

62. Have you ever designed a program on action orientation?
63. Have you ever given a speech on action orientation?
64. Have you ever rewarded or recognized someone for taking action?
65. Have you ever taught a course on taking action?
66. Have you ever tried to help someone deal more effectively with taking action?*
67. Have you ever tried to help someone improve their action-orientation skills?
68. How do you think people develop action orientation skills?
69. How much action orientation is good to have and how much is too much?
70. How much of success do you think is due to action orientation compared with other characteristics?
71. How would you know if someone is bad at taking action?
72. How would you know if someone is good at taking action?
73. If you had to write a book on taking action what would the chapter headings be?
74. What are the benefits to someone who is really good at acting quickly?
75. What are the consequences to someone who is really poor at taking timely action?
76. What do you think the performance standard is on action orientation for someone in your role?
77. What happens if you are too action-oriented?
78. What happens when two people try to work together who have very different levels of action orientation?
79. What wisdom would you pass on to others trying to become better at taking action?
80. When you select others, what do you look for in action orientation?
81. Why do you think people end up being different in their ability to take action?

Dimension 4: Shows personal change and sense-making; learned it one place and applied it in another; can compare and contrast experiences; changes viewpoints across time; can explain personal development or evolution related to the competency

82. Compare and contrast examples of times you've been effective and ineffective at taking action.*
83. Contrast your on- and off-the-job use of an action orientation.*
84. Did you ever pass up a job or assignment because you were not confident in your ability to take action?
85. Do you ever use other skills to cover for your lack of action orientation?*
86. Has getting better at taking quick action ever helped you in other areas?*
87. Has lack of taking action ever been the subject of a development plan for you?
88. Has not taking action ever figured in a failure, struggle, or setback you have had?*
89. Has taking too much action or acting too soon ever figured in a failure, struggle, or setback you have had?*
90. Has your willingness to act always been at the level it is now?
91. Has your willingness to take action, good or bad, ever been the subject of your performance review or a career discussion?
92. Have you ever delegated or assigned someone a task because you didn't know when to take action particularly well?
93. Have you ever made significant strides at becoming more action-oriented?
94. How different are you across situations in taking timely action?*
95. How do you decide how much action to take and when to act?*
96. How much of your success is due to your ability to act quickly?
97. How transferable are your taking-action-skills to other situations?*
98. If you had to become better at taking timely action in a hurry, what would you do?
99. Was there a time when you were not good at taking quick action?

ACTION ORIENTATION

100. What are some times where you took action precipitously? How have you changed how you handle such situations?
101. What caused you to work to improve your skills at taking action?
102. What event or series of events had the most impact on your present action orientation?
103. What's the most varied you can be in taking timely action?*
104. What was the shortest amount of time in which you learned to deal with taking timely action?
105. When did you first realize your level of skill at taking timely action?
106. When you know ahead of time that your usual way of taking action won't work, what do you do?*
107. Why do you think you deal with taking timely action the way you do?
108. Why do you think your action orientation is the way it is?*

D. Follow-up Probes:

1. Are there times when you take action like that and times when you don't?
2. Could you contrast those two bosses for me?
3. Could you give me a few examples of how you've used or applied that?
4. Did you or the other person blink first?
5. Do you suppose if others would just try harder, they could learn to be more action-oriented like you?
6. Do you think this is teachable?
7. Do you think you're better at taking action than most? Why?
8. Do you think you would perform any better if you had a different tack to taking action?
9. Have you ever had to form a relationship with someone you really disliked to get your job done?
10. How did the others react when you did that?
11. How did you come up with that approach to taking action in the first place?
12. How did you know that method of getting over that barrier would work?
13. How do others you have known approach that?
14. How far did you go to try to be a team player?
15. How far will you go before you cut line and try another method?
16. How much did you have to give up to make it work?
17. How often do you use the "Let's meet in the middle" approach?
18. How typical is this for you?
19. How would you approach that same situation today?
20. Is this natural for you or do you really have to dig for it?
21. Was there a time when you didn't understand this about yourself?
22. What did you do after you got that feedback?
23. What did you do to adapt to that?
24. What did you learn from that?
25. Why did you choose that approach?
26. Why did you decide to take the risk?
27. Why did you do it that way?
28. Why did you time your attempt to take action like you did?
29. Why do you suppose organizations work that way?
30. Why do you think that didn't work?
31. Why do you think that happened that way?
32. Why do you think that worked?

ACTION ORIENTATION

33. Why do you think you have difficulties with that sometimes?
34. Would you have done it that way with looser deadlines?
35. Would you have done it that way with tighter deadlines?

E. Themes/Things to Look for:
Frequency
Duration
Consistency across a number of domains
Lots of activity in short bursts
Awareness of impact on others
Driven by a conscientious need to complete things rather than just habit
Tolerance for mistakes
Penchant for doing things and learning from the actions
Can take the heat; plows on when actions aren't well received
High energy for things they enjoy doing

F. Most Likely Résumé:

1. Look for jobs like:

Fix-Its/Turnarounds	Staff to Line Shifts
Staff Leadership (Influencing Without Authority)	Start-Ups

2. Look for develop-in-place assignments like:
Plan for and start up something small (secretarial pool, athletic program, suggestion system, program, etc.).
Launch a new product, service, or process.
Relaunch an existing product or service that's not doing well.
Assign a project to a group with a tight deadline.
Manage an ad hoc, temporary group of people involved in tackling a fix-it or turnaround project.
Help shut down a plant, regional office, product line, business, operation, etc.
Manage a group through a significant business crisis.
Take on a task you dislike or hate to do.

3. Best references to ask about or check:

Direct Boss	Peers and Colleagues
Human Resource Professionals	Spouse
Natural Mentors	Direct Reports
Past Associates/Constituencies	

G. Learning Agility Evaluation:
4. Spectator/Passive vs. Player/Participant
7. Passive vs. Intrigued/Curious
10. Reactive vs. Initiating
14. Sameness vs. Broad Range
17. Avoids Weaknesses vs. Comfortable Facing Weaknesses
18. Stays Close to Home vs. Lots of Curiosity
21. Focus on Self vs. Focus on Others

ACTION ORIENTATION

H. The LEADERSHIP ARCHITECT® Sort Card Connections:

1. Good (positive) if combined with high:
Keeps self under control during high activity periods 11, 41
Cares about impact on others 3, 7, 10, 31, 33
Learns through action; is flexible 30, 32, 45, 51, 58
Follows through; produces results 43, 50, 52, 53, 62
Has a broad range of interests; not a one-activity type 46

2. Bad (negative) if combined with low or high (+):
Either doesn't think or doesn't care about impact on others; runs over or through others 3, 7, 10, 21, 23
Workaholic (+6) 66
Blows up easily 11, 41
Has a set bag of tricks; doesn't learn anything new 30, 32, 45, 46, 51, 58
Loose cannon; shoots self in foot 38, 47, 48 (+13, 43, 57)
Action junkie; flits about; doesn't finish things consistently 43, 53
Doesn't get results; action is wasted 47, 52, 53

3. Too much can contribute to the following Stallers and Stoppers:

A. What too much looks like (overused):
May be a workaholic; may push solutions before adequate analysis; may be non-strategic; may overmanage to get things done too quickly; may have personal and family problems due to disinterest and neglect; may not attend to important but non-challenging duties and tasks; may ignore personal life, burn out.

B. Too much might lead to these Stallers and Stoppers:
Poor administrator (102)   Non-strategic (114)
Overly ambitious (103)   Overmanaging (117)

C. Compensators:
How to compensate for too much of this competency:
    11, 27, 33, 39, 41, 43, 47, 50, 51, 52, 60, 66

D. Things to watch for:
Action junkie   Makes errors; doesn't stop to think or learn
Can't relax/doesn't vacation comfortably   May once in a while run out of gas
Constantly apologizing for premature actions   Volatile
Family problems   Doesn't get results
Loose cannon; runs over others

ACTION ORIENTATION

4. Too little can contribute to the following Stallers and Stoppers:

   A. *What too little looks like (unskilled):*

   Slow to act on an opportunity; may be overly methodical, a perfectionist, or risk averse; may procrastinate; may not set very challenging goals; may lack confidence to act; may know what to do but hesitates to do it; may not be motivated; may be bored with the work or burned out.

   B. *Too little might lead to these Stallers and Stoppers:*

   Performance Problems (118)

   C. *Compensators:*

   How to substitute for too little of this competency:
   9, 12, 16, 27, 32, 34, 36, 43, 50, 52, 53, 57, 62

I. **LEARNING ARCHITECT® Connections:**

Look for people who act like and/or show evidence of:

1a. Pure Action	9. Multiple Sources
1b. Trial and Error	20. Events
2c. Intuition	21. Changer
5. New	22. Experimenter
6. Contentious	25. Personal Change
7. Risks	29. Essence
8. Initiate	35. Breadth

J. **CHOICES ARCHITECT® Connections:**

Look for people who act like and/or show evidence of:

First Edition (Released 1994)	Second Edition (Released 2000)
1. Inquisitive	5. Easy Shifter
12. Experimenter	7. Inquisitive
18. Into Everything	20. Experimenter
19. Tinkerer	23. Visioning
20. Forging Ahead	25. Delivers Results
	26. Drive

K. **Difficulty to Develop:**

17 (of 34)–Easiest

ACTION ORIENTATION

2. DEALING WITH AMBIGUITY

A. Definition:

Can effectively cope with change; can shift gears comfortably; can decide and act without having the total picture; isn't upset when things are up in the air; doesn't have to finish things before moving on; can comfortably handle risk and uncertainty.

B. Arenas/Domains to Explore:

1. A lot going on at once
2. Bosses
3. Career choices
4. Crises
5. External groups
6. Future projection/speculation tasks
7. Life choices
8. Powerless situations
9. Sudden changes
10. Teams and project groups
11. Work problems
12. Work processes

C. Sample Questions:

Dimension 1: Been there, done that–has had direct personal experience(s) involving the competency–candidate was the prime player   Note: * means OK for campus; ** means campus only

1. Do your work habits change when things are up in the air?
2. Have you ever managed anything where the people or units reporting to you were in different locations? How did you get them to be more effective handling ambiguity and uncertainty?
3. How do you get somewhere in a car when you don't know exactly where it is?*
4. How important is it for you to finish what you start?*
5. How much data do you like to have before you act?*
6. Tell me about a time when a crisis made what you had been doing obsolete or ineffective.*
7. Tell me about a time when everything was up in the air.*
8. Tell me about a time when you changed a job, situation, or relationship suddenly.
9. Tell me about a time when you changed schools, majors, went from high school to college.**
10. Tell me about a time when you found yourself with a professor/teacher you didn't know how to deal with.**
11. Tell me about a time when you got a poor grade you weren't expecting.*
12. Tell me about a time when you had a problem relationship that couldn't be worked out.*
13. Tell me about a time when you had a problem where you just didn't know what to do.*
14. Tell me about a time when you had an important school project and you didn't know what to do.*
15. Tell me about a time when you had to act on something important before you had time to come up with a good answer or solution.*
16. Tell me about a time when you had to change something significant in your work environment.
17. Tell me about a time when you inherited a new boss or work group and weren't sure what to do.
18. Tell me about a time when you took a significant personal risk (career, personal).*
19. Tell me about a time when your ability to handle ambiguity worked really well for you.
20. Tell me about a time when your discomfort with uncertainty got you into trouble.
21. Tell me about the time when you had your first real job.
22. Tell me about the time when you had your first really tough course.*
23. Tell me about your first trip to a foreign country with a language other than yours.*

DEALING WITH AMBIGUITY

24. Tell me about your first trip to a foreign country.*
25. What do you do when faced with significant uncertainty as to what to do next?*
26. What do you do when someone asks you to try something completely new to you?*
27. What do you do when someone important asks you a question you can't answer?*
28. What's the goofiest thing you've ever done?*
29. When you are uncertain about what to do, what do you do next?*

Dimension 2: Seen/been around others who were involved with the competency–good and bad; learns from others about self

30. Contrast the most and least able people you know with regard to dealing with uncertainty and ambiguity.*
31. Has dealing with uncertainty and ambiguity ever been in any 360º survey done on you? Was your score among your highest, middle, or lowest?
32. Has someone else's inability to deal with uncertainty and ambiguity ever created an obstacle for you or got in the way of something you were trying to accomplish?*
33. Have you ever talked about your dealing with ambiguity skills with a coach or mentor?
34. Have you ever watched someone fail/get fired because they did not handle ambiguous situations well?*
35. Have you ever watched someone overdo dealing with uncertainty and ambiguity to the point that it backfired?
36. Have you ever watched someone succeed because they were effective at dealing with uncertainty and ambiguity?*
37. Have you ever worked with a coach on dealing with ambiguity?*
38. Have you ever worked with a person who excelled at dealing with uncertainty and ambiguity?
39. Have you ever worked with a skills coach on getting better at dealing with uncertainty and ambiguity?*
40. How do you get feedback about yourself on dealing with ambiguity?
41. How often do you check with multiple sources when you get a piece of critical feedback on how you deal with uncertainty and ambiguity?
42. Is there a historical figure you consider a model of dealing with uncertainty and ambiguity?
43. What do others who are not your fans say about your dealing with uncertainty and ambiguity?
44. What do others who like you say about your dealing with uncertainty and ambiguity?
45. Which boss was the best at dealing with ambiguity?
46. Which boss was the worst at dealing with ambiguity?
47. Which direct report was the best at dealing with ambiguity?
48. Which direct report was the worst at dealing with ambiguity?
49. Which peer was the best at dealing with ambiguity?
50. Which peer was the worst at dealing with ambiguity?
51. Who in your field or business deals the best with ambiguity?
52. Who do you consider a role model of dealing with uncertainty and ambiguity?*
53. Who do you go to for advice on dealing with uncertainty and ambiguity?
54. Who have you learned the most from about dealing with ambiguity?*
55. Who is a higher-management role model for you on dealing with ambiguity?
56. Who is a role model of dealing with ambiguity outside of work?

Dimension 3: Knows how the competency works in theory; shows understanding

57. Are there situations or settings where someone should deal differently with ambiguity and uncertainty?
58. Do you think ambiguity skills can be learned? If so, how do you think people develop these skills?

DEALING WITH AMBIGUITY

59. Do you think there is a way to compensate or work around a low ability to deal with ambiguity and uncertainty?
60. Has anyone asked you for your opinions/advice on dealing with ambiguity and uncertainty?*
61. Have you ever attended a course on dealing with ambiguity and uncertainty?
62. Have you ever been in a situation where you and others put dealing with uncertainty and ambiguity on a success profile?
63. Have you ever been part of an effort to create a policy or a mission statement containing reference to the importance of being able to deal with ambiguity and uncertainty?
64. Have you ever been someone's coach or mentor who had problems dealing well with ambiguous situations?
65. Have you ever created a development plan for someone on dealing more effectively with ambiguity?
66. Have you ever criticized someone for not being able to deal with ambiguity and uncertainty?
67. Have you ever designed a program on dealing with uncertainty and ambiguity?
68. Have you ever given a speech on dealing with uncertainty and ambiguity?
69. Have you ever rewarded or recognized someone for dealing well with ambiguous situations?
70. Have you ever taught a course on dealing with uncertainty and ambiguity?
71. Have you ever tried to help someone deal more effectively with ambiguity?*
72. Have you ever tried to help someone improve their ability to deal with ambiguity and uncertainty?
73. How do you think people develop skills for dealing with ambiguity and uncertainty?
74. How much ability to deal with ambiguity and uncertainty is good to have and how much is too much?
75. How much of success do you think is due to dealing well with ambiguity and uncertainty compared with other characteristics?
76. How would you know if someone is bad at dealing with ambiguity and uncertainty?
77. How would you know if someone is good at dealing with ambiguity and uncertainty?
78. If you had to write a book dealing with ambiguity and uncertainty what would the chapter headings be?
79. What are the benefits to someone who is really good at dealing with ambiguity and uncertainty?
80. What are the consequences to someone who is really poor at dealing with ambiguity and uncertainty?
81. What do you think the performance standard is on dealing with ambiguity and uncertainty for someone in your role?
82. What happens when two people try to work together who are very different in the way they deal with ambiguity and uncertainty?
83. What wisdom would you pass onto others trying to become better at dealing with ambiguity and uncertainty?
84. When you select others, what do you look for in their ability to deal with ambiguity and uncertainty?
85. Why do you think people end up being different in the way they deal with ambiguity and uncertainty?

Dimension 4: Shows personal change and sense-making; learned it one place and applied it in another; can compare and contrast experiences; changes viewpoints across time; can explain personal development or evolution related to the competency

86. Compare and contrast examples of times when you've been effective and ineffective at dealing with change.
87. Contrast your on- and off-the-job ability to deal with change and ambiguity.
88. Did you ever pass up a job or assignment because you were not confident enough in your skills at managing change?
89. Do you ever use other skills to cover for your lack of comfort with ambiguity?
90. Has dealing with change and ambiguity ever figured in a failure, struggle, or setback you have had?
91. Has getting better at dealing with change ever helped you in other areas?
92. Has lack of comfort with change or ambiguity ever been the subject of a development plan for you?

DEALING WITH AMBIGUITY

93. Has your ability to deal with change and ambiguity always been this way?
94. Have you ever delegated or assigned someone a task because you didn't manage change particularly well?
95. Have you ever made significant strides at getting better at dealing with change and ambiguity?
96. Have your change management skills, good or bad, ever been the subject of your performance review or a career discussion?
97. How different are you across situations in your skill at dealing with change and ambiguity?
98. How do you decide how flexible to be?
99. How have you modified the way you manage your feelings of nervousness associated with change or uncertainty over the years?
100. How much of your success is due to your skill at dealing with change and ambiguity?
101. How transferable are your change-management skills to other situations?
102. If you had to become better at dealing with change and ambiguity in a hurry, what would you do?
103. Was there a time when you were not good at dealing with change and ambiguity?
104. What caused you to work to improve your skills at dealing with change and ambiguity?
105. What event or series of events had the most impact on the way you deal with change and ambiguity?
106. What's the most varied you can be in dealing with change and ambiguity?
107. What was the shortest amount of time in which you learned to deal with change and ambiguity?
108. When did you first realize your level of skill at dealing with change and ambiguity?
119. When you know ahead of time that your usual way of dealing with change won't work, what do you do?
110. Where do you think you will be and what will you be doing ten years from now?*
111. Why do you think you deal with change and ambiguity the way you do?
112. Why do you think your skill at dealing with change and ambiguity is the way it is?*

D. Follow-up Probes:

1. Are there times when you're not like this or wouldn't do this?
2. Are there times when you deal with things like that and times when you don't?
3. Could you contrast those two bosses for me?
4. Could you give me a few examples of how you've used or applied that?
5. Do you suppose if others would just try harder, they could learn to deal with the new and different more like you?
6. Do you think this is teachable?
7. Do you think you're better at dealing with change than most? Why?
8. Do you think you would perform any better if you dealt differently with change and ambiguity?
9. Have you ever had to form a relationship with someone you really disliked to get your job done?
10. How did it feel to give up something you wanted to get the project going?
11. How did the others react when you did that?
12. How did you come up with that approach to dealing with this in the first place?
13. How did you know that method of getting over that barrier would work?
14. How do others you have known approach that?
15. How far did you go to try to be a team player?
16. How far will you go before you cut line and try another approach?
17. How much did you have to give up to make it work?
18. How often do you use the "Let's meet in the middle" approach?
19. How typical is this for you?

DEALING WITH AMBIGUITY

20. How would you approach that same situation today?
21. Is this natural for you, or do you really have to dig for it?
22. Was that a fair way to maneuver around them?
23. Was there a time when you didn't understand this about yourself?
24. What changes bothered you most and least?
25. What did you do after you got that feedback?
26. What did you do to adapt to that?
27. What did you learn from that?
28. Why did you choose that approach?
29. Why did you decide to take the risk?
30. Why did you do it that way?
31. Why did you time your attempt like you did?
32. Why do you suppose organizations work that way?
33. Why do you think that didn't work?
34. Why do you think that happened that way?
35. Why do you think that worked?
36. Why do you think you have difficulties with that sometimes?
37. Would you have done it that way with looser deadlines?
38. Would you have done it that way with tighter deadlines?

E. Themes/Things to Look for:

Can work on pieces; doesn't have to have everything packaged first
Comfort with loose ends; doesn't have to finish things to feel good
Comfort with not knowing the answers in advance of the facts
Seeing situations as unique; answers aren't all the same
Taking a chance
Tries things just to see what will happen
Deals effectively with those having trouble with the ambiguity
Flexible, adaptable; admits mistakes and false starts
Learned as they went; didn't have the answers in advance of the facts
Maintains calm in a crisis/uncomfortable situation

F. Most Likely Résumé:

1. Look for jobs like:

Chair of Projects/Task Forces
Cross-Moves
Fix-Its/Turnarounds
Heavy Strategic Demands
International Assignments
Line to Staff Switches
Scope Assignments
Staff Leadership (Influencing Without Authority)
Start-Ups

DEALING WITH AMBIGUITY

2. Look for develop-in-place assignments like:

Integrate diverse systems, processes, or procedures across decentralized and/or dispersed units.

Go on a business trip to a foreign country you've not been to before.

Relaunch an existing product or service that's not doing well.

Manage an ad hoc, temporary group of balky and resisting people through an unpopular change or project.

Manage an ad hoc, temporary group of people where the people in the group are towering experts but the temporary manager is not.

Manage an ad hoc, temporary group of people involved in tackling a fix-it or turnaround project.

Assemble an ad hoc team of diverse people to accomplish a difficult task.

Take on a tough and undoable project, one where others who have tried it have failed.

Take on a task you dislike or hate to do.

Make peace with an enemy or someone you've disappointed with a product or service or someone you've had some trouble with or don't get along well with.

Build a multifunctional project team to tackle a common business issue or problem.

3. Best references to ask about or check:

Natural Mentors

Past Associates/Constituencies

Peers and Colleagues

G. Learning Agility Evaluation:

1. What/Describing vs. Why/Explain
3. Ordinary/Socially Acceptable vs. Insightful/Different
10. Reactive vs. Initiating
11. Generalizations vs. Specific Learnings
13. Simple Views vs. Complex Views
15. Linear vs. Uses Contrasts/Analogies
22. Accomplishments vs. Focusing on Learning from Problems

H. The LEADERSHIP ARCHITECT® Sort Card Connections:

1. Good (positive) if combined with high:

Unafraid to move forward at any time 1, 16, 57

Can deal comfortably with messy situations 8, 37, 38, 40, 48

Good under pressure 11, 41, 50

Deals comfortably with diversity 12, 21, 33, 41, 64

Flexible well organized manager 14, 39, 47, 50, 52, 53

Excellent learner 30, 32, 45, 51

Visionary; good planner 40, 46, 47, 58, 65

DEALING WITH AMBIGUITY

2. **Bad (negative) if combined with low or high (+):**
   Loose cannon, impatient, impulsive (1+) 41
   Lacks functional and/or business depth 5, 24, 46, 61
   Doesn't think things through 30, 51, 52, 53
   Fragments; doesn't know what's going on 35, 47, 50
   Doesn't follow through 39, 53
   Has no work process to handle the confusion 52, 59
   Comfort zone type; won't stand up or out 57

3. **Too much can contribute to the following Stallers and Stoppers:**

   A. *What too much looks like (overused):*

   May move to conclusions without enough data; may fill in gaps by adding things that aren't there; may frustrate others by not getting specific enough; may undervalue orderly problem solving; may reject precedent and history; may err toward the new and risky at the expense of proven solutions; may over-complicate things.

   B. *Too much might lead to these Stallers and Stoppers:*
   Failure to Staff Effectively (111)

   C. *Compensators:*
   How to compensate for too much of this competency:
   5, 17, 24, 30, 35, 39, 40, 47, 50, 51, 52, 59, 61, 63

   D. *Things to watch for:*
   Flitting from flower to flower; doesn't follow through   Rejects the old/current
   Makes half-baked decisions   Renders reactions and opinions too soon
   May make others uncomfortableLacks functional and/or business depth
   May operate in clutter and chaos

4. **Too little can contribute to the following Stallers and Stoppers:**

   A. *What too little looks like (unskilled):*

   Not comfortable with change or uncertainty; may not do well on fuzzy problems with no clear solution or outcome; may prefer more data than others, and structure over uncertainty; prefers things tacked down and sure; less efficient and productive under ambiguity; too quick to close; may have a strong need to finish everything; may like to do things the same way time after time.

   B. *Too little might lead to these Stallers and Stoppers:*
   Unable to Adapt to Differences (101)   Overmanaging (117)
   Blocked Personal Learner (106)   Performance Problems (118)
   Lack of Composure (107)   Political Missteps (119)
   Non-Strategic (114)

   C. *Compensators:*
   How to compensate for too much of this competency:
   1, 5, 12, 14, 16, 21, 28, 30, 32, 36, 39, 40, 46, 47, 50, 51, 52, 58

DEALING WITH AMBIGUITY

I. LEARNING ARCHITECT® Connections:

Look for people who act like and/or show evidence of:

1a. Pure Action	21. Changer
1b. Trial and Error	22. Experimenter
2a. Problem Solving	25. Personal Change
2b. Visioning	27. Conceptualizer
5. New	28. Creator
7. Risks	32. Diversity in Others
9. Multiple Sources	35. Breadth
10. Complexity	36. Comfort With Paradox
11. Why/How	37. Flexibility
12. Rules of Thumb	38. Resilience

J. CHOICES ARCHITECT® Connections:

Look for people who act like and/or show evidence of:

First Edition (Released 1994)
1. Inquisitive
3. Creator
4. Complexity
5. Connector
12. Experimenter
18. Into Everything
19. Tinkerer

Second Edition (Released 2000)
2. Complexity
3. Connector
5. Easy Shifter
7. Inquisitive
14. Open-Minded
20. Experimenter

K. Difficulty to Develop:
28 (of 34)–Harder

3. APPROACHABILITY

A. Definition:

Is easy to approach and talk to; spends the extra effort to put others at ease; can be warm, pleasant, and gracious; is sensitive to and patient with the interpersonal anxieties of others; builds rapport well; is a good listener; is an early knower, getting informal and incomplete information in time to do something about it.

B. Arenas/Domains to Explore:

1. Formal parties
2. Social network
3. Style across various levels/situations
4. Unfamiliar social settings
5. Work and non-work relationships
6. Handling interruptions
7. Meeting visitors
8. Initial work-related meetings
9. Dealing with those of lower status
10. Availability to different levels/groups

C. Sample Questions:

Dimension 1: Been there, done that–has had direct personal experience(s) involving the competency–candidate was the prime player   Note: * means OK for campus

1. Do people tend to seek you out to just talk?*
2. Have you ever managed anything where the people or units reporting to you were in different locations? How did you show your warmth and approachability?
3. How do you build rapport when meeting a new person?*
4. How do you make yourself available to bosses/peers/direct reports/clerical? All the same or different? Why?*
5. How do you make yourself available to parents, friends, classmates, etc? All the same or different? Why?*
6. How quickly do you get to the agenda of a meeting?*
7. How soon do you tend to learn about a piece of juicy work information?*
8. Tell me about a time when you had to communicate something important to someone who did not speak your language very well.
9. Tell me about a time when your lack of warmth and approachability got you into trouble.
10. Tell me about a time when your warmth and approachability worked really well for you.
11. What do you do to put people at ease?*
12. What do you do when people come to tell you something they'd rather not tell you?*
13. What do you do when people come to you with a personal problem?*
14. What do you do when people come to you with a problem, and you think they're wrong?*
15. What do you do when people come to you with a problem that seems unimportant to you?*
16. What do you do when people come to you with a work problem?*
17. What do you do when someone makes you uncomfortable, and you don't want to argue with them?*
18. What is the usual first impression you leave with new people?*
19. What off-work (extracurricular) activities do you engage in?*
20. When and how do you usually get information about important events?*
21. When are you the least approachable?*
22. When are you the most approachable?*
23. When someone walks in with a need to talk, and you absolutely don't have the time, what do you say and do?*

APPROACHABILITY

Dimension 2: Seen/been around others who were involved with the competency–good and bad; learns from others about self

24. Contrast the most and least approachable people you know.*
25. Has approachability ever been in any 360° survey done on you? Was your score among your highest, middle, or lowest?
26. Has poor approachability on someone else's part ever created an obstacle for you or got in the way of something you were trying to accomplish?*
27. Have you ever talked about your approachability with a coach or mentor?
28. Have you ever watched someone fail/get fired because they were not approachable enough?*
29. Have you ever watched someone overdo approachability to the point that it backfired?
30. Have you ever watched someone succeed because they were approachable and able to put people at ease?*
31. Have you ever worked with a coach on being more approachable?*
32. Have you ever worked with a person who excelled at approachability?
33. Have you ever worked with a skills coach on improving your approachability?*
34. How do you get feedback about your approachability?
35. How often do you check with multiple sources when you get a piece of critical feedback on your approachability?
36. Is there a historical figure you consider a model of approachability?
37. What do others who are not your fans say about your approachability?
38. What do others who like you say about your approachability?
39. Which boss was the best at being approachable?
40. Which boss was the worst at being approachable?
41. Which direct report was the best at being approachable?
42. Which direct report was the worst at being approachable?
43. Which peer was the best at being approachable?
44. Which peer was the worst at being approachable?
45. Who in your field or business is the most approachable person?
46. Who do you consider a role model of being approachable?*
47. Who do you go to for advice on being more approachable?
48. Who have you learned the most from about approachability?*
49. Who is a higher-management role model for you on being approachable?
50. Who is a role model of being approachable outside of work?

Dimension 3: Knows how the competency works in theory; shows understanding

51. Are there situations or settings where someone should be more or less approachable?
52. Do you think approachability can be learned? If so, how do you think people develop approachability skills?
53. Do you think there is a way to compensate or work around low approachability skills?
54. Has anyone asked you for your opinions/advice on being approachable?*
55. Have you ever attended a course on approachability?
56. Have you ever been in a situation where you and others put approachability on a success profile?
57. Have you ever been part of an effort to create a policy or a mission statement containing reference to the importance of being approachable?
58. Have you ever been someone's coach or mentor who had problems with approachability?
59. Have you ever created a development plan for someone on approachability?
60. Have you ever criticized someone for not being approachable?

APPROACHABILITY

61. Have you ever designed a program on approachability?
62. Have you ever given a speech on approachability?
63. Have you ever rewarded or recognized someone for being approachable?
64. Have you ever taught a course on approachability?
65. Have you ever tried to help someone become more approachable?*
66. How do you think people develop approachability skills?
67. How much approachability is good to have and how much is too much?
68. How much of success do you think is due to approachability compared with other characteristics?
69. How would you know if someone is unapproachable?
70. How would you know if someone is approachable?
71. If you had to write a book on approachability, what would the chapter headings be?
72. What are the benefits to someone who is really good at being approachable?
73. What are the consequences to someone who is really poor at being approachable?
74. What do you think the performance standard is on approachability for someone in your role?
75. What happens if you are too approachable?
76. What happens when two people try to work together who are very different in their approachability?
77. What wisdom would you pass onto others trying to become better at being approachable?
78. When you select others, what do you look for in approachability?
79. Why do you think people end up being having different approachability skills?

Dimension 4: Shows personal change and sense-making; learned it one place and applied it in another; can compare and contrast experiences; changes viewpoints across time; can explain personal development or evolution related to the competency

80. Compare and contrast examples of times when you've been approachable and unapproachable.
81. Contrast your on- and off-the-job use of approachability.
82. Did you ever pass up a job or assignment because you were not confident enough in your approachability?
83. Do you ever use other skills to cover for your lack of approachability?
84. Has approachability ever figured in a failure, struggle, or setback you have had?
85. Has becoming more approachable ever helped you in other areas?
86. Has approachability ever been the subject of a development plan for you?
87. Has your approachability always been this way?
88. Have you ever delegated or assigned someone a task because you weren't particularly approachable?
89. Have you ever made significant strides at becoming more approachable?
90. Have your approachability skills, good or bad, ever been the subject of your performance review or a career discussion?
91. How different are you across situations in your approachability?
92. How do you decide how approachable to be?
93. How have you adjusted your style or work habits to make yourself more accessible to others?
94. How have you modified the way you set boundaries over the years so that major chunks of time aren't eaten away?
95. How much of your success is due to your approachability?
96. How transferable are your approachability skills to other situations?
97. If you had to become better at becoming approachable in a hurry, what would you do?
98. Was there a time when you were not as approachable?

APPROACHABILITY

99. What caused you to work to change your approachability?
100. What event or series of events had the most impact on your approachability?
101. What's the most varied you can be in approachability?
102. What was the shortest amount of time in which you learned to deal with approachability?
103. When did you first realize your level of skill at being approachable?
104. When you know ahead of time that your usual level of approachability won't work, what do you do?
105. Why do you think you deal with approachability the way you do?
106. Why do you think your approachability is the way it is?*

D. Follow-up Probes:
1. Are there times when you're not like this or wouldn't do this?
2. Are there times when you approach situations like that and times when you don't?
3. Could you contrast those two bosses for me?
4. Could you give me a few examples of how you've used or applied that?
5. Do you suppose if others would just try harder, they could learn to be more approachable like you?
6. Do you think this is teachable?
7. Do you think you're better at approachability than most? Why?
8. Do you think you would perform any better if you took a different tack toward approachability?
9. Have you ever had to form a relationship with someone you really disliked to get your job done?
10. How did the others react when you did that?
11. How did you come up with that approach in the first place?
12. How do others you have known approach that?
13. How far will you go before you cut line and try another approach?
14. How much did you have to give up to make it work?
15. How typical is this for you?
16. How would you approach that same situation today?
17. Is this natural for you, or do you really have to dig for it?
18. Was that a fair way to maneuver around them?
19. Was there a time when you didn't understand this about yourself?
20. What did you do after you got that feedback?
21. What did you do to adapt to that?
22. What did you learn from that?
23. Why did you choose that approach?
24. Why did you decide to take the risk?
25. Why did you do it that way?
26. Why did you time your attempt like you did?
27. Why do you suppose organizations work that way?
28. Why do you think that didn't work?
29. Why do you think that happened that way?
30. Why do you think that worked?
31. Why do you think you have difficulties with that sometimes?
32. Would you have done it that way with looser deadlines?
33. Would you have done it that way with tighter deadlines?

APPROACHABILITY

E. Themes/Things to Look For:

Attracting others without any effort on their part
Graciousness
Making others feel at ease quickly
Optimistic
People give them free things, special opportunities
Positive aura, glow
Protecting others' feelings, whether they agree or not
Revealing a lot of self
Sensitivity and empathy
Sharing information/feelings willingly
Treating others as guests
Warm, welcoming behavior

F. Most Likely Résumé:

1. Look for jobs like:

Staff Leadership (Influencing Without Authority)

2. Look for develop-in-place assignments like:

Study humor in business settings; read books on the nature of humor; collect cartoons you could use in presentations; study funny people around you; keep a log of funny jokes and sayings you hear; read famous speeches and study how humor was used; attend comedy clubs; ask a funny person to act as your tutor; practice funny lines and jokes with others.

Lobby for your organization on a contested issue in local, regional, state, or federal government.

Create employee involvement teams.

Train customers in the use of the organization's products or services.

Manage an ad hoc, temporary group of "green," inexperienced people as their coach, teacher, orienter, etc.

Help shut down a plant, regional office, product line, business, operation, etc.

Manage a dissatisfied internal or external customer; troubleshoot a performance or quality problem with a product or service.

Manage the outplacement of a group of people.

Resolve an issue in conflict between two people, units, geographies, functions, etc.

Make peace with an enemy or someone you've disappointed with a product or service or someone you've had some trouble with or don't get along well with.

3. Best references to ask about or check:

Customers	Past Associates/Constituencies
Human Resource Professionals	Peers and Colleagues
Assigned Mentors	Spouse
Natural Mentors	Direct Reports
Off-Work Associates	

APPROACHABILITY

G. Learning Agility Evaluation:
   4. Spectator/Passive vs. Player/Participant
   7. Passive vs. Intrigued/Curious
   10. Reactive vs. Initiating
   12. Always Has a Rehearsed Answer vs. Candid
   17. Won't Face Weaknesses vs. Comfortable with Weaknesses
   21. Focus on Self vs. Focus on Others

H. The LEADERSHIP ARCHITECT® Sort Card Connections:

1. Good (positive) if combined with high:
Liked by higher management 4, 8, 48
Good counselor/shoulder to cry on 7, 10, 11, 29, 33, 41
More successful negotiator 8, 31, 37, 39, 48
More effective confronter 12, 13, 31, 34, 57
Good getting information from customers 15, 33
Can lighten up tense situations 26, 49
More likely to be listened to 34, 57
More likely to get others to work with them 42, 60

2. Bad (negative) if combined with low or high (+):
May try to get by with being nice 5, 24, 61
More style than substance, slick (+6, 31, 38, 48, 49)
Smoothes over, may need to be liked too much, conflict avoider 7, 10, 12, 13, 34, 57
May become too much of a counselor (+7, 10, 33, 41, 64) 50, 62
Too little structure 18, 20, 34, 39, 47
Doesn't focus on work results 17, 50, 53

3. Too much can contribute to the following Stallers and Stoppers:

A. What too much looks like (overused):
May waste too much time rapport-building in meetings; may be misinterpreted as easygoing or easy to influence; may have too strong a desire to be liked; may avoid necessary negative or unpleasant transactions; may try to smooth over real issues and problems.

B. Too much might lead to these Stallers and Stoppers:
None Apply

C. Compensators:
How to compensate for too much of this competency:
   1, 5, 9, 12, 13, 16, 17, 20, 30, 34, 35, 37, 43, 50, 53, 57, 65

APPROACHABILITY

D. Things to watch for:

Can't inspire groups

Conflict avoider

If people would just talk to each other, there would be no problems

Never met a person I didn't like

Not taken seriously

"They got into it and I just left... ."

Focuses on people results much more than work results

4. Too little can contribute to the following Stallers and Stoppers:

A. What too little looks like (unskilled):

Distant, not easy to be around; not comfortable with first contacts; may be shy, cool, or a person of few words; doesn't reveal much, hard to know what they are really like; doesn't build rapport, may be a "let's get on with it" type; may be a poor listener or appear uninterested; may not pick up on social cues that others would recognize; may be tense; transactions don't go smoothly.

B. Too little might lead to these Stallers and Stoppers:

Arrogant (104)	Insensitive to Others (112)
Defensiveness (108)	Political Missteps (119)
Failure to Build a Team (110)	
Failure to Staff Effectively (111)	

C. Compensators:

How to substitute for too little of this competency:

4, 7, 10, 11, 15, 21, 23, 27, 31, 33, 41, 42, 60

I. LEARNING ARCHITECT® Connections:

Look for people who act like and/or show evidence of:

3a. Checking Feelings	34. Sizing Up Others
3b. Self-Talk	32. Diversity in Others
4a. Getting Information	24. Discloser
4c. Actively Involve	23. Orchestrator
9. Multiple Sources	16. Collaborate

J. CHOICES ARCHITECT® Connections:

Look for people who act like and/or show evidence of:

First Edition (Released 1994)	Second Edition (Released 2000)
14. Transaction Quality	14. Open-Minded
17. Hot/Direct Sources	15. People-Smart

K. Difficulty to Develop:

24 (of 34)–Moderate

APPROACHABILITY

4. BOSS RELATIONSHIPS

A. Definition:

Responds and relates well to bosses; would work harder for a good boss; is open to learning from bosses who are good coaches and who provide latitude; likes to learn from those who have been there before; easy to challenge and develop; is comfortably coachable.

B. Arenas/Domains to Explore:

1. Bosses
2. Coaches
3. Good times/bad times with authority figures
4. Grandparents
5. Law enforcement officers
6. Liked/disliked authority figures
7. Military commanders/officers
8. Older siblings
9. Parents
10. Religious leaders
11. Scout leaders
12. Teachers
13. Team captains
14. Senior managers

C. Sample Questions:

*Dimension 1: Been there, done that–has had direct personal experience(s) involving the competency–candidate was the prime player   Note: * means OK for campus*

1. Have different bosses led you to working differently or harder?
2. Have you and your boss ever been in different locations? How did you maintain your relationship?
3. Have you ever contributed to a boss' downfall?
4. Have you ever contributed to making a boss more successful?
5. Have you ever managed anything where the boss you were reporting to was in a different location? How did you build a relationship?
6. How are you different around bosses?
7. How have you dealt with a boss you don't respect?
8. How have you dealt with a boss you don't like?
9. Tell me about a time when you had to disagree with a boss/teacher/parent/person in authority.
10. Tell me about a time when you had to present bad news to a boss/teacher/parent/person in authority.*
11. Tell me about a time when you helped a boss/teacher/parent/person in authority reach their goals.*
12. Tell me about a time when your ability to relate to your boss worked really well for you.
13. Tell me about a time when your inability to relate to your boss got you into trouble.
14. Tell me about your best boss.
15. Tell me about your worst boss.
16. What do bosses like and dislike about working with you?
17. What do you like and dislike in a boss/teacher/parent/person in authority?*
18. What have your teachers/professors liked and disliked about having you in class?*
19. What kind of a boss/teacher/parent/person in authority are you?*
20. Which boss was the best coach?
21. Which boss was the worst coach?

BOSS RELATIONSHIPS

Dimension 2: Seen/been around others who were involved with the competency–good and bad; learns from others about self

22. Contrast the most and least boss relationship-oriented people you know.*
23. Has boss relationships ever been in any 360° survey done on you? Was your score among your highest, middle, or lowest?
24. Has poor boss relationships on someone else's part ever created an obstacle for you or got in the way of something you were trying to accomplish?*
25. Have you ever talked about your relationships with your bosses with a coach or mentor?
26. Have you ever watched someone fail/get fired because they did not relate well with bosses?*
27. Have you ever watched someone overdo forming a relationship with their boss to the point that it backfired?
28. Have you ever watched someone succeed because they interacted well with bosses?*
29. Have you ever worked with a coach on boss relationships?*
30. Have you ever worked with a person who excelled at boss relationships?
31. Have you ever worked with a skills coach on improving your boss relationships?*
32. How do you get feedback about the relationships you have with your bosses?
33. How often do you check with multiple sources when you get a piece of critical feedback on your relationship with your boss?
34. Is there a historical figure you consider a model of boss relationships?
35. What do others who are not your fans say about your relationship with your boss?
36. What do others who like you say about your relationship with your boss?
37. Which boss was the best at boss relationships?
38. Which boss was the worst at boss relationships?
39. Which direct report was the best at boss relationships?
40. Which direct report was the worst at boss relationships?
41. Which peer was the best at dealing with bosses?
42. Which peer was the worst at dealing with bosses?
43. Who in your field or business deals the best with boss relationships?
44. Who do you consider a role model of effective relationships with bosses?*
45. Who do you go to for advice on relating with your boss?
46. Who have you learned the most from about boss relationships?*
47. Who is a higher-management role model for you on boss relationships?
48. Who is a role model of boss relationships outside of work?

Dimension 3: Knows how the competency works in theory; shows understanding

49. Are there situations or settings where someone should relate to their boss differently?
50. Do you think boss relationship skills can be learned? If so, how do you think people develop these skills?
51. Do you think there is a way to compensate or work around low boss-relationship skills?
52. Has anyone asked you for your opinions/advice on boss relationships?*
53. Have you ever attended a course on boss relationships?
54. Have you ever been in a situation where you and others put boss relationships on a success profile?
55. Have you ever been part of an effort to create a policy or a mission statement containing reference to boss relationships?
56. Have you ever been someone's coach or mentor who had problems with boss relationships?
57. Have you ever created a development plan for someone on boss relationships?
58. Have you ever criticized someone for not relating well with their boss?

BOSS RELATIONSHIPS

59. Have you ever designed a program on boss relationships?
60. Have you ever given a speech on boss relationships?
61. Have you ever rewarded or recognized someone for relating well with their boss?
62. Have you ever taught a course on boss relationships?
63. Have you ever tried to help someone deal with more effectively with their boss?*
64. Have you ever tried to help someone improve their boss relationships?
65. How do you think people develop boss relationship skills?
66. How much of success do you think is due to relating well with your boss compared with other characteristics?
67. How would you know if someone is bad at boss relationships?
68. How would you know if someone is good at boss relationships?
69. If you had to write a book on relating with your boss, what would the chapter headings be?
70. What are the benefits to someone who is really good at boss relationships?
71. What are the consequences to someone who is really poor at boss relationships?
72. What do you think the performance standard is on boss relationships for someone in your role?
73. What happens if you rely too heavily on boss relationships?
74. What happens when two people try to work together who are very different in the way they get along with their bosses?
75. What wisdom would you pass onto others trying to become better at relating well with their boss?
76. When you select others, what do you look for in boss-relationship skills?
77. Why do you think people end up being different in the way they get along with their bosses?

Dimension 4: Shows personal change and sense-making; learned it one place and applied it in another; can compare and contrast experiences; changes viewpoints across time; can explain personal development or evolution related to the competency

78. Compare and contrast examples of times when you've had effective and ineffective boss relationships.
79. Contrast your on- and off-the-job use of boss relationships.
80. Did you ever pass up a job or assignment because you were not confident enough in your boss relationships?
81. Do you ever use other skills to cover for your lack of boss relationship skills?
82. Has getting better at boss relationships ever helped you in other areas?
83. Have your boss relationships always been this way?
84. Have boss relationships ever figured in a failure, struggle, or setback you have had?
85. Have poor boss relationships ever been the subject of a development plan for you?
86. Have you ever delegated or assigned someone a task because you didn't have good relationships with bosses?
87. Have you ever made significant strides at getting better at boss relationships?
88. Have your relationships with bosses, good or bad, ever been the subject of your performance review or a career discussion?
89. How different are you across situations in your boss relationships?
90. How do you decide how focused to be on boss relationships?
91. How have you changed the way you anticipate your bosses' needs over the years?
92. How much of your success is due to your boss relationships?
93. How transferable are your boss relationship skills to other situations?
94. If you had to become better at boss relationships in a hurry, what would you do?

BOSS RELATIONSHIPS

95. Was there a time when you were not good at boss relationships?
96. What caused you to work to change your skill at boss relationships?
97. What event or series of events had the most impact on your relationships with bosses?
98. What's the most varied you can be in boss relationships?
99. What was the shortest amount of time in which you increased your level of skill at boss relationships?
100. When did you first realize your level of skill at boss relationships?
101. When you know ahead of time that your usual way of relating to bosses won't work, what do you do?
102. Why do you think you deal with boss relationships the way you do?
103. Why do you think your boss relationships are the way they are?*
104. Why have you had better relationships with some bosses than others?

D. Follow-up Probes:

1. Are there times when you're not like this or wouldn't do this?
2. Are there times when you deal with bosses/teacher/parent/person in authority like that and times when you don't?
3. Could you contrast those two bosses for me?
4. Could you give me a few examples of how you've used or applied that?
5. Did you or the other person blink first?
6. Do you suppose if others would just try harder, they could learn to deal with those in authority more like you do?
7. Do you think this is teachable?
8. Do you think you're better at dealing with those in authority than most? Why?
9. Do you think you would perform any better if you dealt with those in authority differently?
10. Have you ever had to form a relationship with someone you really disliked to get your job done?
11. Have you changed your initial assessment of this person?
12. How did they react when you did that?
13. How did you come up with that approach in the first place?
14. How did you know that method of getting over that barrier would work?
15. How did you set boundaries in the relationship?
16. How do others you have known approach that?
17. How far did you go to try to be a team player?
18. How far will you go before you cut line and try another approach?
19. How much did you have to give up to make it work?
20. How typical is this for you?
21. How would you approach that same situation today?
22. Is this natural for you, or do you really have to dig for it?
23. Was that a fair way to maneuver around them?
24. Was there a time when you didn't understand this about yourself?
25. What did you do after you got that feedback?
26. What did you do to adapt to that?
27. What did you learn from that?
28. Why did they intimidate you?
29. Why did you choose that approach?

BOSS RELATIONSHIPS

30. Why did you decide to take the risk?
31. Why did you do it that way?
32. Why did you time your attempt like you did?
33. Why do you suppose organizations work that way?
34. Why do you think that didn't work?
35. Why do you think that happened that way?
36. Why do you think that worked?
37. Why do you think you have difficulties like that once in a while?
38. Would you have done it that way with looser deadlines?
39. Would you have done it that way with tighter deadlines?

E. Themes/Things to Look for:

Ability to get through (tolerate/cope with) bad (tense) conflicts with authority

Able to discuss past, bad boss with humor

Awareness of own impact on bosses and people in authority

Candid descriptions of bosses–you can "see" the person described

Complex and varied strategies for dealing with boss issues

Complexity in view of bosses–some good in the bad ones and some bad in the good ones

Empathy for the boss' or person in authority's position and problems

Focuses on helping boss(es) achieve their goals too

Knows how to disagree with authority figures

Can couch issues well

F. Most Likely Résumé:

1. Look for jobs like:

Chair of Projects/Task Forces
Fix-Its/Turnarounds
Heavy Strategic Demands
Line to Staff Switches
Scope (complexity) Assignments
Staff Leadership (Influencing Without Authority)
Start-Ups

2. Look for develop-in-place assignments like:

Manage the renovation of an office, floor, building, meeting room, warehouse, etc.

Plan an off-site meeting, conference, convention, trade show, event, etc.

Write a proposal for a new policy, process, mission, charter, product, service, or system, and present and sell it to top management.

Relaunch an existing product or service that's not doing well.

Serve on a junior or shadow board.

Manage an ad hoc, temporary group of people involved in tackling a fix-it or turnaround project.

Manage the interface between consultants and the organization on a critical assignment.

Prepare and present a proposal of some consequence to top management.

Work on a team that's deciding who to keep and who to let go in a layoff, shutdown, delayering, or divestiture.

Manage a group through a significant business crisis.

Write a speech for someone higher up in the organization.

Build a multifunctional project team to tackle a common business issue or problem.

BOSS RELATIONSHIPS

3. Best references to ask about or check:
Direct Boss
Boss' Boss(es)
Development Professionals
Human Resource Professionals
Natural Mentors

G. Learning Agility Evaluation:
2. All or Nothing vs. Can See Many Sides
6. Reactive/Responsive vs. Adapting
9. Vague/General vs. Sharp/Specific
12. Rehearsed/Socially Acceptable vs. Candid
13. Simple Views vs. Complex Views
19. External Standards vs. Internal Standards
21. View from Self vs. View from Point of View of Others

H. The LEADERSHIP ARCHITECT® Sort Card Connections:

1. Good (positive) if combined with high:
Gets along well with higher management 3, 8, 31, 48
Is able to deliver negative "messages/information" to boss 12, 34, 57
Is able to get support for their direct reports 19, 21, 25, 37, 56
Good team player 42, 60

2. Bad (negative) if combined with low or high (+):
May be given too many opportunities to make excuses 1, 53
Over-relies on boss for sole source of counsel 3, 31, 42, 54, 60, 64
"It's who you know more than what you know" 5, 24, 61
Overambitious; politician (+6, 8, 39, 48)
Uses boss' name/authority to deliver negative messages 9, 12, 57
May not treat the less powerful well (+9, 34, 35) 7, 10
"It's who you know and not how you think" 17, 30, 32, 45, 51, 58

3. Too much can contribute to the following Stallers and Stoppers:

A. *What too much looks like (overused):*
May be overdependent on bosses and high-status figures for advice and counsel; may shut out other sources of feedback and learning; may pick the wrong boss to model.

B. *Too much might lead to these Stallers and Stoppers:*
Overly Ambitious (103)
Overdependence on an Advocate (115)

C. *Compensators:*
How to compensate for too much of this competency:
1, 17, 34, 38, 45, 51, 53, 54, 57

BOSS RELATIONSHIPS

D. Things to watch for:

Defends a bad boss with peers
Doesn't form a network with other potential bosses
May have been fired with their boss in a purge
May model bad characteristics of a boss
"My boss would like you to do this"; name dropper
Few stand-alone achievements
Mentions people and their reactions much more than problem-solving behavior

4. Too little can contribute to the following Stallers and Stoppers:

A. What too little looks like (unskilled):

Not comfortable with bosses; may be tense in boss' presence; may not be open to coaching or direction from bosses; problems dealing comfortably with authority; poor boss relationships get in the way of working productively.

B. Too little might lead to these Stallers and Stoppers:

Unable to Adapt to Differences (101)	Insensitive to Others (122)
Arrogant (104)	Political Missteps (119)

C. Compensators:

How to substitute for too little of this competency:
3, 11, 12, 15, 27, 29, 33, 37, 41, 48

I. LEARNING ARCHITECT® Connections:

Look for people who act like and/or show evidence of:

4a. Getting Information	4c. Actively Involve
4b. Modeling	16. Collaborate

J. CHOICES ARCHITECT® Connections:

Look for people who act like and/or show evidence of:

First Edition (Released 1994)	Second Edition (Released 2000)
14. Transaction Quality	15. People-Smart

K. Difficulty to Develop:

25 (of 34)–Moderate

BOSS RELATIONSHIPS

5. BUSINESS ACUMEN

A. Definition:

Knows how businesses work; knowledgeable in current and possible future policies, practices, trends, technology, and information affecting his/her business and organization; knows the competition; is aware of how strategies and tactics work in the marketplace.

B. Arenas/Domains to Explore:

1. Breadth of business knowledge
2. Classical examples of successful and sailed businesses
3. Financial workings of companies
4. General business tactics
5. Global finance
6. Government/business relationships
7. How things work in business
8. Knowledge of competitors
9. Reading habits in business
10. Understanding of market Forces
11. Wall Street/financial markets

C. Sample Questions:

Dimension 1: Been there, done that–has had direct personal experience(s) involving the competency–candidate was the prime player   Note: * means OK for campus

1. Do you think you are better than others at strategy or tactics ?
2. Does government help or hurt your business?
3. Have you ever started up a business?
4. Have you ever taken over a struggling business?
5. How is doing business around the world different?
6. Tell me about a time when your lack of business knowledge got you into trouble.
7. Tell me about a time when your understanding of business worked really well for you.
8. Tell me about the least successful business you have worked for.
9. Tell me about the most successful business you have worked for.
10. Tell me three business moves you executed that didn't work.
11. Tell me three business moves you executed that worked.
12. Tell me three edges your competitors have.
13. What are the core competencies of your business?
14. What are your major sources of business information?*
15. What newspapers/magazines do you read?*

Dimension 2: Seen/been around others who were involved with the competency–good and bad; learns from others about self

16. Contrast the most and least business savvy people you know.*
17. Has business savvy or acumen ever been in any 360° survey done on you? Was your score among your highest, middle, or lowest?
18. Has poor business savvy or acumen on someone else's part ever created an obstacle for you or got in the way of something you were trying to accomplish?*
19. Have you ever talked about your business acumen with a coach or mentor?
20. Have you ever watched someone fail/get fired because they did not have business acumen?*
21. Have you ever watched someone overdo business savvy to the point that it backfired?

BUSINESS ACUMEN

22. Have you ever watched someone succeed because of their business savvy?*
23. Have you ever worked with a coach on business acumen?*
24. Have you ever worked with a person who excelled at business savvy or acumen?
25. Have you ever worked with a skills coach on improving your business savvy?*
26. How do you get feedback about your business acumen?
27. How often do you check with multiple sources when you get a piece of critical feedback on your business savvy or acumen?
28. Is there a historical figure you consider a model of business savvy?
29. What do others who are not your fans say about your business savvy?
30. What do others who like you say about your business savvy?
31. Which boss was the best at business acumen?
32. Which boss was the worst at business acumen?
33. Which direct report was the best at business acumen?
34. Which direct report was the worst at business acumen?
35. Which peer was the best at business acumen?
36. Which peer was the worst at business acumen?
37. Who in your field or business deals the best with business acumen?
38. Who do you consider a role model of business acumen?*
39. Who do you go to for advice on business acumen?
40. Who have you learned the most from about business acumen?*
41. Who is a higher-management role model for you on business acumen?
42. Who is a role model of business acumen outside of work?

Dimension 3: Knows how the competency works in theory; shows understanding
43. Does government help or hurt business?*
44. How could a business be very profitable but not have any cash?
45. How do new businesses get started?
46. How do the stock, commodity, and bond markets work?*
47. What are the biggest business failures in your view?
48. What are the drivers of a successful business?
49. What difference does it make to organize in a centralized vs. decentralized way?*
50. Are there situations or settings where someone should demonstrate business savvy differently?
51. What happens when there are too many competitors in one market?
52. What is the difference between the leading edge and the bleeding edge?
53. What role does a "corporate culture" play in the success of a company?
54. Which business organizations do you think are doing the best job?*
55. What is the difference between push and pull marketing?
56. Why do number one businesses fail?
57. Why do the majority of startups fail?
58. What are the greatest business successes in your view?
59. Are there situations or settings where someone should use their business acumen skills differently?
60. Do you think business savvy can be learned? If so, how do you think people develop business savvy skills?
61. Do you think there is a way to compensate or work around being low in business acumen skills?
62. Has anyone asked you for your opinions/advice on business acumen?*

BUSINESS ACUMEN

63. Have you ever attended a course on business acumen?
64. Have you ever been in a situation where you and others put business savvy or acumen on a success profile?
65. Have you ever been part of an effort to create a policy or a mission statement containing reference to the importance of business savvy?
66. Have you ever been someone's coach or mentor who had problems with business acumen?
67. Have you ever created a development plan for someone on business acumen?
68. Have you ever criticized someone for not having business savvy?
69. Have you ever designed a program on business acumen?
70. Have you ever given a speech on business acumen?
71. Have you ever rewarded or recognized someone for having business savvy?
72. Have you ever taught a course on business acumen?
73. Have you ever tried to help someone deal with business acumen more effectively?*
74. Have you ever tried to help someone improve their business acumen?
75. How do you think people develop business acumen skills?
76. How much business savvy is good to have and how much is too much?
77. How much of success do you think is due to business savvy compared with other characteristics?
78. How would you know if someone has business savvy?
79. How would you know if someone does not have business savvy?
80. If you had to write a book on business acumen, what would the chapter headings be?
81. Tell me about an unusual market reaction to a product/strategy/service and what this meant to you.
82. What are the benefits to someone who has good business acumen?
83. What are the consequences to someone who has poor business acumen?
84. What do you think the performance standard is on business savvy or acumen for someone in your role?
85. What happens when two people try to work together who have very different business acumen skills?
86. What wisdom would you pass onto others trying to develop business acumen skills?
87. When you select others, what do you look for in business acumen skills?
88. Why do you think people end up having different business acumen skills?

Dimension 4: Shows personal change and sense-making; learned it one place and applied it in another; can compare and contrast experiences; changes viewpoints across time; can explain personal development or evolution related to the competency

89. Compare and contrast examples of times when you've been effective and ineffective at knowing how businesses work.
90. Contrast your on- and off-the-job use of business acumen.
91. Did you ever pass up a job or assignment because you were not confident enough in your business acumen skills?
92. Do you ever use other skills to cover for your lack of business acumen?
93. Has business acumen ever figured in a failure, struggle, or setback you have had?
94. Has getting better at knowing how businesses work ever helped you in other areas?
95. Has poor business acumen ever been the subject of a development plan for you?
96. Has your business acumen always been this way?
97. Have you ever delegated or assigned someone a task because you didn't have the needed level of business acumen?
98. Have you ever made significant strides at getting better at business acumen?

BUSINESS ACUMEN

99. Have your business acumen skills, good or bad, ever been the subject of your performance review or a career discussion?
100. How different are you across situations in your business acumen?
101. How do you decide the appropriate level of business acumen a situation requires?
102. How have you determined the business knowledge needed to be effective in different jobs that you've held?
103. How much of your success is due to your business acumen?
104. How transferable are your business acumen skills to other situations?
105. If you had to become better at business acumen in a hurry, what would you do?
106. Was there a time when you were not good at knowing how businesses works?
107. What caused you to work to change your skills at business acumen?
108. What event or series of events had the most impact on your business acumen?
109. What have you done to enhance your level of business knowledge to make yourself more marketable?
110. What's the most varied you can be in business acumen?
111. What was the shortest amount of time in which you increased your level of business acumen?
112. When did you first realize your level of skill at business acumen?
113. When you know ahead of time that your usual level of business acumen won't work, what do you do?
114. Why do you think you deal with business acumen the way you do?
115. Why do you think your business acumen is the way it is?*

D. Follow-up Probes:
1. Are there times when you're not like this or wouldn't do this?
2. Are there times when you would do that and times when you wouldn't?
3. Can you think of another example of that somewhere else?
4. Could you contrast those two bosses for me?
5. Could you give me a few examples of how you've used or applied that?
6. Do you suppose if others would just try harder, they could learn to be more business-oriented like you?
7. Do you think this is teachable?
8. Do you think you're better at business acumen than most? Why?
9. Do you think you would perform any better if you thought about business issues differently?
10. How did you come up with that approach to that issue in the first place?
11. How do others you have known approach that?
12. How far will you go before you cut line and try another approach?
13. How often do you use the "Let's meet in the middle" approach?
14. How typical is this for you?
15. How would you approach that same situation today?
16. What did you do to adapt to that?
17. What did you learn from that?
18. Why did you choose that approach?
19. Why did you decide to take the risk?
20. Why did you do it that way?
21. Why did you time your attempt like you did?
22. Why do you suppose organizations work that way?
23. Why do you think they are so successful?

BUSINESS ACUMEN

24. Why do you think that didn't work?
25. Why do you think that happened that way?
26. Why do you think that worked?
27. Would you have done it that way with looser deadlines?
28. Would you have done it that way with tighter deadlines?

E. Themes/Things to Look for:

Simultaneous consideration of elements like market business segments, functional matters, related functions, competitors, related/unrelated businesses, unrelated organizations (analogies), the economy, social/demographic trends, knowledge of market psychology

The difference between innovations vs. repeats/me-too variations

Understanding of interrelationships among elements

Understanding trends vs. just stating facts

Analyze and implement rather than just analyze

Looks for principles that are repeatable

F. Most Likely Résumé:

1. Look for jobs like:

Chair of Projects/Task Forces	Scale (size shift) Assignments
Cross-Moves	Scope (complexity) Assignments
Fix-Its/Turnarounds	Staff to Line Shifts
Heavy Strategic Demands	Staff Leadership (Influencing Without Authority)
Member of Projects/Task Forces	Start-Ups
International Assignments	

2. Look for develop-in-place assignments like:

Launch a new product, service, or process.

Relaunch an existing product or service that's not doing well.

Work on a team forming a joint venture or partnership.

Work on a team looking at a reorganization plan where there will be more people than positions.

3. Best references to ask about or check:

Direct Boss	Natural Mentors
Boss' Boss(es)	Past Associates/Constituencies

BUSINESS ACUMEN

G. Learning Agility Evaluation:
1. What/Describing vs. Why/Explain
3. Ordinary/Socially Acceptable vs. Insightful/Different
7. Passive vs. Intrigued/Curious
11. Generalizations vs. Specific Learnings
13. Simple Views vs. Complex Views
14. Sameness vs. Broad Ranging
15. Linear vs. Use Contrasts/Analogies
16. Few Rules of Thumb vs. Many and Varied Rules of Thumb

H. The LEADERSHIP ARCHITECT® Sort Card Connections:

1. Good (positive) if combined with high:
Can get things done 9, 39, 53
Effective visionary 15, 24, 46, 58, 65
Plans accurately, sets good goals 35, 47, 50
Good at designing organizations 38, 52, 59, 63

2. Bad (negative) if combined with low or high (+):
Knows but doesn't act 1, 9, 12, 57
Repetitious, me too; can't act beyond current knowledge 14, 28, 46
Misses the customer; too focused internally 15, 63 (+6, 8, 48)
May rather think and plan than do; may not implement well (+17, 30, 32, 40, 51, 58) 1, 53
Can't consistently get things done 39, 47, 52, 59, 63
Not interested in personal development 45, 54, 55, 61

3. Too much can contribute to the following Stallers and Stoppers:

A. What too much looks like (overused):
May overdevelop or depend upon industry and business knowledge and skills at the expense of personal, interpersonal, managerial, and leadership skills.

B. Too much might lead to these Stallers and Stoppers:
Arrogant (104)	Insensitive to Others (112)
Defensiveness (108)	Overmanaging (117)

C. Compensators:
How to compensate for too much of this competency:
14, 24, 30, 32, 45, 46, 54, 57, 58, 61

D. Things to watch for:
All business/narrow	Too much time learning, too little time doing
Can't reduce down to the here and now/knows too much	Not customer-oriented
Disinterest in the details	

BUSINESS ACUMEN

4. **Too little can contribute to the following Stallers and Stoppers:**

    A. *What too little looks like (unskilled):*

    Doesn't understand how businesses work; not knowledgeable and up-to-date about current and future policies, trends, technology, and information affecting his/her business and organization; doesn't know the competition; is unaware of how strategies and tactics work in the marketplace.

    B. *Too little might lead to these Stallers and Stoppers:*
    Non-Strategic (114)
    Performance Problems (118)

    C. *Compensators:*
    How to substitute for too little of this competency:
    8, 15, 24, 30, 32, 38, 46, 52, 58, 65

I. **LEARNING ARCHITECT® Connections:**

Look for people who act like and/or show evidence of:

2a. Problem Solving	15. Cautious
3c. Personal Experience	17. Selected Sources
4a. Getting Information	18. Straightforward
9. Multiple Sources	19. What
11. Why/How	30. Mastery
12. Rules of Thumb	35. Breadth

J. **CHOICES ARCHITECT® Connections:**

Look for people who act like and/or show evidence of:

First Edition (Released 1994)	Second Edition (Released 2000)
2. Essence	3. Connector
5. Connector	4. Critical Thinker
16. Cold/Indirect Sources	6. Essence

K. **Difficulty to Develop:**
23 (of 34)–Moderate

BUSINESS ACUMEN

6. CAREER AMBITION

A. Definition:

Knows what they want from a career and actively works on it; is career knowledgeable; makes things happen for self; markets self for opportunities; doesn't wait for others to open doors.

B. Arenas/Domains to Explore:

1. Actual advancement
2. Diversity of background
3. Dreams and aspirations
4. Family social/economic background
5. Need/interest for what money can buy
6. Special child/need for resources
7. Spouse's aspirations
8. Values and drivers
9. Career plan/goals
10. Need to achieve

C. Sample Questions:

Dimension 1: Been there, done that–has had direct personal experience(s) involving the competency–candidate was the prime player   Note: * means OK for campus

1. Did you ever get a job a friend wanted? How did you deal with that?
2. Do you have a career plan?*
3. Have you ever changed careers?
4. Have you ever changed jobs just to get a bigger title?
5. Have you ever changed jobs or companies because you were bored?
6. Have you ever followed a boss into a job or a company?
7. Have you ever gotten a job because of a friend?
8. Have you ever gotten a job because you were the first to get there?
9. Have you ever had a written career plan or was it just in your head?
10. Have you ever left a job because of a conflict with a boss?
11. Have you ever moved to a place you didn't like just to get ahead?
12. Have you ever promoted yourself for an open job? What happened?
13. Have you ever taken a decrease in salary to get a job you wanted?
14. Have you ever taken a job in which you didn't want to get ahead?
15. Have you ever worked in different functions/businesses/types of organizations?*
16. Have you pulled one or more people along with you as you moved through your career?
17. Have you worked outside your home country?
18. How close to your early career plan are you?
19. Tell me about a time when you grabbed an opportunity to do something different in your career.*
20. Tell me about a time when you went from one job/career/major to another? What were the toughest transitions? What did you realize about what you want or don't want to do?*
21. Tell me about a time when your ambition worked really well for you.
22. Tell me about a time when your lack of ambition got you into trouble.
23. What do you dislike doing at work?*
24. What do you like to do at work?*
25. What have you done to improve your marketability for promotion?
26. Whose career advice have you followed?

CAREER AMBITION

27. Whose career advice haven't you followed?
28. Would you move to an international location? Where?*

Dimension 2: Seen/been around others who were involved with the competency–good and bad; learns from others about self

29. Contrast the most and least ambitious people you know.*
30. Has career ambition ever been in any 360° survey done on you? Was your score among your highest, middle, or lowest?
31. Has lack of ambition on someone else's part ever created an obstacle for you or got in the way of something you were trying to accomplish?*
32. Have you ever talked about your career ambition with a coach or mentor?
33. Have you ever watched someone fail/get fired because they did not have enough career ambition?*
34. Have you ever watched someone overdo ambition to the point that it backfired?
35. Have you ever watched someone succeed because they were very ambitious?*
36. Have you ever worked with a coach on career ambition?*
37. Have you ever worked with a person who was extremely ambitious?
38. Have you ever worked with a skills coach on improving your career ambition?*
39. How do you get feedback about your career ambition?
40. How often do you check with multiple sources when you get a piece of critical feedback on your career ambition?
41. Is there a historical figure you consider a model of career ambition?
42. What do others who are not your fans say about your career ambition?
43. What do others who like you say about your career ambition?
44. Which boss was the highest on career ambition?
45. Which boss was the lowest on career ambition?
46. Which direct report was the highest on career ambition?
47. Which direct report was the lowest on career ambition?
48. Which peer was the highest on career ambition?
49. Which peer was the worst on career ambition?
50. Who in your field or business deals the best with career ambition?
51. Who do you consider a current role model of career ambition?*
52. Who do you go to for advice on career ambition?
53. Who have you learned the most from about career ambition?*
54. Who is a higher-management role model for you on career ambition?
55. Who is a role model of career ambition outside of work?

Dimension 3: Knows how the competency works in theory; shows understanding

56. Are there situations or settings where someone should demonstrate more or less career ambition?
57. Do you think ambition can be learned? If so, how do you think people develop these skills?
58. Do you think there is a way to compensate or work around low career ambition skills?
59. Has anyone asked you for your opinions/advice on career ambition?*
60. Have you ever attended a course on career ambition?
61. Have you ever been in a situation where you and others put career ambition on a success profile?
62. Have you ever been part of an effort to create a policy or a mission statement containing reference to the importance of being ambitious?
63. Have you ever been someone's coach or mentor who had problems with career ambition skills?

CAREER AMBITION

64. Have you ever created a development plan for someone on career ambition skills?
65. Have you ever criticized someone for not being ambitious?
66. Have you ever designed a program on career ambition skills?
67. Have you ever given a speech on career ambition?
68. Have you ever rewarded or recognized someone for having career ambition?
69. Have you ever taught a course on career ambition?
70. Have you ever tried to help someone deal with career ambition more effectively?*
71. Have you ever tried to help someone improve their career ambition skills?
72. How do you think people develop career ambition skills?
73. How much ambition is good to have and how much is too much?
74. How much of success do you think is due to career ambition compared with other characteristics?
75. How would you know if someone lacks ambition?
76. How would you know if someone is ambitious?
77. If you had to write a book on career ambition, what would the chapter headings be?
78. What are the benefits to someone who has solid career ambition skills?
79. What are the consequences to someone who has poor career ambition skills?
80. What do you think the standard is on career ambition for someone in your role?
81. What happens if you have too much career ambition?
82. What happens when two people try to work together who have very different ambition levels?
83. What wisdom would you pass onto others trying to develop career ambition skills?
84. When you select others, what do you look for in career ambition?
85. Why do you think people end up having different career ambitions?

Dimension 4: Shows personal change and sense-making; learned it one place and applied it in another; can compare and contrast experiences; changes viewpoints across time; can explain personal development or evolution related to the competency

86. Compare and contrast examples of times when you've had effective and ineffective career ambition.
87. Contrast times when you have been focused and not so focused on managing your career.
88. Did you ever pass up a job or assignment because you were not confident enough in your skills at managing your career?
89. Do you ever use other skills to cover for your lack of career ambition?
90. Do you go toward what excites you in a career?
91. Has career ambition ever figured in a failure, struggle, or setback you have had?
92. Has becoming better at career ambition ever helped you in other areas?
93. Has poor career management ever been the subject of a development plan for you?
94. Has your career ambition always been this way?
95. Have you changed personal interests over the years?*
96. Have you done better taking jobs that call on your strengths or that develop your weak or untested areas?
97. Have you ever delegated or assigned someone a task because you didn't manage your career particularly well?
98. Have you ever had a career setback? What did you do?
99. Have you ever made significant strides at becoming better at career management?
100. Have your career management skills, good or bad, ever been the subject of your performance review or a career discussion?
101. How different are you across situations in your career ambition?

CAREER AMBITION

102. How do you decide how career-oriented to be?
103. How much of your success is due to your career ambition?
104. How transferable are your career management skills to other situations?
105. If you could start again, would you follow another career path?
106. If you had to become better at career management in a hurry, what would you do?
107. Was there a time when you were not good at managing your career?
108. What are the next three career steps for you and how long will they take?
109. What career management mistakes do you think you have made?
110. What caused you to work to change your skills at managing your career?
111. What event or series of events had the most impact on your career ambition?
112. What's the most varied you can be in career ambition?
113. What was the shortest amount of time in which you increased your skill level at managing your career?
114. When did you first realize your skill level at managing your career?
115. Where do you think you'll be in five years?*
116. Why do you think you deal with career management the way you do?
117. Why do you think your career ambition is the way it is?*

D. Follow-up Probes:

1. Are there times when you're not like this or wouldn't do this?
2. Are there times when you've been concerned with career advancement and times when you haven't?
3. Could you contrast those two bosses for me?
4. Could you give me a few examples of how you've used or applied that?
5. Do you think this is teachable?
6. Do you think you're more willing to make career changes than most? Why?
7. Do you think you would perform any differently if you were more career-oriented?
8. How did others react when you did that?
9. How did you come up with that approach in the first place?
10. How did you know that method of getting over that barrier would work?
11. How do others you have known approach that?
12. How far did you go to try to be a team player?
13. How much did you have to give up to make it work?
14. How typical is this for you?
15. How would you approach that same situation today?
16. Is this natural for you, or do you really have to dig for it?
17. Was that a fair way to maneuver around them?
18. Was there a time when you didn't understand this about yourself?
19. What did you do after you got that feedback?
20. What did you do to adapt to that?
21. What did you learn from that?
22. What does that imply for the future?
23. Why did you choose that approach?
24. Why did you decide to take the risk?
25. Why did you do it that way?

CAREER AMBITION

26. Why did you time your attempt like you did?
27. Why do you suppose organizations work that way?
28. Why do you think that didn't work?
29. Why do you think that happened that way?
30. Why do you think that worked?
31. Why do you think you are like that?
32. Why do you think you have difficulties with that sometimes?
33. Why is that important to you?

E. Themes/Things to Look for:

Definite likes and dislikes
Drivers, what makes them get up in the morning
Goals set high
Interest in doing something exciting
Interest in skill development

Need to command, build empire
Seizing opportunities
Strong ego, optimism
Achievement ethic; wants to leave a mark
Variety of career interests

F. Most Likely Résumé:

1. Look for jobs like:
International Assignments
Line to Staff Switches
Staff to Line Shifts

2. Look for develop-in-place assignments like:
Do a study of successful executives in your organization and report the findings to top management.
Do a study of failed executives in your organization, including interviewing people still with the organization who knew or worked with them, and report the findings to top management.
Volunteer to fill an open management job temporarily until it's filled.
Manage the outplacement of a group of people.
Write a speech for someone higher up in the organization.

3. Best references to ask about or check:
Assigned Mentors/Sponsors
Natural Mentors
Spouse
Yourself

G. Learning Agility Evaluation:

7. Passive vs. Intrigued/Curious
8. Sameness vs. Diversity
10. Reactive vs. Initiating
11. Generalizations vs. Specific Learnings
14. Sameness vs. Broad Ranging
18. Stays Close to Home vs. Lots of Curiosity

CAREER AMBITION

H. The LEADERSHIP ARCHITECT® Sort Card Connections:

1. Good (positive) if combined with high:
Likes to lead people 9, 20, 36, 60
Effective politician 4, 8, 38, 48
Gets results 16, 17, 50, 51, 53
A personal learner 32, 45, 54
Takes in feedback 33, 41, 45

2. Bad (negative) if combined with low or high (+):
Too self-focused (+9, 43, 53, 57) 42, 60
Gets in trouble promoting self inappropriately 4, 8, 22, 38, 48
Arrogant 7, 10, 41 (+53, 57)
Steps on others to get there (+12, 13, 34, 57)

3. Too much can contribute to the following Stallers and Stoppers:

A. What too much looks like (overused):

May make unwise career choices; may only select jobs in the can-do comfort zone; may be seen as excessively ambitious; may not pay enough attention to the job at hand; may not take career advice comfortably; may not trust the career decisions others make for him/her.

B. Too much might lead to these Stallers and Stoppers:

Overly Ambitious (103)   Lack of Ethics and Values (109)
Betrayal of Trust (105)   Overdependence on an Advocate (115)
Defensiveness (108)   Political Missteps (119)

C. Compensators:
How to compensate for too much of this competency:
    16, 17, 30, 32, 33, 42, 46, 48, 50, 51, 53, 55, 58, 63, 66

D. Things to watch for:
Always looking over the horizon
History of marginal career choices
Markets oneself too much
Not open to career advice
Too rigid a career plan
Idea of a career is more authority and money, not more challenge or newness
Likes the word I; talks about others as objects of their actions
Often compares themselves with others; may tear others down

CAREER AMBITION

4. **Too little can contribute to the following Stallers and Stoppers:**

    A. *What too little looks like (unskilled):*

    Unsure what he/she wants out of a career; may be bored or in the wrong career or the wrong organization; may not want to make sacrifices to get ahead; may not understand how careers really work and how people get ahead; a poor marketer of self; doesn't know how to get noticed; hesitant to speak up on career wants and needs; stuck in his/her career comfort zone; won't take a career risk.

    B. *Too little might lead to these Stallers and Stoppers:*

    Overdependence on an Advocate

    C. *Compensators:*

    How to substitute for too little of this competency:
    1, 4, 8, 9, 15, 24, 28, 43, 46, 48, 49, 53, 57

I. **LEARNING ARCHITECT® Connections:**

Look for people who act like and/or show evidence of:

1a. Pure Action	4a. Getting Information
1c. Following a Plan	25. Personal Change

J. **CHOICES ARCHITECT® Connections:**

Look for people who act like and/or show evidence of:

First Edition (Released 1994)
1. Inquisitive
10. Responds to Feedback
13. Role Flexibility

Second Edition (Released 2000)
7. Inquisitive
17. Responds to Feedback
18. Role Flexibility

K. **Difficulty to Develop:**

24 (of 34)–Moderate

CAREER AMBITION

7. CARING ABOUT DIRECT REPORTS

A. Definition:

Is interested in the work and non-work needs of direct reports; asks about their plans, problems, and desires; knows about their concerns and questions; is available for listening to personal problems; monitors workloads and appreciates extra effort.

B. Arenas/Domains to Explore:

1. Any emotionally charged situation
2. Coaching athletic teams
3. Good samaritan behavior
4. Political persuasion on social issues
5. Situations working with people of lesser status
6. Social role models
7. Team captain
8. Volunteer community work
9. Work/non-work needs
10. Working with children/younger people

C. Sample Questions:

Dimension 1: Been there, done that–has had direct personal experience(s) involving the competency–candidate was the prime player   Note: * means OK for campus

1. Do very many people come to you with their problems?*
2. Have you ever had to fire a friend?
3. Have you ever had to pass a friend over for promotion?
4. Have you ever managed anything where the people or units reporting to you were in different locations? How did you show your concern for them on a personal basis?
5. How do you set boundaries with direct reports? What's too close? Too distant?*
6. How well do you get to know the people you work with?*
7. Tell me about a time when you had to change a person's role (fire, reassign) because they just couldn't do the work.*
8. Tell me about a time when you had to use tough love with a direct report, friend, someone younger/less experienced.*
9. Tell me about a time when you helped a direct report, friend, someone younger/less experienced with a personal problem.*
10. Tell me about a time when you helped a direct report, friend, someone younger/less experienced with a career issue.*
11. Tell me about a time when you helped a direct report, friend, someone younger/less experienced with a conflict they were having with someone else.*
12. Tell me about a time when you helped out someone who needed a boost.*
13. Tell me about a time when you helped a person or a group less fortunate than you.*
14. Tell me about a time when you made peace with a direct report, friend, someone younger/less experienced.*
15. Tell me about a time when you noticed that a direct report, friend, someone younger/less experienced was very overworked.*
16. Tell me about a time when you were left holding the bag and had to do someone else's work for them. Why couldn't they finish it themselves?*
17. Tell me about a time when you wish you had intervened on a work project a direct report, friend, someone younger/less experienced was having trouble with.*
18. Tell me about a time when caring about your direct reports worked really well for you.

CARING ABOUT DIRECT REPORTS

19. Tell me about a time when your closeness to someone had negative consequences.
20. Tell me about a time when your lack of caring about your direct reports got you into trouble.
21. Was there any time when you had to cover the work of a direct report, friend, someone younger/less experienced.*
22. What local, national or global causes do you associate yourself with?

Dimension 2: Seen/been around others who were involved with the competency–good and bad; learns from others about self

23. Contrast the most and least caring people you know with regard to direct reports.*
24. Has caring for direct reports ever been in any 360° survey done on you? Was your score among your highest, middle, or lowest?
25. Has lack of caring for direct reports on someone else's part ever created an obstacle for you or got in the way of something you were trying to accomplish?*
26. Have you ever talked about your level of concern or caring for direct reports with a coach or mentor?
27. Have you ever watched someone fail/get fired because they did not care enough for direct reports?*
28. Have you ever watched someone over caring for direct reports to the point that it backfired?
29. Have you ever watched someone succeed because they cared for direct reports?*
30. Have you ever worked with a coach on caring for your direct reports?*
31. Have you ever worked with a person who excelled at caring for direct reports?
32. Have you ever worked with a skills coach on improving your concern for direct reports?*
33. How do you get feedback about yourself on caring for direct reports?
34. How often do you check with multiple sources when you get a piece of critical feedback on your concern or caring for direct reports?
35. Is there a historical figure you consider a model of caring for direct reports?
36. What do others who are not your fans say about your caring for direct reports?
37. What do others who like you say about your caring for direct reports?
38. Which boss was the best at caring for direct reports?
39. Which boss was the worst at caring for direct reports?
40. Which direct report was the best at caring for direct reports?
41. Which direct report was the worst at caring for direct reports?
42. Which peer was the best at caring for direct reports?
43. Which peer was the worst at caring for direct reports?
44. Who in your field or business deals the best with caring for direct reports?
45. Who do you consider a role model of caring for direct reports?*
46. Who do you go to for advice on caring for direct reports?
47. Who have you learned the most from about caring for direct reports?*
48. Who is a higher-management role model for you on caring for direct reports?
49. Who is a role model of caring for direct reports outside of work?

Dimension 3: Knows how the competency works in theory; shows understanding

50. Are there situations or settings where someone should care for direct reports differently?
51. Do you think caring for direct reports can be learned? If so, how do you think people develop this skill?
52. Do you think there is a way to compensate or work around a lack of concern/caring for direct report skills?
53. Has anyone asked you for your opinions/advice on concern/caring for direct reports?*
54. Have you ever attended a course on demonstrating concern/caring for direct reports?

CARING ABOUT DIRECT REPORTS

55. Have you ever been in a situation where you and others put caring for direct reports on a success profile?
56. Have you ever been part of an effort to create a policy or a mission statement containing reference to the importance of caring for direct reports?
57. Have you ever been someone's coach or mentor who had problems with concern/caring for direct reports?
58. Have you ever created a development plan for someone on concern/caring for direct reports?
59. Have you ever criticized someone for not caring for direct reports?
60. Have you ever designed a program on concern/caring for direct reports?
61. Have you ever given a speech on concern/caring for direct reports?
62. Have you ever rewarded or recognized someone for caring for direct reports?
63. Have you ever taught a course on concern/caring for direct reports?
64. Have you ever tried to help someone deal more effectively with concern/caring for direct reports?*
65. Have you ever tried to help someone improve their concern/caring for direct reports?
66. How do you think people develop concern/caring skills for others?
67. How much caring/concern for direct reports is good to have and how much is too much?
68. How much of success do you think is due to caring for direct reports compared with other characteristics?
69. How would you know if someone is poor at caring for direct reports?
70. How would you know if someone is good at caring for direct reports?
71. If you had to write a book on concern/caring for direct reports, what would the chapter headings be?
72. What are the benefits to someone who is really good at concern/caring for direct reports?
73. What are the consequences to someone who is really poor at concern/caring for direct reports?
74. What do you think the performance standard is on caring for direct reports for someone in your role?
75. What happens when you show too much concern/caring for direct reports?
76. What happens when two people try to work together who are very different on demonstrating caring for direct reports?
77. What wisdom would you pass onto others trying to become better at caring for direct reports?
78. When you select others, what do you look for in the ways they demonstrate concern/caring for others?
79. Why do you think people end up being different in the way they show concern/caring for direct reports?

Dimension 4: Shows personal change and sense-making; learned it one place and applied it in another; can compare and contrast experiences; changes viewpoints across time; can explain personal development or evolution related to the competency

80. Compare and contrast examples of times when you've been effective and ineffective at demonstrating concern for your direct reports.
81. Contrast your on- and off-the-job use of concern/caring about others.
82. Compare and contrast the most effective and ineffective interactions you've had when firing an employee.
83. Did you ever pass up a job or assignment because you were not confident enough in your skills at caring for direct reports?
84. Do you ever use other skills to cover for your lack of concern for direct reports?
85. Has concern/caring about direct reports ever figured in a failure, struggle, or setback you have had?
86. Has becoming better at demonstrating concern for direct reports ever helped you in other areas?
87. Has poor concern/caring about direct reports ever been the subject of a development plan for you?
88. Has your concern/caring about direct reports always been this way?
89. Have you ever delegated or assigned someone a task because you don't demonstrate concern for others particularly well?

CARING ABOUT DIRECT REPORTS

90. Have you ever made significant strides at becoming better at demonstrating concern/caring about direct reports?
91. Have your concern/caring about direct reports skills, good or bad, ever been the subject of your performance review or a career discussion?
92. How different are you across situations in your concern/caring about direct reports?
93. How do you decide how much concern to show for those who report to you?
94. How much of your success is due to the way you show concern for those who report to you?
95. How transferable are your concern/caring about direct reports skills to other situations?
96. If you had to become better at demonstrating concern/caring about direct reports in a hurry, what would you do?
97. Was there a time when you were not good at demonstrating concern/caring for direct reports?
98. What caused you to work to change your skills at demonstrating concern for those who report to you?
99. What event or series of events had the most impact on your concern/caring about direct reports?
100. What's the most varied you can be in demonstrating concern for your direct reports?
101. What was the shortest amount of time in which you increased your skill level at demonstrating concern for those who report to you?
102. When did you first realize your skill level at demonstrating concern/caring for direct reports?
103. When you know ahead of time that your usual level of concern for direct reports won't work, what do you do?
104. Why do you think you deal with concern/caring about direct reports the way you do?
105. Why do you think your concern/caring about direct reports is the way it is?*
106. How has September 11th, 2001 changed the way you feel about your direct reports?

D. Follow-up Probes:

1. Are there times when you're not like this or wouldn't do this?
2. Are there times when you act toward others like that and times when you don't?
3. Could you contrast those two bosses for me?
4. Could you give me a few examples of how you've used or applied that?
5. Did you or the other person blink first?
6. Do you suppose if others would just try harder, they could learn to be more caring like you?
7. Do you think this is teachable?
8. Do you think you're better at concern/caring than most? Why?
9. Do you think you would perform any better if you had a different approach to caring/helpfulness?
10. Have you ever had to form a relationship with someone you really disliked to get your job done?
11. How did it feel to give up something you wanted to get the work going?
12. How did the others react when you did that?
13. How did you come up with that approach in the first place?
14. How did you know that method of getting over that barrier would work?
15. How do others you have known approach that?
16. How far did you go to try to be a team player?
17. How far will you go before you cut line and try another approach?
18. How much did you have to give up to make it work?
19. How typical is this for you?
20. How would you approach that same situation today?
21. Is this natural for you, or do you really have to dig for it?

CARING ABOUT DIRECT REPORTS

22. Was that a fair way to maneuver around them?
23. Was there a time when you didn't understand this about yourself?
24. What did you do after you got that feedback?
25. What did you do to adapt to that?
26. What did you learn from that?
27. Why did you choose that approach?
28. Why did you decide to take the risk?
29. Why did you do it that way?
30. Why did you time your attempt like you did?
31. Why do you suppose organizations work that way?
32. Why do you think that didn't work?
33. Why do you think that happened that way?
34. Why do you think that worked?
35. Why do you think you have difficulties with that sometimes?
36. Would you have done it that way with looser deadlines?
37. Would you have done it that way with tighter deadlines?

E. Themes/Things to Look for:

Ability to articulate feelings and internal views as seen by others
Going out of one's way; caring
Having concerns and caring for people they don't like
Keeping feelings from getting in the way
One size doesn't fit all
Satisfying personal needs or responding to the needs of others
Cares for the few or the many
Simple vs. complex views of human nature and how to solve people problems
Source of the motive to care
Teaching people how to fish rather than just giving them a fish to eat
Trying to help people achieve/solve problems
Seeking to understand what a person is like
Balance concern for the task and concern for the person; kind but firm
Dealing with issues promptly

F. Most Likely Résumé:

1. Look for jobs like:
Fix-Its/Turnarounds
Significant People Demands

2. Look for develop-in-place assignments like:
Create employee involvement teams.
Manage an ad hoc, temporary group of "green," inexperienced people as their coach, teacher, orienter, etc.
Manage an ad hoc, temporary group of low-competence people through a task they couldn't do by themselves.
Help shut down a plant, regional office, product line, business, operation, etc.
Manage a project team of people who are older and more experienced.

CARING ABOUT DIRECT REPORTS

   3. **Best references to ask about or check:**
      Human Resource Professionals
      Direct Reports

G. Learning Agility Evaluation:
   1. What/Describing vs. Why/Explain
   6. Reacting/Responsive vs. Adapting
   8. Sameness vs. Diversity
   13. Simple Views vs. Complex Views
   17. Avoids Discussion of Weaknesses vs. Comfortably Sharing Shortcomings
   20. Avoids Responsibility for Mistakes vs. Admits and Learns from Mistakes
   21. View from Self vs. View from Point of View of Others

H. The LEADERSHIP ARCHITECT® Sort Card Connections:

   1. Good (positive) if combined with high:
   Makes time for others 3, 33, 41
   Kind but firm 12, 13, 23, 35, 53
   Helps others develop 19, 56
   Broadly sensitive 21, 46
   Trusted by others 22, 29
   Would use positive humor 26, 48
   Lets other know what's going on 27
   Team builder 42, 60, 65
   Insightful into people 56, 64

   2. Bad (negative) if combined with low or high (+):
   May overlook poor performance (+10, 21, 22, 23, 64)
   May have trouble with layoffs/tough people decisions 12, 16, 53
   Smoothes over or avoids conflict 12, 13, 34, 57
   Loses sight of targets, may spend too much time with people 17, 50, 53
   Poor judge of talent 25, 56

   3. Too much can contribute to the following Stallers and Stoppers:

   A. What too much looks like (overused):

   > May have trouble being firm with direct reports; may give them too much room for excuses; may not challenge them to perform beyond their comfort zone; may get too deep into their lives; may not be able to make objective calls on performance and potential; may not know when to stop showing care when efforts are rejected.

   B. Too much might lead to these Stallers and Stoppers:
   None Apply

CARING ABOUT DIRECT REPORTS

C. Compensators:
How to compensate for too much of this competency:
9, 12, 13, 17, 18, 20, 23, 27, 34, 35, 56, 57, 64

D. Things to watch for:
Can't separate feelings about people from decisions that have to be made
May know too much about their people
Excuses marginal performers
Poor history of developing people; doesn't size up people well
Rewards everything
Sets standards too low
Group doesn't perform well
Conflict-avoider

4. Too little can contribute to the following Stallers and Stoppers:

A. What too little looks like (unskilled):
May not care much about the personal needs of direct reports; may be too busy to know much about direct reports; may believe work and personal life should be separate; may be more work and task oriented than most; may be very tense and impersonal with direct reports; may lack the listening skills or interest to know people's hopes and problems.

B. Too little might lead to these Stallers and Stoppers:
Arrogant (104)	Failure to Staff Effectively (111)
Lack of Ethics and Values (109)	Insensitive to Others (112)
Failure to Build a Team (110)	Overmanaging (117)

C. Compensators:
How to substitute for too little of this competency:
3, 10, 11, 18, 19, 23, 27, 31, 33, 36, 39, 41, 60, 64

I. LEARNING ARCHITECT® Connections:

Look for people who act like and/or show evidence of:
3a. Checking Feelings	4c. Actively Involve
4a. Getting Information	16. Collaborate

J. CHOICES ARCHITECT® Connections:

Look for people who act like and/or show evidence of:

First Edition (Released 1994)	Second Edition (Released 2000)
14. Transaction Quality	12. Helps Others Succeed
15. Helps Others Succeed	15. People-Smart

K. Difficulty to Develop:
24 (out of 34)–Moderate

CARING ABOUT DIRECT REPORTS

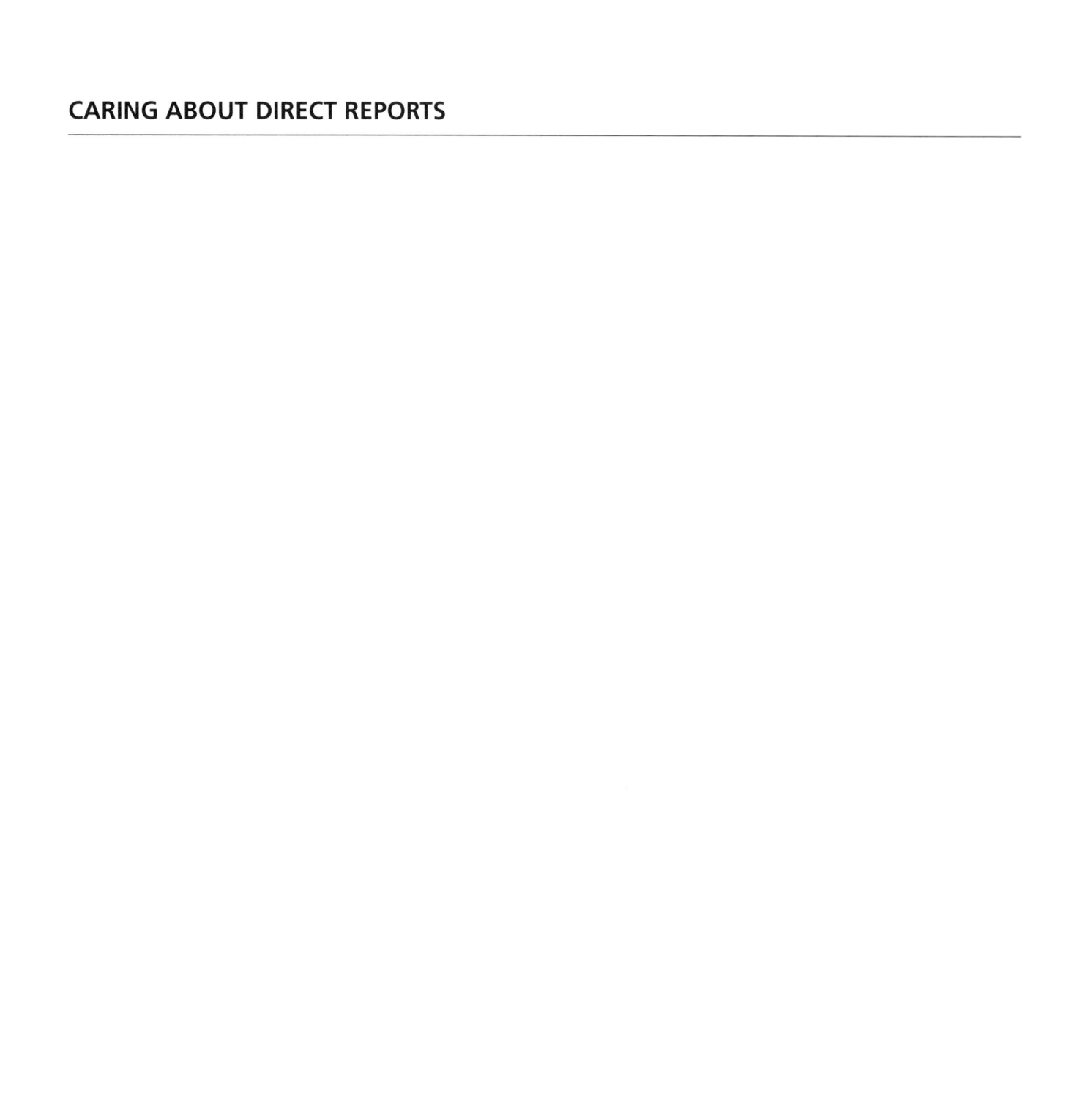

8. COMFORT AROUND TOP MANAGEMENT

A. Definition:

Can deal comfortably with senior managers; can present to more senior managers without undue tension and nervousness; understands how senior managers think and work; can determine the best way to get things done with them by talking their language and responding to their needs; can craft approaches likely to be seen as appropriate and positive.

B. Arenas/Domains to Explore:

1. Attitudes about power/influence
2. Coaches
3. Fear of making mistakes in front of others
4. Foreign dignitaries
5. Good times/bad times with authority figures
6. Government officials
7. Higher-level bosses
8. Liked/disliked authority figures
9. Military commanders/officers
10. Parents
11. Personality–extrovert vs. introvert
12. Perspective
13. Religious leaders
14. Sales technique
15. Scout leaders
16. Self-confidence/ego strength
17. Socio-economic background/exposure growing up
18. Teachers/principals

C. Sample Questions:

Dimension 1: Been there, done that–has had direct personal experience(s) involving the competency–candidate was the prime player   Note: * means OK for campus

1. Did a higher-level manager ever "bark" at you or challenge you? How did you respond?
2. Did you ever have to pick up a VIP from the airport in your own car?
3. Do you present any differently when in front of senior managers?
4. Have you been to business/social events where higher-level managers were present?*
5. Have you been to charity functions where you sat at a table with higher-level managers from inside or outside your organization?*
6. Have you ever had to deliver bad news to someone more senior than yourself?*
7. Have you ever managed anything where the people you reported to were in different locations? How did you get comfortable with them?
8. Have you ever sat next to a higher-level manager on a long plane trip?
9. Have you ever struck a deal with a senior manager only to have them later change their mind and leave you hanging?
10. Tell me about a senior manager you initially had a lot of trouble dealing with.
11. Tell me about a time when you changed your approach because of who was in the room with the other senior managers.
12. Tell me about a time when you had to be political to get something done with senior managers.
13. Tell me about a time when you had to learn to deal with someone much older, more experienced, more senior than you?*
14. Tell me about a time when you lost your confidence in front of a group of senior managers.
15. Tell me about a time when you were seriously challenged in front of a group of senior managers.
16. Tell me about a time when your comfort around senior managers worked really well for you.
17. Tell me about a time when your lack of comfort around more senior management got you into trouble.

COMFORT AROUND TOP MANAGEMENT

18. What's the highest-level, most important person you've met?*
19. When did you have your first prolonged interaction with a significant executive?
20. When you know ahead of time that a senior manager will present a problem with something you want to do, what do you do?

Dimension 2: Seen/been around others who were involved with the competency–good and bad; learns from others about self

21. Contrast people you know who are most and least comfortable around top management.*
22. Has comfort around top management ever been in any 360° survey done on you? Was your score among your highest, middle, or lowest?
23. Has discomfort or nervousness around top management on someone else's part ever created an obstacle for you or got in the way of something you were trying to accomplish?*
24. Have you ever talked about your comfort around top management with a coach or mentor?
25. Have you ever watched someone fail/get fired because they were not comfortable or were nervous around top management?*
26. Have you ever watched someone overstress comfort around top management to the point that it backfired?
27. Have you ever watched someone succeed because they were very comfortable around top management?*
28. Have you ever worked with a coach on being more comfortable around top management?*
29. Have you ever worked with a person who excelled at being comfortable around top management?
30. Have you ever worked with a skills coach on improving your comfort around top management?*
31. How do you get feedback about your level of comfort around top management?
32. How often do you check with multiple sources when you get a piece of critical feedback on your comfort around top management?
33. Is there a historical figure you consider a model of being comfortable around top management?
34. What do others who are not your fans say about your comfort around top management?
35. What do others who like you say about your comfort around top management?
36. Which boss was the best at being comfortable around top management?
37. Which boss was the worst at being comfortable around top management?
38. Which direct report was the best at being comfortable around top management?
39. Which direct report was the worst at being comfortable around top management?
40. Which peer was the best at being comfortable around top management?
41. Which peer was the worst at being comfortable around top management?
42. Who in your field or business deals the best with being comfortable around top management?
43. Who do you consider a role model of being comfortable around top management?*
44. Who do you go to for advice on being comfortable around top management?
45. Who have you learned the most from about being comfortable around top management?*
46. Who is a higher-management role model for you on being comfortable around top management?
47. Who is a role model of being comfortable around top management outside of work?

Dimension 3: Knows how the competency works in theory; shows understanding

48. Are there situations or settings where someone should demonstrate comfort around senior management differently?
49. Do you think comfort around senior management can be learned? If so, how do you think people develop these skills?
50. Do you think there is a way to compensate or work around a low comfort around senior management?
51. Has anyone asked you for your opinions/advice on dealing with senior management?*

COMFORT AROUND TOP MANAGEMENT

52. Have you ever attended a course on dealing with senior management/higher status people?
53. Have you ever been in a situation where you and others put comfort around senior management on a success profile?
54. Have you ever been part of an effort to create a policy or a mission statement containing reference to the importance of being comfortable around senior management?
55. Have you ever been someone's coach or mentor who had problems dealing with senior management?
56. Have you ever created a development plan for someone on building comfortable relationships with senior management?
57. Have you ever criticized someone for not being comfortable around senior management?
58. Have you ever designed a program on becoming comfortable around senior management?
59. Have you ever given a speech on becoming comfortable around senior management?
60. Have you ever rewarded or recognized someone for demonstrating comfort around senior management?
61. Have you ever taught a course on dealing with senior management/higher-status people?
62. Have you ever tried to help someone deal with senior management more effectively?*
63. Have you ever tried to help someone improve their comfort around senior management?
64. How do you think people develop skills to deal with senior management/higher status people?
65. How much comfort around senior management is good to have and how much is too much?
66. How much of success do you think is due to comfort around senior management compared with other characteristics?
67. How would you know if someone is uncomfortable around senior management?
68. How would you know if someone is comfortable around senior management?
69. If you had to write a book on comfort around senior management, what would the chapter headings be?
70. What are the benefits to someone who is really good at dealing with senior management/higher-status people?
71. What are the consequences to someone who is really poor at dealing with senior management/higher-status people?
72. What do you think the performance standard is on comfort around senior management for someone in your role?
73. What happens if you are too comfortable around higher management?
74. What happens when two people try to work together who have very different comfort levels around senior management?
75. What wisdom would you pass onto others trying to develop comfortable relationships with senior management?
76. When you select others, what do you look for in their ability to deal with senior management/higher-status people?
77. Why do you think people end up being different in the way they deal with senior management/higher-status people?

Dimension 4: Shows personal change and sense-making; learned it one place and applied it in another; can compare and contrast experiences; changes viewpoints across time; can explain personal development or evolution related to the competency

78. Compare and contrast your most effective and least effective interaction with a senior executive in a formal setting.
79. Contrast your on- and off-the-job dealings with higher-status people.
80. Did you ever pass up a job or assignment because you were not comfortable enough around senior management?
81. Do you ever use other skills to cover for your lack of comfort around senior managers?

COMFORT AROUND TOP MANAGEMENT

82. Has dealing with senior management ever figured in a failure, struggle, or setback you have had?
83. Has getting more comfortable with senior managers ever helped you in other areas?
84. Has your comfort level around senior management always been this way?
85. Have poor dealings with senior management ever been the subject of a development plan for you?
86. Have you ever delegated or assigned someone a task because you weren't comfortable around senior managers?
87. Have you ever made significant strides at becoming better at dealing with senior management?
88. Has your comfort around senior management skills, good or bad, ever been the subject of your performance review or a career discussion?
89. How different are you across situations in your dealings with senior management?
90. How do you decide how to deal with senior management?
91. How have you changed the way you deal with senior executives when you've switched jobs, been promoted or worked in a different organizational culture? Compare and contrast examples that have led to your personal changes.
92. How much of your success is due to your dealing with senior management?
93. How transferable are your dealing with senior management skills to other situations?
94. If you had to become better at dealing with senior management in a hurry, what would you do?
95. Was there a time when you were not good at being comfortable around top management?
96. What caused you to work to change your comfort around senior managers?
97. What event or series of events had the most impact on your ability to deal with senior management?
98. What's the most varied you can be in dealing with senior management?
99. What was the shortest amount of time in which you increased your skill level at dealing with senior management?
100. When did you first realize your skill level at dealing with senior management?
101. When you know ahead of time that your usual level of comfort around senior managers won't work, what do you do?
102. Why do you think you deal with senior management the way you do?
103. Why do you think your comfort with senior management is the way it is?*

D. Follow-up Probes:

1. Are there times when you're not like this or wouldn't do this?
2. Are there times when you deal with more senior people like that and times when you don't?
3. Could you contrast those two bosses for me?
4. Could you give me a few examples of how you've used or applied that?
5. Did you or the other person blink first?
6. Do you suppose if others would just try harder, they could learn to be more comfortable with higher-level/status people like you are?
7. Do you think this is teachable?
8. Do you think you're better at dealing with higher-level/status people than most? Why?
9. Do you think you would perform any better if you dealt differently with more senior people?
10. Have you changed your initial assessment of this person?
11. Have you ever had to form a relationship with someone you really disliked to get your job done?
12. How did they/they react when you did that?
13. How did you come up with that approach in the first place?

COMFORT AROUND TOP MANAGEMENT

14. How did you know that method of getting over that barrier would work?
15. How do others you have known approach that?
16. How far did you go to try to be a team player?
17. How much did you have to give up to make it work?
18. How typical is this for you?
19. How would you approach that same situation today?
20. Is this natural for you, or do you really have to dig for it?
21. Was that a fair way to maneuver around them?
22. Was there a time when you didn't understand this about yourself?
23. What did you do after you got that feedback?
24. What did you do to adapt to that?
25. What did you learn from that?
26. Why did that person intimidate you? Would they now?
27. Why did you choose that approach?
28. Why did you decide to take the risk?
29. Why did you do it that way?
30. Why did you time your attempt like you did?
31. Why do you suppose organizations work that way?
32. Why do you think that didn't work?
33. Why do you think that happened that way?
34. Why do you think that worked?
35. Why do you think you have difficulties with that once in a while?
36. Would you have done it that way with looser deadlines?
37. Would you have done it that way with tighter deadlines?

E. **Themes/Things to Look for:**
   Ability to get through (tolerate/cope with) bad (tense) conflicts with higher management
   Ability to present
   Ability to sell
   Ability to discuss past mistakes with higher level manager with humor
   Anticipates questions/concerns/perspectives
   Awareness of own impact on people higher up
   Uses complex and varied strategies for dealing with higher-level managers
   Complexity in view of higher-level managers–some good in the bad ones and some bad in the good ones
   Empathy for the boss' or person in authority's position and problems
   Focuses on issues
   Focuses on organizational impact/strategies
   Healthy and balanced attitude toward higher-level management
   History growing up of dealing with important people
   Interpersonal style
   Ease of transition (comfort with language, pace, idea packaging)
   Self-confidence/ego strength and the ability to handle stumbling and making mistakes

COMFORT AROUND TOP MANAGEMENT

F. Most Likely Résumé:

1. Look for jobs like:
Chair of Projects/Task Forces
Fix-Its/Turnarounds
Heavy Strategic Demands
Line to Staff Switches
Scope (complexity) Assignments
Staff Leadership (Influencing Without Authority)
Start-Ups

2. Look for develop-in-place assignments like:
Integrate diverse systems, processes, or procedures across decentralized and/or dispersed units.

Manage the renovation of an office, floor, building, meeting room, warehouse, etc.

Plan a new site for a building (plant, field office, headquarters, etc.).

Represent the concerns of a group of nonexempt, clerical, or administrative employees to higher management to seek resolution of a difficult issue.

Write a proposal for a new policy, process, mission, charter, product, service, or system, and present and sell it to top management.

Relaunch an existing product or service that's not doing well.

Serve on a junior or shadow board.

Manage an ad hoc, temporary group of people involved in tackling a fix-it or turnaround project.

Prepare and present a proposal of some consequence to top management.

Manage a group through a significant business crisis.

Write a speech for someone higher up in the organization.

3. Best references to ask about or check:
Direct Boss
Boss' Boss(es)
Human Resource Professionals
Natural Mentors

G. Learning Agility Evaluation:
2. All or Nothing vs. Can See Many Sides
3. Ordinary/Socially Acceptable vs. Insightful/Different
13. Simple Views vs. Complex Views
21. View from Self vs. View from Point of View of Others
22. Focus on Accomplishments vs. Focus on Solving Problems

COMFORT AROUND TOP MANAGEMENT

H. The LEADERSHIP ARCHITECT® Sort Card Connections:

1. Good (positive) if combined with high:
Can get direct reports developmental opportunities 4, 19
Listened to by higher management 5, 24, 46, 58
More likely to get promoted 6, 49
Good at high-level contact with customers 15
Trusted by higher-level managers 22, 29
Knows things first 32, 33, 42
Courageous 34, 57
Effective selling to higher management 36, 37, 48
Politician 38, 48, 49

2. Bad (negative) if combined with low or high (+):
Politician (+4, 6, 48)
"It's more who you know than what you know" 5, 24, 61
May be too tough on the less powerful (+9, 13, 34, 35) 7, 10
Empty suit; higher management groupie 17, 30, 32, 45, 51, 58
Snake 22, 29
May have loose lips (+27, 44) 48

3. Too much can contribute to the following Stallers and Stoppers:

A. What too much looks like (overused):
May manage up too much; may be seen as too political and ambitious; may spend too much time with more senior managers, parrot their positions, overestimate the meaning and usefulness of the relationships; career may be too dependent on champions; may be too free with confidential information.

B. Too much might lead to these Stallers and Stoppers:
Overly Ambitious (103)
Betrayal of Trust (105)
Overdependence on an Advocate (115)

C. Compensators:
How to compensate for too much of this competency:
5, 9, 12, 17, 22, 24, 29, 30, 45, 51, 53, 57

D. Things to watch for:
Loose lips with confidential information
May lose out in a purge along with top managers
May make fatal political errors at high altitudes
Name-dropper

Others may distrust them
Others may try to use them for access to top management
Hard on the less powerful
Empty suit; few personal ideas/accomplishments

COMFORT AROUND TOP MANAGEMENT

4. Too little can contribute to the following Stallers and Stoppers:

A. *What too little looks like (unskilled):*

Lacks self-confidence in front of more senior people; may appear nervous and tense, not at his/her best; may lose composure or get rattled when questioned by executives; doesn't know how to influence or impress more senior managers; may not understand what top executives are looking for; says and does things that don't fit the situation.

B. *Too little might lead to these Stallers and Stoppers:*

Unable to Adapt to Differences (101)

Political Missteps (119)

C. *Compensators:*

How to substitute for too little of this competency:
3, 4, 5, 9, 12, 27, 33, 34, 37, 38, 48, 49, 57

I. LEARNING ARCHITECT® Connections:

Look for people who act like and/or show evidence of:

1c. Following a Plan	4a. Getting Information
2c. Intuition	16. Collaborate
3b. Self-Talk	

J. CHOICES ARCHITECT® Connections:

Look for people who act like and/or show evidence of:

First Edition (Released 1994)	Second Edition (Released 2000)
9. Self-Aware	9. Agile Communicator
14. Transaction Quality	10. Conflict Manager
23. Communicator	11. Cool Transactor
	15. People-Smart
	19. Self-Aware
	27. Presence

K. Difficulty to Develop:

26 (out of 34)–Moderate

9. COMMAND SKILLS

A. Definition:

Relishes leading; takes unpopular stands if necessary; encourages direct and tough debate but isn't afraid to end it and move on; is looked to for direction in a crisis; faces adversity head on; energized by tough challenges.

B. Arenas/Domains to Explore:

1. Alone in the desert
2. Athletics
3. Crises
4. Early elected leadership positions
5. Fix-its
6. Hard business conditions
7. Impossible deadlines
8. Military experience
9. Mountains to climb
10. Oldest, most experienced in a group under siege
11. Start-ups
12. Step into the breach situations
13. Tough negotiations
14. Unpopular causes

C. Sample Questions:

Dimension 1: Been there, done that–has had direct personal experience(s) involving the competency–candidate was the prime player   Note: * means OK for campus

1. Does your motivation and energy level go up or down when you hit a roadblock?*
2. Have you ever fought for control of a group? What happened?*
3. Have you ever had to lead people who didn't want to be led?*
4. Have you ever managed anything where the people or units reporting to you were in different locations? How did you take control?
5. Have you ever volunteered to lead a stumbling group?*
6. How did you handle the first time your leadership efforts were rejected?*
7. Tell me about a time when you had to follow someone you didn't respect.*
8. Tell me about a time when you have had an open debate on a tough issue and lost.*
9. Tell me about a time when you have had an open debate on a tough issue and won.*
10. Tell me about a time when you managed a crisis.*
11. Tell me about a time when you took charge of a group going nowhere and you led them out of their doldrums.*
12. Tell me about a time when you took charge of a group in which you didn't like how things were going, and you convinced the people to do something different.*
13. Tell me about a time when you were the first to take on a tough issue.*
14. Tell me about a time when your unwillingness to take control of something got you into trouble.
15. Tell me about a time when your willingness to take control of something worked really well for you.
16. Tell me about an impossible situation you had to manage.*
17. Tell me about leading a declining business/downsizing/fix-it.
18. Tell me about managing a shutdown.
19. Tell me about managing a start-up.*
20. Tell me about some tough negotiations you've been in.
21. Were you ever elected to a leadership position you didn't want?*

COMMAND SKILLS

22. What is your go percent–how certain do you need to be to take control?*
23. What kind of leadership positions have you been appointed to or elected for?*
24. What's the least successful crisis you've managed?*
25. What's the most impossible task you've taken on?*
26. What's the most successful crisis you've managed?*
27. What's the most unpopular cause you ever pushed?*
28. What's the most unpopular cause you ever tried to push?

Dimension 2: Seen/been around others who were involved with the competency–good and bad; learns from others about self

29. Contrast the most and least take charge people you know.*
30. Has taking charge or command skills ever been in any 360° survey done on you? Was your score among your highest, middle, or lowest?
31. Has poor command skills or the unwillingness to take charge on someone else's part ever created an obstacle for you or got in the way of something you were trying to accomplish?*
32. Have you ever talked about your taking charge or command skills with a coach or mentor?
33. Have you ever watched someone fail/get fired because they did not take charge?*
34. Have you ever watched someone overdo taking charge or command skills to the point that it backfired?
35. Have you ever watched someone succeed because they were willing to take charge?*
36. Have you ever worked with a coach on taking charge?*
37. Have you ever worked with a person who excelled at taking charge or command skills?
38. Have you ever worked with a skills coach on taking charge or command skills?*
39. How do you get feedback about yourself on taking charge or command skills?
40. How often do you check with multiple sources when you get a piece of critical feedback on taking charge or command skills?
41. Is there a historical figure you consider a model of taking charge or command skills?
42. What do others who are not your fans say about your taking charge or command skills?
43. What do others who like you say about your taking charge or command skills?
44. Which boss was the best at taking charge or command skills?
45. Which boss was the worst at taking charge or command skills?
46. Which direct report was the best at taking charge or command skills?
47. Which direct report was the worst at taking charge or command skills?
48. Which peer was the best at taking charge or command skills?
49. Which peer was the worst at taking charge or command skills?
50. Who in your field or business deals the best with taking charge?
51. Who do you consider a role model of taking charge?*
52. Who do you go to for advice on taking charge or command skills?
53. Who have you learned the most from about taking charge or command skills?*
54. Who is a higher-management role model for you on taking charge?
55. Who is a role model of taking charge or command skills outside of work?

Dimension 3: Knows how the competency works in theory; shows understanding

56. Are there situations or settings where someone should take charge differently?
57. Do you think command skills can be learned? If so, how do you think people develop these skills?
58. Do you think there is a way to compensate or work around low taking-charge or command skills?

COMMAND SKILLS

59. Has anyone asked you for your opinions/advice on taking charge in tough or crisis situations?*
60. Have you ever attended a course on taking charge in tough or crisis situations?
61. Have you ever been in a situation where you and others put taking charge or command skills on a success profile?
62. Have you ever been part of an effort to create a policy or a mission statement containing reference to the importance of taking charge or command skills?
63. Have you ever been someone's coach or mentor who was hesitant to take charge in tough or crisis situations?
64. Have you ever created a development plan for someone to improve their ability to take charge in tough or crisis situations?
65. Have you ever criticized someone for not taking charge of a situation?
66. Have you ever designed a program on leading in tough or crisis situations?
67. Have you ever given a speech on leading in tough or crisis situations?
68. Have you ever rewarded or recognized someone for taking charge of a situation?
69. Have you ever taught a course on leading in tough or crisis situations?
70. Have you ever tried to help someone deal more effectively with taking charge in tough or crisis situations?*
71. Have you ever tried to help someone improve their skills at taking charge in tough or crisis situations?
72. How do you think people develop command skills?
73. How much of success do you think is due to command skills compared with other characteristics?
74. How would you know if someone were bad at taking charge or command skills?
75. How would you know if someone were good at taking charge or command skills?
76. If you had to write a book on taking charge in tough or crisis situations, what would the chapter headings be?
77. What are the benefits to someone who is really good at taking charge in tough or crisis situations?
78. What are the consequences to someone who is really poor at taking charge in tough or crisis situations?
79. What do you think the performance standard is on taking charge or command skills for someone in your role?
80. What happens when two people try to work together who are very different in they way they lead in tough or crisis situations?
81. What wisdom would you pass onto others trying to become better at taking charge or command skills?
82. When you select others, what do you look for relative to their command skills?
83. Why do you think people end up being different in the ways they take charge in tough or crisis situations?

Dimension 4: Shows personal change and sense-making; learned it one place and applied it in another; can compare and contrast experiences; changes viewpoints across time; can explain personal development or evolution related to the competency

84. Compare and contrast examples of times when you've been effective and ineffective at taking charge of a tough situation.
85. Contrast your on- and off-the-job use of your command skills.
86. Did you ever pass up a job or assignment because you were not confident enough in your ability to take charge of a tough situation?
87. Do you ever use other skills to cover for your lack of command skills?
88. Has taking charge ever figured in a failure, struggle, or setback you have had?
89. Has becoming better at taking charge ever helped you in other areas?
90. Have poor command skills ever been the subject of a development plan for you?
91. Has your ability to take charge always been this way?

COMMAND SKILLS

92. Have you ever delegated or assigned someone a task because you don't take charge particularly well?
93. Have you ever made significant strides at becoming better at taking charge?
94. Have your skills at taking charge, good or bad, ever been the subject of your performance review or a career discussion?
95. How different are you across situations in your skill at taking charge?
96. How do you decide how much in charge to be?
97. How do you pick your battles?*
98. How important is it for you to be liked?*
99. How much of your success is due to your ability to take charge of tough situations?
100. How transferable are your taking charge skills to other situations?
101. If you had to become better at taking charge in a hurry, what would you do?
102. Was there a time when you were not good at taking charge of tough situations?
103. What caused you to work to change your skills at taking charge of tough situations?
104. What event or series of events had the most impact on your ability to take charge?
105. What's the most varied you can be in taking charge of tough situations?
106. What was the shortest amount of time in which you increased your skill level at taking charge?
107. When did you first realize your skill level at taking charge of tough situations?
108. When you know ahead of time that your usual level of command skills won't work, what do you do?
109. Why do you think you deal with taking charge the way you do?
110. Why do you think your ability to take charge is the way it is?*

D. Follow-up Probes:

1. Are there times when you're not like this or wouldn't do this?
2. Are there times when you take charge like that and times when you don't?
3. Could you contrast those two bosses for me?
4. Could you give me a few examples of how you've used or applied that?
5. Did you or the other person blink first?
6. Do you suppose if others would just try harder, they could learn to take charge differently?
7. Do you think this is teachable?
8. Do you think you're better at taking charge than most? Why?
9. Do you think you would perform any better if you took charge?
10. Have you ever had to form a relationship with someone you really disliked to get your job done?
11. How did the others react when you did that?
12. How did you come up with that approach in the first place?
13. How did you know that method of getting over that barrier would work?
14. How did you set boundaries or limits on that?
15. How do others you have known approach that?
16. How far did you go to try to be a team player?
17. How far will you go before you cut line and try another approach?
18. How much did you have to give up to make it work?
19. How typical is this for you?
20. How would you approach that same situation today?
21. Is this natural for you, or do you really have to dig for it?

# COMMAND SKILLS

22. Was that a fair way to maneuver around them?
23. Was there a time when you didn't understand this about yourself?
24. What did you do after you got that feedback?
25. What did you do to adapt to that?
26. What did you learn from that?
27. What drives your need to lead/not lead (to see if they understand what drives their behavior)?
28. Why did you choose that approach?
29. Why did you decide to take the risk?
30. Why did you do it that way?
31. Why did you time your attempt like you did?
32. Why do you suppose organizations work that way?
33. Why do you think that didn't work?
34. Why do you think that happened that way?
35. Why do you think that worked?
36. Why do you think you have difficulties like that once in a while (to check for insights into the cause of the problems)?
37. Would you have done it that way with looser deadlines?
38. Would you have done it that way with tighter deadlines?

E. Themes/Things to Look for:

Assertiveness
Career courage
Contention
Gets tougher under conflict
Likes to lead
Low need to be liked when leading

Motivated by the thrill of the hunt
Overcoming obstacles
Quick decisions
Risk-taking
Strong ego
Values and drivers

F. Most Likely Résumé:

1. Look for jobs like:

Fix-Its/Turnarounds
Scale (size shift) Assignments

Significant People Demands
Start-Ups

2. Look for develop-in-place assignments like:

Plan for and start up something small (secretarial pool, athletic program, suggestion system, program, etc.).
Launch a new product, service, or process.
Relaunch an existing product or service that's not doing well.
Assign a project to a group with a tight deadline.
Manage an ad hoc, temporary group of balky and resisting people through an unpopular change or project.
Manage an ad hoc, temporary group of low-competence people through a task they couldn't do by themselves.
Manage an ad hoc, temporary group including former peers to accomplish a task.
Manage an ad hoc, temporary group of people who are older and/or more experienced to accomplish a task.
Manage an ad hoc, temporary group of people involved in tackling a fix-it or turnaround project.
Assemble an ad hoc team of diverse people to accomplish a difficult task.

COMMAND SKILLS

Help shut down a plant, regional office, product line, business, operation, etc.

Prepare and present a proposal of some consequence to top management.

Work on a team that's deciding who to keep and who to let go in a layoff, shutdown, delayering, or divestiture.

Manage a group through a significant business crisis.

Take on a tough and undoable project, one where others who have tried it have failed.

Manage a cost-cutting project.

Resolve an issue in conflict between two people, units, geographies, functions, etc.

Build a multifunctional project team to tackle a common business issue or problem.

3. **Best references to ask about or check:**

   Human Resource Professionals   Past Associates/Constituencies
   Natural Mentors   Direct Reports

G. Learning Agility Evaluation:

   2. All or Nothing vs. Can See Many Sides
   5. Tight/Rigid vs. Loose/Flexible
   10. Reactive vs. Initiating
   12. Rehearsed/Socially Acceptable vs. Candid
   19. External Standards vs. Internal Standards
   22. Focus on Accomplishments vs. Focus on Solving Problems

H. The LEADERSHIP ARCHITECT® Sort Card Connections:

1. Good (positive) if combined with high:

   Quick and fast 1, 16, 32, 57
   Balances leading with concern for others 3, 7, 10
   Works through conflict 12, 43
   Speaks out 34, 57
   Team leader 36, 60
   Gets things done 53

2. Bad (negative) if combined with low or high (+):

   Bull in a china shop (+1) 12, 31, 38, 48
   May step on others to get a better view (+6, 8)
   Runs over people 7, 10, 23
   May lead organizations and people down the wrong path 17, 50
   Doesn't develop, just pushes 18, 19
   Loner 36, 42, 60 (+57)
   Jumps to conclusions; no due process 41, 52, 59

COMMAND SKILLS

3. **Too much can contribute to the following Stallers and Stoppers:**

    A. *What too much looks like (overused):*

    May not be a team player; may not be tolerant of other people's ways of doing things; may choose to strongly lead when other more team-based tactics would do as well or better; may not develop other leaders; may become controversial and be rejected by the team, unit, or organization.

    B. *Too much might lead to these Stallers and Stoppers:*

Unable to Adapt to Differences (101)	Failure to Build a Team (110)
Poor Administrator (102)	Insensitive to Others (112)
Arrogant (104)	Overmanaging (117)
Blocked Personal Learner (106)	

    C. *Compensators:*

    How to compensate for too much of this competency:
    3, 7, 10, 19, 31, 33, 36, 38, 41, 47, 52, 59, 60

    D. *Things to watch for:*

A loner	People may not want to work with them
It's their way or the highway	Poor history of developing talent
May chill the contribution of others	Jumps to conclusions
Only knows one way	Gets in trouble often

4. **Too little can contribute to the following Stallers and Stoppers:**

    A. *What too little looks like (unskilled):*

    More comfortable following; may avoid conflict and crises, be unwilling to take the heat, have problems with taking a tough stand; might be laid back and quiet; too concerned about what others may say or think; may worry too much about being liked, correct or above criticism; may be conflict-shy or lack perseverance; may not be cool under pressure; may not display a sense of urgency.

    B. *Too little might lead to these Stallers and Stoppers:*

    Failure to Build a Team (110)
    Performance Problems (118)

    C. *Compensators:*

    How to substitute for too little of this competency:
    1, 5, 12, 13, 16, 20, 30, 35, 36, 37, 39, 49, 57, 65

I. **LEARNING ARCHITECT® Connections:**

Look for people who act like and/or show evidence of:

1a. Pure Action	8. Initiate
1b. Trial and Error	21. Changer
2a. Problem Solving	23. Orchestrator

COMMAND SKILLS

J. CHOICES ARCHITECT® Connections:

Look for people who act like and/or show evidence of:

First Edition (Released 1994)
- 20. Forging Ahead
- 21. Taking the Heat
- 23. Communicator

Second Edition (Released 2000)
- 9. Agile Communicator
- 10. Conflict Manager
- 22. Taking the Heat
- 23. Visioning
- 24. Inspires Others
- 26. Drive
- 27. Presence

K. Difficulty to Develop:
24 (out of 34)–Moderate

10. COMPASSION

A. Definition:

Genuinely cares about people; is concerned about their work and non-work problems; is available and ready to help; is sympathetic to the plight of others not as fortunate; demonstrates real empathy with the joys and pains of others.

B. Arenas/Domains to Explore:

1. Any emotionally charged event/situation
2. Coaching athletic teams
3. Experience with the handicapped/chronic illnesses
4. Good samaritan behavior
5. Hospital/hospice volunteer work
6. Political persuasion viewpoint on social issues
7. Social role models
8. Team captain for sports
9. Volunteer community work
10. What they read
11. Work/non-work
12. Working with people of lesser status
13. Working with children/younger people

C. Sample Questions:

*Dimension 1: Been there, done that–has had direct personal experience(s) involving the competency–candidate was the prime player   Note: * means OK for campus*

1. Do you volunteer your time for any charity or cause?*
2. Have any of your close friends ever gone through very tough times?*
3. Have you ever been a big brother/sister?
4. Have you ever been in a merger where some people were left without jobs?
5. Have you ever been involved in a layoff?
6. Have you ever been part of a plan to save a struggling employee?
7. Have you ever changed your mind about how you see people based on dealing with a person who was handicapped, mentally ill? What have you done differently?
8. Have you ever dealt with someone with a substance abuse/emotional problem/chronic illness/handicap?*
9. Have you ever had a situation where something was taken away or held back from you and given to someone else?
10. Have you ever had to fire someone who just couldn't do the job?
11. Have you ever managed anything where the people or units reporting to you were in different locations? How did you show your personal concern for them?
12. Have you ever traveled to a Third World country? What were your impressions?
13. Tell me about a time when you have given up something important to you to help someone else.*
14. Tell me about a time when you helped out someone who needed a boost.*
15. Tell me about a time when you helped someone or a group less fortunate than you.*
16. Tell me about a time when you learned to get along with someone you found to be a very difficult person.*
17. Tell me about a time when your lack of concern or feelings for others got you into trouble.
18. Tell me about a time when your concern for others worked really well for you.
19. Tell me about your off-work (school) interests, activities, memberships.* How did you get interested in these off-work activities?*
20. What local, national, or global causes do you associate yourself with?*

COMPASSION

Dimension 2: Seen/been around others who were involved with the competency–good and bad; learns from others about self

21. Contrast the most and least compassionate people you know.*
22. Has compassion/concern for others ever been in any 360° survey done on you? Was your score among your highest, middle, or lowest?
23. Has poor compassion/concern for others on someone else's part ever created an obstacle for you or got in the way of something you were trying to accomplish?*
24. Have you ever talked about your compassion/concern for others with a coach or mentor?
25. Have you ever watched someone fail/get fired because they did not show compassion for others?*
26. Have you ever watched someone exaggerate compassion/concern for others to the point that it backfired?
27. Have you ever watched someone succeed because they showed compassion/concern for others?*
28. Have you ever worked with a coach on compassion/concern for others?*
29. Have you ever worked with a person who excelled at showing compassion/concern for others?
30. Have you ever worked with a skills coach on improving your compassion/concern for others?*
31. How do you get feedback about yourself on showing compassion/concern for others?
32. How often do you check with multiple sources when you get a piece of critical feedback on your compassion/concern for others?
33. Is there a historical figure you consider a model of compassion/concern for others?
34. What do others who are not your fans say about your compassion/concern for others?
35. What do others who like you say about your compassion/concern for others?
36. Which boss was the best at showing compassion/concern for others?
37. Which boss was the worst at showing compassion/concern for others?
38. Which direct report was the best at showing compassion/concern for others?
39. Which direct report was the worst at showing compassion/concern for others?
40. Which peer was the best at showing compassion/concern for others?
41. Which peer was the worst at showing compassion/concern for others?
42. Who in your field or business deals the best with showing compassion/concern for others?
43. Who do you consider a role model of showing compassion/concern for others?*
44. Who do you go to for advice on showing compassion/concern for others?
45. Who have you learned the most from about showing compassion/concern for others?*
46. Who is a higher-management role model for you on showing compassion/concern for others?
47. Who is a role model of showing compassion/concern for others outside of work?

Dimension 3: Knows how the competency works in theory; shows understanding

48. Are there situations or settings where someone should act differently in the way they demonstrate compassion/concern for others?
49. Do you think compassion skills can be learned? If so, how do you think people develop compassion skills?
50. Do you think there is a way to compensate or work around low compassion skills?
51. Has anyone asked you for your opinions/advice on caring or concern for others?*
52. Have you ever attended a course on demonstrating caring or concern for others?
53. Have you ever been in a situation where you and others put compassion/concern for others on a success profile?
54. Have you ever been part of an effort to create a policy or a mission statement containing reference to the importance of being compassionate?
55. Have you ever been someone's coach or mentor who had problems with caring or concern for others?

COMPASSION

56. Have you ever created a development plan for someone on caring or concern for others?
57. Have you ever criticized someone for not demonstrating compassion/concern for others?
58. Have you ever designed a program on demonstrating caring or concern for others?
59. Have you ever given a speech on demonstrating caring or concern for others?
60. Have you ever rewarded or recognized someone for having compassion/concern for others?
61. Have you ever taught a course on caring or concern for others?
62. Have you ever tried to help someone deal more effectively with their concern for others?*
63. Have you ever tried to help someone improve their concern or caring for others?
64. How do you think people develop compassion?
65. How much compassion/concern for others is good to have and how much is too much?
66. How much of success do you think is due to the ability to demonstrate compassion/concern for others compared with other characteristics?
67. How would you know if someone is bad at showing caring/concern for others?
68. How would you know if someone is good at showing caring/concern for others?
69. If you had to write a book on caring or concern for others, what would the chapter headings be?
70. What are the benefits to someone who is really good at demonstrating caring or concern for others?
71. What are the consequences to someone who is really poor at demonstrating caring or concern for others?
72. What do you think the performance standard is on demonstrating caring/concern for others for someone in your role?
73. What happens if you have or use too much compassion?
74. What happens when two people try to work together who are very different on compassion skills?
75. What wisdom would you pass onto others trying to become better at compassion skills?
76. When you select others, what do you look for in their ability to demonstrate compassion/caring for others?
77. Why do you think people end up being different on compassion skills?

Dimension 4: Shows personal change and sense-making; learned it one place and applied it in another; can compare and contrast experiences; changes viewpoints across time; can explain personal development or evolution related to the competency

78. Compare and contrast examples of times when you've been effective and ineffective at showing concern for others.
79. Contrast your on- and off-the-job use of showing compassion for others.
80. Did you ever pass up a job or assignment because you were not confident enough in your ability to show concern for others?
81. Do you ever use other skills to cover for your lack of compassion?
82. Has compassion ever figured in a failure, struggle, or setback you have had?
83. Has becoming better at showing concern for others ever helped you in other areas?
84. Has lack of compassion ever been the subject of a development plan for you?
85. Has your level of concern for others always been this way?
86. Have you ever delegated or assigned someone a task because you don't demonstrate compassionate behavior particularly well?
87. Have you ever made significant strides at becoming better at being compassionate?
88. Have your compassion skills, good or bad, ever been the subject of your performance review or a career discussion?
89. How different are you across situations in your capacity for compassion?
90. How do you decide how much compassion to show?

COMPASSION

91. How has September 11th, 2001 impacted the way you interact with others?
92. How have you adjusted your work habits over time to remain available to people without it interfering with your work?
93. How much of your success is due to your compassionate behavior?
94. How transferable are your compassion skills to other situations?
95. How well do you get to know the people you work with?
96. If you had to become better at being compassionate in a hurry, what would you do?
97. Was there a time when you were not good at being compassionate?
98. What caused you to work to change your skills at showing concern for others?
99. What event or series of events had the most impact on your concern for others?
100. What's the most varied you can be in showing compassion?
101. What was the shortest amount of time in which you increased your skill level at being compassionate?

102. What's your thinking about separating work and personal life?
103. When did you first realize your skill level at being compassionate?
104. When you know ahead of time that your level of compassion won't work, what do you do?
105. Why do you think you deal with showing concern for others the way you do?
106. Why do you think your capacity for compassion is the way it is?*

D. Follow-up Probes:

1. Are there times when you're not like this or wouldn't do this?
2. Are there times when you show concern for others like that and times when you don't?
3. Could you contrast those two bosses for me?
4. Could you give me a few examples of how you've used or applied that?
5. Did you or the other person blink first?
6. Do you suppose if others would just try harder, they could learn to show concern for others as you do?
7. Do you think this is teachable?
8. Do you think you have more concern for others than most? Why?
9. Do you think you would perform any better if your concern for others were different?
10. How did the others react when you did that?
11. How did you come up with that approach in the first place?
12. How did you know that method of getting over that barrier would work?
13. How do others you have known approach that?
14. How far will you go before you cut line and try another approach?
15. How much did you have to give up to make it work?
16. How typical is this for you?
17. How would you approach that same situation today?
18. Is this natural for you, or do you really have to dig for it?
19. Was there a time when you didn't understand this about yourself?
20. What did you do after you got that feedback?
21. What did you do to adapt to that?
22. What did you learn from that?
23. Why did you choose that approach?

COMPASSION

24. Why did you decide to take the risk?
25. Why did you do it that way?
26. Why did you time your attempt like you did?
27. Why do you suppose organizations work that way?
28. Why do you think that didn't work?
29. Why do you think that happened that way?
30. Why do you think that worked?
31. Would you have done it that way with looser deadlines?
32. Would you have done it that way with tighter deadlines?

E. Themes/Things to Look for:

Ability to articulate feelings and internal views as seen by others
Balance between compassion and results/performance
Compassion for the few or the many
Empathy
Gives others the benefit of the doubt
Going out of one's way; compassion
Has compassion for people they don't like
Helps people solve problems
Keeps personal feelings from getting in the way of having compassion for others
One size doesn't fit all; sees differences in others
Satisfying personal needs vs. having true compassion for others
Source of the motive for compassion
Where they place the blame for why people are disadvantaged

F. Most Likely Résumé:

1. Look for jobs like:

Fix-Its/Turnarounds   Staff Leadership (Influencing Without Authority)
Significant People Demands   Staff to Line Shifts

2. Look for develop-in-place assignments like:

Work for a year or more with a charitable organization.
Join a self-help or support group.
Represent the concerns of a group of nonexempt, clerical, or administrative employees to higher management to seek resolution of a difficult issue.
Help shut down a plant, regional office, product line, business, operation, etc.
Work on a team that's deciding who to keep and who to let go in a layoff, shutdown, delayering, or divestiture.
Manage the outplacement of a group of people.

3. Best references to ask about or check:

Development Professionals   Spouse
Human Resource Professionals   Direct Reports
Natural Mentors   Yourself

COMPASSION

G. Learning Agility Evaluation:

2. All or Nothing vs. Can See Many Sides
3. Ordinary/Socially Acceptable vs. Insightful/different
4. Spectator/Passive vs. Player/Participant
15. Linear vs. Use Contrasts/Analogies
19. External Standards vs. Internal Standards
20. Avoids Responsibility for Mistakes vs. Admits and Learns from Mistakes
21. View from Self vs. View from Point of View of Others

H. The LEADERSHIP ARCHITECT® Sort Card Connections:

1. Good (positive) if combined with high:
Balances compassion with doing the job 7, 12, 13, 35, 53
Takes time to listen 7, 19, 33, 41
Mostly uses positive humor 7, 26
Volunteers for community service 7, 46, 66
Takes charge but watches for stress reactions 9, 20, 57
Balances negative messages with compassion for the person 13, 27, 34
Takes people's needs into account when making developmental assignments 17, 19, 25

2. Bad (negative) if combined with low or high (+):
Can't make decisions that negatively affect people 1, 12, 16
Too nice/soft (+3, 7, 23)
Not tough enough 12, 13, 34
Can't make tough management decisions 18, 20, 35
Poor people-decisions 25, 56
Results come second 50, 53

3. Too much can contribute to the following Stallers and Stoppers:

A. What too much looks like (overused):

May smooth over conflict in the interest of harmony; may not be tough enough in the face of malingerers and may make too many concessions; may get so close to people that objectivity is affected and they are able to get away with too much; may have trouble with close calls on people.

B. Too much might lead to these Stallers and Stoppers:
Defensiveness (108)

C. Compensators:
How to compensate for too much of this competency:
12, 13, 16, 18, 20, 34, 37, 50, 53, 57, 59, 62

COMPASSION

D. **Things to watch for:**

Can't separate feelings from tough decisions	May set standards too low
May avoid conflict	May tolerate too many excuses
May get too close to people	Group doesn't perform well
May not be taken seriously when they try to be tough	May have a poor record developing people

4. **Too little can contribute to the following Stallers and Stoppers:**

   A. *What too little looks like (unskilled):*

   May be less caring or empathic than most; doesn't ask personal questions; doesn't respond much when offered; results are all that matters; everything else gets in the way; believes in separation of personal life and business; may find the plight of others an inappropriate topic at work; uncomfortable with people in stress and pain; may not know how to show compassion or how to deal with people in trouble; may have less sympathy than most for the imperfections and problems of others.

   B. *Too little might lead to these Stallers and Stoppers:*

   Arrogant (104)
   Betrayal of Trust (105)
   Lack of Ethics and Values (109)
   Failure to Build a Team (110)
   Insensitive to Others (112)

   C. *Compensators:*

   How to substitute for too little of this competency:
   3, 7, 12, 21, 22, 27, 29, 33, 41, 64

I. **LEARNING ARCHITECT® Connections:**

Look for people who act like and/or show evidence of:

2c. Intuition
3c. Personal Experience
4a. Getting Information
16. Collaborate
32. Diversity in Others

J. **CHOICES ARCHITECT® Connections:**

Look for people who act like and/or show evidence of:

First Edition (Released 1994)
14. Transaction Quality
15. Helps Others Succeed

Second Edition (Released 2000)
12. Helps Others Succeed
15. People-Smart

K. **Difficulty to Develop:**

28 (of 34)–Harder

COMPASSION

11. COMPOSURE

A. Definition:

Is cool under pressure; does not become defensive or irritated when times are tough; is considered mature; can be counted on to hold things together during tough times; can handle stress; is not knocked off balance by the unexpected; doesn't show frustration when resisted or blocked; is a settling influence in a crisis.

B. Arenas/Domains to Explore:

1. A lot going on at once
2. Bad bosses
3. Conflicts with others
4. Crises
5. Disappointments
6. Door slammed in face
7. Goals thwarted
8. Kept waiting
9. Legal testimony
10. Poor treatment
11. Powerless situations
12. Rejection
13. Setbacks
14. Sudden changes
15. Tension between people
16. The unexpected
17. Tough decisions/choices
18. Tough Q & A in front of VIPs
19. Unfairly treated
20. When things go bad
21. With incompetent people

C. Sample Questions:

Dimension 1: Been there, done that–has had direct personal experience(s) involving the competency–candidate was the prime player   Note: * means OK for campus

1. Have you ever been asked a question by a VIP in public you were expected to know but didn't? What did you do?
2. Have you ever been asked to lead a group that did not have the skills you needed?*
3. Have you ever been rejected or turned down by a person or a group?*
4. How do you handle being forced by a person in power to do something that you don't want to do?*
5. How do you handle being unjustly criticized in private?*
6. How do you handle being unjustly criticized in public?*
7. How do you react when someone cuts in front of you on the highway?*
8. Tell me about a crisis you had to manage.*
9. Tell me about a senior manager you initially had a lot of trouble dealing with.
10. Tell me about a time when someone pushed you to the limit.*
11. Tell me about a time when the situation overwhelmed you and you couldn't finish something or couldn't achieve a goal you wanted to achieve.
12. Tell me about a time when you gave a speech or had to push a point to a hostile or unreceptive audience.*
13. Tell me about a time when you had the rug pulled out from under you.*
14. Tell me about a time when you had to deal with an arrogant, condescending person or one who made you angry.*
15. Tell me about a time when you intervened to help settle a heated dispute.
16. Tell me about a time when you lost your composure, and are still glad you did.

COMPOSURE

17. Tell me about a time when you were blind sided by a hostile, personal remark.
18. Tell me about a time when you were caught "red-handed" on something and had no way out.*
19. Tell me about a time when you were publicly embarrassed.*
20. Tell me about a time when your composure worked really well for you.
21. Tell me about a time when your lack of composure got you into trouble.
22. Tell me about a time you believe you were treated unfairly.
23. Tell me about a time you tried your best but failed.*
24. Were you ever in a situation where you had to give a deposition or give testimony in a trial?*
25. What do you do when things just don't go as planned?*
26. What do you do when you absolutely know you're right and someone in power overrules you?*
27. What do you do when you are blamed for something that was not your doing?*
28. What do you generally do when faced with a decision for which there is no clear answer but you have to provide one?*
29. What is your way of getting upset? What do you do?*
30. What's your technique of letting go pent-up steam?*
31. When someone says of you that you lost your cool, what have you probably done?*
32. When you are being defensive, how do you act?*
33. When you are obviously losing a public debate, what do you do?*

Dimension 2: Seen/been around others who were involved with the competency–good and bad; learns from others about self

34. Contrast the most and least composed people you know.*
35. Has composure ever been in any 360° survey done on you? Was your score among your highest, middle, or lowest?
36. Has lack of composure on someone else's part ever created an obstacle for you or got in the way of something you were trying to accomplish?*
37. Have you ever talked with a coach or mentor about your composure?
38. Have you ever watched someone fail/get fired because they lacked composure?*
39. Have you ever watched someone overmaintain composure to the point that it backfired?
40. Have you ever watched someone succeed because they demonstrated composure?*
41. Have you ever worked with a coach on composure?*
42. Have you ever worked with a person who excelled at staying composed?
43. Have you ever worked with a skills coach on your composure, ability to be a calming force, nonverbal behavior, and/or self-control?*
44. How do you get feedback about yourself on composure?
45. How often do you check with multiple sources when you get a piece of critical feedback on your composure?
46. Is there a historical figure you consider a model of composure?
47. What do others who are not your fans say about your composure?
48. What do others who like you say about your composure?
49. Which boss was the best at staying composed?
50. Which boss was the worst at staying composed?
51. Which direct report was the best at staying composed?
52. Which direct report was the worst at staying composed?

COMPOSURE

53. Which peer was the best at staying composed?
54. Which peer was the worst at staying composed?
55. Who in your field or business is the best with staying composed?
56. Who do you consider a role model of composure?*
57. Who do you go to for advice on composure?
58. Who have you learned the most from about composure?*
59. Who is a higher-management role model for you on composure?
60. Who is a role model of composure outside of work?

Dimension 3: Knows how the competency works in theory; shows understanding

61. Are there situations or settings where someone should act differently at maintaining their composure?
62. Do you think composure skills can be learned? If so, how do you think people develop composure skills?
63. Do you think there is a way to compensate or work around being low in composure skills?
64. Has anyone asked you for your opinions/advice on maintaining composure?*
65. Have you ever attended a course on personal composure?
66. Have you ever been in a situation where you and others put composure skills on a success profile?
67. Have you ever been part of an effort to create a policy or a mission statement containing reference to the importance of personal composure?
68. Have you ever been someone's coach or mentor who had problems with maintaining composure?
69. Have you ever created a development plan for someone to improve their personal composure?
70. Have you ever criticized someone for not maintaining composure?
71. Have you ever designed a program on developing composure skills?
72. Have you ever given a speech on maintaining composure?
73. Have you ever rewarded or recognized someone for staying composed?
74. Have you ever taught a course on maintaining personal composure?
75. Have you ever tried to help someone deal more effectively with composure?*
76. Have you ever tried to help someone improve their composure skills?
77. How do you think people develop composure skills?
78. How much composure is good to have and how much is too much?
79. How much of success do you think is due to staying composed compared with other characteristics?
80. How would you know if someone is bad at staying composed?
81. How would you know if someone is good at staying composed?
82. If you had to write a book on maintaining personal composure, what would the chapter headings be?
83. What are the benefits to someone who is really good at staying composed?
84. What are the consequences to someone who is really poor at staying composed?
85. What do you think the performance standard is on demonstrating composure skills for someone in your role?
86. What happens if you overdo staying in control?
87. What happens when two people try to work together who are very different on staying composed?
88. What wisdom would you pass onto others trying to become better at staying composed?
89. When you select others, what do you look for in their ability to stay composed?
90. Why do you think people end up being different in their ability to stay composed?

COMPOSURE

Dimension 4: Shows personal change and sense-making; learned it one place and applied it in another; can compare and contrast experiences; changes viewpoints across time; can explain personal development or evolution related to the competency

91. Compare and contrast examples of times when you've been effective and ineffective at handling stress or staying cool under pressure.
92. Contrast your on- and off-the-job demonstration of composure.
93. Did you ever pass up a job or assignment because you were not confident enough in your ability to stay composed?
94. Do you ever use other skills to cover for your lack of composure?
95. Has composure ever figured in a failure, struggle, or setback you have had?
96. Has becoming better at handling stress or staying cool under pressure ever helped you in other areas?
97. Has poor composure ever been the subject of a development plan for you?
98. Has your ability to remain composed always been this way?
99. Have you ever delegated or assigned someone a task because you didn't stay composed particularly well?
100. Have you ever made significant strides at becoming better at composure?
101. Have your composure skills, good or bad, ever been the subject of your performance review or a career discussion?
102. How different are you across situations in your ability to stay composed?
103. How do you decide how composed to be?
104. How have you adjusted your style to work productively with people you've lost your cool with in the past?
105. How much of your success is due to your skill at handling stress or staying cool under pressure?
106. How transferable are your composure skills to other situations?
107. If you had to become better at handling stress or staying cool under pressure in a hurry, what would you do?
108. Was there a time when you were not good at staying composed?
109. What are your emotional triggers? How do you manage them?
110. What caused you to work to change your ability to stay composed?
111. What event or series of events had the most impact on your ability to handle stress or stay cool under pressure?
112. What's the most varied you can be in staying composed?
113. What was the shortest amount of time in which you increased your skill level at handling stress or staying cool under pressure?
114. When did you first realize your skill level at handling stress or staying cool under pressure?
115. When you know ahead of time that your usual level of composure won't work, what do you do?
116. Why do you think you deal with composure the way you do?
117. Why do you think your composure is the way it is?*

D. Follow-up Probes:

1. Are there times when you're not like this or wouldn't do this?
2. Are there times when you respond like that and times when you don't?
3. Could you contrast those two bosses for me?
4. Could you give me a few examples of how you've used or applied that?
5. Did you or the other person blink first?
6. Do you suppose if others would just try harder, they could learn to be more composed like you?
7. Do you think this is teachable?

COMPOSURE

8. Do you think you're better at staying composed than most? Why?
9. Do you think you would perform any differently if you were more composed?
10. Have you ever had to form a relationship with someone you really disliked to get your job done?
11. How did the others react when you did that?
12. How did you come up with that approach in the first place?
13. How did you get yourself under control in that situation?
14. How did you know that method of getting over that barrier would work?
15. How do others you have known approach that?
16. How do you handle those kinds of frustrations of everyday life?
17. How far did you go to try to be a team player?
18. How far will you go before you cut line and try another approach?
19. How much did you have to give up to make it work?
20. How often do you use the "Let's meet in the middle" approach?
21. How typical is this for you?
22. How would you approach that same situation today?
23. Is this natural for you, or do you really have to dig for it?
24. Was that a fair way to maneuver around them?
25. Was there a time when you didn't understand this about yourself?
26. What did you do after you got that feedback?
27. What did you do to adapt to that?
28. What did you learn from that?
29. What do you do when you think you might lose your cool?
30. Why did that person intimidate you? Would they now?
31. Why did you choose that approach?
32. Why did you decide to take the risk?
33. Why did you do it that way?
34. Why did you time your attempt like you did?
35. Why do you suppose organizations work that way?
36. Why do you think that didn't work?
37. Why do you think that happened that way?
38. Why do you think that worked?
39. Why do you think you have difficulty with that once in a while?
40. Would you have done it that way with looser deadlines?
41. Would you have done it that way with tighter deadlines?

E. Themes/Things to Look for:
   Acknowledges feelings without wallowing in them
   Avoids moodiness; staying even under stress
   Self-awareness–knowing one's tendencies and triggers/controlling reactions
   Comfort with loose ends
   Defers to those in power
   Delay of gratification
   Realistic view of what really is happening
   Selective management of emotions

COMPOSURE

Separates internal feelings from what shows on the outside
Shows flexibility
Sticks to the problem at hand, the facts
Talks about not showing irritation
Knows the danger signs when they are about to blow up

F. Most Likely Résumé:

1. Look for jobs like:

Chair of Projects/Task Forces	Staff to Line Shifts
Line to Staff Switches	Start-Ups
Staff Leadership (Influencing Without Authority)	

2. Look for develop-in-place assignments like:

Study humor in business settings; read books on the nature of humor; collect cartoons you could use in presentations; study funny people around you; keep a log of funny jokes and sayings you hear; read famous speeches and study how humor was used; attend comedy clubs; ask a funny person to act as your tutor; practice funny lines and jokes with others.

Manage an ad hoc, temporary group of "green," inexperienced people as their coach, teacher, orienter, etc.

Manage an ad hoc, temporary group of balky and resisting people through an unpopular change or project.

Manage an ad hoc, temporary group of people where the temporary manager is a towering expert and the people in the group are not.

Manage an ad hoc, temporary group of people where the people in the group are towering experts but the temporary manager is not.

Manage an ad hoc, temporary group of people involved in tackling a fix-it or turnaround project.

Handle a tough negotiation with an internal/external client or customer.

Help shut down a plant, regional office, product line, business, operation, etc.

Prepare and present a proposal of some consequence to top management.

Manage a dissatisfied internal or external customer; troubleshoot a performance or quality problem with a product or service.

Manage the assigning/allocating of office space in a contested situation.

Manage a group through a significant business crisis.

Take on a tough and undoable project, one where others who have tried it have failed.

Manage the outplacement of a group of people.

Manage a cost-cutting project.

Take on a task you dislike or hate to do.

Make peace with an enemy or someone you've disappointed with a product or service or someone you've had some trouble with or don't get along well with.

Manage a project team of people who are older and more experienced.

3. Best references to ask about or check:

Development Professionals	Spouse
Family Members	Direct Reports
Human Resource Professionals	Yourself
Peers and Colleagues	

COMPOSURE

G. Learning Agility Evaluation:
2. All or Nothing vs. Can See Many Sides
5. Tight/Rigid vs. Loose/Flexible
6. Reacting/Responsive vs. Adapting
16. Few Rules of Thumb vs. Many and Varied Rules of Thumb
17. Avoid Discussion of Weaknesses vs. Comfortably Sharing Shortcomings
19. External Standards vs. Internal Standards

H. The LEADERSHIP ARCHITECT® Sort Card Connections:

1. Good (positive) if combined with high:
Low drag coefficient getting airborne 1, 2, 16, 43
Mentally open-minded and flexible 2, 40
Relied on in a crisis 3, 9, 33, 41
Cool and caring 7, 10, 31
Handles conflict with minimal damage 12, 13, 34, 57
Good with emotional customers 12, 15, 33, 41
Doesn't get sidetracked easily 37, 43, 50, 53

2. Bad (negative) if combined with low or high (+):
Lone ranger (+1, 43, 57) 42, 60
Inflexible 2, 40
Uncaring/Cold 3, 7, 10
May be too tough and ride over problems (+9, 34, 35, 53)
May not take "soft" data into account when making decisions about people (+25, 56)
Doesn't show people much 27, 31, 44
Can't show compassion 36, 49

3. Too much can contribute to the following Stallers and Stoppers:

A. What too much looks like (overused):
May not show appropriate emotion; may be seen as cold and uncaring; may seem flat in situations where others show feelings; may be easily misinterpreted; may not be able to relate well to those whose actions and decisions are based more on feelings than on thinking.

B. Too much might lead to these Stallers and Stoppers:
Arrogant (104)
Blocked Personal Learner (106)
Lack of Composure (107)

C. Compensators:
How to compensate for too much of this competency:
3, 10, 14, 26, 27, 31, 44, 60, 66

COMPOSURE

D. Things to watch for:
Can't access emotional language
Can't grieve
Controlled, rigid, inflexible
May "lose it" infrequently but big
May experience physical consequences of holding it in
People feel uncomfortable about not being able to read them

4. Too little can contribute to the following Stallers and Stoppers:

A. What too little looks like (unskilled):
Gets rattled and loses cool under pressure and stress; may blow up, say things he/she shouldn't; gets easily overwhelmed and becomes emotional, defensive or withdrawn; may be defensive and sensitive to criticism; may be cynical or moody; may be knocked off balance by surprises and get easily rattled; may contribute to others losing composure or being unsettled; may let anger, frustration and anxiety show.

B. Too little might lead to these Stallers and Stoppers:
Unable to Adapt to Differences (101)
Betrayal of Trust (105)
Blocked Personal Learner (106)
Lack of Composure (107)
Defensiveness (108)
Lack of Ethics and Values (109)
Failure to Build a Team (110)
Political Missteps (119)

C. Compensators:
How to substitute for too little of this competency:
2, 3, 8, 12, 33, 41, 43, 48, 57

I. LEARNING ARCHITECT® Connections:

Look for people who act like and/or show evidence of:
1c. Following a Plan
3b. Self-Talk
4c. Actively Involve
14. Controlled
24. Discloser
26. Self-Aware
31. Rationality
36. Comfort with Paradox
37. Flexibility
38. Resilience

J. CHOICES ARCHITECT® Connections:

Look for people who act like and/or show evidence of:

First Edition (Released 1994)
8. Cool Transactor
21. Taking the Heat

Second Edition (Released 2000)
10. Conflict Manager
11. Cool Transactor
22. Taking the Heat
27. Presence

K. Difficulty to Develop:
27 (of 34)–Harder

12. CONFLICT MANAGEMENT

A. Definition:

Steps up to conflicts, seeing them as opportunities; reads situations quickly; good at focused listening; can hammer out tough agreements and settle disputes equitably; can find common ground and get cooperation with minimum noise.

B. Arenas/Domains to Explore:

1. Any multi-layer event/situation
2. Assigning blame for a failure
3. Bad bosses
4. Clashes of authority/responsibility
5. Coaching athletic teams
6. Conflicts with others
7. Disputes
8. Door slammed in face
9. Goals thwarted by others
10. Internal bargaining
11. Kept waiting by incompetence
12. Professional association officer
13. Pushing a strongly held belief in the face of resistance
14. Rejection
15. Strained relationships with family
16. Student government
17. Team captain for sports
18. Tension between others
19. Tough negotiations
20. Tough Q & A in front of VIPs
21. Working with incompetent people
22. Working with people of lesser status

C. Sample Questions:

Dimension 1: Been there, done that–has had direct personal experience(s) involving the competency–candidate was the prime player   Note: * means OK for campus

1. Has somebody in power blocking you for no apparent reason ever prevented you from achieving an important goal?
2. Have you ever coached a children's team when the parents were on the sidelines trying to help you do your job?
3. Do you ever fake getting upset to make a point in a conflict?*
4. Has a VIP ever challenged you on a point you knew you were absolutely right about?
5. Have you ever been blamed for something that was not your doing?*
6. Have you ever had to accomplish a tough goal and meet a tight deadline with a group of less experienced or incompetent people?
7. Have you ever had to fight a boss who you knew was wrong in front of others?
8. Have you ever helped others solve a long-standing dispute?*
9. Have you ever managed anything where the people or units reporting to you were in different locations? How did you mange conflict?
10. Have you ever tried to push an unpopular change?*
11. How often do you insert yourself into a conflict that really isn't in your area?*
12. Tell me about a conflict you handled well and one you didn't handle well.*
13. Tell me about a time when someone pushed you to your limit.*
14. Tell me about a time when something went from a harmonious to a conflict-ridden situation.*
15. Tell me about a time when you brought two reluctant people or groups together.*
16. Tell me about a time when you had to give bad news and the receiver didn't take it well.*
17. Tell me about a time when you had to resolve a conflict or you couldn't succeed in what you were doing.*

CONFLICT MANAGEMENT

18. Tell me about a time when you handled a conflict with a group outside the organization.
19. Tell me about a time when you handled a conflict you were having with a parent/friend/schoolmate/boss/peer/direct report.*
20. Tell me about a time when you handled a tough negotiation.
21. Tell me about a time when you made peace with an adversary.*
22. Tell me about a time when you served as a mediator or a neutral third party.*
23. Tell me about a time when you were unwelcome in a group.*
24. Tell me about a time when your ability to deal effectively with conflict worked really well for you.
25. Tell me about a time when your lack of conflict management skills got you into trouble.
26. Tell me about a time you saw a conflict coming.*
27. Tell me about some conflicts you have avoided.*
28. Tell me about some conflicts you waited out.*

Dimension 2: Seen/been around others who were involved with the competency–good and bad; learns from others about self

29. Contrast the people you know who are most and least able to deal with conflict.*
30. Has conflict management ever been in any 360° survey done on you? Was your score among your highest, middle, or lowest?
31. Has poor conflict management on someone else's part ever created an obstacle for you or got in the way of something you were trying to accomplish?*
32. Have you ever talked about your conflict management skills with a coach or mentor?
33. Have you ever watched someone fail/get fired because they did not handle conflict well?*
34. Have you ever watched someone overmanage conflict to the point that it backfired?
35. Have you ever watched someone succeed because they dealt with conflict well?*
36. Have you ever worked with a coach on conflict management?*
37. Have you ever worked with a person who excelled at managing conflict?
38. Have you ever worked with a skills coach on managing conflict?*
39. How do you get feedback about yourself on handling conflict?
40. How often do you check with multiple sources when you get a piece of critical feedback on your ability to manage conflict?
41. Is there a historical figure you consider a model of managing conflict?
42. What do others who are not your fans say about your conflict management skills?
43. What do others who like you say about your conflict management skills?
44. Which boss was the best at managing conflict?
45. Which boss was the worst at managing conflict?
46. Which direct report was the best at managing conflict?
47. Which direct report was the worst at managing conflict?
48. Which peer was the best at managing conflict?
49. Which peer was the worst at managing conflict?
50. Who in your field or business deals the best with conflict?
51. Who do you consider a role model of managing conflict?*
52. Who do you go to for advice on managing conflict?
53. Who have you learned the most from about managing conflict?*
54. Who is a higher-management role model for you on managing conflict?
55. Who is a role model of managing conflict outside of work?

CONFLICT MANAGEMENT

Dimension 3: Knows how the competency works in theory; shows understanding

56. Are there situations or settings where someone should be different on handling conflict?
57. Do you think conflict management skills can be learned? If so, how do you think people develop conflict management skills?
58. Do you think there is a way to compensate or work around low conflict-management skills?
59. Has anyone asked you for your opinions/advice on handling conflict?*
60. Have you ever attended a conflict management course?
61. Have you ever been in a situation where you and others put conflict management skills on a success profile?
62. Have you ever been part of an effort to create a policy or a mission statement containing reference to the importance of being able to handle conflict?
63. Have you ever been someone's coach or mentor who had problems with handling conflict?
64. Have you ever created a development plan for someone on handling conflict?
65. Have you ever criticized someone for not handling conflict well?
66. Have you ever designed a program on handling conflict?
67. Have you ever given a speech on handling conflict?
68. Have you ever rewarded or recognized someone for demonstrating effective conflict-management skills?
69. Have you ever taught a course on handling conflict?
70. Have you ever tried to help someone deal more effectively with conflict?*
71. Have you ever tried to help someone improve their conflict-management skills?
72. To what degree do you think people develop conflict-management skills?
73. How much of success do you think is due to conflict-management skills compared with other characteristics?
74. How would you know if someone is bad at handling conflict?
75. How would you know if someone is good at handling conflict?
76. If you had to write a book on conflict management, what would the chapter headings be?
77. What are the benefits to someone who is really good at handling conflict?
78. What are the consequences to someone who is really poor at handling conflict?
79. What do you think the performance standard is on managing conflict for someone in your role?
80. What happens when two people try to work together who are very different in their ability to handle conflict?
81. What wisdom would you pass onto others trying to become better at handling conflict?
82. When you select others, what do you look for in conflict management skills?
83. Why do you think people end up being different on their ability to handle conflict?

Dimension 4: Shows personal change and sense-making; learned it one place and applied it in another; can compare and contrast experiences; changes viewpoints across time; can explain personal development or evolution related to the competency

84. Compare and contrast examples of times when you've been effective and ineffective at handling conflict.
85. Contrast your on- and off-the-job ability to handle conflict.
86. Did you ever pass up a job or assignment because you were not confident enough in your skills at conflict management?
87. Do you ever use other skills to cover for your lack of conflict management skills?
88. Has becoming better at handling conflict ever helped you in other areas?
89. Has handling conflict ever figured in a failure, struggle, or setback you have had?
90. Has poor conflict management ever been the subject of a development plan for you?

CONFLICT MANAGEMENT

91. Has your ability to handle conflict always been this way?
92. Have you ever delegated or assigned someone a task because you didn't handle conflict particularly well?
93. Have you ever made significant strides at becoming better at handling conflict?
94. Have your conflict management skills, good or bad, ever been the subject of your performance review or a career discussion?
95. How different are you across situations in your handling of conflict?
96. How do you decide how flexible to be?
97. How important is it for you to win an argument?*
98. How much of your success is due to your ability to handle conflict?
99. How transferable are your conflict management skills to other situations?
100. If you had to become better at handling conflict in a hurry, what would you do?
101. Is it important to you to be liked by those you work with?*
102. Was there a time when you were not good at handling conflict?
103. What caused you to work to change your skills at handling conflict?
104. What event or series of events had the most impact on how you handle conflict?
105. What's the most varied you can be in handling conflict?
106. What was the shortest amount of time in which you increased your skill level at handling conflict?
107. When did you first realize your skill level at handling conflict?
108. When you know ahead of time that your usual way of handling conflict won't work, what do you do?
109. Why do you think you handle conflict the way you do?
110. Why do you think your conflict management skills are the way they are?*

D. Follow-up Probes:

1. Are there times when you're not like this or wouldn't do this?
2. Are there times when you handle conflict like that and times when you don't?
3. Could you contrast those two bosses for me?
4. Could you give me a few examples of how you've used or applied that?
5. Did they intimidate you? What would be different now?
6. Did you or the other person blink first?
7. Do you suppose if others would just try harder, they could learn to handle conflict more like you do?
8. Do you think this is teachable?
9. Do you think you're better at handling conflict than most? Why?
10. Do you think you would perform any better if you handled conflict differently?
11. Have you ever had to form a relationship with someone you really disliked to get your job done?
12. How did it feel to give up something you wanted to get the project going?
13. How did the others react when you did that?
14. How did you come up with that approach in the first place?
15. How did you get yourself under control in that situation?
16. How did you know that method of getting over that barrier would work?
17. How do others you have known approach that?
18. How far did you go to try to be a team player?
19. How far will you go before you cut line and try another approach?
20. How much did you have to give up to make it work?

CONFLICT MANAGEMENT

21. How often do you use the "Let's meet in the middle" approach?
22. How typical is this for you?
23. How would you approach that same situation today?
24. Is this natural for you, or do you really have to dig for it?
25. Was that a fair way to maneuver around them?
26. Was there a time when you didn't understand this about yourself?
27. What did you do after you got that feedback?
28. What did you do to adapt to that?
29. What did you learn from that?
30. Why did you choose that approach?
31. Why did you decide to take the risk?
32. Why did you do it that way?
33. Why did you time your attempt like you did?
34. Why do you suppose organizations work that way?
35. Why do you think that didn't work?
36. Why do you think that happened that way?
37. Why do you think that worked?
38. Why do you think you have difficulties with situations/people like that?
39. Would you have done it that way with looser deadlines?
40. Would you have done it that way with tighter deadlines?

E. **Themes/Things to Look for:**
   Ability to admit mistakes
   Able to predict what people are going to do before it happens
   Able to see things through the eyes of others
   Comfortable not having all the answers
   Complex and varied tactics and strategies of getting through tough situations
   Consistency
   Equitable treatment
   Finding an agreement point
   Finding common ground
   Going after the toughest issues/people; not dancing around
   Healthy and balanced attitude toward authority
   In control of their conflict tactics
   Keeping personal feelings from getting in the way
   Letting others save face
   Listening
   One size doesn't fit all
   Selective success
   Understanding others
   Varied tactics
   Willing to lose a battle to win the war

CONFLICT MANAGEMENT

F. Most Likely Résumé:

1. Look for jobs like:

Chair of Projects/Task Forces
Fix-Its/Turnarounds
International Assignments
Line to Staff Switches
Significant People Demands

2. Look for develop-in-place assignments like:

Integrate diverse systems, processes, or procedures across decentralized and/or dispersed units.
Manage the renovation of an office, floor, building, meeting room, warehouse, etc.
Plan an off-site meeting, conference, convention, trade show, event, etc.
Manage the furnishing or refurnishing of new or existing offices.
Coach a children's sports team.
Get involved with the negotiation of a contract or agreement with international consequences.
Relaunch an existing product or service that's not doing well.
Manage an ad hoc, temporary group of balky and resisting people through an unpopular change or project.
Handle a tough negotiation with an internal or external client or customer.
Help shut down a plant, regional office, product line, business, operation, etc.
Manage a dissatisfied internal or external customer; troubleshoot a performance or quality problem with a product or service.
Manage the assigning/allocating of office space in a contested situation.
Work on a team that's deciding who to keep and who to let go in a layoff, shutdown, delayering, or divestiture.
Manage a group through a significant business crisis.
Take on a tough and undoable project, one where others who have tried it have failed.
Manage a cost-cutting project.
Resolve an issue in conflict between two people, units, geographies, functions, etc.
Make peace with an enemy or someone you've disappointed with a product or service or someone you've had some trouble with or don't get along well with.
Do a postmortem on a failed project and present it to the people involved.
Be a member of a union-negotiating or grievance-handling team.
Work on a crisis management team.

3. Best references to ask about or check:

Development Professionals
Family Members
Human Resource Professionals
Natural Mentors
Peers and Colleagues
Spouse
Yourself

CONFLICT MANAGEMENT

G. Learning Agility Evaluation:

2. All or Nothing vs. Can See Many Sides
3. Ordinary/Socially Acceptable vs. Insightful/Different
5. Tight/Rigid vs. Loose/Flexible
6. Reacting/Responsive vs. Adapting
13. Simple Views vs. Complex Views
16. Few Rules of Thumb vs. Many and Varied Rules of Thumb
20. Avoids Responsibility for Mistakes vs. Admits and Learns from Mistakes
21. View from Self vs. View from Point of View of Others

H. The LEADERSHIP ARCHITECT® Sort Card Connections:

1. Good (positive) if combined with high:

Chaos comfortable manager 2, 16, 40, 50, 53
A role model, arbitrator 3, 33, 37, 40, 41, 64
Tough-minded manager 13, 20, 35
Sells well 15, 31, 37
Sells visions 28, 58, 65
Speaks out 34, 57
Makes good deals 36, 37, 49

2. Bad (negative) if combined with low or high (+):

Personal problems get in the way (+3, 7, 10, 11)
Causes pain 3, 7, 23, 31
Ten ton truck (+13, 35, 53)
One sided; not very flexible (+22, 34) 40
Spends a lot of time resolving everybody's conflicts (+31, 42, 60)
Can't finish job, can't resolve tough issues 34, 35, 57
Gets in trouble with higher-ups 38, 48

3. Too much can contribute to the following Stallers and Stoppers:

A. What too much looks like (overused):

May be seen as overly aggressive and assertive; may get in the middle of everyone else's problems; may drive for a solution before others are ready; may have a chilling effect on open debate; may spend too much time with obstinate people and unsolvable problems.

B. Too much might lead to these Stallers and Stoppers:

Failure to Build a Team (110)
Insensitive to Others (112)

C. Compensators:

How to compensate for too much of this competency:
2, 3, 31, 33, 34, 36, 37, 40, 41, 51, 52, 56, 60, 64

CONFLICT MANAGEMENT

D. Things to watch for:
May be a stress/tension carrier making others uncomfortable
May chill the contributions of others
May force others to disclose before they are ready
May have only one direct solution to conflict management
Others may not want to work with them
May be into everybody else's business

4. Too little can contribute to the following Stallers and Stoppers:

A. What too little looks like (unskilled):
Avoids conflict in situations and with people; may accommodate, want everyone to get along; may get upset as a reaction to conflict, takes it personally; can't operate under conflict long enough to get a good deal; gives in and says yes too soon; gets into conflict by accident; doesn't see it coming; will let things fester rather than dealing with them directly; will try to wait long enough for it to go away; may be excessively competitive and have to win every dispute.

B. Too little might lead to these Stallers and Stoppers:
Poor Administrator (102)   Lack of Composure (107)
Arrogant (104)   Defensiveness (108)
Betrayal of Trust (105)   Failure to Staff Effectively (111)

C. Compensators:
How to substitute for too little of this competency:
2, 3, 4, 8, 11, 13, 16, 31, 33, 36, 37, 41, 50, 51, 52

I. LEARNING ARCHITECT® Connections:
Look for people who act like and/or show evidence of:

1a. Pure Action   21. Changer
2a. Problem Solving   22. Experimenter
4a. Getting Information   23. Orchestrator
 6. Contentious   26. Self-Aware
14. Controlled   36. Comfort with Paradox
16. Collaborate   38. Resilience
17. Selected Sources

J. CHOICES ARCHITECT® Connections:
Look for people who act like and/or show evidence of:

First Edition (Released 1994)   **Second Edition (Released 2000)**
 8. Cool Transactor   10. Conflict Manager
11. Open to Diversity   11. Cool Transactor
14. Transaction Quality   14. Open-Minded
20. Forging Ahead   22. Taking the Heat
21. Taking the Heat   23. Visioning

K. Difficulty to Develop:
32 (of 34)–Hardest

13. CONFRONTING DIRECT REPORTS

A. Definition:

Deals with problem direct reports firmly and in a timely manner; doesn't allow problems to fester; regularly reviews performance and holds timely discussions; can make negative decisions when all other efforts fail; deals effectively with troublemakers.

B. Arenas/Domains to Explore:

1. Athletic team captains
2. Attitudes toward competence and hard work
3. Balky/resistant people
4. Clubs, associations, societies
5. Coach/athletes
6. Family issues
7. Hard times
8. Layoffs
9. Marginal performers
10. Mentoring
11. Mergers and acquisitions
12. Military
13. Project teams
14. Student government
15. Task Forces
16. Teacher/students
17. Union experience
18. Volunteer work

C. Sample Questions:

*Dimension 1: Been there, done that–has had direct personal experience(s) involving the competency–candidate was the prime player   Note: * means OK for campus*

1. Describe your procedure for dealing with problem performers.
2. Have you been in a situation where most everyone else feels more negative regarding a person than you?
3. Have you ever been around a purge–when someone new comes in, cleans house, and brings new people in? What did you think of that?
4. Have you ever had to be the messenger of bad news to a person?*
5. Have you ever had to demote or fire a friend?
6. Have you ever had to manage a person that seemed to be sick or absent too much?
7. Have you ever had to turn around a problem performer?*
8. Have you ever had to turn around a quirky/idiosyncratic person?*
9. Have you ever had to turn around a resistant, balky person?*
10. Have you ever inherited a problem performer/troublemaker?
11. Have you ever managed a person who kept going around you to upper management?
12. Have you ever managed anything where the people or units reporting to you were in different locations? How did you confront performance problems?
13. Have you ever managed anything where the people or units reporting to you were in different locations? How did you deal with problem performers?
14. Have you ever used the tactic of assigning someone to a project that would highlight their failings in order to illustrate a point?
15. Have you ever worked for a long time with a problem performer and then given up? What did you do then?
16. How do you typically do performance reviews?
17. How long does it generally take for you to give up on trying to help or save someone?
18. How many people have you fired in your career?

CONFRONTING DIRECT REPORTS

19. Over your career, who was the one person you should have acted on earlier than you did?
20. Tell me about a time when you had to manage one or more direct reports through a downsizing/shutdown.
21. Tell me about a time when you had to manage someone who was an OK performer when OK wasn't good enough.
22. Tell me about a time when you had to manage someone who was an OK performer who, year after year, became slowly more obsolete/under skilled.
23. Tell me about a time when you had to manage someone who wasn't good enough.*
24. Tell me about a time when your hesitation to confront performance problems got you into trouble.
25. Tell me about a time when your willingness to confront performance problems worked really well for you.
26. Tell me about the first person you had to fire.
27. Tell me about the first person you had to lay off.
28. What do you do if someone on a school project/project team/task force isn't pulling their weight?*

Dimension 2: Seen/been around others who were involved with the competency–good and bad; learns from others about self

29. Contrast the people you know who are most and least able to deal with problem performers.*
30. Has dealing with problem performers ever been in any 360° survey done on you? Was your score among your highest, middle, or lowest?
31. Has someone else's inability to deal with problem performers ever created an obstacle for you or got in the way of something you were trying to accomplish?*
32. Have you ever talked about your ability to deal with problem performers with a coach or mentor?
33. Have you ever watched someone fail/get fired because they did not deal with problem performers?*
34. Have you ever watched someone overdo confronting problem performers to the point that it backfired?
35. Have you ever watched someone succeed because they dealt with problem performers well?*
36. Have you ever worked with a coach on dealing with problem performers?*
37. Have you ever worked with a person who excelled at dealing with problem performers?
38. Have you ever worked with a skills coach on dealing with problem performers?*
39. How do you get feedback about yourself on confronting direct reports?
40. How often do you check with multiple sources when you get a piece of critical feedback on your ability to confront problem performers?
41. Is there a historical figure you consider a model of dealing with problem performers?
42. What do others who are not your fans say about your ability to deal with problem performers?
43. What do others who like you say about your ability to deal with problem performers?
44. Which boss was the best at dealing with problem performers?
45. Which boss was the worst at dealing with problem performers?
46. Which direct report was the best at dealing with problem performers?
47. Which direct report was the worst at dealing with problem performers?
48. Which peer was the best at dealing with problem performers?
49. Which peer was the worst at dealing with problem performers?
50. Who in your field or business deals the best with problem performers?
51. Who do you consider a role model of dealing with problem performers?*
52. Who do you go to for advice on dealing with problem performers?
53. Who have you learned the most from about dealing with problem performers?*
54. Who is a higher-management role model for you on dealing with problem performers?
55. Who is a role model of dealing with problem performers outside of work?

CONFRONTING DIRECT REPORTS

Dimension 3: Knows how the competency works in theory; shows understanding

56. Are there situations or settings where someone should act differently when dealing with problem performers?
57. Do you think the ability to deal effectively with problem performers can be learned? If so, how do you think people develop this ability?
58. Do you think there is a way to compensate or work around a low ability to deal with problem performers?
59. Has anyone asked you for your opinions/advice on handling problem performers?*
60. Have you ever attended a course on dealing with problem performers?
61. Have you ever been in a situation where you and others put confronting problem performers on a success profile?
62. Have you ever been part of an effort to create a policy or a mission statement containing reference to the importance of being able to deal with problem performers?
63. Have you ever been someone's coach or mentor who had problems with confronting direct reports?
64. Have you ever created a development plan for someone to improve their skills in handling problem performers?
65. Have you ever criticized someone for the inability to confront direct reports?
66. Have you ever designed a program on handling problem performers?
67. Have you ever given a speech on handling problem performers?
68. Have you ever rewarded or recognized someone for the ability to deal with problem performers?
69. Have you ever taught a course on dealing with problem performers?
70. Have you ever tried to help someone deal more effectively with problem performers?*
71. Have you ever tried to help someone improve their skills in dealing with problem performers?
72. How do you think people develop the skills to deal with problem performers?
73. How much of success do you think is due to the ability to deal with problem performers compared with other characteristics?
74. How would you know if someone is bad at dealing with problem performers?
75. How would you know if someone is good at dealing with problem performers?
76. If you had to write a book on dealing with problem performers, what would the chapter headings be?
77. What are the benefits to someone who is really good at dealing with problem performers?
78. What are the consequences to someone who is really poor at dealing with problem performers?
79. What do you think the performance standard is on the ability to deal with problem performers for someone in your role?
80. What happens when two people try to work together who are very different on their ability to deal with problem performers?
81. What wisdom would you pass onto others trying to become better at dealing with problem performers?
82. When you select others, what do you look for in ability to handle problem performers?
83. Why do you think people end up being different in their ability to confront direct reports?

Dimension 4: Shows personal change and sense-making; learned it one place and applied it in another; can compare and contrast experiences; changes viewpoints across time; can explain personal development or evolution related to the competency

84. Compare and contrast examples of times when you've been effective and ineffective in dealing with problem performers.
85. Contrast your on- and off-the-job methods of dealing with problem performers.
86. Did you ever pass up a job or assignment because you were not confident enough in your skills at dealing with problem performers?
87. Do you ever use other skills to cover for your lack of ability to deal with problem performers?

CONFRONTING DIRECT REPORTS

88. Has dealing with problem performers ever figured in a failure, struggle, or setback you have had?
89. Has becoming better at dealing with problem performers ever helped you in other areas?
90. Has one of your employees ever made you look bad to your boss or the organization? How did you deal with that situation? How did that experience shape the way you manage your staff today?
91. Has poor handling of problem performers ever been the subject of a development plan for you?
92. Has your ability to deal with problem performers always been this way?
93. Have you ever been fired/let go/asked to leave? Why? How did you react?
94. Have you ever delegated or assigned someone a task because you didn't handle problem performers particularly well?
95. Have you ever made significant strides at becoming better at dealing with problem performers?
96. Have you ever received a below-standard performance review? Why? How did you react?
97. Have you ever received a failing grade in school? Why? How did you react?*
98. Has your ability to deal with problem performers, good or bad, ever been the subject of your performance review or a career discussion?
99. How different are you across situations in your dealings with problem performers?
100. How do you decide how confrontational to be with direct reports?
101. How much of your success is due to your ability to deal with problem performers?
102. How transferable are your skills at dealing with problem performers to other situations?
103. If you had to become better at dealing with problem performers in a hurry, what would you do?
104. Was there a time when you were not good at dealing with problem performers?
105. What caused you to work to change your skills at dealing with problem performers?
106. What event or series of events had the most impact on your dealings with problem performers?
107. What's the most varied you can be in dealing with problem performers?
108. What was the shortest amount of time in which you increased your skill level at dealing with problem performers?
109. When did you first realize your skill level at dealing with problem performers?
110. When you know ahead of time that your usual level of skill in dealing with problem performers won't work, what do you do?
111. Why do you think you deal with problem performers the way you do?
112. Why do you think your ability to deal with problem performers is the way it is?*

D. Follow-up Probes:

1. Are there times when you're not like this or wouldn't do this?
2. Are there times when you deal with problem performers like that and times when you don't?
3. Could you contrast those two bosses for me?
4. Could you give me a few examples of how you've used or applied that?
5. Did you later change your assessment of this person?
6. Did you or the other person blink first?
7. Do you suppose if others would just try harder, they could learn to handle performance difficulties more like you do?
8. Do you think that was fair?
9. Do you think this is teachable?
10. Do you think you're better at dealing with problem performers than most? Why?
11. Do you think you would perform any better if you handle problem performers differently?

CONFRONTING DIRECT REPORTS

12. Have you ever had to form a relationship with someone you really disliked to get your job done?
13. How did it feel to give up something you wanted to get the project/work going?
14. How did the others react when you did that?
15. How did you come up with that approach in the first place?
16. How did you deal with the aftermath?
17. How did you know that method of getting over that barrier would work?
18. How do others you have known approach that?
19. How far did you go to try to be a team player?
20. How far will you go before you cut line and try another approach?
21. How much did you have to give up to make it work?
22. How typical is this for you?
23. How would you approach that same situation today?
24. Is this natural for you, or do you really have to dig for it?
25. Was that a fair way to maneuver around them?
26. Was there a time when you didn't understand this about yourself?
27. What did you do after you got that feedback?
28. What did you do to adapt to that?
29. What did you learn from that?
30. What did you lose by not acting sooner?
31. What was your limit with this problem?
32. Why did you choose that approach?
33. Why did you decide to take the risk?
34. Why did you do it that way?
35. Why did you time your attempt like you did?
36. Why do you suppose organizations work that way?
37. Why do you think that didn't work?
38. Why do you think that happened that way?
39. Why do you think that worked?
40. Why do you think you have difficulties with that sometimes?
41. Would you have done it that way with looser deadlines?
42. Would you have done it that way with tighter deadlines?

E. **Themes/Things to Look for:**
   Ability to handle the guilt
   Action balanced with compassion
   Consistency across situations
   Focus on performance
   How soon after the evaluation did they act
   How soon did they make the evaluation
   Incremental improvement
   Keeping feelings from getting in the way
   Not expecting miracles
   Not favoring people they know well over people they know less well

CONFRONTING DIRECT REPORTS

Relationship after separation
Sense of fairness and equity
Sensitivity and empathy
Tough love
Understanding individual motivation
Where they set the performance bar
Working on behalf of the greater good of the organization
Working with wounded puppies
Confronting issues promptly
Sizing people up accurately; understanding their pluses and minuses

F. Most Likely Résumé:

1. Look for jobs like:
Fix-Its/Turnarounds
Significant People Demands

2. Look for develop-in-place assignments like:
Manage an ad hoc, temporary group of balky and resisting people through an unpopular change or project.
Hire and manage a temporary group of people to accomplish a tough or time-tight assignment.
Manage the outplacement of a group of people.

3. Best references to ask about or check:
Direct Boss
Human Resource Professionals

G. Learning Agility Evaluation:
1. What/Describing vs. Why/Explain
2. All or Nothing vs. Can See Many Sides
10. Reactive vs. Initiating
13. Simple Views vs. Complex Views
17. Avoid Discussion of Weaknesses vs. Comfortably Sharing Shortcomings
21. View from Self vs. View from Point of View of Others

H. The LEADERSHIP ARCHITECT® Sort Card Connections:

1. Good (positive) if combined with high:
Timely 1, 16
Velvet glove 3, 10, 26, 31
Good feedback sessions 3, 33, 41
A role model; constructive 7, 10, 19, 36
Know where you stand 18, 27, 29
No favorites 21, 23, 29
Accurate assessor 25, 35, 56, 64
Taskmaster 35, 53
Keeps group on track 39, 60

CONFRONTING DIRECT REPORTS

2. **Bad (negative) if combined with low or high (+):**
   Never acts 1, 12, 16
   Too quick (+1, 16) 41
   Aloof 3, 7
   Cold and impersonal 3, 33, 41
   Too much? (+9, 34, 57)
   Mean 11, 26
   Doesn't understand what to do 19, 36
   Overmanages 18
   Not equitable 21, 23, 29
   Poor judge of people 56

3. **Too much can contribute to the following Stallers and Stoppers:**

   A. What too much looks like (overused):

   May be too quick to act on problem direct reports; may not put enough developmental effort toward the problem; may expect turnarounds in too short a time; may expect miracles.

   B. Too much might lead to these Stallers and Stoppers:
   Arrogant (104)
   Insensitive to Others (112)
   Overmanaging (117)

   C. Compensators:
   How to compensate for too much of this competency:
   3, 7, 12, 19, 20, 21, 23, 31, 33, 36, 41, 56, 60, 64

   D. Things to watch for:
Chills risk-taking	Plays favorites
Done without due compassion	Vindictiveness
Expectations/standards too high	Expects a miracle

4. **Too little can contribute to the following Stallers and Stoppers:**

   A. What too little looks like (unskilled):

   Not comfortable delivering negative messages to direct reports; procrastinates and avoids problems until forced to act; may not communicate clear standards or provide much feedback; lets problems fester hoping they will go away; may give in too soon to excuses; may give people too many chances; can't pull the trigger even when all else has failed; has low standards or plays favorites.

   B. Too little might lead to these Stallers and Stoppers:
Poor Administrator (102)	Failure to Build a Team (110)
Betrayal of Trust (105)	Failure to Staff Effectively (111)
Lack of Composure (107)	Performance Problems (118)

   C. Compensators:
   How to substitute for too little of this competency:
   1, 9, 12, 16, 20, 27, 34, 35, 37, 53, 56, 57

CONFRONTING DIRECT REPORTS

I. LEARNING ARCHITECT® Connections:

Look for people who act like and/or show evidence of:

- 1a. Pure Action
- 1c. Following a Plan
- 2a. Problem Solving
- 4a. Getting Information
- 6. Contentious
- 34. Sizing Up Others

J. CHOICES ARCHITECT® Connections:

Look for people who act like and/or show evidence of:

First Edition (Released 1994)
- 8. Cool Transactor
- 15. Helps Others Succeed

Second Edition (Released 2000)
- 11. Cool Transactor
- 12. Helps Others Succeed

K. Difficulty to Develop:

27 (of 34)–Harder

14. CREATIVITY

A. Definition:

Comes up with a lot of new and unique ideas; easily makes connections among previously unrelated notions; tends to be seen as original and value-added in brainstorming settings.

B. Arenas/Domains to Explore:

1. Academic history
2. Career/life choices
3. Conference management
4. Current event/past parallel connections
5. Event planning
6. Hobbies
7. Meeting facilitation
8. New and unique programs/processes/systems
9. New or unique products/services
10. New or unique team building strategies
11. Reading habits
12. Recreation choices
13. Role models
14. Social network
15. Vacation/touring habits
16. Working out impossible problems
17. Writing/public speaking
18. Design skills
19. Implementation strategies

C. Sample Questions:

*Dimension 1: Been there, done that–has had direct personal experience(s) involving the competency–candidate was the prime player   Note: * means OK for campus*

1. Do you follow the dictum that if it's not broken, don't fix it?*
2. Have you ever managed anything where the people or units reporting to you were in different locations? How did you use your creative skills to improve things?
3. How many of the ideas in your head do you tend to surface and tell others about?* When do you tend to hold back your creative ideas?*
4. Tell me about a new product or service you thought up.
5. Tell me about a new strategy you created.
6. Tell me about a new work process you came up with to solve an old problem.
7. Tell me about a time when you challenged the ideas of others and it led to something new.*
8. Tell me about a time when your creative skills worked really well for you.
9. Tell me about a time when your not being creative enough got you into trouble.
10. Tell me about an unusual way you built a team.
11. Tell me about a time when you came up with a new idea.*
12. Tell me about a time when you tried out one of your ideas and it failed.*
13. Tell me about your greatest brainstorm(s).*
14. Tell me about your most creative area/areas.*
15. What do you think your most creative contribution has ever been?
16. What is your "go" percent before you will take action?*
17. What is your earliest memory of when you offered up something others thought was very creative?*
18. What's the most off-the-wall idea you've ever surfaced that was adopted?*

CREATIVITY

Dimension 2: Seen/been around others who were involved with the competency–good and bad; learns from others about self

19. Contrast the most and least creative people you know.*
20. Has creativity ever been in any 360° survey done on you? Was your score among your highest, middle, or lowest?
21. Has poor creativity on someone else's part ever created an obstacle for you or got in the way of something you were trying to accomplish?*
22. Have you ever talked about your personal creativity with a coach or mentor?
23. Have you ever watched someone fail/get fired because they were not creative?*
24. Have you ever watched someone overextend their creativity to the point that it backfired?
25. Have you ever watched someone succeed because they were creative?*
26. Have you ever worked with a coach on being more creative?*
27. Have you ever worked with a person who was very creative?
28. Have you ever worked with a skills coach on being more creative?
29. How do you get feedback about your creativity?
30. How often do you check with multiple sources when you get a piece of critical feedback on your creativity?
31. Is there a historical figure you consider a model of creativity?
32. What do others who are not your fans say about your creativity?
33. What do others who like you say about your creativity?
34. Which boss was the best at being creative?
35. Which boss was the worst at being creative?
36. Which direct report was the best at being creative?
37. Which direct report was the worst at being creative?
38. Which peer was the best at being creative?
39. Which peer was the worst at being creative?
40. Who in your field or business deals the best with creativity?
41. Who do you consider a role model of personal creativity?*
42. Who do you go to for advice on being more creative?
43. Who have you learned the most from about creativity?*
44. Who is a higher-management role model for you on creativity?
45. Who is a role model of creativity outside of work?

Dimension 3: Knows how the competency works in theory; shows understanding

46. Are there situations or settings where someone should act differently demonstrating creativity?
47. Do you have any favorite examples of very creative products/services/ people? Why do you think they're creative?*
48. Do you think creativity can be learned? If so, how do you think people develop creative skills?
49. Do you think there is a way to compensate or work around low creativity?
50. Has anyone asked you for your opinions/advice on personal creativity?*
51. Have you ever attended a course on creativity?
52. Have you ever been in a situation where you and others put creative skills on a success profile?
53. Have you ever been part of an effort to create a policy or a mission statement containing reference to the importance of being creative?
54. Have you ever been someone's coach or mentor who had problems with personal creativity?
55. Have you ever created a development plan for someone on personal creativity?

CREATIVITY

56. Have you ever criticized someone for not being creative?
57. Have you ever designed a program on the creative process?
58. Have you ever given a speech on the creative process?
59. Have you ever rewarded or recognized someone for being creative?
60. Have you ever taught a course on the creative process?
61. Have you ever tried to help someone deal more effectively with a lack of creativity?*
62. Have you ever tried to help someone improve their creative skills?
63. How do you think people develop creative skills?
64. How much creativity is good to have and how much is too much?
65. How much of success do you think is due to being creative compared with other characteristics?
66. How would you know if someone lacks creativity?
67. How would you know if someone is good at demonstrating creativity?
68. If you had to write a book on creativity, what would the chapter headings be?
69. Tell me your understanding about the nature of creativity/the creative process.*
70. What are the benefits to someone who is really good at personal creativity?
71. What are the consequences to someone who is really poor at personal creativity?
72. What do you think the performance standard is on creativity for someone in your role?
73. What happens if you have or use too much creativity?
74. What happens when two people try to work together who are very different on personal creativity?
75. What wisdom would you pass onto others trying to become better at developing their creative skills?
76. When you select others, what do you look for in personal creativity?
77. Why do you think people end up being different in their ability to demonstrate personal creativity?

Dimension 4: Shows personal change and sense-making; learned it one place and applied it in another; can compare and contrast experiences; changes viewpoints across time; can explain personal development or evolution related to the competency

78. Compare and contrast examples of times when you've effectively and ineffectively used your creativity.
79. Contrast your on- and off-the-job use of creativity.
80. Did you ever pass up a job or assignment because you were not confident enough in your creativity skills?
81. Do you ever use other skills to cover for your lack of creativity?
82. Has lack of creativity ever figured in a failure, struggle, or setback you have had?
83. Has becoming better at creativity ever helped you in other areas?
84. Has poor creativity ever been the subject of a development plan for you?
85. Has your creativity always been this way?
86. Have you ever delegated or assigned someone a task because you weren't particularly creative?
87. Have you ever made significant strides at becoming better at being creative?
88. Have your creativity skills, good or bad, ever been the subject of your performance review or a career discussion?
89. How different are you across situations in your creativity?
90. How do you decide how creative to be?
91. How do you get a group of people to be creative?*
92. How do you know when to give up on a new idea and move on?
93. How do you test whether a new or unique idea has merit?
94. How does the creative process work in you?*

CREATIVITY

95. How much of your success is due to your creativity?
96. How transferable are your creativity skills to other situations?
97. If you had to become better at creativity in a hurry, what would you do?
98. In what situations do you tend to be the least creative?*
99. In what situations do you tend to be the most creative?*
100. Was there a time when you were not good at the creative process?
101. What caused you to work to change your creativity skills?
102. What event or series of events had the most impact on your creative process?
103. What's the most varied you can be in your creativity?
104. What was the shortest amount of time in which you increased your skill level at being creative?
105. When did you first realize your level of skill at being creative?
106. When you know ahead of time that your usual level of creativity won't work, what do you do?
107. Where do you get your ideas from?*
108. Why do you think you deal with creativity the way you do?
109. Why do you think your creativity is the way it is?*

D. Follow-up Probes:
1. Are there times when you're not like this or wouldn't do this?
2. Are there times when you create like that and times when you don't?
3. Could you contrast those two bosses for me?
4. Could you give me a few examples of how you've used or applied that?
5. Do you suppose if others would just try harder, they could learn to be more creative like you?
6. Do you think this is teachable?
7. Do you think you're better at being creative than most? Why?
8. Do you think you would perform any differently if you could be more creative?
9. How did the others react when you did that?
10. How did you come up with that approach in the first place?
11. How did you know that method of getting over that barrier would work?
12. How do others you have known approach that?
13. How far did you go to try to be a team player?
14. How far will you go before you cut line and try another approach?
15. How much did you have to give up to make it work?
16. How typical is this for you?
17. How would you approach that same situation today?
18. Is this natural for you, or do you really have to dig for it?
19. Was that a fair way to maneuver around them?
20. Was there a time when you didn't understand this about yourself?
21. Were there some alternatives you rejected? Were you right?
22. What did you do after you got that feedback?
23. What did you do to adapt to that?
24. What did you learn from that?
25. Why did you choose that approach?
26. Why did you decide to take the risk?

CREATIVITY

27. Why did you do it that way?
28. Why did you time your attempt like you did?
29. Why do you suppose organizations work that way?
30. Why do you think that didn't work?
31. Why do you think that happened that way?
32. Why do you think that worked?
33. Would you have done it that way with looser deadlines?
34. Would you have done it that way with tighter deadlines?

E. Themes/Things to Look for:

Bored with routine	Making unusual connections
Builds off stimuli from others	Many experiments; many failures
Comfortable with complexity	Notices anomalies (things that don't fit)
Comfortable with loose ends	Sees small differences
Comfortable working on pieces	Takes risks
Enjoyment of the new/different/unique	Thinks about what's missing
Focus on the nature of the problem	Tries things just to see what would happen
Immersion/depth in an area	Try anything once
Looking outside organization/business/technical area	Use of parallels/contrasts/metaphors/analogies
Visual imagery	Using trial and error
Lots of question asking	Willing to be/look silly
Loves to explore	Willing to follow feelings/intuition

F. Most Likely Résumé:

1. Look for jobs like:

Heavy Strategic Demands
International Assignments
Line to Staff Switches
Scope (complexity) Assignments
Start-Ups

2. Look for develop-in-place assignments like:

Help someone outside your unit or the organization solve a business problem.
Launch a new product, service, or process.
Relaunch an existing product or service that's not doing well.
Manage an ad hoc, temporary group of balky and resisting people through an unpopular change or project.
Assemble an ad hoc team of diverse people to accomplish a difficult task.
Prepare and present a proposal of some consequence to top management.
Manage a dissatisfied internal or external customer; troubleshoot a performance or quality problem with a product or service.
Manage a group through a significant business crisis.
Take on a tough and undoable project, one where others who have tried it have failed.
Take on a task you dislike or hate to do.

CREATIVITY

3. Best references to ask about or check:
Customers
Past Associates/Constituencies
Peers and Colleagues
Direct Reports

G. Learning Agility Evaluation:
2. All or Nothing vs. Can See Many Sides
3. Ordinary/Socially Acceptable vs. Insightful/Different
7. Passive vs. Intrigued/Curious
8. Sameness vs. Diversity
13. Simple Views vs. Complex Views
15. Linear vs. Use Contrasts/Analogies
18. Stays Close to Home vs. Lots of Curiosity
19. External Standards vs. Internal Standards

H. The LEADERSHIP ARCHITECT® Sort Card Connections:

1. Good (positive) if combined with high:
High idea output 1, 2, 16
Breakthrough visions 5, 46, 58
Useful ideas 15, 17, 46, 58
Knows when to quit 17, 50
On the leading edge of their technology 24, 32, 61
Can put into practical terms 28, 51

2. Bad (negative) if combined with low or high (+):
Thinks but doesn't deliver 1, 16, 53
Doesn't relate to others 3, 7, 64
Poor sense of what's important 5, 46, 50, 51, 58
Only one who knows 18, 20, 27, 44
Rejects the old out of hand (2, +28) 46
Problems selling superior ideas 38, 48, 49
Disorganized 39, 47, 50
Loner (+57) 42, 60

3. Too much can contribute to the following Stallers and Stoppers:

A. What too much looks like (overused):
May get so infatuated with marginally productive ideas that they waste time; may get involved in too many things at once; may not follow through after the idea; may be disorganized or poor at detail; may be a loner and not a good team player; may not relate well to those who are less creative.

B. Too much might lead to these Stallers and Stoppers:
Poor Administrator (102)
Arrogant (104)
Defensiveness (108)
Failure to Build a Team (110)
Overdependence on a Single Skill (116)
Overmanaging (117)
Performance Problems (118)

CREATIVITY

C. Compensators:

How to compensate for too much of this competency:

1, 5, 16, 17, 24, 28, 30, 38, 39, 45, 46, 47, 48, 50, 51, 52, 53, 58, 59, 61, 64

D. Things to watch for:

Too many ideas, too little action	Doesn't finish anything
Time spent being creative out of proportion	Things fall through the cracks
Doesn't relate well to most people	Arrogant
Idiosyncratic	Has a zillion things up in the air
Loses others/leaves people behind	

4. Too little can contribute to the following Stallers and Stoppers:

A. What too little looks like (unskilled):

Narrow, tactical, cautious and conservative; may be more comfortable with the past, prefer the tried and true; narrow perspective may have resulted from narrow background; avoids risk and doesn't seek to be bold or different; doesn't connect with ideas from outside own area; may have no idea how creativity works; uses old solutions for new problems; may chill the creative initiatives of others.

B. Too little might lead to these Stallers and Stoppers:

Non-Strategic (114)

C. Compensators:

How to substitute for too little of this competency:

1, 2, 5, 15, 16, 28, 30, 32, 33, 43, 46, 51, 57, 58, 61

I. LEARNING ARCHITECT® Connections:

Look for people who act like and/or show evidence of:

1b. Trial and Error	12. Rules of Thumb
2b. Visioning	22. Experimenter
2c. Intuition	27. Conceptualizer
4a. Getting Information	28. Creator
7. Risks	30. Mastery
10. Complexity	33. Diversity of Sources
11. Why/How	35. Breadth

CREATIVITY

J. CHOICES ARCHITECT® Connections:

Look for people who act like and/or show evidence of:

First Edition (Released 1994)
1. Inquisitive
2. Essence
3. Creator
4. Complexity
5. Connector
6. Visionary
12. Experimenter
19. Tinkerer

Second Edition (Released 2000)
2. Complexity
3. Connector
4. Critical Thinker
6. Essence
28. Solution Finder
20. Experimenter

K. Difficulty to Develop:
25 (of 34)–Moderate

15. CUSTOMER FOCUS

A. Definition:

Is dedicated to meeting the expectations and requirements of internal and external customers; gets first-hand customer information and uses it for improvements in products and services; acts with customers in mind; establishes and maintains effective relationships with customers and gains their trust and respect.

B. Arenas/Domains to Explore:

1. Association boards
2. Club officer
3. Current external customers
4. Current internal customers
5. Early jobs in service sector
6. Event planning
7. Meeting facilitation
8. Meeting/conference management
9. Religious service
10. Social network
11. Student government
12. Teaching
13. Athletic team captain
14. Volunteer work

C. Sample Questions:

Dimension 1: Been there, done that–has had direct personal experience(s) involving the competency–candidate was the prime player   Note: * means OK for campus

1. Can you be counted on to stick to the procedures in dealing with customers?
2. Do you form personal relationships with your customers?
3. Have you ever "fired" a customer; told them you were no longer interested in their business?
4. Have you ever had a job in direct sales? How did you do?*
5. Have you ever managed anything where the people or units reporting to you were in different locations? How did you get them to be more customer focused.
6. Have you ever violated a policy or a procedure to get something for a customer?
7. How comfortable are you in meeting new people?*
8. How do you divide up your customers into categories?
9. How do you get and keep up-to-date information from customers, and what do you do with it?
10. How do you handle an unjustified complaint from a customer?
11. Tell me about a time when you almost lost some customers and had to turn it around.
12. Tell me about a time when you exceeded your customer's expectations.
13. Tell me about a time when you had to communicate something important to someone who did not speak your language very well.
14. Tell me about a time when you had to deal with unreasonable customer requests.*
15. Tell me about a time when you had to sell something as a school project/job.*
16. Tell me about a time when you lost customers.
17. Tell me about a time when your focus on the customer worked really well for you.
18. Tell me about a time when your lack of customer focus got you into trouble.
19. What do customers do that irritates you? How do you react?
20. When is the last time you were treated badly as a customer?*
21. When was the last time someone lost you as a customer? Why?*

CUSTOMER FOCUS

22. When was the last time you were treated exceptionally well as a customer?*
23. Who are your best and worst customers?

Dimension 2: Seen/been around others who were involved with the competency–good and bad; learns from others about self

24. Contrast the most and least customer focused people you know.*
25. Has customer focus ever been in any 360º survey done on you? Was your score among your highest, middle, or lowest?
26. Has poor customer focus on someone else's part ever created an obstacle for you or got in the way of something you were trying to accomplish?*
27. Have you ever talked about your customer focus with a coach or mentor?
28. Have you ever watched someone fail/get fired because they were not customer focused?*
29. Have you ever watched someone overdo customer focus to the point that it backfired?
30. Have you ever watched someone succeed because they were customer focused?*
31. Have you ever worked with a coach on customer focus?*
32. Have you ever worked with a person who excelled at customer focus?
33. Have you ever worked with a skills coach on customer focus?*
34. How do you get feedback about yourself on customer focus?
35. How often do you check with multiple sources when you get a piece of critical feedback on your customer focus?
36. Is there a historical figure you consider a model of customer focus?
37. What do others who are not your fans say about your customer focus?
38. What do others who like you say about your customer focus?
39. Which boss was the best at customer focus?
40. Which boss was the worst at customer focus?
41. Which direct report was the best at customer focus?
42. Which direct report was the worst at customer focus?
43. Which peer was the best at customer focus?
44. Which peer was the worst at customer focus?
45. Who in your field or business deals the best with customers?
46. Who do you consider a role model of customer focus?*
47. Who do you go to for advice on customer focus?
48. Who have you learned the most from about customer focus?*
49. Who is a higher-management role model for you on customer focus?
50. Who is a role model of customer focus outside of work?

Dimension 3: Knows how the competency works in theory; shows understanding

51. Are there situations or settings where someone should be different on demonstrating customer focus?
52. Do you think customer focus can be learned? If so, how do you think people develop customer focus skills?
53. Do you think there is a way to compensate or work around a lack of customer focus?
54. Has anyone asked you for your opinions/advice on customer focus?*
55. Have you ever attended a course on customer focus?
56. Have you ever been in a situation where you and others put customer focus on a success profile?
57. Have you ever been part of an effort to create a policy or a mission statement containing reference to the importance of being customer focused?

CUSTOMER FOCUS

58. Have you ever been someone's coach or mentor who had problems with customer focus?
59. Have you ever created a development plan for someone on customer focus?
60. Have you ever criticized someone for lack of customer focus?
61. Have you ever designed a program on customer focus?
62. Have you ever given a speech on customer focus?
63. Have you ever rewarded or recognized someone for being customer focused?
64. Have you ever taught a course on customer focus?
65. Have you ever tried to help someone deal more effectively with customer focus?*
66. Have you ever tried to help someone improve their customer service skills?
67. How do you think people develop customer service skills?
68. How much customer focus is good to have and how much is too much?
69. How much of success do you think is due to customer focus compared with other characteristics?
70. How would you know if someone lacks customer focus?
71. How would you know if someone demonstrates customer focus?
72. If you had to write a book on customer focus, what would the chapter headings be?
73. What are the benefits to someone who is really good at customer focus?
74. What are the consequences to someone who is really poor at customer focus?
75. What do you think the performance standard is on customer focus for someone in your role?
76. What happens if you are too customer focused?
77. What happens when two people try to work together who feel very differently about customer focus?
78. What wisdom would you pass onto others trying to become better at customer focus?
79. When you select others, what do you look for in their ability to be responsive to customers?
80. When you think of companies who do well serving their customers, which ones come to mind? Why?*
81. Which companies do badly in customer service? Why?*
82. Why do you think people end up being different in their customer focus skills?

Dimension 4: Shows personal change and sense-making; learned it one place and applied it in another; can compare and contrast experiences; changes viewpoints across time; can explain personal development or evolution related to the competency

83. Compare and contrast examples of times when you've been effective and ineffective at meeting customer expectations.
84. Contrast your on- and off-the-job use of customer orientation.
85. Did you ever pass up a job or assignment because you were not confident enough in your skills at customer focus?
86. Do you ever use other skills to cover for your lack of customer focus skills?
87. Do you treat all of your customers the same?
88. Has customer service ever figured in a failure, struggle, or setback you have had?
89. Has becoming better at customer focus ever helped you in other areas?
90. Has poor customer service ever been the subject of a development plan for you?
91. Has your customer focus always been this way?
92. Have you ever delegated or assigned someone a task because you don't deal with customers particularly well?
93. Have you ever made significant strides at becoming better at customer service?
94. Have your customer service skills, good or bad, ever been the subject of your performance review or a career discussion?

CUSTOMER FOCUS

95. How accurate have you been in predicting what customers will want next?
96. How different are you across situations in your customer service skills?
97. How do you decide how customer focused to be?
98. How much of your success is due to your customer service skills?
99. How transferable are your customer service skills to other situations?
100. If you had to become better at customer service in a hurry, what would you do?
101. Was there a time when you were not good at customer service?
102. What caused you to work to change your customer focus skills?
103. What event or series of events had the most impact on the way you served customers?
104. What's the most varied you can be in serving customers?
105. What was the shortest amount of time in which you increased your level of skill at customer service?
106. When are exceptions to customers justified and not justified?
107. When did you first realize your level of skill at customer service?
108. When you know ahead of time that your usual approach to customer service won't work, what do you do?
109. Who are your internal customers? What is different about the way you deal with internal and external customers?
110. Why do you think you deal with customers the way you do?
111. Why do you think your customer focus is the way it is?*

D. Follow-up Probes:
1. Are there times when you're not like this or wouldn't do this?
2. Are there times when you act like that and times when you don't?
3. Could you contrast those two bosses for me?
4. Could you give me a few examples of how you've used or applied that?
5. Did you or the other person blink first?
6. Do you suppose if others would just try harder, they could learn to be more customer oriented like you?
7. Do you think all customers would react that way?
8. Do you think this is teachable?
9. Do you think you're better at customer focus than most? Why?
10. Do you think you would perform any better if you dealt with customers differently?
11. Have you ever had to form a relationship with a customer you really disliked to get your job done?
12. How did it feel to give up something you wanted to get the project going?
13. How did the others react when you did that?
14. How did you come up with that approach in the first place?
15. How did you know that method of getting over that barrier would work?
16. How did you see that as a customer yourself?
17. How do others you have known approach that?
18. How far will you go before you cut line and try another approach?
19. How much did you have to give up to make it work?
20. How often do you use the "Let's meet in the middle" approach?
21. How typical is this for you?
22. How would you approach that same situation today?
23. Is this natural for you, or do you really have to dig for it?

CUSTOMER FOCUS

24. Was that a fair way to maneuver around them?
25. Was there a time when you didn't understand this about yourself?
26. Were there some alternatives you rejected? Were you right?
27. What did you do after you got that feedback?
28. What did you do to adapt to that?
29. What did you learn about dealing with complaints?
30. What did you learn about how customers are gained?
31. What did you learn about how customers are lost?*
32. What did you learn from that?
33. Why did you choose that approach?
34. Why did you decide to take the risk?
35. Why did you do it that way?
36. Why did you time your attempt like you did?
37. Why do you have difficulties with that sometimes?
38. Why do you suppose organizations work that way?
39. Why do you think that didn't work?
40. Why do you think that happened that way?
41. Why do you think that worked?
42. Would you have done it that way with looser deadlines?
43. Would you have done it that way with tighter deadlines?

E. **Themes/Things to Look for:**
   Asking for the check
   Bone deep belief in serving customers
   Conflict skills with customers
   Frequent product/service improvements based on feedback
   "Going out of one's way" customer service
   Handling irate customers comfortably
   Learning from other organizations
   Likes talking to people
   Marketing and sales agility
   Occasional risk-taking for customers
   Sensitivity and empathy
   Understanding customer policies, practices–a framework to guide the person rather than a one-at-a-time approach
   Understanding product/service benefits
   Understanding product/service features
   Understanding product/service trends
   Understanding sales objections
   Unusual solutions to customer problems

CUSTOMER FOCUS

F. Most Likely Résumé:

1. Look for jobs like:

Chair of Projects/Task Forces
Fix-Its/Turnarounds
Heavy Strategic Demands
International Assignments
Scope (complexity) Assignments
Staff Leadership (Influencing Without Authority)
Staff to Line Shifts
Start-Ups

2. Look for develop-in-place assignments like:

Plan an off-site meeting, conference, convention, trade show, event, etc.

Manage the purchase of a major product, equipment, materials, program, or system.

Study and establish internal or external customer needs, requirements, specifications, and expectations, and present them to the people involved.

Do a customer-satisfaction survey in person or by phone, and present it to the people involved.

Help someone outside your unit or the organization solve a business problem.

Do a feasibility study on an important opportunity, and make recommendations to those who will decide.

Visit Malcolm Baldrige National Quality Award or Deming Prize winners and report back on your findings, showing how they would help your organization.

Work a few shifts in the telemarketing or customer service department, handling complaints and inquiries from customers.

Make speeches/be a spokesperson for the organization on the outside.

Represent the organization at a trade show, convention, exposition, etc.

Spend time with internal or external customers, write a report on your observations, and present it to the people involved with the customers in the organization.

Launch a new product, service, or process.

Be a change agent; create a symbol for change; lead the rallying cry; champion a significant change and implementation.

Relaunch an existing product or service that's not doing well.

Train customers in the use of the organization's products or services.

Manage an ad hoc, temporary group of balky and resisting people through an unpopular change or project.

Manage an ad hoc, temporary group of people involved in tackling a fix-it or turnaround project.

Manage the interface between consultants and the organization on a critical assignment.

Handle a tough negotiation with an internal or external client or customer.

Manage liquidation/sale of products, equipment, materials, a business, furniture, overstock, etc.

Prepare and present a proposal of some consequence to top management.

Manage a dissatisfied internal or external customer; troubleshoot a performance or quality problem with a product or service.

Manage the assigning/allocating of office space in a contested situation.

Manage a cost-cutting project.

Resolve an issue in conflict between two people, units, geographies, functions, etc.

Write a speech for someone higher up in the organization.

Do a postmortem on a failed project, and present it to the people involved.

Build a multifunctional project team to tackle a common business issue or problem.

Work on a crisis management team.

CUSTOMER FOCUS

3. **Best references to ask about or check:**
   Direct Boss
   Customers
   Past Associates/Constituencies

G. Learning Agility Evaluation:
   2. All or Nothing vs. Can See Many Sides
   4. Spectator/Passive vs. Player/Participant
   5. Tight/Rigid vs. Loose/Flexible
   11. Generalizations vs. Specific Learnings
   13. Simple Views vs. Complex Views
   21. View from Self vs. View from Point of View of Others

H. The LEADERSHIP ARCHITECT® Sort Card Connections:

   1. **Good (positive) if combined with high:**
      Satisfies the customer 1, 16, 50, 53
      Good at "hard" customer contact 1, 24, 36, 50, 51, 53
      Good at "soft" customer contact 3, 31, 33, 41, 53
      Services higher management as a customer 4, 8
      Reads the customer 33, 56
      Can stand up to customers when necessary 34, 57
      Makes sense of customer trends, sets up delivery mechanisms 35, 52, 59, 63, 65

   2. **Bad (negative) if combined with low or high (+):**
      Goes through motions, smile school 3, 7, 10
      May not treat internals as customers 8, 42, 60
      Wishy-washy 9, 34, 57
      Poor at customer conflict management 11, 12
      Doesn't read customer needs 33, 56
      Everything's an exception/disorganized 35, 52, 59
      Doesn't improve products/services 53, 63

   3. **Too much can contribute to the following Stallers and Stoppers:**

      A. *What too much looks like (overused):*

      May be overly responsive to customer demands; may be too willing to change established processes and timetables to respond to unreasonable customer requests; may make too many exceptions and not form consistent policies, practices, and processes for others to learn and follow; sticks so close to current customer needs that breakthroughs are missed.

      B. *Too much might lead to these Stallers and Stoppers:*
      None Apply

CUSTOMER FOCUS

C. Compensators:
How to compensate for too much of this competency:

5, 9, 12, 34, 35, 38, 50, 51, 52, 53, 57, 58, 59, 63, 65

D. Things to watch for:

"I'm always right"
"If I ran it, it wouldn't be done that way"
Bad mouthing the company too much
Everything is an exception

Not playing by the rules
Siding with the customer too much
Overreacts to a small sample of complaints

4. Too little can contribute to the following Stallers and Stoppers:

A. What too little looks like (unskilled):
Doesn't think of the customer first; may think he/she already know what they need; may focus on internal operations and get blindsided by customer problems; may not make the first move–won't meet and get to know customers; uncomfortable with new people contacts; may be unwilling to handle criticisms, complaints, and special requests; may not listen well to customers, may be defensive; may not make the time for customer contact.

B. Too little might lead to these Stallers and Stoppers:
Insensitive to Others (112)
Performance Problems (118)

C. Compensators:
How to substitute for too little of this competency:

1, 3, 9, 16, 24, 27, 31, 32, 33, 36, 38, 43, 51, 53, 63

I. LEARNING ARCHITECT® Connections:

Look for people who act like and/or show evidence of:

- 1c. Following a Plan
- 2a. Problem Solving
- 4a. Getting Information
- 9. Multiple Sources
- 16. Collaborate
- 19. What
- 20. Events

J. CHOICES ARCHITECT® Connections:

Look for people who act like and/or show evidence of:

First Edition (Released 1994)
- 7. Helping Others Think
- 13. Role Flexibility
- 14. Transaction Quality
- 23. Communicator

Second Edition (Released 2000)
- 5. Easy Shifter
- 9. Agile Communicator
- 10. Conflict Manager
- 15. People-Smart
- 18. Role Flexibility

K. Difficulty to Develop:
18 (of 34)–Easiest

16. *TIMELY* DECISION MAKING

A. Definition:

Makes decisions in a timely manner, sometimes with incomplete information and under tight deadlines and pressure; able to make a quick decision.

B. Arenas/Domains to Explore:

1. Ambiguous situations
2. Athletic performance
3. Career decisions
4. Conflict situations
5. Daily life choices
6. Direct report decisions
7. Emergencies/crises
8. Layoffs
9. Managing impossible deadlines
10. Managing marginal performers
11. Public decision making in meetings
12. Recreation choices
13. Relationship decisions
14. Sudden changes
15. Task force management
16. Team captain
17. Vacation decisions

C. Sample Questions:

*Dimension 1: Been there, done that–has had direct personal experience(s) involving the competency–candidate was the prime player   Note: * means OK for campus*

1. Do you enjoy analyzing facts and data?*
2. Have you ever avoided making certain kinds of decisions?*
3. Have you ever managed anything where the people or units reporting to you were in different locations? How did you get them to act more quickly?
4. How did you pick the college you went to?*
5. How do you gather information in a hurry?*
6. How do you get through situations where you are overwhelmed with decisions to make?*
7. How do you go about making a capital expenditure decision?*
8. How do you include others when you have to make a fast decision?*
9. How do you know it's time to risk going with a less than well-thought-out decision?*
10. How do you select vacation destinations?*
11. How do/did you select courses to take?*
12. How often do you help or urge others to make quicker decisions than they are normally comfortable with?*
13. How soon have you rescinded or changed a decision after you have made it?*
14. Is there a time to do nothing–just don't decide?*
15. Tell me about a time when making a decision quickly worked really well for you.
16. Tell me about a time when you had to make a decision in less time than you thought was right.*
17. Tell me about a time when your slowness in making a decision got you into trouble.
18. Tell me about some quick decisions that backfired on you.*
19. Tell me about a time when you have made a decision that was against the prevailing opinion of others?*
20. Tell me some snap decisions you had to make/decisions under the gun.*
21. What do you do when faced with an impossible deadline?*
22. What is your "go" percentage before you are willing to make an important decision?*

TIMELY DECISION MAKING

23. What slows you down in decision making?*
24. What was the fastest major decision you have made?*
25. When do you irritate people with your speed of making decisions?*

Dimension 2: Seen/been around others who were involved with the competency–good and bad; learns from others about self

26. Contrast the most and least timely decision makers you know.*
27. Has making timely decisions ever been in any 360° survey done on you? Was your score among your highest, middle, or lowest?
28. Has not making timely decisions on someone else's part ever created an obstacle for you or got in the way of something you were trying to accomplish?*
29. Have you ever talked about your timeliness in making decisions with a coach or mentor?
30. Have you ever watched someone fail/get fired because they did not make timely decisions?*
31. Have you ever watched someone react too decisively/too timely to the point that it backfired?
32. Have you ever watched someone succeed because they made timely decisions?*
33. Have you ever worked with a coach on timely decision making?*
34. Have you ever worked with a person who excelled at making timely decisions?
35. Have you ever worked with a skills coach on making more timely decisions?*
36. How do you get feedback about your ability to make timely decisions?
37. How often do you check with multiple sources when you get a piece of critical feedback indicating that you have not made timely decisions?
38. Is there a historical figure you consider a model of making timely decisions?
39. What do others who are not your fans say about your ability to make timely decisions?
40. What do others who like you say about your ability to make timely decisions?
41. Which boss was the best at making timely decisions?
42. Which boss was the worst at timely decision making?
43. Which direct report was the best at timely decision making?
44. Which direct report was the worst at timely decision making?
45. Which peer was the best at timely decision making?
46. Which peer was the worst at timely decision making?
47. Who in your field or business deals the best with making timely decisions?
48. Who do you consider a role model of making timely decisions?*
49. Who do you go to for advice on making timely decisions?
50. Who have you learned the most from about making timely decisions?*
51. Who is a higher-management role model for you on timely decision making?
52. Who is a role model of timely decision making outside of work?

Dimension 3: Knows how the competency works in theory; shows understanding

53. Are there situations or settings where someone should make timely decisions differently?
54. Do you think timely decision-making skills can be learned? If so, how do you think people develop timely decision-making skills?
55. Do you think there is a way to compensate or work around low timely decision-making skills?
56. Has anyone asked you for your opinions/advice on timely decision making?*
57. Have you ever attended a course on timely decision making?
58. Have you ever been in a situation where you and others put timely decision making on a success profile?

TIMELY DECISION MAKING

59. Have you ever been part of an effort to create a policy or a mission statement containing reference to the importance of making timely decisions?
60. Have you ever been someone's coach or mentor who had problems with timely decision making?
61. Have you ever created a development plan for someone on making timely decisions?
62. Have you ever criticized someone for not making timely decisions?
63. Have you ever designed a program on timely decision making?
64. Have you ever given a speech on making timely decisions?
65. Have you ever rewarded or recognized someone for making timely decisions?
66. Have you ever taught a course on timely decision making?
67. Have you ever tried to help someone deal more effectively with making timely decisions?*
68. Have you ever tried to help someone improve their timely decision-making skills?
69. How do you think people develop timely decision-making skills?
70. How much of success do you think is due to making timely decisions compared with other characteristics?
71. How would you know if someone is bad at making timely decisions?
72. How would you know if someone is good at making timely decisions?
73. If you had to write a book on making timely decisions, what would the chapter headings be?
74. What are the benefits to someone who is really good at making timely decisions?
75. What are the consequences to someone who is really poor at making timely decisions?
76. What do you think the performance standard is on timely decision making for someone in your role?
77. What happens when two people try to work together who are very different on making timely decisions?
78. What wisdom would you pass onto others trying to become better at making timely decisions?
79. Why do you think people end up being different in their ability to make timely decisions?

Dimension 4: Shows personal change and sense-making; learned it one place and applied it in another; can compare and contrast experiences; changes viewpoints across time; can explain personal development or evolution related to the competency

80. Compare and contrast situations where you've been effective and ineffective at making timely decisions.
81. Contrast your on- and off-the-job use of timely decision making skills.
82. Did you ever pass up a job or assignment because you were not confident enough in your ability to make timely decisions?
83. Do you ever use other skills to cover for your lack of timely decision-making skills?
84. Do you have an orderly way to make decisions quickly?*
85. Has timely decision making ever figured in a failure, struggle, or setback you have had?
86. Has becoming better at timely decision making ever helped you in other areas?
87. Has slow decision making ever been the subject of a development plan for you?
88. Has your ability to make timely decisions always been this way?
89. Have you ever delegated or assigned someone a task because you didn't make timely decisions particularly well?
90. Have you ever made significant strides at becoming better at making timely decisions?
91. Has your ability to make timely decisions, good or bad, ever been the subject of your performance review or a career discussion?
92. How different are you across situations in your ability to make timely decisions?
93. How do you decide how much time to spend making a decision?
94. How important is it for you to be right?*
95. How much of your success is due to your ability to make timely decisions?

TIMELY DECISION MAKING

96. How transferable is your ability to make timely decisions to other situations?
97. If you had to become better at timely decision making in a hurry, what would you do?
98. In what situations do you make the slowest decisions?*
99. In what situations do you tend to make the quickest decisions?*
100. Tell me how you go about making big or critical decisions.
101. Was there a time when you were not good at making timely decisions?
102. What caused you to work to make decisions in a more timely fashion?
103. What event or series of events had the most impact on your ability to make timely decisions?
104. What's the most varied you can be in making timely decisions?
105. What was the shortest amount of time in which you increased your level of skill at making timely decisions?
106. When did you first realize your level of skill at making timely decisions?
107. When you know ahead of time that your usual way of making timely decisions won't work, what do you do?
108. Why do you think you make decisions the way you do?
109. Why do you think your decision making speed is the way it is?*

D. **Follow-up Probes:**
1. Are there times when you're not like this or wouldn't do this?
2. Are there times when you decide like that and times when you don't?
3. Could you contrast those two bosses for me?
4. Could you give me a few examples of how you've used or applied that?
5. Did you or the other person blink first?
6. Do you suppose if others would just try harder, they could learn to be more decisive like you?
7. Do you think this is teachable?
8. Do you think you're better at making timely decisions than most? Why?
9. Do you think you would perform any better if you made more timely decisions?
10. Do you think your quick decisions are as good as your thought-through decisions?
11. How did it feel to give up something you wanted to get the decision made?
12. How did the others react when you did that?
13. How did you come up with that approach in the first place?
14. How did you know that method of getting over that barrier would work?
15. How do others you have known approach that?
16. How far did you go to try to be a team player?
17. How far will you go before you cut line and try another approach?
18. How important was it for you to make a quick decision?
19. How much did you have to give up to make it work?
20. How often do you use the "Let's meet in the middle" approach?
21. How typical is this for you?
22. How would you approach that same situation today?
23. Is this natural for you, or do you really have to dig for it?
24. Was that a fair way to maneuver around them?
25. Was there a time when you didn't understand this about yourself?
26. What did you do after you got that feedback?

27. What did you do to adapt to that?
28. What did you learn from that?
29. What do you think would have happened if you had gone with your first impression?
30. Why did you choose that approach?
31. Why did you decide to take the risk?
32. Why did you do it that way?
33. Why did you think it was important for you to make a quick decision?
34. Why did you time your attempt like you did?
35. Why do you suppose organizations work that way?
36. Why do you think that didn't work?
37. Why do you think that happened that way?
38. Why do you think that worked?
39. Why do you think you have difficulties with that once in a while?
40. Would you have done it that way with looser deadlines?
41. Would you have done it that way with tighter deadlines?

E. Themes/Things to Look for:

Admitting mistakes and moving on

Asking focused questions to find the key elements of problems

Awareness of impact of making quick decisions

Being able to get eighty percent of the answers twenty percent of the time/good percent hit rate

Comfort with loose ends; doesn't need to dot the i's

Comfortable not having all the data

Drivers? What drives the speed? Personal needs or requirements of the situation?

Focus on organizing data quickly in categories rather than just gathering data in pieces

Having an orderly way to make decisions (e.g. What are the key elements? What questions would I have to answer to capture the data in efficient categories? Who are the stakeholders? Where can I get information? How will I know what to collect?).

Listening habits

Need for consensus/participation

Need for perfection

Need to be liked

Not avoiding detail if needed

Not avoiding hard to deal with people

Percentage right on first try

Problem definition vs. just doing something

Setting priorities

Taking risks

TIMELY DECISION MAKING

F. Most Likely Résumé:

1. Look for jobs like:
Chair of Projects/Task Forces
Fix-Its/Turnarounds
Scope (complexity) Assignments
Staff to Line Shifts
Start-Ups

2. Look for develop-in-place assignments like:
Manage the renovation of an office, floor, building, meeting room, warehouse, etc.
Plan a new site for a building (plant, field office, headquarters, etc.).
Become a referee for an athletic league or program.
Plan for and start up something small (secretarial pool, athletic program, suggestion system, program, etc.).
Launch a new product, service, or process.
Relaunch an existing product or service that's not doing well.
Manage an ad hoc, temporary group of people involved in tackling a fix-it or turnaround project.
Help shut down a plant, regional office, product line, business, operation, etc.
Manage liquidation/sale of products, equipment, materials, a business, furniture, overstock, etc.
Manage a group through a significant business crisis.
Work on a crisis management team.

3. Best references to ask about or check:
Direct Boss
Customers
Past Associates/Constituencies
Peers and Colleagues
Direct Reports

G. Learning Agility Evaluation:
4. Spectator/Passive vs. Player/Participant
5. Tight/Rigid vs. Loose/Flexible
10. Reacting vs. Initiating
11. Generalizations vs. Specific Learnings
16. Few Rules of Thumb vs. Many and Varied Rules of Thumb
20. Avoids Responsibility for Mistakes vs. Admits and Learns from Mistakes
21. View from Self vs. View from Point of View of Others
22. Focus on Accomplishments vs. Focus on Solving Problems

TIMELY DECISION MAKING

H. **The LEADERSHIP ARCHITECT® Sort Card Connections:**

1. **Good (positive) if combined with high:**
   Can manage through chaos 2, 40
   Feelings don't slow them down 12, 57
   Gets things done 15, 50, 53
   Apt to be right 17, 30, 32, 61
   Thoughtful but fast 17, 41, 47, 51
   Good on feet 27, 49
   Learns from decisions 32, 45
   Can lead a negotiation 36, 37
   Can cycle through a lot at once 47, 50

2. **Bad (negative) if combined with low or high (+):**
   Impulsive/action junkie/disruptive in meetings (+) 11, 41
   Makes decisions quickly to avoid/wipe out ambiguity 2, 40
   Aloof 3, 33
   Doesn't think things through enough 17, 51
   Makes all the decisions themselves 18, 20 (+57)
   Doesn't include others 31, 36, 39, 60
   Disorganized 39, 47
   Seat of the pants 52, 59
   Doesn't learn 32, 45, 51, 58

3. **Too much can contribute to the following Stallers and Stoppers:**

   A. *What too much looks like (overused):*
      May jump to conclusions and take action before reasonable consideration of the information; may get caught up in action for its own sake; may have a chilling effect on getting everyone's input before deciding; might be considered impulsive and impatient; might have some trouble and freeze on issues and problems that are close calls; may make decisions quickly to avoid debate and personal discomfort

   B. *What might it lead to:*
      Unable to Adapt to Differences (101)   Failure to Staff Effectively (111)
      Lack of Ethics and Values (109)   Overmanaging (117)
      Failure to Build a Team (110)

   C. *Compensators:*
      How to compensate for too much of this competency:
           3, 11, 17, 33, 39, 41, 46, 47, 51, 52, 58, 59, 63, 65

TIMELY DECISION MAKING

D. Things to watch for:

"I'd rather just try something than think about it for a long time... ."

"I'm always way out ahead of everybody... ."

"I decided what I wanted to do but had to wait for everyone else to catch up... ."

"I knew what the solution was long before anyone else... ."

"I was ready to act but nobody else was... ."

Impulsiveness (high 1, low 41)

Rigid; has to wipe out uncertainty/ambiguity

Doesn't involve others

Loose cannon

4. Too little can contribute to the following Stallers and Stoppers:

A. What too little looks like (unskilled):

Slow to decide or to declare; conservative and cautious; may procrastinate, seek more information to build confidence and avoid risk; may be a perfectionist, needing to be right, protect strongly against criticism; may be disorganized and always scrambling to meet decision deadlines; may be slow to make decisions on more complex issues.

B. Too little might lead to these Stallers and Stoppers:

Unable to Adapt to Differences (101) Failure to Build a Team (110)
Poor Administrator (102) Performance Problems (118)
Lack of Composure (107)

C. Compensators:

How to substitute for too little of this competency:
1, 2, 12, 27, 32, 37, 40, 43, 50, 51, 52, 53, 62

I. LEARNING ARCHITECT® Connections:

Look for people who act like and/or show evidence of:

1a. Pure Action 4a. Getting Information
1b. Trial and Error 7. Risks
1c. Following a Plan 13. Focused
2a. Problem Solving 22. Experimenter
2c. Intuition 36. Comfort with Paradox

J. CHOICES ARCHITECT® Connections:

Look for people who act like and/or show evidence of:

First Edition (Released 1994) **Second Edition (Released 2000)**
None apply 5. Easy Shifter
 23. Visioning

K. Difficulty to Develop:

18 (of 34)–Easiest

17. DECISION QUALITY

A. Definition:

Makes good decisions (without considering how much time it takes) based upon a mixture of analysis, wisdom, experience, and judgment; most of his/her solutions and suggestions turn out to be correct and accurate when judged over time; sought out by others for advice and solutions.

B. Arenas/Domains to Explore:

1. Association boards/management
2. Big decisions
3. Career decisions
4. Child management
5. Daily management of processes
6. Daily management of tasks
7. Decisions
8. Family finances
9. Financial management at work
10. Helping others solve problems
11. Life decisions
12. Long term decisions
13. Major purchase decisions
14. Mergers/acquisitions/strategic partnerships
15. People decisions
16. Personnel decisions
17. Process improvement decisions
18. Reading habits
19. Student government
20. Tactic and strategy decisions
21. Technical/business decisions
22. White papers/studies/long-term projects
23. Working out of personal problems

C. Sample Questions:

*Dimension 1: Been there, done that–has had direct personal experience(s) involving the competency–candidate was the prime player   Note: * means OK for campus*

1. Do you enjoy collecting and analyzing information?*
2. Do you tend to continue to collect information after you have made a decision?*
3. Give me an example, and lead me through your decision-making process on technical problems.
4. Give me an example, and lead me through your decision-making process on career choices.
5. Give me an example, and lead me through your decision-making process on financial decisions at work.
6. Give me an example, and lead me through your decision-making process on business moves.
7. Give me an example, and lead me through your decision-making process on people problems.*
8. Give me an example, and lead me through your decision-making process on hiring people.
9. Give me an example, and lead me through your decision-making process on process improvement.
10. Have you ever managed anything where the people or units reporting to you were in different locations? How did you make good decisions being that spread out?
11. How often do you tend to be right about major decisions you make?*
12. How sure are you when you make a significant decision?*
13. Tell me about a time when a bad decision got you into trouble.
14. Tell me about a time when a good decision worked really well for you.
15. Tell me about a time when you turned out to be right and others were wrong.*
16. Tell me about a time when you turned out to be wrong and others were right.*
17. What is your "go" percentage before you are willing to make a major decision?*

DECISION QUALITY

Dimension 2: Seen/been around others who were involved with the competency–good and bad; learns from others about self

18. Contrast the people you know who are most and least able to make quality decisions.*
19. Has making quality decisions ever been in any 360° survey done on you? Was your score among your highest, middle, or lowest?
20. Has making poor quality decisions on someone else's part ever created an obstacle for you or got in the way of something you were trying to accomplish?*
21. Have you ever talked about the quality of your decisions with a coach or mentor?
22. Have you ever watched someone fail/get fired because they did not make quality decisions?*
23. Have you ever watched someone overdo making quality decisions to the point that it backfired?
24. Have you ever watched someone succeed because they made quality decisions?*
25. Have you ever worked with a coach on making better quality decisions?*
26. Have you ever worked with a person who excelled at making quality decisions?
27. Have you ever worked with a skills coach on making quality decisions?*
28. How do you get feedback about your ability to make quality decisions?
29. How often do you check with multiple sources when you get a piece of critical feedback on the quality of your decisions?
30. Is there a historical figure you consider a model of making quality decisions?
31. What do others who are not your fans say about your decision quality?
32. What do others who like you say about your decision quality?
33. Which boss was the best at making quality decisions?
34. Which boss was the worst at making quality decisions?
35. Which direct report was the best at making quality decisions?
36. Which direct report was the worst at making quality decisions?
37. Which peer was the best at making quality decisions?
38. Which peer was the worst at making quality decisions?
39. Who in your field or business deals the best with making quality decisions?
40. Who do you consider a role model of making quality decisions?*
41. Who do you go to for advice on making better quality decisions?
42. Who have you learned the most from about making quality decisions?*
43. Who is a higher-management role model for you on making quality decisions?
44. Who is a role model for quality decision making outside of work?

Dimension 3: Knows how the competency works in theory; shows understanding

45. Are there situations or settings where someone should approach making sound decisions differently?
46. Do you think the ability to make sound decisions can be learned? If so, how do you think people develop decision-making skills?
47. Do you think there is a way to compensate or work around poor decision-quality skills?
48. Has anyone asked you for your opinions/advice on making quality decisions?*
49. Have you ever attended a course on making quality decisions?
50. Have you ever been in a situation where you and others put quality decision making on a success profile?
51. Have you ever been part of an effort to create a policy or a mission statement containing reference to the importance of making quality decisions?
52. Have you ever been someone's coach or mentor who had problems with making quality decisions?
53. Have you ever created a development plan for someone on making quality decisions?

DECISION QUALITY

54. Have you ever criticized someone for their inability to make quality decisions?
55. Have you ever designed a program on making quality decisions?
56. Have you ever given a speech on making quality decisions?
57. Have you ever rewarded or recognized someone for having the ability to make quality decisions?
58. Have you ever taught a course on making quality decisions?
59. Have you ever tried to help someone deal more effectively with making quality decisions?*
60. Have you ever tried to help someone improve their decision quality?
61. How do you think people develop decision-making skills?
62. How much of success do you think is due to quality decision making compared with other characteristics?
63. How would you know if someone is bad at making quality decisions?
64. How would you know if someone is good at making quality decisions?
65. If you had to write a book on quality decision making, what would the chapter headings be?
66. What are the benefits to someone who is really good at making quality decisions?
67. What are the consequences to someone who is really poor at making quality decisions?
68. What do you think the performance standard is on making quality decisions for someone in your role?
69. What happens when two people try to work together who are very different in their ability to make quality decisions?
70. What wisdom would you pass onto others trying to become better at making quality decisions?
71. When you select others, what do you look for in their ability to make quality decisions?
72. Why do you think people end up being different in their ability to make quality decisions?

Dimension 4: Shows personal change and sense-making; learned it one place and applied it in another; can compare and contrast experiences; changes viewpoints across time; can explain personal development or evolution related to the competency

73. Compare and contrast examples of times when you've been effective and ineffective at making quality decisions.
74. Contrast a good with a poor decision that you've made.*
75. Contrast your on- and off-the-job ability to make good decisions.
76. Did you ever pass up a job or assignment because you were not confident enough in your ability to make quality decisions?
77. Do you ever use other skills to cover for your inability to make quality decisions?
78. Has decision quality ever figured in a failure, struggle, or setback you have had?
79. Has becoming better at decision quality ever helped you in other areas?
80. Has poor decision quality ever been the subject of a development plan for you?
81. Has your ability to make good decisions always been this way?
82. Have you ever delegated or assigned someone a task because you didn't make decisions particularly well?
83. Have you ever made significant strides at becoming better at making good decisions?
84. Have you become better at making the right decisions the first time?
85. Have your decision quality skills, good or bad, ever been the subject of your performance review or a career discussion?
86. How different are you across situations in your ability to make quality decisions?
87. How do you decide how to make an important decision?
88. How do you know when to stop analyzing/collecting data and make the decision?
89. How important is it to you to be right?*
90. How much of your success is due to your decision quality?

DECISION QUALITY

91. How often does your experience and prior decisions you've made help you make the right decisions today?*
92. How transferable is your decision making ability to other situations?
93. If you had to become better at making good decisions in a hurry, what would you do?
94. Tell me about a time when your experience and prior decisions helped you make the right decision. Have you become better at making the right decisions the first time?
95. Tell me about some of the best decisions you've ever made. How were they similar/different?*
96. Was there a time when you were not good at decision quality?
97. What caused you to work to change your skills at making sound decisions?
98. What event or series of events had the most impact on your decision quality?
99. What is an orderly way to make decisions?*
100. What percent of your decisions do you change, reverse, or take back?*
101. What's the most varied you can be in making decisions?
102. What was the shortest amount of time in which you increased your level of skill at making quality decisions?
103. When did you first realize your level of skill at making quality decisions?
104. When you know ahead of time that your usual level of decision quality won't work, what do you do?
105. Why do you think you deal with making decisions the way you do?
106. Why do you think your decision quality is the way it is?*

D. Follow-up Probes:

1. Are there times when you're not like this or wouldn't do this?
2. Are there times when you make decisions like that and times when you don't?
3. Could you contrast those two bosses for me?
4. Could you give me a few examples of how you've used or applied that?
5. Do you suppose if others would just try harder, they could learn to have better decision quality?
6. Do you think this is teachable?
7. Do you think you're better at this than most? Why?
8. Do you think you would perform any differently if you made more considered decisions?
9. Do you think your quick decisions are as good as your well-thought-through decisions?
10. How certain were you that you were right when you made that decision?
11. How did the others react when you did that?
12. How did you come up with that approach in the first place?
13. How did you know that method of getting over that barrier would work?
14. How do others you have known approach that?
15. How far will you go before you cut line and try another approach?
16. How important was it for you to make a quality decision?
17. How much did you have to give up to make it work?
18. How typical is this for you?
19. How would you approach that same situation today?
20. Is this natural for you, or do you really have to dig for it?
21. Was that a fair way to maneuver around them?
22. Was there a time when you didn't understand this about yourself?
23. Were there some alternatives you rejected? Were you right?
24. What did you do after you got that feedback?
25. What did you do to adapt to that?

DECISION QUALITY

26. What did you learn from that?
27. What do you think would have happened if you had gone with your first impression instead of a well-thought-out decision?
28. Why did you choose that approach?
29. Why did you decide to take the risk?
30. Why did you do it that way?
31. Why did you think it was important for you to make a quality decision?
32. Why did you time your attempt like you did?
33. Why do you suppose organizations work that way?
34. Why do you think that didn't work?
35. Why do you think that happened that way?
36. Why do you think that worked?
37. Why do you think you have difficulties with that sometimes?
38. Would you have done it that way with looser deadlines?
39. Would you have done it that way with tighter deadlines?

E. **Themes/Things to Look for:**
   Can keep feelings out of the data
   Complex and varied tactics and strategies for solving problems
   Good priority-setting skills
   Ability to get to the essence
   Captures meanings; doesn't just rely on a bag of tricks
   Use of parallels/contrasts/analogies
   Need for perfection
   Where they get their data/information
   Drivers? Why do they need to be right? Perfect?
   Orderly process of decision making
   Range of areas/broad perspective
   Organizing data into buckets/categories
   Thorough questions/consideration of the nature of the problem
   Being sought out for quality of thought, not personal support
   Measures outcomes, corrects, doesn't just assume it will work
   Considers stakeholders

DECISION QUALITY

F. Most Likely Résumé:

1. Look for jobs like:

Chair of Projects/Task Forces
Fix-Its/Turnarounds
Member of Projects/Task Forces
Staff Leadership (Influencing Without Authority)
Staff to Line Shifts
Scope (complexity) Assignments
Start-Ups

2. Look for develop-in-place assignments like:

Manage the renovation of an office, floor, building, meeting room, warehouse, etc.
Plan a new site for a building (plant, field office, headquarters, etc.).
Manage the purchase of a major product, equipment, materials, program, or system.
Launch a new product, service, or process.
Relaunch an existing product or service that's not doing well.
Hire/staff a team from outside your unit or organization.
Work on a team forming a joint venture or partnership.
Manage an ad hoc, temporary group of balky and resisting people through an unpopular change or project.
Manage an ad hoc, temporary group of people involved in tackling a fix-it or turnaround project.
Assemble an ad hoc team of diverse people to accomplish a difficult task.
Manage the interface between consultants and the organization on a critical assignment.
Handle a tough negotiation with an internal or external client or customer.
Prepare and present a proposal of some consequence to top management.
Manage a dissatisfied internal or external customer; troubleshoot a performance or quality problem with a product or service.
Manage a group through a significant business crisis.
Take on a tough and undoable project, one where others who have tried it have failed.
Manage a cost-cutting project.
Build a multifunctional project team to tackle a common business issue or problem.
Work on a crisis management team.

3. Best references to ask about or check:

Direct Boss
Past Associates/Constituencies

G. Learning Agility Evaluation:

1. What/Describing vs. Why/Explain
2. All or Nothing vs. Can See Many Sides
3. Ordinary/Socially Acceptable vs. Insightful/Different
7. Passive vs. Intrigued/Curious
9. Vague/General vs. Sharp/Specific
13. Simple Views vs. Complex Views
16. Few Rules of Thumb vs. Many and Varied Rules of Thumb
19. External Standards vs. Internal Standards
22. Focus on Accomplishments vs. Focus on Solving Problems

DECISION QUALITY

H. The LEADERSHIP ARCHITECT® Sort Card Connections:

1. Good (positive) if combined with high:
Flexible problem solver 2, 40, 51
Sought after for advice 3, 31, 33, 41
Good business decisions 5, 46, 50, 58
Good career decisions 6, 45, 54, 55
Good management decisions 20, 35, 39
Trustworthy 22, 29
Good technical decisions 24, 61
Good people decisions 25, 56, 64
Tends to be right 30, 32, 51, 58
Good political decisions 38, 48

2. Bad (negative) if combined with low or high (+):
Right but late 1, 16
Narrow; operates in comfort zone 2, 46
Not sought after for advice 3, 31, 33, 41
Doesn't involve others; arrogant 3, 18, 33, 41
Poor business decisions 5, 46, 50, 58
Poor career decisions 6, 45, 54, 55
Poor management decisions 20, 35, 39
Poor technical decisions 24, 61
Poor people decisions 25, 56, 64
Tends to be wrong 30, 32, 51, 58
Doesn't capture real meaning 32, 45
Poor political decisions 38, 48

3. Too much can contribute to the following Stallers and Stoppers:

A. What too much looks like (overused):
May see him/herself as overly wise or close to perfect, as someone who can't or doesn't make mistakes; may be seen as stubborn and not willing to negotiate or compromise; may get frustrated when advice is rejected; may not relate well to less data-based people.

B. Which Stallers and Stoppers might it lead to:
None Apply

C. Compensators:
How to compensate for too much of this competency:
2, 5, 12, 16, 30, 32, 33, 37, 45, 51, 52, 58, 61, 63

D. Things to watch for:
Conflict avoidance   Perfectionist
Decides too late   Risk avoidance
Inflated ego   Doesn't involve others
Inflexible

DECISION QUALITY

4. Too little can contribute to the following Stallers and Stoppers:

A. What too little looks like (unskilled):
Goes first with quick solutions, conclusions and statements before analysis; may rely too much on self–doesn't ask for help; making decisions may trigger emotions and impatience; may not use orderly decision methods, models or ways to think; may jump to conclusions based on prejudices, historical solutions or narrow perspective; doesn't take the time to define the problem before deciding; may have trouble with complexity; may wait too long, agonize over every detail to avoid risk or error; may go for the big elegant decision when five little ones would be better.

B. Too little might lead to these Stallers and Stoppers:
Failure to Staff Effectively (111)
Performance Problems (118)

C. Compensators:
How to substitute for too little of this competency:
5, 12, 24, 30, 32, 46, 47, 50, 51, 53, 58

I. LEARNING ARCHITECT® Connections:

Look for people who act like and/or show evidence of:

1b. Trial and Error	17. Selected Sources
2a. Problem Solving	18. Straightforward
3c. Personal Experience	19. What
4a Getting Information	29. Essence
11. Why/How	31. Rationality
12. Rules of Thumb	34. Sizing Up Others
15. Cautious	

J. CHOICES ARCHITECT® Connections:

Look for people who act like and/or show evidence of:

First Edition (Released 1994)
2. Essence
4. Complexity
5. Connector
11. Open to Diversity

Second Edition (Released 2000)
2. Complexity
3. Connector
4. Critical Thinker
6. Essence
8. Solution Finder
14. Open-Minded

K. Difficulty to Develop:
20 (of 34)–Easier

18. DELEGATION

A. Definition:
Clearly and comfortably delegates both routine and important tasks and decisions; broadly shares both responsibility and accountability; tends to trust people to perform; lets direct reports and others finish their own work.

B. Arenas/Domains to Explore:
1. Any supervisory role or job
2. Athletic team captains
3. Coaching sports
4. Conference/meeting management
5. Delegating complete tasks/processes
6. Delegating important tasks
7. Event planning
8. Family division of labor/planning family events
9. Managing children
10. Projects/task forces
11. Student government

C. Sample Questions:

*Dimension 1: Been there, done that–has had direct personal experience(s) involving the competency–candidate was the prime player   Note: * means OK for campus*

1. Do you enjoy delegating or doing things yourself?
2. Give me an example of how you divided up a project/assignment in your work group.*
3. Has a direct report ever let you down after you delegated something important to them?
4. Have you been involved in any outsourcing of work you previously did or managed?
5. Have you ever been in trouble for delegating too much?
6. Have you ever been in trouble for not delegating?
7. Have you ever delegated something and had to pull in the reins?*
8. Have you ever delegated something as a test for the person?
9. Have you ever delegated something to provide a developmental opportunity for someone?
10. Have you ever had a direct report outperform what you could have done on a delegated task?
11. Have you ever managed anything where the people or units reporting to you were in different locations? How did you delegate to them?
12. How do you allocate credit for a delegated task you designed and did the major thinking on?*
13. How do you delegate a task where you are the lead expert?
14. How often do you use contract or part-time help?
15. Tell me about a time when someone complained to you that you were delegating too much work to them.
16. Tell me about a time when someone complained to you that you were not delegating enough work to them.
17. Tell me about a time when you delegated something you personally would have enjoyed doing yourself.
18. Tell me about a time when you used someone outside your work group to get something done that your people would have preferred doing themselves.
19. Tell me about a time when your delegation skills worked really well for you.
20. Tell me about a time when your lack of delegating got you into trouble.
21. What was your worst delegation experience?

DELEGATION

Dimension 2: Seen/been around others who were involved with the competency–good and bad; learns from others about self

22. Contrast the people you know who are the most and least effective delegators.*
23. Has delegating ever been in any 360° survey done on you? Was your score among your highest, middle, or lowest?
24. Has poor delegating on someone else's part ever created an obstacle for you or got in the way of something you were trying to accomplish?*
25. Have you ever talked about your delegation skills with a coach or mentor?
26. Have you ever watched someone fail/get fired because they did not delegate?*
27. Have you ever watched someone overdelegate to the point that it backfired?
28. Have you ever watched someone succeed because they delegated?*
29. Have you ever worked with a coach on delegation skills?*
30. Have you ever worked with a person who excelled at delegating?
31. Have you ever worked with a skills coach on delegating?*
32. How do you get feedback about yourself on delegation?
33. How often do you check with multiple sources when you get a piece of critical feedback on your delegation skills?
34. Is there a historical figure you consider a model of delegation?
35. What do others who are not your fans say about your delegation skills?
36. What do others who like you say about your delegation skills?
37. What would your direct reports say about your delegation skills?
38. Which boss was the best at delegation?
39. Which boss was the worst at delegation?
40. Which direct report was the best at delegation?
41. Which direct report was the worst at delegation?
42. Which peer was the best at delegation?
43. Which peer was the worst at delegation?
44. Who in your field or business deals the best with delegation?
45. Who do you consider a role model of delegation?*
46. Who do you go to for advice on delegating?
47. Who have you learned the most from about delegating?*
48. Who is a higher-management role model for you on delegating?
49. Who is a role model of delegation skills outside of work?

Dimension 3: Knows how the competency works in theory; shows understanding

50. Are there situations or settings where someone should delegate differently?
51. Do you think delegation skills can be learned? If so, how do you think people develop delegation skills?
52. Do you think there is a way to compensate or work around low delegation skills?
53. Has anyone asked you for your opinions/advice on delegating to others?*
54. Have you ever attended a course on delegating?
55. Have you ever been in a situation where you and others put delegation skills on a success profile?
56. Have you ever been part of an effort to create a policy or a mission statement containing reference to the importance of demonstrating effective delegation skills?
57. Have you ever been someone's coach or mentor who had problems with delegation?
58. Have you ever created a development plan for someone on delegation skills?

DELEGATION

59. Have you ever criticized someone for not delegating?
60. Have you ever designed a program on delegation skills?
61. Have you ever given a speech on delegating?
62. Have you ever rewarded or recognized someone for being an effective delegator?
63. Have you ever taught a course on delegating?
64. Have you ever tried to help someone deal more effectively with delegation?*
65. Have you ever tried to help someone improve their delegation skills?
66. How do you think people develop delegating skills?
67. How much delegation is good and how much is too much?
68. How much of success do you think is due to effective delegation skills compared with other characteristics?
69. How would you know if someone is bad at delegating?
70. How would you know if someone is good at delegating?
71. If you had to write a book on delegating, what would the chapter headings be?
72. What are the benefits to someone who is really good at delegating?
73. What are the consequences to someone who is really poor at delegating?
74. What do you think the performance standard is on delegating for someone in your role?
75. What happens if you delegate too often?
76. What happens when two people try to work together who are very different in their ability to delegate?
77. What wisdom would you pass on to others who are trying to become better at being effective delegators?
78. When you select others, what do you look for in delegation skills?
79. Why do you think people end up being different in their ability to delegate?

Dimension 4: Shows personal change and sense-making; learned it one place and applied it in another; can compare and contrast experiences; changes viewpoints across time; can explain personal development or evolution related to the competency

80. Compare and contrast examples of times when you've been effective and ineffective at delegating to others.
81. Contrast your on- and off-the-job use of delegation.
82. Did you ever pass up a job or assignment because you were not confident enough in your ability to delegate to others?
83. Do you delegate more or less with tight deadlines and crisis situations?
84. Do you delegate to some and not others?
85. Do you ever use other skills to cover for your lack of delegation skills?
86. Has delegation ever figured in a failure, struggle, or setback you have had?
87. Has becoming better at delegation ever helped you in other areas?
88. Has poor delegation ever been the subject of a development plan for you?
89. Have your delegation skills always been this way?
90. Have you ever assigned someone a task because you didn't delegate particularly well?
91. Have you ever made significant strides at becoming better at delegation?
92. Have your delegation skills, good or bad, ever been the subject of your performance review or a career discussion?
93. How different are you across situations in how you delegate to others?
94. How do you decide how much to delegate to others?
95. How do you divide up the work when you manage others?*
96. How do you give instructions, follow up, and measure after you delegate?

DELEGATION

97. How much of your success is due to your ability to delegate to others?
98. How often do you change or override a delegated task or decision?
99. How transferable are your delegation skills to other situations?
100. If you had to become better at delegating in a hurry, what would you do?
101. Was there a time when you were not good at delegating to others?
102. What caused you to work to develop your skills at delegating to others?
103. What conditions lead you to not delegate?
104. What do you delegate and not delegate?*
105. What event or series of events had the most impact on your delegation skills?
106. What's the most varied you can be in delegating?
107. What's the right level of support when you delegate?*
108. What was the shortest amount of time in which you increased your level of skill at delegating to others?
109. When did you first realize your level of skill at delegating to others?
110. When do you have to intervene after delegating?*
111. When you know ahead of time that your usual way of delegating to others won't work, what do you do?
112. Why do you think you deal with delegation the way you do?
113. Why do you think your delegating skills are the way they are?*

D. Follow-up Probes:
1. Are there times when you're not like this or wouldn't do this?
2. Are there times when you delegate like that and times when you don't?
3. Could you contrast those two bosses for me?
4. Could you give me a few examples of how you've used or applied that?
5. Do you suppose if others would just try harder, they could learn to delegate more like you do?
6. Do you think this is teachable?
7. Do you think you're better at delegation than most? Why?
8. Do you think you would perform any better if you delegated differently?
9. How certain were you that you were right when you made that decision to (not to) delegate?
10. How did it feel to give up something you wanted to get the project going?
11. How did the others react when you did that?
12. How did you come up with that approach in the first place?
13. How did you know that method of getting over that barrier would work?
14. How do others you have known approach that?
15. How far did you go to try to be a team player?
16. How far will you go before you cut line and try another approach?
17. How important was it for you to delegate?
18. How much did you have to give up to make it work?
19. How often do you use the "Let's meet in the middle" approach?
20. How typical is this for you?
21. How would you approach that same situation today?
22. Is this natural for you, or do you really have to dig for it?
23. Was that a fair way to maneuver around them?
24. Was there a time when you didn't understand this about yourself?

DELEGATION

25. Were there some alternatives you rejected? Were you right?
26. What did you do after you got that feedback?
27. What did you do to adapt to that?
28. What did you learn from that?
29. Why did you choose that approach?
30. Why did you decide to take the risk?
31. Why did you do it that way?
32. Why did you think it was important for you to delegate?
33. Why did you time your attempt like you did?
34. Why do you suppose organizations work that way?
35. Why do you think that didn't work?
36. Why do you think that happened that way?
37. Why do you think that worked?
38. Why do you think you delegate like that?
39. Why do you think you have difficulties with that sometimes?
40. Would you have done it that way with looser deadlines?
41. Would you have done it that way with tighter deadlines?

E. Themes/Things to Look for:

Being approachable for help, but not intrusive

Clarity on what the task is, what criteria or elements it contains, and what expectations are

Clear communication style

Complex and varied tactics for delegating

Delegating important, complete tasks

Drivers? Why do they delegate/not delegate?

Interfering when the criteria are not being followed, expectations not being met

Keeping the discussion on criteria/expectations, not the person

Letting people finish their own work if possible

Not specifying how it has to be done

Selective delegating to favorites

Sense of fairness and equity

Tolerance for mistakes

Trusting in others

Using delegation to develop people

DELEGATION

F. Most Likely Résumé:

1. Look for jobs like:

Fix-Its/Turnarounds Significant People Demands
Scale (size shift) Assignments Start-Ups

2. Look for develop-in-place assignments like:

Manage something "remote," away from your location.
Create employee involvement teams.
Assign a project to a group with a tight deadline.
Manage an ad hoc, temporary group of "green," inexperienced people as their coach, teacher, orienter, etc.
Manage an ad hoc, temporary group of balky and resisting people through an unpopular change or project.
Manage an ad hoc, temporary group of low-competence people through a task they couldn't do by themselves.
Manage an ad hoc, temporary group including former peers to accomplish a task.
Manage an ad hoc, temporary group of people who are older and/or more experienced to accomplish a task.
Manage an ad hoc, temporary group of people where the temporary manager is a towering expert and the people in the group are not.
Build a multifunctional project team to tackle a common business issue or problem.

3. Best references to ask about or check:

Human Resource Professionals
Direct Reports

G. Learning Agility Evaluation:

2. All or Nothing vs. Can See Many Sides
8. Sameness vs. Diversity
9. Vague/General vs. Sharp/Specific
20. Avoids Responsibility for Mistakes vs. Admits and Learns from Mistakes
21. View from Self vs. View from Point of View of Others
22. Focus on Accomplishments vs. Focus on Solving Problems

H. The LEADERSHIP ARCHITECT® Sort Card Connections:

1. Good (positive) if combined with high:

Approachable for questions 3, 33, 41
Fair 7, 21, 23
Delegates to the right people 10, 56
Holds people accountable 13, 20
Uses assignments to develop 19
Sets clear expectations 27, 35, 50
Team builder 36, 60, 63, 64

DELEGATION

2. **Bad (negative) if combined with low or high (+):**

   Pushes too hard (+1, 16, 35, 53)

   Cold transfer of tasks to do 3, 26, 33, 36, 41

   Unfair; overloads some, light on others 7, 21, 23

   Delegates the wrong tasks to the wrong people 17, 50, 56

   Doesn't provide clear directions 27, 35, 50

   Looks over shoulder, second guesses (+24, 53, 61)

   One-on-one task master 36, 60, 64

   Delegates in a disorganized manner 47, 38, 52

3. **Too much can contribute to the following Stallers and Stoppers:**

   A. *What too much looks like (overused):*

   May overdelegate without providing enough direction or help; may have unrealistic expectations for direct reports and others, or may overstructure tasks and decisions before delegating them to the point of limiting individual initiatives; may not do enough of the work him/herself.

   B. *Too much might lead to these Stallers and Stoppers:*

   None Apply

   C. *Compensators:*

   How to compensate for too much of this competency:
   7, 19, 20, 21, 23, 33, 35, 36, 57, 60, 63, 64

   D. *Things to watch for:*

   Control freak

   Incomplete communication

   Mosaic instructions

   Sink or swim attitude toward direct reports

   Work avoider

4. **Too little can contribute to the following Stallers and Stoppers:**

   A. *What too little looks like (unskilled):*

   Doesn't believe in or trust delegation; lacks trust and respect in the talent of direct reports and others; does most things by themselves or hoards, keeps the good stuff for themselves; doesn't want or know how to empower others; may delegate but micromanages and looks over shoulders; might delegate but not pass on the authority; may lack a plan of how to work through others; may just throw tasks at people; doesn't communicate the bigger picture.

   B. *Too little might lead to these Stallers and Stoppers:*

   Poor Administrator (102)

   Overmanaging (117)

   C. *Compensators:*

   How to substitute for too little of this competency:
   7, 19, 20, 21, 23, 27, 33, 35, 36, 39, 47, 56, 60, 64

DELEGATION

I. LEARNING ARCHITECT® Connections:

Look for people who act like and/or show evidence of:

- 1c. Following a Plan
- 4c. Actively Involve
- 7. Risks
- 8. Initiate
- 16. Collaborate
- 23. Orchestrator
- 32. Diversity in Others

J. CHOICES ARCHITECT® Connections:

Look for people who act like and/or show evidence of:

First Edition (Released 1994)
- 7. Helping Others Think
- 15. Helps Others Succeed

Second Edition (Released 2000)
- 12. Helps Others Succeed
- 24. Inspires Others

K. Difficulty to Develop:

21 (of 34)–Easier

19. DEVELOPING DIRECT REPORTS AND OTHERS

A. Definition:

Provides challenging and stretching tasks and assignments; holds frequent development discussions; is aware of each person's career goals; constructs compelling development plans and executes them; pushes people to accept developmental moves; will take on those who need help and further development; cooperates with the developmental system in the organization; is a people builder.

B. Arenas/Domains to Explore:

1. Challenging direct reports
2. Coaching
3. Delegation style
4. History of success developing others
5. Knowledge about how development works
6. Mentoring
7. People building
8. Personal career history
9. Personal career interest
10. Putting in the time to develop
11. Selecting/hiring people
12. Teacher/student

C. Sample Questions:

Dimension 1: Been there, done that–has had direct personal experience(s) involving the competency–candidate was the prime player   Note: * means OK for campus

1. Do you know what your direct reports want out of their careers? Is it realistic?
2. Do your people generally over or underestimate what they can do in their careers?
3. Has a boss ever pushed you to take a job you didn't want?
4. Have you ever agreed to take someone into a job below you who really wasn't yet fit for the job?
5. Have you ever coached/worked with a community or charitable group where you had to help people younger and less experienced than you?*
6. Have you ever had someone you were trying to help develop who burned out?
7. Have you ever managed anything where the people or units reporting to you were in different locations? How did you develop them from afar?
8. Have you ever managed someone who has passed you up in the hierarchy?
9. Have you ever worked with a diamond in the rough; taken someone out of their shell and started them down a road of accelerated development?
10. Have your attempts to develop someone ever backfired?
11. How do you make time for developing your people?
12. How many of your people will go to non-technical courses and seminars each year?
13. Tell me about a big challenge you provided for someone else.*
14. Tell me about a time when you put someone in a developmental assignment that failed and the person's career was damaged.
15. Tell me about a time when your efforts at developing your people worked really well for you.
16. Tell me about a time when your lack of developing your people got you into trouble.
17. Tell me about people you helped change jobs/careers/schools/interests.*
18. Tell me about people you helped do something they didn't want to do.*
19. Tell me about people you helped do something they probably didn't think they could do.*
20. What do you think your hit rate is on helping troubled people get back on track and prosper?
21. What is the earliest memory you have of putting someone's development plan in writing?

DEVELOPING DIRECT REPORTS AND OTHERS

Dimension 2: Seen/been around others who were involved with the competency–good and bad; learns from others about self

22. Contrast the most and least effective people-developers you know.*
23. Has developing others ever been in any 360° survey done on you? Was your score among your highest, middle, or lowest?
24. Has poor development of others on someone else's part ever created an obstacle for you or got in the way of something you were trying to accomplish?*
25. Have you ever talked about your ability to develop others with a coach or mentor?
26. Have you ever watched someone fail/get fired because they did not develop others?*
27. Have you ever watched someone overdo developing others to the point that it backfired?
28. Have you ever watched someone succeed because they developed others well?*
29. Have you ever worked with a coach on developing others?*
30. Have you ever worked with a person who excelled at developing others?
31. Have you ever worked with a skills coach on developing others?*
32. How do you get feedback about your development of others?
33. How often do you check with multiple sources when you get a piece of critical feedback on your development of others?
34. Is there a historical figure you consider a model of developing others?
35. What do others who are not your fans say about your development of others?
36. What do others who like you say about your development of others?
37. Which boss was the best at developing others?
38. Which boss was the worst at developing others?
39. Which direct report was the best at developing others?
40. Which direct report was the worst at developing others?
41. Which peer was the best at developing others?
42. Which peer was the worst at developing others?
43. Who in your field or business is the best at developing others?
44. Who do you consider a role model of developing others?*
45. Who do you go to for advice on developing others?
46. Who have you learned the most from about developing others?*
47. Who is a higher-management role model for you on developing others?
48. Who is a role model of developing others outside of work?

Dimension 3: Knows how the competency works in theory; shows understanding

49. Are there situations or settings where someone should develop others differently?
50. Do you think effective people development can be learned? If so, how do you think individuals can build people-development skills?
51. Do you think there is a way to compensate or work around low people-development skills?
52. Has anyone asked you for your opinions/advice on developing others?*
53. Have you ever attended a course on developing others?
54. Have you ever been in a situation where you and others put effective people development on a success profile?
55. Have you ever been part of an effort to create a policy or a mission statement containing reference to the importance of being effective at developing others?
56. Have you ever been someone's coach or mentor who had problems with developing others?

DEVELOPING DIRECT REPORTS AND OTHERS

57. Have you ever created a personal improvement plan for someone on developing others?
58. Have you ever criticized someone for not developing others?
59. Have you ever designed a program on developing others?
60. Have you ever given a speech on developing others?
61. Have you ever rewarded or recognized someone for excelling at developing others?
62. Have you ever taught a course on developing others?
63. Have you ever tried to help someone deal with developing others more effectively?*
64. Have you ever tried to help someone improve their skills at developing others?
65. How do you think people grow the skills needed for developing direct reports?
66. How much of success do you think is due to effectively developing others compared with other characteristics?
67. How would you know if someone is bad at developing others?
68. How would you know if someone is good at developing others?
69. If you had to write a book on developing others, what would the chapter headings be?
70. What are the benefits to someone who is really good at developing others?
71. What are the consequences to someone who is really poor at developing others?
72. What do you think the performance standard is on developing direct reports for someone in your role?
73. What happens if you focus too much on developing others?
74. What happens when two people try to work together who are very different in their ability to develop others?
75. What wisdom would you pass onto others trying to become better at developing direct reports?
76. When you select others, what do you look for in developing direct report skills?
77. Why do you think people end up being different in their ability to develop others?

Dimension 4: Shows personal change and sense-making; learned it one place and applied it in another; can compare and contrast experiences; changes viewpoints across time; can explain personal development or evolution related to the competency

78. Compare and contrast examples of times when you've been effective and ineffective at developing your direct reports.
79. Contrast your on- and off-the-job development of other people.
80. Did you ever pass up a job or assignment because you were not confident enough in your ability to develop others?
81. Do you ever use other skills to cover for your lack of skill at developing others?
82. Do you work on the development of some and not on others?
83. Has lack of developing others ever figured in a failure, struggle, or setback you have had?
84. Has becoming better at developing others ever helped you in other areas?
85. Has poor development of others ever been the subject of a development plan for you?
86. Has your development of others always been this way?
87. Have you ever delegated or assigned someone a task because you don't develop others particularly well?
88. Have you ever made significant strides at becoming better at developing others?
89. Have your development-of-others skills, good or bad, ever been the subject of your performance review or a career discussion?
90. How different are you across situations in your development of others?
91. How do you decide how much effort you should spend in developing others?
92. How do you know when it's time to give up and stop trying to help someone develop?

DEVELOPING DIRECT REPORTS AND OTHERS

93. How far out do you think about the careers of your people?
94. How much of your success is due to developing others?
95. How transferable is your ability to develop direct reports to other situations?
96. If you had to become better at developing others in a hurry, what would you do?
97. Was there a time when you were not good at developing others?
98. What caused you to work to change your skills at developing others?
99. What event or series of events had the most impact on your development of others?
100. What's the most varied you can be in developing others?
101. What was the shortest amount of time in which you increased your level of skill at developing others?
102. When did you first realize your level of skill at developing others?
103. When you know ahead of time that your usual level of developing others won't work, what do you do?
104. Why do you think you deal with development of others the way you do?
105. Why do you think your development of others is the way it is?*

D. Follow-up Probes:

1. Are there times when you're not like this or wouldn't do this?
2. Are there times when you develop others like that and times when you don't?
3. Could you contrast those two bosses for me?
4. Could you give me a few examples of how you've used or applied that?
5. Do you do that for everyone or just one or a few?
6. Do you suppose if others would just try harder, they could learn to be more developmental?
7. Do you think this is teachable?
8. Do you think you're better at developing others than most? Why?
9. Do you think you would perform any better if you developed others differently?
10. How certain were you that you were right when you made that decision to (not to) develop?
11. How did others react when you did that?
12. How did you come up with that approach in the first place?
13. How did you know that method of getting over that barrier would work?
14. How do others you have known approach that?
15. How far will you go before you cut line and try another approach?
16. How important was it for you to develop your direct reports?
17. How much did you have to give up to make it work?
18. How typical is this for you?
19. How would you approach that same situation today?
20. Is this natural for you, or do you really have to dig for it?
21. Was that a fair way to maneuver around them?
22. Was there a time when you didn't understand this about yourself?
23. Were there some alternatives you rejected? Were you right?
24. What did you do after you got that feedback?
25. What did you do to adapt to that?
26. What did you learn from that?
27. Why did you choose that approach?
28. Why did you decide to take the risk?

DEVELOPING DIRECT REPORTS AND OTHERS

29. Why did you do it that way?
30. Why did you think it was important for you to develop your direct reports?
31. Why did you time your attempt like you did?
32. Why do you suppose organizations work that way?
33. Why do you think that didn't work?
34. Why do you think that happened that way?
35. Why do you think that worked?
36. Why do you think you develop direct reports like that?
37. Why do you think you have difficulties with that sometimes?
38. Would you have done it that way with looser deadlines?
39. Would you have done it that way with tighter deadlines?

E. **Themes/Things to Look for:**

Ability to inspire others to reach high
Balancing getting today's job done and preparing for the future
Being there to help
Bone deep belief in the value of people
Complex and varied tactics and strategies for developing others
Drivers? Why are they developing (not developing) people?
Going out of one's way development
Keeping personal feelings out of decisions
Making personal sacrifices for the benefit of others
Not expecting miracles
Personal history of being (not being) developed
Providing whole challenges, not pieces
Pushing people out of their comfort zone
Rewarding improvement
No selective development of favorites
Sense of fairness and equity
Setting high developmental goals for others
Sizing up people as to what they need, where they can improve
Success rate/history of developing others
Taking risks with people
Taking the longer view of getting people ready for the future
Understanding the process
Providing support and encouragement but not doing it for them
Focusing people on the goal of development, not the obstacles, frustrations, and mistakes along the way

DEVELOPING DIRECT REPORTS AND OTHERS

F. Most Likely Résumé:

1. Look for jobs like:
Scale (size shift) Assignments
Significant People Demands
Staff to Line Shifts

2. Look for develop-in-place assignments like:
Manage an ad hoc, temporary group of "green," inexperienced people as their coach, teacher, orienter, etc.
Manage an ad hoc, temporary group of low-competence people through a task they couldn't do by themselves.
Manage an ad hoc, temporary group of people where the temporary manager is a towering expert and the people in the group are not.

3. Best references to ask about or check:
Direct Boss
Human Resource Professionals
Past Associates/Constituencies
Direct Reports

G. Learning Agility Evaluation:
1. What/Describing vs. Why/Explain
2. All or Nothing vs. Can See Many Sides
3. Ordinary/Socially Acceptable vs. Insightful/Different
10. Reactive vs. Initiating
13. Simple Views vs. Complex Views
14. Sameness vs. Broad Ranging
19. External Standards vs. Internal Standards
21. View from Self vs. View from Point of View of Others

H. The LEADERSHIP ARCHITECT® Sort Card Connections:

1. Good (positive) if combined with high:
Listens to direct reports about their development 3, 33, 41
Gets development opportunities for their people 4, 8, 38
Fair with everyone's development 7, 21, 23
Urges people to develop 13, 36
Accurately assesses development needs 17, 56, 64
Planful, orderly 18, 47
Technical role model 24, 61
Rewards appropriately 35
Takes a long-term view of development 46, 58

DEVELOPING DIRECT REPORTS AND OTHERS

2. **Bad (negative) if combined with low or high (+):**

   Doesn't take the time to develop (+1, 16, 53, 57) 62

   Impatient with progress (+1, 13, 53) 41

   Doesn't take action 1, 16, 57

   Doesn't take assignment risks 2, 40

   Cold impersonal career discussions 3, 31, 33, 41

   Can't make things happen for their people 4, 8, 38 ,48

   Concentrate development on a few; may be arbitrary 7, 21, 23

   Doesn't think of the long-term view of development 46, 58 ,65

   Over or under optimistic about people; not accurate 56, 64

   Means well, but doesn't deliver 18, 47

3. **Too much can contribute to the following Stallers and Stoppers:**

    A. *What too much looks like (overused):*

    May concentrate on the development of a few at the expense of many; may create work inequities as challenging assignments are parceled out; may be overly optimistic about how much people can grow; may endorse the latest developmental fad within the organization and cooperate with the system even when it doesn't make sense for an individual.

    B. *Too much might lead to these Stallers and Stoppers:*

    None Apply

    C. *Compensators:*

    How to compensate for too much of this competency:
    7, 12, 18, 20, 21, 23, 25, 35, 36, 47, 54, 56

    D. *Things to watch for:*

    | Playing favorites | Disorderly application |
    | A development junkie | Overly reliant on training courses for development |
    | Impossible expectations/goals | Unrealistic about who can grow and how much |

4. **Too little can contribute to the following Stallers and Stoppers:**

    A. *What too little looks like (unskilled):*

    Not a people developer or builder; very results driven and tactical; no time for long-term development; doesn't see long-term development as his/her job; plays it safe–can't bring him/herself to assign really stretching (risky) work; thinks development is going to a course–doesn't know how development really happens; may not know the aspirations of people, may not hold career discussions or provide coaching, may not push people to take their development seriously; may prefer to select talent rather than develop it; doesn't support or cooperate with the developmental system in the organization.

    B. *Too little might lead to these Stallers and Stoppers:*

    Overly Ambitious (103)

    Failure to Build a Team (110)

    Overmanaging (117)

    C. *Compensators:*

    How to substitute for too little of this competency:
    7, 10, 13, 18, 20, 27, 33, 36, 56, 60, 64

DEVELOPING DIRECT REPORTS AND OTHERS

I. LEARNING ARCHITECT® Connections:

Look for people who act like and/or show evidence of:

- 1c. Following a Plan
- 2a. Problem Solving
- 4c. Actively Involve
- 11. Why/How
- 21. Changer

J. CHOICES ARCHITECT® Connections:

Look for people who act like and/or show evidence of:

First Edition (Released 1994)
- 15. Helps Others Succeed

Second Edition (Released 2000)
- 11. Cool Transactor
- 12. Helps Others Succeed
- 15. People-Smart

K. Difficulty to Develop:

27 (of 34)–Harder

20. DIRECTING OTHERS

A. Definition:

Is good at establishing clear directions; sets stretching objectives; distributes the workload appropriately; lays out work in a well-planned and organized manner; maintains two-way dialogue with others on work and results; brings out the best in people; is a clear communicator.

B. Arenas/Domains to Explore:

1. Any supervisory event
2. Club/association management
3. Coaching
4. Event/conference management
5. Family management
6. Managing children
7. Meeting facilitation
8. Scout leader
9. Student government
10. Study groups
11. Taskforce management
12. Teacher/student
13. Team captain
14. Volunteer work

C. Sample Questions:

Dimension 1: Been there, done that–has had direct personal experience(s) involving the competency–candidate was the prime player   Note: * means OK for campus

1. Has anyone ever accused you of playing favorites?
2. Have units you have managed won any awards?
3. Have you ever had to direct a team of people who did not report to you on a permanent basis?*
4. Have you ever had to manage a team that was not up to the task?*
5. Have you ever managed anything where the people or units reporting to you were in different locations? How were you able to manage them?
6. Have you ever really failed as a manager?*
7. Have you ever taken over a team that was badly managed?*
8. Have you ever taken over a team that was very well managed?*
9. How do you deal with a direct report struggling with a task?
10. How do you detect that someone is struggling to keep up?
11. How do you determine what a stretch objective is for someone?
12. How do you explain what needs to be done?*
13. How do you judge when it's time to stop listening and just get on with it?
14. How do you keep things on track in your group (on a school or service project) when everyone is very busy, facing a tight deadline, confused?*
15. How do you make the time to listen to your people?
16. How do you manage when you are the lead expert?
17. How hard or easy is it to fill open jobs on your team?
18. Tell me about a time when your ability to manage others worked really well for you.
19. Tell me about a time when your lack of skills in managing others got you into trouble.
20. Tell me about the best unit you have ever managed.
21. Tell me about the worst unit you have ever managed.
22. What's your method of administering tough love?

DIRECTING OTHERS

23. When the group is confused or working on many things at once, what do you do to restore focus?*
24. When you set goals and objectives, at what level do you set them?
25. When you were in a leadership position/running a task force or project, tell me about how you organized the work load, followed up, set objectives, checked in with people.*

Dimension 2: Seen/been around others who were involved with the competency–good and bad; learns from others about self

26. Contrast the people you know who are most and least effective at managing others.*
27. Has managing others ever been in any 360° survey done on you? Was your score among your highest, middle, or lowest?
28. Has poor management of others on someone else's part ever created an obstacle for you or got in the way of something you were trying to accomplish?*
29. Have you ever talked with a coach or mentor about how you manage others?
30. Have you ever watched someone fail/get fired because they did not manage others well?*
31. Have you ever watched someone overmanage others to the point that it backfired?
32. Have you ever watched someone succeed because they effectively managed others?*
33. Have you ever worked with a coach on managing others?*
34. Have you ever worked with a person who excelled at managing others?
35. Have you ever worked with a skills coach on managing others?*
36. How do you get feedback about how you manage others?
37. How often do you check with multiple sources when you get a piece of critical feedback on your ability to manage others?
38. Is there a historical figure you consider a model of managing others?
39. What do others who are not your fans say about your ability to manage others?
40. What do others who like you say about your ability to manage others?
41. Which boss was the best at managing others?
42. Which boss was the worst at managing others?
43. Which direct report was the best at managing others?
44. Which direct report was the worst at managing others?
45. Which peer was the best at managing others?
46. Which peer was the worst at managing others?
47. Who in your field or business is the best at managing others?
48. Who do you consider a role model of managing others?*
49. Who do you go to for advice on managing others?
50. Who have you learned the most from about managing others?*
51. Who is a higher-management role model for you on managing others?
52. Who is a role model of managing others outside of work?

Dimension 3: Knows how the competency works in theory; shows understanding

53. Are there situations or settings where someone should direct others differently?
54. Do you think effective people management skills can be learned? If so, how do you think individuals develop these people management skills?
55. Do you think there is a way to compensate or work around a low ability to manage or direct others?
56. Has anyone asked you for your opinions/advice on directing others?*
57. Have you ever attended a course on directing others?

DIRECTING OTHERS

58. Have you ever been in a situation where you and others put management of direct reports on a success profile?
59. Have you ever been part of an effort to create a policy or a mission statement containing reference to the importance of effectively directing others?
60. Have you ever been someone's coach or mentor who had problems with directing others?
61. Have you ever created a development plan for someone on directing others?
62. Have you ever criticized someone for not directing others effectively?
63. Have you ever designed a program on directing others?
64. Have you ever given a speech on directing others?
65. Have you ever rewarded or recognized someone for effectively directing others?
66. Have you ever taught a course on directing others?
67. Have you ever tried to help someone deal more effectively with directing others?*
68. Have you ever tried to help someone improve their ability to direct others?
69. How do you think people develop the capability to direct others?
70. How much of success do you think is due to effectively directing others compared with other characteristics?
71. How would you know if someone is bad at directing others?
72. How would you know if someone is good at directing others?
73. If you had to write a book on directing others, what would the chapter headings be?
74. What are the benefits to someone who is really good at directing others?
75. What are the consequences to someone who is really poor at directing others?
76. What do you think the performance standard is on directing others for someone in your role?
77. What happens if you direct others too much?
78. What happens when two people try to work together who are very different in their ability to direct others?
79. What wisdom would you pass onto others trying to become better at directing others?
80. When you select individuals, what do you look for in ability to direct others?
81. Why do you think people end up being different in their ability to direct others?

Dimension 4: Shows personal change and sense-making; learned it one place and applied it in another; can compare and contrast experiences; changes viewpoints across time; can explain personal development or evolution related to the competency

82. Compare and contrast examples of times when you've been effective and ineffective at directing others.
83. Contrast your on- and off-the-job methods of directing others.
84. Did you ever pass up a job or assignment because you were not confident enough in your skills at directing others?
85. Do you communicate more with some and less with others?
86. Do you delegate to some and not others?
87. Do you ever use other skills to cover for your lack of ability to direct others?
88. Has directing others ever figured in a failure, struggle, or setback you have had?
89. Has becoming better at directing others ever helped you in other areas?
90. Has giving poor direction to others ever been the subject of a development plan for you?
91. Has your skill at directing others always been this way?
92. Have you ever delegated or assigned someone a task because you didn't direct others particularly well?
93. Have you ever made significant strides at becoming better at directing others?
94. Has your skill at directing others, good or bad, ever been the subject of your performance review or a career discussion?

DIRECTING OTHERS

95. How different are you across situations in the way you direct others?
96. How do you decide how much direction to give to others?
97. How do you tell what's a right or fair direction to give someone?*
98. How much of your success is due to your ability to direct others?
99. How transferable is your skill at directing others to other situations?
100. If you had to become better at directing others in a hurry, what would you do?
101. Was there a time when you were not good at directing others?
102. What caused you to work to change your skills at directing others?
103. What event or series of events had the most impact on how you direct others?
104. What's the most varied you can be in directing others?
105. What was the shortest amount of time in which you increased your level of skill at directing others?
106. When did you first realize your level of skill at directing others?
107. When you know ahead of time that your usual level of directing others won't work, what do you do?
108. Why do you think you deal with directing others the way you do?
109. Why do you think your skill at directing others is the way it is?*

D. Follow-up Probes:
1. Are there times when you're not like this or wouldn't do this?
2. Are there times when you manage like that and times when you don't?
3. Could you contrast those two bosses for me?
4. Could you give me a few examples of how you've used or applied that?
5. Do you suppose if others would just try harder, they could learn to manage more like you?
6. Do you think this is teachable?
7. Do you think you're better at managing/directing others than most? Why?
8. Do you think you would perform any better if you directed others differently?
9. Have you ever had to form a relationship with someone you really disliked to get your job done?
10. How did it feel to give up something you wanted to get the project going?
11. How did the others react when you did that?
12. How did you come up with that approach in the first place?
13. How did you know that method of getting over that barrier would work?
14. How do others you have known approach that?
15. How important was it for you to manage your direct reports that way?
16. How much did you have to give up to make it work?
17. How typical is this for you?
18. How would you approach that same situation today?
19. Is this natural for you, or do you really have to dig for it?
20. Was that a fair way to maneuver around them?
21. Was there a time when you didn't understand this about yourself?
22. Were there some alternatives you rejected? Were you right?
23. What did you do after you got that feedback?
24. What did you do to adapt to that?
25. What did you learn from that?
26. Why did you choose that approach?

DIRECTING OTHERS

27. Why did you decide to take the risk?
28. Why did you do it that way?
29. Why did you think it was important for you to manage your direct reports that way?
30. Why did you time your attempt like you did?
31. Why do you suppose organizations work that way?
32. Why do you think that didn't work?
33. Why do you think that happened that way?
34. Why do you think that worked?
35. Why do you think you have difficulties with that sometimes?
36. Would you have done it that way with looser deadlines?
37. Would you have done it that way with tighter deadlines?

E. Themes/Things to Look for:

Ability to motivate people to work hard
Ability to motivate people to work right
Able to see things through the eyes of others
Balance between command and participation
Balance between organization and people needs
Problem-solving rather than blame-placing
Checking in with people often
Clarity of directions
Communicating the larger picture
Complex and varied tactics and strategies for managing
Drivers, why do they manage the way they do
High standards
Likes/enjoys managing
Listening
Listening skills
Methods for relieving tension/stress
One size doesn't fit all, sees differences among people
Playing favorites
Sensing mechanisms for people's needs/stresses
Sensitivity and empathy
Taking risks; stretching people

F. Most Likely Résumé:

1. Look for jobs like:

Fix-Its/Turnarounds Staff to Line Shifts
Scale (size shift) Assignments Start-Ups
Significant People Demands

DIRECTING OTHERS

2. Look for develop-in-place assignments like:

Assign a project to a group with a tight deadline.

Manage an ad hoc, temporary group of balky and resisting people through an unpopular change or project.

Manage an ad hoc, temporary group of low-competence people through a task they couldn't do by themselves.

Manage an ad hoc, temporary group including former peers to accomplish a task.

Manage an ad hoc, temporary group of people who are older and/or more experienced to accomplish a task.

Manage an ad hoc, temporary group of people where the temporary manager is a towering expert and the people in the group are not.

Manage an ad hoc, temporary group of people involved in tackling a fix-it or turnaround project.

Manage an ad hoc, temporary group of people in a rapidly expanding operation.

Assemble an ad hoc team of diverse people to accomplish a difficult task.

Build a multifunctional project team to tackle a common business issue or problem.

3. Best references to ask about or check:

Human Resource Professionals

Direct Reports

G. Learning Agility Evaluation:

2. All or Nothing vs. Can See Many Sides
5. Tight/Rigid vs. Loose/Flexible
8. Sameness vs. Diversity
12. Rehearsed/Socially Acceptable vs. Candid
20. Avoids Responsibility for Mistakes vs. Admits and Learns from Mistakes
21. View from Self vs. View from Point of View of Others

H. The LEADERSHIP ARCHITECT® Sort Card Connections:

1. Good (positive) if combined with high:

Receptive, listens to all 3, 7, 33

Charismatic manager 9, 14, 36, 49

Tells it like it is 12, 13

Equitable 18, 21, 23

Uses assignments partially for development 19, 56

Measures appropriately 35, 53

Team-oriented 36, 60

Very efficient manager of work 38, 47, 50, 52

Focus on grander purpose 58, 65

2. Bad (negative) if combined with low or high (+):

Lots of pressure (+1, 16, 9, 43, 53)

Intervenes too soon (+1, 16) 41

Too loose for most (+2, 40)

Drops work on others without consideration 3, 7, 33

May not be able to make tough decisions (+7, 10) 12

Too top down (+9, 34, 57)

Doesn't distribute the load appropriately 18, 21, 23

DIRECTING OTHERS

Knows more than direct reports (+24, 61)
One way today, another way tomorrow 47, 52
Activities, but little purpose 50, 58, 65
"Just do your own work" (+57) 36, 60

3. **Too much can contribute to the following Stallers and Stoppers:**

   A. *What too much looks like (overused):*

   May be overly controlling; may have a chilling effect on others, discouraging input and ideas, intolerant of disagreements; may only delegate pieces and not share the larger picture; may be overly directive and stifle creativity and initiative.

   B. *Too much might lead to these Stallers and Stoppers:*

Arrogant (104)	Insensitive to Others (112)
Failure to Build a Team (110)	Overmanaging (117)

   C. *Compensators:*
   How to compensate for too much of this competency:
   3, 7, 14, 18, 19, 21, 23, 28, 31, 33, 35, 36, 60, 64

   D. *Things to watch for:*

Control freak	Perfectionist
Looking over everyone's shoulder	Doesn't listen to others
My way and the wrong way	Too much structure, too little left for people to determine
My way or the highway	Lots of activity, little focus

4. **Too little can contribute to the following Stallers and Stoppers:**

   A. *What too little looks like (unskilled):*

   Unclear or cryptic communicator to direct reports; doesn't set goals, targets, mileposts and objectives; not very planful giving out work–just gives out tasks; mostly tells and sells; doesn't listen much; plays favorites and is tough on others; may be too impatient to structure work for others; doesn't delegate well; doesn't take the time to manage; may lack interest in managing and be more eager to work on own assignments.

   B. *Too little might lead to these Stallers and Stoppers:*

Poor Administrator (102)	Overmanaging (117)
Failure to Build a Team (110)	Performance Problems (118)

   C. *Compensators:*
   How to substitute for too little of this competency:
   9, 12, 13, 18, 21, 23, 27, 33, 35, 36, 39, 47, 60

I. **LEARNING ARCHITECT® Connections:**

Look for people who act like and/or show evidence of:

1c. Following a Plan	21. Changer
18. Initiate	23. Orchestrator

DIRECTING OTHERS

J. CHOICES ARCHITECT® Connections:

Look for people who act like and/or show evidence of:

First Edition (Released 1994)
- 7. Helping Others Think
- 14. Transaction Quality
- 21. Taking the Heat

Second Edition (Released 2000)
- 9. Agile Communicator
- 11. Cool Transactor
- 22. Taking the Heat
- 24. Inspires Others

K. Difficulty to Develop:

21 (of 34)–Easier

21. *MANAGING* DIVERSITY

A. Definition:

Manages all kinds and classes of people equitably; deals effectively with all races, nationalities, cultures, disabilities, ages and both sexes; hires variety and diversity without regard to class; supports equal and fair treatment and opportunity for all.

B. Arenas/Domains to Explore:

1. Athletic teams
2. College dorms
3. College curriculum
4. Disaster/emergency relief
5. Equity
6. Foreign travel
7. Fraternity/sorority life
8. Geographies lived in
9. Language study
10. Military service
11. Neighborhoods of childhood
12. Political campaigns
13. Social service
14. Trips/tours/vacations
15. Volunteer work

C. Sample Questions:

Dimension 1: Been there, done that–has had direct personal experience(s) involving the competency–candidate was the prime player   Note: * means OK for campus

1. Have you ever been the first to hire a member of a minority in an organization?
2. Have you ever fired anyone who would be considered a minority?
3. Have you ever had a boss who was a member of a minority? Did you find it any different to work for this person than any other boss?
4. Have you ever had to be a "champion" for people not like you?
5. Have you ever had to manage someone who was older or more experienced than you?*
6. Have you ever integrated someone who was different into your group?*
7. Have you ever made allowances for someone who was not yet part of the mainstream to account for a different kind of background?*
8. Have you ever managed anything where the people or units reporting to you were in different locations? How did you get them to act quickly, deal with change, etc., or how did you show your openness to diversity?
9. How many languages do you speak?*
10. How much have you traveled outside your home country?*
11. Tell me about a time when managing diversity backfired on you and produced a worse work outcome.
12. Tell me about a time when you had to communicate something important to someone who did not speak your language very well.*
13. Tell me about a time when you managed a diverse group, and how this diversity contributed to some different accomplishments.
14. Tell me about a time when you went from being an outsider to an insider.*
15. Tell me about a time when your openness to diversity got you into trouble.
16. Tell me about a time when your openness to diversity worked really well for you.
17. What's the longest you have been in a country that does not speak your language?*
18. What cultural practice do you know of that is the most different from your own?*

MANAGING DIVERSITY

19. Who is the most different-from-you person you consider a close friend?*
20. What is the most diverse team you have been a part of?*
21. When you were the "new kid on the block" (personally, school, work), how did you get integrated into the group?*

Dimension 2: Seen/been around others who were involved with the competency–good and bad; learns from others about self

22. Contrast the most and least effective managers of diversity you know.*
23. Has managing diversity ever been in any 360° survey done on you? Was your score among your highest, middle, or lowest?
24. Has not being open to diversity on someone else's part ever created an obstacle for you or got in the way of something you were trying to accomplish?*
25. Have you ever talked about your openness to diversity with a coach or mentor?
26. Have you ever watched someone fail/get fired because they were not open to diversity?*
27. Have you ever watched someone exaggerate openness to diversity to the point that it backfired?
28. Have you ever watched someone succeed because they were very open to diversity?*
29. Have you ever worked with a coach on managing diversity?*
30. Have you ever worked with a person who excelled at managing diversity?
31. Have you ever worked with a skills coach on managing diversity?*
32. How do you get feedback about your effectiveness in managing diversity?
33. How often do you check with multiple sources when you get a piece of critical feedback on your willingness to be open to diversity?
34. Is there a historical figure you consider a model of managing diversity?
35. What do others who are not your fans say about your being open to diversity?
36. What do others who like you say about your being open to diversity?
37. Which boss was the best at managing diversity?
38. Which boss was the worst at managing diversity?
39. Which direct report was the best at managing diversity?
40. Which direct report was the worst at managing diversity?
41. Which peer was the best at managing diversity?
42. Which peer was the worst at managing diversity?
43. Who in your field or business deals the best with managing diversity?
44. Who do you consider a current role model of managing diversity?*
45. Who do you go to for advice on managing diversity?
46. Who have you learned the most from about managing diversity?*
47. Who is a higher-management role model for you on managing diversity?
48. Who is a role model of managing diversity outside of work?

Dimension 3: Knows how the competency works in theory; shows understanding

49. Are there situations or settings where someone should manage diversity differently?
50. Do you think effective diversity-management can be learned? If so, how do you think people develop diversity-management skills?
51. Do you think there is a difference between equal opportunity and equal treatment?*
52. Do you think there is a way to compensate or work around low diversity-management skills?
53. Has anyone asked you for your opinions/advice on managing diversity?*

MANAGING DIVERSITY

54. Have you ever attended a course on managing diversity?
55. Have you ever been in a situation where you and others put diversity management on a success profile?
56. Have you ever been part of an effort to create a policy or a mission statement containing reference to the importance of effectively managing diversity?
57. Have you ever been someone's coach or mentor who had problems with managing diversity?
58. Have you ever created a development plan for someone on managing diversity?
59. Have you ever criticized someone for not effectively managing diversity?
60. Have you ever designed a program on managing diversity?
61. Have you ever given a speech on managing diversity?
62. Have you ever rewarded or recognized someone for effectively managing diversity?
63. Have you ever taught a course on managing diversity?
64. Have you ever tried to help someone more effectively manage diversity?*
65. Have you ever tried to help someone improve their diversity-management skills?
66. How do you think people develop diversity-management skills?
67. How important is it to treat all people equally?*
68. How much of success do you think is due to effectively managing diversity compared with other characteristics?
69. How would you know if someone is bad at managing diversity?
70. How would you know if someone is good at managing diversity?
71. If you had to write a book on managing diversity, what would the chapter headings be?
72. To what extent do you think all people around the world are the same?*
73. To what extent do you think people around the world are different?*
74. What are the advantages and disadvantages of people diversity?*
75. What are the benefits to someone who is really good at managing diversity?
76. What are the consequences to someone who is really poor at managing diversity?
77. What do you think the standard is on managing diversity for someone in your role?
78. What happens when two people try to work together who are very different in their ability to manage diversity?
79. What mix of people do you think makes for an ideal working (social, community, project, job) group?*
80. Which parts of diversity matter and which do not?*
81. What wisdom would you pass onto others trying to become better at managing diversity?
82. When you select others, what do you look for in diversity-management skills?
83. Why do you think people end up being different in their ability to manage diversity?

Dimension 4: Shows personal change and sense-making; learned it one place and applied it in another; can compare and contrast experiences; changes viewpoints across time; can explain personal development or evolution related to the competency

84. Compare and contrast examples of times when you've been effective and ineffective at managing diversity.
85. Contrast your on- and off-the-job methods of managing diversity.
86. Did you ever pass up a job or assignment because you were not confident enough in your skills at managing diversity?
87. Do you ever use other skills to cover for your lack of diversity management skills?
88. Has managing diversity ever figured in a failure, struggle, or setback you have had?
89. Has becoming better at managing diversity ever helped you in other areas?
90. Has poor diversity management ever been the subject of a development plan for you?

MANAGING DIVERSITY

91. Has the way you've managed diversity always been this way?
92. Have you ever delegated or assigned someone a task because you didn't manage diversity particularly well?
93. Have you ever made significant strides at becoming better at managing diversity?
94. Have your diversity management skills, good or bad, ever been the subject of your performance review or a career discussion?
95. How different are you across situations in how you manage diversity?
96. How do you decide how diversity-oriented to be?
97. How much of your success is due to your skill level at managing diversity?
98. How transferable are your diversity management skills to other situations?
99. If you had to become better at managing diversity in a hurry, what would you do?
100. Was there a time when you were not good at managing diversity?
101. What are the key issues to resolve in building a diverse group that can work together?*
102. What are your diversity hiring practices? Who are you looking for and why? What do you do? In what ways is this the same as any other work situation? Different?
103. What caused you to work to change your skills at managing diversity?
104. What event or series of events had the most impact on how you manage diversity?
105. What's the most varied you can be in the way you manage diversity?
106. What was the shortest amount of time in which you increased your level of skill at managing diversity?
107. When did you first realize your level of skill at managing diversity?
108. When you know ahead of time that your usual level of diversity management won't work, what do you do?
109. Why do you think you deal with diversity the way you do?
110. Why do you think your management of diversity is the way it is?*

D. Follow-up Probes:

1. Are there times when you're not like this or wouldn't do this?
2. Are there times when you manage diversity like that and times when you don't?
3. Could you contrast those two bosses for me?
4. Could you give me a few examples of how you've used or applied that?
5. Did you or the other person blink first?
6. Do you suppose if others would just try harder, they could learn to manage diversity more like you?
7. Do you think this is teachable?
8. Do you think you're better at dealing with diversity than most? Why?
9. Do you think you would perform any better if you managed diversity differently?
10. Have you ever had to form a relationship with someone you really disliked to get your job done?
11. How did it feel to give up something you wanted to get the project going?
12. How did the others react when you did that?
13. How did you come up with that approach in the first place?
14. How did you know that method of getting over that barrier would work?
15. How do others you have known approach that?
16. How much did you have to give up to make it work?
17. How typical is this for you?
18. How would you approach that same situation today?
19. Is this natural for you, or do you really have to dig for it?
20. Was that a fair way to maneuver around them?
21. Was there a time when you didn't understand this about yourself?

MANAGING DIVERSITY

22. What did you do after you got that feedback?
23. What did you do to adapt to that?
24. What did you learn from that?
25. Why did you choose that approach?
26. Why did you decide to take the risk?
27. Why did you do it that way?
28. Why did you time your attempt like you did?
29. Why do you suppose organizations work that way?
30. Why do you think that didn't work?
31. Why do you think that happened that way?
32. Why do you think that worked?
33. Would you have done it that way with looser deadlines?
34. Would you have done it that way with tighter deadlines?
35. Did that make you more or less sympathetic to their cause?
36. Do you do that for everyone or just certain people?
37. Do you think that's fair?
38. How important was it for you to manage your direct reports that were members of a minority that way?
39. Were there some alternatives you rejected? Were you right?
40. Why did you think it was important for you to manage diversity that way?
41. Why do you think you deal with diversity like that?

E. Themes/Things to Look for:
Balance between "everybody's the same" and "everybody's different"
Championing diversity
Diversity history in childhood
Diversity history in college
Diversity history of family
Drivers, why do they do what they do
Enjoyment of diversity
False acceptance of everyone with no real experience
Getting to know people as individuals, getting past class
High standards combined with fair treatment
Narrow view of diversity
Negative diversity experiences and their effect
No favoritism
Political/social viewpoint
Selective diversity acceptance
Significant early diversity events/experiences
Socially acceptable/rehearsed statements
Valuing different viewpoints; seeing them as benefits
Viewpoint of organization they belong to

F. Most Likely Résumé:

1. Look for jobs like:

MANAGING DIVERSITY

    International Assignments
    Scope (complexity) Assignments
    Significant People Demands

2. Look for develop-in-place assignments like:

    Serve for a year or more with a community agency.

    Work for a year or more with a charitable organization.

    Represent the concerns of a group of nonexempt, clerical, or administrative employees to higher management to seek resolution of a difficult issue.

    Assemble an ad hoc team of diverse people to accomplish a difficult task.

    Build a multifunctional project team to tackle a common business issue or problem.

    Be a member of a union-negotiating or grievance-handling team.

3. Best references to ask about or check:

    Human Resource Professionals   Past Associates/Constituencies
    Natural Mentors   Direct Reports

G. Learning Agility Evaluation:

    2. All or Nothing vs. Can See Many Sides
    5. Tight/Rigid vs. Loose/Flexible
    8. Sameness vs. Diversity
   11. Generalizations vs. Specific Learnings
   13. Simple Views vs. Complex Views
   20. Avoids Responsibility for Mistakes vs. Admits and Learns from Mistakes
   21. View from Self vs. View from Point of View of Others

H. The LEADERSHIP ARCHITECT® Sort Card Connections:

1. Good (positive) if combined with high:

    Good at bringing in outsiders 3, 31, 33, 41
    Makes a business case for diversity 5, 8, 46, 58
    Single standard 13, 20, 35, 53
    Tries to provide equal opportunity 19, 23
    Fights for what's right 22, 34, 57
    Hires the best regardless of class 25, 56

2. Bad (negative) if combined with low or high (+):

    Believes but has a tough time handling 2, 40
    Doesn't help them in personally 3, 31, 33, 41, 64
    May be too much of a sympathizer, not a manager (+7, 10, 23)
    Goes through the motions 7, 10, 64
    Can't resolve disagreements/conflict about diversity 12
    Compromises, won't take a stand 13, 34, 57
    Hires but doesn't develop 19 (+25)
    Zealot (+22, 29)
    Plays favorites 23

MANAGING DIVERSITY

Manages individual differences; doesn't build or balance a team 25, 60
Accepts on the outside, but not inside personally 45, 54
Doesn't size up diverse people well 56

3. **Too much can contribute to the following Stallers and Stoppers:**

   A. *What too much looks like (overused):*

   May make too many allowances for members of a particular class; may not apply equal standards and criteria to all classes; may show an inappropriate preference for a single class of people; may compromise standards to achieve diversity.

   B. *Too much might lead to these Stallers and Stoppers:*

Overly Ambitious (103)	Lack of Ethics and Values (109)
Betrayal of Trust (105)	Failure to Build a Team (110)
Defensiveness (108)	

   C. *Compensators:*

   How to compensate for too much of this competency:
   9, 12, 13, 18, 19, 20, 25, 34, 35, 36, 37, 56, 57, 60, 64

   D. *Things to watch for:*

May be an advocate rather than a developer	Group doesn't perform well
Differential standards	Plays favorites
Selective acceptance	

4. **Too little can contribute to the following Stallers and Stoppers:**

   A. *What too little looks like (unskilled):*

   Not effective with groups much different from him/her; may be uncomfortable with those not like him/her; may act inappropriately with those different from him/her; defends turf from outsiders; avoids conflict and the noise of differing views and agendas; doesn't see the business value of diversity; treats everybody the same without regard to their differences; very narrow and ethnocentric; believes his/her group to be superior; may carry around negative and demeaning stereotypes he/she has trouble getting rid of.

   B. *Too little might lead to these Stallers and Stoppers:*

Unable to Adapt to Differences (101)	Insensitive to Others (112)
Arrogant (104)	Non-Strategic (114)
Lack of Ethics and Values (109)	Performance Problems (118)
Failure to Build a Team (110)	Political Missteps (119)
Failure to Staff Effectively (111)	

   C. *Compensators:*

   How to substitute for too little of this competency:
   7, 10, 18, 22, 23, 29, 33, 35, 40, 41, 46, 53, 56, 60, 64

MANAGING DIVERSITY

I. LEARNING ARCHITECT® Connections:

Look for people who act like and/or show evidence of:

- 2a. Problem Solving
- 3b. Self-Talk
- 4a. Getting Information
- 5. New
- 7. Risks
- 8. Initiate
- 9. Multiple Sources
- 23. Orchestrator
- 28. Creator
- 32. Diversity in Others
- 34. Sizing Up Others
- 35. Breadth
- 36. Comfort with Paradox

J. CHOICES ARCHITECT® Connections:

Look for people who act like and/or show evidence of:

First Edition (Released 1994)
- 8. Cool Transactor
- 11. Open to Diversity
- 17. Hot/Direct Sources

Second Edition (Released 2000)
- 11. Cool Transactor
- 14. Open-Minded
- 15. People-Smart

K. Difficulty to Develop:

28 (of 34)–Harder

22. ETHICS AND VALUES

A. Definition:

Adheres to an appropriate (for the setting) and effective set of core values and beliefs during both good and bad times; acts in line with those values; rewards the right values and disapproves of others; practices what he/she preaches.

B. Arenas/Domains to Explore:

1. Calls on the margins
2. Choices
3. Contract negotiations
4. Customs/immigration contacts
5. Foreign country experiences
6. Hard times
7. Labor disputes
8. Layoffs
9. Legal tangles
10. Political views on values issues
11. Project bidding
12. Public relations fiascoes
13. Role models
14. Under stress
15. Union transactions
16. Value/action consistency (walking the talk)
17. Values conflicts
18. Wall street transactions
19. Whistleblowing
20. Working for an unethical boss/organization

C. Sample Questions:

Dimension 1: Been there, done that–has had direct personal experience(s) involving the competency–candidate was the prime player   Note: * means OK for campus

1. Do you know anybody you like who lives on the margins of ethics? How do you deal with this person without compromising yourself?
2. Have you ever been around a major breach of ethics?
3. Have you ever been around when a scandal took place?*
4. Have you ever been involved in a scandal?*
5. Have you ever had to do something in a foreign country that would have been illegal or unethical back in your home country?*
6. Have you ever had to present an unpopular proposal/point of view that you believed in?*
7. Have you ever had to represent a position you didn't totally agree with?*
8. Have you ever known someone who did something bad that really surprised you?* Did you deal with them differently after that?
9. Have you ever left a job or company over a matter of ethics or values?*
10. Have you ever managed anything where the people or units reporting to you were in different locations? How did you handle questions of ethics?
11. Have you ever taken on anyone in public on a matter of ethics or values?*
12. How in line are your values and ethics compared to the people around you?*
13. How much are you willing to bend your values and ethics to fit in better?*
14. How often do you find yourself calling someone on their values or ethics?*
15. How often do you find yourself the lone voice or a member of the minority on a matter of values or ethics?*
16. How well do you know the values and ethics of those around you?
17. Tell me about a senior manager you initially had a lot of trouble dealing with due to differences in ethics or values.

ETHICS AND VALUES

18. Tell me about a time when you felt pulled both ways.*
19. Tell me about a time when you had to deal with two antagonistic people, and you thought both were right or both were wrong.*
20. Tell me about a time when you had to manage a crisis situation.*
21. Tell me about a time when you stood alone for what was right.*
22. Tell me about a time when you took on a peer on a matter of ethics and values. Tell me about a time when you were asked to do something against your beliefs.*
23. Tell me about a time when your ethics or values got you into trouble.
24. Tell me about a time when your ethics and values worked really well for you.
25. What's it like for you when your basic values and ethics are challenged by those around you?*
26. What's the largest difference in values or ethics between you and one of your closest friends?

Dimension 2: Seen/been around others who were involved with the competency–good and bad; learns from others about self

27. Contrast the most and least ethical/values-based people you know.*
28. Has ethics and values ever been in any 360° survey done on you? Was your score among your highest, middle, or lowest?
29. Has marginal ethics and values on someone else's part ever created an obstacle for you or got in the way of something you were trying to accomplish?*
30. Have you ever talked about your ethics and values with a coach or mentor?
31. Have you ever watched someone fail/get fired because of a lack of ethics and values?*
32. Have you ever watched someone exaggerate ethics and values to the point that it backfired?
33. Have you ever watched someone succeed because they had strong ethics and values?*
34. Have you ever worked with a coach on ethics and values?*
35. Have you ever worked with a person who exemplified ethics and values?
36. Have you ever worked with a skills coach on ethics and values or walking your talk?*
37. How do you get feedback about your ethics and values?
38. How often do you check with multiple sources when you get a piece of critical feedback on your ethics and values?
39. Is there a historical figure you consider a model of strong ethics and values?
40. What do others who are not your fans say about your ethics and values?
41. What do others who like you say about your ethics and values?
42. Which boss was the best at practicing ethics and values?
43. Which boss was the worst at practicing ethics and values?
44. Which direct report was the best at practicing ethics and values?
45. Which direct report was the worst at practicing ethics and values?
46. Which peer was the best at practicing ethics and values?
47. Which peer was the worst at practicing ethics and values?
48. Who in your field or business deals the best with proper ethics and values?
49. Who do you consider a current role model of strong ethics and values?*
50. Who do you go to for advice on ethics and values?
51. Who have you learned the most from about ethics and values?*
52. Who is a higher-management role model for you on ethics and values?
53. Who is a role model of ethics and values outside of work?

ETHICS AND VALUES

Dimension 3: Knows how the competency works in theory; shows understanding

54. Are there situations or settings where someone should act differently in the way they demonstrate ethics and values?
55. Do you think ethics and values can be learned? If so, how do you think people develop ethics and values?
56. Do you think there is a way to compensate or work around a lack of ethics and values?
57. Has anyone asked you for your opinions/advice on ethics and values?*
58. Have you ever attended a course on ethics and values?
59. Have you ever been in a situation where you and others put ethics and values on a success profile?
60. Have you ever been part of an effort to create a policy or a mission statement containing reference to being ethical/values-based?
61. Have you ever been someone's coach or mentor who had problems with ethics and values?
62. Have you ever created a development plan for someone regarding ethics and values?
63. Have you ever criticized someone for not being ethical/values-based?
64. Have you ever designed a program on ethics and values?
65. Have you ever given a speech on ethics and values?
66. Have you ever rewarded or recognized someone for being ethical/values-based?
67. Have you ever taught a course on ethics and values?
68. Have you ever tried to help someone deal more effectively with ethics and values?*
69. Have you ever tried to help someone improve their ethics and values?
70. How do you think people develop ethics and values?
71. How much of success do you think is due to ethics and values compared with other characteristics?
72. How would you know if someone is bad at demonstrating ethics and values?
73. How would you know if someone is good at demonstrating ethics and values?
74. If you had to write a book on ethics and values, what would the chapter headings be?
75. What are the benefits to someone who is really good at demonstrating ethics and values?
76. What are the consequences to someone who is really poor at walking their talk?
77. What do you think the performance standard is on demonstrating ethics and values for someone in your role?
78. What happens when two people try to work together who are very different in the way they demonstrate ethics and values?
79. What wisdom would you pass onto others trying to become better at demonstrating ethics and values?
80. When you select others, what do you look for in the way they demonstrate ethics and values?
81. Why do you think people end up being different in the way they demonstrate ethics and values?

Dimension 4: Shows personal change and sense-making; learned it one place and applied it in another; can compare and contrast experiences; changes viewpoints across time; can explain personal development or evolution related to the competency

82. Compare and contrast examples of times when you've been effective and ineffective at practicing what you preach.
83. Contrast your on- and off-the-job use of ethics and values.
84. Did you ever pass up a job or assignment because you were not confident enough in your ability to practice what you preach?
85. Do you always act in line with your beliefs?*
86. Do you ever use other skills to cover for your problems with communicating your ethics or values?
87. Has ethics and values ever figured in a failure, struggle, or setback you have had?

ETHICS AND VALUES

88. Has becoming better at practicing what you preach ever helped you in other areas?
89. Has poor ethics and values ever been the subject of a development plan for you?
90. Have your ethics and values always been this way?
91. Have you ever delegated or assigned someone a task because you don't practice what you preach particularly well?
92. Have you ever made a life/career choice/decision based on values or ethics?*
93. Have you ever made significant strides at becoming better at walking the talk?
94. Have your ethics and values, good or bad, ever been the subject of your performance review or a career discussion?
95. Have your ethics and values always been this way?
96. How consistent are you in applying your values and ethics across situations?
97. How different are you across situations in your ethical stance?
98. How do you decide how ethical to be?
99. How much of your success is due to your ethics and values?
100. How transferable are your ethics and values to other situations?
101. If you had to become better at walking the talk in a hurry, what would you do?
102. Was there a time when you were not good at walking the talk?
103. What caused you to work to change your skills at walking the talk?
104. What event or series of events had the most impact on your ethics and values?
105. What's the latest change you have made to your values or ethics?*
106. What's the most varied you can be in taking an ethical stance?
107. What was the shortest amount of time in which you increased your level of skill at adhering to ethics and values?
108. When did you first realize your level of skill at adhering to ethics and values?
109. When did your current ethics and values form and remain consistent?
110. When you know ahead of time that your usual level of ethics and values won't work, what do you do?
111. Why do you think you deal with ethics and values the way you do?
112. Why do you think your ethics and values are the way they are?*

D. Follow-up Probes:

1. Are there times when you're not like this or wouldn't do this?
2. Are there times when you act out your values like that and times when you don't?
3. Could you contrast those two bosses for me?
4. Could you give me a few examples of how you've used or applied that?
5. Did that make you more or less sympathetic to their values?
6. Did you or the other person blink first?
7. Do you do that for everyone, just one, or a few?
8. Do you think that's fair?
9. Do you think that was the right thing to do?
10. Do you think this is teachable?
11. Do you think you're better at sticking to your values than most? Why?
12. Do you think you would perform any better if you had a different way of showing your ethics and values?
13. Have you ever had to form a relationship with someone you really disliked to get your job done?
14. How certain were you that you were right when you made that decision on how to (how not to) act that way?

ETHICS AND VALUES

15. How did it feel to give up something you wanted to get the project/work going?
16. How did the others react when you did that?
17. How did those values form?
18. How did you come up with that approach in the first place?
19. How did you know that method of getting over that barrier would work?
20. How do others you have known approach that?
21. How far will you go before you cut line and try another approach?
22. How much did you have to give up to make it work?
23. How typical is this for you?
24. How would you approach that same situation today?
25. Is this natural for you, or do you really have to dig for it?
26. Was that a fair way to maneuver around them?
27. Was there a time when you didn't understand this about yourself?
28. Were there some alternatives you rejected? Were you right?
29. What did you do after you got that feedback?
30. What did you do to adapt to that?
31. What did you learn from that?
32. Why did you choose that approach?
33. Why did you decide to take the risk?
34. Why did you do it that way?
35. Why did you think it was important for you to play out your values that way?
36. Why did you time your attempt like you did?
37. Why do you suppose organizations work that way?
38. Why do you think that didn't work?
39. Why do you think that happened that way?
40. Why do you think that worked?
41. Would you have done it that way with looser deadlines?
42. Would you have done it that way with tighter deadlines?

E. Themes/Things to Look For:
   Ability to articulate values
   Ability to see things through the eyes of others
   Ability to take the context into consideration
   Admitting to changing values over time
   Balance between the letter and what's real
   Complex view of the world/values
   Courage
   Direct and diplomatic
   Doesn't attack people, attacks problems
   Drivers/source of the values
   Extent of situational ethics/values
   Flexibility with those they don't totally agree with
   Knowing where their values came from

ETHICS AND VALUES

Knows how to depersonalize (can present a rationale for something)
Knows how to keep focus on issues
Has been in personal jeopardy over value stance
Real vs. rehearsed/socially acceptable values
Selective ethics
Sensitivity to personal impact
No shifts in values during crises/tough times
Tolerance of values other than their own
Walking the talk
Picks battles wisely

F. Most Likely Résumé:

1. Look for jobs like:

Chair of Projects/Task Forces
Fix-Its/Turnarounds
Line to Staff Switches
Scale (size shift) Assignments
Scope (complexity) Assignments
Staff Leadership (Influencing Without Authority)
Start-Ups

2. Look for develop-in-place assignments like:

Handle a tough negotiation with an internal or external client or customer.
Help shut down a plant, regional office, product line, business, operation, etc.
Prepare and present a proposal of some consequence to top management.
Manage a dissatisfied internal or external customer; troubleshoot a performance or quality problem with a product or service.
Manage the assigning/allocating of office space in a contested situation.
Manage a group through a significant business crisis.
Take on a tough and undoable project, one where others who have tried it have failed.
Manage the outplacement of a group of people.
Resolve an issue in conflict between two people, units, geographies, functions, etc.
Make peace with an enemy or someone you've disappointed with a product or service or someone you've had some trouble with or don't get along well with.
Be a member of a union-negotiating or grievance-handling team.

3. Best references to ask about or check:

Natural Mentors
Past Associates/Constituencies
Peers and Colleagues
Spouse
Direct Reports
Yourself

G. Learning Agility Evaluation:

1. What/Describing vs. Why/Explain
2. All or Nothing vs. Can See Many Sides
6. Reactive/Responsive vs. Adapting
9. Vague/General vs. Sharp/Specific
12. Rehearsed/Socially Acceptable vs. Candid
14. Sameness vs. Broad Ranging

ETHICS AND VALUES

15. Linear vs. Use Contrasts/Analogies
17. Avoid Discussion of Weaknesses vs. Comfortably Sharing Shortcomings
19. External Standards vs. Internal Standards
21. View from Self vs. View from Point of View of Others

H. The LEADERSHIP ARCHITECT® Sort Card Connections:

1. Good (positive) if combined with high:
Flexible/situational 2, 12, 40
Deep belief in people 7, 10, 21, 23
Values based decision maker 23, 16, 50
Understands diversity of values/ethics 21, 46
Trusted 29
Courage, does the right thing 29, 34, 57
Extracts lessons from tough situations 32, 45
Knows how to couch issues 48, 49
Understands their personal values 55
Quality family time 66

2. Bad (negative) if combined with low or high (+):
Strong values hold up production 1, 16, 53
Values never change 2, 32, 40, 46
Somebody else's values (+6, 8, 48)
Everyone will hear about their values (+13, 34, 44, 57)
Out of date values 21, 23
Selects people on values 25, 56
Strong but wrong 29
May push issues in a vacuum 31, 33, 64
Bullying or rigid 48

3. Too much can contribute to the following Stallers and Stoppers:

A. What too much looks like (overused):
May go to battle based on beliefs and values when not appropriate; may be overly sensitive to situations he/she see as litmus tests of principles, values, and beliefs; may be seen as stubborn and insensitive to the need for change and compromise; may be overly critical of those who do not hold the same values; may use ethics statements to close off discussion.

B. Too much might lead to these Stallers and Stoppers:
Unable to Adapt to Differences (101)   Failure to Staff Effectively (111)
Blocked Personal Learner (106)   Political Missteps (119)
Defensiveness (108)

C. Compensators:
How to compensate for too much of this competency:
10, 11, 12, 17, 21, 32, 33, 37, 41, 45, 46, 48, 55, 56, 58, 64, 65

ETHICS AND VALUES

D. Things to watch for:

Devalues values of others	Sees the world from the inside out
Has never changed values	Stuck on old values
Input jack is broken	Opinionated; rigid
My way and the wrong way	Surrounds self with clones
Ranks people on values	Sees values issues where others don't

4. Too little can contribute to the following Stallers and Stoppers:

A. What too little looks like (unskilled):

Values may be out of sync with those of the organization; strong individualist with low concern for values of others; may set his/her own rules; make others uncomfortable; may play too close or over the edge for the organization; may not think about own values much and have no idea how he/she comes across; behavior may vary too much across situations; values may be seen as too self serving; he/she doesn't walk the talk; says one thing, does another.

B. Too little might lead to these Stallers and Stoppers:

Overly Ambitious (103)	Lack of Ethics and Values (109)
Betrayal of Trust (105)	Political Missteps (119)

C. Compensators:

How to substitute for too little of this competency:
5, 7, 10, 21, 24, 46, 47, 50, 52, 53, 58, 63

I. LEARNING ARCHITECT® Connections:

Look for people who act like and/or show evidence of:

1c. Following a Plan	13. Focused
3b. Self-Talk	15. Cautious
3c. Personal Experience	

J. CHOICES ARCHITECT® Connections:

Look for people who act like and/or show evidence of:

First Edition (Released 1994)	**Second Edition (Released 2000)**
8. Cool Transactor	11. Cool Transactor
9. Self-Aware	19. Self-Aware
	27. Presence

K. Difficulty to Develop:

26 (of 34)–Moderate

23. FAIRNESS TO DIRECT REPORTS

A. Definition:

Treats direct reports equitably; acts fairly; has candid discussions; doesn't have hidden agenda; doesn't give preferential treatment.

B. Arenas/Domains to Explore:

1. Allocation of resources
2. Allocation of rime/attention
3. Clubs/associations
4. Coaching
5. Conflicts
6. Delivering bad news
7. Disagreements
8. Distribution of access/exposure to top management
9. Distribution of awards/rewards
10. Distribution of development opportunities
11. Distribution of information
12. Emotional support
13. Equity of work load
14. Equity standards
15. Helping with a personal problem
16. Military
17. Project teams
18. Sharing of confidential information
19. Task forces
20. Teaching
21. Team captains
22. Volunteer community work

C. Sample Questions:

Dimension 1: Been there, done that–has had direct personal experience(s) involving the competency–candidate was the prime player   Note: * means OK for campus

1. Have you ever had negative information about a direct report that you decided not to share with them?
2. Have you ever had to choose to keep one of two individuals and let the other one go?
3. Have you ever had to shift funding from one person's project to someone else's?
4. Have you ever had to take a task away from one person and give it to another?
5. Have you ever had two or more direct reports fight over an assignment they all wanted?
6. Have you ever managed anything where the people or units reporting to you were in different locations? How did you manage issues of fairness and equity?
7. How much of what you really know and think about a person do you disclose to them?*
8. Tell me about a time when tight deadlines or tight resources caused you to be less than fair to everyone.
9. Tell me about a time when you did not effectively handle a person who disagreed with you.*
10. Tell me about a time when you distributed the work load on a complex task to several different people.*
11. Tell me about a time when you effectively handled a person who disagreed with you.*
12. Tell me about a time when you had to deliver an unpopular message to your work group.*
13. Tell me about a time when you helped settle a conflict between two direct reports (friends).*
14. Tell me about a time when you let some of your people go in a downsizing or shutdown.
15. Tell me about a time when you managed people less experienced than you.*
16. Tell me about a time when you ran a project and had to deal with troublesome direct reports.*
17. Tell me about a time when you thought you were treated unfairly but now, looking back, you understand it better.
18. Tell me about a time when you went from managing harmony to managing conflict when you changed work groups.

FAIRNESS TO DIRECT REPORTS

19. Tell me about a time when you went from managing harmony to managing conflict within the same group.
20. Tell me about a time when you were unpopular in a group you had to manage.
21. Tell me about a time when your attempts to be fair got you into trouble.
22. Tell me about a time when your attempts to be fair worked really well for you.
23. Tell me times when you treated someone more fairly than others because you thought they deserved it.
24. What's the most unfair treatment you have been subjected to in your career?

Dimension 2: Seen/been around others who were involved with the competency–good and bad; learns from others about self

25. Contrast the most and least fair people you know.*
26. Has fairness to direct reports ever been in any 360° survey done on you? Was your score among your highest, middle, or lowest?
27. Has unfairness to direct reports on someone else's part ever created an obstacle for you or got in the way of something you were trying to accomplish?*
28. Have you ever talked about your fairness to direct reports with a coach or mentor?
29. Have you ever watched someone fail/get fired because they did not treat direct reports fairly?*
30. Have you ever watched someone overextend fairness to direct reports to the point that it backfired?
31. Have you ever watched someone succeed because they treated direct reports fairly?*
32. Have you ever worked with a coach on fairness to direct reports?*
33. Have you ever worked with a person who excelled at being fair to direct reports?
34. Have you ever worked with a skills coach on fairness to direct reports?*
35. How do you get feedback about your fairness to direct reports?
36. How often do you check with multiple sources when you get a piece of critical feedback on treating direct reports fairly?
37. Is there a historical figure you consider a model of treating direct reports fairly?
38. What do others who are not your fans say about your fairness to direct reports?
39. What do others who like you say about your fairness to direct reports?
40. Which boss was the best at being fair to direct reports?
41. Which boss was the worst at being fair to direct reports?
42. Which direct report was the best at being fair to others?
43. Which direct report was the worst at being fair to others?
44. Which peer was the best at being fair to others?
45. Which peer was the worst at being fair to others?
46. Who in your field or business deals the best with being fair to direct reports?
47. Who do you consider a current role model of treating direct reports fairly?*
48. Who do you go to for advice on fairness to direct reports?
49. Who have you learned the most from about fairness to direct reports?*
50. Who is a higher-management role model for you on fairness to direct reports?
51. Who is a role model of fairness to direct reports outside of work?

Dimension 3: Knows how the competency works in theory; shows understanding

52. Are there situations or settings where someone should act differently in being fair to direct reports?
53. Do you think fairness to direct reports can be learned? If so, how do you think people develop these skills?
54. Do you think fairness means equal, or each according to their means? Needs? Abilities?*
55. Do you think some people should be treated more fairly than others?*

FAIRNESS TO DIRECT REPORTS

56. Do you think there is a difference between equal opportunity and equal treatment?*
57. Do you think there is a way to compensate or work around being unfair to direct reports?
58. Has anyone asked you for your opinions/advice on fairness to direct reports?*
59. Have you ever attended a course on fairness to direct reports?
60. Have you ever been in a situation where you and others put fairness to direct reports on a success profile?
61. Have you ever been part of an effort to create a policy or a mission statement containing reference to the importance of being fair to direct reports?
62. Have you ever been someone's coach or mentor who had problems with fairness to direct reports?
63. Have you ever created a development plan for someone on demonstrating fairness to direct reports?
64. Have you ever criticized someone for not being fair to direct reports?
65. Have you ever designed a program on fairness to direct reports?
66. Have you ever given a speech on fairness and direct reports?
67. Have you ever rewarded or recognized someone for demonstrating fairness to direct reports?
68. Have you ever taught a course on fairness to direct reports?
69. Have you ever tried to help someone with demonstrating fairness to direct reports?*
70. Have you ever tried to help someone improve at being fair to direct reports?
71. How do you think people develop the ability to treat direct reports fairly?
72. How much of success do you think is due to being fair to direct reports compared with other characteristics?
73. How would you know if someone is not fair with direct reports?
74. How would you know if someone is fair with direct reports?
75. If you had to write a book on fairness to direct reports what would the chapter headings be?
76. What are the benefits to someone who is really good at fairness to direct reports?
77. What are the consequences to someone who is really poor at fairness to direct reports?
78. What do you think the performance standard is on fairness to direct reports for someone in your role?
79. What happens when two people try to work together who are very different at being fair to direct reports?
80. What wisdom would you pass onto others trying to become better at showing fairness to direct reports?
81. When you select others, what do you look for in treating direct reports fairly?
82. Why do you think people end up acting differently in treating direct reports fairly?

Dimension 4: Shows personal change and sense-making; learned it one place and applied it in another; can compare and contrast experiences; changes viewpoints across time; can explain personal development or evolution related to the competency

83. Compare and contrast examples of times when you've been effective and ineffective at being fair to people who report to you.
84. Contrast your on- and off-the-job use of fairness to others.
85. Did you ever pass up a job or assignment because you were not confident enough in your ability to be fair to direct reports?
86. Do you ever use other skills to cover for your lack of fairness to others?
87. Do you listen to all of your people equally in terms of time and attention?
88. Has fairness to direct reports ever figured in a failure, struggle, or setback you have had?
89. Has becoming better at fairness to direct reports ever helped you in other areas?
90. Has unfairness to direct reports ever been the subject of a development plan for you?
91. Has your fairness to direct reports always been this way?
92. Have you ever delegated or assigned someone a task because you didn't demonstrate fairness to others particularly well?

FAIRNESS TO DIRECT REPORTS

93. Have you ever made significant strides at becoming better at being more fair to your direct reports?
94. Has your fairness to direct reports, good or bad, ever been the subject of your performance review or a career discussion?
95. How different are you across situations in your fairness to direct reports?
96. How do you decide how fair to be to direct reports?
97. How important is it for you to be liked by the people you manage?
98. How much of your success is due to your fairness to direct reports?
99. How transferable to other situations is your ability to be fair to your staff?
100. If you had to become better at fairness to direct reports in a hurry, what would you do?
101. Was there a time when you were not as fair to your direct reports?
102. What caused you to work to change your skills at demonstrating fairness to your direct reports?
103. What event or series of events had the most impact on the way you demonstrated fairness to direct reports?
104. What's the most varied you can be in demonstrating fairness to direct reports?
105. What was the shortest amount of time in which you increased your level of skill at demonstrating fairness to direct reports?
106. When did you first realize your level of skill at demonstrating fairness to direct reports?
107. When you know ahead of time that your usual level of fairness to direct reports won't work, what do you do?
108. Why do you think you deal with demonstrating fairness to direct reports the way you do?
109. Why do you think the way you demonstrate fairness to direct reports is the way it is?*

D. Follow-up Probes:

1. Are there times when you're not like this or wouldn't do this?
2. Are there times when you consider that to be fair and times when you don't?
3. Could you contrast those two bosses for me?
4. Could you give me a few examples of how you've used or applied that?
5. Did that make you more or less sympathetic to their cause?
6. Did you or the other person blink first?
7. Do you suppose if others would just try harder, they could learn to be more fair?
8. Do you think that's fair?
9. Do you think this is teachable?
10. Do you think you're better at fairness than most? Why?
11. Do you think you would perform any better if you treated people differently?
12. Have you ever had a boss who was unfair and treated people differently?
13. Have you ever had a boss who was exceptionally fair and even-handed in the way they managed people?
14. Have you ever had to form a relationship with someone you really disliked to get your job done?
15. How did it feel to give up something you wanted to get the project going?
16. How did the others react when you did that?
17. How did you come up with that approach in the first place?
18. How did you know that method of getting over that barrier would work?
19. How do others you have known approach that?
20. How far will you go before you cut line and try another approach?
21. How important was it for you to treat your direct reports that way?
22. How much did you have to give up to make it work?

FAIRNESS TO DIRECT REPORTS

23. How often do you use the "Let's meet in the middle" approach?
24. How typical is this for you?
25. How would you approach that same situation today?
26. Is this natural for you, or do you really have to dig for it?
27. Was that a fair way to maneuver around them?
28. Was there a time when you didn't understand this about yourself?
29. Were there some alternatives you rejected? Were you right?
30. What did you do after you got that feedback?
31. What did you do to adapt to that?
32. What did you learn from that?
33. Why did you choose that approach?
34. Why did you decide to take the risk?
35. Why did you do it that way?
36. Why did you think it was important for you to treat people that way?
37. Why did you time your attempt like you did?
38. Why do you suppose organizations work that way?
39. Why do you think that didn't work?
40. Why do you think that happened that way?
41. Why do you think that worked?
42. Why do you think you deal with fairness like that?
43. Why do you think you have difficulties with that sometimes?
44. Would you have done it that way with looser deadlines?
45. Would you have done it that way with tighter deadlines?

E. Themes/Things to Look For:

Applying equity beyond reality
Awareness of impact
Balance between equity and getting the work out
Candor with everyone
Changing tactics and methods over time
Complex views of equity
Concern for both equity and maintaining standards
Denial of the fact of an inequitable world
Drivers for fairness, where did it come from
Engaging conflict when it arises
Inviting candor

Knowing the value of fairness
Means testing
Not playing favorites
Not trying to please everyone
Personal experiences with unfair treatment
Rehearsed/socially acceptable statements
Selective fairness
Talk but no real experience under fire
Unafraid of facing conflict
Understanding others

F. Most Likely Résumé:

1. Look for jobs like:

Fix-Its/Turnarounds
Scale (size shift) Assignments
Significant People Demands

FAIRNESS TO DIRECT REPORTS

2. Look for develop-in-place assignments like:

Represent the concerns of a group of nonexempt, clerical, or administrative employees to higher management to seek resolution of a difficult issue.

Manage an ad hoc, temporary group of "green," inexperienced people as their coach, teacher, orienter, etc.

Manage an ad hoc, temporary group of balky and resisting people through an unpopular change or project.

Manage an ad hoc, temporary group of low-competence people through a task they couldn't do by themselves.

Manage an ad hoc, temporary group including former peers to accomplish a task.

Manage an ad hoc, temporary group of people who are older and/or more experienced to accomplish a task.

Manage an ad hoc, temporary group of people where the temporary manager is a towering expert and the people in the group are not.

Manage an ad hoc, temporary group of people involved in tackling a fix-it or turnaround project.

Help shut down a plant, regional office, product line, business, operation, etc.

Manage a project team of people who are older and more experienced.

3. Best references to ask about or check:

Human Resource Professionals
Past Associates/Constituencies
Direct Reports

G. Learning Agility Evaluation:

2. All or Nothing vs. Can See Many Sides
6. Reactive/Responsive vs. Adapting
8. Sameness vs. Diversity
12. Rehearsed/Socially Acceptable vs. Candid
13. Simple Views vs. Complex Views
20. Avoids Responsibility for Mistakes vs. Admits and Learns from Mistakes
21. View from Self vs. View from Point of View of Others

H. The LEADERSHIP ARCHITECT® Sort Card Connections:

1. Good (positive) if combined with high:

Keeps personal feelings out 11, 33
Balanced approach 12, 13, 34, 35, 53
Everybody gets feedback 13
Everybody's busy 18, 20
Develops as many as possible 19
Good job at affirmative action 21, 56
Trusted by all 22, 29
Fairness outside of work 46, 66
Means testing 56

2. Bad (negative) if combined with low or high (+):

Slow to make direct report decisions 1, 16
Spends too much time worrying about fairness (+3, 7, 10, 21)
Can't make the business case for equity 5, 46, 58
May be mechanical, no passion for equity 7, 10, 21

FAIRNESS TO DIRECT REPORTS

Doesn't lead 9, 57
Avoids conflict, doesn't act on beliefs 12, 13, 34
May not assess people challenges well 19, 56
May only deal with selected groups fairly 21
May lack high standards of performance 35, 53

3. **Too much can contribute to the following Stallers and Stoppers:**

   A. *What too much looks like (overused):*

   May spend too much time pleasing everyone; may worry about distributing the work evenly and not using, challenging, or developing the best; his/her need to be fair may mask real problems and differences.

   B. *Too much might lead to these Stallers and Stoppers:*
   None Apply

   C. *Compensators:*
   How to compensate for too much of this competency:
   9, 12, 13, 18, 19, 20, 21, 25, 34, 35, 36, 37, 51, 52, 56, 57, 64

   D. *Things to watch for:*
   Being overly direct and candid, chilling others in the process
   Downplaying real differences
   Equity zealot
   Makes too many compromises to achieve equity
   Need to be liked
   Poor at developing people
   Conflict avoider
   Group doesn't perform well

4. **Too little can contribute to the following Stallers and Stoppers:**

   A. *What too little looks like (unskilled):*

   Is not equitable toward direct reports; doesn't listen to direct reports' concerns and needs; may not read people's needs well and not be able to tell how they are responding to their treatment; hides or keeps things from their people they have a right to know; may be inconsistent and play favorites; may not think about it or be too busy to pay attention to equity; may bucket people into good and bad buckets and treat them accordingly.

   B. *Too little might lead to these Stallers and Stoppers:*

Poor Administrator (102)	Failure to Build a Team (110)
Betrayal of Trust (105)	Insensitive to Others (112)

   C. *Compensators:*
   How to substitute for too little of this competency:
   7, 10, 18, 20, 21, 22, 29, 35, 53, 56, 60

FAIRNESS TO DIRECT REPORTS

I. LEARNING ARCHITECT® Connections:

Look for people who act like and/or show evidence of:

1c. Following a Plan
4a. Getting Information
34. Sizing Up Others

J. CHOICES ARCHITECT® Connections:

Look for people who act like and/or show evidence of:

First Edition (Released 1994)
8. Cool Transactor
15. Helps Others Succeed

Second Edition (Released 2000)
11. Cool Transactor
12. Helps Others Succeed

K. Difficulty to Develop:

22 (of 34)–Easier

24. FUNCTIONAL/TECHNICAL SKILLS

A. Definition:
Has the functional and technical knowledge and skills to do the job at a high level of accomplishment.

B. Arenas/Domains to Explore:
1. Academic background
2. Conference attendance
3. Courses/seminars
4. Expertise
5. Exposures to technology
6. Military training
7. Problem solving in their area
8. Professional association memberships
9. Reading habits
10. Rotational assignments
11. Self-study
12. Social/technical network
13. Technical hobbies
14. Technical mentors
15. Work experience

C. Sample Questions:

*Dimension 1: Been there, done that–has had direct personal experience(s) involving the competency–candidate was the prime player   Note: * means OK for campus*

1. Are you skilled technically in more than one function?*
2. Do you attend professional meetings and conferences in your area?
3. Do you belong to any professional groups in your functional or technical area?
4. Does your current function match your education?
5. Have you ever been in a job where you stumbled because you were not up to speed with the technology of the job?
6. Have you ever been in a situation where you knew more about the technical aspects of the job than your boss did?
7. Have you ever managed a team where they knew the technology and you didn't?*
8. Have you ever managed a team where you knew the technology and they didn't?*
9. Have you ever managed anything where the people or units reporting to you were in different locations? How did you provide technical/functional coaching and tutoring?
10. Have you ever misapplied your technical skills to a problem?*
11. Have you received any awards for your technical skills?*
12. Have you represented your technology in a project/taskforce?
13. Have you written any articles about your technology?
14. How do you keep up-to-date in your technology?
15. How many functions have you worked in?
16. Tell me about a time when you weren't up to the technical part of the task. Why?*
17. Tell me about a time when your functional or technical skills got you into trouble.
18. Tell me about a time when your functional or technical skills worked really well for you.
19. What are your best and worst technical skills?*
20. What are your core technical competencies?*
21. What do you like and not like to do at work?*
22. What percent of your technical area changes each year?*

FUNCTIONAL TECHNICAL SKILLS

23. What's coming next in your technical area? What's at the leading edge?*
24. What's the latest new technical trick or skill you have learned and applied?*
25. What's the latest significant book in your technical area?*

Dimension 2: Seen/been around others who were involved with the competency–good and bad; learns from others about self

26. Contrast the most and least functionally/technically skilled people you know.*
27. Has functional or technical skills ever been in any 360° survey done on you? Was your score among your highest, middle, or lowest?
28. Has weak functional or technical skills on someone else's part ever created an obstacle for you or got in the way of something you were trying to accomplish?*
29. Have you ever talked about your functional or technical skills with a coach or mentor?
30. Have you ever watched someone fail/get fired because they did not have sufficient functional/technical skills?*
31. Have you ever watched someone exaggerate functional or technical skills to the point that it backfired?
32. Have you ever watched someone succeed because they had strong functional/technical skills?*
33. Have you ever worked with a coach on functional/technical skills?*
34. Have you ever worked with a person who excelled at functional or technical skills?
35. Have you ever worked with a skills coach on functional or technical skills?*
36. How do you get feedback about your functional/technical skills?
37. How often do you check with multiple sources when you get a piece of critical feedback on your functional or technical skills?
38. Is there a historical figure you consider a model of functional or technical skills?
39. What do others who are not your fans say about your functional or technical skills?
40. What do others who like you say about your functional or technical skills?
41. Which boss was the most functionally or technically skilled?
42. Which boss was the least functionally or technically skilled?
43. Which direct report was the most functionally or technically skilled?
44. Which direct report was the least functionally or technically skilled?
45. Which peer was the most functionally or technically skilled?
46. Which peer was the least functionally or technically skilled?
47. Who in your field or business is the most functionally or technically skilled?
48. Who do you consider a current role model of functional or technical skills?*
49. Who do you go to for advice on functional/technical skills?
50. Who have you learned the most from about functional/technical skills?*
51. Who is a higher-management role model for you on functional/technical skills?
52. Who is a role model of functional/technical skills outside of work?

Dimension 3: Knows how the competency works in theory; shows understanding

53. Are there situations or settings where someone should be different in how they demonstrates functional or technical skills?
54. Do you think functional/technical skills can be learned? If so, how do you think people develop functional/technical skills?
55. Do you think there is a way to compensate or work around low functional/technical skills?
56. Has anyone asked you for your opinions/advice on functional/technical skills?*
57. Have you ever attended a course on functional or technical skills?

FUNCTIONAL TECHNICAL SKILLS

58. Have you ever been in a situation where you and others put functional/technical skills on a success profile?
59. Have you ever been part of an effort to create a policy or a mission statement containing reference to the importance of being functionally or technically skilled?
60. Have you ever been someone's coach or mentor who had problems with functional/technical skills?
61. Have you ever created a plan to help someone develop functional/technical skills?
62. Have you ever criticized someone for not having functional or technical skills?
63. Have you ever designed a program on functional/technical skills?
64. Have you ever given a speech on functional/technical skills?
65. Have you ever rewarded or recognized someone for having functional or technical skills?
66. Have you ever taught a course on functional/technical skills?
67. Have you ever tried to help someone deal more effectively with functional/technical skills?*
68. Have you ever tried to help someone improve their functional/technical skills?
69. How do you think people develop functional/technical skills?
70. How much of success do you think is due to being functionally or technically skilled compared with other characteristics?
71. How would you know if someone lacks functional or technical skills?
72. How would you know if someone possesses functional or technical skills?
73. If you had to write a book on functional or technical skills, what would the chapter headings be?
74. What are the benefits to someone who has really good functional/technical skills?
75. What are the consequences to someone who has really poor functional/technical skills?
76. What do you think the performance standard is on functional or technical skills for someone in your role?
77. What happens if you are too dependent on functional/technical skills?
78. What happens when two people try to work together who are very different at demonstrating functional/technical skills?
79. What wisdom would you pass onto others trying to become better at demonstrating functional/technical skills?
80. When you select others, what do you look for in functional/technical skills?
81. Why do you think people end up being different at demonstrating functional/technical skills?

Dimension 4: Shows personal change and sense-making; learned it one place and applied it in another; can compare and contrast experiences; changes viewpoints across time; can explain personal development or evolution related to the competency

82. Compare and contrast examples of times when your functional or technical skills have been effective and ineffective.
83. Contrast your on- and off-the-job use of functional or technical skills.
84. Did you ever pass up a job or assignment because you were not confident enough in the functional or technical skills that were required?
85. Do you ever use other skills to cover for your lack of functional or technical skills?
86. Has becoming better at any functional or technical skills ever helped you in other areas?
87. Has poor functional or technical skills ever been the subject of a development plan for you?
88. Have your functional or technical skills always been at this level?
89. Have functional or technical skills ever figured in a failure, struggle, or setback you have had?
90. Have you ever delegated or assigned someone a task because you didn't have the required functional or technical skills?
91. Have you ever made significant strides at becoming better at functional or technical skills?

FUNCTIONAL TECHNICAL SKILLS

92. Have your functional or technical skills, good or bad, ever been the subject of your performance review or a career discussion?
93. How different are you across situations in your functional or technical skills?
94. How do you decide what kind of and how much functional or technical skill to build?
95. How much of your success is due to your functional or technical skills?
96. How transferable are your functional or technical skills to other situations?
97. If you had to become better at functional or technical skills in a hurry, what would you do?
98. Was there a time when you did not have good functional or technical skills?
99. What caused you to work to improve your functional or technical skills?
100. What event or series of events had the most impact on your present functional or technical skills?
101. What was the shortest amount of time in which you improved your functional or technical skills?
102. When did you first realize your level of ability to learn functional or technical skills?
103. When you know ahead of time that your usual level of functional or technical skills isn't adequate, what do you do?
104. Why do you think you use functional or technical skills the way you do?
105. Why do you think your functional or technical skills are the way they are?*
106. How do you integrate state of the art technology into your job?
107. How transferable are your technical skills to other functional areas?

D. Follow-up Probes:

1. Are there times when you're not like this or wouldn't do this?
2. Could you contrast those two bosses for me?
3. Could you give me a few examples of how you've used or applied that?
4. Do you suppose if others would just try harder, they could learn to be more technically proficient like you?
5. Do you think this is teachable?
6. Do you think you're better at technical matters than most? Why?
7. Do you think you would perform any differently if you had more or less technical skill?
8. Have your technical skills ever gotten in the way? How did that make you feel?
9. How did it feel to give up something you wanted to get the project going?
10. How did the others react when you did that?
11. How did you come up with that approach in the first place?
12. How did you know that method of getting over that barrier would work?
13. How do others you have known approach that?
14. How do you know when technical skills alone won't help the problem any further?
15. How much did you have to give up to make it work?
16. How typical is this for you?
17. How would you approach that same situation today?
18. Is this natural for you, or do you really have to dig for it?
19. Was there a time when you didn't understand this about yourself?
20. What did you do after you got that feedback?
21. What did you do to adapt to that?
22. What did you learn from that?
23. What do you use these technical skills for?
24. What kinds of problems have you solved/what accomplishments?*

FUNCTIONAL TECHNICAL SKILLS

25. Why did you choose that approach?
26. Why did you decide to take the risk?
27. Why did you do it that way?
28. Why did you think it was important for you to use your technical skills that way?
29. Why did you time your attempt like you did?
30. Why do you suppose organizations work that way?
31. Why do you think that didn't work?
32. Why do you think that happened that way?
33. Why do you think that worked?
34. Why do you think you have difficulties with that sometimes?
35. Would you have done it that way with looser deadlines?
36. Would you have done it that way with tighter deadlines?

E. Themes/Things to Look For:

Appreciation of the technical skills of others	Sought after for technical knowledge
Balance between technology and other skills	Staying state of the art
Deep knowledge	Technology from the lessons of experience
Emotional commitment to technology	Time allocation to technology
Integrating new technologies	Understanding/rules of thumb
Putting technology to use	Up to speed
Reliance on technology alone	Where the rubber meets the road
Skilled in more than one area	Can explain technical matters in plain language

F. Most Likely Résumé:

1. Look for jobs like:

Chair of Projects/Task Forces	Member of Projects/Task Forces
Fix-Its/Turnarounds	Scope (complexity) Assignments
Heavy Strategic Demands	Staff Leadership (Influencing Without Authority)
Line to Staff Switches	Start-Ups

2. Look for develop-in-place assignments like:

Plan a new site for a building (plant, field office, headquarters, etc.)

Manage the purchase of major product, equipment, materials, program, or system.

Manage an ad hoc, temporary group of people where the people in the group are towering experts but the temporary manager is not.

Manage a cost-cutting project.

Audit cost overruns to assess the problem, and present your findings to the person or people involved.

3. Best references to ask about or check:

Direct Boss	Peers and Colleagues
Natural Mentors	Direct Reports
Past Associates/Constituencies	

FUNCTIONAL TECHNICAL SKILLS

Learning Agility Evaluation:

1. What/Describing vs. Why/Explain
7. Passive vs. Intrigued/Curious
9. Vague/General vs. Sharp/Specific
11. Generalizations vs. Specific Learnings
18. Stays Close to Home vs. Lots of Curiosity
19. External Standards vs. Internal Standards
22. Focus on Accomplishments vs. Focus on Solving Problems

H. The LEADERSHIP ARCHITECT® Sort Card Connections:

1. Good (positive) if combined with high:

Understands ultimate complexity of technology 2, 30, 61
Can make money with technical advancements 14, 28, 61
Can be a technical resource to customers 15, 33, 41
Can teach others 19, 36, 49
Learns from experience 32, 45, 61
Puts expertise to use 51, 52, 53
Knows likes and dislikes 55
Stays up to date 61

2. Bad (negative) if combined with low or high (+):

Doesn't know how it fits 5, 46, 58
Has the answers but can't deliver the message 8, 49
Overmanages the technical aspect of the work (+13, 20) 18
Theoretical or removed 17, 52, 53
Hires on technology and surface characteristics 25, 56
Encyclopedia; doesn't put it all together 32, 45
Loner 36, 42, 60

3. Too much can contribute to the following Stallers and Stoppers:

A. What too much looks like (overused):

May be seen as too narrow; may overdevelop or depend upon technical and functional knowledge and skills at the expense of personal, interpersonal and managerial skills; may use deep technical knowledge and skills to avoid ambiguity and risk.

B. Too much might lead to these Stallers and Stoppers:

Poor Administrator (102)
Blocked Personal Learner (106)
Defensiveness (108)
Overmanaging (117)
Performance Problems (118)

C. Compensators:

How to compensate for too much of this competency:
14, 28, 30, 32, 45, 46, 51, 57, 58

FUNCTIONAL TECHNICAL SKILLS

   D. *Things to watch for:*
   Arrogance over those less skilled
   Blames others when their technology solutions didn't work
   Can't leave technical comfort zone
   Hides behind technical skills in conflicts
   Overvalues self just for technical expertise
   Spends too much time on technology
   Thinks technical skills are synonymous with high performance
   Technology can solve anything
   Doesn't get results
   Poor judge of people
   Surrounds self with technical types

4. **Too little can contribute to the following Stallers and Stoppers:**

   A. *What too little looks like (unskilled):*

   Not up to functional or technical proficiency; makes technical/functional errors; judgment and decision making marginal because of lack of knowledge; may be stuck in past skills and technologies; may be inexperienced, new to the area, or lack interest in it; lack of detail orientation to go deep; may not make the time to learn.

   B. *Too little might lead to these Stallers and Stoppers:*
   Poor Administrator (102)
   Performance Problems (118)

   C. *Compensators:*
   How to substitute for too little of this competency:
   5, 18, 20, 30, 32, 33, 35, 46, 50, 56, 61

I. LEARNING ARCHITECT® Connections:

Look for People Who Act Like and/or show Evidence of:

2a. Problem Solving	15. Cautious
4a. Getting Information	18. Straightforward
4b. Modeling	19. What
5. New	20. Events
9. Multiple Sources	35. Breadth
13. Focused	

J. CHOICES ARCHITECT® Connections:

Look for people who act like and/or show evidence of:

First Edition (Released 1994)
   4. Complexity

Second Edition (Released 2000)
   2. Complexity

FUNCTIONAL TECHNICAL SKILLS

K. Difficulty to Develop:
13 (of 34)–Easiest

25. HIRING AND STAFFING

A. Definition:

Has a nose for talent; hires the best people available from inside or outside; is not afraid of selecting strong people; assembles talented staffs.

B. Arenas/Domains to Explore:

1. Athletic team captains
2. Coaches
3. Filling jobs from inside the organization
4. Filling jobs from outside the organization
5. Fraternity/sorority management
6. Layoffs
7. Managing an event/conference/off-site
8. Mergers/acquisitions
9. Military command
10. Nominating people for boards
11. Picking friends
12. Picking people for project teams
13. Picking people for task forces
14. Picking travel companions
15. Professional association management
16. Selecting consultants
17. Selecting temporaries
18. Selecting vendors/suppliers
19. Start-ups
20. Student government
21. Teachers

C. Sample Questions:

Dimension 1: Been there, done that–has had direct personal experience(s) involving the competency–candidate was the prime player   Note: * means OK for campus

1. Can you tell me about a time when the reference checks were right on target?
2. Can you tell me about a time when the reference checks were wrong?
3. Has anyone ever accused you of messing something up because of poor hiring or staffing?
4. Has anyone you supported for an open job been turned down?
5. Have you been on an interview team and had the only negative vote?
6. Have you been on an interview team and had the only positive vote?
7. Have you ever filled an open job reporting to you with a compromise candidate?
8. Have you ever had to replace someone because they lacked hiring or staffing skills?
9. Have you ever had to work longer and harder because someone else on the team wasn't qualified or up to the task?*
10. Have you ever hired anyone stronger than you were in some aspect of the job?
11. Have you ever hired anyone who later passed you up?
12. Have you ever hired someone from the outside when others thought an internal candidate should have gotten the job?
13. Have you ever hired someone who you or someone else had to let go?
14. Have you ever managed anything where the people or units reporting to you were in different locations? How did you handle remote hiring and staffing?
15. Have you ever passed on someone you found out later was quite successful?
16. Have you ever passed someone over for promotion because they didn't hire or staff well?
17. Have you ever run a group where you selected the membership? Who did you pick and why?*
18. Have you ever staffed a group from scratch? Describe what you did and why.

HIRING AND STAFFING

19. Have you ever taken on a troubled person who later had to be let go?
20. Have you ever taken on a troubled person who later turned out to be very successful?
21. Have you ever taken over a team where you had to replace most of the people over time?
22. Have you ever worked for a company that freely recruited from outside the organization for experienced talent?
23. Have you ever worked for a company that totally promoted from within? What did you think of that?
24. How hard is it for you to fill open positions on your team?
25. How much information do you generally need to make a hiring decision?
26. What do you think your long-term hit rate is for hiring successful people?
27. What's the biggest chance you have taken in hiring someone?
28. What is your approach to interviewing internal candidates?
29. What is your approach to interviewing outside candidates?
30. What's your hit rate been on predicting long term career success?
31. What's the most diverse team you have ever assembled?
32. Who has turned out to be your best hire?
33. Who was your worst hire?

Dimension 2: Seen/been around others who were involved with the competency–good and bad; learns from others about self

34. Contrast the people you know who are most and least skilled at hiring and staffing with strong talent.*
35. Has hiring or staffing success ever been in any 360° survey done on you? Was your score among your highest, middle, or lowest?
36. Has poor hiring or staffing results on someone else's part ever created an obstacle for you or got in the way of something you were trying to accomplish?*
37. Have you ever talked about your hiring and staffing skills with a coach or mentor?
38. Have you ever watched someone fail/get fired because they did not hire and staff with talent?*
39. Have you ever watched someone overhire or staff with talent to the point that it backfired?
40. Have you ever watched someone succeed because they had strong hiring and staffing skills?*
41. Have you ever worked with a coach on improving your hiring and staffing skills?*
42. Have you ever worked with a person who excelled at hiring or staffing with strong talent?
43. Have you ever worked with a skills coach on improving your hiring or staffing results?*
44. How do you get feedback about yourself on hiring and staffing success?
45. How often do you check with multiple sources when you get a piece of critical feedback on your hiring or staffing results?
46. Is there a historical figure you consider a model of hiring or staffing with strong talent?
47. What do others who are not your fans say about your hiring and staffing success?
48. What do others who like you say about your hiring and staffing success?
49. Which boss was the best at hiring or staffing with strong talent?
50. Which boss was the worst at hiring and staffing?
51. Which direct report was the best at hiring or staffing with strong talent?
52. Which direct report was the worst at hiring and staffing?
53. Which peer was the best at hiring or staffing with strong talent?
54. Which peer was the worst at hiring and staffing?
55. Who in your field or business is the best at hiring and staffing with strong talent?
56. Who do you consider a current role model of hiring or staffing with strong talent?*

HIRING AND STAFFING

57. Who do you go to for advice on improving hiring and staffing results?
58. Who have you learned the most from about hiring and staffing?*
59. Who is a higher-management role model for you on hiring and staffing?
60. Who is a role model of hiring and staffing outside of work?

Dimension 3: Knows how the competency works in theory; shows understanding

61. Are there situations or settings where someone would hire and staff talent differently?
62. Do you think hiring and staffing skills can be learned? If so, how do you think people develop hiring and staffing skills?
63. Do you think there is a way to compensate or work around low hiring and staffing skills?
64. Has anyone asked you for your opinions/advice on hiring and staffing?*
65. Have you ever attended a course on hiring and staffing?
66. Have you ever been in a situation where you and others put hiring and staffing on a success profile?
67. Have you ever been part of an effort to create a policy or a mission statement containing reference to the importance of effective hiring and staffing?
68. Have you ever been someone's coach or mentor who had problems with hiring and staffing?
69. Have you ever created a hiring and staffing talent development plan for someone?
70. Have you ever criticized someone for not effectively hiring and staffing talent?
71. Have you ever designed a program on hiring and staffing?
72. Have you ever given a speech on hiring and staffing?
73. Have you ever rewarded or recognized someone for effectively hiring or staffing strong talent?
74. Have you ever taught a course on hiring and staffing?
75. Have you ever tried to help someone deal more effectively with hiring and staffing?*
76. Have you ever tried to help someone improve their hiring and staffing skills?
77. How do you determine if someone is talented?*
78. How do you think people develop hiring and staffing skills?
79. How is finding a person outside the organization different than finding one inside?
80. How much of success do you think is due to hiring and staffing compared with other characteristics?
81. How would you know if someone is bad at hiring and staffing?
82. How would you know if someone is good at hiring and staffing?
83. If you had to write a book on hiring and staffing, what would the chapter headings be?
84. What are the benefits to someone who is really good at hiring and staffing?
85. What are the consequences to someone who is really poor at hiring and staffing?
86. What do you think the performance standard is on hiring and staffing for someone in your role?
87. What happens when two people try to work together who are very different at hiring and staffing talent?
88. What wisdom would you pass onto others trying to become better at hiring and staffing?
89. When you select others, what do you look for in hiring and staffing talent?
90. Why do you think people end up having different hiring and staffing skills?

Dimension 4: Shows personal change and sense-making; learned it one place and applied it in another; can compare and contrast experiences; changes viewpoints across time; can explain personal development or evolution related to the competency

91. Compare and contrast examples of being effective and ineffective at hiring and staffing?
92. Contrast your on- and off-the-job use of effective hiring and staffing procedures.
93. Did you ever pass up a job or assignment because you were not confident enough in your skills at hiring and staffing with strong talent?

HIRING AND STAFFING

94. Do you ever use other skills to cover for your poor hiring and staffing skills?
95. Has poor hiring and staffing success ever figured in a failure, struggle, or setback you have had?
96. Has becoming more successful at hiring and staffing ever helped you in other areas?
97. Has poor hiring and staffing success ever been the subject of a development plan for you?
98. Has your ability to hire and staff with talent always been at this level?
99. Have you ever delegated or assigned or shared with someone the task of hiring and staffing because you don't do particularly well at it?
100. Have you ever made significant strides at improving your hiring and staffing success?
101. Have your hiring and staffing skills, good or bad, ever been the subject of your performance review or a career discussion?
102. How different are you across situations in your hiring and staffing success?
103. How much of your success is due to your ability to hire and staff with strong people?
104. How transferable are your hiring and staffing skills to other situations?
105. If you had to become better at hiring and staffing with stronger people in a hurry, what would you do?

106. Was there a time when your success at hiring and staffing was poor?
107. What caused you to work to improve your skills at hiring and staffing?
108. What event or series of events had the most impact on your hiring and staffing success?
109. What's the most varied you have been at hiring and staffing successes and failures?
110. What was the shortest amount of time in which you increased your level of skill and success at hiring and staffing?
111. When did you first realize your level of skill and success at hiring and staffing?
112. When you know ahead of time that your usual way of hiring and staffing won't work, what do you do?
113. Why do you think you hire and staff the way you do?
114. Why do you think your hiring and staffing abilities are the way they are?*
115. Who are the best people you've ever assembled? Why? What happened to them later?*
116. Who's the best person to replace you for your job?
117. Have you played any team sports? What have you learned from this about how to pick and mold together talent?*

D. Follow-up Probes:

1. Are there times when you don't hire people like that or that way?
2. Could you contrast those two bosses for me?
3. Could you give me a few examples of how you've used or applied that?
4. Do you always hire people that way or was that a special situation?
5. Do you do treat everyone like that or just one or a few?
6. Do you suppose if others would just try harder, they could learn to judge talent more like you?
7. Do you think it's fair to hire people based on that?
8. Do you think this is teachable?
9. Do you think you're better at judging talent than most? Why?
10. Do you think you would perform any better if you had different hiring and staffing skills?
11. How certain were you that you were right when you made that decision on whether to (or not to) hire?
12. How did the others react when you did that?
13. How did you come up with that approach in the first place?

HIRING AND STAFFING

14. How did you know that approach to hiring would work?
15. How do others you have known approach that?
16. How much did you have to give up to make it work?
17. How often do you use the "Let's meet in the middle" approach?
18. How typical is this for you?
19. How would you approach that same situation today?
20. Is hiring talented staff natural for you, or do you really have to dig for it?
21. Was there a time when you didn't understand this about yourself?
22. Were there some alternatives you rejected? Were you right?
23. What did you do after you got that feedback?
24. What did you do to adapt to that?
25. What did you learn from that?
26. Why did you choose that approach?
27. Why did you decide to take the risk?
28. Why did you do it that way?
29. Why did you time your attempt like you did?
30. Why do you suppose organizations work that way?
31. Why do you think that didn't work?
32. Why do you think that happened that way?
33. Why do you think that worked?
34. Why do you think you have difficulties with that sometimes?
35. Why do you think you hire people like that?
36. Would you have done it that way with looser deadlines?
37. Would you have done it that way with tighter deadlines?

E. Themes/Things to Look For:

- Bone deep belief that talent always wins
- Always on the hunt for talent
- Will hire against the grain of the culture
- Cutting losses quickly
- Takes risks with people
- Fighting for the right hire
- Using structured hiring technology
- Not afraid to hire future boss
- Setting high goals
- Fighting compromises
- Complex view of talent
- Elitist
- Short term vs. long view
- Looking broadly
- Variety of skill and personal criteria
- Admitting mistakes
- Cloning, not selecting in own image

F. Most Likely Résumé:

1. Look for jobs like:
  Fix-Its/Turnarounds
  Significant People Demands
  Start-Ups

HIRING AND STAFFING

2. Look for develop-in-place assignments like:

Go to a campus as a recruiter.

Train and work as an assessor in an assessment center.

Plan for and start up something small (secretarial pool, athletic program, suggestion system, program, etc.).

Hire/staff a team from outside your unit or organization.

Work on a team that's deciding who to keep and who to let go in a layoff, shutdown, delayering, or divestiture.

Manage the outplacement of a group of people.

Work on a team looking at a reorganization plan where there will be more people than positions.

3. Best references to ask about or check:

Direct Boss	Natural Mentors
Human Resource Professionals	Past Associates/Constituencies

G. Learning Agility Evaluation:

2. All or Nothing vs. Can See Many Sides
3. Ordinary/Socially Acceptable vs. Insightful/Different
7. Passive vs. Intrigued/Curious
8. Sameness vs. Diversity
9. Vague/General vs. Sharp/Specific
13. Simple Views vs. Complex Views
14. Sameness vs. Broad Ranging
19. External Standards vs. Internal Standards
20. Avoids Responsibility for Mistakes vs. Admits and Learns from Mistakes

H. The LEADERSHIP ARCHITECT® Sort Card Connections:

1. Good (positive) if combined with high:

People calls accurate 17, 56, 64

Uses the talent well 18, 20, 39, 60

Likely to build a team 5, 19, 21, 60

Thinks long term in hiring 21, 46, 58

Goes where the talent is, even outside the organization 34, 57

2. Bad (negative) if combined with low or high (+):

People-user 7, 10, 23 (+53)

Loses them after they're hired 18, 19, 20, 35

Doesn't mold a team 19, 60

Hires only some classes/groups 21

Criteria are too local/short term 5, 46, 58

Doesn't admit mistakes; may select in own image 55

Superficial 56 (+24)

HIRING AND STAFFING

3. **Too much can contribute to the following Stallers and Stoppers:**

   A. *What too much looks like (overused):*

   May overlook slow starters; may select on a surface or a limited number of characteristics; may assemble a team of individual performers who aren't good team players; may prefer currently talented people who aren't broad enough for further growth; may be too quick to replace rather than work with a person.

   B. *Too much might lead to these Stallers and Stoppers:*

   Failure to Staff Effectively (111)

   C. *Compensators:*

   How to compensate for too much of this competency:
   21, 30, 33, 41, 52, 56, 60, 64

   D. *Things to watch for:*

Assembles hard-to-manage talent	Poor morale/cooperation in the team
Cloning	Too few decision criteria
Their people don't get promoted	Turnover under them
No or little time on development	

4. **Too little can contribute to the following Stallers and Stoppers:**

   A. *What too little looks like (unskilled):*

   Doesn't have a good track record in hiring and/or staffing; may clone him/herself or focus on one or two preferred characteristics; may look narrowly for people who are similar to them; may play it safe with selections; doesn't select much diversity; may not know what competence looks like, lack criteria, or assume he/she just knows; may lack the patience to wait for a better candidate.

   B. *Too little might lead to these Stallers and Stoppers:*

   Failure to Staff Effectively (111)

   C. *Compensators:*

   How to substitute for too little of this competency:
   5, 17, 19, 20, 21, 23, 35, 39, 53, 56, 60, 63, 64

I. LEARNING ARCHITECT® Connections:

Look for people who act like and/or show evidence of:

2c. Intuition	12. Rules of Thumb
3c. Personal Experience	30. Mastery
4c. Actively Involve	32. Diversity in Others
11. Why/How	34. Sizing Up Others

HIRING AND STAFFING

J. CHOICES ARCHITECT® Connections:

Look for people who act like and/or show evidence of:

First Edition (Released 1994)
15. Helps Others Succeed

Second Edition (Released 2000)
11. Cool Transactor
12. Helps Others Succeed

K. Difficulty to Develop:
24 (of 34)–Moderate

26. HUMOR

A. Definition:

Has a positive and constructive sense of humor; can laugh at him/herself and with others; is appropriately funny and can use humor to ease tension.

B. Arenas/Domains to Explore:

1. Across different groups
2. Acting
3. Behavior in the interview
4. Entertainment preferences
5. Hosting/participating in roasts
6. Negotiating style
7. Performing
8. Presentation style
9. Reading habits
10. Role models
11. Role played in work group
12. Social events
13. Social events at work
14. Tense situations
15. Writing style

C. Sample Questions:

Dimension 1: Been there, done that–has had direct personal experience(s) involving the competency–candidate was the prime player   Note: * means OK for campus

1. Are you asked to host roasts/give presentations at roasts?
2. Are you good at telling jokes?
3. Do you do any public speaking? How do you use humor?
4. Do you ever use humor as a defense mechanism to get out of a jam?*
5. Do you ever use humor to deliver a serious message?*
6. Do you generally spend time with people who are more serious or more humorous?*
7. Do you use any cartoons or humorous material in your presentations?*
8. Do you use physical humor much; doing funny things?*
9. Has anyone ever accused you of messing something up because of lack of a sense of humor?
10. Has anyone ever accused you of messing something up because you used inappropriate humor?*
11. Has anyone ever had to tell you to get serious?*
12. Have you ever managed anything where the people or units reporting to you were in different locations? How did you use your humor?
13. Have you ever tried to use your humor in a foreign country?*
14. Tell me about a time when an attempt at humor backfired for you.*
15. Tell me about a time when something really funny happened at work (school). What benefit did it serve?*
16. Tell me about a time when you criticized someone for an inappropriate use of humor.*
17. Tell me about a time when you used humor to defuse a tense situation.*
18. Tell me about a time when your humor got you into trouble.
19. Tell me about a time when your humor worked really well for you.
20. Were you ever considered to be the class clown?*
21. What role do you play in your work group?
22. What style of humor is the most attractive to you?* How do you react when the joke is on you?*
23. What were some of your best and worst uses of humor?*
24. Who are your favorite comedians?*

HUMOR

Dimension 2: Seen/been around others who were involved with the competency–good and bad; learns from others about self

25. Contrast the most and least humorous people you know.*
26. Has humor ever been in any 360° survey done on you? Was your score among your highest, middle, or lowest?
27. Has lack of humor on someone else's part ever created an obstacle for you or got in the way of something you were trying to accomplish?*
28. Have you ever talked about your use of humor with a coach or mentor?
29. Have you ever watched someone fail/get fired because they did not use humor?*
30. Have you ever watched someone fail/get fired because they used inappropriate humor?*
31. Have you ever watched someone be too humorous to the point that it backfired?
32. Have you ever watched someone succeed because they had a good sense of humor?*
33. Have you ever worked with a coach on using humor?*
34. Have you ever worked with a person who excelled at having a sense of humor?
35. Have you ever worked with a skills coach on using humor?*
36. How do you get feedback about your use of humor?
37. How often do you check with multiple sources when you get a piece of critical feedback on your use of humor?
38. Is there a historical figure you consider a model of using humor?*
39. What do others who are not your fans say about your use of humor?
40. What do others who like you say about your use of humor?
41. Which boss was the best at using humor?
42. Which boss was the worst at using humor?
43. Which direct report was the best at using humor?
44. Which direct report was the worst at using humor?
45. Which peer was the best at using humor?
46. Which peer was the worst at using humor?
47. Who in your field or business is the best at using humor?
48. Who do you consider a role model of using humor?*
49. Who do you go to for advice on using humor?
50. Who have you learned the most from about using humor?*
51. Who is a higher-management role model for you on using humor?
52. Who is a role model of using humor outside of work?

Dimension 3: Knows how the competency works in theory; shows understanding

53. Are there situations or settings where someone should use humor differently?
54. Do you think humor can be learned? If so, how do you think people develop humor skills?
55. Do you think there is a way to compensate or work around low humor skills?
56. Has anyone asked you for your opinions/advice on using humor?*
57. Have you ever attended a course on using humor?
58. Have you ever been in a situation where you and others put using humor on a success profile?
59. Have you ever been part of an effort to create a policy or a mission statement containing reference to the importance of using humor or having fun?
60. Have you ever been someone's coach or mentor who had problems with humor?
61. Have you ever created a development plan for someone on using humor?

HUMOR

62. Have you ever criticized someone for not using humor?
63. Have you ever designed a program on using humor?
64. Have you ever given a speech on using humor?
65. Have you ever rewarded or recognized someone for using humor?
66. Have you ever taught a course on using humor?
67. Have you ever tried to help someone deal with the use of humor more effectively?*
68. Have you ever tried to help someone improve their use of humor?
69. How do you think people develop humor skills?
70. How much use of humor is good and how much is too much?
71. How much of success do you think is due to using humor compared with other characteristics?
72. How would you know if someone is bad at using humor?
73. How would you know if someone is good at using humor?
74. If you had to write a book on using humor, what would the chapter headings be?
75. What are the benefits to someone who is really good at using humor?
76. What are the consequences to someone who is really poor at using humor?
77. What do you think the performance standard is on using humor for someone in your role?
78. What happens if you have or use too much humor?
79. What happens when two people try to work together who are very different in the way they use humor?
80. What wisdom would you pass onto others trying to become better at using humor?
81. When you select others, what do you look for in the use of humor?
82. Why do you think people end up being different in the way they use humor?

Dimension 4: Shows personal change and sense-making; learned it one place and applied it in another; can compare and contrast experiences; changes viewpoints across time; can explain personal development or evolution related to the competency

83. Compare and contrast examples of how you've been effective and ineffective at using humor.
84. Contrast your on- and off-the-job use of humor.
85. Did you ever pass up a job or assignment because you were not confident enough in your ability to use humor?
86. Do you ever use other skills to cover for your lack of skill at using humor?
87. Has lack of or inappropriate humor ever figured in a failure, struggle, or setback you have had?
88. Has becoming better at using humor ever helped you in other areas?
89. Has poor or inappropriate use of humor ever been the subject of a development plan for you?
90. Has your sense and use of humor always been this way?
91. Have you ever delegated or assigned someone a task because you didn't have the required sense of humor?
92. Have you ever made significant strides at becoming better at using humor?
93. Has your sense of humor, good or bad, ever been the subject of a performance review or career discussion?
94. How different are you across situations in your sense and use of humor?
95. How do you decide how much humor to use?
96. How much of your success is due to your sense of humor?
97. How transferable is your sense of humor to other situations?
98. If you had to become better at using humor in a hurry, what would you do?
99. Was there a time when you were not as good at using humor?
100. What caused you to work to improve your sense of humor?

HUMOR

101. What event or series of events had the most impact on your sense of humor?
102. What's the most varied you can be in your use of humor?
103. What was the shortest amount of time in which you increased your level of skill at using humor?
104. When did you first realize your level of skill at using humor?
105. When you know ahead of time that your usual use of humor won't work, what do you do?
106. Why do you think you use humor the way you do?
107. Why do you think your sense of humor is the way it is?*
108. When can humor un-stick a stalled group? When can it disrupt?*
109. How have you changed your humor through the years as sensitivities have increased?*

D. Follow-up Probes:

1. Are there times when you don't use your humor like that or that way?
2. Could you contrast those two bosses for me?
3. Could you give me a few examples of how you've used or applied that?
4. Do you always use your humor that way or was that a special situation?
5. Do you think that kind of humor hurts others or at least makes them feel bad?
6. Do you think this is teachable?
7. Do you think you're better at using humor than most? Why?
8. Do you think you were using your humor to make a serious point?
9. Do you think you would perform any differently if you were able to use humor more effectively?
10. Do you use your humor with everyone or just one or a few?
11. Have you always used humor that way or is this a more recent development in you?
12. How certain were you that you were right when you made that decision on whether to (or not to) use humor in that situation?
13. How did others react when you did that?
14. How did that make you feel?
15. How did you come up with that approach to humor in the first place?
16. How do others you have known approach that?
17. How typical is this for you?
18. How would you approach that same situation today?
19. Is humor and being funny natural for you, or do you really have to dig for it?
20. Was there a time when you didn't understand this about yourself?
21. What did you do after you got that feedback?
22. What did you do to adapt to that?
23. What did you learn from that experience?
24. What did you learn from that?
25. What do you think you do differently today because of that experience?
26. What impact did that have on you?
27. Why did you decide to take the risk?
28. Why did you do it that way?
29. Why did you time your attempt like you did?
30. Why do you think that didn't work?
31. Why do you think that happened that way?

32. Why do you think that worked?
33. Why do you think you have difficulties with that sometimes?
34. Why do you think you use your humor like that?
35. Why were you hesitant to use your humor in a situation like that?

E. Themes/Things to Look For:

Can poke fun at self
Carefully using humor with people one doesn't know well
Deadpan humor
Did they make you laugh in the interview?
Drivers–what's the purpose of the humor
Helping move work forward, not deflecting it with humor
Humor as tension relief
Humor in service of a purpose
Idiosyncratic humor
Joke telling vs. being humorous vs. physical humor
Not using humor as a weapon
Not using humor as conflict avoidance
Odd sense of humor
Poking fun at human foibles, not picking on individuals
"Performer" capabilities–enjoys staging and telling you about it
Rehearsed humor vs. natural
Relieving tension
Sarcasm delivered as humor
Serious points delivered humorously
Whimsical humor

F. Most Likely Résumé:

1. Look for jobs like:

None Apply (Note: humor isn't learned from jobs)

2. Look for develop-in-place assignments like:

Study humor in business settings; read books on the nature of humor; collect cartoons you could use in presentations; study funny people around you; keep a log of funny jokes and sayings you hear; read famous speeches and study how humor was used; attend comedy clubs; ask a funny person to act as your tutor; practice funny lines and jokes with others.

Try to learn something frivolous and fun to see how good you can get (e.g., juggling, square dancing, magic).

3. Best references to ask about or check:

Family Members	Past Associates/Constituencies
Human Resource Professionals	Peers and Colleagues
Natural Mentors	Spouse
Off-Work Associates	

HUMOR

G. Learning Agility Evaluation:

2. All or Nothing vs. Can See Many Sides
3. Ordinary/Socially Acceptable vs. Insightful/Different
5. Tight/Rigid vs. Loose/Flexible
6. Reacting/Responsive vs. Adapting
7. Passive vs. Intrigued/Curious
15. Linear vs. Use Contrasts/Analogies
17. Avoid Discussion of Weaknesses vs. Comfortably Sharing Shortcomings
21. View from Self vs. View from Point of View of Others

H. The LEADERSHIP ARCHITECT® Sort Card Connections:

1. Good (positive) if combined with high:

Uses humor to help people through tension 2, 12
Engaging 3, 31
Sensitive to the feelings of others 7, 10, 21
Softens the blow/light touch 13, 27, 34, 48
Humor used to mold team 36, 60
Uses self-humor 44
Uses humor in presentations 49
Uses humor in writing 67

2. Bad (negative) if combined with low or high (+):

Loose humor (+1, 16) 48
Avoids dealing with tough, ambiguous situations 2, 51
May be sarcastic, attacking 7, 10, 21
Uses humor as a cover to avoid dealing directly with conflicts 12, 34
Politically incorrect humor 21, 48
Humor as a weapon 22, 29
Too much share of conversation 33
Uses humor to express impatience 41

3. Too much can contribute to the following Stallers and Stoppers:

A. What too much looks like (overused):

May disrupt group process with untimely or inappropriate humor; may use humor to deflect real issues and problems; may use humor to criticize others and veil an attack; may use humor to deliver sarcasm or cynicism; may be perceived as immature or lacking in appropriate seriousness; his/her humor may be misinterpreted.

B. Too much might lead to these Stallers and Stoppers:

Arrogant (104)	Insensitive to Others (112)
Failure to Build a Team (110)	Overdependence on a Single Skill (116)

HUMOR

C. Compensators:
How to compensate for too much of this competency:
7, 10, 11, 22, 31, 33, 41, 43, 48, 52, 55

D. Things to watch for:
Bad timing	Poor judgment
Humor as a mask	Primal humor
Humor at the expense of others	Unsuccessful attempts at humor
Mean humor	Humor as attack
Past trouble due to humor	Humor to deflect or avoid
Politically insensitive humor	

4. Too little can contribute to the following Stallers and Stoppers:

A. What too little looks like (unskilled):
Appears humorless; doesn't know how or doesn't want to use humor in the workplace; may have problems telling a joke; may chill humor in others; thinks humor is out of place in the workplace; may be too serious and want to avoid looking or sounding silly; may lack a light touch; may use sarcastic or politically offensive humor; may use humor in the wrong time or wrong place or in the wrong way.

B. Too little might lead to these Stallers and Stoppers:
Arrogant (104)

C. Compensators:
How to substitute for too little of this competency:
3, 14, 31, 44, 49

I. LEARNING ARCHITECT® Connections:

Look for people who act like and/or show evidence of:

- 2b. Visioning
- 2c. Intuition
- 3a. Checking Feelings
- 4c. Actively Involve
- 7. Risks
- 24. Discloser
- 38. Comfort with Paradox

J. CHOICES ARCHITECT® Connections:

Look for people who act like and/or show evidence of:

First Edition (Released 1994)
None Apply

Second Edition (Released 2000)
13. Light Touch

K. Difficulty to Develop:
24 (of 34)–Moderate

HUMOR

27. INFORMING

A. Definition:

Provides the information people need to know to do their jobs and to feel good about being a member of the team, unit, and/or the organization; provides individuals information so that they can make accurate decisions; is timely with information.

B. Arenas/Domains to Explore:

1. Before delegating
2. Career discussions
3. Corrective discussions
4. Crisis communication
5. Customer communication
6. Downward communication
7. Family communication
8. Formal presentations
9. Frequency
10. Group communication
11. Late-breaking news
12. Lateral communication
13. Mission/vision/values messages
14. One-on-ones
15. Outside communication
16. Performance appraisals
17. Proprietary communications
18. Purpose
19. Reports
20. Setting goals/time frames
21. Supportive communication during personal problems
22. Timing
23. Upward communication
24. White papers
25. Written communication

C. Sample Questions:

*Dimension 1: Been there, done that–has had direct personal experience(s) involving the competency–candidate was the prime player   Note: * means OK for campus*

1. Do you ever keep some people more informed than others?*
2. Do you manage people who work at other sites? How do you keep them up-to-date?
3. Has a boss ever disclosed a piece of information about you or from you that you expected them to keep confidential?
4. Has anyone ever accused you of messing something up because you didn't inform others?
5. Has disclosing a piece of information ever backfired on you?*
6. Have you ever been briefed by the legal or public affairs function as to the security of certain information?
7. Have you ever been embarrassed in public when you disclosed a piece of proprietary/confidential information you didn't know was confidential?
8. Have you ever been in an organization going through a tense period like a merger or downsizing? How did you handle the information you had as part of management?
9. Have you ever communicated something you weren't supposed to?*
10. Have you ever given a deposition?
11. Have you ever made a bad decision because a boss did not share a piece of information they had?
12. Have you ever managed anything where the people or units reporting to you were in different locations? How did you keep people informed?
13. Have you ever not communicated something you should have?*
14. Have you ever testified in a court proceeding?

INFORMING

15. How do you know who not to overwhelm with a lot of information?
16. How do you react when someone starts a conversation with "You can't tell anyone what I'm going to tell you?"*
17. How do you set aside the time necessary to inform everyone?*
18. How do you keep others informed at work while you travel?*
19. How good are you at hiding information you know you have but others only suspect?*
20. Tell me about a time when communication was essential. How did you keep people apprised of what was going on?*
21. Tell me about a time when you had to communicate something important to someone who did not speak your language.
22. Tell me about a time when informing got you into trouble.
23. Tell me about a time when informing worked really well for you.
24. Tell me about how you organize and run staff meetings.
25. What are your e-mail–answering habits?*
26. When you were managing a project, how did you communicate with project members?*

Dimension 2: Seen/been around others who were involved with the competency–good and bad; learns from others about self

27. Contrast the most and least informing people you know.*
28. Has keeping others informed ever been in any 360º survey done on you? Was your score among your highest, middle, or lowest?
29. Has not keeping others informed on someone else's part ever created an obstacle for you or got in the way of something you were trying to accomplish?*
30. Have you ever talked about improving your skill in keeping others informed with a coach or mentor?
31. Have you ever watched someone fail/get fired because they didn't keep others informed?*
32. Have you ever watched someone overdo informing others to the point that it backfired?
33. Have you ever watched someone succeed because they kept others informed?*
34. Have you ever worked with a coach on your skill in keeping others informed?*
35. Have you ever worked with a person who excelled at keeping others informed?
36. Have you ever worked with a skills coach on keeping others informed?*
37. How do you get feedback about yourself on keeping others informed?
38. How often do you check with multiple sources when you get a piece of critical feedback on your informing skills?
39. Is there a historical figure you consider a model of keeping others informed?
40. What do others who are not your fans say about how well you keep others informed?
41. What do others who like you say about how well you keep others informed?
42. Which boss was the best at keeping others informed?
43. Which boss was the worst at keeping others informed?
44. Which direct report was the best at keeping others informed?
45. Which direct report was the worst at keeping others informed?
46. Which peer was the best at keeping others informed?
47. Which peer was the worst at keeping others informed?
48. Who in your field or business deals the best with keeping others informed?
49. Who do you consider a role model of keeping others informed?*
50. Who do you go to for advice on keeping others informed?
51. Who have you learned the most from about keeping others informed?*
52. Who is a higher-management role model for you on keeping others informed?
53. Who is a role model of keeping others informed outside of work?

INFORMING

Dimension 3: Knows how the competency works in theory; shows understanding

54. Are there situations or settings where someone should use informing skills differently?
55. Do you think informing skills can be learned? If so, how do you think people develop informing skills?
56. Do you think there is a way to compensate or work around low informing skills?
57. Has anyone asked you for your opinions/advice on keeping others informed?*
58. Have you ever attended a course on keeping others informed?
59. Have you ever been in a situation where you and others put keeping others informed on a success profile?
60. Have you ever been part of an effort to create a policy or a mission statement containing reference to the importance of keeping others well informed?
61. Have you ever been someone's coach or mentor who had problems with keeping others well informed?
62. Have you ever created a development plan for someone on keeping others informed?
63. Have you ever criticized someone for not keeping others informed?
64. Have you ever designed a program on keeping others informed?
65. Have you ever given a speech on keeping others informed?
66. Have you ever rewarded or recognized someone for keeping others informed?
67. Have you ever taught a course on keeping others informed?
68. Have you ever tried to help someone keep others informed more effectively?*
69. Have you ever tried to help someone improve their informing skills?
70. How do you think people develop informing skills?
71. How much of success do you think is due to keeping others informed compared with other characteristics?
72. How would you know if someone is bad at keeping others informed?
73. How would you know if someone is good at keeping others informed?
74. If you had to write a book on keeping others well informed, what would the chapter headings be?
75. What are the benefits to someone who is really good at keeping others well informed?
76. What are the consequences to someone who is really poor at keeping others well informed?
77. What do you think the performance standard is on keeping others informed for someone in your role?
78. What happens when two people try to work together who are very different in the way they keep others informed?
79. What wisdom would you pass onto others trying to become better at keeping others well informed?
80. When you select others, what do you look for in the way they keep others informed?
81. Why do you think people end up being different in the way they keep others informed?

Dimension 4: Shows personal change and sense-making; learned it one place and applied it in another; can compare and contrast experiences; changes viewpoints across time; can explain personal development or evolution related to the competency

82. Compare and contrast examples of how you've been effective and ineffective at keeping others informed?
83. Contrast your on- and off-the-job use of keeping others informed.
84. Did you ever pass up a job or assignment because you were not confident enough in your skills at keeping others well informed?
85. Do you ever use other skills to cover for your lack of informing skills?
86. Has becoming better at keeping others informed ever helped you in other areas?
87. Has not keeping others informed ever been the subject of a development plan for you?
88. Has not keeping others informed ever figured in a failure, struggle, or setback you have had?
89. Have you ever delegated or assigned someone a task because you didn't keep others informed particularly well?
90. Have you ever made significant strides at becoming better at informing others?

INFORMING

91. Have your informing skills always been this way?
92. Have your informing skills skills, good or bad, ever been the subject of your performance review or a career discussion?
93. How different are you across situations in your practice of keeping people informed?
94. How do you decide how much information to share?
95. How much of your success is due to keeping others well informed?
96. How transferable are your information sharing skills to other situations?
97. If you had to become better at keeping others informed in a hurry, what would you do?
98. Was there a time when you were not good at keeping people informed?
99. What caused you to work to improve your skills at keeping others informed?
100. What event or series of events had the most impact on your habit of keeping people informed?
101. What's the most varied you can be at keeping people informed?
102. What was the shortest amount of time in which you increased your level of skill at keeping others informed?
103. When did you first realize your level of skill at keeping people informed?
104. When you know ahead of time that your usual level of keeping others informed isn't adequate, what do you do?
105. Why do you think you keep people informed the way you do?
106. Why do you think your skill of keeping people informed is the way it is?*
107. How do you decide what to tell people and what to hold back?*
108. Tell me when, how often, and why you use written communications. What topics do you most often cover?

D. Follow-up Probes:

1. Are there times when you don't inform people like that or that way?
2. Could you contrast those two bosses for me?
3. Do you always inform people that way or was that a special situation?
4. Do you inform everyone like that or just one or a few?
5. Do you think this is teachable?
6. Do you think you're better at informing skills than most? Why?
7. Do you think you would perform any differently if you were able to inform better?
8. Have you always communicated with people that way or is this a recent development in you?
9. How certain were you that you were right when you made that decision on whether to (or not to) inform?
10. How did that make you feel?
11. How did the others react when you did that?
12. How did you come up with that approach to informing people in the first place?
13. How did you know that approach to informing would work?
14. How do others you have known approach that?
15. How typical is this for you?
16. How would you approach that same situation today?
17. Is informing natural for you, or do you really have to dig for it?
18. Was there a time when you didn't understand this about yourself?
19. Were there some alternatives you rejected? Were you right?
20. What did you do after you got that feedback?
21. What did you learn from that experience?
22. What do you think you do differently today because of that experience?
23. What impact did that have on you?

INFORMING

24. Why did you choose that approach?
25. Why did you do it that way?
26. Why did you time your attempt like you did?
27. Why didn't you take action?
28. Why do suppose organizations work that way?
29. Why do you think that didn't work?
30. Why do you think that happened that way?
31. Why do you think that worked?
32. Why do you think you inform people like that?
33. Why do you think you prefer to inform people like that?
34. Would you have done it that way with looser deadlines?
35. Would you have done it that way with tighter deadlines?

E. Themes/Things to Look For:

Admitting mistakes
Candor
Communication style
Cuing information
Disclosure decision making
Drivers; why do they inform
Equity of information distribution
Formal information mechanisms (memo format, policies)
Informing people to help them understand practices and policies
Need to know vs. want to know
Sensitivity and empathy
Sifting out the important from the less so
Speed and timing
Strategies and potential disasters
Thoughtful forewarning
Understanding the emotional component
Knowing what constitutes a confidence

F. Most Likely Résumé:

1. Look for jobs like:

Fix-Its/Turnarounds	Scope (complexity) Assignments
Line to Staff Switches	Staff Leadership (Influencing Without Authority)
Significant People Demands	Start-Ups

2. Look for develop-in-place assignments like:

Integrate diverse systems, processes, or procedures across decentralized and/or dispersed units.
Manage the renovation of an office, floor, building, meeting room, warehouse, etc.
Establish security procedures for a building or floor.
Manage something "remote," away from your location.

INFORMING

- Plan a new site for a building (plant, field office, headquarters, etc.).
- Lobby for your organization on a contested issue in local, regional, state, or federal government.
- Make speeches/be a spokesperson for the organization on the outside.
- Represent the organization at a trade show, convention, exposition, etc.
- Represent the concerns of a group of nonexempt, clerical, or administrative employees to higher management to seek resolution of a difficult issue.
- Write a proposal for a new policy, process, mission, charter, product, service, or system, and present and sell it to top management.
- Spend time with internal or external customers, write a report on your observations, and present it to the people involved with the customers in the organization.
- Draft a mission statement, policy proposal, charter, or goal statement and get feedback from others.
- Be a change agent; create a symbol for change; lead the rallying cry; champion a significant change and implementation.
- Relaunch an existing product or service that's not doing well.
- Seek out and use a seed budget to create and pursue a personal idea, product, or service.
- Create employee involvement teams.
- Run (chair) a taskforce on a pressing problem.
- Manage a study/project team on a significant issue and present the results to key people.
- Serve on a product/service/project review committee.
- Manage a joint project with another unit, function, geography, etc.
- Teach a course, seminar, or workshop on something you know a lot about.
- Teach a course, seminar, or workshop on something you don't know well.
- Teach/coach someone how to do something you are not an expert in.
- Teach/coach someone how to do something you're an expert in.
- Become someone's assigned mentor, coach, sponsor, champion, or orienter.
- Train customers in the use of the organization's products or services.
- Present the strategy of your unit to others not familiar with your business.
- Manage an ad hoc, temporary group of people involved in tackling a fix-it or turnaround project.
- Take over for someone on vacation or a long trip.
- Help shut down a plant, regional office, product line, business, operation, etc.
- Manage a group through a significant business crisis.
- Take on a tough and undoable project, one where others who have tried it have failed.
- Manage the outplacement of a group of people.
- Work on a team looking at a reorganization plan where there will be more people than positions.
- Work on a crisis management team.

3. **Best references to ask about or check:**
   Customers
   Peers and Colleagues
   Direct Reports

INFORMING

G. Learning Agility Evaluation:

1. What/Describing vs. Why/Explain
4. Spectator/Passive vs. Player/Participant
9. Vague/General vs. Sharp/Specific
19. External Standards vs. Internal Standards
20. Avoids Responsibility for Mistakes vs. Admits and Learns from Mistakes
21. View from Self vs. View from Point of View of Others
22. Focus on Accomplishments vs. Focus on Solving Problems

H. The LEADERSHIP ARCHITECT® Sort Card Connections:

1. Good (positive) if combined with high:

Timely communications 1, 16
Can make sense out of chaos 2, 30, 50, 51
Sift through data well 2, 50, 58, 65
Clear upward communications 8, 34, 57
Inspiring 9, 14, 36, 65
Good performance discussions 13, 33, 35
Good dealing with customer problems 15, 33, 53
Good career discussions 19, 33
Trusted source 22, 29, 48
With a light touch 26
Scopes out what people need to know 39, 47
Clear presenter 49
Clear writing 67

2. Bad (negative) if combined with low or high (+):

Loose lips (+1, 16) 41
Insensitive communication 7, 10, 21
Spends too much time communicating (+7, 10, 23)
Waters a plant with a fire hose (+13, 34) 11
Hard time deciding what to communicate 17, 40
Withholds or misuses information 22, 29
Not tuned in to what people need to know 3, 33, 56, 64
May overwhelm; be scattered 39, 47, 50
Inappropriate disclosure 39, 48

3. Too much can contribute to the following Stallers and Stoppers:

A. What too much looks like (overused):

May provide too much information; may upset people by giving them information they can't handle or preliminary information that turns out not to be true.

B. Too much might lead to these Stallers and Stoppers:

Overly Ambitious (103)   Insensitive to Others (112)
Betrayal of Trust (105)   Political Missteps (119)
Lack of Ethics and Values (109)

INFORMING

C. Compensators:
How to compensate for too much of this competency:
2, 8, 11, 12, 22, 29, 33, 38, 41, 47, 48, 50, 52, 64

D. Things to watch for:
Sharing proprietary information
Using information sharing just for personal purposes
Using information sharing as a weapon
Using information sharing for personal gain
Misjudging what information people need
Misjudging what information people want
Misjudging the capacity of people for information
Sharing information to make self feel important
Sharing information to release tension
Indiscriminate communicator

4. Too little can contribute to the following Stallers and Stoppers:

A. What too little looks like (unskilled):
Not a consistent communicator; tells too little or too much; tells too late; timing is off; may be unclear; may inform some better than others; may not think through who needs to know by when; doesn't seek or listen to the data needs of others; may inform but lack follow-through; may either hoard information or not see informing as important; may only have one mode–written or oral or e-mail.

B. Too little might lead to these Stallers and Stoppers:
Poor Administrator (102)
Failure to Build a Team (110)
Insensitive to Others (112)

C. Compensators:
How to substitute for too little of this competency:
1, 3, 13, 18, 20, 31, 33, 34, 44, 60

I. LEARNING ARCHITECT® Connections:

Look for people who act like and/or show evidence of:

1c. Following a Plan
3b. Self-Talk
8. Initiate
15. Cautious
16. Collaborate
18. Straightforward
24. Discloser

J. CHOICES ARCHITECT® Connections:

Look for people who act like and/or show evidence of:

First Edition (Released 1994)
8. Cool Transactor
23. Communicator

Second Edition (Released 2000)
9. Agile Communicator
11. Cool Transactor

K. Difficulty to Develop:
17 (of 34)–Easiest

28. INNOVATION MANAGEMENT

A. Definition:

Is good at bringing the creative ideas of others to market; has good judgment about which creative ideas and suggestions will work; has a sense about managing the creative process of others; can facilitate effective brainstorming; can project how potential ideas may play out in the marketplace.

B. Arenas/Domains to Explore:

1. Acquisitions
2. Awards for innovation
3. Club/association management
4. Coaching
5. Event/conference programming
6. Management of the creative process
7. Mergers
8. Need to Idea to marketplace
9. New products/services
10. Producing new ideas
11. Results of project teams/task forces
12. Teaching
13. Volunteer community work
14. Work process design

C. Sample Questions:

*Dimension 1: Been there, done that–has had direct personal experience(s) involving the competency–candidate was the prime player   Note: * means OK for campus*

1. Do you enjoy working around creative people who are a bit different?*
2. Do you have any copyrights or patents on anything?
3. Do you have any current ideas running around in your head that might be successful innovations?*
4. Do you manage (have you ever managed) creative people?
5. Has anyone ever accused you of messing something up because of a lack of innovation?
6. Have you ever been around a failed attempt to innovate?
7. Have you ever been around a major successful innovation?
8. Have you ever had to tell someone that that's enough creativity for now, get back to work?
9. Have you ever invented anything?*
10. Have you ever managed anything where the people or units reporting to you were in different locations? How did you manage/promote innovation?
11. Have you ever written anything that was considered an innovation at the time?
12. How do you size up an idea for marketability?
13. In your experience, what is the eventual success rate of raw creative ideas?
14. Tell me about a time when you managed an idea to market that was not yours.
15. Tell me about a time when you managed your own idea to market.
16. Tell me about a time when you took a good idea from inception to market.
17. Tell me about a time when innovating got you into trouble.
18. Tell me about a time when innovating worked really well for you.
19. What do you consider your best innovation?*
20. What kinds of experiments go on in your department?

INNOVATION MANAGEMENT

Dimension 2: Seen/been around others who were involved with the competency–good and bad; learns from others about self

21. Contrast the most and least innovative people you know.*
22. Has innovation management ever been in any 360° survey done on you? Was your score among your highest, middle, or lowest?
23. Has lack of innovation management on someone else's part ever created an obstacle for you or got in the way of something you were trying to accomplish?*
24. Have you ever talked about your ability to manage innovation with a coach or mentor?
25. Have you ever watched someone fail/get fired because they could not manage innovation?*
26. Have you ever watched someone overextend innovation management to the point that it backfired?
27. Have you ever watched someone succeed because they effectively managed innovation?*
28. Have you ever worked with a coach on your ability to manage innovation?*
29. Have you ever worked with a person who excelled at managing innovation?
30. Have you ever worked with a skills coach on managing innovation?*
31. How do you get feedback about yourself on managing innovation?
32. How often do you check with multiple sources when you get a piece of critical feedback on your ability to manage innovation?
33. Is there a historical figure you consider a model of the ability to manage innovation?
34. What do others who are not your fans say about your ability to manage innovation?
35. What do others who like you say about your ability to manage innovation?
36. Which boss was the best at managing innovation?
37. Which boss was the worst at managing innovation?
38. Which direct report was the best at managing innovation?
39. Which direct report was the worst at managing innovation?
40. Which peer was the best at managing innovation?
41. Which peer was the worst at managing innovation?
42. Who in your field or business is the best at managing innovation?
43. Who do you consider a current role model of managing innovation?*
44. Who do you go to for advice on managing innovation?
45. Who have you learned the most from about managing innovation?*
46. Who is a higher-management role model for you on managing innovation?
47. Who is a role model of managing innovation outside of work?

Dimension 3: Knows how the competency works in theory; shows understanding

48. Are there situations or settings where someone should be different in how they manage innovation?
49. As you look at the world as a customer, what do you think were recent innovations that you have appreciated?*
50. Do you think innovation management can be learned? If so, how do you think people develop innovation management skills?
51. Do you think the people who can manage an innovation are the same as the people with the ideas?
52. Do you think there is a way to compensate or work around low innovation-management skills?
53. Has anyone asked you for your opinions/advice on managing innovation?*
54. Have you ever attended a course on managing innovation?
55. Have you ever been in a situation where you and others put innovation management on a success profile?

INNOVATION MANAGEMENT

56. Have you ever been part of an effort to create a policy or a mission statement containing reference to the importance of managing innovation?
57. Have you ever been someone's coach or mentor who had problems with innovation management?
58. Have you ever created a development plan for someone on managing innovation?
59. Have you ever criticized someone for not managing innovation?
60. Have you ever designed a program on managing innovation?
61. Have you ever given a speech on managing innovation?
62. Have you ever rewarded or recognized someone for their ability to manage innovation?
63. Have you ever taught a course on managing innovation?
64. Have you ever tried to help someone deal more effectively with innovation management?*
65. Have you ever tried to help someone improve their innovation-management skills?
66. How do good innovators get a sense of the future market for an idea, product, or service?
67. How do you think people develop innovation skills?
68. How much innovation is good to have and how much is too much?
69. How much of success do you think is due to innovation management compared with other characteristics?
70. How would you know if someone is bad at managing innovation?
71. How would you know if someone is good at managing innovation?
72. If you had to write a book on managing innovation, what would the chapter headings be?
73. What are the benefits to someone who is really good at managing innovation?
74. What are the consequences to someone who is really poor at managing innovation?
75. What do successful innovations have in common?*
76. What do you see as the three or four major trends that are going to affect your business?
77. What do you think is the biggest or most significant innovation going on at the moment?*
78. What do you think the performance standard is on managing innovation for someone in your role?
79. What happens if you have or use too much innovation?
80. What happens when two people try to work together who are very different in the way they manage innovation?
81. What promotes an innovative and non-innovative climate?*
82. What wisdom would you pass onto others trying to become better at managing innovation?
83. When you select others, what do you look for in innovation-management skills?
84. Why do you think people end up being different in the way they manage innovation?

Dimension 4: Shows personal change and sense-making; learned it one place and applied it in another; can compare and contrast experiences; changes viewpoints across time; can explain personal development or evolution related to the competency

85. Compare and contrast examples of how you've been effective and ineffective at managing innovation.
86. Contrast your on- and off-the-job success at managing innovation.
87. Did you ever pass up a job or assignment because you were not confident enough in your skills at managing innovation?
88. Do you ever use other skills to cover for your lack of innovation-management skills?
89. Has becoming better at managing innovation ever helped you in other areas?
90. Has not being able to manage innovation ever figured in a failure, struggle, or setback you have had?
91. Has poor innovation management ever been the subject of a development plan for you?
92. Have you ever delegated or assigned someone a task because you didn't manage innovation particularly well?

INNOVATION MANAGEMENT

93. Have you ever made significant strides at becoming better at managing innovation?
94. Have your innovation-management skills always been this way?
95. Have your innovation-management skills, good or bad, ever been the subject of your performance review or a career discussion?
96. How different are your innovation-management skills across situations?
97. How do you decide how innovative to be?
98. How much of your success is due to your innovation-management skills?
99. How transferable are your innovation-management skills to other situations?
100. If you had to become better at managing innovation in a hurry, what would you do?
101. Was there a time when you were not as good at managing innovation?
102. What caused you to work to improve your skills at managing innovation?
103. What event or series of events had the most impact on your innovation-management skills?
104. What's the most varied you can be in innovation management?
105. What was the shortest amount of time in which you learned to become better at managing innovation?
106. When did you first realize your level of skill at managing innovation?
107. When you know ahead of time that your usual level of innovation management isn't adequate, what do you do?
108. Why do you think you manage innovation the way you do?
109. Why do you think your ability to manage innovation is the way it is?*
110. How do you tell a good idea from a not so good one?*
111. How do you go about selecting one idea from among many to push forward?

D. Follow-up Probes:
1. Are there times when you don't innovate like that or that way?
2. Could you contrast those two bosses for me?
3. Could you give me a few examples of how you've used or applied that?
4. Do you always innovate that way or was that a special situation?
5. Do you think this is teachable?
6. Do you think you're better at innovating skills than most? Why?
7. Do you think you would perform any differently if you were able to innovate better?
8. Have you always innovated that way or is this a recent development in you?
9. How certain were you that you were right when you made that decision on whether to (or not to) innovate?
10. How did it feel to give up something you wanted to get the project going?
11. How did others react when you did that?
12. How did that make you feel?
13. How did you come up with that approach to innovation in the first place?
14. How did you know that method of getting over that barrier would work?
15. How did you know that approach to innovation would work?
16. How do others you have known approach that?
17. How far will you go before you cut line and try another approach?
18. How typical is this for you?
19. How would you approach that same situation today?
20. Is innovating natural for you, or do you really have to dig for it?
21. Were there some alternatives you rejected? Were you right?

22. What did you learn from that experience?
23. What do you think you do differently today because of that experience?
24. What impact did that have on you?
25. Why didn't you take action?
26. Why do you think that didn't work?
27. Why do you think that happened that way?
28. Why do you think that worked?
29. Why do you think you innovate like that?
30. Why do you think you prefer to innovate like that?
31. Was there a time when you didn't understand this about yourself?
32. What did you do after you got that feedback?
33. What did you do to adapt to that?
34. Why did you decide to take the risk?
35. Why did you do it that way?
36. Why did you time your attempt like you did?
37. Why do you suppose organizations work that way?

E. Themes/Things to Look for:

Appreciation of creative people
Broadening the issue from the original problem
Change master
Enjoyment of watching the creative process
Facilitation with the new and the bold
Focus on interesting problems–go into depth, really try to understand the problem uniquely
Having failures, learning from them
Not dictating process; monitoring and learning from process
Openness to many ideas
Picking out the one idea among many
Realistic expectation of success
Rigorous look at and definition of problems
Sense of how things/processes work
Sense of the customer
Sense of the marketplace
Sense of timing
Student of inventions and innovations
Tolerance for failure
Tolerance of seeing ten bad ideas to wait for the good one
Understanding of creative people
Understanding the process of innovation
Visionary, ability to see ahead
Visualizing outcomes/how something might be used
Appreciation for underdeveloped ideas
Experiment/learn/experiment
Looking outside one's business for ideas/parallels

INNOVATION MANAGEMENT

F. Most Likely Résumé:

1. Look for jobs like:
Heavy Strategic Demands
Scope (complexity) Assignments
Start-Ups

2. Look for develop-in-place assignments like:
Monitor and follow a new product or service through the entire idea, design, test market, and launch cycle.
Launch a new product, service, or process.
Relaunch an existing product or service that's not doing well.
Seek out and use a seed budget to create and pursue a personal idea, product, or service.

3. Best references to ask about or check:
Direct Boss
Past Associates/Constituencies

G. Learning Agility Evaluation:
1. What/Describing vs. Why/Explain
2. All or Nothing vs. Can See Many Sides
3. Ordinary/Socially Acceptable vs. Insightful/Different
7. Passive vs. Intrigued/Curious
18. Stays Close to Home vs. Lots of Curiosity
19. External Standards vs. Internal Standards
20. Avoids Responsibility for Mistakes vs. Admits and Learns from Mistakes

H. The LEADERSHIP ARCHITECT® Sort Card Connections:

1. Good (positive) if combined with high:
Pushes innovation constantly 1, 16, 34, 53, 5 7
Can get the ideas from the creative 3, 31, 33, 41
Good sense of what will sell 5, 15, 24, 46, 53
Balances the old with the new 5, 40
Can sell ideas through a system 12, 36, 38, 48, 59
Good sense of what's important 15, 50, 51, 58, 65
Can create their own innovative ideas 30, 14
Learns as they go 32, 61
Organizes chaos 39, 47, 52
Can see the grand scheme 46, 58, 65

INNOVATION MANAGEMENT

2. **Bad (negative) if combined with low or high (+):**

   Knows what to do but doesn't do it 1, 16, 53
   Ideas may not always be possible at the detail level 5, 24, 52
   Poor sense of what's important 5, 50, 51, 58
   In the service of whom 15
   Doesn't have ways to capture learning 32, 61
   Can't sell ideas through the system 38, 48
   Disorganized execution 39, 47, 52
   One person show 42, 60 (+57)

3. **Too much can contribute to the following Stallers and Stoppers:**

   A. *What too much looks like (overused):*

   May err toward the new and reject the old; may prefer creative people and undervalue those less creative; may get too far out in front of others in thinking and planning.

   B. *Too much might lead to these Stallers and Stoppers:*

   Poor Administrator (102)

   C. *Compensators:*

   How to compensate for too much of this competency:
   16, 17, 24, 27, 33, 47, 50, 52, 53, 59, 61, 64

   D. *Things to watch for:*

   Flitting from flower to flower without finishing anything
   Just using others without appreciation of contribution
   Leaving people behind
   Playing favorites
   Short attention span
   Stresses others by always pushing ahead of the wave
   Unrealistic expectations
   Doesn't use scarce resources wisely

4. **Too little can contribute to the following Stallers and Stoppers:**

   A. *What too little looks like (unskilled):*

   Not a good judge of what's creative; doesn't understand the marketplace for innovation; can't select from among creative ideas which one would work the best; doesn't innovate; may not be open to the creative suggestions of others; may be stuck in his/her comfort zone of tasks and methods of doing them; may not understand creativity or the process of innovation; may close too soon with solutions and conclusions; may be a perfectionist avoiding risk and fearing failures and mistakes; may not use experiments to learn and improve, and may block the innovations of others.

   B. *Too little might lead to these Stallers and Stoppers:*

   Non-Strategic (114)

INNOVATION MANAGEMENT

C. *Compensators:*
How to substitute for too little of this competency:
2, 5, 12, 14, 16, 24, 30, 32, 34, 37, 38, 46, 48, 49, 51, 53, 57, 58, 61, 63

I. LEARNING ARCHITECT® Connections:

Look for people who act like and/or show evidence of:

1b. Trial and Error	9. Multiple Sources
1c. Following a Plan	10. Complexity
2a. Problem Solving	21. Changer
2b. Visioning	22. Experimenter
2c. Intuition	28. Creator
5. New	33. Diversity of Sources
7. Risks	

J. CHOICES ARCHITECT® Connections:

Look for people who act like and/or show evidence of:

First Edition (Released 1994)
1. Inquisitive
6. Visionary
12. Experimenter
19. Tinkerer
20. Forging Ahead
21. Taking the Heat

Second Edition (Released 2000)
7. Inquisitive
20. Experimenter
21. Innovation Manager
22. Taking the Heat
23. Visioning
25. Delivers Results

K. Difficulty to Develop:
29 (of 34)–Hardest

29. INTEGRITY AND TRUST

A. Definition:

Is widely trusted; is seen as a direct, truthful individual; can present the unvarnished truth in an appropriate and helpful manner; keeps confidences; admits mistakes; doesn't misrepresent him/herself for personal gain.

B. Arenas/Domains to Explore:

1. Advice to associates
2. Being an officer of an organization
3. Career discussions
4. Club/association management
5. Coaching
6. Communication to the public
7. Communications to shareholders/Wall Street
8. Completing 360° surveys
9. Consistency
10. Consistency of messaging across people/groups
11. Contract negotiations
12. Counseling
13. Customer relations
14. During crises
15. Family communications
16. Feedback to bosses/higher-level management
17. Feedback to direct reports
18. Government reporting
19. Hard times
20. Holding proprietary information
21. Legal testimony
22. Mentoring
23. Peer appraisal
24. Performance appraisals
25. Personal gain at stake
26. Project team/taskforce meetings
27. Solicited feedback
28. Staff meetings
29. Teaching
30. Union relations
31. Unsolicited feedback
32. Up-against-the wall times
33. Vendor/supplier relations
34. Whistleblowing

C. Sample Questions:

Dimension 1: Been there, done that–has had direct personal experience(s) involving the competency–candidate was the prime player   Note: * means OK for campus

1. Are you uncomfortable when you have information you cannot disclose?*
2. Has anyone ever accused you of messing something up because of lack of integrity?
3. Has anyone ever asked you to stop giving them any more information on a topic?*
4. Have you ever been asked for some feedback in a public forum that would have been more negative than the requester was expecting? What did you do?
5. Have you ever been caught between a rock and a hard place, where whatever you said or did would anger one group or person?*
6. Have you ever been in a situation where you needed to say something although you knew that it was not correct?*
7. Have you ever been in a situation where you turned down obtaining information because you didn't want to be responsible for it?*
8. Have you ever been involved in a whistleblower type of incident to higher management outside the formal chain of command?
9. Have you ever changed your mind about something, or said something different to one person than another, and had this come back to haunt you?*

INTEGRITY AND TRUST

10. Have you ever completed a 360° survey on someone you didn't think much of? What did you say?
11. Have you ever had to present material you were not really in support of in your role as a manager or reporting out from a taskforce when you did not support the conclusions?
12. Have you ever kept a confidence even though it cost you?*
13. Have you ever kept a confidence that you wish you hadn't?*
14. Have you ever managed anything where the people or units reporting to you were in different locations? How did you communicate that you could be trusted?
15. Have you ever used information for personal gain?*
16. Have you ever witnessed a significant breach of security in an organization? What did you do about it?
17. Have you ever worked for someone you did not trust?*
18. How do you handle possessing confidential information a requester knows you have but you can't or won't disclose?*
19. How do you react when someone starts a conversation with "You can't tell anyone what I'm going to tell you?"*
20. Tell me about a time when you delivered bad news poorly.*
21. Tell me about a time when you delivered bad news well.*
22. Tell me about a time when you publicly admitted a mistake or failure.
23. What percent of what you know do you generally pass on to bosses?
24. What percent of what you know do you generally pass on to customers?
25. What percent of what you know do you generally pass on to direct reports?
26. What percent of what you know do you generally pass on to higher management?
27. What percent of what you know do you generally pass on to peers/colleagues?
28. What were a couple of your larger mistakes?*

Dimension 2: Seen/been around others who were involved with the competency–good and bad; learns from others about self

29. Contrast the most and least trustworthy people you know.*
30. Has integrity and trust ever been in any 360° survey done on you? Was your score among your highest, middle, or lowest?
31. Has lack of integrity and trust on someone else's part ever created an obstacle for you or got in the way of something you were trying to accomplish?*
32. Have you ever talked with a coach or mentor about your integrity and trust?
33. Have you ever watched someone fail/get fired because they lacked integrity or were not trustworthy?*
34. Have you ever watched someone exaggerate integrity and trust to the point that it backfired?
35. Have you ever watched someone succeed because they demonstrated integrity and trust?*
36. Have you ever worked with a coach on integrity and trust?*
37. Have you ever worked with a person who excelled at having integrity and being trustworthy?
38. Have you ever worked with a skills coach on improving integrity and trust?*
39. How do you get feedback about your integrity and trust?
40. How often do you check with multiple sources when you get a piece of critical feedback on your integrity and trust?
41. Is there a historical figure you consider a model of integrity and trust?
42. What do others who are not your fans say about your integrity and trust?
43. What do others who like you say about your integrity and trust?
44. Which boss was the best at having integrity and being trustworthy?

INTEGRITY AND TRUST

45. Which boss was the worst at having integrity and being trustworthy?
46. Which direct report was the best at having integrity and being trustworthy?
47. Which direct report was the worst at having integrity and being trustworthy?
48. Which peer was the best at having integrity and being trustworthy?
49. Which peer was the worst at having integrity and being trustworthy?
50. Who in your field or business deals the best with integrity and trust?
51. Who do you consider a role model of integrity and trust?*
52. Who do you go to for advice on integrity and trust?
53. Who have you learned the most from about integrity and trust?*
54. Who is a higher-management role model for you on integrity and trust?
55. Who is a role model of integrity and trust outside of work?

Dimension 3: Knows how the competency works in theory; shows understanding

56. Are there situations or settings where someone should be different in demonstrating integrity and trust?
57. Do you think integrity and trust can be learned? If so, how do you think people develop integrity and trust skills?
58. Do you think there is a way to compensate or work around low integrity and trust?
59. Has anyone asked you for your opinions/advice on integrity and trust?*
60. Have you ever attended a course on integrity and trust?
61. Have you ever been in a situation where you and others put integrity and trust on a success profile?
62. Have you ever been part of an effort to create a policy or a mission statement containing reference to the importance of having integrity and being trustworthy?
63. Have you ever been someone's coach or mentor who had problems with integrity and trust?
64. Have you ever created a development plan for someone on integrity and trust?
65. Have you ever criticized someone for not having integrity and being trustworthy?
66. Have you ever designed a program on integrity and trust?
67. Have you ever given a speech on integrity and trust?
68. Have you ever rewarded or recognized someone for having integrity and being trustworthy?
69. Have you ever taught a course on integrity and trust?
70. Have you ever tried to help someone deal with integrity and trust issues more effectively?*
71. Have you ever tried to help someone improve their integrity and trustworthiness?
72. How do you think people develop integrity and trust?
73. How much of success do you think is due to having integrity and being trustworthy compared with other characteristics?
74. How would you know if someone does not have integrity and is untrustworthy?
75. How would you know if someone has integrity and is trustworthy?
76. If you had to write a book on integrity and trust, what would the chapter headings be?
77. What are the benefits to someone who has integrity and is trustworthy?
78. What are the consequences to someone who does not have integrity and is untrustworthy?
79. What do you think the performance standard is on integrity and trust for someone in your role?
80. What happens when two people try to work together who have very different levels of integrity and trust?
81. What wisdom would you pass on to others trying to improve their level of integrity and trust?
82. When you select others, what do you look for in integrity and trustworthiness?
83. Why do you think people end up being different in the way they demonstrate integrity and trust?

INTEGRITY AND TRUST

Dimension 4: Shows personal change and sense-making; learned it one place and applied it in another; can compare and contrast experiences; changes viewpoints across time; can explain personal development or evolution related to the competency

84. Compare and contrast examples of time when you've been strong and weak at demonstrating integrity and trust.
85. Contrast your on- and off-the-job methods of demonstrating integrity and trust.
86. Did you ever pass up a job or assignment because you were not confident enough in your level of straightforwardness or trustworthiness?
87. Do you ever use other skills to cover for your lack of straightforwardness or trustworthiness?
88. Has becoming better at being straightforward or trustworthy ever helped you in other areas?
89. Has lack of integrity and trust ever figured in a failure, struggle, or setback you have had?
90. Has poor integrity and trust ever been the subject of a development plan for you?
91. Has your level of being straightforward or trustworthy always been this way?
92. Have you ever delegated or assigned someone a task because you didn't feel you were straightforward enough?
93. Have you ever made significant strides at becoming better at integrity and trust?
94. Have your integrity and trust skills, good or bad, ever been the subject of your performance review or a career discussion?
95. How different are you across situations in demonstrating integrity and trust?
96. How do you decide how truthful to be?
97. How much of your success is due to the way you demonstrate integrity and trust?
98. How transferable are your integrity and trust skills to other situations?
99. If you had to become better at demonstrating integrity and trust in a hurry, what would you do?
100. Was there a time when you were not as good at demonstrating integrity and trust?
101. What caused you to work to improve your skills at demonstrating integrity and trust?
102. What event or series of events had the most impact on your level of integrity and trust?
103. What's the most varied you can be in demonstrating integrity and trust?
104. What was the shortest amount of time in which you learned to become better at being straightforward or trustworthy?
105. When did you first realize your level of skill at being straightforward or trustworthy?
106. When you know ahead of time that your usual level of integrity and trust won't work, what do you do?
107. Why do you think you deal with integrity and trust the way you do?
108. Why do you think your integrity and trust is the way it is?*
109. How trusted do you think you are in terms of people believing what you say?*
110. Are there times when you don't walk your talk?
111. Under what conditions do you say less than you know?*
112. Do you disclose more to some and less to others?*
113. How do you judge when to be direct and when to hedge?*

INTEGRITY AND TRUST

D. Follow-up Probes:

1. Are there times when you're honest like that or that way and other times when you are not?
2. Could you contrast those two bosses for me?
3. Could you give me a few examples of how you've used or applied that?
4. Did you or the other person blink first?
5. Do you always operate that way or was that a special situation?
6. Do you think that was fair to do?
7. Do you think this is teachable?
8. Do you think you're more trusted than most? Why?
9. Do you think you would perform any differently if you were seen as more trustworthy?
10. Have you always operated that way or is this a recent development in you?
11. How certain were you that you were right when you made that decision on whether to (or not to) be open and honest?
12. How did that make you feel?
13. How did the others react when you did that?
14. How did you come up with that approach to operating in the first place?
15. How did you know that approach to operating would work?
16. How did you resolve that dilemma?
17. How do others you have known approach that?
18. How typical is this for you?
19. How would you approach that same situation today?
20. Is candor natural for you, or do you really have to dig for it?
21. Were there some alternatives you rejected? Were you right?
22. What could you have gained by sharing that information?
23. What could you have gained by withholding that information?
24. What did you do after you got that feedback?
25. What did you do to adapt to that?
26. What did you learn from that experience?
27. What do you think you do differently today because of that experience?
28. What impact did that have on you?
29. What were the moral issues involved?
30. Why did they give you that information in the first place?
31. Why did you think holding back information would be right to do in that situation?
32. Why did you time your attempt like you did?
33. Why do you suppose organizations work that way?
34. Why do you think that didn't work?
35. Why do you think that happened that way?
36. Why do you think that worked?
37. Why do you think you chose to operate like that?
38. Why do you think you have difficulty with that sometimes?
39. Why do you think you prefer to operate like that?
40. Would you have done it that way with looser deadlines?
41. Would you have done it that way with tighter deadlines?

INTEGRITY AND TRUST

E. Themes/Things to Look For:

Acknowledging real dilemmas with vague answers
Candor disguising conflict avoidance; "Don't ask me if you don't really want to know"
Complex tactics and strategies for dealing with candor and trust
Courage
Direct but diplomatic
Drivers–why candid
During hard times/crises
Exchanging information for personal advantage
Handling of proprietary information
Holding self/others accountable
Keeping confidences
No win situations–lose something no matter what
Candor with some but not others
Tough personal decisions with consequences
Treating others equitably
Unvarnished truth (doesn't smooth over, shade)
Walking their talk
When they know but can't say
Witnessing integrity breaches

F. Most Likely Résumé:

1. Look for jobs like:

Chair of Projects/Task Forces	Scale Assignments
Fix-Its/Turnarounds	Scope Assignments
Line to Staff Switches	Staff Leadership (Influencing Without Authority)

2. Look for develop-in-place assignments like:

Handle a tough negotiation with an internal or external client or customer.
Help shut down a plant, regional office, product line, business, operation, etc.
Prepare and present a proposal of some consequence to top management.
Manage a dissatisfied internal or external customer; troubleshoot a performance or quality problem with a product or service.
Manage the assigning/allocating of office space in a contested situation.
Manage a group through a significant business crisis.
Take on a tough and undoable project, one where others who have tried it have failed.
Manage the outplacement of a group of people.
Resolve an issue in conflict between two people, units, geographies, functions, etc.
Make peace with an enemy or someone you've disappointed with a product or service or someone you've had some trouble with or don't get along well with.
Be a member of a union-negotiating or grievance-handling team.
Manage a project team of people who are older and more experienced.

INTEGRITY AND TRUST

3. **Best references to ask about or check:**

   Direct Boss

   Human Resource Professionals

   Natural Mentors

   Past Associates/Constituencies

   Spouse

   Direct Reports

G. Learning Agility Evaluation:

   2. All or Nothing vs. Can See Many Sides
   12. Rehearsed/Socially Acceptable vs. Candid
   19. External Standards vs. Internal Standards
   20. Avoids Responsibility for Mistakes vs. Admits and Learns from Mistakes
   21. View from Self vs. View from Point of View of Others

H. The LEADERSHIP ARCHITECT® Sort Card Connections:

   1. **Good (positive) if combined with high:**

      Flexible 2, 12, 40

      Gets more information than others 3, 22, 33, 41

      Shows more candor up than most 4, 8

      Does means testing for capacity to handle candor 10, 56

      Shows more candor to customers than most 15

      Shows more candor down than most 18, 19, 23, 27

      Sensitive 31, 64

      Learns from litmus test experiences 32, 45

      Courage 34, 57

      Knows how to couch issues 38, 48

      Shows more candor to peers/colleagues than most 42, 60

   2. **Bad (negative) if combined with low or high (+):**

      Lacks sense of nuance or complexity 2, 40, 46

      May roll over people 31, 33, 48, 64

      May hedge/not direct 9, 34, 57

   3. **Too much can contribute to the following Stallers and Stoppers:**

      ### A. *What too much looks like (overused):*

      May be too direct at times, which may catch people off guard and make them uncomfortable; may push openness and honesty to the point of being disruptive; may be so "only the facts" driven as to omit drawing reasonable conclusions, rendering opinions, fixing blame, even when it's reasonable.

      ### B. *Too much might lead to these Stallers and Stoppers:*

      Unable to Adapt to Differences (101)

      Arrogant (104)

      Blocked Personal Learner (106)

INTEGRITY AND TRUST

C. Compensators:
How to compensate for too much of this competency:
2, 5, 14, 22, 26, 31, 33, 38, 40, 42, 46, 48, 52, 54, 56, 64

D. Things to watch for:
Aberrant style

Candor actually hiding a fear of being tentative

Disclosure as a weapon to harm those who disagree

Only informing when absolutely sure–yes, the Titanic is sinking, that's why we are under water

Poor timing

Raw data without frosting

Single-minded bluntness; one size fits all

Gets in trouble by making others uncomfortable

4. Too little can contribute to the following Stallers and Stoppers:

A. What too little looks like (unskilled):
Is not widely trusted; may hedge or not take a stand; may treat others differently or indifferently at times; may not walk his/her talk and be seen as inconsistent; may have trouble keeping confidences and talks out of school; makes promises he/she doesn't or can't keep; may lack follow-through and causes problems for others; blames others for own mistakes; seen as just out for him/herself.

B. Too little might lead to these Stallers and Stoppers:
Overly Ambitious (103)   Lack of Ethics and Values (109)

Betrayal of Trust (105)   Political Missteps (119)

Defensiveness (108)

C. Compensators:
How to substitute for too little of this competency:
3, 22, 23, 27, 33, 34, 44, 57

I. LEARNING ARCHITECT® Connections:
Look for people who act like and/or show evidence of:

3b. Self-Talk   9. Multiple Sources

J. CHOICES ARCHITECT® Connections:
Look for people who act like and/or show evidence of:

First Edition (Released 1994)   **Second Edition (Released 2000)**

8. Cool Transactor   10. Conflict Manager

9. Self-Aware   11. Cool Transactor

                                  19. Self-Aware

                                  27. Presence

K. Difficulty to Develop:
20 (of 34)–Easier

30. INTELLECTUAL HORSEPOWER

A. Definition:

Is bright and intelligent; deals with concepts and complexity comfortably; described as intellectually sharp, capable, and agile.

B. Arenas/Domains to Explore:

1. Academic achievement history
2. Academic awards
3. Analytical tasks
4. Cognitive speed
5. Complex concepts
6. Computer literacy
7. Course selection
8. Crossword puzzles
9. Debating
10. Entrance exam performance (GRE, SAT)
11. Filling-dead-time habits
12. Heavy cognitive challenges
13. Heavy problem solving
14. Hobbies
15. Mensa membership
16. Mentors
17. Number crunching/understanding
18. Puzzles
19. Range of intellectual interests
20. Reading selections
21. Role models
22. Technical prowess
23. Tested IQ
24. Tough Q & A
25. TV viewing habits

C. Sample Questions:

Dimension 1: Been there, done that–has had direct personal experience(s) involving the competency–candidate was the prime player   Note: * means OK for campus

1. Are you on any national panels or study groups looking into tough issues in your field?
2. Did you receive any academic achievement awards?*
3. Do you belong to any professional associations in your field? Have you ever been an officer or board member? Do you give addresses at the national conferences? On what?
4. Do you belong to Mensa? Have you ever thought about applying?
5. Do you do crossword puzzles?*
6. Do you enjoy doing mental puzzles?*
7. Do you hold any copyrights or patents?
8. Do you turn your intellectual skills on and off depending upon the situation?*
9. Has anyone ever accused you of messing something up because you lacked the intellectual skills to do it?
10. Have you ever managed anything where the people or units reporting to you were in different locations? How did you use your intellectual skills?
11. Have you ever said in a staff meeting, "Would you please go over that again, I didn't quite get it?"
12. Have you published anything in your field?
13. Have your intellectual skills ever been tested? Do you remember your scores?*
14. How are you at manipulating solid (spatial) objects in your head?*
15. How computer literate are you? How extensively do you use the Internet?*
16. How good are you at finding the essence of an issue?
17. How good are you at math?*

INTELLECTUAL HORSEPOWER

18. How good is your memory for facts and past events?*
19. Tell me about a time when you were not the smartest person on the team.*
20. Tell me about a time when you were the smartest person on the team.*
21. Tell me about a time when your intelligence got you into trouble.
22. Tell me about a time when your intelligence worked really well for you.
23. Was getting good grades easy for you or did you really have to work for them?*
24. Were you a National Merit Scholar?*
25. What was the toughest intellectual problem you couldn't quite handle?*
26. What was your performance on college entrance exams?*
27. What were your grades in high school and college?*
28. What's the toughest purely intellectual problem you've solved?*
29. What's your shifting gears speed? Faster or slower than most?*
30. What's your vocabulary like?*
31. When you and your peers work on tough analytical problems, where do you usually come out in the order of getting it? First? Last? Middle?
32. Where did you graduate in your class?*

Dimension 2: Seen/been around others who were involved with the competency–good and bad; learns from others about self

33. Contrast the most and least intelligent people you know.*
34. Has intelligence ever been in any 360° survey done on you? Was your score among your highest, middle, or lowest?
35. Has lack of intelligence on someone else's part ever created an obstacle for you or got in the way of something you were trying to accomplish?*
36. Have you ever talked with a coach or mentor about your intellectual skills?
37. Have you ever watched someone fail/get fired because they were not smart enough?*
38. Have you ever watched someone overintellectualize to the point that it backfired?
39. Have you ever watched someone succeed because they were highly intelligent?*
40. Have you ever worked with a coach on honing your intellectual skills?*
41. Have you ever worked with a person who was exceedingly smart?
42. Have you ever worked with a skills coach on improving your intellectual skills?*
43. How do you get feedback about your intellectual skills?
44. How often do you check with multiple sources when you get a piece of critical feedback on your intellectual skills?
45. Is there a historical figure you consider a model of intellectual skills?
46. What do others who are not your fans say about your intellectual skills?
47. What do others who like you say about your intellectual skills?
48. Which boss was the least intelligent?
49. Which boss was the smartest?
50. Which direct report was the least intelligent?
51. Which direct report was the smartest?
52. Which peer was the least intelligent?
53. Which peer was the smartest?
54. Who is the most intelligent person in your field or business?
55. Who do you consider a role model of using intellectual skills?*

INTELLECTUAL HORSEPOWER

56. Who do you go to for advice on honing your intellectual skills?
57. Who have you learned the most from about intellectual skills?*
58. Who is a higher-management role model for you on intellectual horsepower?
59. Who is a role model of intellectual horsepower outside of work?

Dimension 3: Knows how the competency works in theory; shows understanding

60. Are there situations or settings where someone should be different in demonstrating their intellectual skills?
61. How do you think people develop intellectual skills?
62. Do you think there is a way to compensate or work around being less intelligent?
63. Has anyone asked you for your opinions/advice on developing intellectual skills?*
64. Have you ever attended a course on honing intellectual skills?
65. Have you ever been in a situation where you and others put intellectual horsepower on a success profile?
66. Have you ever been part of an effort to create a policy or a mission statement containing reference to the importance of being intelligent?
67. Have you ever been someone's coach or mentor who had problems with intelligence?
68. Have you ever created a development plan for someone on developing intellectual skills?
69. Have you ever criticized someone for not having intellectual horsepower?
70. Have you ever designed a program on developing intellectual horsepower?
71. Have you ever given a speech on intellectual horsepower?
72. Have you ever rewarded or recognized someone for having intellectual horsepower?
73. Have you ever taught a course on intellectual horsepower?
74. Have you ever tried to help someone develop their intellectual horsepower?*
75. How do you think people develop intelligence?
76. How much intellectual horsepower is good to have and how much is too much?
77. How much of success do you think is due to intellectual horsepower compared with other characteristics?
78. How would you know if someone lacks intellectual horsepower?
79. How would you know if someone demonstrates intellectual horsepower?
80. If you had to write a book on intellectual horsepower, what would the chapter headings be?
81. What are the benefits to someone who is really intelligent?
82. What are the consequences to someone who lacks intellectual horsepower?
83. What do you think the performance standard is on intellectual horsepower for someone in your role?
84. What happens when two people try to work together who have very different intelligence levels?
85. What wisdom would you pass on to others trying to develop intellectual skills?
86. When you select others, what do you look for in intellectual horsepower?
87. Why do you think people end up having different intellectual skills?

Dimension 4: Shows personal change and sense-making; learned it one place and applied it in another; can compare and contrast experiences; changes viewpoints across time; can explain personal development or evolution related to the competency

88. Compare and contrast examples of times you've been very bright and just been smart.
89. Contrast your on- and off-the-job use of your intellectual skills.
90. Did you ever pass up a job or assignment because you didn't think you were smart enough?
91. Do you ever use other skills to cover for your lack of intellectual skills?
92. Has not being smart enough ever figured in a failure, struggle, or setback you have had?
93. Has becoming better at intellectual skills ever helped you in other areas?

INTELLECTUAL HORSEPOWER

94. Have less-than-required intellectual skills ever been the subject of a development plan for you?
95. Have your intellectual skills always been this way?
96. Have you ever delegated or assigned someone a task because they were smarter than you?
97. Have you ever made significant strides at becoming better at intellectual skills?
98. Have your intellectual skills, high or low, ever been the subject of your performance review or a career discussion?
99. How different are you across situations in your intellectual skills?
100. How do you decide how much intellectual horsepower to apply?
101. How much of your success is due to your intelligence?
102. How transferable are your intellectual skills to other situations?
103. If you had to become better at intellectual skills in a hurry, what would you do?
104. Was there a time when you were not as intelligent?
105. What caused you to work to improve your intellectual skills?
106. What event or series of events had the most impact on your intellectual skills?
107. What's the most varied you can be with your intellectual skills?
108. What was the shortest amount of time in which you increased your level of intelligence?
109. When did you first realize your level of intelligence?
110. When you know ahead of time that your usual level of intelligence isn't adequate, what do you do?
111. Why do you think your intellectual skills are what they are?*
112. Tell me about your last three successful projects or accomplishments in your area. How were they the same, different; what's repeatable?*
113. Are there times when you purposefully play dumb? When do you do that?*

D. Follow-up Probes:

1. Are there times when you can turn it off and just go with the flow?
2. Could you give me a few examples of how you've used or applied that?
3. Do those kinds of insights come in spurts or are they consistent?
4. Do you have those same kinds of insights in other areas?
5. Do you think intelligence is overrated?
6. Do you think you're better at doing that than most?
7. Do you use your intellectual skills that way with everyone or with a more select group of people?
8. Have you always been like that?
9. How did that make you feel?
10. How did the others react when you did that?
11. How did you come up with that approach in the first place?
12. How did you react to knowing you scored the way you did on the test?
13. How typical is this for you?
14. Was that easy for you to do or were you pushing on all cylinders?
15. What could you do better in your job if you had ten more IQ points?
16. What did you do after you received that feedback?
17. What did you learn from that?
18. What would have happened if you were not as smart as you are?
19. What would have happened to you if you were much smarter?
20. When did you first realize you were smart/bright/brilliant?

INTELLECTUAL HORSEPOWER

21. Where did you learn that way of approaching problems?
22. Why did you choose that approach?
23. Why do you think that didn't work?
24. Why do you think that worked?
25. Why do you think you have difficulties with that sometimes?

E. Themes/Things to Look for:

Abstract concept capacity
Adjusts to your style and pace in the interview
Broad sourcing
Catches on to humor quickly
Cognitive curiosity
Comfort with abstraction or complexity
Concepts vs. facts
Crunches large data bases of facts/numbers/concepts at once
Doesn't overvalue the importance of intelligence–doesn't see it as equalling performance
Draws parallels
Four-deep answers when peeling the onion
Interest in how things work behind the screen/behind the curtain
Looks under rocks
Makes connections
Many only partially related principles/rules of thumb/insights
Metaphors/analogies
More than one area
Pushes back at you intellectually in the interview
Quick on the uptake
Social intelligence
Spatial intelligence
Switches gears rapidly and comfortably
Technical depth
Unusual sourcing
Verbal intelligence/agility
Works through a new concept
You learn a lot from the interview about what the person knows

F. Most Likely Résumé:

1. Look for jobs like:

Fix-Its/Turnarounds
Heavy Strategic Demands
Scope Assignments
Staff Leadership (Influencing Without Authority)
Start-Ups

INTELLECTUAL HORSEPOWER

2. Look for develop-in-place assignments like:

Do a competitive analysis of your organization's products or services or your position in the marketplace and present it to the people involved.

Train and work as an assessor in an assessment center.

Relaunch an existing product or service that's not doing well.

Teach a course, seminar, or workshop on something you don't know well.

Teach/coach someone how to do something you are not an expert in.

Manage an ad hoc, temporary group of people where the people in the group are towering experts but the temporary manager is not.

Assemble an ad hoc team of diverse people to accomplish a difficult task.

Manage a group through a significant business crisis.

Take on a tough and undoable project, one where others who have tried it have failed.

Do a postmortem on a failed project, and present it to the people involved.

Audit cost overruns to assess the problem, and present your findings to the person or people involved.

Work on a crisis management team.

3. Best references to ask about or check:

Direct Boss

Boss' Boss

Development Professionals

Human Resource Professionals

Natural Mentors

G. Learning Agility Evaluation:

1. What/Describing vs. Why/Explain
2. All or Nothing vs. Can See Many Sides
3. Ordinary/Socially Acceptable vs. Insightful/Different
7. Passive vs. Intrigued/Curious
9. Vague/General vs. Sharp/Specific
13. Simple Views vs. Complex Views
15. Linear vs. Use Contrasts/Analogies
16. Few Rules of Thumb vs. Many and Varied Rules of Thumb
18. Stays Close to Home vs. Lots of Curiosity

H. The LEADERSHIP ARCHITECT® Sort Card Connections:

1. Good (positive) if combined with high:

Bright but still approachable 3, 7, 10

Has breadth 5, 40, 46, 58

In service of a grander purpose 15, 46, 65

Passes it on to others; teaches others 18, 19, 44

Technically deep 24, 61

Articulate 27, 49, 67

Sensitive to others; doesn't overwhelm them 31, 64

Can solve tough problems 32, 51

Easily accessible 33, 41

Can see the future 46, 58, 65

Orderly 47, 50

Can set agenda and use intellect to get things done (doesn't just dispense wisdom) 50, 51, 53

INTELLECTUAL HORSEPOWER

2. **Bad (negative) if combined with low or high (+):**

   Too fast for most (+1, 16) 41
   Just thinking, no action 1, 53
   Loner; individual contributor (+57) 3, 31, 42, 60
   Limited to narrow technology 5 (+24, 61) 46
   Insensitive to others 3, 7, 10, 33
   Not enough life tapes to come to correct decisions 17, 51
   Overmanages 18
   Stuck in the past 32, 61
   Limited to things and concepts 33, 56, 64
   Disorganized thinking/wasted effort 47, 50, 62
   Doesn't understand why others can't keep up 55
   Machine; never sleeps 66

3. **Too much can contribute to the following Stallers and Stoppers:**

   A. What too much looks like (overused):

   May use intelligence to dominate and intimidate others; may not be able to relate to those less intelligent; may only accept own solutions; may be impatient with due process.

   B. Too much might lead to these Stallers and Stoppers:

   Arrogant (104)   Failure to Build a Team (110)
   Blocked Personal Learner (106)   Overdependence on a Single Skill (116)
   Defensiveness (108)

   C. Compensators:

   How to compensate for too much of this competency:
   3, 4, 7, 10, 15, 18, 19, 26, 31, 33, 36, 41, 42, 44

   D. Things to watch for:

   Can't relate to those less skilled   Skips steps others need to know to understand
   Chills input from others   Too fast
   Could not assemble a jury of their peers   Unrealistic expectation for others
   Intelligence as a weapon   Impractical
   My way or the wrong way   Thinks too much, acts too little

4. **Too little can contribute to the following Stallers and Stoppers:**

   A. What too little looks like (unskilled):

   May be intellectually lazy or disorganized; may not think things through carefully; always wants everything to be simple; emotions may get in the way of careful consideration; impatience may get in the way of careful consideration; may be mentally inflexible or stale–believing that their way is the best and virtually only way to do things or solve problems; may get frustrated when others are talking conceptually; may be slow to catch on to things.

INTELLECTUAL HORSEPOWER

B. Too little might lead to these Stallers and Stoppers:
Lack of Composure (107)

Non-Strategic (114)

C. Compensators:
How to substitute for too little of this competency:

1, 5, 14, 17, 24, 32, 33, 46, 51, 58, 61

I. LEARNING ARCHITECT® Connections:

Look for people who act like and/or show evidence of:

2a. Problem Solving

10. Complexity

27. Conceptualizer

28. Creator

J. CHOICES ARCHITECT® Connections:

Look for people who act like and/or show evidence of:

First Edition (Released 1994)

2. Essence

5. Connector

Second Edition (Released 2000)

1. Broad Scanner

3. Connector

6. Essence

K. Difficulty to Develop:
22 (of 34)–Easier

31. INTERPERSONAL SAVVY

A. Definition:

Relates well to all kinds of people, up, down, and sideways, inside and outside the organization; builds appropriate rapport; builds constructive and effective relationships; uses diplomacy and tact; can diffuse even high-tension situations comfortably.

B. Arenas/Domains to Explore:

1. Across different groups
2. Coaching
3. Conferences/meetings/workshops
4. Conflict/tension/stress events
5. Customer service jobs
6. Delivering bad news
7. During tough Q & A
8. Early service jobs
9. First three minutes of the interview
10. Foreign visitors
11. Formal parties
12. Friend network
13. Handicapped
14. Inside/outside relationships
15. Marketing calls
16. Meeting facilitation
17. Meeting people for the first-time
18. Negotiating disagreements
19. New people to the group
20. Non-native tongue speakers
21. On stage
22. Sales calls
23. Social networks
24. Style across various levels/settings
25. Teaching
26. Team captain
27. Unfamiliar social settings
28. Visiting VIPs
29. Volunteer work
30. With people they don't like
31. With people they don't trust
32. With people they are trying to get rid of/away from
33. With customers
34. Work and non-work relationships

C. Sample Questions:

Dimension 1: Been there, done that–has had direct personal experience(s) involving the competency–candidate was the prime player   Note: * means OK for campus

1. Has anyone ever accused you of messing something up because of poor interpersonal skills?
2. Has having a relationship ever gotten you out of a bad situation?*
3. Has using your interpersonal skills to get out of a problem ever backfired and gotten you in trouble?*
4. Have you ever brought two people together who were having problems with each other?*
5. Have you ever coached a children's team with parents on the sidelines?*
6. Have you ever gotten out of a tough problem with your charm?*
7. Have you ever had to negotiate with people you didn't like or didn't trust?*
8. Have you ever made peace with an enemy?*
9. Have you ever managed anything where the people or units reporting to you were in different locations? How did you form interpersonal relationships at a distance?
10. Have you ever talked your way out of a traffic ticket?*
11. How close do you get to customers?
12. How close do you get to your direct reports?
13. How do you deal with people you don't like?*

INTERPERSONAL SAVVY

14. How do you get out of situations you don't want to be in anymore?*
15. How do you get to know new coworkers (students, classmates)?*
16. How do you prepare when you know ahead of time you are probably going to have trouble with a person?*
17. How good are you at entertaining visiting VIPs?
18. How much do you use humor to make contact and build relationships?*
19. How much of a network outside your work group have you built?
20. How well do you know people above your boss in the organization?
21. In one-to-one meetings, how often do you talk first?*
22. Tell me about a time when you built strong relationships where none previously existed.*
23. Tell me about a time when you changed your interpersonal style midstream because something wasn't working?*
24. Tell me about a time when you had to communicate something important to someone who did not speak your language very well.
25. Tell me about a time when you handled a community service project.*
26. Tell me about a time when you handled a crisis.*
27. Tell me about a time when you handled a dispute with a customer.
28. Tell me about a time when you handled a tough negotiation.
29. Tell me about a time when you handled an arrogant person or one who made you angry.*
30. Tell me about a time your interpersonal skills were put to the toughest test.*
31. What do you do when you feel the sale slipping away from you?
32. What do you normally do with new people in an unfamiliar setting or gathering?*
33. What kind of a network do you have laterally in the organization?
34. When new people are introduced into your group, are you the first or last to make contact?*
35. When you travel on business, do you call friends and acquaintances to go out to dinner or meet after you're done working?

Dimension 2: Seen/been around others who were involved with the competency–good and bad; learns from others about self

36. Contrast the most and least interpersonally skilled people you know.*
37. Has interpersonal skills ever been in any 360° survey done on you? Was your score among your highest, middle, or lowest?
38. Has poor interpersonal skills on someone else's part ever created an obstacle for you or got in the way of something you were trying to accomplish?*
39. Have you ever talked with a coach or mentor about your interpersonal skills?
40. Have you ever watched someone fail /get fired because they lacked interpersonal skills?*
41. Have you ever watched someone overuse their interpersonal skills to the point that it backfired?
42. Have you ever watched someone succeed because they had excellent interpersonal skills?*
43. Have you ever worked with a coach on your interpersonal skills?*
44. Have you ever worked with a person who excelled at interpersonal skills?
45. Have you ever worked with a skills coach on improving your interpersonal skills?*
46. How do you get feedback about your interpersonal skills?
47. How often do you check with multiple sources when you get a piece of critical feedback on your interpersonal skills?
48. Is there a historical figure you consider a model of interpersonal skills?
49. What do others who are not your fans say about your interpersonal skills?

INTERPERSONAL SAVVY

50. What do others who like you say about your interpersonal skills?
51. Which boss was the best at interpersonal skills?
52. Which boss was the worst at interpersonal skills?
53. Which direct report was the best at interpersonal skills?
54. Which direct report was the worst at interpersonal skills?
55. Which peer was the best at interpersonal skills?
56. Which peer was the worst at interpersonal skills?
57. Who in your field or business has the best interpersonal skills?
58. Who do you consider a role model of effective interpersonal savvy?*
59. Who do you go to for advice on interpersonal skills?
60. Who have you learned the most from about interpersonal skills?*
61. Who is a higher-management role model for you on effective interpersonal skills?
62. Who is a role model of effective interpersonal skills outside of work?

Dimension 3: Knows how the competency works in theory; shows understanding

63. Are there situations or settings where someone should use interpersonal skills differently?
64. Do you think interpersonal skills can be learned? If so, how do you think people develop interpersonal skills?
65. Do you think there is a way to compensate or work around low interpersonal skills?
66. Has anyone asked you for your opinions/advice on interpersonal skills?*
67. Have you ever attended a course on interpersonal skills?
68. Have you ever been in a situation where you and others put interpersonal skills on a success profile?
69. Have you ever been part of an effort to create a policy or a mission statement containing reference to the importance of being interpersonally skilled?
70. Have you ever been someone's coach or mentor who had problems with interpersonal skills?
71. Have you ever created a development plan for someone on interpersonal skills?
72. Have you ever criticized someone for not being interpersonally skilled?
73. Have you ever designed a program on interpersonal skills?
74. Have you ever given a speech on interpersonal skills?
75. Have you ever rewarded or recognized someone for having interpersonal skills?
76. Have you ever taught a course on interpersonal skills?
77. Have you ever tried to help someone deal more effectively with interpersonal skills?*
78. Have you ever tried to help someone improve their interpersonal savvy?
79. How do you think people develop interpersonal skills?
80. How much of success do you think is due to interpersonal skills compared with other characteristics?
81. How would you know if someone lacks interpersonal skills?
82. How would you know if someone has good interpersonal skills?
83. If you had to write a book on interpersonal skills, what would the chapter headings be?
84. What are the benefits to someone who is interpersonally skilled?
85. What are the consequences to someone who is not interpersonally skilled?
86. What do you think the performance standard is on interpersonal skills for someone in your role?
87. What happens when two people try to work together who have very different interpersonal skills?
88. What wisdom would you pass on to others trying to develop interpersonal skills?
89. When you select others, what do you look for in interpersonal skills?
90. Why do you think people end up having different levels of interpersonal skills?

INTERPERSONAL SAVVY

Dimension 4: Shows personal change and sense-making; learned it one place and applied it in another; can compare and contrast experiences; changes viewpoints across time; can explain personal development or evolution related to the competency

91. Compare and contrast examples of times you've been effective and ineffective at using interpersonal skills.
92. Contrast your on- and off-the-job use of interpersonal skills.
93. Did you ever pass up a job or assignment because you were not confident enough in your interpersonal skills?
94. Do you ever use other skills to cover for your lack of interpersonal skills?
95. Has becoming better at interpersonal skills ever helped you in other areas?
96. Has your interpersonal savvy always been this way?
97. Have interpersonal skills ever figured in a failure, struggle, or setback you have had?
98. Have poor interpersonal skills ever been the subject of a development plan for you?
99. Have you ever delegated or assigned someone a task because you didn't have adequate interpersonal skills?
100. Have you ever made significant strides at becoming better at interpersonal skills?
101. Have your interpersonal skills, good or bad, ever been the subject of your performance review or a career discussion?
102. How different are you across situations in your interpersonal skills?
103. How do you decide how much interpersonal savvy to use?
104. How much of your success is due to your interpersonal skills?
105. How transferable are your interpersonal skills across situations?
106. If you had to become better at interpersonal skills in a hurry, what would you do?
107. Was there a time when you were not as good at interpersonal skills?
108. What caused you to work to improve your interpersonal skills?
109. What event or series of events had the most impact on your interpersonal skills?
110. What's the most varied you can be with your interpersonal skills?
111. What was the shortest amount of time in which you increased your level of interpersonal skills?
112. When did you first realize the level of your interpersonal skills?
113. When you know ahead of time that your usual level of interpersonal skills won't work, what do you do?
114. Why do you think you demonstrate interpersonal skills the way you do?
115. Why do you think your interpersonal skills are the way they are?*
116. Does your interpersonal style differ depending upon who you're with?*
117. How much of your interpersonal skills is real and how much is practiced and rehearsed?*
118. Are there situations where you are more or less interpersonally comfortable?*

D. Follow-up Probes:

1. Are there times when you don't interact with people like that?
2. Could you contrast those two people for me?
3. Could you give me a few examples of how you've used or applied that?
4. Did you or the other person blink first?
5. Do you act that way with everyone, just one, or a few?
6. Do you always interact that way or was that a special situation?
7. Do you ever turn off your interpersonal skills and just hibernate?
8. Do you think it was right/fair for you to act that way?
9. Do you think this is teachable?

INTERPERSONAL SAVVY

10. Do you think you're better at interpersonal skills than most? Why?
11. Do you think you would perform any differently if you had better interpersonal skills?
12. Have you always interacted that way or is this a recent development in you?
13. Have you ever had to form a relationship with someone you really disliked to get your job done?
14. How certain were you that you were right when you made that decision on how to (how not to) deal with a person?
15. How did the others react when you did that?
16. How did you come up with that approach to dealing with people in the first place?
17. How did you know that interpersonal style would work?
18. How do others you have known approach that?
19. How important was it for you to interact with your direct reports that way?
20. How typical is this for you?
21. How would you approach that same situation today?
22. Is this natural for you, or do you really have to dig for it?
23. Were there some alternatives you rejected? Were you right?
24. What did you do after you got that feedback?
25. What did you do to adapt to that?
26. Why did you do it that way?
27. Why did you time your attempt like you did?
28. Why do you suppose organizations work that way?
29. Why do you think that didn't work?
30. Why do you think that happened that way?
31. Why do you think that worked?
32. Why do you think you have difficulties with that sometimes?
33. Why do you think you prefer to act that way?
34. Would you have done it that way with looser deadlines?
35. Would you have done it that way with tighter deadlines?

E. Themes/Things to Look for:

Ability to anticipate what others will do	Made you feel comfortable
Ability to defuse	Makes others feel at ease
Attracts others easily	Observes/studies people
Awareness of impact	One size doesn't fit all
Balances personal with organization needs	Orchestrating the engagement
Complex and varied tactics for relationship building	Personal packaging
Complex view of people differences	Rehearsed vs. natural
Contours to the situation	Satisfying personal needs vs. in the service of others
Differentiation/doesn't generalize a lot	Selective interpersonal savvy–good with some, not with others
Drivers–why they use the skills	Selling skills
Empathy	Tap dancing out of a problem
Finding common ground	Tension relief skills; humor
Keeping personal feelings out of the situation	Values being with people
Letting others save face	Values learning from others
Listening for cues	Works from the outside in

INTERPERSONAL SAVVY

F. Most Likely Résumé:

1. Look for jobs like:
Cross-Moves
Fix-Its/Turnarounds
International Assignments
Line to Staff Switches
Member of Projects/Task Forces
Scale Assignments
Start-Ups

2. Look for develop-in-place assignments like:

Integrate diverse systems, processes, or procedures across decentralized and/or dispersed units.

Be a change agent; create a symbol for change; lead the rallying cry; champion a significant change and implementation.

Manage an ad hoc, temporary group of "green," inexperienced people as their coach, teacher, orienter, etc.

Manage an ad hoc, temporary group of low-competence people through a task they couldn't do by themselves.

Manage an ad hoc, temporary group including former peers to accomplish a task.

Manage an ad hoc, temporary group of people who are older and/or more experienced to accomplish a task.

Manage an ad hoc, temporary group of people where the temporary manager is a towering expert and the people in the group are not.

Manage an ad hoc, temporary group of people where the people in the group are towering experts but the temporary manager is not.

Help shut down a plant, regional office, product line, business, operation, etc.

Manage a dissatisfied internal or external customer; troubleshoot a performance or quality problem with a product or service.

Manage the assigning/allocating of office space in a contested situation.

Take on a tough and undoable project, one where others who have tried it have failed.

Manage the outplacement of a group of people.

Resolve an issue in conflict between two people, units, geographies, functions, etc.

Make peace with an enemy or someone you've disappointed with a product or service or someone you've had some trouble with or don't get along well with.

Manage a project team of people who are older and more experienced.

3. Best references to ask about or check:
Human Resource Professionals
Natural Mentors
Off-Work Associates
Past Associates/Constituencies
Peers and Colleagues
Spouse

G. Learning Agility Evaluation:
4. Spectator/Passive vs. Player/Participant
5. Tight/Rigid vs. Loose/Flexible
6. Reacting/Responsive vs. Adapting
10. Reactive vs. Initiating
11. Generalizations vs. Specific Learnings
13. Simple Views vs. Complex Views
15. Linear vs. Use Contrasts/Analogies
16. Few Rules of Thumb vs. Many and Varied Rules of Thumb
21. View from Self vs. View from Point of View of Others

INTERPERSONAL SAVVY

H. The LEADERSHIP ARCHITECT® Sort Card Connections:

1. Good (positive) if combined with high:
Attracts others 3, 33, 41
Does well with higher-ups 8, 48
Helps outsiders gain entry 10, 21
Can maneuver 12, 37
Softens the blow 13, 34
Effective at selling 15, 36, 49, 53
Engaging 26
Balances personal and organizational goals 40, 58, 65
Facilitates well; gets lateral cooperation 42, 60
Adjusts to the audience 56, 64

2. Bad (negative) if combined with low or high (+):
May freeze facing tough decisions/actions 1, 9, 34, 57
Too soft; need to be liked (+3, 7, 10, 23)
Lacks substance 5, 24, 58
Can't be effective with enemies 10, 12, 40
Can't get the product out 12, 20, 35, 53
Slimy 22, 29, 33
Doesn't adjust for the audience 32, 56, 64
Wanders into dangerous waters 38, 48
Doesn't organize people's efforts 38, 50, 60
Spends too much time relating 50, 62
Can't use skills as a tool 55
Political animal (+4, 6, 8, 48)

3. Too much can contribute to the following Stallers and Stoppers:

A. What too much looks like (overused):
May be able to get by with just smooth interpersonal skills; may spend too much time building networks and glad-handing; may not be taken as substantive by some; may not be a credible take-charge leader when that's necessary; may have some trouble and freeze when facing serious conflict.

B. Too much might lead to these Stallers and Stoppers:
Betrayal of Trust (105)
Overdependence on a Single Skill (116)

C. Compensators:
How to compensate for too much of this competency:
1, 5, 9, 12, 13, 20, 24, 34, 36, 50, 51, 52, 57, 62, 65

INTERPERSONAL SAVVY

D. Things to watch for:
Can't pull off being tough
Can't say no
May attract too many time-wasting transactions
May try to cover for other deficits rather than working on them
Overconfidence in interpersonal skills
Skills hide underlying problem dealing with conflict
Strong need to be liked
Low substance
Seen as a politician
Seen as a ladder-climber

4. Too little can contribute to the following Stallers and Stoppers:

A. What too little looks like (unskilled):
Doesn't relate smoothly to a variety of people; may not build relationships easily–may lack approachability or good listening skills; doesn't take the time to build rapport; may be too raw and direct at times; may be excessively work oriented or intense; may be impatient to get on with the agenda; judgmental or arrogant toward others; may not read others well; may freeze or panic in the face of conflict, attack, or criticism; may be shy or lack confidence around others.

B. Too little might lead to these Stallers and Stoppers:
Arrogant (104)
Failure to Build a Team (110)
Failure to Staff Effectively (111)
Insensitive to Others (112)
Political Missteps (119)

C. Compensators:
How to substitute for too little of this competency:
1, 3, 7, 10, 12, 15, 21, 27, 33, 37, 39, 41, 42, 49, 60

I. LEARNING ARCHITECT® Connections:

Look for people who act like and/or show evidence of:

1c. Following a Plan
2a. Problem Solving
2c. Intuition
3a. Checking Feelings
3b. Self-Talk
4a. Getting Information
4c. Actively Involve
9. Multiple Sources
16. Collaborate
23. Orchestrator

J. CHOICES ARCHITECT® Connections:

Look for people who act like and/or show evidence of:

First Edition (Released 1994)
14. Transaction Quality

Second Edition (Released 2000)
13. Light Touch
15. People-Smart

K. Difficulty to Develop:
24 (of 34)–Moderate

32. LEARNING ON THE FLY

A. Definition:

Learns quickly when facing new problems; a relentless and versatile learner; open to change; analyzes both successes and failures for clues to improvement; experiments and will try anything to find solutions; enjoys the challenge of unfamiliar tasks; quickly grasps the essence and the underlying structure of anything.

B. Arenas/Domains to Explore:

1. A lot going on at once
2. Academic record
3. Any new or unfamiliar exposure
4. Can program their VCR
5. Computer literary
6. Exposure outside their home area
7. First exposure to new culture
8. First to break through
9. Foreign travel experiences
10. Hobbies
11. How quick do they understand your interview questions
12. New countries
13. New industries
14. New people
15. New problems
16. New sport
17. New strategies
18. New technical system
19. On their feet thinking
20. Picks up on jokes quickly
21. Quick on the uptake
22. Short time to explain a complex thing
23. Starting a new job
24. Starting a new major
25. Studying a problem for the first-time
26. Sudden changes
27. Tough Q & A
28. Transitions

C. Sample Questions:

Dimension 1: Been there, done that–has had direct personal experience(s) involving the competency–candidate was the prime player   Note: * means OK for campus

1. Do you have any interest in mental puzzles/crossword puzzles?*
2. Has anyone ever accused you of messing something up because of not picking up on things quickly enough?
3. Have you ever managed anything where the people or units reporting to you were in different locations? How did you quickly learn what they were doing?
4. Have you ever tried to learn a foreign language?*
5. How easy is it for you to get to the essence of an issue?*
6. How important is it to you to finish what you start?*
7. In terms of catching on to a complex presentation, where are you generally in the order of getting it? First? Last? Middle?*
8. Tell me about a time when a change/crisis made what you had been doing irrelevant.*
9. Tell me about a time when you changed jobs to a new area.
10. Tell me about a time when you didn't know what to do at work.*
11. Tell me about a time when you had a problem relationship that couldn't be worked out and one that could.*
12. Tell me about a time when you had to learn a new technical area quickly.*
13. Tell me about a time when you inherited a new boss (teacher, advisor) or work group and weren't sure what to do.*
14. Tell me about a time when you moved to a different physical environment.*

LEARNING ON THE FLY

15. Tell me about a time when you took a risk (career/investment/ strategy/process).*
16. Tell me about a time when you were alone and stranded without a solution and had to make things up as you went.*
17. Tell me about a time when learning quickly got you into trouble.
18. Tell me about a time when learning quickly went really well for you.
19. Tell me about your last three successful projects.*
20. What do you do when everybody else seems to have caught on to something and you haven't?*
21. What do you do when you have caught on to something and nobody else has?*
22. What happens to your efficiency when you are working against tight time lines?*
23. What happens to your efficiency when you have a lot of balls in the air at once?*
24. What's the quickest and the toughest mental transition you have ever had to make?*
25. What's your tolerance for routine and task repetition?*

Dimension 2: Seen/been around others who were involved with the competency–good and bad; learns from others about self

26. Contrast the most and least learning agile or quick learning people you know.*
27. Has learning on the fly or being a quick study ever been in any 360° survey done on you? Was your score among your highest, middle, or lowest?
28. Has someone else's inability to learn things quickly ever created an obstacle for you or got in the way of something you were trying to accomplish?*
29. Have you ever talked with a coach or mentor about learning on the fly or being a quick study?
30. Have you ever watched someone fail/get fired because they did not learn new things quickly enough?*
31. Have you ever watched someone exaggerate learning on the fly or being a quick study to the point that it backfired?
32. Have you ever watched someone succeed because they were able to learn new things quickly?*
33. Have you ever worked with a coach on learning on the fly or being a quick study?*
34. Have you ever worked with a person who excelled at learning on the fly or being a quick study?
35. Have you ever worked with a skills coach on being more learning agile or a quicker learner?*
36. How do you get feedback about yourself on your ability to learn on the fly?
37. How often do you check with multiple sources when you get a piece of critical feedback on your ability to learn things quickly?
38. Is there a historical figure you consider a model of learning on the fly or being a quick study?
39. What do others who are not your fans say about your ability to learn on the fly?
40. What do others who like you say about your ability to learn on the fly?
41. Which boss was the best at learning on the fly?
42. Which boss was the worst at learning on the fly?
43. Which direct report was the best at learning on the fly?
44. Which direct report was the worst at learning on the fly?
45. Which peer was the best at learning on the fly?
46. Which peer was the worst at learning on the fly?
47. Who in your field or business is the quickest learner?
48. Who do you consider a role model of learning on the fly?*
49. Who do you go to for advice on learning on the fly or being a quick study?
50. Who have you learned the most from about learning on the fly?*
51. Who is a higher-management role model for you on learning on the fly?
52. Who is a role model of learning on the fly outside of work?

LEARNING ON THE FLY

Dimension 3: Knows how the competency works in theory; shows understanding

53. Are there situations or settings where someone should be different in the way they demonstrate an ability to learn quickly?
54. Do you think being a quick study can be learned? If so, how do you think people develop these skills?
55. Do you think there is a way to compensate or work around low the ability to learn quickly?
56. Has anyone asked you for your opinions/advice on learning quickly?*
57. Have you ever attended a course on learning quickly?
58. Have you ever been in a situation where you and others put learning on the fly on a success profile?
59. Have you ever been part of an effort to create a policy or a mission statement containing reference to being a quick study?
60. Have you ever been someone's coach or mentor who had problems with learning quickly?
61. Have you ever created a development plan for someone on learning quickly?
62. Have you ever criticized someone for not learning quickly?
63. Have you ever designed a program on ways to improve learning speed?
64. Have you ever given a speech on learning on the fly?
65. Have you ever rewarded or recognized someone for being a quick study?
66. Have you ever taught a course on learning on the fly?
67. Have you ever tried to help someone deal more effectively with learning on the fly?*
68. Have you ever tried to help someone improve their learning speed?
69. How do you think people develop the skill to learn quickly?
70. How much of success do you think is due to learning on the fly compared with other characteristics?
71. How would you know if someone learns quickly?
72. How would you know if someone doesn't learn quickly?
73. If you had to write a book on learning on the fly, what would the chapter headings be?
74. What are the benefits to someone who is really good at learning quickly?
75. What are the consequences to someone who is really poor at learning quickly?
76. What do you think the performance standard is on learning speed for someone in your role?
77. What happens when two people try to work together who are very different in their learning speeds?
78. What wisdom would you pass on to others trying to become better at learning on the fly?
79. When you select others, what do you look for in ability to learn quickly?
80. Why do you think people end up being different on how fast they learn?

Dimension 4: Shows personal change and sense-making; learned it one place and applied it in another; can compare and contrast experiences; changes viewpoints across time; can explain personal development or evolution related to the competency

81. Compare and contrast examples of when you've been effective and ineffective at learning new things quickly.
82. Contrast your on- and off-the-job use of learning on the fly or being a quick study.
83. Did you ever pass up a job or assignment because you were not confident enough in your ability to learn new things quickly?
84. Do you ever use other skills to cover for your lack of learning new things quickly?
85. Has becoming better at learning new things quickly ever helped you in other areas?
86. Has not learning things quickly enough ever figured in a failure, struggle, or setback you have had?
87. Has poor learning on the fly ever been the subject of a development plan for you?
88. Has your ability to learn new things quickly always been this way?
89. Have you ever delegated or assigned someone a task because you didn't learn new things quickly enough?
90. Have you ever made significant strides at becoming better at learning new things quickly?

LEARNING ON THE FLY

91. Has your skill at learning new things quickly, good or bad, ever been the subject of your performance review or a career discussion?
92. How different are you across situations in your ability to learn new things quickly?
93. How much of your success is due to your ability to learn new things quickly?
94. How transferable are your learning agility skills to other situations?
95. If you had to become better at learning agility in a hurry, what would you do?
96. Was there a time when you were not as good at learning on the fly?
97. What caused you to work to improve your skills at learning new things quickly?
98. What event or series of events had the most impact on your ability to learn quickly?
99. What's the most varied you can be in your ability to learn quickly?
100. What was the shortest amount of time in which you increased your level of skill at learning something new?
101. When did you first realize your level of skill at learning quickly?
102. When you know ahead of time that your usual level of learning new things isn't fast enough, what do you do?
103. Why do you think you learn quickly the way you do?
104. Why do you think your learning agility is the way it is?*
105. What's your risk boundary? What won't you try?
106. How many failures will stop you from trying any more?*
107. Do you ever get an unstoppable obsession to learn something and you don't stop until you do it?*

D. Follow-up Probes:

1. Are there times when you pick up on things quickly and times when you don't?
2. Could you give me a few examples of how you've used or applied that?
3. Did you get bored with it after you solved it?
4. Do you always learn that quickly or was that a special situation?
5. Do you ever turn off your quick study skills and just hibernate?
6. Do you suppose if others would just try harder, they could learn faster?
7. Do you think that's teachable?
8. Do you think you're better at learning things quickly than most? Why?
9. Do you think you would perform any differently if you could pick up on things more quickly?
10. Have you always learned that way or is this a recent development in you?
11. How did the others react when you did that?
12. How did you come up with that approach to learning quickly in the first place?
13. How did you know that method of quick learning would work?
14. How did you react when you began to understand how fast you learned things compared to others?
15. How do others you have known approach that?
16. How do you feel when others have caught on and you haven't?
17. How do you feel when you get it before others do?
18. How typical is this for you?
19. How would you approach that same situation today?
20. Is this natural for you, or do you really have to dig for it?
21. Was there a time when you didn't understand this about yourself?
22. What did you do after you got that feedback?
23. What did you do to adapt to that?
24. Why did you do it that way?

LEARNING ON THE FLY

25. Why do you suppose organizations work that way?
26. Why do you think that didn't work?
27. Why do you think that happened that way?
28. Why do you think that worked?
29. Why do you think you have difficulty with that sometimes?
30. Why do you think you prefer to learn that way?
31. Would you have done it that way with looser deadlines?
32. Would you have done it that way with tighter deadlines?

E. Themes/Things to Look for:

Adjusts to your style and speed in the interview
Analyzing successes and failures
Broad perspective
Can simplify
Catches on first
Cognitive flexibility
Cognitive speed
Comfort with abstractions
Comparisons and contrasts
Each answer leads to a question
Enjoys the thrill of the intellectual hunt
Experimental
Finds parallels
Gets to the essence/root quickly

Intellectual openness; listens to anything for awhile
Likes new challenges
Looks under rocks
Makes connections
Metaphors/analogies
No path not worth running down for awhile
Not stopped by dead ends
Really bothered by not knowing something
Runs scenarios
Switches gears rapidly and comfortably
Takes intellectual risks
Taught you some things in the interview
Thinks in transitional terms

F. Most Likely Résumé:

1. Look for jobs like:

Chair of Projects/Task Forces
Cross-Moves
Fix-Its/Turnarounds
Heavy Strategic Demands
International Assignments
Line to Staff Switches

Member of Projects/Task Forces
Scope (complexity) Assignments
Staff Leadership (Influencing Without Authority)
Staff to Line Shifts
Start-Ups

2. Look for develop-in-place assignments like:

Plan a new site for a building (plant, field office, headquarters, etc.).
Plan an off-site meeting, conference, convention, trade show, event, etc.
Work short rotations in other units, functions, or geographies you've not been exposed to before.
Study and summarize a new trend, product, service, technique, or process and present and sell it to others.
Benchmark innovative practices, processes, products, or services of competitors, vendors, suppliers, or customers, and present a report to others to create recommendations for change.
Work on a project that involves travel and study of an issue, acquisition, or joint venture off-shore or overseas, with a report back to management.
Manage a project team made up of nationals from a number of countries.

LEARNING ON THE FLY

Relaunch an existing product or service that's not doing well.
Teach a course, seminar, or workshop on something you don't know well.
Teach/coach someone how to do something you are not an expert in.
Design a training course in an area you're not an expert in.
Manage an ad hoc, temporary group of "green," inexperienced people as their coach, teacher, orienter, etc.
Manage an ad hoc, temporary group of people where the people in the group are towering experts but the temporary manager is not.
Manage an ad hoc, temporary group of people involved in tackling a fix-it or turnaround project.
Manage an ad hoc, temporary group of people in a rapidly expanding operation.
Assemble an ad hoc team of diverse people to accomplish a difficult task.
Volunteer to fill an open management job temporarily until it's filled.
Handle a tough negotiation with an internal or external client or customer.
Help shut down a plant, regional office, product line, business, operation, etc.
Work on a team that's deciding who to keep and who to let go in a layoff, shutdown, delayering, or divestiture.
Manage a group through a significant business crisis.
Take on a tough and undoable project, one where others who have tried it have failed.
Take on a task you dislike or hate to do.
Resolve an issue in conflict between two people, units, geographies, functions, etc.
Do a postmortem on a failed project, and present it to the people involved.
Be a member of a union-negotiating or grievance-handling team.

3. Best references to ask about or check:

Direct Boss

Natural Mentors

G. Learning Agility Evaluation:

1. What/Describing vs. Why/Explain
2. All or Nothing vs. Can See Many Sides
3. Ordinary/Socially Acceptable vs. Insightful/Different
6. Reacting/Responsive vs. Adapting
7. Passive vs. Intrigued/Curious
9. Vague/General vs. Sharp/Specific
11. Generalizations vs. Specific Learnings
13. Simple Views vs. Complex Views
14. Sameness vs. Broad Ranging
15. Linear vs. Use Contrasts/Analogies
16. Few Rules of Thumb vs. Many and Varied Rules of Thumb
22. Focus on Accomplishments vs. Focus on Solving Problems

H. The LEADERSHIP ARCHITECT® Sort Card Connections:

1. Good (positive) if combined with high:

Blazing 1, 16
Comfortable with chaos 2, 14
First to spot trends 5, 15, 46, 58
Quick with a retort 26
Formidable problem solver 30, 51, 61

LEARNING ON THE FLY

Good on their feet 31, 49
Reacts to feedback 33, 45
Reads and pushes hot buttons 36, 56
Maze bright 39, 48
Quick to spot opportunities for improvement 51, 63
Reads people quickly 56, 64

2. Bad (negative) if combined with low or high (+):
May jump to conclusions; leave others behind (+1, 16) 33, 41
In service of what 5, 15, 53
Not technically deep; not much content 5, 24, 61
Does too much themselves 18, 20
Doesn't pass it on to others 19
Can't explain themselves 27, 33, 49
May be disorganized 35, 39, 47
Gets into trouble wandering into other people's territory 39, 48
No process 47, 50, 52
Blind spot with people 56, 64

3. Too much can contribute to the following Stallers and Stoppers:

A. What too much looks like (overused):

May leave others behind; may frustrate others with his/her need for change; may tend to change things too often; people may interpret openness as indecisiveness or being wishy-washy; may seek out change for change's sake regardless of the situation; may not be good at routine administration or unchallenging tasks or jobs.

B. Too much might lead to these Stallers and Stoppers:

Unable to Adapt to Differences (101)

C. Compensators:

How to compensate for too much of this competency:
27, 33, 39, 41, 43, 47, 52, 59

D. Things to watch for:

Change for change's sake	Needs an external challenge to stay alert
Impractical	Short attention span
Insensitive to the intellectual speed of others	Takes people down unproductive paths
Makes others uncomfortable	Unnecessarily rejects the old/current

4. Too little can contribute to the following Stallers and Stoppers:

A. What too little looks like (unskilled):

Not agile or versatile in learning to deal with first time or unusual problems; may not analyze problems carefully or search for multiple clues and parallels; may be afraid to take a chance on the unknown; learns new things slowly; may be stuck in historical, tried and true methods, uncomfortable with ambiguity and quick to jump to a solution; doesn't look under rocks, just sticks to the obvious; looks for the simplest explanation too soon; gives up too soon and accepts a marginal solution; functions on the surface, doesn't go deep.

LEARNING ON THE FLY

B. Too little might lead to these Stallers and Stoppers:

Unable to Adapt to Differences (101)
Arrogant (104)
Blocked Personal Learner (106)
Failure to Staff Effectively (111)
Key Skill Deficiencies (113)
Non-Strategic (114)
Political Missteps (119)

C. Compensators:

How to substitute for too little of this competency:
1, 2, 5, 14, 16, 24, 28, 30, 33, 45, 46, 50, 51, 61

I. LEARNING ARCHITECT® Connections:

Look for people who act like and/or show evidence of:

1b. Trial and Error
2a. Problem Solving
2c. Intuition
3c. Personal Experience
5. New
7. Risks
8. Initiate
9. Multiple Sources
10. Complexity
11. Why/How
22. Experimenter
25. Personal Change
26. Self-Aware
27. Conceptualizer
28. Creator
29. Essence
30. Mastery
31. Rationality
32. Diversity in Others
33. Diversity of Sources
34. Sizing Up Others
35. Breadth
37. Flexibility

J. CHOICES ARCHITECT® Connections:

Look for people who act like and/or show evidence of:

First Edition (Released 1994)
1. Inquisitive
2. Essence
3. Creator
4. Complexity
5. Connector
7. Helping Others Think
11. Open to Diversity
12. Experimenter
16. Cold/Indirect
17. Hot/Direct Sources
18. Into Everything
22. Self-Talk

Second Edition (Released 2000)
2. Complexity
3. Connector
4. Critical Thinker
5. Easy Shifter
6. Essence
7. Inquisitive
8. Solution Finder
14. Open-Minded
16. Personal Learner
21. Innovation Manager
25. Delivers Results

K. Difficulty to Develop:

27 (of 34)–Harder

33. LISTENING

A. Definition:

Practices attentive and active listening; has the patience to hear people out; can accurately restate the opinions of others even when he/she disagree.

B. Arenas/Domains to Explore:

1. Across different cultures
2. Club/association management
3. Coaching/teaching
4. Conferences/meetings/workshops
5. Counseling
6. Customer service
7. During Q & A
8. Early customer service jobs
9. Employee assistance programs
10. Helping someone with a personal problem
11. Listening behavior you can see in the interview
12. Listening opportunities down
13. Listening opportunities up
14. Listening opportunities with customers
15. Listening opportunities with outsiders
16. Listening opportunities with peers/colleagues
17. Listening opportunities with people they don't know
18. Listening opportunities with people they know
19. Listening to people of lesser status
20. Marketing
21. Meeting people for the first-time
22. Mentoring
23. Negotiating
24. Professional 360° facilitation
25. Selling
26. Team head
27. Under pressure
28. When they are really not interested
29. With people forced to be with
30. With people they don't like
31. With people who don't speak the language well
32. With people who have little to offer
33. With strangers

C. Sample Questions:

Dimension 1: Been there, done that–has had direct personal experience(s) involving the competency–candidate was the prime player Note: * means OK for campus

1. Are you certified to give feedback on any instrument or tool? If so, how much time do you spend letting the learner talk during the feedback session?
2. Do you ever just listen as a tactic to defuse a situation?*
3. Do you have a habit of interrupting others before they are finished or finishing sentences for them?*
4. Has anyone ever accused you of messing something up because of not listening?*
5. Have you ever been on a debate team? Did you usually win?*
6. Have you ever managed anything where the people or units reporting to you were in different locations? How did you listen from a distance?
7. How do you attend workshops and seminars? How do you take in information? Do you ask questions?*
8. How do you listen in career discussions?
9. How do you listen in performance reviews?
10. How do you shut down people when you're done with them?*
11. How do you think you signal your complete attention to others?
12. Tell me about a time when listening kept you out of trouble.*
13. Tell me about a time when not listening got you into trouble.*

LISTENING

14. Tell me about a time when others were missing the key points in a discussion and you jumped in and helped.*
15. Tell me about a time when you came to terms with a person or group you didn't agree with.*
16. Tell me about a time when you had to communicate something important to someone who did not speak your language very well.*
17. Tell me about a time when you had to have a substantive discussion with someone who struggled with your language or meaning.*
18. Tell me about a time when you managed a conflict with your boss (teacher, parents).*
19. Tell me about a time when you were in a negotiation with balky or angry people.*
20. Tell me about a time when you were managing a work group who didn't know much about the task.*
21. Tell me about a time when you were managing a work group who were experts in the task and you weren't.*
22. Tell me about a time when you were really angry with someone.*
23. Tell me about a time when you were working with peers (students) who hadn't done their homework.*
24. Tell me about a time when your listening worked really well for you.
25. What do you do when you think someone is not listening to you?*
26. What's the longest you can usually listen without talking?*
27. What's your response when someone says to you that you're not listening?*
28. When you and your workmates debate what someone has just said, do you find yourself agreeing or did you come away with a different message?

Dimension 2: Seen/been around others who were involved with the competency–good and bad; learns from others about self

29. Contrast the people you know who are the best and worst listeners.*
30. Has listening ever been in any 360° survey done on you? Was your score among your highest, middle, or lowest?
31. Has poor listening on someone else's part ever created an obstacle for you or got in the way of something you were trying to accomplish?*
32. Have you ever talked with a coach or mentor about your listening skills?
33. Have you ever watched someone fail/get fired because they did not listen enough?*
34. Have you ever watched someone overdo listening to the point that it backfired?
35. Have you ever watched someone succeed because they listened to others?*
36. Have you ever worked with a coach on listening skills?*
37. Have you ever worked with a person who excelled at listening skills?
38. Have you ever worked with a skills coach on improving your listening skills?*
39. How do you get feedback about your listening skills?
40. How often do you check with multiple sources when you get a piece of critical feedback on your listening skills?
41. Is there a historical figure you consider a model of listening skills?
42. What do others who are not your fans say about your listening skills?
43. What do others who like you say about your listening skills?
44. Which boss was the best at listening to others?
45. Which boss was the worst at listening to others?
46. Which direct report was the best at listening to others?
47. Which direct report was the worst at listening to others?

LISTENING

48. Which peer was the best at listening to others?
49. Which peer was the worst at listening to others?
50. Who is the best listener in your field or business?
51. Who do you consider a role model of listening to others?*
52. Who do you go to for advice on listening skills?
53. Who have you learned the most from about listening skills?*
54. Who is a higher-management role model for you on listening skills?
55. Who is a role model of listening skills outside of work?

Dimension 3: Knows how the competency works in theory; shows understanding

56. Are there situations or settings where someone should listen differently?
57. Do you think listening skills can be learned? If so, how do you think people develop listening skills?
58. Do you think there is a way to compensate or work around low listening skills?
59. Has anyone asked you for your opinions/advice on listening?*
60. Have you ever attended a course on listening skills?
61. Have you ever been in a situation where you and others put listening skills on a success profile?
62. Have you ever been part of an effort to create a policy or a mission statement containing reference to the importance of having good listening skills?
63. Have you ever been someone's coach or mentor who had problems with listening?
64. Have you ever created a plan for someone on developing listening skills?
65. Have you ever criticized someone for not listening to others?
66. Have you ever designed a program on listening skills?
67. Have you ever given a speech on listening skills?
68. Have you ever rewarded or recognized someone for having listening skills?
69. Have you ever taught a course on listening skills?
70. Have you ever tried to help someone deal with listening more effectively?*
71. Have you ever tried to help someone improve their listening skills?
72. How do you think people develop listening skills?
73. How much of success do you think is due to listening skills compared with other characteristics?
74. How would you know if someone is bad at listening?
75. How would you know if someone is good at listening?
76. If you had to write a book on listening skills, what would the chapter headings be?
77. What are the benefits to someone who is really good at listening?
78. What are the consequences to someone who is really poor at listening?
79. What do you think the performance standard is on listening skills for someone in your role?
80. What happens when two people try to work together who are very different listeners?
81. What wisdom would you pass onto others trying to become better at listening to others?
82. When you select others, what do you look for in listening skills?
83. Why do you think people end up being different in the way they listen to others?

Dimension 4: Shows personal change and sense-making; learned it one place and applied it in another; can compare and contrast experiences; changes viewpoints across time; can explain personal development or evolution related to the competency

84. Compare and contrast examples of when you've been effective and ineffective at listening
85. Contrast your on- and off-the-job use of listening skills.

LISTENING

86. Did you ever pass up a job or assignment because you were not a good enough listener?
87. Do you ever use other skills to cover for your lack of listening skills?
88. Have poor listening skills ever figured in a failure, struggle, or setback you have had?
89. Has becoming better at listening ever helped you in other areas?
90. Have poor listening skills ever been the subject of a development plan for you?
91. Have your listening skills always been this way?
92. Have you ever delegated or assigned someone a task because you didn't listen particularly well?
93. Have you ever made significant strides at becoming better at listening?
94. Have your listening skills, good or bad, ever been the subject of your performance review or a career discussion?
95. How different are you across situations in how you listen?
96. How do you decide how much of a listener to be?
97. How much of your success is due to listening?
98. How transferable are your listening skills to other situations?
99. If you had to become better at listening in a hurry, what would you do?
100. Was there a time when you were not as good at listening?
101. What caused you to work to improve your listening skills?
102. What event or series of events had the most impact on your listening skills?
103. What's the most varied you can be as a listener?
104. What was the shortest amount of time in which you increased your level of skill at listening?
105. When did you first realize your level of skill at listening?
106. When you know ahead of time that your usual way of listening won't work, what do you do?
107. Why do you think you listen the way you do?
108. Why do you think your listening skill is the way it is?*
109. How have you learned to suffer fools gladly without letting them know what you're doing?* Do you do this sometimes and not others?
110. Do you make an effort to listen more to some and less to others?*

D. Follow-up Probes:

1. Are there times when you listen and times when you don't?
2. Could you give me a few examples of how you've used or applied that?
3. Do you always listen or was that a special situation?
4. Do you ever turn off your listening skills and just hibernate?
5. Do you suppose if others would just try harder, they could learn to listen better?
6. Do you think that's teachable?
7. Do you think you're better at listening than most? Why?
8. Do you think you would perform any differently if you could be a better listener?
9. Have you always listened that well or is this a recent development in you?
10. How did others react when you did that?
11. How did you come up with that approach to listening in the first place?
12. How did you know that method of listening would work?
13. How do others you have known approach that?
14. How do you feel when others have caught on and you haven't?

LISTENING

15. How do you feel when you "get it" before others do?
16. How typical is this for you?
17. How would you approach that same situation today?
18. Is this natural for you, or do you really have to dig for it?
19. Was there a time when you didn't understand this about yourself?
20. What did you do after you got that feedback?
21. What did you do to adapt to that?
22. Why did you choose that approach?
23. Why did you do it that way?
24. Why do you think that didn't work?
25. Why do you think that happened that way?
26. Why do you think that worked?
27. Why do you think you have difficulties with that sometimes?
28. Why do you think you prefer to listen that way?

E. Themes/Things to Look for:

A physical listening credibility
Always has time
Asks lots of open-ended questions
Can listen to understand without having to cave in and agree with the person
Can separate personal feelings from the need to listen
Deep interest in understanding
Did they listen to you in the interview
Disengagement skills–can get out of a conversation
Gain from listening to people they don't like or don't agree with
Doesn't reject anything without debate
Doesn't run over people regardless of how justified it might appear
Gives feedback to the speaker
Good eye contact; physically receptive
Lets others save face
Listens under extreme time pressure
Optimistic about getting value from everyone
Patience with those of lesser skills
Selective listening vs. giving anyone an ear
Summarizes; can present the other side before adding a new thought
Talk/listen ratio
Talks about feelings as data

F. Most Likely Résumé:

1. **Look for jobs like:**

   Cross-Moves   Significant People Demands
   Fix-Its/Turnarounds   Staff Leadership (Influencing Without Authority)
   International Assignments   Start-Ups
   Scope (complexity) Assignments

LISTENING

2. Look for develop-in-place assignments like:

Attend a self-awareness/assessment course that includes feedback.

Find and spend time with an expert to learn something new to you.

Integrate diverse systems, processes, or procedures across decentralized and/or dispersed units.

Manage the renovation of an office, floor, building, meeting room, warehouse, etc.

Plan an off-site meeting, conference, convention, trade show, event, etc.

Go to a campus as a recruiter.

Manage the furnishing or refurnishing of new or existing offices.

Study and establish internal or external customer needs, requirements, specifications, and expectations, and present it to the people involved.

Do a customer-satisfaction survey in person or by phone and present it to the people involved.

Do a study of successful executives in your organization, and report the findings to top management.

Do a study of failed executives in your organization, including interviewing people still with the organization who knew or worked with them, and report the findings to top management.

Do a feasibility study on an important opportunity, and make recommendations to those who will decide.

Go on a business trip to a foreign country you've not been to before.

Lobby for your organization on a contested issue in local, regional, state, or federal government.

Work short rotations in other units, functions, or geographies you've not been exposed to before.

Benchmark innovative practices, processes, products, or services of competitors, vendors, suppliers, or customers, and present a report to others to create recommendations for change.

Interview outsiders on their view of your organization and present your findings to management.

Train and work as an assessor in an assessment center.

Work a few shifts in the telemarketing or customer service department, handling complaints and inquiries from customers.

Represent the concerns of a group of nonexempt, clerical, or administrative employees to higher management to seek resolution of a difficult issue.

Spend time with internal or external customers, write a report on your observations, and present it to the people involved with the customers in the organization.

Draft a mission statement, policy proposal, charter, or goal statement and get feedback from others.

Be a change agent; create a symbol for change; lead the rallying cry; champion a significant change and implementation.

Relaunch an existing product or service that's not doing well.

Create employee involvement teams.

Teach a course, seminar, or workshop on something you don't know well.

Design a training course in an area you're not an expert in.

Become someone's assigned mentor, coach, sponsor, champion, or orienter.

Train customers in the use of the organization's products or services.

Manage an ad hoc, temporary group of balky and resisting people through an unpopular change or project.

Manage an ad hoc, temporary group of people where the people in the group are towering experts but the temporary manager is not.

Take over for someone on vacation or a long trip.

Handle a tough negotiation with an internal or external client or customer.

Help shut down a plant, regional office, product line, business, operation, etc.

Manage a dissatisfied internal or external customer; troubleshoot a performance or quality problem with a product or service.

LISTENING

Manage the assigning/allocating of office space in a contested situation.

Take on a tough and undoable project, one where others who have tried it have failed.

Manage the outplacement of a group of people.

Resolve an issue in conflict between two people, units, geographies, functions, etc.

Make peace with an enemy or someone you've disappointed with a product or service or someone you've had some trouble with or don't get along well with.

Write a speech for someone higher up in the organization.

Be a member of a union-negotiating or grievance-handling team.

3. Best references to ask about or check:

Customers
Development Professionals
Human Resource Professionals
Natural Mentors
Past Associates/Constituencies
Peers and Colleagues
Spouse
Direct Reports

G. Learning Agility Evaluation:

3. Ordinary/Socially Acceptable vs. Insightful/Different
4. Spectator/Passive vs. Player/Participant
7. Passive vs. Intrigued/Curious
11. Generalizations vs. Specific Learnings
20. Avoids Responsibility for Mistakes vs. Admits and Learns from Mistakes
21. View from Self vs. View from Point of View of Others

H. The LEADERSHIP ARCHITECT® Sort Card Connections:

1. Good (positive) if combined with high:

Good counselor 3, 7, 29, 41

Can shut down unproductive transactions 12, 50, 62

Good at customer service 15, 31

Takes others' needs into account 19

Understands the problems 21

May make better hiring decisions 25, 56

Learns a lot from others 32, 61

Maze safe 39, 48

Builds team cooperation 42, 60

Lifelong improver 45, 54, 55

Understands the message in the context of the person 56, 64

2. Bad (negative) if combined with low or high (+):

Freezes; doesn't ask 1, 9, 12, 13, 16, 34, 57

Cares too much; wastes time (+3, 7, 10, 23) 62

Attracts all the negative information and gossip 10, 21

Can't say no; can't close someone down 12

Can't use it personally 32, 45, 55

LISTENING

Doesn't sort through issues to reach resolution 37, 50
Doesn't know what to pass on and what not to repeat 39, 48
Selective listening 41
Can't really empathize 56, 64

3. **Too much can contribute to the following Stallers and Stoppers:**

   A. *What too much looks like (overused):*

   May spend too much time listening; may avoid necessary action; others may confuse listening with agreement.

   B. *Too much might lead to these Stallers and Stoppers:*

   Failure to Build a Team (110)

   C. *Compensators:*

   How to compensate for too much of this competency:
   1, 9, 12, 13, 16, 17, 27, 34, 37, 38, 50, 57

   D. *Things to watch for:*

Wastes time	Doesn't say "Thank you but no thank you, I don't agree"
Attracts problems	Listens to avoid conflict
Can't tell/signal someone to stop	Doesn't finish; loose ends abound

4. **Too little can contribute to the following Stallers and Stoppers:**

   A. *What too little looks like (unskilled):*

   Doesn't listen well; cuts people off and finishes their sentences if they hesitate; interrupts to make a pronouncement or render a solution or decision; doesn't learn much from interactions with others; appears not to listen or be too busy constructing his/her own response; many times misses the point others are trying to make; may appear arrogant, impatient or uninterested; may listen to some groups/people and not to others; inaccurate in restating the case of others.

   B. *Too little might lead to these Stallers and Stoppers:*

Unable to Adapt to Differences (101)	Failure to Build a Team (110)
Arrogant (104)	Failure to Staff Effectively (111)
Blocked Personal Learner (106)	Insensitive to Others (112)
Lack of Composure (107)	Overmanaging (117)
Defensiveness (108)	Political Missteps (119)

   C. *Compensators:*

   How to substitute for too little of this competency:
   3, 7, 12, 18, 19, 21, 23, 31, 36, 41, 60

LISTENING

I. LEARNING ARCHITECT® Connections:

Look for people who act like and/or show evidence of:

- 3b. Self-Talk
- 4a. Getting Information
- 5. New
- 9. Multiple Sources
- 11. Why/How
- 12. Rules of Thumb
- 13. Focused
- 15. Cautious
- 16. Collaborate
- 17. Selected Sources
- 19. What
- 20. Events
- 25. Personal Change
- 26. Self-Aware
- 29. Essence
- 32. Diversity in Others
- 33. Diversity of Sources
- 34. Sizing Up Others

J. CHOICES ARCHITECT® Connections:

Look for people who act like and/or show evidence of:

First Edition (Released 1994)
- 7. Helping Others Think
- 8. Cool Transactor
- 10. Responds to Feedback
- 11. Open to Diversity
- 14. Transaction Quality
- 17. Hot/Direct Sources
- 22. Self-Talk

Second Edition (Released 2000)
- 11. Cool Transactor
- 14. Open-Minded
- 15. People-Smart
- 17. Responds to Feedback

K. Difficulty to Develop:

20 (of 34)–Moderate

LISTENING

34. MANAGERIAL COURAGE

A. Definition:

Doesn't hold back anything that needs to be said; provides current, direct, complete, and "actionable" positive and corrective feedback to others; lets people know where they stand; faces up to people problems with any person or situation (not including direct reports) quickly and directly; is not afraid to take negative action when necessary.

B. Arenas/Domains to Explore:

1. Asked for feedback in a public forum
2. Asked to take over stumbling group/area
3. Athlete/coach
4. Breach of ethics
5. Complaining about poor service
6. Completing 360° feedback on someone
7. Direct one-to-one feedback
8. Doing audits
9. Equity disputes
10. Feedback passed through channels
11. Feedback to bosses team
12. Feedback to customers
13. Feedback to higher management
14. Feedback to peers/colleagues
15. Going against the culture
16. Going against prevailing opinion
17. Judging people outside their own direct report team
18. Leaving no tip
19. Leaving/withdrawing from an unacceptable situation
20. Lunch with VIP circuit
21. Marginal performers
22. Negative feedback across boundaries
23. Pointing out incompetence
24. Refusing to pay for something below standard
25. Scandal
26. Sending restaurant food back
27. Service on a project
28. Service on a taskforce
29. Solicited criticism
30. Someone else's low performance hurts them/
31. Student/teacher
32. Taking on someone in power
33. Timeliness
34. Tough, negative situations
35. Unsolicited criticism
36. Whistleblowing
37. Writing/e-mailing to government officials
38. Written critique

C. Sample Questions:

Dimension 1: Been there, done that–has had direct personal experience(s) involving the competency–candidate was the prime player   Note: * means OK for campus

1. Have you ever asked a peer to take one of their direct reports off a project you were managing?
2. Have you ever been around a failing business where someone in higher management just didn't get it?
3. Have you ever been in a situation where many people were let go? Were you caught up in it?
4. Have you ever been on a team chartered to audit something and report back negative news to higher management?
5. Have you ever been punished for calling someone on an ethical or performance issue?
6. Have you ever challenged a teacher in a class or workshop?*
7. Have you ever held anything back that you now think you should have passed on?*
8. Have you ever managed anything where your peers and bosses were in different locations? How did you communicate your criticisms at a distance?

MANAGERIAL COURAGE

9. Have you ever put your job or a promotion at risk by going outside the chain of command with some negative information?
10. Have you ever stepped in to defend someone (other than a direct report) you felt was being unfairly treated?*
11. Have you ever uncovered fraud or a serious breach of conduct?*
12. Have you lived through a scandal or significant breach of ethics where you worked?
13. Have you written letters complaining about anything to a company?*
14. Have you written letters complaining about anything to a congressman?*
15. How do you respond in a public meeting when asked for your opinion when you know your answer will be more negative than the requester wants or expects?*
16. How much criticism do you generally pass on to peers/colleagues?*
17. How much criticism do you generally pass on to customers?
18. How much criticism do you generally pass on to bosses?
19. How much criticism do you generally pass on to higher management?
20. How much criticism do you generally pass on to higher authorities?
21. How often do you send back or refuse food in a restaurant?*
22. How often do your criticisms come with solutions attached?*
23. Tell me about a time when criticizing the status quo got you in trouble.
24. Tell me about a time when you challenged a coach.*
25. Tell me about a time when you contributed to getting someone fired or put on probation.
26. Tell me about a time when you delivered bad news to someone of higher status than you.*
27. Tell me about a time when you delivered bad news to someone of lower status than you (someone else's direct report, a younger/less experienced person).*
28. Tell me about a time when you had to blow the whistle on someone or some practice.*
29. Tell me about a time when you had to shut down or downsize an operation.
30. Tell me about a time when you have criticized someone higher up, and offered a solution that actually worked better.*
31. Tell me about a time you got into political trouble for something you said about someone or something outside your own work unit.
32. When you were not first to criticize, when do you generally join in?*

Dimension 2: Seen/been around others who were involved with the competency–good and bad; learns from others about self

33. Contrast the people you know who are most and least willing to take a stand or challenge the status quo.*
34. Has challenging the status quo or managerial courage ever been in any 360° survey done on you? Was your score among your highest, middle, or lowest?
35. Has lack of the willingness to take a stand or challenge the status quo on someone else's part ever created an obstacle for you or got in the way of something you were trying to accomplish?*
36. Have you ever talked with a coach or mentor about your willingness to take a stand or challenge the status quo?
37. Have you ever watched someone fail/get fired because they did not take a stand or challenge the status quo?*
38. Have you ever watched someone overdo challenging the status quo to the point that it backfired?
39. Have you ever watched someone succeed because they spoke up?*
40. Have you ever worked with a coach on your managerial courage?*
41. Have you ever worked with a person who excelled at taking a stand and challenging the status quo?

MANAGERIAL COURAGE

42. Have you ever worked with a skills coach on improving your ability to take a stand or challenge the status quo?*
43. How do you get feedback about your managerial courage?
44. How often do you check with multiple sources when you get a piece of critical feedback on your managerial courage?
45. Is there a historical figure you consider a model of managerial courage?
46. What do others who are not your fans say about your managerial courage?
47. What do others who like you say about your managerial courage?
48. Which boss was the best at taking a stand and challenging the status quo?
49. Which boss was the worst at taking a stand and challenging the status quo?
50. Which direct report was the best at taking a stand and challenging the status quo?
51. Which direct report was the worst at taking a stand and challenging the status quo?
52. Which peer was the best at taking a stand and challenging the status quo?
53. Which peer was the worst at taking a stand and challenging the status quo?
54. Who in your field or business is the best at taking a stand and challenging the status quo?
55. Who do you consider a current role model of managerial courage?*
56. Who do you go to for advice on managerial courage?
57. Who have you learned the most from about managerial courage?*
58. Who is a higher-management role model for you on managerial courage?
59. Who is a role model of managerial courage outside of work?

Dimension 3: Knows how the competency works in theory; shows understanding

60. Are there situations or settings where someone should be different in the way they take a stand or challenges the status quo?
61. Do you think managerial courage can be learned? If so, how do you think people develop managerial courage skills?
62. Do you think there is a way to compensate or work around low managerial courage?
63. Has anyone asked you for your opinions/advice on taking a stand or challenging the status quo?*
64. Have you ever attended a course on taking a courageous stand?
65. Have you ever been in a situation where you and others put managerial courage on a success profile?
66. Have you ever been part of an effort to create a policy or a mission statement containing reference to taking a stand or challenging the status quo?
67. Have you ever been someone's coach or mentor who had problems with taking a courageous stand?
68. Have you ever created a development plan for someone on taking a courageous stand?
69. Have you ever criticized someone for not taking a stand or challenging the status quo?
70. Have you ever designed a program on taking a stand or challenging the status quo?
71. Have you ever given a speech on taking a courageous stand?
72. Have you ever rewarded or recognized someone for taking a stand or challenging the status quo?
73. Have you ever taught a course on managerial courage?
74. Have you ever tried to help someone deal more effectively with taking a stand or challenging the status quo?*
75. Have you ever tried to help someone improve their managerial courage?
76. How do you think people develop managerial courage skills?
77. How much managerial courage is good to have and how much is too much?
78. How much of success do you think is due to managerial courage compared with other characteristics?

MANAGERIAL COURAGE

79. How would you know if someone is bad at taking a stand or challenging the status quo?
80. How would you know if someone is good at taking a stand or challenging the status quo?
81. If you had to write a book on managerial courage, what would the chapter headings be?
82. What are the benefits to someone who is really good at taking a courageous stand?
83. What are the consequences to someone who is really poor at taking a courageous stand?
84. What do you think the performance standard is on taking a stand or challenging the status quo for someone in your role?
85. What happens when two people try to work together who are very different on taking a stand or challenging the status quo?
86. What wisdom would you pass onto others trying to become better at challenging the status quo?
87. When you select others, what do you look for in managerial courage?
88. Why do you think people end up being different on taking a stand or challenging the status quo?

Dimension 4: Shows personal change and sense-making; learned it one place and applied it in another; can compare and contrast experiences; changes viewpoints across time; can explain personal development or evolution related to the competency

89. Compare and contrast examples times you've been effective and ineffective at taking stands or challenging the status quo.
90. Contrast your on- and off-the-job demonstration of taking courageous stands.
91. Did you ever pass up a job or assignment because you were not confident enough in your skills at taking stands or challenging the status quo?
92. Do you ever use other skills to cover for your lack of willingness to take a stand or challenge the status quo?
93. Has not taking a stand or challenging the status quo ever figured in a failure, struggle, or setback you have had?
94. Has becoming better at managerial courage ever helped you in other areas?
95. Has taking stands or challenging the status quo ever been the subject of a development plan for you?
96. Has your willingness to take a stand or challenge the status quo always been this way?
97. Have you ever delegated or assigned someone a task because you didn't take tough stands or challenge the status quo particularly well?
98. Have you ever made significant strides at becoming better at taking courageous stands?
99. Have your taking stands or challenging the status quo skills, good or bad, ever been the subject of your performance review or a career discussion?
100. How different are you across situations in taking stands or challenging the status quo?
101. How do you decide when to take a courageous stand or challenge the status quo?
102. How much of your success is due to your willingness to take courageous stands?
103. How transferable are your managerial-courage skills to other situations?
104. If you had to become better at taking courageous stands in a hurry, what would you do?
105. Was there a time when you were not as good at taking courageous stands?
106. What caused you to work to improve your skills taking stands or challenging the status quo?
107. What event or series of events had the most impact on your managerial courage?
108. What's the most varied you can be in demonstrating managerial courage?
109. What was the shortest amount of time in which you increased your level of skill at taking stands or challenging the status quo?
110. When did you first realize your level of skill at taking courageous stands?
111. When you know ahead of time that your usual skill level of taking stands or challenging the status quo won't work, what do you do?

MANAGERIAL COURAGE

112. Why do you think you take courageous stands the way you do?
113. Why do you think your managerial courage is the way it is?*
114. How direct do you get when you have something negative to say about someone else?*
115. How do you determine which battles to fight and when to just remain silent?*

D. Follow-up Probes:
1. Are there times when you challenge others and times when you don't?
2. Could you contrast those two bosses for me?
3. Could you give me a few examples of how you've used or applied that?
4. Did anyone else join you or were you on your own?
5. Did you lose sleep over that?
6. Did you or the other person blink first?
7. Do you always challenge or was that a special situation?
8. Do you ever turn off your need to challenge and just hibernate?
9. Do you suppose if others would just try harder, they could learn to be more comfortable with aggressively challenging others?
10. Do you think that's teachable?
11. Do you think you're better at challenging than most? Why?
12. Do you think you would perform any differently if you could be more comfortable criticizing others?
13. Have you always challenged others that way or is this a recent development in you?
14. How did the others react when you did that?
15. How did you come up with that approach to challenging others in the first place?
16. How did you know that method of challenging would work?
17. How do others you have known approach that?
18. How do you feel when others challenge and you haven't?
19. How do you feel when you challenge before others do?
20. How typical is this for you?
21. How would you approach that same situation today?
22. Is this natural for you, or do you really have to dig for it?
23. Was there a time when you didn't understand this about yourself?
24. Were you emotionally involved or was it just business?
25. What did you do after you got that feedback?
26. What did you do to adapt to that?
27. Why did you choose that approach?
28. Why did you decide to take the risk?
29. Why did you do it that way?
30. Why did you time your challenge like that?
31. Why do you suppose organizations work that way?
32. Why do you think that didn't work?
33. Why do you think that happened that way?
34. Why do you think that worked?
35. Why do you think you have difficulty with that sometimes?
36. Why do you think you prefer to challenge in that way?
37. Would you have done it that way with looser deadlines?
38. Would you have done it that way with tighter deadlines?

MANAGERIAL COURAGE

E. Themes/Things to Look for:

Able to take the heat	Performance focus
Admits errors of judgment	Political sensitivity
Awareness of impact on others	Resilience
Balance between positive and negative feedback	Risk tolerance
Candor and caring	Satisfying personal needs vs. the common good
Clear and clean purpose	Feedback in some directions but not others
Couching skills	Feedback to some people but not others
Courage	Sense of equity and fairness
Drivers–why the criticism	Sense of fairness
Giving people a fair chance to respond	Sense of priorities
Keeping personal feelings out of the equation	Sense of timing
Not expecting miracles	Specificity
Not procrastinating	Varied tactics of delivering feedback
Passionate commitment to what's right	Perspective–doesn't tilt at windmills

F. Most Likely Résumé:

1. Look for jobs like:
Fix-Its/Turnarounds
Significant People Demands

2. Look for develop-in-place assignments like:
Manage an ad hoc, temporary group of balky and resisting people through an unpopular change or project.
Manage an ad hoc, temporary group of people involved in tackling a fix-it or turnaround project.
Help shut down a plant, regional office, product line, business, operation, etc.
Manage a group through a significant business crisis.
Take on a tough and undoable project, one where others who have tried it have failed.
Manage a cost-cutting project.
Do a postmortem on a failed project, and present it to the people involved.
Work on a team looking at a reorganization plan where there will be more people than positions.

3. Best references to ask about or check:
Development Professionals
Past Associates/Constituencies
Direct Reports

G. Learning Agility Evaluation:

4. Spectator/Passive vs. Player/Participant
9. Vague/General vs. Sharp/Specific
10. Reactive vs. Initiating
12. Rehearsed/Socially Acceptable vs. Candid
19. External Standards vs. Internal Standards
22. Focus on Accomplishments vs. Focus on Solving Problems

MANAGERIAL COURAGE

H. The LEADERSHIP ARCHITECT® Sort Card Connections:

1. Good (positive) if combined with high:
Criticizes but is sensitive 7, 10, 23
Can fire up safely 8, 39, 48
Can/will defend 11, 12
Criticizes but develops 19
Can go outside the chain of command safely 22, 29
Light touch 26
Listened to 32, 51, 53, 57
High standards 35, 53
Has accurate concerns 35, 56, 64
Doesn't expect miracles 41
Good sideways 38, 42, 60
Knows when, how, who, and what 52, 63
Knows what's important 50, 51, 53

2. Bad (negative) if combined with low or high (+):
Too quick with criticism (+1, 16) 41
Delivered with a hammer 3, 10, 31
Gets into boss conflicts 4
Motives questioned (+6)
Gets in trouble for candor 8, 39, 48
Doesn't line up allies (+9, 57)
Not accepted well 22, 29
Could be sarcastic 26
Won't take any advice 33, 45
Doesn't do means testing before shooting 56, 64
Tilts at windmills 50, 51, 53

3. Too much can contribute to the following Stallers and Stoppers:

A. *What too much looks like (overused):*
May be overly critical; may be too direct and heavy-handed when providing feedback or addressing issues; may provide too much negative and too little positive feedback; may put too much emphasis on the dark side; may fight too many battles.

B. *Too much might lead to these Stallers and Stoppers:*
Insensitive to Others (112)
Overmanaging (117)

C. *Compensators:*
How to compensate for too much of this competency:
3, 7, 10, 11, 12, 19, 23, 26, 31, 33, 36, 41, 56, 60, 64

D. *Things to watch for:*
Always negative; never anything good to say
Always speaks regardless of the context or consequences
An overestimate of the worth of their views
Can't leave anything alone
Only has a high, inside, fast ball
Will never relent on anything
Doesn't pick their battles well

MANAGERIAL COURAGE

4. Too little can contribute to the following Stallers and Stoppers:

A. What too little looks like (unskilled):

Doesn't take tough stands with others; holds back in tough feedback situations; doesn't know how to present a tough position; knows but doesn't disclose; doesn't step up to issues; intimidated by others in power; hangs back and lets others take the lead; is a conflict avoider unwilling to take the heat of controversy; afraid to be wrong, get in a win/lose situation, or make a tough personnel call.

B. Too little might lead to these Stallers and Stoppers:

Poor Administrator (102)
Betrayal of Trust (105)
Lack of Composure (107)
Failure to Build a Team (110)
Failure to Staff Effectively (111)
Performance Problems (118)

C. Compensators:

How to substitute for too little of this competency:
1, 4, 8, 9, 12, 27, 38, 43, 48, 57

I. LEARNING ARCHITECT® Connections:

Look for people who act like and/or show evidence of:

1c. Following a Plan
3b. Self-Talk
4a. Getting Information
4c. Actively Involve
6. Contentious
7. Risks
8. Initiate
34. Sizing Up Others
38. Resilience

J. CHOICES ARCHITECT® Connections:

Look for people who act like and/or show evidence of:

First Edition (Released 1994)
20. Forging Ahead
21. Taking the Heat

Second Edition (Released 2000)
22. Taking the Heat
23. Visioning
27. Presence

K. Difficulty to Develop:

29 (of 34)–Hardest

35. MANAGING AND MEASURING WORK

A. Definition:

Clearly assigns responsibility for tasks and decisions; sets clear objectives and measures; monitors process, progress, and results; designs feedback loops into work.

B. Arenas/Domains to Explore:

1. Any supervisory Event
2. Club/association management
3. Coaching
4. Elected leadership positions
5. Event/conference management
6. Family management
7. Group/team leader
8. Installing feedback loops
9. Managing consultants
10. Managing outside contractors
11. Managing suppliers/vendors
12. Meeting facilitation
13. Military background
14. Project/taskforce leader
15. Responsible for work flow
16. Student government
17. Teacher
18. Team captain

C. Sample Questions:

Dimension 1: Been there, done that–has had direct personal experience(s) involving the competency–candidate was the prime player   Note: * means OK for campus

1. Do you have your people report progress verbally or in writing?
2. Do you manage any differently under tight deadlines or pressure from higher management?
3. Do you monitor progress personally or do you set up self-running checklists and systems for keeping track?
4. Do you set different levels of goals for different people?
5. Do you use PERT or GANTT or other planning/measuring tools to plot progress?
6. Do you write out instructions or do you deliver them verbally?
7. Have you ever gotten in trouble for not being clear about who was responsible?*
8. Have you ever had a project/process failure as a manager/project leader?*
9. Have you ever managed anything where the people or units reporting to you were in different locations? How did you monitor work and measure progress?
10. Have you ever taken over a team that was badly managed? What did you do?
11. How do you allocate credit for a task you designed and delegated?
12. How do you check for understanding of the goals and objectives you have set?
13. How do you communicate and manage when there is a significant shift in goals and objectives midway through a project?
14. How do you explain to a direct report what it is you want?
15. How do you keep things on track when everyone is busy facing a tight deadline where everything has to be perfect?*
16. How have past direct reports reacted to your goal-setting style?
17. Tell me about a time when you had to communicate and manage when there was a significant shift in goals and objectives midway through a project.
18. Tell me about a time when you organized and managed others on a complex task from start to finish.*
19. Tell me about a time when you've involved others in the goal-setting process.

MANAGING AND MEASURING WORK

20. Tell me generally how you divide up the work, assign tasks and responsibility, monitor progress, and give corrective feedback.*
21. What have you found most effective in measuring progress toward task completion?
22. What triggers you to intervene and provide corrective instructions?
23. When you set goals and objectives, at what level do you set them?*

Dimension 2: Seen/been around others who were involved with the competency–good and bad; learns from others about self

24. Contrast the people you know who are the best and worst at managing, monitoring, and measuring results.*
25. Has managing, monitoring, and measuring results ever been in any 360° survey done on you? Was your score among your highest, middle, or lowest?
26. Has not managing, monitoring, and measuring results on someone else's part ever created an obstacle for you or got in the way of something you were trying to accomplish?*
27. Have you ever talked with a coach or mentor about managing, monitoring, and measuring progress and results?
28. Have you ever watched someone fail/get fired because they did not manage work and measure progress and results well?*
29. Have you ever watched someone overdo managing, monitoring, and measuring results to the point that it backfired?
30. Have you ever watched someone succeed because they managed work and measured progress and results well?*
31. Have you ever worked with a coach on monitoring and measuring work progress and results?*
32. Have you ever worked with a person who excelled at managing, monitoring, and measuring progress and results?
33. Have you ever worked with a skills coach on managing, monitoring, and measuring progress and results?*
34. How do you get feedback about yourself on managing, monitoring, and measuring progress and results?
35. How often do you check with multiple sources when you get a piece of critical feedback on your skills at managing, monitoring, and measuring progress and results?
36. Is there a historical figure you consider a model of managing, monitoring, and measuring progress and results?
37. What do others who are not your fans say about your skills at managing, monitoring, and measuring progress and results?
38. What do others who like you say about your skills at managing, monitoring, and measuring progress and results?
39. Which boss was the best at monitoring work and measuring progress?
40. Which boss was the worst at monitoring work and measuring progress?
41. Which direct report was the best at monitoring work and measuring progress?
42. Which direct report was the worst at monitoring work and measuring progress?
43. Which peer was the best at monitoring work and measuring progress?
44. Which peer was the worst at monitoring work and measuring progress?
45. Who in your field or business is the best at monitoring work and measuring progress?
46. Who do you consider a role model of monitoring work and measuring progress?*
47. Who do you go to for advice on monitoring work and measuring progress?
48. Who have you learned the most from about monitoring work and measuring progress?*
49. Who is a higher-management role model for you on managing work and measuring progress?
50. Who is a role model of managing work and measuring progress outside of work?

MANAGING AND MEASURING WORK

Dimension 3: Knows how the competency works in theory; shows understanding

51. Are there situations or settings where someone should be different on monitoring work and measuring progress?
52. Do you think managing work and measuring progress can be learned; how do you think people develop managing, monitoring, and measuring results skills?
53. Do you think there is a way to compensate or work around being low in skills at monitoring work and measuring progress?
54. Has anyone asked you for your opinions/advice on monitoring work and measuring progress?*
55. Have you ever attended a course on monitoring work and measuring progress?
56. Have you ever been in a situation where you and others put managing work and measuring progress on a success profile?
57. Have you ever been part of an effort to create a policy or a mission statement containing reference to managing, monitoring, and measuring results?
58. Have you ever been someone's coach or mentor who had problems with monitoring work and measuring progress?
59. Have you ever created a development plan for someone on monitoring work and measuring progress?
60. Have you ever criticized someone for not managing, monitoring, and measuring results?
61. Have you ever designed a program on monitoring work and measuring progress?
62. Have you ever given a speech on monitoring work and measuring progress?
63. Have you ever rewarded or recognized someone for the ability to manage work and measure progress and results?
64. Have you ever taught a course on monitoring work and measuring progress?
65. Have you ever tried to help someone deal more effectively with monitoring work and measuring progress?*
66. Have you ever tried to help someone improve their skill at monitoring work and measuring progress?
67. How do you think people develop skills for monitoring work and measuring progress?
68. How much ability to manage work and measure progress and results is good to have and how much is too much?
69. How much of success do you think is due to managing, monitoring, and measuring results compared with other characteristics?
70. How would you know if someone is bad at managing, monitoring, and measuring results?
71. How would you know if someone is good at managing, monitoring, and measuring results?
72. If you had to write a book on monitoring work and measuring progress, what would the chapter headings be?
73. What are the benefits to someone who is really good at monitoring work and measuring progress?
74. What are the consequences to someone who is really poor at monitoring work and measuring progress?
75. What do you think the standard is on managing, monitoring, and measuring results for someone in your role?
76. What happens if you do too much monitoring of work and measuring progress?
77. What happens when two people try to work together who are very different in their ability to manage work and measure progress and results?
78. What wisdom would you pass on to others trying to become better at managing, monitoring, and measuring results?
79. When you select others, what do you look for in ability to monitor work and measure progress?
80. Why do you think people end up being different in their ability to monitor work and measure progress?

MANAGING AND MEASURING WORK

Dimension 4: Shows personal change and sense-making; learned it one place and applied it in another; can compare and contrast experiences; changes viewpoints across time; can explain personal development or evolution related to the competency

81. Compare and contrast examples of times you've been effective and ineffective at managing, monitoring, and measuring progress and results.
82. Contrast your on- and off-the-job use of your ability to manage work and measure progress and results.
83. Did you ever pass up a job or assignment because you were not confident enough in your skills at managing, monitoring, and measuring results?
84. Do you ever use other skills to cover for your not managing, monitoring, and measuring results well enough?
85. Has becoming better at managing work and measuring results ever been the subject of a development plan for you?
86. Has becoming better at managing, monitoring, and measuring results ever helped you in other areas?
87. Has not managing, monitoring, and measuring results ever figured in a failure, struggle, or setback you have had?
88. Has your ability to manage work and measure progress and results always been this way?
89. Have you ever delegated or assigned someone a task because you didn't manage work and measure progress and results particularly well?
90. Have you ever made significant strides at becoming better at managing work and measuring progress?
91. Have your managing and measuring work skills, good or bad, ever been the subject of your performance review or a career discussion?
92. How different are you across situations in your managing of work and measuring of progress?
93. How do you decide how much measuring of progress and results should be applied?
94. How much of your success is due to your ability to manage work and measure results?
95. How transferable are your managing work and measuring progress skills to other situations?
96. If you had to become better at managing work and measuring progress in a hurry, what would you do?
97. Was there a time when you were not as good at managing work and measuring progress?
98. What caused you to work to improve your skills at managing, monitoring, and measuring progress and results?
99. What event or series of events had the most impact on your ability to manage work and measure progress?
100. What's the most varied you can be in managing work and measuring progress?
101. What was the shortest amount of time in which you increased your level of skill at managing, monitoring, and measuring progress and results?
102. When did you first realize your level of skill at managing work and measuring progress?
103. When you know ahead of time that your usual level of managing work and measuring results won't work, what do you do?
104. Why do you think you deal with managing work and measuring progress the way you do?
105. Why do you think your managing work and measuring progress skills are the way they are?*
106. How do you balance control of the task with letting people find their way through it?*
107. When a group is off track and confused, what do you do to restore focus?

MANAGING AND MEASURING WORK

D. Follow-up Probes:

1. Are there times when you set goals/assign responsibility/monitor progress/provide task feedback like that and times when you don't?
2. Could you contrast those two bosses for me?
3. Could you give me a few examples of how you've used or applied that?
4. Do you always set goals/assign responsibility/monitor progress/provide task feedback like that or was that a special situation?
5. Do you ever turn off your need to set goals/assign responsibility/monitor progress/provide task feedback and just go with the flow?
6. Do you suppose if others would just try harder, they could learn to be more effective setting goals/assigning responsibility/monitoring progress/providing task feedback like you do?
7. Do you think that's all teachable?
8. Do you think you're better at setting goals/assigning responsibility/monitoring progress/providing task feedback than most? Why?
9. Do you think you would perform any differently if you could be more effective setting goals/assigning responsibility/monitoring progress/providing task feedback?
10. Have you always set goals/assigned responsibility/monitored progress/provided task feedback that way or is this a recent development in you?
11. How did the others react when you did that?
12. How did you come up with that approach to setting goals/assigning responsibility/monitoring progress/providing task feedback in the first place?
13. How did you know that method of setting goals/assigning responsibility/monitoring progress/providing task feedback would work?
14. How do others you have known approach that?
15. How typical is this for you?
16. How would you approach that same situation today?
17. Is this natural for you, or do you really have to dig for it?
18. Was that a fair way to do that?
19. Was there a time when you didn't understand this about yourself?
20. What did you do after you got that feedback?
21. What did you do to adapt to that?
22. What did you learn from that?
23. Why did you choose that approach?
24. Why did you decide to take the risk?
25. Why did you do it that way?
26. Why did you time your corrective feedback like that?
27. Why do you suppose organizations work that way?
28. Why do you think that didn't work?
29. Why do you think that happened that way?
30. Why do you think that worked?
31. Why do you think you have difficulties with that sometimes?
32. Why do you think you prefer to set goals/assign responsibility/monitor progress/provide task feedback that way?
33. Would you have done it that way with looser deadlines?
34. Would you have done it that way with tighter deadlines?

MANAGING AND MEASURING WORK

E. Themes/Things to Look for:
Ability to motivate
Communicating the big picture
Balance between command and empowerment
No blame-placing when something doesn't work
Clarity of directions
Clear communication style
Complex and varied tactics for assigning tasks
Drivers–why do they do it that way
Empowerment
Empowerment tolerance
Feedback for growth and correction
Good teacher
In service of what
Keeping personal feelings out of the feedback
Keeping the task feedback focused on the work, not the person
Letting people finish their own work
Methods for relieving stress/tension
More specification of problems/parameters/questions to be answered/feedback to insure progress and expected outcomes than trying to lay out every step of the process
Non-intrusive methods of checking in
One size doesn't fit all; sees differences
Orderly thought process
Not playing favorites
Sense of fairness and equity
Sensing people's personal needs
Setting goals too high
Setting goals too low
Taking risks
Tasking without responsibility
Telling more what than how
Trust in others to do the job
Using assignments for development

F. Most Likely Résumé:

1. Look for jobs like:
Fix-Its/Turnarounds
Scale (size shift) Assignments
Significant People Demands
Staff to Line Shifts
Start-Ups

2. Look for develop-in-place assignments like:
Manage an ad hoc, temporary group of balky and resisting people through an unpopular change or project.
Manage an ad hoc, temporary group of low-competence people through a task they couldn't do by themselves.
Manage an ad hoc, temporary group of people involved in tackling a fix-it or turnaround project.
Manage an ad hoc, temporary group of people in a stable and static operation.

MANAGING AND MEASURING WORK

Manage an ad hoc, temporary group of people in a rapidly expanding operation.
Assemble an ad hoc team of diverse people to accomplish a difficult task.
Manage a cost-cutting project.
Build a multifunctional project team to tackle a common business issue or problem.
Audit cost overruns to assess the problem, and present your findings to the person or people involved.
Work on a team looking at a reorganization plan where there will be more people than positions.

3. Best references to ask about or check:
Direct Reports

G. Learning Agility Evaluation:
9. Vague/General vs. Sharp/Specific
16. Few Rules of Thumb vs. Many and Varied Rules of Thumb
19. External Standards vs. Internal Standards
22. Focus on Accomplishments vs. Focus on Solving Problems

H. The LEADERSHIP ARCHITECT® Sort Card Connections:

1. Good (positive) if combined with high:
Delivers instructions smoothly; people not afraid to ask for help 3, 31, 33, 41
Does means testing for task size/complexity 7, 10, 23
Direct tough feedback 13
Spreads the work out 21, 18, 23
Uses assignments to develop 19, 56
Good workflow manager 20, 47, 50, 52
Good meeting/project group/taskforce task head 39, 47
Accurately sizes tasks and people 56
Can articulate the grander purpose 58, 65

2. Bad (negative) if combined with low or high (+):
May be overly controlling (+1, 9, 57)
Intervenes too soon (+1, 16) 41
Lots of pressure (+1, 16, 43, 53)
Doesn't empower 3, 33, 36, 60
Just talks; doesn't listen 3, 33, 41
May not be able to make the tough calls 12, 13, 34
Too mechanical 14, 19, 28
Distributes the load unevenly 18, 21, 23
Knows too much to empower (+24, 61)
Doesn't excite 36
Work assignments lack context 50, 58, 65
Structure but no output 50, 53
Doesn't do accurate means testing 56, 64

3. Too much can contribute to the following Stallers and Stoppers:

A. What too much looks like (overused):
May be overcontrolling; may look over people's shoulders; may prescribe too much and not empower people.

MANAGING AND MEASURING WORK

B. Too much might lead to these Stallers and Stoppers:
Poor Administrator (102)
Failure to Build a Team (110)
Performance Problems (118)

C. Compensators:
How to compensate for too much of this competency:
3, 14, 18, 19, 26, 33, 36, 44, 57, 60, 63, 64, 65

D. Things to watch for:
As a shield against having to deal with conflict
Control freak
Doesn't admit errors of judgment
Responsibility but no empowerment
Structure but without meaning
Pressures too much

4. Too little can contribute to the following Stallers and Stoppers:

A. What too little looks like (unskilled):
Doesn't use goals and objectives to manage self or others; not orderly in assigning and measuring work; isn't clear about who is responsible for what; may be disorganized, just throw tasks at people, or lack goals or priorities; may manage time poorly and not get around to managing in an orderly way; doesn't provide work in progress feedback; doesn't set up benchmarks and ways for people to measure themselves.

B. Too little might lead to these Stallers and Stoppers:
Poor Administrator (102)
Failure to Build a Team (110)
Performance Problems (118)

C. Compensators:
How to substitute for too little of this competency:
5, 9, 12, 13, 20, 24, 27, 39, 47, 52, 53, 56, 63

I. LEARNING ARCHITECT® Connections:

Look for people who act like and/or show evidence of:

1c. Following a Plan	18. Straightforward
6. Contentious	19. What
8. Initiate	30. Mastery
13. Focused	31. Rationality
14. Controlled	34. Sizing Up Others
15. Cautious	

J. CHOICES ARCHITECT® Connections:

Look for people who act like and/or show evidence of:

First Edition (Released 1994)
15. Helps Others Succeed

Second Edition (Released 2000)
12. Helps Others Succeed

K. Difficulty to Develop:
20 (of 34)–Easier

36. MOTIVATING OTHERS

A. Definition:
Creates a climate in which people want to do their best; can motivate many kinds of direct reports and team or project members; can assess each person's hot button and use it to get the best out of him/her; pushes tasks and decisions down; empowers others; invites input from each person and shares ownership and visibility; makes each individual feel their work is important; is someone people like working for and with.

B. Arenas/Domains to Explore:
1. Any supervisory event
2. Career discussions
3. Club/association management
4. Coaching
5. During crises
6. During tough times
7. Elected leadership positions
8. Event/conference management
9. Fund-raising
10. Getting people to take assignments they don't want
11. Group/team leader
12. In presentations
13. In writing
14. Lobbying
15. Managing outside contractors
16. Meeting facilitation
17. Mentoring
18. Military leadership positions
19. Project/taskforce leader
20. Something nobody wants to do
21. Sports team captain
22. Student government
23. Teacher
24. Under impossible deadlines
25. United Way chair/captain
26. Where people volunteer to work with them
27. Working political campaigns

C. Sample Questions:

Dimension 1: Been there, done that–has had direct personal experience(s) involving the competency–candidate was the prime player   Note: * means OK for campus

1. Do you create and give out awards?
2. Do you directly help people with personal problems or do you get them the help they need?
3. Do you use time off, dinner vouchers, theater tickets or other small trinkets to reward someone?
4. Give me an example of a time you've had to give up on trying to motivate someone. How did you know it was time to give up?
5. Has anyone ever accused you of messing something up because you failed to motivate others?
6. Have you ever been a team captain, United Way chair, or community service volunteer?*
7. Have you ever been in direct marketing?
8. Have you ever been in direct sales?
9. Have you ever lobbied for yourself or for an organization?*
10. Have you ever managed a fix-it?
11. Have you ever managed a start-up?
12. Have you ever managed anything where the people or units reporting to you were in different locations? How did you motivate people at a distance?
13. Have you ever managed people from a foreign country? Was it different?

MOTIVATING OTHERS

14. Have you ever saved a good employee who was on the verge of quitting?
15. Have you ever taken over a team from a bad boss?
16. Have you ever taken over a team that was in trouble?
17. Have you ever taken over a team whose spirit was broken/had poor morale?
18. Have you ever worked to raise funds for a cause or for a politician?*
19. How do you celebrate successes of others on your team or work group?
20. How do you generally measure your impact on individuals, teams or the entire organization?
21. How do you use delegation as a motivational technique?
22. How hard is it to fill open jobs on your team?
23. Tell me about a time when you changed a group's mind on something big.*
24. Tell me about a time when you failed as a manager/project manager.*
25. Tell me about a time when you had to communicate something important to someone who did not speak your language very well.
26. Tell me about a time when you had to fight to keep one of your programs/projects going.*
27. Tell me about a time when you had to motivate someone not from your country or culture.*
28. Tell me about a time when you have been in a position to argue for something to higher management that you knew they didn't like.
29. Tell me about a time when you managed a work project (group) of very different people. How did you appeal to each?*
30. Tell me about a time when you took charge of a group going nowhere and you led them out of their doldrums.*
31. Tell me about a time when you've collected input from multiple people on a project or goal.
32. Tell me about a time when your attempt to motivate a person/group was rejected.*
33. Tell me about a time when your attempt to motivate others got you into trouble.
34. Tell me about a time when your attempt to motivate others worked really well for you.
35. Tell me about an impossible situation you had to manage.*
36. What do you do with a demoralized team/person?*
37. What's the most unpopular cause you've ever pushed?*

Dimension 2: Seen/been around others who were involved with the competency–good and bad; learns from others about self

38. Contrast the people you know who are the most and least able to motivate others.*
39. Has motivating others ever been in any 360° survey done on you? Was your score among your highest, middle, or lowest?
40. Has lack of the ability to motivate others on someone else's part ever created an obstacle for you or got in the way of something you were trying to accomplish?*
41. Have you ever talked with a coach or mentor about your ability to motivate others?
42. Have you ever watched someone fail/get fired because they could not motivate others?*
43. Have you ever watched someone overmotivate others to the point that it backfired?
44. Have you ever watched someone succeed because they were able to motivate others?*
45. Have you ever worked with a coach on motivating others?*
46. Have you ever worked with a person who excelled at motivating others?
47. Have you ever worked with a skills coach on motivating others?*
48. How do you get feedback about yourself on motivating others?
49. How often do you check with multiple sources when you get a piece of critical feedback on motivating others?

MOTIVATING OTHERS

50. Is there a historical figure you consider a model of motivating others?
51. What do others who are not your fans say about your ability to motivate others?
52. What do others who like you say about your ability to motivate others?
53. Which boss was the best at motivating others?
54. Which boss was the worst at motivating others?
55. Which direct report was the best at motivating others?
56. Which direct report was the worst at motivating others?
57. Which peer was the best at motivating others?
58. Which peer was the worst at motivating others?
59. Who in your field or business is the best at motivating others?
60. Who do you consider a role model of motivating others?*
61. Who do you go to for advice on motivating others?
62. Who have you learned the most from about motivating others?*
63. Who is a higher-management role model for you on motivating others?
64. Who is a role model of motivating others outside of work?

Dimension 3: Knows how the competency works in theory; shows understanding

65. Are there situations or settings where someone should motivate others differently?
66. Do you think the ability to motivate others can be learned; how do you think people develop motivation skills?
67. Do you think there is a way to compensate or work around a low ability to motivate others?
68. Has anyone asked you for your opinions/advice on motivating others?*
69. Have you ever attended a course on motivating others?
70. Have you ever been in a situation where you and others put motivating others on a success profile?
71. Have you ever been part of an effort to create a policy or a mission statement containing reference to motivating others?
72. Have you ever been someone's coach or mentor who had problems with motivating others?
73. Have you ever created a development plan for someone on motivating others?
74. Have you ever criticized someone for not motivating others?
75. Have you ever designed a program on motivating others?
76. Have you ever given a speech on motivating others?
77. Have you ever rewarded or recognized someone for motivating others?
78. Have you ever taught a course on motivating others?
79. Have you ever tried to help someone deal more effectively with motivating others?*
80. Have you ever tried to help someone improve their motivational skills?
81. How do you think people develop the skills to motivate others?
82. How much ability at motivating others is good to have and how much is too much?
83. How much of success do you think is due to the ability to motivate others compared with other characteristics?
84. How would you know if someone is bad at motivating others?
85. How would you know if someone is good at motivating others?
86. If you had to write a book on motivating others, what would the chapter headings be?
87. What are the benefits to someone who is really good at motivating others?
88. What are the consequences to someone who is really poor at motivating others?

MOTIVATING OTHERS

89. What do you think the standard is on motivating others for someone in your role?
90. What happens when two people try to work together who are very different in their ability to motivate others?
91. What wisdom would you pass on to others trying to become better at motivating others?
92. When you select others, what do you look for in motivational skills?
93. Why do you think people end up being different in their ability to motivate others?

Dimension 4: Shows personal change and sense-making; learned it one place and applied it in another; can compare and contrast experiences; changes viewpoints across time; can explain personal development or evolution related to the competency

94. Compare and contrast examples of times you've been effective and ineffective at motivating others.
95. Contrast your on- and off-the-job success at motivating others.
96. Did you ever pass up a job or assignment because you were not confident enough in your skills at motivating others?
97. Do you ever use other skills to cover for your inability to motivate others?
98. Has not being able to motivate others ever figured in a failure, struggle, or setback you have had?
99. Has becoming better at motivating others ever helped you in other areas?
100. Has your ability to motivate others ever been the subject of a development plan for you?
101. Has your ability to motivate others always been this way?
102. Have you ever delegated or assigned someone a task because you didn't motivate others particularly well?
103. Have you ever made significant strides at becoming better at motivating others?
104. Have your skills at motivating others, good or bad, ever been the subject of your performance review or a career discussion?
105. How different are you across situations in your ability to motivate others?
106. How do you decide how motivating to be?
107. How much of your success is due to your ability to motivate others?
108. How transferable is your skill level at motivating others to different situations?
109. If you had to become better at motivating others in a hurry, what would you do?
110. Was there a time when you were not as good at motivating others?
111. What caused you to work to improve your skills at motivating others?
112. What event or series of events had the most impact on your ability to motivate others?
113. What's the most varied you can be in motivating others?
114. What was the shortest amount of time in which you increased your level of skill at motivating others?
115. When did you first realize your level of skill at motivating others?
116. When you know ahead of time that your usual skill level of motivating others won't work, what do you do?
117. Why do you think you deal with motivating others the way you do?
118. Why do you think your ability to motivate others is the way it is?*
119. How do you balance hard and soft rewards and methods of motivating?
120. How do you balance individual rights with team/organizational rights?*
121. How have you determined what turns people on?*
122. When do you stop trying to motivate.*
123. Do you use different motivational techniques for different people?*

MOTIVATING OTHERS

D. Follow-up Probes:

1. Are there times when you motivate people like that and times when you don't?
2. Could you contrast those two bosses for me?
3. Could you give me a few examples of how you've used or applied that?
4. Do you always motivate people like that or was that a special situation?
5. Do you ever turn off your need to motivate others and just go with the flow and let self-motivation take over?
6. Do you suppose if others would just try harder, they could learn to more effectively motivate people like you do?
7. Do you think that's all teachable?
8. Do you think you're better at motivating people than most? Why?
9. Do you think you would perform any differently if you could be more effective motivating others?
10. Have you always motivated that way or is this a recent development in you?
11. How did the others react when you did that?
12. How did you come up with that approach to motivating others in the first place?
13. How did you know that method of motivating would work?
14. How do others you have known approach that?
15. How far will you go before you cut line and try another approach?
16. How much did you have to give up to make it work?
17. How typical is this for you?
18. How would you approach that same situation today?
19. Is this natural for you, or do you really have to dig for it?
20. Was that a fair way to motivate them?
21. Was there a time when you didn't understand this about yourself?
22. What did you do after you got that feedback?
23. What did you do to adapt to that?
24. What did you learn from that?
25. Why did you choose that approach?
26. Why did you decide to take the risk?
27. Why did you do it that way?
28. Why did you time your attempt to motivate like that?
29. Why do you suppose organizations work that way?
30. Why do you think that didn't work?
31. Why do you think that happened that way?
32. Why do you think that worked?
33. Why do you think you have difficulty with that sometimes?
34. Why do you think you prefer to motivate that way?
35. Would you have done it that way with looser deadlines?
36. Would you have done it that way with tighter deadlines?

MOTIVATING OTHERS

E. Themes/Things to Look for:

Able to predict what people will respond to
Assessing people as individuals
Being approachable
Charisma
Complex and varied tactics to motivate
Drivers–why they motivate
Empathy
Extrovert
Inviting input
Likes to lead
One size doesn't fit all; sees differences
Passion
Patience with the unconverted
Interested in personal gain or the common good
Playing favorites
Pushing tasks/decisions down
Role model
Selective motivating
Sharing visibility and credit
Taking risks
Understanding others
Using both hard and soft motivators
Willingness to push
Working with troubled people

F. Most Likely Résumé:

1. Look for jobs like:

Fix-Its/Turnarounds
Scale (size shift) Assignments
Significant People Demands
Staff Leadership (Influencing Without Authority)
Scope (complexity) Assignments
Start-Ups

2. Look for develop-in-place assignments like:

Integrate diverse systems, processes, or procedures across decentralized and/or dispersed units.

Be a change agent; create a symbol for change; lead the rallying cry; champion a significant change and implementation.

Relaunch an existing product or service that's not doing well.

Create employee involvement teams.

Teach a course, seminar, or workshop on something you know a lot about.

Teach a course, seminar, or workshop on something you don't know well.

Assign a project to a group with a tight deadline.

Manage an ad hoc, temporary group of "green," inexperienced people as their coach, teacher, orienter, etc.

Manage an ad hoc, temporary group of balky and resisting people through an unpopular change or project.

Manage an ad hoc, temporary group including former peers to accomplish a task.

Manage an ad hoc, temporary group of people who are older and/or more experienced to accomplish a task.

Manage an ad hoc, temporary group of people where the temporary manager is a towering expert and the people in the group are not.

Manage an ad hoc, temporary group of people involved in tackling a fix-it or turnaround project.

Handle a tough negotiation with an internal or external client or customer.

Prepare and present a proposal of some consequence to top management.

Manage a group through a significant business crisis.

Take on a tough and undoable project, one where others who have tried it have failed.

Resolve an issue in conflict between two people, units, geographies, functions, etc.

Make peace with an enemy or someone you've disappointed with a product or service or someone you've had some trouble with or don't get along well with.

Manage a project team of people who are older and more experienced.

MOTIVATING OTHERS

3. **Best references to ask about or check:**
   Human Resource Professionals
   Past Associates/Constituencies
   Direct Reports

G. Learning Agility Evaluation:
1. What/Describing vs. Why/Explain
4. Spectator/Passive vs. Player/Participant
5. Tight/Rigid vs. Loose/Flexible
6. Reacting/Responsive vs. Adapting
9. Vague/General vs. Sharp/Specific
11. Generalizations vs. Specific Learnings
13. Simple Views vs. Complex Views
15. Linear vs. Use Contrasts/Analogies
21. View from Self vs. View from Point of View of Others

H. The LEADERSHIP ARCHITECT® Sort Card Connections:

1. Good (positive) if combined with high:
Inspiring 1, 16, 53
Good up 4, 8, 48
Charismatic 9, 14, 49
Takes stands 9, 57
Faces and resolves disagreements 12, 13, 34
Good with customers 15, 53
Can get people to take developmental assignments 19, 56
Good down 18, 20, 21, 23
Listened to 22, 29
Can get people to take the job 25
Can get others to sign 37
Good sideways 38, 42, 60
Finds hot buttons 56, 64
Can sell strategy/mission 58, 65
Promotes the team 60

2. Bad (negative) if combined with low or high (+):
May overpower/chill initiative (+1, 9, 16, 53)
Only uses soft techniques (+3, 7, 10, 21, 23)
Doesn't know when to stop pushing 10, 56
Questionable motives 22, 29
One way 33, 41
Only uses hard techniques (+35, 43, 53)
Doesn't deliver 47, 50, 53
Everything is the number one priority 50
Uses wrong techniques 56, 64

MOTIVATING OTHERS

3. Too much can contribute to the following Stallers and Stoppers:

A. What too much looks like (overused):

May not be good at building team spirit because of an overemphasis on motivating individuals; may be seen as providing preferential treatment by treating each person individually; may not take tough stands when the situation calls for it; may be reluctant to assign work with tough deadlines.

B. Too much might lead to these Stallers and Stoppers:
Overmanaging (117)

C. Compensators:
How to compensate for too much of this competency:
9, 12, 13, 18, 19, 20, 34, 35, 37, 50, 52, 56, 57, 60

D. Things to watch for:
Believing some class needs more motivating than others
Cheerleader
Playing favorites
The belief that everyone needs to "be motivated"
Smothers
Doesn't deliver consistent results

4. Too little can contribute to the following Stallers and Stoppers:

A. What too little looks like (unskilled):

Doesn't know what motivates others or how to do it; people under him/her don't do their best; not empowering and not a person many people want to work for, around or with; may be a one style fits all person, have simplistic models of motivation, or may not care as much as most others do; may be a driver just interested in getting the work out; may have trouble with people not like him/her; may be a poor reader of others, may not pick up on their needs and cues; may be judgmental and put people in stereotypical categories; intentionally or unintentionally demotivates others.

B. Too little might lead to these Stallers and Stoppers:
Poor Administrator (102)   Insensitive to Others (112)
Arrogant (104)   Performance Problems (118)
Failure to Build a Team (110)

C. Compensators:
How to substitute for too little of this competency:
1, 7, 12, 13, 16, 18, 19, 20, 21, 27, 31, 33, 37, 39, 47, 49, 53

MOTIVATING OTHERS

I. LEARNING ARCHITECT® Connections:

Look for people who act like and/or show evidence of:

- 2a. Problem Solving
- 4a. Getting Information
- 4c. Actively Involve
- 6. Contentious
- 8. Initiate
- 16. Collaborate
- 21. Changer
- 23. Orchestrator
- 34. Sizing Up Others

J. CHOICES ARCHITECT® Connections:

Look for people who act like and/or show evidence of:

First Edition (Released 1994)
- 14. Transaction Quality
- 15. Helps Others Succeed
- 23. Communicator

Second Edition (Released 2000)
- 9. Agile Communicator
- 12. Helps Others Succeed
- 15. People-Smart
- 21. Innovation Manager
- 24. Inspires Others

K. Difficulty to Develop:

26 (of 34)–Moderate

MOTIVATING OTHERS

37. NEGOTIATING

A. Definition:

Can negotiate skillfully in tough situations with both internal and external groups; can settle differences with minimum noise; can win concessions without damaging relationships; can be both direct and forceful as well as diplomatic; gains trust quickly of other parties to the negotiations; has a good sense of timing.

B. Arenas/Domains to Explore:

1. Bargaining for a fee/royalty/commission/override
2. Bargaining for headcount
3. Bargaining for office space
4. Bargaining for project funding
5. Bargaining for resources
6. Bargaining to get out of something
7. Bargaining with customs
8. Bargaining with immigration
9. Buying a business
10. Consultant/vendor/supplier bargaining
11. Contract negotiations
12. Disputes
13. Knowing when to close
14. Managing an acquisition
15. Marketing events
16. Mediating a dispute
17. Negotiating a deadline
18. Negotiating a strategic partnership
19. Negotiating a termination package
20. Negotiating for a legal settlement
21. Negotiating for a VIPs time
22. Negotiating for job arrangements
23. Negotiating for land
24. Negotiating to buy a car/house/major purchase
25. Negotiating with a customer
26. Negotiating with a group to do something they don't want to do
27. Negotiating with someone to take a job they don't want
28. Negotiations with the government
29. Sales events
30. Union bargaining

C. Sample Questions:

*Dimension 1: Been there, done that–has had direct personal experience(s) involving the competency–candidate was the prime player   Note: * means OK for campus*

1. Do you generally offer less than you are willing to settle for when you are negotiating for something?*
2. Has anyone ever accused you of messing something up because you didn't negotiate well?
3. Has anyone ever negotiated with you in bad faith?
4. Have you ever bargained to keep headcount?
5. Have you ever been involved in bargaining with a union?
6. Have you ever had a car that was a lemon and had to bargain with a dealership over a settlement?
7. Have you ever had to bargain with a peer over resources when the result was win/lose?*
8. Have you ever managed anything where the people or units reporting to you were in different locations? How did you negotiate from a distance?
9. Have you ever negotiated for a grade change in school?*
10. Have you ever negotiated for additional resources to complete a project?*
11. Have you ever settled a pay dispute with a vendor/supplier/consultant when the result was less money than they asked for?
12. Have you ever walked out during a negotiation?

NEGOTIATING

13. How do you buy your cars?
14. How do you handle customs/immigration when you travel internationally?
15. How do you tell when you need to stop bargaining and cut your losses?*
16. How have you done buying/selling land/houses/cars?
17. Tell me about a time when you brought two reluctant groups together.*
18. Tell me about a time when you conducted a formal negotiation with an outside group.
19. Tell me about a time when you were able to get a good deal for yourself or your organization because the other party was a weak negotiator.
20. Tell me about a time when you've negotiated with multiple peers.*
21. Tell me about a time when you've made peace with an adversary.*
22. Tell me about a time when you've served as a mediator.*
23. Tell me about a time when your attempt to negotiate got you into trouble.
24. Tell me about a time when your attempt to negotiate worked really well for you.
25. Was there ever a time when a blunder on your part harmed a negotiation?
26. What do you do to prepare when you know ahead of time that the negotiation will be difficult?*
27. What's the biggest negotiation you've lost?*
28. What's the biggest negotiation you've won?*
29. What's your bargaining strategy at garage and estate sales?*
30. When you are part of a negotiating team, what role do you usually play?

Dimension 2: Seen/been around others who were involved with the competency–good and bad; learns from others about self

31. Contrast the best and worst negotiators you know.*
32. Has negotiating ever been in any 360° survey done on you? Was your score among your highest, middle, or lowest?
33. Has poor negotiating skills on someone else's part ever created an obstacle for you or got in the way of something you were trying to accomplish?*
34. Have you ever talked with a coach or mentor about your negotiating skills?
35. Have you ever watched someone fail/get fired because they did not negotiate well?*
36. Have you ever watched someone overnegotiate to the point that it backfired?
37. Have you ever watched someone succeed because they negotiated well?*
38. Have you ever worked with a coach on negotiating?*
39. Have you ever worked with a person who excelled at negotiating?
40. Have you ever worked with a skills coach on negotiating?*
41. How do you get feedback about yourself on negotiating?
42. How often do you check with multiple sources when you get a piece of critical feedback on your negotiating skills?
43. Is there a historical figure you consider a model of negotiating?
44. What do others who are not your fans say about your negotiating skills?
45. What do others who like you say about your negotiating skills?
46. Which boss was the best at negotiating?
47. Which boss was the worst at negotiating?
48. Which direct report was the best at negotiating?
49. Which direct report was the worst at negotiating?
50. Which peer was the best at negotiating?

NEGOTIATING

51. Which peer was the worst at negotiating?
52. Who in your field or business is the best at negotiating?
53. Who do you consider a role model of negotiating skills?*
54. Who do you go to for advice on negotiating?
55. Who have you learned the most from about negotiating?*
56. Who is a higher-management role model for you on negotiating?
57. Who is a role model of negotiating skills outside of work?

Dimension 3: Knows how the competency works in theory; shows understanding

58. Are there situations or settings where someone should negotiate differently?
59. Do you think negotiating skills can be learned; how do you think people develop negotiating skills?
60. Do you think there is a way to compensate or work around low negotiating skills?
61. Has anyone asked you for your opinions/advice on negotiating?*
62. Have you ever attended a course on negotiating skills?
63. Have you ever been in a situation where you and others put negotiating skills on a success profile?
64. Have you ever been part of an effort to create a policy or a mission statement containing reference to being a good negotiator?
65. Have you ever been someone's coach or mentor who had problems with negotiating?
66. Have you ever created a development plan for someone on negotiating?
67. Have you ever criticized someone for not negotiating well?
68. Have you ever designed a program on negotiating skills?
69. Have you ever given a speech on negotiating skills?
70. Have you ever rewarded or recognized someone for having negotiating skills?
71. Have you ever taught a course negotiating skills?
72. Have you ever tried to help someone deal with negotiating more effectively?*
73. Have you ever tried to help someone improve their negotiating skills?
74. How do you think people develop negotiating skills?
75. How much negotiating is good and how much is too much?
76. How much of success do you think is due to negotiating skills compared with other characteristics?
77. How would you know if someone is bad at negotiating?
78. How would you know if someone is good at negotiating?
79. If you had to write a book on negotiating skills, what would the chapter headings be?
80. What are the benefits to someone who is really good at negotiating?
81. What are the consequences to someone who is really poor at negotiating?
82. What do you think the standard is on negotiating skills for someone in your role?
83. What happens if you negotiate too much?
84. What happens when two people try to work together who are very different in their negotiating abilities?
85. What wisdom would you pass on to others trying to become better at negotiating?
86. When you select others, what do you look for in negotiating skills?
87. Why do you think people end up having different negotiating abilities?

NEGOTIATING

Dimension 4: Shows personal change and sense-making; learned it one place and applied it in another; can compare and contrast experiences; changes viewpoints across time; can explain personal development or evolution related to the competency

88. Compare and contrast times when you've been effective and ineffective at negotiating with others.
89. Contrast your on- and off-the-job use of negotiating skills.
90. Did you ever pass up a job or assignment because you were not confident enough in your negotiating skills?
91. Do you ever use other skills to cover for your lack of negotiating skills?
92. Has becoming better at negotiating ever helped you in other areas?
93. Have negotiating skills ever figured in a failure, struggle, or setback you have had?
94. Have poor negotiating skills ever been the subject of a development plan for you?
95. Have you ever delegated or assigned someone a negotiating task because you didn't do particularly well at it?
96. Have you ever made significant strides at becoming better at negotiating?
97. Have your negotiating skills always been this way?
98. Have your negotiating skills, good or bad, ever been the subject of your performance review or a career discussion?
99. How different are you across situations in your negotiating skills?
100. How do you decide how much negotiating to do?
101. How much of your success is due to your negotiating skills?
102. How transferable are your negotiating skills to other situations?
103. If you had to become better at negotiating in a hurry, what would you do?
104. Was there a time when you were not as good at negotiating?
105. What caused you to work to improve your negotiating skills?
106. What event or series of events had the most impact on your negotiating skills?
107. What's the most varied you can be in negotiating?
108. What was the shortest amount of time in which you increased your level of skill at negotiating?
109. When did you first realize your level of skill at negotiating?
110. When you know ahead of time that your usual level of negotiating won't work, what do you do?
111. Why do you think you negotiate the way you do?
112. Why do you think your negotiating skills are the way they are?*
113. How do you think others negotiate with you?*
114. When do you stop trying to negotiate and cut line?*
115. Tell me about a time you negotiated well. Contrast this with a time you didn't negotiate well.*
116. Do you bargain differently with different people/groups?*
117. How important is it for you personally to win every negotiation?*

D. Follow-up Probes:

1. Are there times when you negotiate like that and times when you don't?
2. Could you contrast those two bosses for me?
3. Could you give me a few examples of how you've used or applied that?
4. Did you or the other person blink first?
5. Do you always negotiate like that or was that a special situation?
6. Do you ever turn off your need to negotiate with others and just go with the flow and let others take over?
7. Do you suppose if others would just try harder, they could learn to be a more effective negotiator?
8. Do you think that's all teachable?

NEGOTIATING

9. Do you think you're better at negotiating than most? Why?
10. Do you think you would perform any differently if you could be a more effective negotiator?
11. Have you always negotiated that way or is this a recent development in you?
12. Have you ever had to negotiate with someone you really disliked?
13. How did the others react when you did that?
14. How did you come up with that approach to negotiating in the first place?
15. How did you know that method of negotiating would work?
16. How do others you have known approach that?
17. How far will you go before you turn and try another approach?
18. How much did you have to give up to make it work?
19. How often do you use the "Let's meet in the middle" approach?
20. How typical is this for you?
21. How would you approach that same situation today?
22. Is this natural for you, or do you really have to dig for it?
23. Was that a fair way to negotiate with them?
24. Was there a time when you didn't understand this about yourself?
25. What did you do after you got that feedback?
26. What did you do to adapt to that?
27. What did you learn from that?
28. Why did you choose that approach?
29. Why did you decide to take the risk?
30. Why did you do it that way?
31. Why did you time your attempt to negotiate like that?
32. Why do you suppose organizations work that way?
33. Why do you think that didn't work?
34. Why do you think that happened that way?
35. Why do you think that worked?
36. Why do you think you have difficulty with that sometimes?
37. Why do you think you prefer to negotiate that way?
38. Would you have done it that way with looser deadlines?
39. Would you have done it that way with tighter deadlines?

E. Themes/Things to Look for:

Ability to predict what other people are going to do	Lets others save face
Able to take heat	Listens well
Awareness of impact on others	Noise/damage control skills
Calmness under stress/pressure	Not afraid to cut line
Can keep personal feeling from getting in the way	Not afraid to intimidate when necessary
Can play a hand without signaling what they've got	Political sensitivity
Can tolerate losing a battle to win the war	Pushes at the right times
Can walk away	Seeing feelings and emotions as data points
Clear communicator	Negotiates in some directions (levels, groups) better than others
Complex and varied negotiation tactics	Sense of equity

NEGOTIATING

Doesn't dodge tough issues but doesn't run over others
Finding common ground
Finds an agreement point
Good couching skills
Understanding the other side
Willing to lose something to gain elsewhere
Wins the deal but maintains the relationship
Redirects the discussion

F. Most Likely Résumé:

1. Look for jobs like:
International Assignments
Line to Staff Switches
Scope Assignments
Staff Leadership (Influencing Without Authority)
Start-Ups

2. Look for develop-in-place assignments like:
Integrate diverse systems, processes, or procedures across decentralized and/or dispersed units.
Manage the renovation of an office, floor, building, meeting room, warehouse, etc.
Plan a new site for a building (plant, field office, headquarters, etc.).
Plan an off-site meeting, conference, convention, trade show, event, etc.
Manage the purchase of a major product, equipment, materials, program, or system.
Work on a project that involves travel and study of an issue, acquisition, or joint venture off-shore or overseas, with a report back to management.
Get involved with the negotiation of a contract or agreement with international consequences.
Manage an ad hoc, temporary group of balky and resisting people through an unpopular change or project.
Manage the interface between consultants and the organization on a critical assignment.
Handle a tough negotiation with an internal or external client or customer.
Help shut down a plant, regional office, product line, business, operation, etc.
Manage liquidation/sale of products, equipment, materials, a business, furniture, overstock, etc.
Manage a dissatisfied internal or external customer; troubleshoot a performance or quality problem with a product or service.
Manage the assigning/allocating of office space in a contested situation.
Work on a team that's deciding who to keep and who to let go in a layoff, shutdown, delayering, or divestiture.
Manage a cost-cutting project.
Resolve an issue in conflict between two people, units, geographies, functions, etc.
Make peace with an enemy or someone you've disappointed with a product or service or someone you've had some trouble with or don't get along well with.
Be a member of a union-negotiating or grievance-handling team.

3. Best references to ask about or check:
Customers
Natural Mentors
Past Associates/Constituencies
Peers and Colleagues

G. Learning Agility Evaluation:
4. Spectator/Passive vs. Player/Participant
5. Tight/Rigid vs. Loose/Flexible
6. Reacting/Responsive vs. Adapting
10. Reactive vs. Initiating

NEGOTIATING

   11. Generalizations vs. Specific Learnings
   16. Few Rules of Thumb vs. Many and Varied Rules of Thumb
   21. View from Self vs. View from Point of View of Others
   22. Focus on Accomplishments vs. Focus on Solving Problems

H. The LEADERSHIP ARCHITECT® Sort Card Connections:

   1. Good (positive) if combined with high:
   Flexible; doesn't walk over people 2, 41
   Good up 4, 8, 48
   Gets career advantages 6
   Good down 7, 10, 21, 23
   Tough 9, 57
   Good with customers 15, 53
   Eyes on the goal 17, 50, 51, 53
   Gets people to take development assignments 19, 36
   Savvy; maze bright 33, 38, 48, 56
   Picks up the other sides point quickly 32, 33
   Light touch available as a tool 26
   Good spokesperson 27, 49
   Good sideways 38, 42, 60
   Accurately scopes out the other side 56, 64

   2. Bad (negative) if combined with low or high (+):
   Takes forever 1, 16, 62
   Not good up 4, 8
   For personal gain (+6)
   Overpowering (+9, 16, 35, 43, 53)
   Can't handle the pressure/stress 11
   Can't add value to initial positions 14, 30, 51
   Not good with customers 15
   Used for ill purposes 22, 29
   One way 33
   Commits political errors 38, 48
   Not good sideways 38, 42, 60
   Sometimes picks the wrong tactic 56, 64

   3. Too much can contribute to the following Stallers and Stoppers:

   A. What too much looks like (overused):

   May leave people-damage in his/her wake; may walk over people's feelings; may always need to win; may hang on to a position too long; may become overly accommodating and be reluctant to walk away; may need to smooth over everything; may take too long to get things decided.

   B. Too much might lead to these Stallers and Stoppers:
   Lack of Ethics and Values (109)

NEGOTIATING

C. Compensators:
How to compensate for too much of this competency:
2, 12, 16, 17, 30, 38, 41, 48, 50, 51, 52, 53, 56, 57, 63

D. Things to watch for:
Enjoys the process so much they lose sight of the goal
May win negotiation; lose relationship
Unrealistic need to close
Win/lose mentality
Won't lose a battle to win the war

4. Too little can contribute to the following Stallers and Stoppers:

A. What too little looks like (unskilled):
Not a good deal maker; doesn't come away with much; may use ineffective tactics–too hard or too soft; may have to win every battle or gives away too much to get the agreement; poor conflict manager, trouble dealing with attack, contention or non-negotiable points; may hold back and be afraid to take tough stands; poor listener; may not seek or know how to find common ground; may be too noisy and do too much damage to relationships; may not know how to be diplomatic, direct and polite.

B. Too little might lead to these Stallers and Stoppers:
None Apply

C. Compensators:
How to substitute for too little of this competency:
2, 9, 11, 12, 16, 27, 30, 32, 33, 36, 38, 48, 50, 51, 52, 56, 57, 64

I. LEARNING ARCHITECT® Connections:

Look for people who act like and/or show evidence of:

- 1c. Following a Plan
- 2a. Problem Solving
- 4a. Getting Information
- 4c. Actively Involve
- 6. Contentious
- 16. Collaborate
- 23. Orchestrator
- 36. Comfort with Paradox
- 38. Resilience

J. CHOICES ARCHITECT® Connections:

Look for people who act like and/or show evidence of:

First Edition (Released 1994)
- 8. Cool Transactor
- 14. Transaction Quality
- 21. Taking the Heat
- 22. Self-Talk
- 23. Communicator

Second Edition (Released 2000)
- 9. Agile Communicator
- 10. Conflict Manager
- 11. Cool Transactor
- 15. People-Smart
- 22. Taking the Heat

K. Difficulty to Develop:
27 (of 34)–Harder

38. ORGANIZATIONAL AGILITY

A. Definition:
Knowledgeable about how organizations work; knows how to get things done both through formal channels and the informal network; understands the origin and reasoning behind key policies, practices, and procedures; understands the cultures of organizations.

B. Arenas/Domains to Explore:
1. Academic program
2. Any multi-layer initiative
3. Benchmarking visit
4. Case studies in courses/workshops
5. Club/association management
6. Cross-organizational boundary initiatives
7. Dealing with unions
8. Entering new culture for the first-time
9. Event planning
10. Formal/informal systems
11. Insight into fallen organizations
12. Lobbying
13. Managing academic program/getting things done
14. Managing Total Quality Management/ process re-engineering
15. Meeting/conference management
16. Need to use other people's resources
17. Organizational development background/exposure
18. Outside consultant
19. Reading habits (Peters, Drucker, Jacques, Argyris, etc.)
20. Short-term assignment in alien unit
21. Small start-ups within a larger organization
22. Student government
23. Studies/projects/task forces studying cross-boundary processes
24. Successful cross-move
25. Understanding *Fortune/WSJ* articles on organizations
25. Understanding *Fortune/WSJ* articles on organizations
26. Visiting foreign businesses/organizations
27. Visitor to new organization

C. Sample Questions:

Dimension 1: Been there, done that–has had direct personal experience(s) involving the competency–candidate was the prime player   Note: * means OK for campus

1. Did you ever stumble at doing something important because you didn't understand how an organization worked?*
2. Do you ever do lunch or meet just to form alliances?
3. Has a gatekeeper who wouldn't let you through ever blocked you from getting something you wanted in an organization? What did you do?*
4. Has anyone ever accused you of messing something up because you didn't understand how to maneuver through the organization?
5. Have you ever been a part of a merger or acquisition where the two parties had quite different cultures?
6. Have you ever been an outside consultant?
7. Have you ever been involved in a court proceeding?
8. Have you ever been involved with a police investigation as a witness?
9. Have you ever been on the board of a professional organization?
10. Have you ever been part of a group writing a constitution or bylaws for a professional group?
11. Have you ever been part of a merger or acquisition team studying possible partners?

ORGANIZATIONAL AGILITY

12. Have you ever been part of forming an organization?*
13. Have you ever been part of settling an estate?
14. Have you ever had any significant dealings with the administrative side of a government organization?
15. Have you ever had material you needed in a foreign country hung up in customs?
16. Have you ever lodged a formal complaint with a brokerage?
17. Have you ever managed a unit located in a foreign country?
18. Have you ever managed anything where the people or units reporting to you were in different locations? How did you help them get things done inside the organization?
19. Have you ever provided testimony in front of a government body?
20. Have you ever sought special funding for a project in an organization?*
21. Have you ever worked for a charity/community service group?*
22. Have you ever worked on a political campaign?
23. Tell me about a time when you got a new or revised policy/practice/ procedure approved.*
24. Tell me about a time when you had to settle something of some complexity with a hospital administration.
25. Tell me about a time when you needed information quickly and couldn't get it through formal channels.*
26. Tell me about a time when you needed to use a lawyer to help you deal with a situation and an organization you couldn't handle yourself.
27. Tell me about a time when you created something from nothing.*
28. Tell me about a time when you tried to get something significant done through the government.
29. Tell me about a time when you tried to get something significant done through a school system.
30. Tell me about a time when you were in the role of a gatekeeper for a VIP/boss/executive.
31. Tell me about a time when you were under time pressure and had to get something approved.*
32. Tell me about a time when your knowledge of how to maneuver through an organization got you into trouble.
33. Tell me about a time when your knowledge of how to maneuver through an organization worked really well for you.
34. Tell me about a time you visited an organization in a foreign country.
35. What kind of a network do you have outside your own workgroup?
36. When you are new to an organization, how do you find out who the key players and gatekeepers are?

Dimension 2: Seen/been around others who were involved with the competency–good and bad; learns from others about self

37. Contrast the best and worst people you know at understanding and maneuvering through organizations.*
38. Has understanding and maneuvering through organizations ever been in any 360° survey done on you? Was your score among your highest, middle, or lowest?
39. Has the lack of understanding and maneuvering through organizations on someone else's part ever created an obstacle for you or got in the way of something you were trying to accomplish?*
40. Have you ever talked with a coach or mentor about your understanding and maneuvering through organizations?
41. Have you ever watched someone fail/get fired because they did not understand or maneuver through organizations well?*
42. Have you ever watched someone exaggerate understanding and maneuvering through organizations to the point that it backfired?
43. Have you ever watched someone succeed because they understood and maneuvered through organizations well?*
44. Have you ever worked with a coach on understanding and maneuvering through organizations?*

ORGANIZATIONAL AGILITY

45. Have you ever worked with a person who excelled at understanding and maneuvering through organizations?
46. Have you ever worked with a skills coach on understanding and maneuvering through organizations?*
47. How do you get feedback about yourself on understanding and maneuvering through organizations?
48. How often do you check with multiple sources when you get a piece of critical feedback on understanding and maneuvering through organizations?
49. Is there a historical figure you consider a model of understanding and maneuvering through organizations?
50. What do others who are not your fans say about your ability to understand and maneuver through organizations?
51. What do others who like you say about your ability to understand and maneuver through organizations?
52. Which boss was the best at understanding and maneuvering through organizations?
53. Which boss was the worst at understanding and maneuvering through organizations?
54. Which direct report was the best at understanding and maneuvering through organizations?
55. Which direct report was the worst at understanding and maneuvering through organizations?
56. Which peer was the best at understanding and maneuvering through organizations?
57. Which peer was the worst at understanding and maneuvering through organizations?
58. Who in your field or business is the best at understanding and maneuvering through organizations?
59. Who do you consider a current role model of understanding and maneuvering through organizations?*
60. Who do you go to for advice on understanding and maneuvering through organizations?
61. Who have you learned the most from about understanding and maneuvering through organizations?*
62. Who is a higher-management role model for you on understanding and maneuvering through organizations?
63. Who is a role model of understanding and maneuvering through organizations outside of work?

Dimension 3: Knows how the competency works in theory; shows understanding

64. Are there situations or settings where someone should be different on understanding and maneuvering through organizations?
65. Do you think the ability to understand and maneuver through organizations can be learned; how do you think people develop these skills?
66. Do you think there is a way to compensate or work around a low ability to understand and maneuver through organizations?
67. Has anyone asked you for your opinions/advice on understanding and maneuvering through organizations?*
68. Have you ever attended a course on understanding and maneuvering through organizations?
69. Have you ever criticized someone for not having understood and maneuvered through organizations well?*
70. Have you ever rewarded or recognized someone for having understood and maneuvered through organizations well?
71. Have you ever been in a situation where you and others put understanding and maneuvering through organizations on a success profile?
72. Have you ever been part of an effort to create a policy or a mission statement containing reference to being able to understand and maneuver through organizations?
73. Have you ever been someone's coach or mentor who had problems with understanding and maneuvering through organizations?
74. Have you ever created a development plan for someone on understanding and maneuvering through organizations?
75. Have you ever designed a program on understanding and maneuvering through organizations?
76. Have you ever given a speech on understanding and maneuvering through organizations?
77. Have you ever taught a course on understanding and maneuvering through organizations?

ORGANIZATIONAL AGILITY

78. Have you ever tried to help someone deal more effectively with understanding and maneuvering through organizations?*
79. Have you ever tried to help someone improve their ability to understand and maneuver through organizations?
80. How do you think people develop organizational agility skills?
81. How much organizational agility is good to have and how much is too much?
82. How much of success do you think is due to being able to understand and maneuver through organizations compared with other characteristics?
83. How would you know if someone is bad at being able to understand and maneuver through organizations?
84. How would you know if someone is good at being able to understand and maneuver through organizations?
85. If you had to write a book on organizational agility, what would the chapter headings be?
86. What are the benefits to someone who is really good at understanding and maneuvering through organizations?
87. What are the consequences to someone who is really poor at understanding and maneuvering through organizations?
88. What do you think the standard is on organizational agility for someone in your role?
89. What happens if you have or use too much organizational agility?
90. What happens when two people try to work together who have very different levels of organizational agility?
91. What wisdom would you pass on to others trying to become better at understanding and maneuvering through organizations?
92. When you select others, what do you look for in organizational agility?
93. Why do you think people end up being different in their ability to understand and maneuver through organizations?

Dimension 4: Shows personal change and sense-making; learned it one place and applied it in another; can compare and contrast experiences; changes viewpoints across time; can explain personal development or evolution related to the competency

94. Compare and contrast examples of when you've been effective and ineffective at understanding and maneuvering through organizations.
95. Contrast your on- and off-the-job ability to understand and maneuver through organizations.
96. Did you ever pass up a job or assignment because you were not confident enough in your skills at understanding and maneuvering through complex organizations?
97. Do you ever use other skills to cover for the lack of the ability to understand and maneuver through organizations?
98. Has becoming better at understanding and maneuvering through organizations ever helped you in other areas?
99. Has not having understood and maneuvered through organizations well ever figured in a failure, struggle, or setback you have had?
100. Has poor understanding and maneuvering through organizations ever been the subject of a development plan for you?
101. Has your organizational understanding always been this way?
102. Have you ever delegated or assigned someone a task because you didn't understand and maneuver through organizations particularly well?
103. Have you ever made significant strides at becoming better at understanding and maneuvering through organizations?
104. Have your organizational agility skills, good or bad, ever been the subject of your performance review or a career discussion?

ORGANIZATIONAL AGILITY

105. How different are you across situations in your ability to understand and maneuver through organizations?
106. How do you decide how much organizational maneuvering to do?
107. How much of your success is due to your ability to understand and maneuver through organizations?
108. How transferable are your maneuvering skills to other situations?
109. If you had to become better at maneuvering through organizations in a hurry, what would you do?
110. Was there a time when you were not as good at maneuvering through organizations?
111. What caused you to work to improve your skills at understanding and maneuvering through organizations?
112. What event or series of events had the most impact on your ability to understand and maneuver through organizations?
113. What's the most varied you can be in your ability to maneuver through organizations?
114. What was the shortest amount of time in which you increased your level of skill at understanding and maneuvering through organizations?
115. When did you first realize your level of skill at maneuvering through organizations?
116. When you know ahead of time that your usual ability to maneuver through organizations isn't adequate, what do you do?
117. Why do you think you maneuver through organizations the way you do?
118. Why do you think your ability to maneuver through organizations is the way it is?*
119. How do you wend your way through the organizational systems (purchasing, real estate, policies, construction) to get things done?
120. What do think some smart and dumb organizational (school) policies are? What do you do about the dumb policies?*

D. Follow-up Probes:

1. Are there times when you maneuver like that and times when you don't?
2. Could you contrast those two bosses for me?
3. Could you give me a few examples of how you've used or applied that?
4. Do you always maneuver like that or was that a special situation?
5. Do you suppose if others would just try harder, they could learn to be more effective at maneuvering through organizations like you do?
6. Do you think that's all teachable?
7. Do you think you're better at maneuvering than most? Why?
8. Do you think you would perform any differently if you could be more effective at understanding and maneuvering through the maze of organizations?
9. Have you always understood organizations that way or is this a recent development in you?
10. Have you ever had to maneuver around someone you really disliked?
11. Have you ever had to form a relationship with someone you really disliked to get things done in an organization?
12. How did the others react when you did that?
13. How did you come up with that approach to working your way through organizations in the first place?
14. How did you know that method of getting over that barrier would work?
15. How do others you have known approach that?
16. How far will you go before you cut line and try another approach?
17. How much did you have to give up to make it work?
18. How typical is this for you?
19. How would you approach that same situation today?

ORGANIZATIONAL AGILITY

20. Is this natural for you, or do you really have to dig for it?
21. Was that a fair way to maneuver around them?
22. Was there a time when you didn't understand this about yourself?
23. What did you do after you got that feedback?
24. What did you do to adapt to that?
25. What did you learn from that?
26. Why did you choose that approach?
27. Why did you decide to take the risk?
28. Why did you do it that way?
29. Why did you time your attempt to maneuver like that?
30. Why do you think that didn't work?
31. Why do you think that happened that way?
32. Why do you think you have difficulty with that sometimes?
33. Why do you suppose organizations work that way?
34. Why do you think that worked?
35. Would you have done it that way with looser deadlines?
36. Would you have done it that way with tighter deadlines?

E. Themes/Things to Look for:

Complex views of how organizations function
Drawing parallels between dissimilar organizations
Exposure to Organizational Development training
Exposure to the best and worst organizations have to offer
Exposure to varied organizations
Has a generalized model of how organizations work
Keeps people informed
Knows what must be followed and what to end around (understands the norms)
Knows who the stakeholders are
Opportunities to establish practices
Opportunities to set policies
Takes calculated risks to get things done
Understanding of what goes on at different layers of an organization
Understands the gatekeeper function in organizations
Working through large informal network

F. Most Likely Résumé:

1. Look for jobs like:

Chair of Projects/Task Forces
Cross-Moves
Fix-Its/Turnarounds
International Assignments
Line to Staff Switches
Scope (complexity) Assignments
Staff to Line Shifts
Staff Leadership (Influencing Without Authority)
Start-Ups

ORGANIZATIONAL AGILITY

2. **Look for develop-in-place assignments like:**

   Integrate diverse systems, processes, or procedures across decentralized and/or dispersed units.

   Manage the renovation of an office, floor, building, meeting room, warehouse, etc.

   Plan a new site for a building (plant, field office, headquarters, etc.).

   Plan for and start up something small (secretarial pool, athletic program, suggestion system, program, etc.).

   Launch a new product, service, or process.

   Be a change agent; create a symbol for change; lead the rallying cry; champion a significant change and implementation.

   Relaunch an existing product or service that's not doing well.

   Help shut down a plant, regional office, product line, business, operation, etc.

   Manage the assigning/allocating of office space in a contested situation.

   Manage a group through a significant business crisis.

   Work on a team looking at a reorganization plan where there will be more people than positions.

3. **Best references to ask about or check:**

   Boss' Boss(es)   Natural Mentors
   Human Resource Professionals   Past Associates/Constituencies

G. Learning Agility Evaluation:

   2. All or Nothing vs. Can See Many Sides
   3. Ordinary/Socially Acceptable vs. Insightful/Different
   7. Passive vs. Intrigued/Curious
   11. Generalizations vs. Specific Learnings
   13. Simple Views vs. Complex Views
   21. View from Self vs. View from Point of View of Others
   22. Focus on Accomplishments vs. Focus on Solving Problems

H. The LEADERSHIP ARCHITECT® Sort Card Connections:

1. **Good (positive) if combined with high:**

   Smooth operator 12, 31, 48

   Extensive network 4, 8, 42, 60

   Knows where to look 5, 24

   Puts organization first 27, 51, 53, 63, 65

   Maneuvers well around specific people 56, 64

   Can get the resources to get things done 39, 42, 53, 60

   Meets and gets through barriers 9, 12, 34

   Understands the customer's organization 15

   More likely to get ideas through the systems 28

   Advanced knowledge about how organizations function 52, 59

ORGANIZATIONAL AGILITY

2. **Bad (negative) if combined with low or high (+):**
   Doesn't wait long enough for knowledge to guide actions (+1, 16, 53) 41
   Too simple a viewpoint 2, 40
   Distrusted motives (+6, 8, 48)
   For own ends only 7, 21, 23
   Knows but can't deal with the maze 12, 34
   Distrusted motives 22, 29
   Takes a long time to learn new organizations 30, 32, 51
   All knees and elbows 12, 31, 48

3. **Too much can contribute to the following Stallers and Stoppers:**

   A. *What too much looks like (overused):*

   May spend too much time maneuvering for advantage; may spend too much time and energy working on issues that lack substance; may be seen as too political.

   B. *Too much might lead to these Stallers and Stoppers:*
   Overly Ambitious (103)   Overmanaging (117)
   Betrayal of Trust (105)   Political Missteps (119)
   Lack of Ethics and Values (109)

   C. *Compensators:*
   How to compensate for too much of this competency:
   4, 5, 8, 12, 17, 22, 27, 29, 51, 52, 53, 57, 63

   D. *Things to watch for:*
   Making everything more complex than it needs to be
   Need to "couch" everything
   Seeing everything through a political filter
   Seeing mazes where none exist
   Too much in love with figuring out the one best way through the maze
   Just a process person
   Too much in love with figuring out the one best way through the maze
   Just a process person

4. **Too little can contribute to the following Stallers and Stoppers:**

   A. *What too little looks like (unskilled):*

   Doesn't get things done in organizations beyond his/her area; may lack the interpersonal skills to get things done across boundaries; may not negotiate well within organizations; may be too timid and laid back to maneuver through organizations; may reject the complexity of organizations; may lack the experience or simply not know who and where to go; may be too impatient to learn; may neither know nor care to know the origins of how things work around the organization.

ORGANIZATIONAL AGILITY

B. *Too little might lead to these Stallers and Stoppers:*

Poor Administrator (102)

Performance Problems (118)

Political Missteps (119)

C. *Compensators:*

Competencies that substitute for too little of this competency:

5, 8, 32, 39, 48, 52, 59, 64

I. LEARNING ARCHITECT® Connections:

Look for people who act like and/or show evidence of:

1b. Trial and Error	11. Why/How
1c. Following a Plan	12. Rules of Thumb
2a. Problem Solving	15. Cautious
4a. Getting Information	21. Changer
9. Multiple Sources	23. Orchestrator

J. CHOICES ARCHITECT® Connections:

Look for people who act like and/or show evidence of:

First Edition (Released 1994)	Second Edition (Released 2000)
13. Role Flexibility	9. Agile Communicator
17. Hot/Direct Sources	15. People-Smart
23. Communicator	18. Role Flexibility

K. Difficulty to Develop:

28 (of 34)–Harder

ORGANIZATIONAL AGILITY

39. ORGANIZING

A. Definition:

Can marshal resources (people, funding, material, support) to get things done; can orchestrate multiple activities at once to accomplish a goal; uses resources effectively and efficiently; arranges information and files in a useful manner.

B. Arenas/Domains to Explore:

1. Any cross-boundary event
2. Any supervisory event
3. Arrange/manage a trip/tour
4. Case study groups/projects
5. Club/association management
6. Coaching
7. Consulting
8. Coordinating vendors/suppliers
9. Elected leadership positions
10. Event/conference planning/management
11. Family event management
12. Fund drives
13. Major grant proposal
14. Major presentation preparation
15. Meeting facilitation
16. Military experiences
17. Mixing private/public organizations
18. New processes
19. Political campaigns
20. Prepare a legal case
21. Putting together resources
22. Simultaneous activities
23. Starting up a product/service
24. Starting up an organization
25. Student government
26. Taskforce management
27. Teaching
28. Team captain
29. United Way
30. Using resources that aren't your own
31. Using union members
32. Volunteer groups

C. Sample Questions:

*Dimension 1: Been there, done that–has had direct personal experience(s) involving the competency–candidate was the prime player   Note: * means OK for campus*

1. Has anyone ever accused you of messing something up because of poor organizational skills?
2. Have you ever been responsible for shipping material to a foreign country on a tight time schedule?
3. Have you ever been stopped from doing something because you couldn't get others to share their resources with you? How did you recover?
4. Have you ever done a project that mixed union and non-union members together?
5. Have you ever had to depend upon volunteers to get something significant done?*
6. Have you ever managed a consulting project with team members from other offices/practices?
7. Have you ever managed a major conference or meeting?
8. Have you ever managed anything where the people or units reporting to you were in different locations? How did you get things organized at a distance?
9. Have you ever run a taskforce with representatives from many diverse units in the organization (school)?*
10. Have you ever straightened out someone else's mess?
11. How many major projects have you ever managed at the same time?
12. In your school work, did you get things done at the last moment or were you more planful?*
13. Tell me about a time when you had a project dropped on you (United Way, party, convention, trade show) that you'd never done before.*

ORGANIZING

14. Tell me about a time when you put together a deal.*
15. Tell me about a time when you put together a funding proposal.*
16. Tell me about a time when you put together a start-up.*
17. Tell me about a time when you put together and managed a project team.*
18. Tell me about a time when you traded something with a colleague to get a resource you needed.
19. Tell me about a time when your attempt to organize got you into trouble.
20. Tell me about a time when your attempt to organize worked really well for you.
21. What's the longest lead-time project you've ever managed?
22. What's the most complex set of logistics you've ever managed?

Dimension 2: Seen/been around others who were involved with the competency–good and bad; learns from others about self

23. Contrast the best and worst people you know at organizing people and resources to get things done.*
24. Has organizing people and resources to get things done ever been in any 360° survey done on you? Was your score among your highest, middle, or lowest?
25. Has the lack of ability to organize people and resources to get things done on someone else's part ever created an obstacle for you or got in the way of something you were trying to accomplish?*
26. Have you ever talked with a coach or mentor about organizing people and resources to get things done?
27. Have you ever watched someone fail/get fired because they did not organize people and resources well?*
28. Have you ever watched someone overdo organizing people and resources to get things done to the point that it backfired?
29. Have you ever watched someone succeed because they organized people and resources well?*
30. Have you ever worked with a coach on organizing people and resources to get things done?*
31. Have you ever worked with a person who excelled at organizing people and resources to get things done?
32. Have you ever worked with a skills coach on organizing people and resources to get things done?*
33. How do you get feedback about yourself on organizing people and resources to get things done?
34. How often do you check with multiple sources when you get a piece of critical feedback on organizing people and resources to get things done?
35. Is there a historical figure you consider a model of organizing people and resources to get things done?
36. What do others who are not your fans say about your ability to organize people and resources to get things done?
37. What do others who like you say about your ability to organize people and resources to get things done?
38. Which boss was the best at organizing people and resources to get things done?
39. Which boss was the worst at organizing people and resources to get things done?
40. Which direct report was the best at organizing people and resources to get things done?
41. Which direct report was the worst at organizing people and resources to get things done?
42. Which peer was the best at organizing people and resources to get things done?
43. Which peer was the worst at organizing people and resources to get things done?
44. Who in your field or business is best at organizing people and resources to get things done?
45. Who do you consider a current role model of organizing people and resources to get things done?*
46. Who do you go to for advice on organizing people and resources to get things done?
47. Who have you learned the most from about organizing people and resources to get things done?*
48. Who is a higher-management role model for you on organizing people and resources to get things done?
49. Who is a role model of organizing people and resources to get things done outside of work?

ORGANIZING

Dimension 3: Knows how the competency works in theory; shows understanding

50. Are there situations or settings where someone should be different in organizing people and resources to get things done?
51. Do you think organizing skills can be learned; how do you think people develop organizing skills?
52. Do you think there is a way to compensate or work around a low ability to organize people and resources to get things done?
53. Has anyone asked you for your opinions/advice on organizing people and resources to get things done?*
54. Have you ever attended a course on organizing skills?
55. Have you ever been in a situation where you and others put organizing skills on a success profile?
56. Have you ever been part of an effort to create a policy or a mission statement containing reference to having the ability to organize the people and resources to get things done?
57. Have you ever criticized someone for not organizing people and resources well?*
58. Have you ever rewarded or recognized someone for having organized people and resources well?
59. Have you ever been someone's coach or mentor who had problems with organizing skills?
60. Have you ever created a development plan for someone on organizing people and resources to get things done?
61. Have you ever designed a program on organizing people and resources to get things done?
62. Have you ever given a speech on organizing people and resources to get things done?
63. Have you ever taught a course on organizing people and resources to get things done?
64. Have you ever tried to help someone deal with organizing people and resources to get things done more effectively?*
65. Have you ever tried to help someone improve their organizing skills?
66. How do you think people develop organizational skills?
67. How much organizing ability is good to have and how much is too much?
68. How much of success do you think is due to organizing skills compared with other characteristics?
69. How would you know if someone is bad at organizing people and resources to get things done?
70. How would you know if someone is good at organizing people and resources to get things done?
71. If you had to write a book on organizing people and resources to get things done, what would the chapter headings be?
72. What are the benefits to someone who is really good at organizing people and resources to get things done?
73. What are the consequences to someone who is really poor at organizing people and resources to get things done?
74. What do you think the standard is on organizing people and resources to get things done for someone in your role?
75. What happens if you have or use too much of your organizing skills?
76. What happens when two people try to work together who are very different in their ability to organize the people and resources to get things done?
77. What wisdom would you pass on to others trying to become better at organizing people and resources to get things done?
78. When you select others, what do you look for in ability to organize people and resources to get things done?
79. Why do you think people end up being different in their ability to organize people and resources to get things done?

ORGANIZING

Dimension 4: Shows personal change and sense-making; learned it one place and applied it in another; can compare and contrast experiences; changes viewpoints across time; can explain personal development or evolution related to the competency

80. Compare and contrast examples when you've been effective and ineffective at organizing people and resources to get things done.
81. Contrast your on- and off-the-job use of your ability to organize people and resources to get things done.
82. Did you ever pass up a job or assignment because you were not confident enough in your skills at organizing people and resources?
83. Do you ever use other skills to cover for your lack of organization?
84. Has becoming better at organizing people and resources ever helped you in other areas?
85. Has poor organization of people and resources ever figured in a failure, struggle, or setback you have had?
86. Has poor organization of people and resources ever been the subject of a development plan for you?
87. Has your ability to organize people and resources always been at this level?
88. Have you ever delegated or assigned someone a task because you didn't organize people and resources particularly well?
89. Have you ever made significant strides at becoming better at organizing people and resources to get things done?
90. Have your resource organization skills, good or bad, ever been the subject of your performance review or a career discussion?
91. How different are you across situations in your organization of people and resources to get things done?
92. How do you decide how much organizing is needed?
93. How much of your success is due to your skills at organizing people and resources to get things done?
94. How transferable are your organizing skills to other situations?
95. If you had to become better at organization of people and resources in a hurry, what would you do?
96. Was there a time when you were not as good at organizing people and resources to get things done?
97. What caused you to work to improve your organizing people and resources to get things done skills?
98. What event or series of events had the most impact on your at organizing people and resources to get things done?
99. What's the most varied you can be in your organization of resources?
100. What was the shortest amount of time in which you increased your level of skill at organizing people and resources to get things done?
101. When did you first realize your level of skill at organizing resources?
102. When you know ahead of time that your skills at organizing people and resources to get things done aren't enough, what do you do?
103. Why do you think you deal with organizing people and resources to get things done the way you do?
104. Why do you think your skills at organizing people and resources to get things done are what they are?*
105. What do you think are some smart and dumb ways to organize resources that are outside of your direct control?*
106. How do you determine when you need to stop yourself from acting and spend the time organizing/ delegating and/or planning instead?

D. Follow-up Probes:

1. Are there times when you organize resources like that and times when you don't?
2. Could you contrast those two bosses for me?
3. Could you give me a few examples of how you've used or applied that?
4. Do you always organize resources like that or was that a special situation?
5. Do you suppose if others would just try harder, they could learn to be more effective at organize resources like you do?

ORGANIZING

6. Do you think that's all teachable?
7. Do you think you're better at organizing resources than most? Why?
8. Do you think you would perform any differently if you could be more effective at organizing resources?
9. Have you always organized resources that way or is this a recent development in you?
10. Have you ever had to organize resources with someone you really disliked?
11. How did the others react when you did that?
12. How did you come up with that approach to organizing resources in the first place?
13. How did you know that method of getting over that barrier would work?
14. How do others you have known approach that?
15. How far will you go before you cut line and try another approach?
16. How typical is this for you?
17. How would you approach that same situation today?
18. Is there a difference between managing people who report to you and people you borrow from other managers?
19. Is this natural for you, or do you really have to dig for it?
20. Was that a fair way to organize resources?
21. Was there a time when you didn't understand this about yourself?
22. What did you do after you got that feedback?
23. What did you do to adapt to that?
24. What did you learn from that?
25. Why did you choose that approach?
26. Why did you decide to take the risk?
27. Why did you do it that way?
28. Why did you time your attempt to organize resources like that?
29. Why do you think that didn't work?
30. Why do you think that happened that way?
31. Why do you think you have difficulty with that sometimes?
32. Why do you suppose organizations work that way?
33. Why do you think that worked?
34. Would you have done it that way with looser deadlines?
35. Would you have done it that way with tighter deadlines?

E. Themes/Things to Look for:

A sense of timing	Gets tougher when blocked
Ability to motivate others	Good teacher/instructor
Ability to project task completion schedules	Keeping personal feelings out of the task
Ability to relieve tensions	Keeps people informed
Ability to see things through the eyes of others	Knows policies, systems of suppliers/customers
Able to run internal simulations/scenarios	Knows policies, systems, stakeholders
Able to track simultaneous tasks/activities	Likes to coordinate/lead
Assertiveness	Listening
Being approachable	More specifying of what to do; less how to do
Not placing blame when something doesn't work	Orderly thought process
Checking in with people often	Overcoming obstacles
Clarity of directions	Taking risks
Clear communication style	Tasking without the responsibility

ORGANIZING

Communicating the larger picture
Complex and varied tactics for organizing resources
Effective and timely decisions
Empowerment
Tracking all components (people, funds, materials, support)
Trusting others
Willingness to delegate and trust

F. Most Likely Résumé:

1. Look for jobs like:

Chair of Projects/Task Forces
Cross-Moves
Fix-Its/Turnarounds
International Assignments
Scale Assignments
Scope (complexity) Assignments
Significant People Demands
Staff to Line Shifts
Start-Ups

2. Look for develop-in-place assignments like:

Integrate diverse systems, processes, or procedures across decentralized and/or dispersed units.
Manage the renovation of an office, floor, building, meeting room, warehouse, etc.
Plan a new site for a building (plant, field office, headquarters, etc.).
Plan an off-site meeting, conference, convention, trade show, event, etc.
Manage the purchase of a major product, equipment, materials, program, or system.
Manage the visit of a VIP (member of top management, government official, outside customer, foreign visitor, etc.).
Relaunch an existing product or service that's not doing well.
Manage an ad hoc, temporary group of "green," inexperienced people as their coach, teacher, orienter, etc.
Manage an ad hoc, temporary group of balky and resisting people through an unpopular change or project.
Manage an ad hoc, temporary group of low-competence people through a task they couldn't do by themselves.
Manage an ad hoc, temporary group of people involved in tackling a fix-it or turnaround project.
Manage an ad hoc, temporary group of people in a rapidly expanding operation.
Assemble an ad hoc team of diverse people to accomplish a difficult task.
Help shut down a plant, regional office, product line, business, operation, etc.
Manage liquidation/sale of products, equipment, materials, a business, furniture, overstock, etc.
Prepare and present a proposal of some consequence to top management.
Manage a dissatisfied internal or external customer; troubleshoot a performance or quality problem with a product or service.
Work on a team that's deciding who to keep and who to let go in a layoff, shutdown, delayering, or divestiture.
Manage a group through a significant business crisis.
Take on a tough and undoable project, one where others who have tried it have failed.
Manage the outplacement of a group of people.
Manage a cost-cutting project.
Build a multifunctional project team to tackle a common business issue or problem.
Audit cost overruns to assess the problem, and present your findings to the person or people involved.
Work on a team looking at a reorganization plan where there will be more people than positions.

3. Best references to ask about or check:

Direct Boss
Customers
Direct Reports

ORGANIZING

G. Learning Agility Evaluation:

1. What/Describing vs. Why/Explain
5. Tight/Rigid vs. Loose/Flexible
6. Reacting/Responsive vs. Adapting
9. Vague/General vs. Sharp/Specific
10. Reactive vs. Initiating
11. Generalizations vs. Specific Learnings
19. External Standards vs. Internal Standards
22. Focus on Accomplishments vs. Focus on Solving Problems

H. The LEADERSHIP ARCHITECT® Sort Card Connections:

1. Good (positive) if combined with high:

Flexible 2, 12, 40
In service of getting it done 15, 53
Keeps cool 11, 12, 33
Gives out important pieces 18
Model task manager 18, 20, 35
Picks the right people 25, 56
Can push ideas through the organization 28
Can rally a volunteer force 36, 60
Can organize across boundaries 38, 42
Gets the resources from anywhere 51, 53

2. Bad (negative) if combined with low or high (+):

May lose the team (+1, 16) 33, 41
Rigid (+22) 2, 12, 40
For who's benefit (+6, 8, 48)
May fold under pressure 9, 37, 57
Loner; may want things their own way (+9, 57) 33
May lose composure 11, 12, 33
Picks the wrong people 25, 56
Can't get the resources from some 29
Has trouble getting the resources 38, 42, 60

3. Too much can contribute to the following Stallers and Stoppers:

A. What too much looks like (overused):

May not be tolerant of normal chaos; may too often want to do things his/her own way; may not be open to suggestions and input; may lose their effectiveness when things don't go as planned.

B. Too much might lead to these Stallers and Stoppers:

Unable to Adapt to Differences (101)
Blocked Personal Learner (106)
Defensiveness (108)
Failure to Build a Team (110)
Insensitive to Others (112)

ORGANIZING

    C. Compensators:
       How to compensate for too much of this competency:
          2, 11, 12, 26, 32, 33, 36, 40, 46, 52, 60

    D. Things to watch for:

Rigid	Does for personal power
Not open to input	Too much into detail
Loner	Controlling

4. Too little can contribute to the following Stallers and Stoppers:

    A. What too little looks like (unskilled):

    Doesn't pull resources together effectively; may not know how to find and arrange people, materials, budget, etc.; may be a poor delegator and planner and not very motivating to work with; performance decreases as the number of simultaneous activities increase; may rely too much on self; may scramble at the last minute and have to work long hours to finish; may not anticipate or be able to see how multiple activities come together.

    B. Too little might lead to these Stallers and Stoppers:
    Poor Administrator (102)
    Failure to Build a Team (110)
    Performance Problems (118)

    C. Compensators:
       How to substitute for too little of this competency:
          9, 18, 20, 25, 36, 47, 52, 60

I. LEARNING ARCHITECT® Connections:

Look for people who act like and/or show evidence of:

1c. Following a Plan	15. Cautious
4a. Getting Information	16. Collaborate
4c. Actively Involve	23. Orchestrator
9. Multiple Sources	32. Diversity in Others
13. Focused	34. Sizing Up Others

J. CHOICES ARCHITECT® Connections:

Look for people who act like and/or show evidence of:

First Edition (Released 1994)	**Second Edition (Released 2000)**
22. Self-Talk	8. Solution Finder
	10. Conflict Manager

K. Difficulty to Develop:

20 (of 34)–Easier

40. *DEALING WITH* PARADOX

A. Definition:

Can act in ways that seem contradictory; is very flexible and adaptable when facing tough calls; can combine seeming opposites like being compassionately tough, stand up for self without trampling others, set strong but flexible standards; can act differently depending upon the situation; is seen as balanced despite the conflicting demands of the situation.

B. Arenas/Domains to Explore:

1. A leader at 10 AM; a follower at 11 AM
2. Acting counter to the available information; acting on gut feel
3. Actively listening to a view you already have decided to reject
4. Being a responsible member of the loyal opposition
5. Blowing the whistle on a friend
6. Contradicting a prior stance in front of the same audience
7. Crises
8. Dealing with a bad boss
9. Deferring to others
10. Disciplinary situations
11. Ethical problems
12. Exposure to an unfamiliar set of norms/cultural rituals
13. Firing friends
14. Fix-its
15. Forgives and forgets quickly; it's just business
16. Helping an enemy
17. Job change
18. Legal testimony
19. Life choices
20. Losing battles to win wars
21. Moral dilemmas
22. On/off-work personality differences
23. Operating in a foreign environment far removed from home norms
24. Overplaying a weak hand
25. Performance appraisal discussions
26. Personal challenges
27. Quitting a job you like over a principle
28. Sometimes democratic/participative; sometimes command
29. Spokesperson for a position they don't fully support
30. Take contradictory stands on issues within different contexts
31. The velvet hammer
32. Tough love
33. Underplaying a strong hand

C. Sample Questions:

Dimension 1: Been there, done that–has had direct personal experience(s) involving the competency–candidate was the prime player   Note: * means OK for campus

1. Has anyone ever accused you of messing something up because of inflexibility or inability to adapt?
2. Have you ever agreed to something you really didn't believe in just to win another point later?*
3. Have you ever been required to tell a customer something that really wasn't true to save the sale?
4. Have you ever changed jobs/gotten a promotion and found that your former way of managing was half effective?*
5. Have you ever had a work (or school) associate who was significantly different socially?*
6. Have you ever had to give a speech or inform a group on something you personally didn't agree with?
7. Have you ever had to give legal testimony for your organization where you knew more than you answered?
8. Have you ever had to manage a fix-it or crisis? Tell me what tight wires you had to walk.*

DEALING WITH PARADOX

9. Have you ever managed anything where the people or units reporting to you were in different locations? How did you handle the conflicting demands of different locations?
10. Have you ever not told the whole story to someone in a career discussion or a performance appraisal?
11. Have you ever significantly helped an enemy or someone you dislike?*
12. How do you deal with having proprietary information others need but you can't disclose?*
13. How do you react when you hear a politician say one thing and then do/vote another way?*
14. In a foreign country, have you ever done or said anything you would never say or do back in your home country?*
15. Tell me about a time when you had to act one way, and then a few minutes later act in a totally different way.*
16. Tell me about a time when you have had to administer tough love.*
17. Tell me about a time when you were under personal attack and caught between wanting to maintain a relationship with someone and maintain your dignity as well.*
18. Tell me about a time when your attempts to be flexible got you into trouble.
19. Tell me about a time when your attempts to be flexible worked really well for you.
20. Tell me about an ethical dilemma where you felt trapped.*
21. What do you do when you find yourself at odds over issues or principles of upper management but you want to continue with the organization?

Dimension 2: Seen/been around others who were involved with the competency–good and bad; learns from others about self

22. Contrast the most and least flexible or adaptable people you know.*
23. Has flexibility or adaptability ever been in any 360° survey done on you? Was your score among your highest, middle, or lowest?
24. Has lack of flexibility or adaptability on someone else's part ever created an obstacle for you or got in the way of something you were trying to accomplish?*
25. Have you ever talked with a coach or mentor about your flexibility or adaptability?
26. Have you ever watched someone fail/get fired because they lacked flexibility or adaptability?*
27. Have you ever watched someone overdo flexibility and adaptability to the point that it backfired?
28. Have you ever watched someone succeed because they were very flexible or adaptable?*
29. Have you ever worked with a coach on flexibility or adaptability?*
30. Have you ever worked with a person who excelled at being flexible or adaptable?
31. Have you ever worked with a skills coach on flexibility or adaptability?*
32. How do you get feedback about yourself on flexibility or adaptability?
33. How often do you check with multiple sources when you get a piece of critical feedback on your flexibility or adaptability?
34. Is there a historical figure you consider a model of flexibility or adaptability?
35. What do others who are not your fans say about your flexibility or adaptability?
36. What do others who like you say about your flexibility or adaptability?
37. Which boss was the best at being flexible or adaptable?
38. Which boss was the worst at being flexible or adaptable?
39. Which direct report was the best at being flexible or adaptable?
40. Which direct report was the worst at being flexible or adaptable?
41. Which peer was the best at being flexible or adaptable?
42. Which peer was the worst at being flexible or adaptable?

DEALING WITH PARADOX

43. Who in your field or business is the best at being flexible or adaptable?
44. Who do you consider a current role model of being flexible or adaptable?*
45. Who do you go to for advice on being flexible or adaptable?
46. Who have you learned the most from about dealing with paradox and being flexible or adaptable?*
47. Who is a higher-management role model for you on being flexible or adaptable?
48. Who is a role model of being flexible or adaptable outside of work?

Dimension 3: Knows how the competency works in theory; shows understanding

49. Are there situations or settings where someone should be different on dealing with paradox and being flexible or adaptable?
50. Do you think flexibility or adaptability can be learned; how do you think people develop flexibility or adaptability skills?
51. Do you think there is a way to compensate or work around low flexibility or adaptability?
52. Has anyone asked you for your opinions/advice on dealing with paradox and being flexible or adaptable?*
53. Have you ever attended a course on dealing with paradox and being flexible or adaptable?
54. Have you ever been in a situation where you and others put dealing with paradox and being flexible or adaptable on a success profile?
55. Have you ever been part of an effort to create a policy or a mission statement containing reference to being flexible or adaptable?
56. Have you ever been someone's coach or mentor who had problems with flexibility or adaptability?
57. Have you ever created a development plan for someone on dealing with paradox and being flexible or adaptable?
58. Have you ever criticized someone for not dealing with paradox and being flexible or adaptable?
59. Have you ever designed a program on dealing with paradox and being flexible or adaptable?
60. Have you ever given a speech on dealing with paradox and being flexible or adaptable?
61. Have you ever rewarded or recognized someone for dealing with paradox and being flexible or adaptable?
62. Have you ever taught a course on dealing with paradox and being flexible or adaptable?
63. Have you ever tried to help someone deal more effectively with paradox?*
64. Have you ever tried to help someone improve their ability to deal with paradox?
65. Have you ever tried to help someone improve their flexibility or adaptability?
66. How much flexibility or adaptability is good to have and how much is too much?
67. How much of success do you think is due to the ability to deal with paradox compared with other characteristics?
68. How would you know if someone is bad at dealing with paradox?
69. How would you know if someone is good at dealing with paradox?
70. If you had to write a book on dealing with paradox, what would the chapter headings be?
71. What are the benefits to someone who is really good at dealing with paradox?
72. What are the consequences to someone who is really poor at dealing with paradox?
73. What do you think the standard is on dealing with paradox for someone in your role?
74. What happens if you are too flexible or adaptable?
75. What happens when two people try to work together who are very different on how they deal with paradox?
76. What wisdom would you pass on to others trying to become better at dealing with paradox?
77. When you select others, what do you look for in ability to deal with paradox?
78. Why do you think people end up being different in their ability to deal with paradox?

DEALING WITH PARADOX

Dimension 4: Shows personal change and sense-making; learned it one place and applied it in another; can compare and contrast experiences; changes viewpoints across time; can explain personal development or evolution related to the competency

79. Compare and contrast examples of times you've been flexible and adaptable and times you've been inflexible and rigid.
80. Contrast your on- and off-the-job flexibility or adaptability.
81. Did you ever pass up a job or assignment because you were not confident enough in your ability to be flexible and adaptable?
82. Do you ever use other skills to cover for your lack of flexibility or adaptability?
83. Has becoming more flexible or adaptable ever helped you in other areas?
84. Has not being flexible or adaptable enough ever figured in a failure, struggle, or setback you have had?
85. Has poor personal flexibility and adaptability ever been the subject of a development plan for you?
86. Has your flexibility or adaptability always been this way?
87. Have you ever delegated or assigned someone a task because you weren't flexible or adaptable enough for the task?
88. Have you ever made significant strides at becoming better at being flexible or adaptable?
89. Have your flexibility or adaptability, good or bad, ever been the subject of your performance review or a career discussion?
90. How different are you across situations with your flexibility or adaptability?
91. How do you decide how flexible or adaptable to be?
92. How much of your success is due to your flexibility or adaptability?
93. How transferable is your flexibility or adaptability to other situations?
94. If you had to become more flexible or adaptable in a hurry, what would you do?
95. Was there a time when you were not as flexible or adaptable?
96. What caused you to work at being more flexible or adaptable?
97. What event or series of events had the most impact on your flexibility or adaptability?
98. What's the most varied you can be in personal flexibility?
99. What was the shortest amount of time in which you increased your level of skill at being flexible or adaptable?
100. When did you first realize your level of skill at being flexible or adaptable?
101. When you know ahead of time that your usual level of flexibility or adaptability won't work, what do you do?
102. Why do you think you deal with personal flexibility the way you do?
103. Why do you think your flexibility or adaptability is the way it is?*
104. What are the most important balances to maintain?*
105. Are you a walking contradiction?*
106. Have the terms two-faced or wishy-washy ever been applied to you?*
107. What are some of the toughest transitions you've made?*
108. How consistent are you across situations?*
109. Do you overdo and underdo certain behaviors?

D. Follow-up Probes:

1. Are there times when you act like that and times when you don't?
2. Could you contrast those two bosses for me?
3. Could you give me a few examples of how you've used or applied that?
4. Do you always act like that or was that a special situation?
5. Do you suppose if others would just try harder, they could learn to be more effective at being able to act in seemingly contradictory ways?

DEALING WITH PARADOX

6. Do you think that's teachable?
7. Do you think you're better at dealing with paradox than most? Why?
8. Do you think you would perform any differently if you could be more effective at dealing with paradox?
9. Have you always been able to deal with acting in paradoxical ways or is this a recent development in you?
10. How did the others react when you did that?
11. How did you come up with that approach to dealing with paradox in the first place?
12. How did you know that method of getting over that paradox would work?
13. How do others you have known approach that?
14. How typical is this for you?
15. How would you approach that same situation today?
16. Is this natural for you, or do you really have to dig for it?
17. Was that a fair way to act around them?
18. Was there a time when you didn't understand this about yourself?
19. What did you do after you got that feedback?
20. What did you do to adapt to that?
21. What did you learn from that?
22. Why did you choose that approach?
23. Why did you decide to take the risk?
24. Do you enjoy paradoxes?
25. Does it bother you to be seen differently by different people?
26. How do you feel about acting differently across situations?
27. Why did you do it that way?
28. Why did you time your attempt to deal with paradox like that?
29. Why do you suppose organizations work that way?
30. Why do you think that didn't work?
31. Why do you think that happened that way?
32. Why do you think that worked?
33. Why do you think you have difficulty with that sometimes?
34. Would you have acted that way with looser deadlines?
35. Would you have acted that way with tighter deadlines?

E. Themes/Things to Look for:

Ability and willingness to take the context into consideration

Has a number of gradations of style to apply depending upon the situation

No blind adherence to consistency

Not searching for a just world

Realism; lack of bland, socially acceptable responses

Sees situations as different; answers aren't always the same

Thinks in balances

Tolerance and understanding of other people being different across settings

Understands the difference between what politicians say and what they do/vote

Willing to change views

Speaks of times for this, times for that

Doesn't overdo anything

DEALING WITH PARADOX

F. Most Likely Résumé:

1. Look for jobs like:

Chair of Projects/Task Forces
Cross-Moves
Fix-Its/Turnarounds
Heavy Strategic Demands
International Assignments
Line to Staff Switches
Scope (complexity) Assignments
Staff Leadership (Influencing Without Authority)
Start-Ups

2. Look for develop-in-place assignments like:

Make speeches/be a spokesperson for the organization.

Manage an ad hoc, temporary group of balky and resisting people through an unpopular change or project.

Manage an ad hoc, temporary group of people where the people in the group are towering experts but the temporary manager is not.

Manage an ad hoc, temporary group of people involved in tackling a fix-it or turnaround project.

Manage an ad hoc, temporary group of people in a rapidly expanding operation.

Assemble an ad hoc team of diverse people to accomplish a difficult task.

Take on a tough and undoable project, one where others who have tried it have failed.

Take on a task you dislike or hate to do.

Make peace with an enemy or someone you've disappointed with a product or service or someone you've had some trouble with or don't get along well with.

Build a multifunctional project team to tackle a common business issue or problem.

Audit cost overruns to assess the problem, and present your findings to the person or people involved.

Work on a team looking at a reorganization plan where there will be more people than positions.

3. Best references to ask about or check:

Direct Boss
Natural Mentors

G. Learning Agility Evaluation:

2. All or Nothing vs. Can See Many Sides
5. Tight/Rigid vs. Loose/Flexible
6. Reacting/Responsive vs. Adapting
13. Simple Views vs. Complex Views
15. Linear vs. Use Contrasts/Analogies
16. Few Rules of Thumb vs. Many and Varied Rules of Thumb
17. Avoid Discussion of Weaknesses vs. Comfortably Sharing Shortcomings
20. Avoids Responsibility for Mistakes vs. Admits and Learns from Mistakes

H. The LEADERSHIP ARCHITECT® Sort Card Connections:

1. Good (positive) if combined with high:

Flexible problem solver 2, 37, 51
Knowledgeable about how business works 5, 46, 58
Can take charge 9, 12, 34
Can think their way out of boxes 30, 50, 51
Good call on needs 56, 64

DEALING WITH PARADOX

2. **Bad (negative) if combined with low or high (+):**

   Wishy-washy (+2) 1, 16, 57

   May scare/confuse others (+1, 2, 16)

   Knows it but doesn't act on it 1, 16, 50

   Gets in trouble with higher management; they see different people 8, 48

   Seen as political, self-serving, or a chameleon 22, 29

   Doesn't make it easy on others to figure it out 27, 44

   Knows it but doesn't speak out 34, 57

   Bad reads on what's required 56, 64

3. **Too much can contribute to the following Stallers and Stoppers:**

   A. *What too much looks like (overused):*

   May be seen as two-faced or wishy-washy; may change too easily from one style or mode to another; may misread what skills are called for; may confuse people who observe them across different settings; may be misinterpreted.

   B. *Too much might lead to these Stallers and Stoppers:*

   Lack of Ethics and Values (109)

   C. *Compensators:*

   How to compensate for too much of this competency:
   5, 9, 12, 17, 29, 30, 34, 37, 38, 47, 50, 51, 52, 53, 58

   D. *Things to watch for:*

Impulsivity (a false showing)	Unaware of their impact
Internally driven change; not adjusting to conditions	Wishy-washy
So busy matching conditions that original purpose lost	Confuses others

4. **Too little can contribute to the following Stallers and Stoppers:**

   A. *What too little looks like (unskilled):*

   Not very flexible; can't shift gears readily; one-trick pony (although may be very good at that one trick); believes strongly in personal consistency and following a few principles; tries to get everything done one way; doesn't take a balanced approach; may be seen as rigidly following and overdoing their one best way; may rely too much on personal strengths; has trouble shifting modes of behavior in the same meeting or situation.

   B. *Too little might lead to these Stallers and Stoppers:*

Unable to Adapt to Differences (101)	Lack of Ethics and Values (109)
Lack of Composure (107)	Non-Strategic (114)
Defensiveness (108)	Overmanaging (117)

   C. *Compensators:*

   How to substitute for too little of this competency:
   2, 12, 16, 32, 57

DEALING WITH PARADOX

I. LEARNING ARCHITECT® Connections:

Look for people who act like and/or show evidence of:

1a. Pure Action
1b. Trial and Error
1c. Following a Plan
2a. Problem Solving
2b. Visioning
2c. Intuition
3a. Checking Feelings
3b. Self-Talk
3c. Personal Experience
4a. Getting Information
4b. Modeling
4c. Actively Involve
10. Complexity
22. Experimenter
27. Conceptualizer
28. Creator
36. Comfort with Paradox
37. Flexibility

J. CHOICES ARCHITECT® Connections:

Look for people who act like and/or show evidence of:

First Edition (Released 1994)
2. Essence
6. Visionary
8. Cool Transactor
11. Open to Diversity
13. Role Flexibility
18. Into Everything

Second Edition (Released 2000)
5. Easy Shifter
6. Essence
7. Inquisitive
11. Cool Transactor
14. Open-Minded
18. Role Flexibility

K. Difficulty to Develop:

28 (of 34)–Harder

41. PATIENCE

A. Definition:

Is tolerant with people and processes; listens and checks before acting; tries to understand the people and the data before making judgments and acting; waits for others to catch up before acting; sensitive to due process and proper pacing; follows established process.

B. Arenas/Domains to Explore:

1. A lot going on at once
2. Bad bosses
3. Being in the audience
4. Conflict with others
5. Counseling
6. Door slammed in face
7. Feedback facilitation
8. Goals thwarted
9. Impossible deadlines
10. In a Bad Job
11. In the face of incompetence
12. Kept waiting
13. Late projects
14. Learning the computer
15. Long-drawn-out meetings
16. Older people
17. Opposite opinion
18. Outmaneuvered
19. People they dislike
20. Poor treatment
21. Powerless situations
22. Rejection
23. Setbacks
24. Slow negotiation
25. Slow talkers
26. Tasks they dislike
27. Unanswered complaint
28. Under stress
29. Unfairly treated
30. Waiting on acts of nature
31. Waiting your political turn
32. With children
33. With different styles
34. With less-skilled people
35. With the handicapped
36. With the unmotivated

C. Sample Questions:

*Dimension 1: Been there, done that–has had direct personal experience(s) involving the competency–candidate was the prime player   Note: * means OK for campus*

1. Compared to other people, how much air time do you usually take up in a meeting?
2. Do you doodle during meetings?
3. Do you drum your fingers in meetings?
4. Do you finish other people's sentences?*
5. Do you generally give suggestions to meeting managers and facilitators on how to move things along?*
6. Do you interrupt others while they are still talking?*
7. Do you usually talk first or second when meeting someone for the first time?*
8. Has anyone ever accused you of messing something up because of being impatient?
9. Have you ever asked someone to skip ahead in their presentation?
10. Have you ever managed anything where the people or units reporting to you were in different locations? How did you stay patient/tolerant with diverse people and processes at a distance?
11. Have you ever maneuvered to get ahead of others in a line?*
12. Have you ever walked out of a store because the service was slow?*

PATIENCE

13. How are you at waiting in line/in traffic/for a delayed plane?*
14. How do you check for understanding what others have said?*
15. How do you feel when you have something you really want to say and your political sense tells you to just keep it to yourself?*
16. How do you feel when you have something you want badly to say but someone else is taking up all the air time?*
17. How do you make time for listening to people?
18. How do you manage people who interrupt others a lot?
19. How do you react when your patience is really tested?*
20. How do you regain your composure after you lose it?*
21. How do you respond when people say they don't understand what you just said or what you meant?*
22. How good are you at suffering fools wisely?*
23. How long can you listen once you get it?*
24. How much of a rule follower are you?*
25. How much of what occurs to you to say in your head do you eventually say?*
26. How soon after you have come to a conclusion in a meeting do you tell others about it?*
27. Tell me about a time when you coached a team or individual.*
28. Tell me about a time when you had to communicate something important to someone who did not speak your language very well.
29. Tell me about a time when you had to deal with a person or group who could only see their side of the issue.*
30. Tell me about a time when you had to deal with someone who was very unreasonable.*
31. Tell me about a time when you had to get along with someone with a very different cadence (very slow, fast, detail-oriented, mercurial).
32. Tell me about a time when you had to learn a new skill.*
33. Tell me about a time when you had to work on a project with less skilled/less knowledgeable people.*
34. Tell me about a time when you taught someone to do something new.*
35. Tell me about a time when your patience got you into trouble.
36. Tell me about a time when your patience worked really well for you.
37. What do you do in a group when one person is holding all the others from moving forward?
38. What do you do when you're bored in a meeting?
39. What do you do when your audience just isn't getting it?

Dimension 2: Seen/been around others who were involved with the competency–good and bad; learns from others about self

40. Contrast the most and least patient people you know.*
41. Has patience ever been in any 360° survey done on you? Was your score among your highest, middle, or lowest?
42. Has lack of patience on someone else's part ever created an obstacle for you or got in the way of something you were trying to accomplish?*
43. Have you ever talked with a coach or mentor about patience?
44. Have you ever watched someone fail/get fired because they were not patient?*
45. Have you ever watched someone exaggerate patience to the point that it backfired?
46. Have you ever watched someone succeed because they were patient?*
47. Have you ever worked with a coach on patience?*

PATIENCE

48. Have you ever worked with a person who excelled at patience?
49. Have you ever worked with a skills coach on being more patient?*
50. How do you get feedback about yourself on patience?
51. How often do you check with multiple sources when you get a piece of critical feedback on your patience?
52. Is there a historical figure you consider a model of patience?
53. What do others who are not your fans say about your patience?
54. What do others who like you say about your patience?
55. Which boss was the best at being patient?
56. Which boss was the worst at being patient?
57. Which direct report was the best at being patient?
58. Which direct report was the worst at being patient?
59. Which peer was the best at being patient?
60. Which peer was the worst at being patient?
61. Who in your field or business is best at being patient?
62. Who do you consider a role model of being patient?*
63. Who do you go to for advice on patience?
64. Who have you learned the most from about patience?*
65. Who is a higher-management role model for you on being patient?
66. Who is a role model of being patient outside of work?

Dimension 3: Knows how the competency works in theory; shows understanding

67. Are there situations or settings where someone should be different on patience levels?
68. Do you think patience can be learned; how do you think people develop patience?
69. Do you think there is a way to compensate or work around being impatient?
70. Has anyone asked you for your opinions/advice on patience?*
71. Have you ever attended a course on patience?
72. Have you ever been in a situation where you and others put patience on a success profile?
73. Have you ever been part of an effort to create a policy or a mission statement containing reference to being patient?
74. Have you ever been someone's coach or mentor who had problems with patience?
75. Have you ever created a development plan for someone on patience?
76. Have you ever criticized someone for not being patient?
77. Have you ever designed a program on patience?
78. Have you ever given a speech on patience?
79. Have you ever rewarded or recognized someone for having patience?
80. Have you ever taught a course on patience?
81. Have you ever tried to help someone deal with being patient more effectively?*
82. Have you ever tried to help someone improve their ability to be patient?
83. How do you think people develop patience skills?
84. How much patience is good to have and how much is too much?
85. How much of success do you think is due to patience compared with other characteristics?
86. How would you know if someone is bad at being patient?
87. How would you know if someone is good at being patient?

PATIENCE

88. If you had to write a book on patience, what would the chapter headings be?
89. What are the benefits to someone who is really good at being patient?
90. What are the consequences to someone who is really poor at being patient?
91. What do you think the standard is on patience for someone in your role?
92. What happens if you have or use too much patience?
93. What happens when two people try to work together who are very different on being patient?
94. What wisdom would you pass on to others trying to become better at being patient?
95. When you select others, what do you look for in patience levels?
96. Why do you think people end up being different in demonstrating patience?

Dimension 4: Shows personal change and sense-making; learned it one place and applied it in another; can compare and contrast experiences; changes viewpoints across time; can explain personal development or evolution related to the competency

97. Compare and contrast examples of times you've been effective and ineffective at demonstrating patience.
98. Contrast your patience on and off the job.
99. Did you ever pass up a job or assignment because you were not patient enough?
100. Do you ever use other skills to cover for your lack of patience?
101. Has being too impatient ever been the subject of a development plan for you?
102. Has becoming better at being patient ever helped you in other areas?
103. Has lack of patience ever figured in a failure, struggle, or setback you have had?
104. Has your patience level always been this way?
105. Have patience, good or bad, ever been the subject of your performance review or a career discussion?
106. Have you ever delegated or assigned someone a task because you weren't patient enough?
107. Have you ever made significant strides at becoming more patient?
108. How different are you across situations at being patient?
109. How do you decide how patient to be?
110. How much of your success is due to your patience?
111. How transferable are your patience skills to other situations?
112. If you had to become more patient in a hurry, what would you do?
113. Was there a time when you were not good at being patient?
114. What caused you to work to improve your skill at being patient?
115. What event or series of events had the most impact on your patience?
116. What's the most varied you can be at demonstrating patience?
117. What was the shortest amount of time in which you increased your level of skill at being patient?
118. When did you first realize your level of skill at being patient?
119. When you know ahead of time that your usual level of patience won't work, what do you do?
120. Why do you think you deal with being patient the way you do?
121. Why do you think your patience is the way it is?*
122. When are some times you've found it useful to be impatient?
123. Give some examples of people you are most and least patient with.

PATIENCE

D. Follow-up Probes:
1. Are there times when you are patient like that and times when you aren't?
2. Could you contrast those two bosses for me?
3. Could you give me a few examples of how you've used or applied that?
4. Do you always react like that or was that a special situation?
5. Do you suppose if others would just try harder, they could learn to be more patient like you?
6. Do you think that's teachable?
7. Do you think you're better at patience than most? Why?
8. Do you think you would perform any differently if you could be more patient?
9. Have you always been that way or is this a recent development in you?
10. Have you ever had to be patient around someone you really disliked?
11. How did the others react when you did that?
12. How did you come up with that approach to being patient in the first place?
13. How did you know that method of getting over that situation would work?
14. How do others you have known approach that?
15. How far will you go before you cut line and try another approach?
16. How typical is this for you?
17. How would you approach that same situation today?
18. Is this natural for you, or do you really have to dig for it?
19. Was there a time when you didn't understand this about yourself?
20. What did you do after you got that feedback?
21. What did you do to adapt to that?
22. What did you learn from that?
23. Why did you choose that approach?
24. Why did you decide to take the risk?
25. Why did you do it that way?
26. Why did you time your reaction like that?
27. Why do you think that didn't work?
28. Why do you think that happened that way?
29. Why do you think that worked?
30. Why do you think you have difficulties with that sometimes?
31. How did you get yourself under control in that situation?
32. Would you have done it that way with looser deadlines?
33. Would you have done it that way with tighter deadlines?

E. Themes/Things to Look for:

Acknowledging frustration but managing it	Listening skills
Can defer	Not expecting perfection
Can turn oneself off for awhile	Pace
Comfort with loose ends	Selective patience
Comfort with not knowing everything in advance	Separating internal feelings from what's showing on the outside
Composure when frustrated	Situational patience
Control techniques at the edges	Tolerance for mistakes and differences
Delay of gratification	Triggers for loosing patience

PATIENCE

Directional patience
Finding common ground
Having reasonable standards for processes
Interrupts you in the interview

Understanding others
Doesn't reject others quickly
Satisfied with bit by bit understanding

F. Most Likely Résumé:

1. Look for jobs like:

International Assignments
Staff Leadership (Influencing Without Authority)

2. Look for develop-in-place assignments like:

Integrate diverse systems, processes, or procedures across decentralized and/or dispersed units.
Manage the renovation of an office, floor, building, meeting room, warehouse, etc.
Plan a new site for a building (plant, field office, headquarters, etc.).
Teach a child a new skill (e.g., reading, running a computer, a sport).
Seek out and use a seed budget to create and pursue a personal idea, product, or service.
Create employee involvement teams.
Manage an ad hoc, temporary group of "green," inexperienced people as their coach, teacher, orienter, etc.
Manage an ad hoc, temporary group of balky and resisting people through an unpopular change or project.
Manage an ad hoc, temporary group of low-competence people through a task they couldn't do by themselves.
Manage an ad hoc, temporary group of people where the temporary manager is a towering expert and the people in the group are not.
Manage an ad hoc, temporary group of people where the people in the group are towering experts but the temporary manager is not.
Manage an ad hoc, temporary group of people involved in tackling a fix-it or turnaround project.
Assemble an ad hoc team of diverse people to accomplish a difficult task.
Handle a tough negotiation with an internal or external client or customer.
Help shut down a plant, regional office, product line, business, operation, etc.
Manage a dissatisfied internal or external customer; troubleshoot a performance or quality problem with a product or service.
Manage the assigning/allocating of office space in a contested situation.
Manage a group through a significant business crisis.
Take on a tough and undoable project, one where others who have tried it have failed.
Manage the outplacement of a group of people.
Manage a cost-cutting project.
Take on a task you dislike or hate to do.
Resolve an issue in conflict between two people, units, geographies, functions, etc.
Make peace with an enemy or someone you've disappointed with a product or service or someone you've had some trouble with or don't get along well with.
Be a member of a union-negotiating or grievance-handling team.
Manage a project team of people who are older and more experienced.

3. Best references to ask about or check:

Development Professionals
Family Members

Spouse
Direct Reports

PATIENCE

G. Learning Agility Evaluation:

   2. All or Nothing vs. Can See Many Sides
   5. Tight/Rigid vs. Loose/Flexible
   6. Reacting/Responsive vs. Adapting
   17. Avoid Discussion of Weaknesses vs. Comfortably Sharing Shortcomings
   20. Avoids Responsibility for Mistakes vs. Admits and Learns from Mistakes
   21. View from Self vs. View from Point of View of Others

H. The LEADERSHIP ARCHITECT® Sort Card Connections:

   ### 1. Good (positive) if combined with high:
   Can wait out chaos 2, 40
   Easy to talk to 3, 33
   Has time for personal problems 7, 10
   Deals calmly with conflict 11, 12
   High patience; respect for others 11, 33, 64
   Can wait them out 12, 37
   Good to have in customer service 15, 33
   Gives people time 19
   Tolerant 55

   ### 2. Bad (negative) if combined with low or high (+):
   May freeze up under pressure 1, 9, 12, 13, 34, 57
   Waits too long; needs too much data 1, 16
   Has trouble with complex issues 2, 40
   Goes through the motions 11, 33, 64
   Encourages customers to complain (+15, 33)
   Wastes time (+33) 62
   Doesn't understand impact on others 55
   Doesn't match pace 56

   ### 3. Too much can contribute to the following Stallers and Stoppers:

   #### A. What too much looks like (overused):
   May wait too long to act; may try to please everyone; others may confuse attentive listening with acceptance of their position; may waste time when faced with issues too close to a 50/50 proposition; may let things fester without acting.

   #### B. Too much might lead to these Stallers and Stoppers:
   None Apply

   #### C. Compensators:
   How to compensate for too much of this competency:
   1, 2, 9, 12, 13, 16, 34, 40, 53, 57

PATIENCE

D. Things to watch for:

Attracts flies/complainers
Misunderstood
Patience hiding conflict avoidance
One hundred percent right but one hundred percent late
Freezes; does little
Smoother
Mole hills become mountains

4. Too little can contribute to the following Stallers and Stoppers:

A. What too little looks like (unskilled):

Acts before it's time to act; intolerant of the slow pace and cumbersome processes of others; may be seen as a self-centered do it my way and at my speed type; doesn't take the time to listen or understand; thinks almost everything needs to be faster and shorter; disrupts those facilitating meetings with his/her need to finish sooner; frequently interrupts and finishes other people's sentences; makes their own process rules; doesn't wait for others; may appear to others as arrogant, uninterested or a know-it-all; may be action-oriented and resist process and problem complexity; may just jump to conclusions rather than thinking things through.

B. Too little might lead to these Stallers and Stoppers:

Poor Administrator (102)
Arrogant (104)
Blocked Personal Learner (106)
Lack of Composure (107)
Failure to Build a Team (110)
Failure to Staff Effectively (111)
Insensitive to Others (112)
Non-Strategic (114)
Overmanaging (117)
Political Missteps (119)

C. Compensators:

How to substitute for too little of this competency:
3, 11, 17, 33, 48

I. LEARNING ARCHITECT® Connections:

Look for people who act like and/or show evidence of:

1c. Following a Plan
4c. Actively Involve
11. Why/How
14. Controlled
15. Cautious
16. Collaborate
32. Diversity in Others
33. Diversity of Sources
37. Flexibility
38. Resilience

J. CHOICES ARCHITECT® Connections:

Look for people who act like and/or show evidence of:

First Edition (Released 1994)
8. Cool Transactor
11. Open to Diversity
15. Helps Others Succeed
22. Self-Talk

Second Edition (Released 2000)
10. Conflict Manager
11. Cool Transactor
12. Helps Others Succeed
14. Open-Minded

K. Difficulty to Develop:

23 (of 34)–Moderate

42. PEER RELATIONSHIPS

A. Definition:

Can quickly find common ground and solve problems for the good of all; can represent their own interests and yet be fair to other groups; can solve problems with peers with a minimum of noise; is seen as a team player and is cooperative; easily gains trust and support of peers; encourages collaboration; can be candid with peers.

B. Arenas/Domains to Explore:

1. Cross-boundary implementations
2. Any lateral cooperation event
3. Assigning blame across boundaries
4. Blended sports events (All-stars)
5. Cooperative event planning
6. Dispute/conflict resolution
7. External like-level peers
8. Fraternal organizations
9. Internal like-level customers
10. Joint problem solving
11. Joint product/service promotions
12. Limited resource battles
13. Managing trade shows
14. Merger/acquisition management
15. Negotiating a contract
16. Office space allocation
17. Professional association peers/colleagues
18. Project groups
19. Resource sharing
20. Selection of common tools/software
21. Staff meetings
22. Task forces
23. United Way
24. Volunteer work
25. Working political campaigns
26. Working with consultants
27. Working with suppliers
28. Working with vendors

C. Sample Questions:

Dimension 1: Been there, done that–has had direct personal experience(s) involving the competency–candidate was the prime player   Note: * means OK for campus

1. Do you do lunch or meet just to form alliances?
2. Has anyone ever accused you of messing something up because of your being a poor team player?
3. Have you ever managed anything where your peers were in different locations? How did you form relationships with them?
4. Have you ever traded a resource with a peer in exchange for something you needed?*
5. Have you moved across business units or geographical locations in your current organization?
6. How competitive do you tend to be?*
7. How many functions have you spent time in?
8. Tell me about a time when a peer thought you went back on a deal.*
9. Tell me about a time when one or more peers ganged up on you with a grievance.
10. Tell me about a time when you handled a conflict with an individual or group outside your organization (school, place of work).*
11. Tell me about a time when you made peace with an adversary.*
12. Tell me about a time when you negotiated an agreement over resources with peers.*
13. Tell me about a time when you resolved a conflict you were having with peers.*
14. Tell me about a time when you served as a mediator between two peers.*

PEER RELATIONSHIPS

15. Tell me about a time when you were able to get something you probably shouldn't have because you had formed a good relationship with someone.*
16. Tell me about a time when you were able to head off a problem because you had a relationship with someone outside your unit.
17. Tell me about a time when you were at odds with peers over resources or policies.*
18. Tell me about a time when you were stopped from getting something you needed because you didn't have a good relationship with the person controlling it.*
19. Tell me about a time when your peer relationships got you into trouble.
20. Tell me about a time when your peer relationships worked really well for you.
21. Was there a time when you gave up control you could have had for the good of teamwork?*
22. Was there a time when you had to hold in your own thoughts or ideas for the good of the team/group?*
23. What kind of a network have you formed outside your own work unit?
24. What's the worst peer conflict you can remember?*
25. When you meet with a group of peers, what role do you usually play?
26. Where would you put yourself on a loner-to-team-player scale?*

Dimension 2: Seen/been around others who were involved with the competency–good and bad; learns from others about self

27. Contrast the best and worst people you know at peer relationships.*
28. Has peer relationships ever been in any 360° survey done on you? Was your score among your highest, middle, or lowest?
29. Has poor peer relationships on someone else's part ever created an obstacle for you or got in the way of something you were trying to accomplish?*
30. Have you ever talked with a coach or mentor about your peer relationships?
31. Have you ever watched someone fail/get fired because they did not have good peer relationships?*
32. Have you ever watched someone over-relate to peers to the point that it backfired?
33. Have you ever watched someone succeed because they had very good peer relationships?*
34. Have you ever worked with a coach on peer relationships?*
35. Have you ever worked with a person who excelled at peer relationships?
36. Have you ever worked with a skills coach on peer relationships?*
37. How do you get feedback about yourself on peer relationships?
38. How often do you check with multiple sources when you get a piece of critical feedback on your peer relationships?
39. Is there a historical figure you consider a model of relating well to peers?
40. What do others who are not your fans say about your peer relationships?
41. What do others who like you say about your peer relationships?
42. Which boss was the best at peer relationships?
43. Which boss was the worst at peer relationships?
44. Which direct report was the best at peer relationships?
45. Which direct report was the worst at peer relationships?
46. Which peer was the best at peer relationships?
47. Which peer was the worst at peer relationships?
48. Who in your field or business deals with peer relationships the best?
49. Who do you consider a role model of effective peer relationships?*
50. Who do you go to for advice on peer relationships?

PEER RELATIONSHIPS

51. Who have you learned the most from about peer relationships?*
52. Who is a higher-management role model for you on peer relationships?
53. Who is a role model of peer relationships outside of work?

Dimension 3: Knows how the competency works in theory; shows understanding

54. Are there situations or settings where someone should be different on dealing with peer relationships?
55. Do you think peer relationship skills can be learned; how do you think people develop peer relationship skills?
56. Do you think there is a way to compensate or work around low peer relationship skills?
57. Has anyone asked you for your opinions/advice on peer relationships?*
58. Have you ever attended a course on dealing with peer relationships?
59. Have you ever been in a situation where you and others put dealing with peer relationships on a success profile?
60. Have you ever been part of an effort to create a policy or a mission statement containing reference to dealing with peer relationships?
61. Have you ever been someone's coach or mentor who had problems with peer relationships?
62. Have you ever created a development plan for someone on dealing with peer relationships?
63. Have you ever criticized someone for not dealing well with peer relationships?
64. Have you ever designed a program on peer relationships?
65. Have you ever given a speech on dealing with peer relationships?
66. Have you ever rewarded or recognized someone for having good peer relationships?
67. Have you ever taught a course on dealing with peer relationships?
68. Have you ever tried to help someone deal more effectively with peer relationships?*
69. Have you ever tried to help someone improve their peer relationships?
70. How do you think people develop peer relationship skills?
71. How much of success do you think is due to peer relationships compared with other characteristics?
72. How would you know if someone is bad at peer relationships?
73. How would you know if someone is good at peer relationships?
74. If you had to write a book on peer relationships, what would the chapter headings be?
75. What are the benefits to someone who is really good at peer relationships?
76. What are the consequences to someone who is really poor at peer relationships?
77. What do you think the standard is on dealing with peer relationships for someone in your role?
78. What happens when two people try to work together who are very different in dealing with peer relationships?
79. What wisdom would you pass on to others trying to become better at peer relationships?
80. When you select others, what do you look for in their peer relationship skills?
81. Why do you think people end up being different in peer relationship skills?

Dimension 4: Shows personal change and sense-making; learned it one place and applied it in another; can compare and contrast experiences; changes viewpoints across time; can explain personal development or evolution related to the competency

82. Compare and contrast examples of times when you've been effective and ineffective at having relationships with peers.
83. Contrast your on- and off-the-job relationships with peers.
84. Did you ever pass up a job or assignment because you were not confident enough in your skills at relating well with peers?

PEER RELATIONSHIPS

85. Do you ever use other skills to cover for your lack of ability to relate well to peers?
86. Has becoming better at peer relationships ever helped you in other areas?
87. Has having poor peer relationships ever been the subject of a development plan for you?
88. Has having poor peer relationships ever figured in a failure, struggle, or setback you have had?
89. Have your relationships with peers always been this way?
90. Have you ever delegated or assigned someone a task because you didn't relate to peers particularly well?
91. Have you ever made significant strides in your ability to relate well with peers?
92. Have your relationships with peers, good or bad, ever been the subject of your performance review or a career discussion?
93. How different are you across situations in your relationships with peers?
94. How do you decide how much relating to peers you need?
95. How much of your success is due to your ability to relate well to peers?
96. How transferable to other situations is your ability to relate with peers?
97. If you had to become better at relating to peers in a hurry, what would you do?
98. Was there a time when you were not as good at having peer relationships?
99. What caused you to work to improve your peer relationships?
100. What event or series of events had the most impact on your relationships with peers?
101. What's the most varied you can be in your relationships with peers?
102. What was the shortest amount of time in which you increased your level of skill at relating to peers?
103. When did you first realize your level of skill at relating well with peers?
104. When you know ahead of time that your usual level of peer relationships isn't sufficient, what do you do?
105. Why do you think you deal with peers the way you do?
106. Why do you think your relationships with peers are the way they are?*
107. How do you do generally in situations where you have to share space/resources with another peer or colleague?
108. How do you generally go about forming relationships with peers and colleagues?
109. How have your relationships with peers improved or eroded over the years?

D. Follow-up Probes:

1. Are there times when you form relationships like that and times when you don't?
2. Could you contrast those two bosses for me?
3. Could you give me a few examples of how you've used or applied that?
4. Did you or the other person blink first?
5. Do you always try to form relationships like that or was that a special situation?
6. Do you suppose if others would just try harder, they could learn to be more effective at forming good peer and colleague relationships like you do?
7. Do you think that's teachable?
8. Do you think you're better at forming relationships than most? Why?
9. Do you think you would perform any differently if you could be more effective at forming peer and colleague relationships?
10. Have you ever had to form a relationship with someone you really disliked to get your job done?
11. How did it feel to give up something you wanted to get the project going?
12. How did the others react when you did that?
13. How did you come up with that approach to forming relationships in the first place?

PEER RELATIONSHIPS

14. How did you know that method of getting over that barrier would work?
15. How do others you have known approach that?
16. How far did you go to try to be a team player?
17. How far will you go before you cut line and try another approach?
18. How much did you have to give up to make it work?
19. How often do you use the "let's meet in the middle" approach to settling disputes?
20. How typical is this for you?
21. How would you approach that same situation today?
22. Is this natural for you, or do you really have to dig for it?
23. Was that a fair way to maneuver around them?
24. Was there a time when you didn't understand this about yourself?
25. What did you do after you got that feedback?
26. What did you do to adapt to that?
27. What did you learn from that?
28. Why did you choose that approach?
29. Why did you decide to take the risk?
30. Why did you do it that way?
31. Why did you time your attempt to form a relationship like you did?
32. Why do you suppose organizations work that way?
33. Why do you think that didn't work?
34. Why do you think that happened that way?
35. Why do you think that worked?
36. Why do you think you have difficulties with that sometimes?
37. Would you have done it that way with looser deadlines?
38. Would you have done it that way with tighter deadlines?

E. Themes/Things to Look for:

- A range of styles/approaches to use
- Ability to predict what other people are going to do
- Able to take the heat if necessary
- Appreciation of due process
- Appropriately straight with others
- Arrogance
- Awareness of impact on others
- Calmness under stress
- Can follow other people's lead
- Can keep personal feelings from getting in the way
- Clear communicator
- Delay of gratification
- Equitable treatment
- Finds common ground/points of agreement
- Going after tough issues/people
- Good couching skills
- Lets others save face
- Listening skills
- Loses a battle to win a war
- Loyalty to the greater good
- Mental rehearsal of things people might say or do
- More problem focused; less people focused
- Noise management/damage control techniques
- Patience
- Pushes at the right time
- Seeing the other side
- Sees differences; one size doesn't fit all
- Sense of fairness
- Sensitivity and empathy
- Takes the strategic view
- Tolerance of diversity of views
- Understands the other side of arguments
- Win/win skills
- Wins agreement and keeps the relationship

PEER RELATIONSHIPS

F. Most Likely Résumé:

1. Look for jobs like:
Chair of Projects/Task Forces
Cross-Moves
Fix-Its/Turnarounds
Scope Assignments
Staff Leadership (Influencing Without Authority)

2. Look for develop-in-place assignments like:
Integrate diverse systems, processes, or procedures across decentralized and/or dispersed units.
Manage the renovation of an office, floor, building, meeting room, warehouse, etc.
Join a self-help or support group.
Join a community board.
Manage the assigning/allocating of office space in a contested situation.
Manage a cost-cutting project.
Resolve an issue in conflict between two people, units, geographies, functions, etc.
Work on a team looking at a reorganization plan where there will be more people than positions.

3. Best references to ask about or check:
Human Resource Professionals
Off-Work Associates
Past Associates/Constituencies
Peers

G. Learning Agility Evaluation:
2. All or Nothing vs. Can See Many Sides
4. Spectator/Passive vs. Player/Participant
5. Tight/Rigid vs. Loose/Flexible
6. Reacting/Responsive vs. Adapting
9. Vague/General vs. Sharp/Specific
10. Reactive vs. Initiating
15. Linear vs. Use Contrasts/Analogies
16. Few Rules of Thumb vs. Many and Varied Rules of Thumb
19. External Standards vs. Internal Standards
22. Focus on Accomplishments vs. Focus on Solving Problems

H. The LEADERSHIP ARCHITECT® Sort Card Connections:

1. Good (positive) if combined with high:
Flexible 2, 40
A model team player 3, 33, 37, 41, 60, 64
Cares about peers/colleague 7, 10, 11
Can resolve tough issues among/between peers/colleagues 9, 12, 34, 57
Informal team leader 9, 36, 39, 60
Can give away parts of the project 18
With a variety of people 21, 23
Assembles good network 25, 56
Accurate in gauging approach 56, 64

PEER RELATIONSHIPS

2. **Bad (negative) if combined with low or high (+):**

   Too much of a good thing (+3, 31, 48, 60)

   In service of self (+6) 22, 29

   Just goes along 9, 12, 34, 57

   Selective 21, 23

   Wrong approaches; wrong people 25, 56, 64

   Doesn't take advantage of the network 39, 52

   One person at a time 60

   Superficial 3, 10, 11

3. **Too much can contribute to the following Stallers and Stoppers:**

   A. *What too much looks like (overused):*

   May touch base with too many peers and be overly concerned with making everyone happy; may be too accommodating; may invest too much in peer relationships at the expense of others; may be uncomfortable with relationships where everyone's not equal; may share sensitive information inappropriately just to solidify a relationship; may get in trouble by being too candid with peers.

   B. *Too much might lead to these Stallers and Stoppers:*

   Overly Ambitious

   C. *Compensators:*

   How to compensate for too much of this competency:

   4, 8, 9, 12, 16, 23, 29, 34, 37, 43, 50, 53, 57

   D. *Things to watch for:*

   May get things done through their network that should have been rejected

   Pays/trades too much just to form relationships

   Poor time/priority management

   Relationships cloud judgment on tough issues

   Too strong a need to please and be liked

   Works on issues not worth working on

4. **Too little can contribute to the following Stallers and Stoppers:**

   A. *What too little looks like (unskilled):*

   Not good at lateral cross boundary relations; doesn't strike fair bargains or understand what peers expect or need; not open to negotiation; a loner, not seen as a team player, doesn't have the greater good in mind; may withhold resources from the other team members; may not respect their functions or disciplines and somehow communicates that; may be very competitive, play and maneuver for advantage and withhold information; may have a chilling effect on the entire unit because they won't play; may deal with lateral conflict noisily or uncooperatively.

   B. *Too little might lead to these Stallers and Stoppers:*

   Overly Ambitious (103)   Overdependence on an Advocate (115)

   Arrogant (104)   Political Missteps (119)

   Insensitive to Others (112)

PEER RELATIONSHIPS

C. Compensators:
How to substitute for too little of this competency:
3, 9, 12, 21, 27, 33, 36, 39, 52, 60

I. LEARNING ARCHITECT® Connections:

Look for people who act like and/or show evidence of:

2a. Problem Solving	9. Multiple Sources
3b. Self-Talk	16. Collaborate
4a. Getting Information	34. Sizing Up Others
4c. Actively Involve	

J. CHOICES ARCHITECT® Connections:

Look for people who act like and/or show evidence of:

First Edition (Released 1994)	Second Edition (Released 2000)
8. Cool Transactor	9. Agile Communicator
11. Open to Diversity	11. Cool Transactor
15. Helps Others Succeed	12. Helps Others Succeed
23. Communicator	14. Open-Minded

K. Difficulty to Develop:
22 (of 34)–Easier

43. PERSEVERANCE

A. Definition:

Pursues everything with energy, drive, and a need to finish; seldom gives up before finishing, especially in the face of resistance or setbacks.

B. Arenas/Domains to Explore:

1. Bargaining in a tense union situation
2. Collecting bad debts
3. Cost/benefit analysis of energy vs. payback
4. Door slammed in face
5. Expediting late payments
6. Facing resistance
7. Finishing long books
8. Fixing a strained relationship
9. Frustrating drawn-out negotiation
10. Goals thwarted
11. Helping someone with a personal problem
12. Hobbies
13. In the face of rejection
14. Keeping at a hard sale
15. Kept waiting
16. Physical challenges
17. Pursuing a complaint
18. Pushing an unpopular idea/program
19. Reworks requested by doubters
20. Rising from the ashes phoenix projects/resurrection attempts
21. Staying with something others have given up on
22. Time management
23. Trying to save a dying project
24. Working in very ambiguous situations
25. Working on long lead-time projects
26. Working through a legal process
27. Working through an athletic injury
28. Working through chaos
29. Working through conflicts
30. Working through disputes
31. Working with a problem employee
32. Working with a slow government agency
33. Working with people of lesser skills

C. Sample Questions:

*Dimension 1: Been there, done that–has had direct personal experience(s) involving the competency–candidate was the prime player   Note: * means OK for campus*

1. Do you generally stay home or go to school/work when you have a cold or the flu?*
2. Do you think there was a time when you gave up too soon on something?*
3. Do you think there was a time when you kept pushing beyond reason?*
4. Has anyone ever accused you of messing something up because of lack of perseverance?
5. Have you ever called someone on not persevering on something?*
6. Have you ever managed anything where the people or units reporting to you were in different locations? How did you push through obstacles from a distance?
7. Have you had a direct sales or telephone solicitation job in your career?*
8. How are you at dropping a project in the middle and moving on to some other priority?*
9. How does it make you feel when you have to give up on something you felt strongly about that just isn't going to happen?*
10. How far did you progress in the scouts/4H/hobbies?*
11. In athletics, was there a time when you had to play through pain?*
12. Tell me about a time when everything you tried got resisted/blocked.*
13. Tell me about a time when you accomplished something against the odds.*

PERSEVERANCE

14. Tell me about a time when you started up and ran with an idea/project no matter what got in your way.*
15. Tell me about a time when you tried your best and failed.*
16. Tell me about a time when your perseverance got you into trouble.
17. Tell me about a time when your perseverance worked really well for you.
18. What do you generally do when you're blocked from achieving something important?*
19. What happens to your performance when a lot of things are up in the air?*
20. What's the farthest you have taken a hobby?*
21. What's the most unpopular thing you have ever tried to push? What happened?*
22. Would others label you a perfectionist?*

Dimension 2: Seen/been around others who were involved with the competency–good and bad; learns from others about self

23. Contrast the most and least persevering people you know.*
24. Has perseverance or stick-to-itiveness ever been in any 360° survey done on you? Was your score among your highest, middle, or lowest?
25. Has lack of perseverance on someone else's part ever created an obstacle for you or got in the way of something you were trying to accomplish?*
26. Have you ever talked with a coach or mentor about your perseverance or stick-to-itiveness?
27. Have you ever watched someone fail/get fired because they did not persevere through resistance or adversity?*
28. Have you ever watched someone overpersevere to the point that it backfired?
29. Have you ever watched someone succeed because they persevered through resistance or adversity?*
30. Have you ever worked with a coach on perseverance?*
31. Have you ever worked with a person who excelled at perseverance or stick-to-itiveness?
32. Have you ever worked with a skills coach on perseverance or stick-to-itiveness?*
33. How do you get feedback about yourself on perseverance or stick-to-itiveness?
34. How often do you check with multiple sources when you get a piece of critical feedback on your perseverance or stick-to-itiveness?
35. Is there a historical figure you consider a model of perseverance or stick-to-itiveness?
36. What do others who are not your fans say about your perseverance or stick-to-itiveness?
37. What do others who like you say about your perseverance or stick-to-itiveness?
38. Which boss was the best at perseverance?
39. Which boss was the worst at perseverance?
40. Which direct report was the best at perseverance?
41. Which direct report was the worst at perseverance?
42. Which peer was the best at perseverance?
43. Which peer was the worst at perseverance?
44. Who in your field or business is the best at perseverance or stick-to-itiveness?
45. Who do you consider a role model of perseverance or stick-to-itiveness?*
46. Who do you go to for advice on perseverance?
47. Who have you learned the most from about perseverance?*
48. Who is a higher-management role model for you on perseverance?
49. Who is a role model of perseverance outside of work?

PERSEVERANCE

Dimension 3: Knows how the competency works in theory; shows understanding

50. Are there situations or settings where someone should be different on demonstrating perseverance skills?
51. Do you think perseverance can be learned; how do you think people develop perseverance skills?
52. Do you think there is a way to compensate or work around low perseverance skills?
53. Has anyone asked you for your opinions/advice on perseverance?*
54. Have you ever attended a course on perseverance?
55. Have you ever been in a situation where you and others put perseverance or stick-to-itiveness on a success profile?
56. Have you ever been part of an effort to create a policy or a mission statement containing reference to persevering?
57. Have you ever been someone's coach or mentor who had problems with perseverance?
58. Have you ever created a plan for someone on developing perseverance skills?
59. Have you ever criticized someone for not persevering?
60. Have you ever designed a program on perseverance?
61. Have you ever given a speech on perseverance?
62. Have you ever rewarded or recognized someone for persevering?
63. Have you ever taught a course on perseverance?
64. Have you ever tried to help someone more effectively persevere?*
65. Have you ever tried to help someone improve their perseverance skills?
66. How do you think people develop perseverance skills?
67. How much perseverance or stick-to-itiveness is good to have and how much is too much?
68. How much of success do you think is due to perseverance or stick-to-itiveness compared with other characteristics?
69. How would you know if someone is bad at persevering?
70. How would you know if someone is good at persevering?
71. If you had to write a book on perseverance or stick-to-itiveness, what would the chapter headings be?
72. What are the benefits to someone who is really good at persevering?
73. What are the consequences to someone who is really poor at persevering?
74. What do you think the standard is on perseverance or stick-to-itiveness for someone in your role?
75. What happens if you persevere too much?
76. What happens when two people try to work together who are very different in their ability to persevere?
77. What wisdom would you pass on to others trying to become better at persevering?
78. When you select others, what do you look for in perseverance level?
79. Why do you think people end up being different in perseverance skills?

Dimension 4: Shows personal change and sense-making; learned it one place and applied it in another; can compare and contrast experiences; changes viewpoints across time; can explain personal development or evolution related to the competency

80. Compare and contrast examples of time when you've been effective and ineffective at perseverance or stick-to-itiveness?
81. Contrast your on- and off-the-job perseverance.
82. Did you ever pass up a job or assignment because of your lack of perseverance or stick-to-itiveness?
83. Do you ever use other skills to cover for your lack of perseverance or stick-to-itiveness?
84. Has becoming better at persevering through adversity ever helped you in other areas?
85. Has not persevering through adversity ever been the subject of a development plan for you?

PERSEVERANCE

86. Has not persevering through adversity ever figured in a failure, struggle, or setback you have had?
87. Has your perseverance or stick-to-itiveness always been this way?
88. Have you ever delegated or assigned someone a task because of your lack of perseverance or stick-to-itiveness?
89. Have you ever made significant strides at becoming better at perseverance?
90. Have your perseverance or stick-to-itiveness, good or bad, ever been the subject of your performance review or a career discussion?
91. How different are you across situations in persevering in the face of adversity?
92. How do you decide how perseverant to be?
93. How much of your success is due to your ability to persevere through resistance or adversity?
94. How transferable are your perseverance skills to other situations?
95. If you had to become better at perseverance in a hurry, what would you do?
96. Was there a time when you were not as good at being perseverant?
97. What caused you to work on getting more perseverant?
98. What event or series of events had the most impact on your perseverance?
99. What's the most varied you can be in demonstrating your perseverance?
100. What was the shortest amount of time in which you increased your level of skill at persevering through resistance or adversity?
101. When did you first realize your level of perseverance?
102. When you know ahead of time that your usual level of perseverance or stick-to-itiveness isn't sufficient, what do you do?
103. Why do you think you deal with perseverance the way you do?
104. Why do you think your perseverance is the way it is?*
105. How important is it for you to finish everything you start?*
106. How do you decide which battles are worth fighting and which are a lost cause?*

D. Follow-up Probes:

1. Are there times when you persevere like that and times when you don't?
2. Could you contrast those two bosses for me?
3. Could you give me a few examples of how you've used or applied that?
4. Do you always persevere like that or was that a special situation?
5. Do you suppose if others would just try harder, they could learn to persevere more like you?
6. Do you think that's teachable?
7. Do you think you're better at persevering than most? Why?
8. Do you think you would perform any differently if you could be better at persevering?
9. Do you think your approach caused any of the resistance?
10. Have you always had the strong need to finish everything you started?
11. Have you ever had to persevere with someone you really disliked?
12. How did the others react when you did that?
13. How did you come up with that approach to persevering in the first place?
14. How did you know that method of getting over that barrier would work?
15. How do others you have known approach that?
16. How far did you go to try to be a team player?
17. How far will you go before you cut line and try another approach?

PERSEVERANCE

18. How much did you have to give up to make it work?
19. How typical is this for you?
20. How would you approach that same situation today?
21. Is this natural for you, or do you really have to dig for it?
22. Was that a fair way to maneuver around them?
23. Was the resistance you encountered normal?
24. Was there a time when you didn't understand this about yourself?
25. Were others blocked as well or only you?
26. What did you do after you got that feedback?
27. What did you do to adapt to that?
28. What did you learn from that?
29. What signs do you read to know when to stop?
30. When is the last time you changed how you do this?
31. Why did you choose that approach?
32. Why did you decide to take the risk?
33. Why did you do it that way?
34. Why did you keep pushing?
35. Why did you stop pushing when you did?
36. Why did you time your attempt to pursue the issue like that?
37. Why do you think that didn't work?
38. Why do you think that happened that way?
39. Why do you think that worked?
40. Why do you think you have difficulty with that sometimes?
41. Would you have done it that way with looser deadlines?
42. Would you have done it that way with tighter deadlines?

E. **Themes/Things to Look for:**
   Able to take the heat
   Anticipates roadblocks/questions
   Doesn't personalize rejection
   Drivers–why they expend so much energy
   Gets tougher under conflict
   Goal gradient–works harder as the the goal gets closer
   Goes back at dead issues, but only when they have a different slant on them
   Keeping personal feelings from getting in the way
   Leaves no stone unturned
   Loses sleep over getting it done
   Loves a challenge
   Mentally flexible–knows many ways to go after what they want
   Within reason; no obsession with perfection
   Optimism
   Passionate commitment to what's right
   Pride in workmanship

PERSEVERANCE

Resilience
Results-driven
Sees resistance as a challenge
Selective application
Self-motivated
Self-rewarding
Sell and sell again–knows the stakeholders
Sets priorities; fights the best battles

F. Most Likely Résumé:

1. Look for jobs like:

Fix-Its/Turnarounds	Staff Leadership (Influencing Without Authority)
International Assignments	Start-Ups

2. Look for develop-in-place assignments like:

Plan a new site for a building (plant, field office, headquarters, etc.).
Draft a mission statement, policy proposal, charter, or goal statement and get feedback from others.
Manage an ad hoc, temporary group of "green," inexperienced people as their coach, teacher, orienter, etc.
Manage an ad hoc, temporary group of balky and resisting people through an unpopular change or project.
Manage an ad hoc, temporary group of people where the people in the group are towering experts but the temporary manager is not.
Manage an ad hoc, temporary group of people involved in tackling a fix-it or turnaround project.
Handle a tough negotiation with an internal or external client or customer.
Help shut down a plant, regional office, product line, business, operation, etc.
Take on a tough and undoable project, one where others who have tried it have failed.
Manage the outplacement of a group of people.
Take on a task you dislike or hate to do.
Resolve an issue in conflict between two people, units, geographies, functions, etc.
Work on a crisis management team.

3. Best references to ask about or check:

Human Resource Professionals	Spouse
Natural Mentors	Direct Reports

G. Learning Agility Evaluation:

4. Spectator/Passive vs. Player/Participant
6. Reacting/Responsive vs. Adapting
7. Passive vs. Intrigued/Curious
10. Reactive vs. Initiating
12. Rehearsed/Socially Acceptable vs. Candid
19. External Standards vs. Internal Standards
22. Focus on Accomplishments vs. Focus on Solving Problems

PERSEVERANCE

H. The LEADERSHIP ARCHITECT® Sort Card Connections:

1. **Good (positive) if combined with high:**
   Knows many ways to get something done 2, 14, 46, 51
   Not stopped by chaos 2, 40
   Gets support of stakeholders 4, 8, 42, 60
   Has courage 9, 34, 57
   Can take the heat 11, 12
   Makes the sale eventually 15, 53
   Waits for slow starters 19
   Selects appropriate tactics 33, 56, 64
   Good in drawn-out negotiations 37
   Doesn't have to win the first time 41
   Plans orderly attack on target 47, 51
   Strives for continuous improvement 63

2. **Bad (negative) if combined with low or high (+):**
   A runaway train (+1, 9, 16, 53)
   Crawls over people to get there 3, 7, 10, 23
   Doesn't push hard enough 9, 13, 34
   Won't ask for help (+9, 57) 60
   Personally motivated 22, 29
   Gets stuck on lost cause (+22, 57) 50
   Doesn't adjust tactics to fit the person accurately 33, 56, 64
   Crude techniques 38, 48, 49
   On the wrong track 46, 58, 65
   Wastes time 50, 62

3. **Too much can contribute to the following Stallers and Stoppers:**

   A. *What too much looks like (overused):*

   May stick to efforts beyond reason, in the face of overwhelming odds and evidence to the contrary; may be seen as stubborn and unyielding; may not set appropriate priorities; may find it difficult to change course; may confuse personal have-to-do's with what most needs to be done.

   B. *Too much might lead to these Stallers and Stoppers:*
   Overly Ambitious (103)

   C. *Compensators:*
   How to compensate for too much of this competency:
   2, 14, 26, 33, 41, 45, 46, 50, 51, 54, 60

   D. *Things to watch for:*
   Can't/won't admit they can't get it done
   Get too upset at setbacks
   Lets it get personal
   Obsessive/compulsive
   Perfectionist beyond reason
   Too readily blames others
   Works on everything at high pitch
   Little sense of effort to reward
   Likes fighting the sea

PERSEVERANCE

4. Too little can contribute to the following Stallers and Stoppers:

A. *What too little looks like (unskilled):*

Gives up too soon or moves on to something that's going better; doesn't push hard enough to get things done; doesn't go back with different strategies for the third and fourth try; may take rejection too personally; may hesitate to push when met with conflict, disagreement or attacks; may agree too early just to get it over with; may compromise for less than the original goal or objective; may simply not want to take charge and be out front.

B. *Too little might lead to these Stallers and Stoppers:*

Lack of Composure (107)

Performance Problems (118)

C. *Compensators:*

How to substitute for too little of this competency:

1, 9, 12, 16, 34, 39, 47, 53

I. LEARNING ARCHITECT® Connections:

Look for people who act like and/or show evidence of:

1a. Pure Action	13. Focused
1b. Trial and Error	21. Changer
1c. Following a Plan	29. Essence
2a. Problem Solving	31. Rationality
6. Contentious	38. Resilience

J. CHOICES ARCHITECT® Connections:

Look for people who act like and/or show evidence of:

First Edition (Released 1994)
20. Forging Ahead
21. Taking the Heat

Second Edition (Released 2000)
22. Taking the Heat
23. Visioning
25. Delivers Results
26. Drive
27. Presence

K. Difficulty to Develop:

18 (of 34)–Easiest

44. PERSONAL DISCLOSURE

A. Definition:

Shares his/her thoughts about personal strengths, weaknesses, and limitations; admits mistakes and shortcomings; is open about personal beliefs and feelings; is easy to get to know for those who interact with him/her regularly.

B. Arenas/Domains to Explore:

1. Career discussions
2. Coaching situations
3. Confusing situations
4. Convincing someone to take a job they don't want
5. Counseling/facilitating 360° feedback
6. Developmental situations
7. Director of ceremonies
8. Disciplinary actions
9. Giving advice
10. Giving tough feedback
11. Hardships
12. Helping someone through a hardship
13. Helping someone with a personal problem
14. High emotions
15. Hiring and staffing
16. Inspirational presentations
17. Mentoring
18. Motivating the troops
19. Performance appraisals
20. Roast host
21. Team building
22. Tense situations
23. With new boss
24. With new direct report
25. With new team member
26. Working with children

C. Sample Questions:

Dimension 1: Been there, done that–has had direct personal experience(s) involving the competency–candidate was the prime player   Note: * means OK for campus

1. Do people around you know your political affiliation?*
2. Has anyone ever accused you of messing something up because didn't disclose enough about yourself?
3. Has anyone ever taken advantage of you because you are so open about everything?*
4. Have you ever been hurt by disclosing a negative piece of information about yourself?*
5. Have you ever called someone on not being willing to disclose something about themselves?*
6. Have you ever disclosed a piece of confidential personal information you shouldn't have?*
7. Have you ever gained an advantage by disclosing a negative piece of information about yourself?*
8. Have you ever managed anything where the people or units reporting to you were in different locations? How did you help them get to know you personally?
9. How many people know how you voted for president or state office?*
10. How much about you do people who work with you get to know?*
11. How much do you know about the lives of people you work with?
12. How much do you know about the personal lives of the people who work for you?
13. How well can you hold proprietary information?*
14. Tell me about a time when you decided to say what you were really thinking.*
15. Tell me about a time when you didn't explain why you were doing something and it backfired on you.*
16. Tell me about a time when you made some of your larger mistakes and what you did about them.*
17. Tell me about a time when you shared something about yourself you were reluctant to share. How did this work out?*

PERSONAL DISCLOSURE

18. Tell me about a time when you successfully coached or developed someone.*
19. Tell me about a time when disclosures about yourself got you into trouble.
20. Tell me about a time when disclosures about yourself worked really well for you.
21. Where are you on a very-private-to-totally-open-person scale?*

Dimension 2: Seen/been around others who were involved with the competency–good and bad; learns from others about self

22. Contrast the most and least personally open people you know.*
23. Has personal disclosure or being personally open ever been in any 360° survey done on you? Was your score among your highest, middle, or lowest?
24. Has not being personally open on someone else's part ever created an obstacle for you or got in the way of something you were trying to accomplish?*
25. Have you ever talked with a coach or mentor about being more open about yourself?
26. Have you ever watched someone fail/get fired because they did not disclose enough about themselves?*
27. Have you ever watched someone be too personally open to the point that it backfired?
28. Have you ever watched someone succeed because they disclosed personal information?*
29. Have you ever worked with a coach on personal disclosure?*
30. Have you ever worked with a person who excelled at personal disclosure?
31. Have you ever worked with a skills coach on personal disclosure?*
32. How do you get feedback about yourself on personal disclosure?
33. How often do you check with multiple sources when you get a piece of critical feedback on not being personally open?
34. Is there a historical figure you consider a model of personal disclosure?
35. What do others who are not your fans say about your being personally open?
36. What do others who like you say about your being personally open?
37. Which boss was the best at personal disclosure?
38. Which boss was the worst at personal disclosure?
39. Which direct report was the best at personal disclosure?
40. Which direct report was the worst at personal disclosure?
41. Which peer was the best at personal disclosure?
42. Which peer was the worst at personal disclosure?
43. Who in your field or business is the best at disclosing personal information about themselves?
44. Who do you consider a current role model of personal disclosure?*
45. Who do you go to for advice on personal disclosure?
46. Who have you learned the most from about personal disclosure?*
47. Who is a higher-management role model for you on personal disclosure?
48. Who is a role model of personal disclosure outside of work?

Dimension 3: Knows how the competency works in theory; shows understanding

49. Are there situations or settings where someone should disclose personal information differently?
50. Do you think personal disclosure skills can be learned; how do you think people develop personal disclosure skills?
51. Do you think there is a way to compensate or work around low personal disclosure skills?
52. Has anyone asked you for your opinions/advice on personal disclosure?*
53. Have you ever attended a course on personal disclosure?

PERSONAL DISCLOSURE

54. Have you ever been in a situation where you and others put personal disclosure on a success profile?
55. Have you ever been part of an effort to create a policy or a mission statement containing reference to being personally open?
56. Have you ever been someone's coach or mentor who had problems with personal disclosure?
57. Have you ever created a development plan for someone on personal disclosure?
58. Have you ever criticized someone for not being personally open?
59. Have you ever designed a program on personal disclosure?
60. Have you ever given a speech on personal disclosure?
61. Have you ever rewarded or recognized someone for being personally open?
62. Have you ever taught a course on personal disclosure?
63. Have you ever tried to help someone deal more effectively with personal disclosure?*
64. Have you ever tried to help someone improve their personal disclosure skills?
65. How do you think people develop personal disclosure skills?
66. How much personal disclosure is good and how much is too much?
67. How much of success do you think is due to personal disclosure compared with other characteristics?
68. How would you know if someone is bad at personal disclosure?
69. How would you know if someone is good at personal disclosure?
70. If you had to write a book on personal disclosure, what would the chapter headings be?
71. What are the benefits to someone who is really good at personal disclosure?
72. What are the consequences to someone who is really poor at personal disclosure?
73. What do you think the standard is on personal disclosure for someone in your role?
74. What happens if you are too personally open?
75. What happens when two people try to work together who are very different in the way they disclose personal information?
76. What wisdom would you pass on to others trying to become better at being personally open?
77. When you select others, what do you look for in personal disclosure skills?
78. Why do you think people end up being different in the way they disclose personal information?

Dimension 4: Shows personal change and sense-making; learned it one place and applied it in another; can compare and contrast experiences; changes viewpoints across time; can explain personal development or evolution related to the competency

79. Compare and contrast examples of times when you've been effective and ineffective at disclosing your personal opinions, beliefs or feelings.
80. Contrast the way you are personally open on and off the job.
81. Did you ever pass up a job or assignment because you were not confident enough in your ability to be personally open?
82. Do you ever use other skills to cover for your lack of ability to be personally open?
83. Has becoming better at being personally open ever helped you in other areas?
84. Has not being personally open ever been the subject of a development plan for you?
85. Has personal disclosure ever figured in a failure, struggle, or setback you have had?
86. Has your personal disclosure or ability to be personally open always been this way?
87. Have you ever delegated or assigned someone a task because you lack the ability to be personally open?
88. Have you ever made significant strides to improve your ability to be personally open?
89. Have your personal disclosure skills, good or bad, ever been the subject of your performance review or a career discussion?

PERSONAL DISCLOSURE

90. How different are you across situations in how much you disclose about yourself?
91. How do you decide how much to disclose about yourself?
92. How much of your success is due to your being personally open?
93. How transferable are your personal disclosure skills to other situations?
94. If you had to become better at being personally open in a hurry, what would you do?
95. Was there a time when you were not as good at personal disclosure?
96. What caused you to work to try to disclose more about yourself?
97. What event or series of events had the most impact on your level of personal disclosure?
98. What's the most varied you can be in how much you personally disclose?
99. What was the shortest amount of time in which you increased your level of comfort at being personally open?
100. When did you first realize your level of comfort at personal disclosure?
101. When you know ahead of time that your usual level of personal disclosure isn't sufficient, what do you do?
102. Why do you think you deal with personal disclosure the way you do?
103. Why do you think your personal disclosure attitude is the way it is?*
104. Do you share your personal and political views with those around you at work?*
105. How much do the people around you know about you?*
106. Do you share personal information more with some and less with others?*
107. What do you feel about keeping personal life and work separate?*

D. Follow-up Probes:

1. Are there times to disclose and times not to?
2. Are there times when you're open like that and times when you aren't?
3. Could you contrast those two bosses for me?
4. Could you give me a few examples of how you've used or applied that?
5. Did that disclosure shock anyone?
6. Did they think you were too open?
7. Do you always disclose information about yourself like that or was that a special situation?
8. Do you find it hard to share feelings?
9. Do you suppose if others would just try harder, they could learn to be more comfortable disclosing negative information about themselves like you do?
10. Do you think that's teachable?
11. Do you think that harmed you in any way?
12. Do you think that was the right person to share that with?
13. Do you think you're better at openness about yourself than most? Why?
14. Do you think you would perform any differently if you could learn to be more comfortable disclosing negative information about yourself?
15. Have you ever had to disclose something about yourself to someone you really disliked?
16. How did the others react when you did that?
17. How did you come up with that approach to sharing negative information about yourself in the first place?
18. How did you know that method of getting over that barrier would work?
19. How do others you have known approach that?
20. How typical is this for you?
21. How would you approach that same situation today?

PERSONAL DISCLOSURE

22. Is this natural for you, or do you really have to dig for it?
23. Was there a time when you didn't understand this about yourself?
24. What did you do after you got that feedback?
25. What did you do to adapt to that?
26. What did you gain by disclosing that about yourself?
27. What did you learn from that?
28. Why did you choose that approach?
29. Why did you decide to take the risk?
30. Why did you do it that way?
31. Why did you time your disclosure like that?
32. Why do you think that didn't work?
33. Why do you think that happened that way?
34. Why do you think that worked?
35. Would you have done it that way with looser deadlines?
36. Would you have done it that way with tighter deadlines?

E. Themes/Things to Look for:
Ability to articulate feelings
Admits mistakes
Candor
Compensates for weaknesses
Defensiveness
Did they disclose more than others usually do in the interview
Drivers–why share
Embellishes the truth
Gets stronger by sharing
Makes others feel at ease
Relieves tension
Secure ego
Seeks feedback
Selective sharing
Self-awareness
Sense of appropriateness
Sense of timing
Sharing in order to teach
Not sharing only for personal gain
Sharing to ease someone else's pain
Sharing to entertain
Sharing to inspire
Sharing when it will explain why something is being done
Team building
Humor
Humility
Sharing to help someone feel more competent

PERSONAL DISCLOSURE

F. Most Likely Résumé:

1. Look for jobs like:
None Apply (Not learned from categories of jobs)

2. Look for develop-in-place assignments like:
Attend a self-awareness/assessment course that includes feedback.

Attend a course or event which will push you personally beyond your usual limits or outside your comfort zone (e.g., Outward Bound, language immersion training, sensitivity group, public speaking).

Join a self-help or support group.

Try to learn something frivolous and fun to see how good you can get (e.g., juggling, square dancing, magic).

Assemble an ad hoc team of diverse people to accomplish a difficult task.

Make peace with an enemy or someone you've disappointed with a product or service or someone you've had some trouble with or don't get along well with.

3. Best references to ask about or check:
Development Professionals

Natural Mentors

Spouse

G. Learning Agility Evaluation:
1. What/Describing vs. Why/Explain
3. Ordinary/Socially Acceptable vs. Insightful/Different
9. Vague/General vs. Sharp/Specific
10. Reactive vs. Initiating
12. Rehearsed/Socially Acceptable vs. Candid
16. Few Rules of Thumb vs. Many and Varied Rules of Thumb
17. Avoid Discussion of Weaknesses vs. Comfortably Sharing Shortcomings
20. Avoids Responsibility for Mistakes vs. Admits and Learns from Mistakes
21. View from Self vs. View from Point of View of Others

H. The LEADERSHIP ARCHITECT® Sort Card Connections:

1. Good (positive) if combined with high:
Invites reciprocal sharing; easy to share with 3, 33

Creates feeling of belonging 7, 36, 60

Can disclose up 8, 48

Knows who to share with and how to do it 15, 56, 64

Likes to teach 19

Trusted to share with 22, 29

Disclosure as a communication tool 26, 49

Can disclose laterally 42, 48

Doesn't overdo it; has good reasons 45, 48, 55

Does something about it 45, 54

PERSONAL DISCLOSURE

2. **Bad (negative) if combined with low or high (+):**

   Discloses too quickly (+1, 16) 41

   Too melodramatic 11, 26

   Can't take the heat when it backfires 11, 12

   Is it the truth 22, 29

   Doesn't do anything about it 45, 54

   Inappropriate disclosure 48, 50

   Discloses to the wrong people or in the wrong way 56, 64

   May not be accurate 55

3. **Too much can contribute to the following Stallers and Stoppers:**

   A. *What too much looks like (overused):*

   May turn off some people by excessive directness; may leave him/herself open for criticism because of his/her honesty; openness and directness may actually lead to a lack of trust; open style may lack credibility with some.

   B. *Too much might lead to these Stallers and Stoppers:*

   Blocked Personal Learner (106)

   Political Missteps (119)

   C. *Compensators:*

   How to compensate for too much of this competency:

   15, 22, 27, 29, 45, 48, 55, 56, 64

   D. *Things to watch for:*

Doesn't gauge the impact	Shocks others too much
Dumps everything	Talks, but doesn't do anything
Indiscriminate sharing	Cheap therapy
Makes others uncomfortable	Political missteps
No mystery left	

4. **Too little can contribute to the following Stallers and Stoppers:**

   A. *What too little looks like (unskilled):*

   A private person who does not discuss personal information; a closed book to most; hard to tell where he/she is coming from; may not believe in sharing personal views and foibles; works to keep personal and business separate; may fear what will happen if he/she discloses; may be shy; doesn't ask others for personal information; doesn't know what is helpful to share or why people find it valuable; may believe he/she has something to hide; may be defensive and unwilling to share much.

   B. *Too little might lead to these Stallers and Stoppers:*

Arrogant (104)	Failure to Build a Team (110)
Blocked Personal Learner (106)	Key Skill Deficiencies (113)
Defensiveness (108)	

   C. *Compensators:*

   How to substitute for too little of this competency:

   27, 29, 45, 54, 55

PERSONAL DISCLOSURE

I. LEARNING ARCHITECT® Connections:

Look for people who act like and/or show evidence of:

3a. Checking Feelings	15. Cautious
3b. Self-Talk	24. Discloser
7. Risks	38. Resilience

J. CHOICES ARCHITECT® Connections:

Look for people who act like and/or show evidence of:

First Edition (Released 1994)	Second Edition (Released 2000)
None Apply	None Apply

K. Difficulty to Develop:

27 (of 34)–Harder

45. PERSONAL LEARNING

A. Definition:

Picks up on the need to change personal, interpersonal, and managerial behavior quickly; watches others for their reactions to his/her attempts to influence and perform, and adjusts; seeks feedback; is sensitive to changing demands and responds accordingly.

B. Arenas/Domains to Explore:

1. 360° feedback
2. Advice from friends
3. Analyzing failures
4. Analyzing successes
5. Assessments in courses/workshops
6. Attitude survey results
7. Being asked to leave
8. Being fired
9. Career discussions
10. Changes in jobs/companies
11. Discussions with mentors
12. Getting feedback on giving feedback
13. Grades
14. Monitoring the reactions of others
15. On-line real-time feedback
16. Outside audits
17. Performance appraisals
18. Reflective (internal self-talk) feedback
19. Role model reading
20. Self-development reading
21. Self-talk
22. Solicited feedback
23. Spouse/family feedback
24. Trying something for the first-time
25. Watching bad role models
26. Watching good role models
27. Watching themselves on tape
28. Watching others adjust to circumstances
29. Watching others get public feedback
30. Working in foreign countries
31. Written critiques

C. Sample Questions:

*Dimension 1: Been there, done that–has had direct personal experience(s) involving the competency–candidate was the prime player   Note: * means OK for campus*

1. Give me some examples of situations where you had to adjust your style to get something done.
2. Has anyone ever accused you of messing something up because of being insensitive to the need to change behavior/not being receptive to negative feedback?*
3. Has anyone ever accused you of messing something up because of lack of adaptability?
4. Have you ever been through an assessment center process?
5. Have you ever found yourself in a situation where your current strengths weren't going to get you through?*
6. Have you ever joined a group or organization where you had to learn a new set of norms/behaviors to do well?*
7. Have you ever managed anything where the people or units reporting to you were in different locations? How did you change your behavior to adjust to them from a distance?
8. Have you ever received feedback you did not consider to be accurate?*
9. Have you ever volunteered for an evaluation or assessment event or process?
10. Have you ever worked in a foreign country? How was it different?
11. How do you check whether your style or approach is having the desired effect?*
12. How do you go about getting feedback about yourself?*

PERSONAL LEARNING

13. How do you react to courses and workshops that have assessment linked to them?
14. How do you respond when a single person has seen you be quite different across situations and calls you on it?*
15. Tell me about a time when you changed jobs/schools, and your behavior needed to change along with it to survive.*
16. Tell me about a time when you had no idea why people were acting the way they were, and you wondered what it had to do with you.*
17. Tell me about a time when you had to communicate something important to someone who did not speak your language very well.*
18. Tell me about a time when you joined a group with different norms.*
19. Tell me about a time when you realized a person/people weren't responding well to what you were trying to do.*
20. Tell me about a time when you realized things you had done in the past weren't working anymore.*
21. Tell me about a time when you realized you lacked a skill that you needed to do a task.*
22. Tell me about a time when you successfully coached or developed someone.*
23. Tell me about a time when you watched people closely to see how they were reacting to you. How did you respond.*
24. Tell me about a time when your flexibility or adaptability got you into trouble.
25. Tell me about a time when your flexibility or adaptability worked really well for you.
26. When you think you need some feedback, what do you do?

Dimension 2: Seen/been around others who were involved with the competency–good and bad; learns from others about self

27. Contrast the most and least willing people you know with regard to making personal changes in response to feedback.*
28. Has personal flexibility ever been in any 360° survey done on you? Was your score among your highest, middle, or lowest?
29. Has poor personal flexibility on someone else's part ever created an obstacle for you or got in the way of something you were trying to accomplish?*
30. Have you ever talked with a coach or mentor about personal flexibility?
31. Have you ever watched someone fail/get fired because they did not respond to feedback and change their behavior?*
32. Have you ever watched someone overrespond to feedback and changing their behavior to the point that it backfired?
33. Have you ever watched someone succeed because they responded to feedback and changed their behavior?*
34. Have you ever worked with a coach on making personal changes in response to feedback?*
35. Have you ever worked with a person who excelled at making personal changes in response to feedback?
36. Have you ever worked with a skills coach on making personal changes in response to feedback?*
37. How do you get feedback about yourself on personal flexibility?
38. How often do you check with multiple sources when you get a piece of critical feedback on not making personal changes in response to feedback?
39. Is there a historical figure you consider a model of making personal changes in response to feedback?
40. What do others who are not your fans say about your making personal changes in response to feedback?
41. What do others who like you say about your making personal changes in response to feedback?
42. Which boss was the best at making personal changes in response to feedback?
43. Which boss was the worst at making personal changes in response to feedback?

PERSONAL LEARNING

44. Which direct report was the best at making personal changes in response to feedback?
45. Which direct report was the worst at making personal changes in response to feedback?
46. Which peer was the best at making personal changes in response to feedback?
47. Which peer was the worst at making personal changes in response to feedback?
48. Who in your field or business is the best at making personal changes in response to feedback?
49. Who do you consider a role model of making personal changes in response to feedback?*
50. Who do you go to for advice on making personal changes in response to feedback?
51. Who have you learned the most from about making personal changes in response to feedback?*
52. Who is a higher-management role model for you on making personal changes in response to feedback?
53. Who is a role model of making personal changes in response to feedback outside of work?

Dimension 3: Knows how the competency works in theory; shows understanding

54. Are there situations or settings where someone should be different in the way they make personal changes in response to feedback?
55. Do you think being able to make personal changes in response to feedback can be learned; how do you think people develop these skills?
56. Do you think there is a way to compensate or work around low personal learning skills?
57. Has anyone asked you for your opinions/advice on making personal changes in response to feedback?*
58. Has anyone asked you for your opinions/advice on seeking feedback and changing behavior?*
59. Have you ever attended a course on seeking feedback and changing behavior?
60. Have you ever been in a situation where you and others put seeking feedback and changing behavior on a success profile?
61. Have you ever been part of an effort to create a policy or a mission statement containing reference to personal learning?
62. Have you ever been someone's coach or mentor who had problems with seeking feedback and changing behavior?
63. Have you ever created a development plan for someone on seeking feedback and changing behavior?
64. Have you ever criticized someone for not seeking feedback and changing behavior?
65. Have you ever designed a program on seeking feedback and changing behavior?
66. Have you ever given a speech on seeking feedback and changing behavior?
67. Have you ever rewarded or recognized someone for seeking feedback and changing behavior?
68. Have you ever taught a course on seeking feedback and changing behavior?
69. Have you ever tried to help someone deal more effectively with seeking feedback and changing behavior?*
70. Have you ever tried to help someone improve their willingness to seek feedback and change behavior?
71. How do you think people develop personal learning skills?
72. How much personal change in response to feedback is good and how much is too much?
73. How much of success do you think is due to personal learning skills compared with other characteristics?
74. How would you know if someone is bad at seeking feedback and changing behavior?
75. How would you know if someone is good at seeking feedback and changing behavior?
76. If you had to write a book on personal learning, what would the chapter headings be?
77. What are the benefits to someone who is really good at seeking feedback and changing behavior?
78. What are the consequences to someone who is really poor at seeking feedback and changing behavior?
79. What do you think the standard is on personal learning for someone in your role?
80. What happens if you make too many personal changes in response to feedback?
81. What happens when two people try to work together who are very different in their personal learning skills?

PERSONAL LEARNING

82. What wisdom would you pass on to others trying to become better at seeking feedback and changing behavior?
83. When you select others, what do you look for in personal learning skills?
84. Why do you think people end up being different in the way they make personal changes in response to feedback?

Dimension 4: Shows personal change and sense-making; learned it one place and applied it in another; can compare and contrast experiences; changes viewpoints across time; can explain personal development or evolution related to the competency

85. Compare and contrast examples of times when you've been effective and ineffective at making personal changes in response to feedback.
86. Contrast your on- and off-the-job methods of making personal changes in response to feedback.
87. Did you ever pass up a job or assignment because you were not confident enough that you could adjust your behavior to fit the situation?
88. Do you ever use other skills to cover for your lack of ability to make personal changes in response to feedback?
89. Has becoming better at making personal changes in response to feedback ever helped you in other areas?
90. Has making personal changes in response to feedback, good or bad, ever been the subject of your performance review or a career discussion?
91. Has not responding to feedback and changing your behavior ever been the subject of a development plan for you?
92. Has not responding to feedback and changing your behavior ever figured in a failure, struggle, or setback you have had?
93. Has your personal adaptability always been this way?
94. Have you ever delegated or assigned someone a task because you didn't make personal changes in response to feedback particularly well?
95. Have you ever made significant strides at improving your ability to make personal changes in response to feedback?
96. How different are you across situations in your ability to make personal changes in response to feedback?
97. How do you decide how much you are willing to change in response to feedback?
98. How much of your success is due to your ability to respond to feedback and change behavior?
99. How transferable are your skills at responding to feedback and changing behavior to other situations?
100. If you had to become better at making personal changes in response to feedback in a hurry, what would you do?
101. Was there a time when you were not as good at making personal changes in response to feedback?
102. What caused you to work to increase your ability to make personal changes in response to feedback?
103. What event or series of events had the most impact on your willingness and ability to make personal changes in response to feedback?
104. What's the most varied you can be in making personal changes in response to feedback?
105. What was the shortest amount of time in which you increased your level of skill at making personal changes in response to feedback?
106. When did you first realize your level of skill at making personal changes in response to feedback?
107. When you know ahead of time that your usual level of making personal changes in response to feedback isn't sufficient, what do you do?
108. Why do you think you deal with making personal changes in response to feedback the way you do?
109. Why do you think your personal flexibility is the way it is?*
110. Do you look to your failures for hints about what you could have done better?*

PERSONAL LEARNING

111. Do you look to your successes for hints about what you could have done better?*
112. When you learn about something you need to do better, what do you do?
113. How important is it for you to be true to yourself all the time?*
114. How different are you willing to be to get to where you want to go?*
115. Over your career, what's the greatest difference between who you are today and who you were when you started?

D. Follow-up Probes:

1. Are there times when you listen to and do something about the feedback you get and times when you don't?
2. Could you contrast those two bosses for me?
3. Could you give me a few examples of how you've used or applied that?
4. Do you always listen to and do something about the feedback you get like that or was that a special situation?
5. Do you suppose if others would just try harder, they could learn to be more effective at listening to and doing something about the feedback they get like you do?
6. Do you think that's teachable?
7. Do you think you're better at listening to and doing something about the feedback you get than most? Why?
8. Do you think you would perform any differently if you could be more effective at listening to and doing something about the feedback you get?
9. Have you ever had to listen to feedback from someone you really disliked?
10. How did that make you feel?
11. How did the others react when you did that?
12. How did you come up with that approach to listening to and doing something about the feedback you get in the first place?
13. How did you fight back at the inaccurate feedback?
14. How did you know that method of getting feedback would work?
15. How did you react to that negative criticism?
16. How do others you have known approach that?
17. How typical is this for you?
18. How would you approach that same situation today?
19. Is this natural for you, or do you really have to dig for it?
20. Was that a fair way to get feedback from them?
21. Was there a time when you didn't understand this about yourself?
22. What did you do after you got that feedback?
23. What did you do to adapt to that?
24. What did you learn from that?
25. Why did you choose that approach to getting feedback?
26. Why did you decide to take the risk?
27. Why did you do it that way?
28. Why did you time your attempt to get feedback like that?
29. Why do you think that didn't work?
30. Why do you think that happened that way?
31. Why do you think that worked?
32. Why do you think you have difficulties with that sometimes?
33. Would you have done it that way with looser deadlines?
34. Would you have done it that way with tighter deadlines?

PERSONAL LEARNING

E. Themes/Things to Look for:

Accepting the need for personal change–admitting mistakes or weak areas
Can they gain from feedback from people they dislike
Comparing situations/people
Drive to do it better
Eager to experiment and learn
Keeping feelings from blocking the message
Learns from experience
Lifelong commitment to continuous incremental improvement
Listening skills
Listening to unjustified criticism calmly
Looks forward to testing new skills
Mental rehearsal before entering tough situations
Observing others
Optimism about getting feedback from everyone
Seeking feedback
Self knowledge
Studies failures
Studies successes
Takes chances
Takes the heat
Using role models
Watching for their reactions

F. Most Likely Résumé:

1. Look for jobs like:

International Assignments
Scope (complexity) Assignments

2. Look for develop-in-place assignments like:

Attend a self-awareness/assessment course that includes feedback.
Attend a course or event which will push you personally beyond your usual limits or outside your comfort zone (e.g., Outward Bound, language immersion training, sensitivity group, public speaking).
Interview or work with a tutor or mentor on a skill you need to develop.
Do a study of successful executives in your organization, and report the findings to top management.
Join a self-help or support group.
Try to learn something frivolous and fun to see how good you can get (e.g., juggling, square dancing, magic).
Go on a business trip to a foreign country you've not been to before.
Relaunch an existing product or service that's not doing well.
Teach/coach someone how to do something you are not an expert in.
Assemble an ad hoc team of diverse people to accomplish a difficult task.
Take on a tough and undoable project, one where others who have tried it have failed.
Take on a task you dislike or hate to do.
Make peace with an enemy or someone you've disappointed with a product or service or someone you've had some trouble with or don't get along well with.

PERSONAL LEARNING

3. **Best references to ask about or check:**
   Human Resource Professionals
   Natural Mentors

G. Learning Agility Evaluation:
   1. What/Describing vs. Why/Explain
   4. Spectator/Passive vs. Player/Participant
   7. Passive vs. Intrigued/Curious
   15. Linear vs. Use Contrasts/Analogies
   16. Few Rules of Thumb vs. Many and Varied Rules of Thumb
   18. Stays Close to Home vs. Lots of Curiosity
   21. View from Self vs. View from Point of View of Others

H. The LEADERSHIP ARCHITECT® Sort Card Connections:

1. Good (positive) if combined with high:
   Does something with the feedback 1, 16, 43, 51, 53
   Gets top-down feedback 3, 4, 8
   Gets upward feedback 3, 33, 7, 23
   Gets lateral feedback 3, 33, 42, 60
   Committed to self-betterment 6, 44, 54, 55
   Can take criticism calmly 11, 12
   Picks up on subtle criticism 32, 33
   Picks up on need to behave differently across situations 31, 32, 46
   Can both take and give accurate criticism 56, 64

2. Bad (negative) if combined with low or high (+):
   Doesn't do anything about the feedback 1, 6, 43, 51, 54
   People don't offer enough feedback 3, 31
   Doesn't know how to graciously accept feedback from higher levels 4, 8
   Doesn't always react well to criticism 11, 12, 41
   Doesn't pick up on subtle criticism 32, 33
   Doesn't know how to get help from higher ups 39, 48
   Doesn't admit to it 44
   Can't judge the accuracy 55

3. Too much can contribute to the following Stallers and Stoppers:

   A. What too much looks like (overused):

   May be seen as too changeable; may shift situationally too easily and leave the impression of being wishy-washy; may err toward doing things differently rather than remaining the same; may confuse people by experimenting and being so adaptable.

   B. Too much might lead to these Stallers and Stoppers:
   Arrogant (104)

   C. Compensators:
   How to compensate for too much of this competency:
   5, 16, 17, 39, 46, 47, 50, 51, 52, 53, 58, 59, 62, 65

PERSONAL LEARNING

D. Things to watch for:

Doesn't have a keel in the water
Has a coat of too many colors
High need to please and be liked
Overreacts to feedback
Spends too much time adjusting to others

4. Too little can contribute to the following Stallers and Stoppers:

A. What too little looks like (unskilled):

Doesn't change or adapt to his/her surroundings or the situation; may have a view that being true to oneself is all that matters; may see adjusting to others as a sign of weakness; may be a one thing at a time person or a person who only thinks about what he/she is doing, not how others are responding or what they need; doesn't pick up on the need for personal change; doesn't seek or listen to personal on-line feedback; not a people watcher or studier, doesn't see or understand their reactions to him/her; may be arrogant or defensive.

B. Too little might lead to these Stallers and Stoppers:

Unable to Adapt to Differences (101)
Blocked Personal Learner (106)
Defensiveness (108)
Key Skill Deficiencies (113)
Political Missteps (119)

C. Compensators:

How to substitute for too little of this competency:
32, 33, 44, 54, 55

I. LEARNING ARCHITECT® Connections:

Look for people who act like and/or show evidence of:

2a. Problem Solving
3b. Self-Talk
3c. Personal Experience
4a. Getting Information
5. New
7. Risks
9. Multiple Sources
10. Complexity

12. Rules of Thumb
15. Cautious
25. Personal Change
26. Self-Aware
33. Diversity of Sources
37. Flexibility
38. Resilience

J. CHOICES ARCHITECT® Connections:

Look for people who act like and/or show evidence of:

First Edition (Released 1994)

10. Responds to Feedback
11. Open to Diversity
13. Role Flexibility
22. Self-Talk

Second Edition (Released 2000)

5. Easy Shifter
14. Open-Minded
16. Personal Learner
17. Responds to Feedback
18. Role Flexibility

K. Difficulty to Develop:

30 (of 34)–Hardest

46. PERSPECTIVE

A. Definition:

Looks toward the broadest possible view of an issue/challenge; has broad-ranging personal and business interests and pursuits; can easily pose future scenarios; can think globally; can discuss multiple aspects and impacts of issues and project them into the future.

B. Arenas/Domains to Explore:

1. Academic background
2. Assumption challenging events/experiences
3. Brainstorming
4. Business associate network
5. Family background in childhood
6. Foreign country exposure
7. Hobbies
8. Journals
9. Military experience
10. Personal network
11. Political history
12. Professional association memberships
13. Public/private/government/military employment
14. Range of business interests
15. Range of personal interests
16. Reads case studies
17. Religious history
18. Role models
19. Sense of history
20. Simulations/scenarios/projections
21. Strategic planning off-sites
22. TV viewing habits
23. What they read
24. Where they lived
25. Where they travel
26. Where they vacation
27. Where they went to school
28. Who they associate with
29. Who they work for
30. Work in international division
31. Workshops/courses/seminars

C. Sample Questions:

Dimension 1: Been there, done that–has had direct personal experience(s) involving the competency–candidate was the prime player   Note: * means OK for campus

1. Are you a history/biography/autobiography reader?
2. Are you a science fiction fan?*
3. Did your family move around when you were still living at home?*
4. Do you generally read the editorial page of your newspaper?*
5. Do you use the Internet?*
6. Has anyone ever accused you of messing something up because of your lack of perspective?
7. Have you ever done business in a foreign country? How was it different?
8. Have you ever done business in Mexico? What was different?
9. Have you ever done business in Canada? How was it different?
10. Have you ever managed anything where the people or units reporting to you were in different locations? How did you communicate what issues outside the organization should be monitored and considered for impact?
11. Have you ever worked in an international job?
12. How many different businesses have you worked for?
13. How many foreign countries have you spent any time in?*
14. How many foreign nationals have you worked with?

PERSPECTIVE

15. In how many places have you lived?*
16. Tell me about a time when your perspective got you into trouble.
17. Tell me about a time when your perspective worked really well for you.
18. What are the best three books you've read?*
19. What are the last three books you've read?*
20. What are your tastes in music and art?*
21. What hobbies/interests do you have?*
22. What kind of architecture do you like?*
23. What periodicals/magazines do you read regularly?*

Dimension 2: Seen/been around others who were involved with the competency–good and bad; learns from others about self

24. Contrast the people you know who have the broadest and narrowest range of perspective.*
25. Has perspective ever been in any 360° survey done on you? Was your score among your highest, middle, or lowest?
26. Has lack of broad perspective on someone else's part ever created an obstacle for you or got in the way of something you were trying to accomplish?*
27. Have you ever talked with a coach or mentor about improving your perspective?
28. Have you ever watched someone fail/get fired because they had a narrow perspective?*
29. Have you ever watched someone overextend their perspective to the point that it backfired?
30. Have you ever watched someone succeed because they had a broad perspective?*
31. Have you ever worked with a coach on broadening your perspective?*
32. Have you ever worked with a person who excelled at having a broad perspective?
33. Have you ever worked with a skills coach on perspective?*
34. How do you get feedback about yourself on your perspective?
35. How often do you check with multiple sources when you get a piece of critical feedback on your lack of perspective?
36. Is there a historical figure you consider a model of broad perspective?
37. What do others who are not your fans say about your perspective?
38. What do others who like you say about your perspective?
39. Which boss was the best at having a broad perspective?
40. Which boss was the worst at having a broad perspective?
41. Which direct report was the best at having a broad perspective?
42. Which direct report was the worst at having a broad perspective?
43. Which peer was the best at having a broad perspective?
44. Which peer was the worst at having a broad perspective?
45. Who in your field or business has the broadest perspective?
46. Who do you consider a current role model of having a broad perspective?*
47. Who do you go to for advice on broadening your perspective?
48. Who have you learned the most from about perspective?*
49. Who is a higher-management role model for you on having a broad perspective?
50. Who is a role model of perspective outside of work?

Dimension 3: Knows how the competency works in theory; shows understanding

51. Are there situations or settings where someone should have a different perspective?
52. Could the U.S. government actually go bankrupt?*
53. Do you think perspective can be learned; how do you think people develop this skill?

PERSPECTIVE

54. Do you think there is a way to compensate or work around having too broad or narrow a perspective?
55. Has anyone asked you for your opinions/advice on range of perspective?*
56. Have you ever attended a course on perspective?
57. Have you ever been in a situation where you and others put range of perspective on a success profile?
58. Have you ever been part of an effort to create a policy or a mission statement containing reference to range of perspective?
59. Have you ever been someone's coach or mentor who had problems with their range of perspective?
60. Have you ever created a development plan for someone on changing their range of perspective?
61. Have you ever criticized someone for lack of perspective?
62. Have you ever designed a program on perspective?
63. Have you ever given a speech on perspective?
64. Have you ever rewarded or recognized someone for having too broad or narrow a perspective?
65. Have you ever taught a course on perspective?
66. Have you ever tried to help someone deal more effectively with changing their perspective?*
67. Have you ever tried to help someone improve their range of perspective?
68. How do the financial markets work? Who do you buy a stock or bond from? Who gets the money?*
69. How do you think people develop perspective?
70. How does doing business around the world differ?*
71. How much perspective is good to have and how much is too much?
72. How much of success do you think is due to range of perspective compared with other characteristics?
73. How would you know if someone lacks perspective?
74. How would you know if someone demonstrates perspective?
75. If you had to write a book on perspective, what would the chapter headings be?
76. What are one or two things that are going to happen beyond the current year that are going to make a big difference in how we do business?*
77. What are the benefits to someone who is really good at having a broad perspective?
78. What are the consequences to someone who is really poor at having a broad perspective?
79. What do you think of the world's immigration issues?*
80. What do you think the standard is on range of perspective for someone in your role?
81. What does balance of trade mean?*
82. What does the FTC do?*
83. What happens if you have too broad or narrow a perspective?
84. What happens when two people try to work together who have very different perspectives?
85. What is this TQM/Process Re-engineering/Six Sigma stuff all about?
86. What will happen at that point in the future when there are equal numbers of men and women in senior management jobs?*
87. What wisdom would you pass onto others trying to develop a broader range of perspective?
88. What's a service economy?*
89. What's an information worker?*
90. What's industrial policy? Do we have it in the U.S.?*
91. What's the difference between a patent, a trademark and a copyright?*
92. What's the effect of the E.U. on your business?
93. What's the negative effect of terrorism on your business? Can this be turned into a positive?
94. When you select others, what do you look for in how they demonstrate a broad range of perspective?
95. Why do you think people end up being different in how they demonstrate a broad range of perspective?

PERSPECTIVE

96. With the U.S. moving labor-intensive factories to foreign countries, what do you think will eventually happen?*

Dimension 4: Shows personal change and sense-making; learned it one place and applied it in another; can compare and contrast experiences; changes viewpoints across time; can explain personal development or evolution related to the competency

97. Compare and contrast examples of times when you've been broad and narrow in perspective.
98. Contrast your on- and off-the-job perspective.
99. Did you ever pass up a job or assignment because you were not broad enough in your perspective?
100. Do you ever use other skills to cover for your lack of a broad perspective?
101. Has building a broader perspective ever helped you in other areas?
102. Has having a narrow perspective ever figured in a failure, struggle, or setback you have had?
103. Has lack of perspective ever been the subject of a development plan for you?
104. Has perspective, good or bad, ever been the subject of your performance review or a career discussion?
105. Has your perspective always been this way?
106. Have you ever delegated or assigned someone a task because you didn't have a broad enough perspective for the task?
107. Have you ever made significant strides at broadening your perspective?
108. How different is your perspective across situations?
109. How do you decide how broad a perspective to have?
110. How much of your success is due to your having a broad perspective?
111. How transferable is your perspective to other situations?
112. If you had to have a broader perspective in a hurry, what would you do?
113. Was there a time when your perspective was not as broad as it is today?
114. What caused you to work to broaden your perspective?
115. What event or series of events had the most impact on your perspective?
116. What's the most varied you can be in perspective?
117. What was the shortest amount of time in which you increased your level of skill at broadening your perspective?
118. When did you first realize your level of perspective is what it is?
119. When you know ahead of time that your usual level of perspective isn't adequate, what do you do?
120. Why do you think you deal with perspective the way you do?
121. Why do you think your perspective is the way it is?*
122. What are the two most varied company cultures you have worked in so far?
123. How have your successes and failures modified your perspective on doing business?

D. Follow-up Probes:

1. Are there times when you use a broad perspective like that and times when you don't?
2. Could you contrast those two bosses for me?
3. Could you give me a few examples of how you've used or applied that?
4. Do you always look at things that broadly or was that a special situation?
5. Do you suppose if others would just try harder, they could learn to look at issue and problem more broadly like you do?
6. Do you think that's teachable?
7. Do you think you're better at viewing things broadly than most? Why?
8. Do you think you would perform any differently if you could be more effective at taking a broader view?

PERSPECTIVE

9. Have you always understood the world that way or is this a recent development in you?
10. How did the others react when you said/did that?
11. How did you come up with that approach to taking the broader view in the first place?
12. How did you learn that?
13. How do others you have known approach that?
14. How do you determine how broad a view to take?
15. How typical is this for you?
16. How would you approach that same situation today?
17. Is this natural for you, or do you really have to dig for it?
18. Was there a time when you didn't understand this about yourself?
19. What did you do after you got that feedback?
20. What did you do to adapt to that?
21. What did you learn from that?
22. Why did you choose that approach?
23. Why did you decide to take that risk?
24. Why did you do it that way?
25. Why did you time your attempt to apply a broader view like that?
26. Why do you suppose that works that way?
27. Why do you think that didn't work?
28. Why do you think that happened that way?
29. Why do you think you have difficulty with that sometimes?
30. Why did you decide to read that?
31. Why did you decide to go to that?
32. Why do you think that worked?
33. Would you have done it that way with looser deadlines?
34. Would you have done it that way with tighter deadlines?

E. Themes/Things to Look for:
   Able to run scenarios in their head
   Abstract concept capability
   Asks lots of questions
   Broad sourcing
   Capacity for complexity
   Comfort with projecting into the future
   Contrasts dissimilar domains
   Drawing parallels
   Global view
   Good at making connections
   Interest in how things work behind the screen/behind the curtain
   Internalizes, relates, draws parallels
   Knows why things are like they are
   Looking outside their normal area
   Loves to explore the new/unique/different/foreign
   Narrow vs. broad
   Range of disconnected, marginally connected interests

PERSPECTIVE

Sense of history

Simultaneous consideration of business, cultural, economic, political, social, market, demographic, historical, and future elements of an issue/problem

Staying state of the art in their field

Transfers learning from one area into another

Understands trends

Unusual sourcing

Uses metaphors/analogies

Visionary; ability to see out in front of the headlights

Visualizing likely outcomes

F. Most Likely Résumé:

1. Look for jobs like:

Cross-Moves

Heavy Strategic Demands

International Assignments

Scope (complexity) Assignments

2. Look for develop-in-place assignments like:

Manage the renovation of an office, floor, building, meeting room, warehouse, etc.

Serve for a year or more with a community agency.

Become a volunteer for a year or more for an outside organization.

Work for a year or more with a charitable organization.

Lobby for your organization on a contested issue in local, regional, state, or federal government.

Act as a loaned executive to a charity, government, agency, etc.

Work short rotations in other units, functions, or geographies you've not been exposed to before.

Work on a project that involves travel and study of an issue, acquisition, or joint venture off-shore or overseas, with a report back to management.

Manage a project team made up of nationals from a number of countries.

Get involved with the negotiation of a contract or agreement with international consequences.

Join a community board.

Manage an ad hoc, temporary group of people where the people in the group are towering experts but the temporary manager is not.

Assemble an ad hoc team of diverse people to accomplish a difficult task.

3. Best references to ask about or check:

Boss' Boss(es)

Natural Mentors

All Other Superiors

G. Learning Agility Evaluation:

1. What/Describing vs. Why/Explain
2. All or Nothing vs. Can See Many Sides
3. Ordinary/Socially Acceptable vs. Insightful/Different
7. Passive vs. Intrigued/Curious
8. Sameness vs. Diversity
9. Vague/General vs. Sharp/Specific
13. Simple Views vs. Complex Views
14. Sameness vs. Broad Ranging

PERSPECTIVE

15. Linear vs. Use Contrasts/Analogies
18. Stays Close to Home vs. Lots of Curiosity

H. The LEADERSHIP ARCHITECT® Sort Card Connections:

1. Good (positive) if combined with high:
Willing to act on perspective 1, 9, 16, 57
Will contemplate the long-term future 2, 40, 58
Balances perspective with here and now 5, 24, 58, 65
Uses perspective to come up with something new 14, 28
Broad perspective on diversity 21
Expert in their field 24, 61
Really understands the maze 39, 48
Puts perspective to good business use 50, 51, 52, 53, 63
Complex diagnostic perspective on people 56, 64

2. Bad (negative) if combined with low or high (+):
Too much perspective for most to handle; confuses people (+2, 40)
May not understand things above their level 4, 8
Not focused on task at hand 5, 24
Can't translate above average knowledge into outcomes 14, 28
Broad perspective doesn't include people differences 21
Can't articulately tell others 27, 49, 67
Doesn't add new perspectives easily 32, 33
Broad perspective doesn't include how organizations work 38, 48, 59
Broad perspective doesn't include self 45, 55

3. Too much can contribute to the following Stallers and Stoppers:

A. What too much looks like (overused):
Might have some trouble concentrating on the here and now; may leave others behind when he/she speculates in the broad view of an issue; may not set practical priorities; may always be reaching for too much and/or the ideal; may see connections that aren't there.

B. Too much might lead to these Stallers and Stoppers:
Poor Administrator (102)
Performance Problems (118)

C. Compensators:
How to compensate for too much of this competency:
5, 16, 17, 24, 35, 38, 47, 50, 51, 52, 53, 58, 59, 63, 65

D. Things to watch for:
Complexities things into uselessness
Doesn't do means testing for the capacity to understand the broader perspective
Gets lost on unproductive tangents

PERSPECTIVE

Nothing is ever simple enough to act on
Wanders too widely for the task at hand
Somewhere out there

4. Too little can contribute to the following Stallers and Stoppers:

A. What too little looks like (unskilled):

Is narrow and parochial; has narrow views of issues and challenges; uses only one or a few lenses to view problems and opportunities; doesn't have far ranging interests, not well read; background may be narrow; isn't good at running "what if" scenarios; lacks interest in maybe's and the future and how world events do and will affect his/her organization; won't be a good strategist or visionary; a here and now person who is often surprised by unexpected change; may be a single function/profession/technical area/skill person.

B. Too little might lead to these Stallers and Stoppers:

Unable to Adapt to Differences (101)   Non-strategic (114)
Blocked Personal Learner (106)   Overdependence on a Single Skill (116)
Defensiveness (108)

C. Compensators:

How to substitute for too little of this competency:
5, 15, 21, 32, 38, 58, 61

I. LEARNING ARCHITECT® Connections:

Look for people who act like and/or show evidence of:

2a. Problem Solving   12. Rules of Thumb
2b. Visioning   17. Selected Sources
2c. Intuition   18. Straightforward
 5. New   27. Conceptualizer
 9. Multiple Sources   28. Creator
10. Complexity   33. Diversity of Sources
11. Why/How   35. Breadth

J. CHOICES ARCHITECT® Connections:

Look for people who act like and/or show evidence of:

First Edition (Released 1994)   **Second Edition (Released 2000)**
 1. Inquisitive   1. Broad Scanner
 5. Connector   3. Connector
 6. Visionary   7. Inquisitive
11. Open to Diversity   14. Open-Minded
16. Cold/Indirect
18. Into Everything

K. Difficulty to Develop:

25 (of 34)–Moderate

47. PLANNING

A. Definition:

Accurately scopes out length and difficulty of tasks and projects; sets objectives and goals; breaks down work into the process steps; develops schedules and task/people assignments; anticipates and adjusts for problems and roadblocks; measures performance against goals; evaluates results.

B. Arenas/Domains to Explore:

1. Any supervisory event
2. Arrange/manage a tour/trip
3. Building a facility
4. Building office space
5. Club/association management
6. Coordinating vendors/suppliers
7. Deploying resources across geographies
8. Event/conference planning/management
9. Fund drives
10. Giving out assignments
11. Group/team leader
12. Implementing new programs
13. Installing new systems
14. Introducing new policies
15. Managing simultaneous activities
16. Managing the work of volunteers
17. Military experiences
18. Planning an off-site event
19. Planning and managing a company function
20. Planning consulting projects
21. Planning for obstacles
22. Preparing for a Legal proceeding
23. Preparing for meetings
24. Preparing for significant presentations
25. Preparing grant proposals
26. Process Re-engineering
27. Project/taskforce leader
28. Ramping up to make a major data-based decision
29. Renovations
30. Schedules
31. TQM
32. United Way Captain/Chair
33. Working for Political Campaigns

C. Sample Questions:

Dimension 1: Been there, done that–has had direct personal experience(s) involving the competency–candidate was the prime player   Note: * means OK for campus

1. Do you have a written career plan?*
2. Do you have a written financial plan?
3. Do you use PERT or GANTT or other project-charting techniques?
4. Do you use project planning software?
5. Has anyone ever accused you of messing something up because of poor planning?
6. Have you ever managed anything where the people or units reporting to you were in different locations? How did you handle planning from a distance?
7. Have you ever set project goals and targets too high?*
8. Have you ever set project goals and targets too low?*
9. Have you ever stumbled because you didn't anticipate a roadblock/obstacle?*
10. How do you design benchmarks to measure progress?
11. How much time do you think you should spend planning against the time it takes to do the projects?
12. Tell me about a time when you designed an early warning system for a project/task you were doing.*

PLANNING

13. Tell me about a time when you designed some problem prevention procedures for a project/task you were doing.*
14. Tell me about a time when you organized and managed others on a complex task from start to finish.*
15. Tell me about a time when you planned and pulled off a complex assignment.*
16. Tell me about a time when you used some mid-course correction measures for a project/task you were doing.*
17. Tell me about a time when your attempt to plan got you into trouble.
18. Tell me about a time when your attempt to plan worked really well for you.
19. Tell me about the project where you missed the deadline the most.
20. Tell me about your most over-budget project.
21. What is your hit rate at predicting how long projects will take? Give me some examples of hits and misses.
22. What is your hit rate at predicting project costs? Give me some examples of hits and misses.
23. What is your hit rate of assigning the right people to the right tasks? Give me some examples of hits and misses.
24. What's the largest cost project you've ever managed?
25. What's the largest number of simultaneous projects you've managed at one time?
26. What's the longest, lead-time project you've worked on?
27. Why did you go to the schools you did?*
28. Why did you pick the major you did?*

Dimension 2: Seen/been around others who were involved with the competency–good and bad; learns from others about self

29. Contrast the best and worst planners you know.*
30. Has planning ever been in any 360° survey done on you? Was your score among your highest, middle, or lowest?
31. Has poor planning skills on someone else's part ever created an obstacle for you or got in the way of something you were trying to accomplish?*
32. Have you ever talked with a coach or mentor about your planning skills?
33. Have you ever watched someone fail/get fired because they did not plan well?*
34. Have you ever watched someone overplan to the point that it backfired?
35. Have you ever watched someone succeed because they planned well?*
36. Have you ever worked with a coach on planning skills?*
37. Have you ever worked with a person who excelled at planning?
38. Have you ever worked with a skills coach on planning skills?*
39. How do you get feedback about yourself on planning skills?
40. How often do you check with multiple sources when you get a piece of critical feedback on your planning skills?
41. Is there a historical figure you consider a model of planning?
42. What do others who are not your fans say about your planning skills?
43. What do others who like you say about your planning skills?
44. Which boss was the best at planning?
45. Which boss was the worst at planning?
46. Which direct report was the best at planning?
47. Which direct report was the worst at planning?
48. Which peer was the best at planning?

PLANNING

49. Which peer was the worst at planning?
50. Who in your field or business is the best planner?
51. Who do you consider a current role model of planning?*
52. Who do you go to for advice on planning?
53. Who have you learned the most from about planning?*
54. Who is a higher-management role model for you on planning?
55. Who is a role model of planning outside of work?

Dimension 3: Knows how the competency works in theory; shows understanding

56. Are there situations or settings where someone should plan differently?
57. Do you think planning skills can be learned; how do you think people develop planning skills?
58. Do you think there is a way to compensate or work around ineffective planning skills?
59. Has anyone asked you for your opinions/advice on planning?*
60. Have you ever attended a course on effective planning?
61. Have you ever been in a situation where you and others put planning skills on a success profile?
62. Have you ever been part of an effort to create a policy or a mission statement containing reference to being an effective planner?
63. Have you ever been someone's coach or mentor who had problems with planning?
64. Have you ever created a development plan for someone on planning?
65. Have you ever criticized someone for not planning?
66. Have you ever designed a program on effective planning?
67. Have you ever given a speech on effective planning?
68. Have you ever rewarded or recognized someone for having planning skills?
69. Have you ever taught a course on effective planning?
70. Have you ever tried to help someone deal more effectively with planning?*
71. Have you ever tried to help someone improve their planning skills?
72. How do you think people develop effective planning skills?
73. How much planning is good to have and how much is too much?
74. How much of success do you think is due to planning compared with other characteristics?
75. How would you know if someone is bad at planning?
76. How would you know if someone is good at planning?
77. If you had to write a book on effective planning, what would the chapter headings be?
78. What are the benefits to someone who is really good at effective planning?
79. What are the consequences to someone who is really poor at effective planning?
80. What do you think the standard is on effective planning for someone in your role?
81. What happens if you plan too much?
82. What happens when two people try to work together who have very different planning skills?
83. What wisdom would you pass on to others trying to become better at planning?
84. When you select others, what do you look for in planning skills?
85. Why do you think people end up having different planning skills?

PLANNING

Dimension 4: Shows personal change and sense-making; learned it one place and applied it in another; can compare and contrast experiences; changes viewpoints across time; can explain personal development or evolution related to the competency

86. Compare and contrast examples of times you've been effective and ineffective at planning.
87. Contrast your on- and off-the-job use of planning.
88. Did you ever pass up a job or assignment because you were not confident enough in your planning skills?
89. Do you ever use other skills to cover for your lack of planning abilities?
90. Has becoming better at planning ever helped you in other areas?
91. Has poor planning ever been the subject of a development plan for you?
92. Have poor planning skills ever figured in a failure, struggle, or setback you have had?
93. Have you ever delegated or assigned someone a task because you didn't plan particularly well?
94. Have you ever made significant strides at improving your planning skills?
95. Have your planning skills always been this way?
96. Have your planning skills, good or bad, ever been the subject of your performance review or a career discussion?
97. How different are you across situations in your planning?
98. How do you decide how much planning to do?
99. How much of your success is due to your planning skills?
100. How transferable are your planning skills to other situations?
101. If you had to become better at planning in a hurry, what would you do?
102. Was there a time when you were not as good at planning?
103. What caused you to work to improve your planning skills?
104. What event or series of events had the most impact on your planning skills?
105. What's the most varied you can be in planning?
106. What was the shortest amount of time in which you increased your level of skill at planning?
107. When did you first realize your level of skill at planning?
108. When you know ahead of time that your usual level of planning isn't adequate, what do you do?
109. Why do you think you plan the way you do?
110. Why do you think your planning skills are the way they are?*
111. How do you balance achieving results against plan with letting people take initiative and find their own ways to do things?
112. How good are you at predicting how projects will turn out?*

D. Follow-up Probes:

1. Are there times when you plan like that and times when you don't?
2. Could you contrast those two bosses for me?
3. Could you give me a few examples of how you've used or applied that?
4. Do you always plan like that or was that a special situation?
5. Do you suppose if others would just try harder, they could learn to be more effective at planning like you do?
6. Do you think that's teachable?
7. Do you think you're better at planning than most? Why?
8. Do you think you overplanned that?
9. Do you think you would perform any differently if you could be more effective at planning?

PLANNING

10. Have you ever had to plan around someone you really disliked?
11. How did the others react when you did that?
12. How did you come up with that approach to planning in the first place?
13. How did you know that method of planning would work?
14. How did you react when the project steps didn't work out as you had designed them?
15. How do others you have known approach that?
16. How much time did you spend planning?
17. How typical is this for you?
18. How would you approach that same situation today?
19. Is this natural for you, or do you really have to dig for it?
20. Was that a fair way to plan around them?
21. Was there a time when you didn't understand this about yourself?
22. What did you do after you got that feedback?
23. What did you do to adapt to that?
24. What did you learn from that?
25. Why did you choose that approach?
26. Why did you decide to take the risk?
27. Why did you do it that way?
28. Why did you time your attempt to plan like that?
29. Why do you think that didn't work?
30. Why do you think that happened that way?
31. Why do you think that worked?
32. Why do you think you have difficulty with that sometimes?
33. Would you have done it that way with looser deadlines?
34. Would you have done it that way with tighter deadlines?

E. Themes/Things to Look for:

- A good sense of timing
- Ability to estimate time
- Ability to estimate costs
- Ability to realistically project how things play out
- Ability to run internal simulations/scenarios
- Ability to run/track simultaneous projects
- Anticipating problems
- Breaking things down into steps
- Checking progress techniques
- Clarity of communication
- Complex and varied tactics for getting resources
- Effective and timely decisions
- Enjoys being orderly
- Vision of the end result
- Gets tougher when blocked
- Goal driven
- Keeping people informed
- Keeping personal feelings from getting in the way
- Orderly thought process
- Overcoming obstacles
- Placing blame when something doesn't work as planned
- Providing timely actionable feedback to those in the project
- Putting feedback loops in place
- Setting goals too high
- Setting goals too low
- Sharing the big picture
- Understands vendors/suppliers/consultants
- Willingness to delegate

PLANNING

F. Most Likely Résumé:

1. Look for jobs like:

Chair of Projects/Task Forces
Fix-Its/Turnarounds
Line to Staff Switches
Scale (size shift) Assignments
Staff to Line Shifts
Start-Ups

2. Look for develop-in-place assignments like:

Install a new process or system (computer system, new policies, new process, new procedures, etc.).

Integrate diverse systems, processes, or procedures across decentralized and/or dispersed units.

Manage the renovation of an office, floor, building, meeting room, warehouse, etc.

Plan a new site for a building (plant, field office, headquarters, etc.).

Plan an off-site meeting, conference, convention, trade show, event, etc.

Manage the purchase of a major product, equipment, materials, program, or system.

Run a company or unit picnic or annual outing.

Manage the visit of a VIP (member of top management, government official, outside customer, foreign visitor, etc.).

Launch a new product, service, or process.

Relaunch an existing product or service that's not doing well.

Seek out and use a seed budget to create and pursue a personal idea, product, or service.

Work on a team writing a proposal to obtain significant government or foundation grants or funding of an activity.

Teach a course, seminar, or workshop on something you don't know well.

Design a training course in an area you're not an expert in.

Manage an ad hoc, temporary group of balky and resisting people through an unpopular change or project.

Manage an ad hoc, temporary group of low-competence people through a task they couldn't do by themselves.

Manage an ad hoc, temporary group of people involved in tackling a fix-it or turnaround project.

Manage an ad hoc, temporary group of people in a rapidly expanding operation.

Assemble an ad hoc team of diverse people to accomplish a difficult task.

Help shut down a plant, regional office, product line, business, operation, etc.

Manage liquidation/sale of products, equipment, materials, a business, furniture, overstock, etc.

Prepare and present a proposal of some consequence to top management.

Work on a team that's deciding who to keep and who to let go in a layoff, shutdown, delayering, or divestiture.

Manage a cost-cutting project.

Build a multifunctional project team to tackle a common business issue or problem.

Work on a team looking at a reorganization plan where there will be more people than positions.

3. Best references to ask about or check:

Direct Boss
Direct Reports

G. Learning Agility Evaluation:

1. What/Describing vs. Why/Explain
2. All or Nothing vs. Can See Many Sides
3. Ordinary/Socially Acceptable vs. Insightful/Different
5. Tight/Rigid vs. Loose/Flexible
6. Reacting/Responsive vs. Adapting

PLANNING

   9. Vague/General vs. Sharp/Specific
   11. Generalizations vs. Specific Learnings
   16. Few Rules of Thumb vs. Many and Varied Rules of Thumb
   19. External Standards vs. Internal Standards

H. The LEADERSHIP ARCHITECT® Sort Card Connections:

1. Good (positive) if combined with high:
   Carries out the plan 1, 16, 53
   Flexible; can organize chaos 2, 40
   Good content 5, 24, 30, 46, 51
   Takes people's needs into account 7, 10, 23
   Takes on the obstacles directly 9, 12, 34, 57
   Uses plans to create something new 14, 28
   Empowers 33, 36, 60
   Couched well 39, 48
   Plans actually work out 39, 52
   Extends to strategic planning 46, 58
   Good at writing plans down 67

2. Bad (negative) if combined with low or high (+):
   Nothing comes from the plan 1, 16, 53
   Where's the beef 5, 15, 24
   Short term planning only (+5, 24) 46, 58, 65
   Doesn't take people's needs into account 7, 10, 23
   Can't sell others on the plan 8, 27, 36, 49
   Overreacts when things don't go as planned 11, 12, 41
   Uninspired plans 14, 28
   May be too controlling 18 (+35, 39)
   Won't use others 18, 33 (+57)
   Plans run into obstacles from above 38, 48, 52
   Spends too much time planning 50, 62

3. Too much can contribute to the following Stallers and Stoppers:

A. What too much looks like (overused):

   May be overly dependent on rules, regulations, procedures, and structure; may leave out the human element of the work; may be inflexible and have trouble with rapid change.

B. Too much might lead to these Stallers and Stoppers:
   Unable to Adapt to Differences (101)   Failure to Build a Team (110)
   Blocked Personal Learner (106)   Insensitive to Others (112)
   Defensiveness (108)   Overmanaging (117)

PLANNING

C. Compensators:
How to compensate for too much of this competency:
2, 3, 10, 14, 15, 26, 31, 32, 33, 40, 46, 57, 60, 64

D. Things to watch for:

Leads to people being unmotivated	Sticks with it over the cliff
Narrow	The magic is gone
Obsessive/compulsive	Too mired in detail
Perfectionist	Knows the results before the facts

4. Too little can contribute to the following Stallers and Stoppers:

A. What too little looks like (unskilled):
Doesn't plan for much; may be a seat-of-the-pants performer scratching it out at the last minute; doesn't follow an orderly method of setting goals and laying out work; may be uncomfortable with structure and process flow; may be disdainful of planning and come across to others as loose or too simple; may not have the patience to establish goals and objectives, scope out difficulties, plan for task completion, develop schedules, and do roadblock management; may be confusing to work for and with; may be demotivating for others who work with him/her.

B. Too little might lead to these Stallers and Stoppers:

Poor Administrator (102)	Failure to Build a Team (110)
Blocked Personal Learner (106)	Performance Problems (118)

C. Compensators:
How to substitute for too little of this competency:
18, 20, 24, 35, 39, 51, 52

I. LEARNING ARCHITECT® Connections:

Look for people who act like and/or show evidence of:

1c. Following a Plan	18. Straightforward
2a. Problem Solving	19. What
13. Focused	20. Events
14. Controlled	23. Orchestrator
15. Cautious	

J. CHOICES ARCHITECT® Connections:

Look for people who act like and/or show evidence of:

First Edition (Released 1994)	Second Edition (Released 2000)
4. Complexity	2. Complexity
13. Role Flexibility	18. Role Flexibility

K. Difficulty to Develop:
18 (of 34)–Easier

48. POLITICAL SAVVY

A. Definition:

Can maneuver through complex political situations effectively and quietly; is sensitive to how people and organizations function; anticipates where the land mines are and plans his/her approach accordingly; views corporate politics as a necessary part of organizational life and works to adjust to that reality; is a maze-bright person.

B. Arenas/Domains to Explore:

1. Any multi-layer Event
2. Black Tie social/business events
3. Club/association management
4. Cross-boundary initiatives
5. Dealing with government officials
6. Dealing with the board of directors
7. Dealing with the press
8. Dealing with unions
9. Entering new culture for the first-time
10. Event/conference management with mixed organization attendance
11. Getting things done when you don't have the power
12. Key account marketing
13. Lobbying
14. Managing a cross-division meeting/initiative
15. Managing a merger/acquisition
16. Managing foreign dignitaries
17. Managing outside consultants inside the organization
18. Managing proprietary information
19. Managing VIP visitors
20. Need to use other people's resources
21. Negotiating vendor/supplier relationships
22. Public relations assignment
23. Selling a major initiative to top management
24. Short-term assignments/visits to alien units
25. Small start-ups inside larger organization
26. Staff jobs in corporate with powerful divisions
27. Strategic partnerships
28. Student government
29. Volunteer work in outside agency
30. Working on a political campaign

C. Sample Questions:

Dimension 1: Been there, done that–has had direct personal experience(s) involving the competency–candidate was the prime player   Note: * means OK for campus

1. Has anyone ever accused you of messing something up because of poor political skills?
2. Have you ever been a United Way captain/community service/club leader?*
3. Have you ever been an outside consultant in an organization serving more than one division?
4. Have you ever been involved in fund-raising outside the company (for a school or charity, for example)?*
5. Have you ever been part of an affirmative action audit?
6. Have you ever been the spokesperson for your organization in front of the press?
7. Have you ever been the spokesperson for your organization in front of the shareholders?
8. Have you ever been the spokesperson for your organization in front of the union?
9. Have you ever had a corporate job in a heavily divisionalized company?
10. Have you ever had shipped material hung up in customs that you had to have?
11. Have you ever had to give a speech containing material you did not agree with?*
12. Have you ever marketed yourself for a job with your boss' boss or higher?
13. Have you ever had to mediate something between two people more powerful than you?*

POLITICAL SAVVY

14. Have you ever had to report bad news to management two or more levels above you?
15. Have you ever lobbied for an organization?
16. Have you ever managed a visit by a foreign senior manager or dignitary?
17. Have you ever managed anything where the people or units reporting to you were in different locations? How did you deal with the differing political situations of the various locations?
18. Have you ever managed key accounts?
19. Have you ever stretched the truth a bit to keep a customer?
20. Have you ever testified or been deposed in a legal proceeding when you needed to say as little as possible?
21. Have you ever worked on a political campaign?*
22. How much that's on your mind to do you actually tell your boss?
23. Tell me about a successful experience you've had implementing something across organization boundaries.
24. Tell me about a time when you didn't use your political skills when you should have.*
25. Tell me about a time when you got a major policy/practice/procedure approved.*
26. Tell me about a time when you got something approved under time pressure that was out of the ordinary.*
27. Tell me about a time when you got something changed that was a long-standing practice/policy.*
28. Tell me about a time when you had to deal with some dumb policies.*
29. Tell me about a time when you overcame resistance inside to get a project done.*
30. Tell me about a time when you overused your political skills.*
31. Tell me about a time when you were called for using a political maneuver.
32. Tell me about a time when you were outmaneuvered by a competitor.
33. Tell me about a time when your attempts to be political got you into trouble.
34. Tell me about a time when your attempts to be political worked really well for you.
35. Tell me about an unsuccessful experience you've had implementing something across organization boundaries.
36. What portion of your time do you spend having to be political in your job?
37. What's the highest level person you have ever presented to?
38. When you have gained something you wanted by using a political maneuver, how does that make you feel?

Dimension 2: Seen/been around others who were involved with the competency–good and bad; learns from others about self

39. Contrast the most and least politically savvy people you know.*
40. Has political savvy ever been in any 360° survey done on you? Was your score among your highest, middle, or lowest?
41. Has lack of political savvy on someone else's part ever created an obstacle for you or got in the way of something you were trying to accomplish?*
42. Have you ever talked with a coach or mentor about your political skills?
43. Have you ever watched someone fail/get fired because they did not have sufficient political skills?*
44. Have you ever watched someone overdo political savvy to the point that it backfired?
45. Have you ever watched someone succeed because they had political skills?*
46. Have you ever worked with a coach on political savvy?*
47. Have you ever worked with a person who excelled at political savvy?
48. Have you ever worked with a skills coach on political skills?*
49. How do you get feedback about yourself on political savvy?
50. How often do you check with multiple sources when you get a piece of critical feedback on your political skills?

POLITICAL SAVVY

51. Is there a historical figure you consider a model of political savvy?
52. What do others who are not your fans say about your political skills?
53. What do others who like you say about your political skills?
54. Which boss was the best at political savvy?
55. Which boss was the worst at political savvy?
56. Which direct report was the best at political savvy?
57. Which direct report was the worst at political savvy?
58. Which peer was the best at political savvy?
59. Which peer was the worst at political savvy?
60. Who in your field or business is the best at political savvy?
61. Who do you consider a role model of political savvy?*
62. Who do you go to for advice on political savvy?
63. Who have you learned the most from about political savvy?*
64. Who is a higher-management role model for you on political savvy?
65. Who is a role model of political savvy outside of work?

Dimension 3: Knows how the competency works in theory; shows understanding

66. Are there situations or settings where someone should demonstrate political skills differently?
67. Do you think political savvy can be learned; how do you think people develop political skills?
68. Do you think there is a way to compensate or work around low political skills?
69. Has anyone asked you for your opinions/advice on political savvy?*
70. Have you ever attended a course on political savvy?
71. Have you ever been in a situation where you and others put political savvy on a success profile?
72. Have you ever been part of an effort to create a policy or a mission statement containing reference to being politically savvy?
73. Have you ever been someone's coach or mentor who had problems with political savvy?
74. Have you ever created a development plan for someone on political savvy?
75. Have you ever criticized someone for not being politically savvy?
76. Have you ever designed a program on political savvy?
77. Have you ever given a speech on political savvy?
78. Have you ever rewarded or recognized someone for having political savvy?
79. Have you ever taught a course on political savvy?
80. Have you ever tried to help someone deal more effectively with politics?*
81. Have you ever tried to help someone improve their political savvy?
82. How do you think people develop political skills?
83. How much political savvy is good to have and how much is too much?
84. How much of success do you think is due to political savvy compared with other characteristics?
85. How would you know if someone lacks political savvy?
86. How would you know if someone has good political skills?
87. If you had to write a book on political savvy, what would the chapter headings be?
88. What are the benefits to someone who has really good political skills?
89. What are the consequences to someone who has really poor political skills?
90. What do you think the standard is on political savvy for someone in your role?
91. What happens if you have or use too much political savvy?

POLITICAL SAVVY

92. What happens when two people try to work together who have very different political skills?
93. What wisdom would you pass on to others trying to develop political savvy?
94. When you select others, what do you look for in political savvy?
95. Why do you think people end up having different levels of political savvy?

Dimension 4: Shows personal change and sense-making; learned it one place and applied it in another; can compare and contrast experiences; changes viewpoints across time; can explain personal development or evolution related to the competency

96. Compare and contrast examples of times you've been effective and ineffective at dealing with the politics in an organization.
97. Contrast your on- and off-the-job use of political savvy.
98. Did you ever pass up a job or assignment because you were not confident enough in your political savvy?
99. Do you ever use other skills to cover for your lack of political savvy?
100. Has becoming better at political skills ever helped you in other areas?
101. Has lack of political savvy ever figured in a failure, struggle, or setback you have had?
102. Has poor political savvy ever been the subject of a development plan for you?
103. Has your political savvy always been this way?
104. Have you ever delegated or assigned someone a task because you did not have sufficient political skills?
105. Have you ever made significant strides to improve your political savvy?
106. Have your political skills, good or bad, ever been the subject of your performance review or a career discussion?
107. How different are you across situations in your political savvy?
108. How do you decide how political to be?
109. How much of your success is due to your political savvy?
110. How transferable are your political skills to other situations?
111. If you had to become better at political skills in a hurry, what would you do?
112. Was there a time when your political skills were not as good as they are now?
113. What caused you to work to improve your political skills?
114. What event or series of events had the most impact on your political skills?
115. What's the most varied you can be in political savvy?
116. What was the shortest amount of time in which you increased your level of skill at political savvy?
117. When did you first realize your level of skill at political savvy?
118. When you know ahead of time that your usual level of political savvy isn't sufficient, what do you do?
119. Why do you think you deal with political situations the way you do?
120. Why do you think your political savvy is the way it is?*
121. In your experience is politics the "art of the possible?"
122. How do feel about people who play "corporate/school politics?"* Why do you have those feelings?
123. Do you tell some people more of what you know than others?
124. How important is it for you to be trusted?*
125. Have you changed the kind of jokes you tell as sensitivities have changed?*
126. Have you changed your language and the words you use as sensitivities have changed?

D. Follow-up Probes:

1. Are there times when you use your political skills like that and times when you don't?

POLITICAL SAVVY

2. Could you contrast those two bosses for me?
3. Could you give me a few examples of how you've used or applied that?
4. Did that person outmaneuver you that time?
5. Do you always maneuver through situations like that or was that a special situation?
6. Do you suppose if others would just try harder, they could learn to be more effective at maneuvering through organizations like you do?
7. Do you think that's all teachable?
8. Do you think that's dishonest in any way?
9. Do you think you have better political skills than most? Why?
10. Do you think you would perform any differently if you could be more effective at understanding and maneuvering through the maze of organizations?
11. Have you always understood organizations that way or is this a recent development in you?
12. Have you ever had to maneuver around someone you really disliked to get what you wanted?
13. How did that make you feel about yourself?
14. How did the others react when you did that?
15. How did you come up with that approach to working your way through organizations in the first place?
16. How did you know that method of getting over that barrier would work?
17. How do others you have known approach that?
18. How do you feel about having to say something not quite in line with what you really believe?
19. How typical is this for you?
20. How would you approach that same situation today?
21. Is this natural for you, or do you really have to dig for it?
22. Was that a fair way to maneuver around them?
23. Was there a time when you didn't understand this about yourself?
24. What did you do after you got that feedback?
25. What did you do to adapt to that?
26. What did you learn from that?
27. Why did you choose an indirect approach?
28. Why did you choose that approach?
29. Why did you decide to take the risk?
30. Why did you do it that way?
31. Why did you time your attempt to maneuver like that?
32. Why do you suppose organizations work that way?
33. Why do you think that didn't work?
34. Why do you think that happened that way?
35. Why do you think that worked?
36. Why do you think you have difficulty with that sometimes?
37. Would you have done it that way with looser deadlines?
38. Would you have done it that way with tighter deadlines?

POLITICAL SAVVY

E. Themes/Things to Look for:

Ability to market and sell
Anticipating questions/concerns/perspectives/land mines
Awareness of own impact
Being outmaneuvered and learning from it
Complex views of power
Composure during tense political struggles
Getting through gatekeepers
Has seen politics pay off
Healthy skepticism
Identifies stakeholders early
Influence without authority skills
Knows stakeholders
Knows who to involve and when on what
Losing battles to win wars
Maneuvering skills
Networking
Packaging skills
Peace with moral paradoxes in politics (saying one thing, knowing another)
Positive attitude toward "politics" as a necessary evil
Sense of timing
Senses trouble before it happens
Staging capabilities
Takes calculated risks
Thinking several moves ahead
Understanding of power relationships
Understands gatekeeping
Understands why there is resistance
Using political skills to get out of tight situations
Using political skills to get things done
Using political skills to cover a shortage of content
Working through a variety of political situations

F. Most Likely Résumé:

1. Look for jobs like:

Chair of Projects/Task forces
Cross-Moves
Fix-Its/Turnarounds
International Assignments
Scope (size shift) Assignments
Staff Leadership (Influencing Without Authority)
Start-Ups

2. Look for develop-in-place assignments like:

Integrate diverse systems, processes, or procedures across decentralized and/or dispersed units.
Manage the renovation of an office, floor, building, meeting room, warehouse, etc.
Plan a new site for a building (plant, field office, headquarters, etc.).

POLITICAL SAVVY

Plan an off-site meeting, conference, convention, trade show, event, etc.

Serve for a year or more with a community agency.

Go on a business trip to a foreign country you've not been to before.

Lobby for your organization on a contested issue in local, regional, state, or federal government.

Write a proposal for a new policy, process, mission, charter, product, service, or system, and present and sell it to top management.

Plan for and start up something small (secretarial pool, athletic program, suggestion system, program, etc.).

Launch a new product, service, or process.

Be a change agent; create a symbol for change; lead the rallying cry; champion a significant change and implementation.

Relaunch an existing product or service that's not doing well.

Eke out and use a seed budget to create and pursue a personal idea, product, or service.

Serve on a junior or shadow board.

Join a community board.

Work on a team forming a joint venture or partnership.

Manage an ad hoc, temporary group of balky and resisting people through an unpopular change or project.

Manage an ad hoc, temporary group of people involved in tackling a fix-it or turnaround project.

Assemble an ad hoc team of diverse people to accomplish a difficult task.

Manage the interface between consultants and the organization on a critical assignment.

Prepare and present a proposal of some consequence to top management.

Manage the assigning/allocating of office space in a contested situation.

Take on a tough and undoable project, one where others who have tried it have failed.

Manage a cost-cutting project.

Do a postmortem on a failed project and present it to the people involved.

Build a multifunctional project team to tackle a common business issue or problem.

Work on a team looking at a reorganization plan where there will be more people than positions.

3. Best references to ask about or check:

Direct Boss

Boss' Boss(es)

Human Resource Professionals

Natural Mentors

Past Associates/Constituencies

G. Learning Agility Evaluation:

1. What/Describing vs. Why/Explain
2. All or Nothing vs. Can See Many Sides
3. Ordinary/Socially Acceptable vs. Insightful/Different
5. Tight/Rigid vs. Loose/Flexible
7. Passive vs. Intrigued/Curious
8. Sameness vs. Diversity
11. Generalizations vs. Specific Learnings
13. Simple Views vs. Complex Views
21. View from Self vs. View from Point of View of Others
22. Focus on Accomplishments vs. Focus on Solving Problems

POLITICAL SAVVY

H. The LEADERSHIP ARCHITECT® Sort Card Connections:

1. Good (positive) if combined with high:
Uses political skills to get things done 1, 16, 38, 53
Can use charm as a political tactic 3, 31
Strong network 4, 8 , 42, 60
Never to harm 7, 10, 21, 23
Smooth 12, 31, 38
Stands up when necessary 13, 34, 57
Can maneuver outside organization 15, 38, 53
Trusted use of political skills as positive 22, 29
Can use humor as a political tactic 26
Can craft messages 27, 49, 51, 67
Puts organization first 27, 51, 53, 63
Picks up signs quickly 32, 56, 64
Can politic across boundaries 36, 38, 42, 60

2. Bad (negative) if combined with low or high (+):
Has trouble in paradoxical situations 2, 40
Interpersonal skills not available as an option 3, 31, 33
Limited to people 5, 38, 52
May not care who gets hurt/used 7, 10, 21, 23
Used to promote self (+6)
Wilts quickly when challenged 11, 12
In service of inappropriate or personal motives 22, 29
May pick wrong tactic 30, 51
May have trouble across boundaries 42, 60
All situations have political ramifications 50

3. Too much can contribute to the following Stallers and Stoppers:

A. *What too much looks like (overused):*
May be seen as excessively political; may not be trusted; may tell others what they are expecting to hear rather than what he/she knows to be true; may overstate what they know; may be seen as manipulative and scheming.

B. *Too much might lead to these Stallers and Stoppers:*
Overly Ambitious (103)   Overdependence on an Advocate (115)
Betrayal of Trust (105)   Overdependence on a Single Skill (116)

C. *Compensators:*
How to compensate for too much of this competency:
4, 8, 12, 17, 22, 27, 29, 30, 34, 38, 44, 51, 53, 57, 63

POLITICAL SAVVY

D. Things to watch for:

Overvaluing style over substance
Seeing everything as political
Spending excessive time plotting, staging and packaging
Using easy to read political tactics
Using political skills primarily for personal gain
Using political skills primarily to get out of tight situations
Using political skills to cover for missing content/substance
Little sense of priorities
Wastes effort in turf considerations

4. Too little can contribute to the following Stallers and Stoppers:

A. What too little looks like (unskilled):

Doesn't know how to navigate smoothly and quietly through political waters; says and does things that cause political problems; doesn't understand how to deal with not invented here and territory protection; rejects politics and may view self as apolitical; others might see this as naive; may not deal with upper management persuasively; may be impatient with political process and make procedural errors; may be too direct and not consider impact on others; may not project out consequences of their actions well.

B. Too little might lead to these Stallers and Stoppers:

Unable to Adapt to Differences (101)   Insensitive to Others (112)
Lack of Composure (107)   Political Missteps (119)
Lack of Ethics and Values (109)

C. Compensators:

How to substitute for too little of this competency:
3, 4, 8, 12, 22, 31, 32, 33, 36, 38, 42, 47, 52, 56, 64

I. LEARNING ARCHITECT® Connections:

Look for people who act like and/or show evidence of:

2a. Problem Solving   11. Why/How
3b. Self-Talk   12. Rules of Thumb
4a. Getting Information   15. Cautious
 9. Multiple Sources   34. Sizing Up Others

J. CHOICES ARCHITECT® Connections:

Look for people who act like and/or show evidence of:

First Edition (Released 1994)   **Second Edition (Released 2000)**
13. Role Flexibility   5. Easy Shifter
23. Communicator   9. Agile Communicator
                                          15. People-Smart
                                          18. Role Flexibility

POLITICAL SAVVY

K. Difficulty to Develop:
32 (of 34)–Hardest

49. PRESENTATION SKILLS

A. Definition:

Is effective in a variety of formal presentation settings: one-on-one, small and large groups, with peers, direct reports, and bosses; is effective both inside and outside the organization, on both cool data and controversial topics; commands attention and can manage group process during the presentation; can change tactics midstream when something isn't working.

B. Arenas/Domains to Explore:

1. Annual plan presentations
2. Appearing on TV/radio
3. Board presentations
4. Case study reports
5. Church sermons
6. Coaching
7. Commencement addresses
8. Community work
9. Customer training
10. Fund-Raising
11. Hosting conferences
12. Human resource Reviews
13. Interviewed by the press
14. Introducing VIPs to audiences
15. Lecturing
16. Marketing and selling
17. Master of ceremonies
18. Press conferences
19. Product/Service presentations
20. Professional association speeches
21. Project progress reviews
22. Running tours
23. Shareholder meeting presentations
24. Simultaneous translation speeches
25. Staff meeting presentations
26. Strategic plan reviews
27. Taskforce/project reports
28. Teaching
29. Testifying before regulators
30. Toastmasters
31. United Way appeals
32. Wall Street Briefings

C. Sample Questions:

Dimension 1: Been there, done that–has had direct personal experience(s) involving the competency–candidate was the prime player   Note: * means OK for campus

1. Did you take speech classes in school?*
2. Do you ever rehearse your presentations?*
3. Do you get butterflies before major presentations?*
4. Do you give presentations to customers?
5. Do you script your speeches?*
6. Do you speak on behalf of your organization?
7. Do you speak to Wall Street analysts about your organization?
8. Do you tend to use a podium or do you walk around?
9. Do you use humor in your presentations?*
10. Has anyone ever accused you of messing something up because you didn't present it well?*
11. Have you been part of a panel of speakers?
12. Have you been videotaped?
13. Have you ever forgotten what you were going to say in front of an audience?*

PRESENTATION SKILLS

14. Have you ever given a speech where someone else handled your visuals?
15. Have you ever had a slip of the tongue, and said something you shouldn't have in front of an audience?*
16. Have you ever had the audio or visual breakdown during a speech?
17. Have you ever managed anything where the people or units reporting to you were in different locations? How did you present information to them?
18. Have you ever received a standing ovation after a speech?*
19. Have you ever stopped a presentation midstream, asked the audience whether it was working or not, and then continued in a different direction?
20. Have you ever used a TelePrompTer?
21. Have you presented in a video conference?
22. Have you used a wireless microphone?
23. How do you manage hecklers?*
24. How do you shut off people in audiences who talk too much?*
25. How frequently do you give presentations to groups of more than twenty-five?*
26. Tell me about a time when you had to communicate something important to someone who did not speak your language very well.
27. Tell me about a time when you ran into a resistant audience.*
28. Tell me about a time when you were positively surprised by an audience.*
29. Tell me about a time when you were surprised by a negative audience.*
30. Were you ever on a debate team?*
31. What kind of visuals do you usually use when making presentations?
32. What's the highest level person you've presented to?
33. What's the largest group you've ever addressed?*
34. What's the toughest Q & A you've ever had to handle?*

Dimension 2: Seen/been around others who were involved with the competency–good and bad; learns from others about self

35. Contrast the best and worst presenters you know.*
36. Has presentation skills ever been in any 360° survey done on you? Was your score among your highest, middle, or lowest?
37. Has poor presentation skills on someone else's part ever created an obstacle for you or got in the way of something you were trying to accomplish?*
38. Have you ever talked with a coach or mentor about your presentation skills?
39. Have you ever watched someone fail /get fired because they did not present well?*
40. Have you ever watched someone overdo presentation skills to the point that it backfired?
41. Have you ever watched someone succeed because they presented well?*
42. Have you ever worked with a coach on presentation skills?*
43. Have you ever worked with a person who excelled at presenting?
44. Have you ever worked with a skills coach on presentation skills?*
45. How do you get feedback about yourself on how well you present?
46. How often do you check with multiple sources when you get a piece of critical feedback on your presentation skills?
47. Is there a historical figure you consider a model of presenting?
48. What do others who are not your fans say about your presentation skills?
49. What do others who like you say about your presentation skills?

PRESENTATION SKILLS

50. Which boss was the best at presenting?
51. Which boss was the worst at presenting?
52. Which direct report was the best at presenting?
53. Which direct report was the worst at presenting?
54. Which peer was the best at presenting?
55. Which peer was the worst at presenting?
56. Who in your field or business is the best presenter?
57. Who do you consider a role model of presentation skills?*
58. Who do you go to for advice on presentation skills?
59. Who have you learned the most from about presenting?*
60. Who is a higher-management role model for you on presentation skills?
61. Who is a role model of presentation skills outside of work?

Dimension 3: Knows how the competency works in theory; shows understanding

62. Are there situations or settings where someone should present differently?
63. Do you think presentation skills can be learned; how do you think people develop presentation skills?
64. Do you think there is a way to compensate or work around low presentation skills?
65. Has anyone asked you for your opinions/advice on presentation skills?*
66. Have you ever attended a course on presentation skills?
67. Have you ever been in a situation where you and others put presentation skills on a success profile?
68. Have you ever been part of an effort to create a policy or a mission statement containing reference to presentation skills?
69. Have you ever been someone's coach or mentor who had problems with presenting?
70. Have you ever created a development plan for someone on presentation skills?
71. Have you ever criticized someone for not presenting well?
72. Have you ever designed a program on presentation skills?
73. Have you ever given a speech on presentation skills?
74. Have you ever rewarded or recognized someone for having presentation skills?
75. Have you ever taught a course on presentation skills?
76. Have you ever tried to help someone present more effectively?*
77. Have you ever tried to help someone improve their presentation skills?
78. How do you think people develop presentation skills?
79. How much of success do you think is due to presentation skills compared with other characteristics?
80. How would you know if someone is bad at presenting?
81. How would you know if someone is good at presenting?
82. If you had to write a book on presentation skills, what would the chapter headings be?
83. What are the benefits to someone who is really good at presenting?
84. What are the consequences to someone who is really poor at presenting?
85. What do you think the standard is on presentation skills for someone in your role?
86. What happens when two people try to work together who have very presentation skills?
87. What wisdom would you pass on to others trying to become better at presenting?
88. When you select others, what do you look for in presentation skills?
89. Why do you think people end up having different presentation skills?

PRESENTATION SKILLS

Dimension 4: Shows personal change and sense-making; learned it one place and applied it in another; can compare and contrast experiences; changes viewpoints across time; can explain personal development or evolution related to the competency

90. Compare and contrast examples of being effective and ineffective at presenting.
91. Contrast your on- and off-the-job presentation skills.
92. Did you ever pass up a job or assignment because you were not confident enough in your presentation skills?
93. Do you ever use other skills to cover for your lack of presentation skills?
94. Do you present differently to inside groups than outside groups even if the topic is the same? How? Why?*
95. Has becoming better at presentation skills ever helped you in other areas?
96. Have poor presentation skills ever been the subject of a development plan for you?
97. Have you ever delegated or assigned someone a presentation because you don't do presentations particularly well?
98. Have you ever made significant strides at becoming better at presentation skills?
99. Have your presentation skills always been basically this way?
100. Have your presentation skills ever figured in a failure, struggle, or setback you have had?
101. Have your presentation skills, good or bad, ever been the subject of your performance review or a career discussion?
102. How different are you across situations in your presentation skills?
103. How do you decide how much or which presentation skills to use?
104. How much of your success is due to your presentation skills?
105. How transferable are your presentation skills to other situations?
106. If you had to become better at presentation skills in a hurry, what would you do?
107. Was there a time when your presentation skills were not as good as they are now?
108. What caused you to work to improve your presentation skills?
109. What do you do differently when you're presenting one-on-one?*
110. What event or series of events had the most impact on your presentation skills?
111. What's the difference between small and large group presentations?*
112. What's the most varied you can be in presentation skills?
113. What was the shortest amount of time in which you increased your presentation skills?
114. When did you first realize your level of skill at presenting?
115. When you know ahead of time that your usual way of presenting won't work, what do you do?
116. Why do you think you deal with presenting the way you do?
117. Why do you think your presentation skills are the way they are?*

D. Follow-up Probes:

1. Are there times when you present like that and times when you don't?
2. Could you contrast those two bosses for me?
3. Could you give me a few examples of how you've used or applied that?
4. Did making that presentation make you anxious?
5. Did your presentation skills help you get through that situation?
6. Do you always present like that or was that a special situation?
7. Do you suppose if others would just try harder, they could learn to be more effective at presenting like you do?

PRESENTATION SKILLS

8. Do you think that's all teachable?
9. Do you think you have better presentation skills than most? Why?
10. Do you think you would perform any differently if you could be more effective at presenting?
11. How did that make you feel?
12. How did the heckler react when you took them on?
13. How did the others react when you did that?
14. How did you come up with that approach to making presentations in the first place?
15. How did you know that method of presenting would work?
16. How do others you have known approach that?
17. How typical is this for you?
18. How would you approach that same situation today?
19. Is this natural for you, or do you really have to dig for it?
20. Was there a time when you didn't understand this about yourself?
21. What did you do after you got that feedback?
22. What did you do to adapt to that?
23. What did you learn from that?
24. Why did you choose that approach?
25. Why did you decide to take the risk?
26. Why did you do it that way?
27. Why did you time your presentation like that?
28. Why do you think that didn't work?
29. Why do you think that happened that way?
30. Why do you think that worked?
31. Why do you think you have difficulty with that sometimes?
32. Would rehearsing ahead of time have helped?
33. Would you have done it that way with looser deadlines?
34. Would you have done it that way with tighter deadlines?
35. Would you have prepared differently had you known that ahead of time?

E. **Themes/Things to Look for:**

Ability to handle tough questions
Able to change pace to match the audience
Accent
Acting training
Actual rehearsal
Agility with audio/visual aids
Audience responses
Butterflies
Enjoyment of speaking/presenting
Facilitating discussions
Handling hecklers by drawing them out, taking their questions seriously, giving their views status rather than blasting them
Humor

PRESENTATION SKILLS

Matching level of content to audience
Mental rehearsal
Methods to calm themselves before going on stage
Physical presence
Quick change if something doesn't work
Reading audiences
Sensitivity to audiences
Shutting someone off smoothly
Student government leadership positions
Using scripts
Varied tactics
Voice strength

F. Most Likely Résumé:

1. Look for jobs like:

Chair of Projects/Task Forces
Heavy Strategic Demands
Line to Staff Switches
Scale Assignments
Staff Leadership (Influencing Without Authority)
Start-Ups

2. Look for develop-in-place assignments like:

Integrate diverse systems, processes, or procedures across decentralized and/or dispersed units.

Plan a new site for a building (plant, field office, headquarters, etc.).

Study humor in business settings; read books on the nature of humor; collect cartoons you could use in presentations; study funny people around you; keep a log of funny jokes and sayings you hear; read famous speeches and study how humor was used; attend comedy clubs; ask a funny person to act as your tutor; practice funny lines and jokes with others.

Study and summarize a new trend, product, service, technique, or process and present and sell it to others.

Make speeches/be a spokesperson for the organization on the outside.

Represent the organization at a trade show, convention, exposition, etc.

Represent the concerns of a group of nonexempt, clerical, or administrative employees to higher management to seek resolution of a difficult issue.

Write a proposal for a new policy, process, mission, charter, product, service, or system, and present and sell it to top management.

Be a change agent; create a symbol for change; lead the rallying cry; champion a significant change and implementation.

Relaunch an existing product or service that's not doing well.

Seek out and use a seed budget to create and pursue a personal idea, product, or service.

Teach a course, seminar, or workshop on something you know a lot about.

Teach a course, seminar, or workshop on something you don't know well.

Train customers in the use of the organization's products or services.

Present the strategy of your unit to others not familiar with your business.

Prepare and present a proposal of some consequence to top management.

Manage a group through a significant business crisis.

PRESENTATION SKILLS

3. **Best references to ask about or check:**
   Direct Boss
   Boss' Boss(es)
   Customers
   Natural Mentors
   Past Associates/Constituencies
   Peers and Colleagues
   All Other Superiors

G. Learning Agility Evaluation:
   4. Spectator/Passive vs. Player/Participant
   5. Tight/Rigid vs. Loose/Flexible
   6. Reacting/Responsive vs. Adapting
   9. Vague/General vs. Sharp/Specific
   10. Reactive vs. Initiating
   15. Linear vs. Use Contrasts/Analogies
   16. Few Rules of Thumb vs. Many and Varied Rules of Thumb
   21. View from Self vs. View from Point of View of Others

H. The LEADERSHIP ARCHITECT® Sort Card Connections:

1. **Good (positive) if combined with high:**
   Charismatic 1, 9, 36, 65
   Engaging 3, 26, 60
   Knows topics 5, 24, 30, 46, 61
   Uses humor constructively 7, 10, 21, 23, 26
   Comfortable presenting up 8, 48
   Can handle tough Q & A 11, 12
   Can think on their feet 32, 51
   Understands what people want to hear 33, 36, 56, 64
   Courage to present controversial subjects 34, 57
   Comfortable presenting to peers 42, 60

2. **Bad (negative) if combined with low or high (+):**
   Has trouble with tough Q & A 2, 11, 12
   Flat presenter 3, 31
   Content light 5, 24, 61
   Humor may hurt others 7, 10, 21, 23 (+26)
   Can't think on their feet 16, 30, 32, 51
   Misses the meaning of questions 33
   Says things they shouldn't have 38, 48
   Bad sense of timing 47, 50, 62
   Misreads audiences 56, 64
   May write ineffective content 67
   Snake 22, 29
   Doesn't understand personal impact 45

PRESENTATION SKILLS

3. Too much can contribute to the following Stallers and Stoppers:

A. What too much looks like (overused):

May try to win with style and presentation skills over fact and substance; may be able to wing it and dance/perform without really being prepared; may be able to sell things that shouldn't be sold.

B. Too much might lead to these Stallers and Stoppers:

Lack of Ethics and Values (109)   Political Missteps (119)

C. Compensators:

How to compensate for too much of this competency:
5, 17, 22, 24, 30, 32, 33, 46, 51, 53, 57, 58, 61, 63, 65

D. Things to watch for:

Hidden motives
Procrastinates; waits until the last minute to prepare
Style over substance
Uses skills once too often and loses credibility
Using skills to hurt others
Uses skills for personal gain

4. Too little can contribute to the following Stallers and Stoppers:

A. What too little looks like (unskilled):

Not a skilled presenter in varying situations; may be shy; may be disorganized, presentations lack focus; may have a flat or grating style; doesn't listen to audience; may have personal idiosyncrasies and habits that get in the way; may be unprepared for or unable to handle tough questions; may always present the same way, not adjusting to audiences; may lose his/her cool during hot debate; may be nervous, even scared when speaking.

B. Too little might lead to these Stallers and Stoppers:

None Apply

C. Compensators:

How to substitute for too little of this competency:
3, 8, 9, 12, 24, 26, 31, 36, 48, 65

I. LEARNING ARCHITECT® Connections:

Look for people who act like and/or show evidence of:

1b. Trial and Error
2c. Intuition
3b. Self-Talk
4c. Actively Involve
19. What

J. CHOICES ARCHITECT® Connections:

Look for people who act like and/or show evidence of:

First Edition (Released 1994)
23. Communicator

Second Edition (Released 2000)
9. Agile Communicator
27. Presence

K. Difficulty to Develop:

24 (of 34)–Moderate

50. PRIORITY SETTING

A. Definition:

Spends his/her time and the time of others on what's important; quickly zeros in on the critical few and puts the trivial many aside; can quickly sense what will help or hinder accomplishing a goal; eliminates roadblocks; creates focus.

B. Arenas/Domains to Explore:

1. A lot going on at once
2. Allocating resources across projects
3. Allocation of office space
4. Ambiguous situations
5. Assigning people to tasks
6. Assignment choices
7. Balance between life/work
8. Being two places at once
9. Blowing the whistle on a friend
10. Can't win them all
11. Career choices
12. Competing demands on time/resources
13. Doing fix-its
14. Doing start-ups
15. During crises
16. Funding competing charities
17. Giving out plum assignments
18. Lose a battle; win the war
19. Major purchases
20. Managing a layoff
21. Many attractive options
22. Moral/ethics conflicts
23. Organizing activities
24. Personal money management
25. Personal time management
26. Priorities on the fly
27. Reorganizations
28. Selecting projects
29. Tight deadlines
30. Too many things to do at once
31. Two people want your time
32. Vacation destination choices
33. Where to do family holidays
34. Which customers to attend to

C. Sample Questions:

Dimension 1: Been there, done that–has had direct personal experience(s) involving the competency–candidate was the prime player   Note: * means OK for campus

1. Has anyone ever accused you of messing something up because of a poor ability to set priorities?*
2. Have you ever managed anything where the people or units reporting to you were in different locations? How did you set priorities from afar? Was this different for different locations?
3. How do you allot your personal time?*
4. How do you allot your work time?*
5. How do you balance work and personal life?
6. How do you decide which charities to give time or money to?
7. How do you determine what is mission critical and what's less critical?
8. How do you determine who you are willing to spend time with?*
9. How do you generally choose friends?*
10. How do you give out assignments among your people?
11. How do you involve others in helping determine priorities? Give me some examples.*
12. On what basis do you make career choices?
13. On what basis do you make major capital expenditure decisions?

PRIORITY SETTING

14. On what basis do you make vacation plans?*
15. Tell me about a time when a crisis made what you had been doing obsolete.*
16. Tell me about a time when organization priorities shifted and threw everything up in the air for you and your group.
17. Tell me about a time when you faced a moral/ethical dilemma?*
18. Tell me about a time when you had to cut back and lay off people.
19. Tell me about a time when you had to set overall direction for a group.*
20. Tell me about a time when you had to trim projects due to budget restrictions.
21. Tell me about a time when you inherited a new work group.
22. Tell me about a time when you managed a fix-it.
23. Tell me about a time when you managed a reorganization.
24. Tell me about a time when you managed a start-up.
25. Tell me about a time when you ran out of time and had to choose what to finish.*
26. Tell me about a time when you were overwhelmed with obligations.*
27. Tell me about a time when you weren't willing to say no to a request and got overloaded.*
28. Tell me about a time when your attempt to set priorities got you into trouble.
29. Tell me about a time when your attempt to set priorities worked really well for you.
30. What do you do when your priorities don't match with those around you?*
31. What do you do when your priorities don't match with your boss'?
32. What do you generally do when faced with two equally attractive alternatives?*
33. When dealing with two important things to do at once, how do you respond?*
34. When do you take a back seat and let someone else set priorities?*
35. When two people need you at the same time, what do you do?*

Dimension 2: Seen/been around others who were involved with the competency–good and bad; learns from others about self

36. Contrast the best and worst priority-setters you know.*
37. Has setting priorities ever been in any 360° survey done on you? Was your score among your highest, middle, or lowest?
38. Has poor priority setting on someone else's part ever created an obstacle for you or got in the way of something you were trying to accomplish?*
39. Have you ever talked with a coach or mentor about your priority setting?
40. Have you ever watched someone fail/get fired because they did not set good priorities?*
41. Have you ever watched someone overdo setting priorities to the point that it backfired?
42. Have you ever watched someone succeed because they set good priorities?*
43. Have you ever worked with a coach on priority setting?*
44. Have you ever worked with a person who excelled at priority setting?
45. Have you ever worked with a skills coach on setting priorities?*
46. How do you get feedback about yourself on setting priorities?
47. How often do you check with multiple sources when you get a piece of critical feedback on your priority setting?
48. Is there a historical figure you consider a model of setting the right priorities?
49. What do others who are not your fans say about your priority setting?
50. What do others who like you say about your priority setting?
51. Which boss was the best at setting priorities?

PRIORITY SETTING

52. Which boss was the worst at setting priorities?
53. Which direct report was the best at setting priorities?
54. Which direct report was the worst at setting priorities?
55. Which peer was the best at setting priorities?
56. Which peer was the worst at setting priorities?
57. Who in your field or business is the best at setting priorities?
58. Who do you consider a role model of setting priorities?*
59. Who do you go to for advice on setting priorities?
60. Who have you learned the most from about setting priorities?*
61. Who is a higher-management role model for you on setting priorities?
62. Who is a role model of setting priorities outside of work?

Dimension 3: Knows how the competency works in theory; shows understanding

63. Are there situations or settings where someone should be setting different priorities?
64. Do you think priority setting can be learned; how do you think people develop priority setting skills?
65. Do you think there is a way to compensate or work around low priority-setting skills?
66. Has anyone asked you for your opinions/advice on setting priorities?*
67. Have you ever attended a course on priority setting?
68. Have you ever been in a situation where you and others put priority setting on a success profile?
69. Have you ever been part of an effort to create a policy or a mission statement containing reference to setting priorities?
70. Have you ever been someone's coach or mentor who had problems with setting priorities?
71. Have you ever created a development plan for someone on setting priorities?
72. Have you ever criticized someone for not setting priorities?
73. Have you ever designed a program on setting priorities?
74. Have you ever given a speech on setting priorities?
75. Have you ever rewarded or recognized someone for setting sound priorities?
76. Have you ever taught a course on setting priorities?
77. Have you ever tried to help someone deal with more effectively with priority setting?*
78. Have you ever tried to help someone improve their priority-setting skills?
79. How do you think people develop priority setting skills?
80. How much priority setting is good to do and how much is too much?
81. How much of success do you think is due to setting priorities compared with other characteristics?
82. How would you know if someone is bad at setting priorities?
83. How would you know if someone is good at setting priorities?
84. If you had to write a book on priority setting, what would the chapter headings be?
85. What are the benefits to someone who is really good at setting priorities?
86. What are the consequences to someone who is really poor at setting priorities?
87. What do you think the standard is on setting priorities for someone in your role?
88. What happens if you set too many priorities?
89. What happens when two people try to work together who are have very different priority-setting skills?
90. What wisdom would you pass onto others trying to become better at setting priorities?
91. Why do you think people end up having different priority-setting skills?

PRIORITY SETTING

Dimension 4: Shows personal change and sense-making; learned it one place and applied it in another; can compare and contrast experiences; changes viewpoints across time; can explain personal development or evolution related to the competency

92. Compare and contrast examples of your being effective and ineffective at setting priorities.
93. Contrast your on- and off-the-job use of priority setting skills.
94. Did you ever pass up a job or assignment because you were not confident enough in your priority setting skills?
95. Do you ever use other skills to cover for your lack of priority setting abilities?
96. Has becoming better at setting priorities ever helped you in other areas?
97. Has poor priority setting ever been the subject of a development plan for you?
98. Has priority setting ever figured in a failure, struggle, or setback you have had?
99. Has your ability to set priorities always been this way?
100. Have you ever delegated or assigned someone a task because you didn't set priorities particularly well?
101. Have you ever made significant strides at improving your priority setting abilities?
102. Have your priority setting skills, good or bad, ever been the subject of your performance review or a career discussion?
103. How different are you across situations in your priority setting?
104. How do you decide how much or when to use priority setting?
105. How do you determine what's most important?*
106. How important is it for you to please others with your work and productivity?*
107. How much of your success is due to your priority setting skills?
108. How transferable are your priority setting skills to other situations?
109. If you had to become better at setting priorities in a hurry, what would you do?
110. Was there a time when you were not good at setting priorities?
111. What caused you to work to change your skills at priority setting?
112. What event or series of events had the most impact on your priority setting?
113. What's the most varied you can be in setting priorities?
114. What was the shortest amount of time in which you increased your level of skill at setting priorities?
115. When did you first realize your level of skill at setting priorities?
116. When two things compete for your time, how do you decide?*
117. When you know ahead of time that your usual way of priority setting won't work, what do you do?
118. Why do you think you deal with priority setting the way you do?
119. Why do you think your priority setting is the way it is?*

D. Follow-up Probes:

1. Are there times when you set priorities like that and times when you don't?
2. Could you contrast those two bosses for me?
3. Could you give me a few examples of how you've used or applied that?
4. Do you always set priorities like that or was that a special situation?
5. Do you suppose if others would just try harder, they could learn to be more effective at setting priorities like you do?
6. Do you think that's all teachable?
7. Do you think you're better at setting priorities than most? Why?
8. Do you think you would perform any differently if you could be more effective at setting priorities?

PRIORITY SETTING

9. Do you think your spouse and family would agree with that?
10. Have you always set priorities that way or is this a recent development in you?
11. How did the others react when you did that?
12. How did you come up with that approach to setting priorities in the first place?
13. How did you feel about the option you couldn't get to?
14. How did you know that method of setting priorities would work?
15. How do others you have known approach that?
16. How do you feel when you can't do everything?
17. How much weight did you give to your personal needs?
18. How typical is this for you?
19. How would you approach that same situation today?
20. Is this natural for you, or do you really have to dig for it?
21. Was there a time when you didn't understand this about yourself?
22. What did you do after you got that feedback?
23. What did you do to adapt to that?
24. What did you learn from that?
25. Why did you choose that approach?
26. Why did you decide to take the risk?
27. Why did you do it that way?
28. Why did you time your priorities like that?
29. Why did you weigh the factors that way?
30. Why do you suppose organizations work priorities that way?
31. Why do you think that didn't work?
32. Why do you think that happened that way?
33. Why do you think that worked?
34. Why do you think you have difficulty with that sometimes?
35. Would you have done it that way with looser deadlines?
36. Would you have done it that way with tighter deadlines?

E. **Themes/Things to Look for:**

Ability to estimate costs
Ability to project consequences
Ability to run internal simulations
Ability to sift and focus
Broad perspective on what's important
Can handle complexity
Can make decision and move on
Changes priorities when context changes
Comfortable not having all the answers
Complex and varied schemes to assign values
Consistency across venues
Deciding too quickly
Driver of their priorities

Essence detector
Flexible in setting priorities
Mental priority checklist
Moving ahead without complete agreement
Open to input from others
Organizing available data quickly
Seeing the big picture
Sensitive to priorities of others
Taking risks
Unafraid to place a value on activities, outcomes, and tasks
Values time
Weight assigned to options

PRIORITY SETTING

F. Most Likely Résumé:

1. Look for jobs like:
Chair of Projects/Task forces
Fix-Its/Turnarounds
Heavy Strategic Demands
International Assignments
Line to Staff Switches
Scale (size shift) Assignments
Scope (complexity) Assignments
Staff Leadership (Influencing Without Authority)
Start-Ups

2. Look for develop-in-place assignments like:
Manage the renovation of an office, floor, building, meeting room, warehouse, etc.
Plan a new site for a building (plant, field office, headquarters, etc.).
Manage the purchase of a major product, equipment, materials, program, or system.
Assign a project to a group with a tight deadline.
Manage an ad hoc, temporary group of "green," inexperienced people as their coach, teacher, orienter, etc.
Manage an ad hoc, temporary group of balky and resisting people through an unpopular change or project.
Manage an ad hoc, temporary group of low-competence people through a task they couldn't do by themselves.
Manage an ad hoc, temporary group including former peers to accomplish a task.
Manage an ad hoc, temporary group of people who are older and/or more experienced to accomplish a task.
Manage an ad hoc, temporary group of people where the temporary manager is a towering expert and the people in the group are not.
Manage an ad hoc, temporary group of people where the people in the group are towering experts but the temporary manager is not.
Manage an ad hoc, temporary group of people involved in tackling a fix-it or turnaround project.
Manage an ad hoc, temporary group of people in a rapidly expanding operation.
Assemble an ad hoc team of diverse people to accomplish a difficult task.
Manage the interface between consultants and the organization on a critical assignment.
Help shut down a plant, regional office, product line, business, operation, etc.
Manage liquidation/sale of a business, products, equipment, materials, furniture, overstock, etc.
Prepare and present a proposal of some consequence to top management.
Manage a dissatisfied internal or external customer; troubleshoot a performance or quality problem with a product or service.
Manage a group through a significant business crisis.
Take on a tough and undoable project, one where others who have tried it have failed.
Manage a cost-cutting project.
Take on a task you dislike or hate to do.
Build a multifunctional project team to tackle a common business issue or problem.
Work on a team looking at a reorganization plan where there will be more people than positions.
Work on a crisis management team.

3. Best references to ask about or check:
Direct Boss
Past Associates/Constituencies
Direct Reports

PRIORITY SETTING

G. Learning Agility Evaluation:

9. Vague/General vs. Sharp/Specific
10. Reactive vs. Initiating
13. Simple Views vs. Complex Views
14. Sameness vs. Broad Ranging
19. External Standards vs. Internal Standards
22. Focus on Accomplishments vs. Focus on Solving Problems

H. The LEADERSHIP ARCHITECT® Sort Card Connections:

1. Good (positive) if combined with high:

Warp drive 1, 16, 32
Makes changes on the run 2, 32
Can handle complexity 2, 40
Open to other views 3, 12, 33
Sets right business priorities 5, 17, 24
Makes good career choices 6, 17, 55
Gives people and their issues time 7, 10, 21, 23
Gets ideas to market 28, 38, 53
Knows when to hold 'em and when to play 'em 38, 48
Eye on goals 39, 47, 51, 53
Eye on bigger picture 46, 58, 65
Doesn't waste time 62

2. Bad (negative) if combined with low or high (+):

Too quick to judge (+1, 16) 41
May not act on choices 1, 53
Uses old priorities 2, 32, 46, 61
Trouble when chaos present 2, 40
None of the choices may be right 5, 24
People are always second 7, 10, 21, 23
May not make difficult calls 12, 34, 57
Poor or inconsistent judgment 22, 29
Selects people on wrong criteria 25, 56
Own best counsel 33
Priorities free from political realities 38, 48
Sets poor personal priorities 45, 55
In service of what? 53
Out of balance 66

3. Too much can contribute to the following Stallers and Stoppers:

A. What too much looks like (overused):

May let the trivial accumulate into a critical problem; may too quickly reject the priorities of others; may have a chilling effect on necessary complexity by requiring everything to be reduced to the simple; may confuse simple with simplistic; may be too dominant a force on priorities for the team.

PRIORITY SETTING

    B. **Too much might lead to these Stallers and Stoppers:**
       None Apply

    C. **Compensators:**
       How to compensate for too much of this competency:
          2, 3, 12, 15, 17, 27, 30, 33, 38, 46, 52, 63, 65

    D. **Things to watch for:**

Can only do one thing at a time	Thinks less is always better
Numbers everything	Thinks simple is always best
Only accepts their own priorities	Mole hills become mountains
Sets priorities before everything is known	

4. **Too little can contribute to the following Stallers and Stoppers:**

    A. *What too little looks like (unskilled):*

       Has little sense of what's mission critical and what's just nice to do; doesn't identify the critical few well for self or others; may believe that everything's equally important, may overwhelm others with unfocused activities; may be addicted to action, do a little bit of everything quickly; may be a poor time manager; may not say no; wants to do everything; not good at figuring out how to eliminate a roadblock.

    B. **Too little might lead to these Stallers and Stoppers:**

Being a Poor Administrator (102)	Overmanaging (117)
Non-Strategic (114)	Performance Problems (118)

    C. **Compensators:**
       How to substitute for too little of this competency:
          16, 17, 24, 33, 39, 47, 51, 52

I. LEARNING ARCHITECT® Connections:

Look for people who act like and/or show evidence of:

1c. Following a Plan	17. Selected Sources
2a. Problem Solving	18. Straightforward
2c. Intuition	20. Events
8. Initiate	29. Essence
13. Focused	36. Comfort with Paradox
14. Controlled	

J. CHOICES ARCHITECT® Connections:

Look for people who act like and/or show evidence of:

First Edition (Released 1994)	Second Edition (Released 2000)
2. Essence	6. Essence
13. Role Flexibility	10. Conflict Manager
	18. Role Flexibility

K. Difficulty to Develop:
20 (of 34)–Easier

51. PROBLEM SOLVING

A. Definition:

Uses rigorous logic and methods to solve difficult problems with effective solutions; probes all fruitful sources for answers; can see hidden problems; is excellent at honest analysis; looks beyond the obvious and doesn't stop at the first answers.

B. Arenas/Domains to Explore:

1. Academic awards
2. Academic history
3. Analytical tasks
4. Can program their VCR
5. Complex problems
6. Computer literacy
7. Crossword puzzles
8. Debate team
9. Entrance exam performance (GRE, SAT)
10. Facing dilemmas
11. First-time tasks
12. First to make a break through
13. Fix-its
14. Getting out of tough spots
15. Group problem solving
16. Heavy strategic challenge
17. Helping others out of problems
18. High stakes
19. Intellectually challenging hobbies
20. Joining a new company
21. Looking up data on the internet
22. Making transitions
23. New or unfamiliar situations
24. No precedents
25. Number crunching
26. On-their-feet problem solving
27. Reading selections
28. Starting a new job
29. Tested IQ
30. Tight deadlines
31. Using a reference library
32. Working out personal problems

C. Sample Questions:

Dimension 1: Been there, done that–has had direct personal experience(s) involving the competency–candidate was the prime player   Note: * means OK for campus

1. Has anyone ever accused you of messing something up because of poor problem solving?
2. Have you been in brain storming sessions?*
3. Have you ever faced a problem you just couldn't solve?*
4. Have you ever had to solve a problem twice, when the first solution wasn't right?*
5. Have you ever managed anything where the people or units reporting to you were in different locations? How did you help them solve problems?
6. Have you ever solved a problem others around you couldn't?*
7. How do you make the time to stop and really look at the data and analyze the problem?*
8. How much time do you generally spend defining the elements of a problem?*
9. Tell me about a time when the final solution to a problem was quite different than your first impression?*
10. Tell me about a time when you came up with a process or procedure to solve a problem.*
11. Tell me about a time when you delegated solving a problem where you didn't know the answer.
12. Tell me about a time when you delegated solving a problem you already knew the answer to.
13. Tell me about a time when you didn't select your first or second solution?*
14. Tell me about a time when you found that a work problem was more than it appeared to be at first.*

PROBLEM SOLVING

15. Tell me about a time when you had a work problem and didn't know what to do.*
16. Tell me about a time when you selected a solution that worked in the past but didn't work this time.
17. Tell me about a time when you solved one problem but created others.*
18. Tell me about a time when you stopped a group from selecting its favorite solution and walked it through a thorough analysis leading to a different solution.
19. Tell me about a time when you went with a partial solution and decided to come back to it later when you had more time.
20. Tell me about a time when your mistakes caught up with you.*
21. Tell me about a time when your attempt to solve a problem got you into trouble.
22. Tell me about a time when your attempt to solve a problem worked really well for you.
23. Was there ever a time that the solution you used actually made things worse?*
24. What are some of the toughest problems you ever solved?*
25. When you are part of a team solving a problem, what role do you usually play?*
26. Where are you generally in the order of solving problems a group is working on? First? Last? In the middle?*

Dimension 2: Seen/been around others who were involved with the competency–good and bad; learns from others about self

27. Contrast the best and worst problem solvers you know.*
28. Has problem solving ever been in any 360° survey done on you? Was your score among your highest, middle, or lowest?
29. Has poor problem solving on someone else's part ever created an obstacle for you or got in the way of something you were trying to accomplish?*
30. Have you ever talked with a coach or mentor about improving your problem-solving skills?
31. Have you ever watched someone fail/get fired because they did not have good problem-solving skills?*
32. Have you ever watched someone exaggerate their ability to solve problems to the point that it backfired?
33. Have you ever watched someone succeed because they had good problem-solving skills?*
34. Have you ever worked with a coach on problem solving?*
35. Have you ever worked with a person who excelled at problem solving?
36. Have you ever worked with a skills coach on problem solving?*
37. How do you get feedback about yourself on problem-solving skills?
38. How often do you check with multiple sources when you get a piece of critical feedback on your problem-solving skills?
39. Is there a historical figure you consider a model of solving tough problems?
40. What do others who are not your fans say about your problem-solving skills?
41. What do others who like you say about your problem-solving skills?
42. Which boss was the best at solving tough problems?
43. Which boss was the worst at problem solving?
44. Which direct report was the best at solving tough problems?
45. Which direct report was the worst at problem solving?
46. Which peer was the best at solving tough problems?
47. Which peer was the worst at problem solving?
48. Who in your field or business is the best at solving tough problems?
49. Who do you consider a role model of solving tough problems?*
50. Who do you go to for advice on problem solving?

PROBLEM SOLVING

51. Who have you learned the most from about problem solving?*
52. Who is a higher-management role model for you on problem solving?
53. Who is a role model of problem solving outside of work?

Dimension 3: Knows how the competency works in theory; shows understanding

54. Are there situations or settings where someone should solve problems differently?
55. Do you think problem-solving skills can be learned; how do you think people develop problem-solving skills?
56. Do you think there is a way to compensate or work around low problem-solving skills?
57. Has anyone asked you for your opinions/advice on problem solving?*
58. Have you ever attended a course on problem solving?
59. Have you ever been in a situation where you and others put problem solving on a success profile?
60. Have you ever been part of an effort to create a policy or a mission statement containing reference to problem solving?
61. Have you ever been someone's coach or mentor who had problems with problem solving?
62. Have you ever created a development plan for someone on problem solving?
63. Have you ever criticized someone for not solving problems?
64. Have you ever designed a program on problem solving?
65. Have you ever given a speech on problem solving?
66. Have you ever rewarded or recognized someone for having problem-solving skills?
67. Have you ever taught a course on problem solving?
68. Have you ever tried to help someone deal with problem solving more effectively?*
69. Have you ever tried to help someone improve their problem-solving abilities?
70. How do you think people develop problem-solving skills?
71. How much of success do you think is due to problem-solving skills compared with other characteristics?
72. How would you know if someone is bad at solving tough problems?
73. How would you know if someone is good at solving tough problems?
74. If you had to write a book on problem solving, what would the chapter headings be?
75. What are the benefits to someone who is really good at problem solving?
76. What are the consequences to someone who is really poor at problem solving?
77. What do you think the standard is on problem solving for someone in your role?
78. What happens when two people try to work together who have very different problem-solving skills?
79. What wisdom would you pass onto others trying to become better at problem solving?
80. When you select others, what do you look for in problem-solving abilities?
81. Why do you think people end up being different at solving problems?

Dimension 4: Shows personal change and sense-making; learned it one place and applied it in another; can compare and contrast experiences; changes viewpoints across time; can explain personal development or evolution related to the competency

82. Compare and contrast examples of your being effective and ineffective at problem solving.
83. Contrast your on- and off-the-job use of problem solving.
84. Did you ever pass up a job or assignment because you were not confident enough in your problem-solving skills?
85. Do you ever use other skills to cover for your lack of problem-solving skill?
86. Has becoming better at problem solving ever helped you in other areas?

PROBLEM SOLVING

87. Has poor problem solving ever been the subject of a development plan for you?
88. Has poor problem solving ever figured in a failure, struggle, or setback you have had?
89. Have you ever delegated or assigned someone a task because you didn't solve problems well enough?
90. Have you ever made significant strides in your problem-solving abilities?
91. Have your problem-solving skills always been this way?
92. Have your problem-solving skills, good or bad, ever been the subject of your performance review or a career discussion?
93. How different are you across situations in your problem-solving ability?
94. How do you decide how much of a problem solver to be?
95. How much of your success is due to your problem-solving skills?
96. How transferable are your problem-solving skills to other situations?
97. If you had to become better at problem solving in a hurry, what would you do?
98. Was there a time when you were not good at problem solving?
99. What caused you to work to change your skills at problem solving?
100. What do you do when a problem stops you in your tracks?*
101. What do you enjoy most about the problem-solving process?*
102. What event or series of events had the most impact on your problem-solving skills?
103. What's the most varied you can be in problem-solving ability?
104. What was the shortest amount of time in which you increased your level of skill at problem solving?
105. When did you first realize your level of skill at problem solving?
106. When you know ahead of time that your usual way of problem solving won't work, what do you do?
107. Why do you think you deal with problem solving the way you do?
108. Why do you think your problem solving ability is the way it is?*

D. Follow-up Probes:

1. Are there times when you solve problems like that and times when you don't?
2. Could you contrast those two bosses for me?
3. Could you give me a few examples of how you've used or applied that?
4. Do you always solve problems like that or was that a special situation?
5. Do you suppose if others would just try harder, they could learn to be a better problem solver like you?
6. Do you think that's teachable?
7. Do you think you're better at solving problems than most? Why?
8. Do you think you would perform any differently if you could be more effective at solving problems?
9. Have you always solved problems that way or is this a recent development in you?
10. How did the others react when you did that?
11. How did you come up with that approach to solving problems in the first place?
12. How did you know that method of solving the problem would work?
13. How did you know what problem solving technique to use?
14. How do others you have known approach that?
15. How much of that was you and how much was the group?
16. How typical is this for you?
17. How would you approach that same situation today?
18. Is this natural for you, or do you really have to dig for it?

PROBLEM SOLVING

19. Was there a time when you didn't understand this about yourself?
20. What did you do after you got that feedback?
21. What did you do to adapt to that?
22. What did you learn from that?
23. Where did you look for the answer?
24. Where did you come up with the questions to ask?
25. Why did you choose that approach?
26. Why did you decide to take the risk?
27. Why did you do it that way?
28. Why did you time your attempt to solve the problem like that?
29. Why do you suppose organizations work that way?
30. Why do you think that didn't work?
31. Why do you think that happened that way?
32. Why do you think that worked?
33. Why do you think you have difficulty with that sometimes?
34. Would you have done it that way with looser deadlines?
35. Would you have done it that way with tighter deadlines?

E. Themes/Things to Look for:

Always wanting to improve things
Asking what's missing
Can't let things alone
Challenges the solutions of others
Enjoying the hunt
Focusing on the nature of the problem
Getting better when things get tougher
Immersion/depth
Inquisitive
Looking outside one's area of expertise
Looking to multiple sources
Looking under rocks
Not happy with other people's solutions without checking
Not interested in the credit; just the solution
Not satisfied with the first solution
Patient to find the best answer
Question asking
Seeing beneath the surface (hidden problems and patterns)
Taking intellectual risks
Using varied techniques
Willing to ask the stupid question
Zeroing in

PROBLEM SOLVING

F. Most Likely Résumé:

1. Look for jobs like:
Heavy Strategic Demands
Scope (complexity) Assignments

2. Look for develop-in-place assignments like:
Integrate diverse systems, processes, or procedures across decentralized and/or dispersed units.

Plan a new site for a building (plant, field office, headquarters, etc.).

Study history and draw parallels for a current business issue or problem, and present your findings to others for comment.

Relaunch an existing product or service that's not doing well.

Manage an ad hoc, temporary group of people where the people in the group are towering experts but the temporary manager is not.

Manage an ad hoc, temporary group of people involved in tackling a fix-it or turnaround project.

Assemble an ad hoc team of diverse people to accomplish a difficult task.

Handle a tough negotiation with an internal or external client or customer.

Manage a group through a significant business crisis.

Take on a tough and undoable project, one where others who have tried it have failed.

Take on a task you dislike or hate to do.

Resolve an issue in conflict between two people, units, geographies, functions, etc.

Build a multifunctional project team to tackle a common business issue or problem.

Audit cost overruns to assess the problem, and present your findings to the person or people involved.

3. Best references to ask about or check:
Direct Boss   Natural Mentors
Boss' Boss(es)   Past Associates/Constituencies
Human Resource Professionals

G. Learning Agility Evaluation:
1. What/Describing vs. Why/Explain
2. All or Nothing vs. Can See Many Sides
3. Ordinary/Socially Acceptable vs. Insightful/Different
7. Passive vs. Intrigued/Curious
13. Simple Views vs. Complex Views
14. Sameness vs. Broad Ranging
15. Linear vs. Use Contrasts/Analogies
16. Few Rules of Thumb vs. Many and Varied Rules of Thumb
18. Stays Close to Home vs. Lots of Curiosity
22. Focus on Accomplishments vs. Focus on Solving Problems

PROBLEM SOLVING

H. The LEADERSHIP ARCHITECT® Sort Card Connections:

1. Good (positive) if combined with high:
Creates motion 1, 16, 53
May get overly complex 2, 30, 40
Helps others solve problems 3, 33, 62
Knows what's important 5, 24, 50, 58
Solves career problems 6, 45, 55
Takes on the tougher problems 12, 34, 57
Comes up with unique solutions 14
Inspires team to solve problems 18, 36, 60, 65
Picks and develops the best 19, 25, 56
Captures meaning quickly 32
Solves complex organizational problems 38, 48
Efficient organizer 39, 47, 52
Seeks the broadest counsel/sources 46

2. Bad (negative) if combined with low or high (+):
Needs too much data 1, 16 (+24, 47)
Leaves others behind (+1, 16) 41
Too narrow 2, 14, 40, 46
No room for others to contribute (+5, 9, 24, 53, 57, 61)
Does too much themselves 18, 33, 42, 60
Inconsistent quality 22, 29
Can't go deep 30, 32
Not applied to self 45, 55, 54
May solve the wrong problem 50, 62

3. Too much can contribute to the following Stallers and Stoppers:

A. What too much looks like (overused):
May tend toward analysis paralysis; may wait too long to come to a conclusion; may not set analysis priorities; may get hung up in the process and miss the big picture; may make things overly complex; may do too much of the analysis personally.

B. Too much might lead to these Stallers and Stoppers:
Overmanaging (117)

C. Compensators:
How to compensate for too much of this competency:
1, 16, 18, 20, 35, 36, 50, 52, 55, 60

D. Things to watch for:
Avoids trial and error; won't shoot from the hip
Breaks down everything into pieces; misses the whole
Solves all problems anew; doesn't use past solutions
See a problem under every rock
Slows everyone else down
Spends too much time solving; too little time acting
Loner

PROBLEM SOLVING

4. Too little can contribute to the following Stallers and Stoppers:

A. *What too little looks like (unskilled):*

Not a disciplined problem solver; may be stuck in the past, wed to what worked before; many times has to come back and rework the problem a second time; may be a fire-ready-aim type; may get impatient and jump to conclusions too soon; may not stop to define and analyze the problem; doesn't look under rocks; may have a set bag of tricks and pull unfit solutions from it; may miss the complexity of the issue and force fit it to what he/she is most comfortable with; unlikely to come up with the second and better solution, ask penetrating questions, or see hidden patterns.

B. *Too little might lead to these Stallers and Stoppers:*

Blocked Personal Learner (106)
Lack of Composure (107)
Non-Strategic (114)

C. *Compensators:*

How to substitute for too little of this competency:
5, 14, 17, 24, 30, 32, 33, 46, 50, 58

I. LEARNING ARCHITECT® Connections:

Look for people who act like and/or show evidence of:

2a. Problem Solving	20. Events
4a. Getting Information	27. Conceptualizer
5. New	28. Creator
8. Initiate	29. Essence
10. Complexity	30. Mastery
11. Why/How	31. Rationality
12. Rules of Thumb	33. Diversity of Sources
18. Straightforward	36. Comfort with Paradox

J. CHOICES ARCHITECT® Connections:

Look for people who act like and/or show evidence of:

First Edition (Released 1994)	Second Edition (Released 2000)
2. Essence	2. Complexity
3. Creator	3. Connector
4. Complexity	4. Critical Thinker
5. Connector	6. Essence
6. Visionary	8. Solution Finder
7. Helping Others Think	10. Conflict Manager
8. Cool Transactor	11. Cool Transactor
19. Tinkerer	20. Experimenter
22. Self-Talk	21. Innovation Manager

K. Difficulty to Develop:

24 (of 34)–Moderate

52. PROCESS MANAGEMENT

A. Definition:

Good at figuring out the processes necessary to get things done; knows how to organize people and activities; understands how to separate and combine tasks into efficient work flow; knows what to measure and how to measure it; can see opportunities for synergy and integration where others can't; can simplify complex processes; gets more out of fewer resources.

B. Arenas/Domains to Explore:

1. Any cross-division event
2. Arranging major meeting across organizations
3. Complex processes
4. Coordinating large projects
5. Creating a study/project plan
6. Creating an audit/consulting assignment
7. First-time work flow tasks
8. Fund-raising
9. Getting disparate groups working together
10. Getting government funding
11. Getting things done across boundaries
12. Influencing without authority
13. Logical tasks
14. Meeting facilitation
15. Multiple demands
16. No precedents
17. Process re-engineering projects
18. Professional association committees
19. Regulatory processes
20. Resources spread out
21. Sending/shipping things internationally
22. Setting up production systems
23. Simultaneous tracks
24. Start-ups
25. Tight deadlines
26. Total quality efforts
27. Using resources that aren't theirs
28. Volunteer work
29. Work design
30. Working through a government agency
31. Working with unions

C. Sample Questions:

Dimension 1: Been there, done that–has had direct personal experience(s) involving the competency–candidate was the prime player   Note: * means OK for campus

1. Do you find yourself criticizing other people's workflow processes?*
2. Has anyone ever accused you of messing something up because of poor workflow design?
3. Have you ever been on a cost cutting taskforce?
4. Have you ever been on a re-engineering taskforce?
5. Have you ever been part of a Six Sigma effort?
6. Have you ever been part of a TQM effort?
7. Have you ever been part of an ISO effort?
8. Have you ever diagrammed out a process?*
9. Have you ever inherited a broken-down process you had to fix in a hurry?*
10. Have you ever managed anything where the people or units reporting to you were in different locations? How did you streamline the workflow at a distance?
11. Have you ever used process design software?*
12. How do you go about getting resources to get something done that are not under your direct control?*
13. How do you react when you find yourself hung up in an inefficient process?*
14. How good are you at estimating how long something takes to do?*

PROCESS MANAGEMENT

15. How often do you write letters complaining of badly handled processes?
16. How orderly are your work habits and workspace?*
17. Tell me about a time when you designed and installed a process measurement system.
18. Tell me about a time when you had to install a new system.*
19. Tell me about a time when you had to make some mid-course corrections in a process.*
20. Tell me about a time when you had to organize and implement a system/ work process.*
21. Tell me about a time when you organized and managed others on a complex task from start to finish.*
22. Tell me about a time when you reordered the steps in a process.
23. Tell me about a time when you took steps out of a process someone else designed.
24. Tell me about a time when your attempt to design an efficient process got you into trouble.
25. Tell me about a time when your attempt to design an efficient process worked really well for you.
26. When you are part of a team designing a new process, what role do you usually play?
27. When you attack a process and find it very complex, what do you do first?*
28. When you design a work process, how do you determine where to start?*

Dimension 2: Seen/been around others who were involved with the competency–good and bad; learns from others about self

29. Contrast the best and worst people you know at designing and managing workflow processes to get things done.*
30. Has workflow design and management ever been in any 360° survey done on you? Was your score among your highest, middle, or lowest?
31. Has poor workflow design and management on someone else's part ever created an obstacle for you or got in the way of something you were trying to accomplish?*
32. Have you ever talked with a coach or mentor about your workflow design and management skills?
33. Have you ever watched someone fail/get fired because they did not design and manage workflow well?*
34. Have you ever watched someone exaggerate workflow design and management to the point that it backfired?
35. Have you ever watched someone succeed because they designed and managed workflow well?*
36. Have you ever worked with a coach on designing and managing more effective and efficient workflow?*
37. Have you ever worked with a person who excelled at designing and managing workflow processes that got things done?
38. Have you ever worked with a skills coach on workflow design and management?*
39. How do you get feedback about yourself on workflow design and management skills?
40. How often do you check with multiple sources when you get a piece of critical feedback on your workflow design and management skills?
41. Is there a historical figure you consider a model of designing and managing processes to get things done?
42. What do others who are not your fans say about your workflow design and management skills?
43. What do others who like you say about your workflow design and management skills?
44. Which boss was the best at designing and managing workflow?
45. Which boss was the worst at designing and managing workflow?
46. Which direct report was the best at designing and managing workflow?
47. Which direct report was the worst at designing and managing workflow?
48. Which peer was the best at designing and managing workflow?
49. Which peer was the worst at designing and managing workflow?
50. Who in your field or business is the best at workflow design and management?
51. Who do you consider a current role model of workflow design and management skills?*

PROCESS MANAGEMENT

52. Who do you go to for advice on designing and managing workflow?
53. Who have you learned the most from about designing and managing workflow?*
54. Who is a higher-management role model for you on designing and managing workflow?
55. Who outside of work is a role model of designing and managing workflow?

Dimension 3: Knows how the competency works in theory; shows understanding

56. Are there situations or settings where someone should design and manage workflow differently?
57. Do you think workflow design and management can be learned; how do you think people develop workflow design and management skills?
58. Do you think there is a way to compensate or work around low workflow design and management skills?
59. Has anyone asked you for your opinions/advice on designing and managing workflow?*
60. Have you ever attended a course on designing and managing workflow?
61. Have you ever been in a situation where you and others put workflow design and management on a success profile?
62. Have you ever been part of an effort to create a policy or a mission statement containing reference to workflow design and management skills?
63. Have you ever been someone's coach or mentor who had problems with designing and managing workflow?
64. Have you ever created a development plan for someone on designing and managing workflow?
65. Have you ever criticized someone for not designing and managing more effective and efficient workflow?
66. Have you ever designed a program on designing and managing workflow?
67. Have you ever given a speech on designing and managing workflow?
68. Have you ever rewarded or recognized someone for designing and managing effective and efficient workflow?
69. Have you ever taught a course on designing and managing workflow?
70. Have you ever tried to help someone deal more effectively with designing and managing workflow?*
71. Have you ever tried to help someone improve their workflow design and management skills?
72. How do you think people develop workflow design and management skills?
73. How much workflow design and management is good to have and how much is too much?
74. How much of success do you think is due to workflow design and management compared with other characteristics?
75. How would you know if someone is bad at designing and managing workflow?
76. How would you know if someone is good at designing and managing workflow?
77. If you had to write a book on workflow design and management, what would the chapter headings be?
78. What are the benefits to someone who is really good at designing and managing workflow?
79. What are the consequences to someone who is really poor at designing and managing workflow?
80. What do you think the standard is on workflow design and management for someone in your role?
81. What happens if you design and manage workflow too much?
82. What happens when two people try to work together who are very different workflow design and management?
83. What wisdom would you pass onto others trying to become better at workflow design and management?
84. When you select others, what do you look for in workflow design and management skills?
85. Why do you think people end up being different on designing and managing effective and efficient workflow?

Dimension 4: Shows personal change and sense-making; learned it one place and applied it in another; can compare and contrast experiences; changes viewpoints across time; can explain personal development or evolution related to the competency

86. Compare and contrast examples of your being effective and ineffective at designing and managing workflow.

PROCESS MANAGEMENT

87. Contrast your on- and off-the-job use of workflow design and management.
88. Did you ever pass up a job or assignment because you were not confident enough in your skills at designing and managing workflow processes?
89. Do you ever use other skills to cover for your lack of ability to design and manage workflow processes?
90. Has designing and managing workflow processes ever figured in a failure, struggle, or setback you have had?
91. Has designing and managing workflow processes, good or bad, ever been the subject of your performance review or a career discussion?
92. Has becoming better at designing and managing workflow processes ever helped you in other areas?
93. Has poor design and management of workflow processes ever been the subject of a development plan for you?
94. Has your ability to design and manage workflow processes always been this way?
95. Have you ever delegated or assigned someone a task because you didn't design and manage workflow processes particularly well?
96. Have you ever made significant strides at becoming better at designing and managing workflow processes?
97. How different are you across situations in your ability to design and manage workflow processes?
98. How do you decide how much design and management of workflow processes to use?
99. How do you get people not under your control to work on your project?*
100. How much of your success is due to your ability to design and manage effective workflow processes?
101. How transferable are your skills at designing and managing workflow to other situations?
102. If you had to become better at designing and managing workflow processes in a hurry, what would you do?
103. Was there a time when you were not as good at designing and managing workflow processes?
104. What caused you to work to improve your skills at designing and managing workflow processes?
105. What event or series of events had the most impact on your ability to design and manage workflow processes?
106. What's the most varied you can be in the design and management of workflow processes?
107. What was the shortest amount of time in which you increased your level of skill at designing and managing workflow processes?
108. When did you first realize your level of skill at designing and managing workflow processes?
109. When you design a process to get something done, how do you go about lining up the steps?*
110. When you know ahead of time that your usual way of designing and managing workflow processes won't work, what do you do?
111. Why do you think you deal with designing and managing workflow processes the way you do?
112. Why do you think your design and management of workflow processes is the way it is?*

D. Follow-up Probes:

1. Are there times when you manage processes like that and times when you don't?
2. Could you contrast those two bosses for me?
3. Could you give me a few examples of how you've used or applied that?
4. Did you anticipate that resistance ahead of time?
5. Do you always manage processes like that or was that a special situation?
6. Do you suppose if others would just try harder, they could learn to be more effective at managing processes like you do?
7. Do you think that's teachable?
8. Do you think you're better at managing processes than most? Why?
9. Do you think you would perform any differently if you could be more effective at managing processes?
10. Have you always managed processes or is this a recent development in you?

PROCESS MANAGEMENT

11. Have you ever had to manage a process around someone you really disliked?
12. How did the others react when you did that?
13. How did you come up with that approach to managing processes in the first place?
14. How did you know that method of getting over that barrier would work?
15. How do others you have known approach that?
16. How much time did that take to do?
17. How typical is this for you?
18. How would you approach that same situation today?
19. Is this natural for you, or do you really have to dig for it?
20. Was that worth the amount of time you put into that?
21. Was there a time when you didn't understand this about yourself?
22. What did you do after you got that feedback?
23. What did you do to adapt to that?
24. What did you learn from that?
25. Why did you choose that approach?
26. Why did you choose that method of handling the problem?
27. Why did you decide to take the risk?
28. Why did you do it that way?
29. Why did you time your management of that process like that?
30. Why do you think that didn't work?
31. Why do you think that happened that way?
32. Why do you think that worked?
33. Why do you think you have difficulty with that sometimes?
34. Would you design the process that way today?
35. Would you have done it that way with looser deadlines?
36. Would you have done it that way with tighter deadlines?

E. **Themes/Things to Look for:**

A feel for how people are impacted by process
A feel for person/machine interaction
A natural feel for sequence; what follows what
Able to run different flow scenarios in their head
An eye for process detail
Anticipating consequences and problems
Anticipating problems
Begins with end uses/users/outcomes in mind
Belief in incremental improvement
Can describe process
Efficient use of resources
Essence detector
Goal driven
Has high process standards
Influencing without authority skills
Interest in how things work outside their normal range
Knows the difference between simple and simplistic
Managing multiple processes at once
Motivated to learn how things work
Running internal simulations
Scavenger for resources
Sensitive to what people are good at
Can make cold, impersonal calls on assignments
Patience with other people's understanding of their processes
Learns from other people's processes
Sensitive to what people want to do
Setting up feedback loops
Simplifying complex processes
Synergy and integration
Thinks in terms of cost/benefit
Upset with bad work flow

PROCESS MANAGEMENT

F. Most Likely Résumé:

1. Look for jobs like:

Chair of Projects/Task forces
Fix-Its/Turnarounds
Heavy Strategic Demands
Line to Staff Switches
Scale (size shift) Assignments (9, 24)
Significant People Demands
Staff Leadership (Influencing Without Authority)
Start-Ups

2. Look for develop-in-place assignments like:

Install a new process or system (computer system, new policies, new process, new procedures, etc.).

Integrate diverse systems, processes, or procedures across decentralized and/or dispersed units.

Manage the renovation of an office, floor, building, meeting room, warehouse, etc.

Plan a new site for a building (plant, field office, headquarters, etc.).

Monitor and follow a new product or service through the entire idea, design, test market, and launch cycle.

Visit Malcolm Baldrige National Quality Award or Deming Prize winners and report back on your findings, showing how they would help your organization.

Launch a new product, service, or process.

Relaunch an existing product or service that's not doing well.

Manage an ad hoc, temporary group of people in a stable and static operation.

Manage an ad hoc, temporary group of people in a rapidly expanding operation.

Help shut down a plant, regional office, product line, business, operation, etc.

Manage liquidation/sale of products, equipment, materials, a business, furniture, overstock, etc.

Manage the assigning/allocating of office space in a contested situation.

Work on a team that's deciding who to keep and who to let go in a layoff, shutdown, delayering, or divestiture.

Manage a group through a significant business crisis.

Manage a cost-cutting project.

Build a multifunctional project team to tackle a common business issue or problem.

3. Best references to ask about or check:

Customers
Natural Mentors
Past Associates/Constituencies
Direct Reports

G. Learning Agility Evaluation:

1. What/Describing vs. Why/Explain
3. Ordinary/Socially Acceptable vs. Insightful/Different
7. Passive vs. Intrigued/Curious
9. Vague/General vs. Sharp/Specific
11. Generalizations vs. Specific Learnings
13. Simple Views vs. Complex Views
16. Few Rules of Thumb vs. Many and Varied Rules of Thumb
19. External Standards vs. Internal Standards

H. The LEADERSHIP ARCHITECT® Sort Card Connections:

1. Good (positive) if combined with high:

Makes up process on the go 1, 16, 32, 51
Can organize chaos 2, 40, 47

PROCESS MANAGEMENT

Listens to input 3, 33, 31, 41
State of the art processes 5, 24, 61
Sensitive to the needs of people in the processes 7, 10, 21, 23
Fights for the right process 12, 34, 57, 63
Inventive with processes 14, 28
Empowers others to design and work the process 18, 19, 36, 60
Handles people/resources well 20, 35, 36
Can articulate the process 27, 47, 49, 67
Can handle more complex processes 30, 32, 51
Can design in the maze; get around political issues 38, 48
Builds in measurements 35, 53
Spends time on the most important strategic issues 46, 50, 58, 63

2. **Bad (negative) if combined with low or high (+):**

   Too controlling, too hands on (+1, 9, 35, 57) 18
   Doesn't always wait for data or other people to catch up (+1, 16, 53) 41
   Gets stuck under too much uncertainty 2, 32, 40
   Misjudges others' capacity to deal with change 2, 56, 64
   Process may be out of context 5, 24
   Doesn't take people's needs into account 7, 10, 21, 23
   Unimaginative process 14, 28
   Unproductive process 17, 53, 63
   Not open to input 18, 33, 42, 60
   Can't explain the process 27, 49, 67
   Processes run afoul of the political realities 38, 48

3. **Too much can contribute to the following Stallers and Stoppers:**

   A. *What too much looks like (overused):*

   May always be tinkering and refining–nothing is ever the same for long; may have trouble explaining his/her vision of a process; may never finish anything; may always be dissatisfied because of unreasonably high standards and expectations of self and others; may attempt to put too much together at once; may misjudge the capacity of others to absorb change.

   B. *Too much might lead to these Stallers and Stoppers:*

Unable to Adapt to Differences (101)	Failure to Build a Team (110)
Lack of Composure (107)	Insensitive to Others (112)
Defensiveness (108)	Non-Strategic (114)
Lack of Ethics and Values (109)	Political Missteps (119)

   C. *Compensators:*

   How to compensate for too much of this competency:
   3, 14, 15, 19, 27, 33, 36, 41, 46, 47, 50, 56, 57, 58, 60, 63

PROCESS MANAGEMENT

D. Things to watch for:

Never finishes	Glass is always half empty
Leaves no mystery or sense of adventure	Process standards always zero defects
Leaves others behind and wondering	Rejects the processes of others
Needs a process for everything	

4. Too little can contribute to the following Stallers and Stoppers:

A. What too little looks like (unskilled):

Not good at figuring out effective and efficient ways to get things done; works in a disorganized fashion; doesn't take advantage of opportunities for synergy and efficiency with others; can't visualize effective processes in his/her head; lays out tasks for self and others in a helter skelter way; doesn't work to simplify things; uses more resources than others to get the same thing done; lacks attention to detail; doesn't anticipate the problems that will arise; not a systemic thinker.

B. Too little might lead to these Stallers and Stoppers:

Being a Poor Administrator (102)	Performance Problems (118)
Failure to Build a Team (110)	Political Missteps (119)

C. Compensators:

How to substitute for too little of this competency:
17, 18, 20, 24, 30, 32, 33, 35, 39, 47, 50, 51, 59

I. LEARNING ARCHITECT® Connections:

Look for people who act like and/or show evidence of:

1c. Following a Plan	27. Conceptualizer
2a. Problem Solving	28. Creator
4a. Getting Information	29. Essence
12. Rules of Thumb	30. Mastery
14. Controlled	31. Rationality
15. Cautious	33. Diversity of Sources
16. Collaborate	36. Comfort with Paradox
19. What	

J. CHOICES ARCHITECT® Connections:

Look for people who act like and/or show evidence of:

First Edition (Released 1994)
4. Connector
5. Complexity
6. Visionary
7. Helping Others Think
21. Taking The Heat
23. Communicator

Second Edition (Released 2000)
2. Complexity
3. Connector
9. Agile Communicator
22. Taking the Heat

K. Difficulty to Develop:

24 (of 34)–Moderate

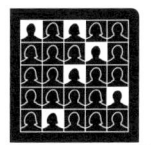

53. *DRIVE FOR* RESULTS

A. Definition:

Can be counted on to exceed goals successfully; is constantly and consistently one of the top performers; very bottom-line oriented; steadfastly pushes self and others for results.

B. Arenas/Domains to Explore:

1. Against impossible odds
2. Any goal
3. Any job
4. Any task
5. Asking for the check
6. Athletic history
7. Buying a business
8. Career goals
9. Career progress
10. Closing the sale
11. Coaching athletic teams
12. Collecting bad debts
13. Consulting projects
14. During crisis
15. Financial situation
16. Finishing something others have given up on
17. Fraternal organizations
18. Fund-raising
19. Goals thwarted by others
20. Grant proposals
21. Group/team leader
22. Hard times
23. Hobbies
24. In the face of reluctant customers
25. In the face of resistance
26. Inspiring others to produce
27. Ladder height
28. Life goals
29. Managing an acquisition
30. Military experiences
31. Political campaigns
32. Professional associations
33. Projects
34. Pushing an unpopular idea/program
35. Quests
36. Sales Contests
37. Student government
38. Task forces
39. Winning big by losing small
40. Working with a union
41. Working with people they dislike

C. Sample Questions:

Dimension 1: Been there, done that–has had direct personal experience(s) involving the competency–candidate was the prime player   Note: * means OK for campus

1. Are there times when you can slack off because your people are working harder?
2. Are there times when you drive yourself harder than you drive your people?
3. Has anyone ever accused you of messing something up because of lack of focus on results?
4. Have you ever been a team captain for United Way?
5. Have you ever been assigned to a fix-it situation?
6. Have you ever done fund-raising?*
7. Have you ever failed to pull something out of the hat at the last minute?*
8. Have you ever inherited a dispirited team?
9. Have you ever inherited a poorly performing group?
10. Have you ever managed anything where the people or units reporting to you were in different locations? How did you focus on results?
11. Have you ever run a business?*
12. Have you ever tried to champion a cause others had abandoned?*

DRIVE FOR RESULTS

13. Have you ever worked in a political campaign?*
14. Have you ever worked in direct sales?
15. Have you won any performance or sales contests?
16. How consistent is your drive for getting things done in other areas of your life?*
17. How do you go about celebrating wins?*
18. How do you hold costs in check?
19. How do you select what's the next important thing for you to do?*
20. How hard is it for you to say no when your card is full?*
21. How many people who worked under you have quit in the last five years? How many have you fired? Promoted?
22. Tell me about a time when you got results against the odds.*
23. Tell me about a time when you got results even though some major external factor shifted on you (budgets cut, competitor moves, market changed). What did you do that others didn't?
24. Tell me about a time when you got results that far exceeded everyone's expectations.*
25. Tell me about a time when you got results that far exceeded your own expectations.*
26. Tell me about a time when you got results when others tried and failed.*
27. Tell me about a time when you just had to give up and move on to something else.*
28. Tell me about a time when you went with a partial solution because you thought it was more important to move on to something else.
29. Tell me about a time when your drive for results got you into trouble.
30. Tell me about a time when your drive for results worked really well for you.
31. When dealing with two important things to do at once, what do you do?*

Dimension 2: Seen/been around others who were involved with the competency–good and bad; learns from others about self

32. Contrast the most and least results oriented people you know.*
33. Has being results driven ever been in any 360° survey done on you? Was your score among your highest, middle, or lowest?
34. Has poor drive for results on someone else's part ever created an obstacle for you or got in the way of something you were trying to accomplish?*
35. Have you ever talked with a coach or mentor about your drive for results?
36. Have you ever watched someone fail/get fired because they did not get results?*
37. Have you ever watched someone overdo a drive for results to the point that it backfired?
38. Have you ever watched someone succeed because they got results?*
39. Have you ever worked with a coach on drive for results and getting things done?*
40. Have you ever worked with a person who excelled at drive for results?
41. Have you ever worked with a skills coach on drive for results?*
42. How do you get feedback about yourself on drive for results and getting things done?
43. How often do you check with multiple sources when you get a piece of critical feedback on your focus on results?
44. Is there a historical figure you consider a model of being results driven?
45. What do others who are not your fans say about your drive for results?
46. What do others who like you say about your drive for results?
47. Which boss was the best at driving for results?
48. Which boss was the worst at driving for results?
49. Which direct report was the best at driving for results?
50. Which direct report was the worst at driving for results?

DRIVE FOR RESULTS

51. Which peer was the best at driving for results?
52. Which peer was the worst at driving for results?
53. Who in your field or business is the best at focusing on results?
54. Who do you consider a current role model of drive for results?*
55. Who do you go to for advice on how to focus on results?
56. Who have you learned the most from about focusing on results?*
57. Who is a higher-management role model for you on getting results?
58. Who is a role model of getting results outside of work?

Dimension 3: Knows how the competency works in theory; shows understanding

59. Are there situations or settings where someone should be different in their drive for results?
60. Do you think a results orientation can be learned; how do you think people develop results-oriented skills?
61. Do you think there is a way to compensate or work around a low drive for results?
62. Has anyone asked you for your opinions/advice on getting results?*
63. Have you ever attended a course on getting results?
64. Have you ever been in a situation where you and others put drive for results on a success profile?
65. Have you ever been part of an effort to create a policy or a mission statement containing reference to being results-driven?
66. Have you ever been someone's coach or mentor who had problems with getting results?
67. Have you ever created a development plan for someone on getting results?
68. Have you ever criticized someone for not getting results?
69. Have you ever designed a program on getting results?
70. Have you ever given a speech on getting results?
71. Have you ever rewarded or recognized someone for being results-driven?
72. Have you ever taught a course on getting results?
73. Have you ever tried to help someone deal more effectively with getting results?*
74. Have you ever tried to help someone improve their results orientation?
75. How do you think people develop results orientation skills?
76. How much results orientation is good to have and how much is too much?
77. How much of success do you think is due to a drive for results compared with other characteristics?
78. How would you know if someone is bad at getting results?
79. How would you know if someone is good at getting results?
80. If you had to write a book on getting results, what would the chapter headings be?
81. What are the benefits to someone who is really good at getting results?
82. What are the consequences to someone who is really poor at getting results?
83. What do you think the standard is on results orientation for someone in your role?
84. What happens if you have or use too much of drive for results?
85. What happens when two people try to work together who have very different results orientations?
86. What wisdom would you pass on to others trying to become better at getting results?
87. When you select others, what do you look for in results orientation?
88. Why do you think people end up being different at getting results?

Dimension 4: Shows personal change and sense-making; learned it one place and applied it in another; can compare and contrast experiences; changes viewpoints across time; can explain personal development or evolution related to the competency

89. Compare and contrast examples of being effective and ineffective at driving for results.
90. Contrast your on- and off-the-job use of getting things done.

DRIVE FOR RESULTS

91. Did you ever pass up a job or assignment because you were not confident enough in your skills at getting things done?
92. Do you ever use other skills to cover for your lack of a drive for results?
93. Has becoming better at getting results ever helped you in other areas?
94. Has not getting results ever been the subject of a development plan for you?
95. Has your ability to get things done always been this way?
96. Has your drive for results ever figured in a failure, struggle, or setback you have had?
97. Has your drive for results, good or bad, ever been the subject of your performance review or a career discussion?
98. Have you ever delegated or assigned someone a task because you didn't get things done at a high enough level?
99. Have you ever made significant strides in your ability to get things done?
100. How competitive are you; how important is it for you to win?*
101. How different are you across situations in your ability to get things done?
102. How do you balance your needs to get results against the needs of others and the needs of your team?
103. How do you decide how results-oriented to be?
104. How do you get results, build team spirit, and not burn out people all at the same time?
105. How much of your success is due to your ability to get things done?
106. How transferable are your results orientation skills to other situations?
107. If you had to become better at getting results in a hurry, what would you do?
108. Was there a time when you were not as good at getting things done?
109. What caused you to work to improve your skills at getting things done?
110. What do you generally do when a door is slammed in your face?*
111. What event or series of events had the most impact on your drive for results?
112. What's the most varied you can be in getting things done?
113. What was the shortest amount of time in which you increased your level of skill at getting things done?
114. When did you first realize your level of skill at getting things done?
115. When you know ahead of time that your usual way of getting results won't work, what do you do?
116. Why do you think you deal with getting things done the way you do?
117. Why do you think your results orientation is the way it is?*

D. Follow-up Probes:
1. Are there times when you drive for results like that and times when you don't?
2. Could you contrast those two bosses for me?
3. Could you give me a few examples of how you've used or applied that?
4. Do you always drive for results like that or was that a special situation?
5. Do you suppose if others would just try harder, they could learn to be results-oriented like you?
6. Do you think that's teachable?
7. Do you think you're better at getting things done than most? Why?
8. Do you think you would perform any differently if you could be more effective at getting things done?
9. Have you always been able to get results like that or is this a recent development in you?
10. Have you ever had to get results despite having to work with someone you really disliked?
11. How did the others react when you did that?
12. How did you come up with that approach to getting results in the first place?
13. How did you know that method of getting over that barrier would work?
14. How do others you have known approach that?

DRIVE FOR RESULTS

15. How do you feel after you've achieved something significant?
16. How do you feel when you come up a little short on your goal?
17. How typical is this for you?
18. How would you approach that same situation today?
19. Is this natural for you, or do you really have to dig for it?
20. Was there a time when you didn't understand this about yourself?
21. What did you do after you got that feedback?
22. What did you do to adapt to that?
23. What did you learn from that?
24. Why did you choose that approach?
25. Why did you decide to take the risk?
26. Why did you do it that way?
27. Why did you time your attempt to maneuver like that?
28. Why do you think that didn't work?
29. Why do you think that happened that way?
30. Why do you think that worked?
31. Why do you think you have difficulty with that sometimes?
32. Would you have done it that way with looser deadlines?
33. Would you have done it that way with tighter deadlines?

E. Themes/Things to Look for:

- Balance between results and teamwork/development/caring
- Can reward self internally
- Complex and varied tactics to get things done
- End justifies the means
- Enjoying the thrill of the hunt
- Even plays social games with intensity
- Fights through barriers
- Gets impossible things done
- Gets through resistance
- High need for achievement
- High standards
- Ingenuity
- Inspires others
- Looks for laurels
- Modesty–gives credit where it's due; doesn't gloat
- Need to win
- Passion for results
- Perseverance
- Perspective–doesn't blindly pursue results, results, results
- Tackles big mountains
- Tougher under stress
- Try, try, try again
- Wins contests

F. Most Likely Résumé:

1. Look for jobs like:

- Chair of Projects/Task forces
- Fix-Its/Turnarounds
- Scale Assignments
- Scope Assignments
- Staff Leadership (Influencing Without Authority)
- Staff to Line Shifts

2. Look for develop-in-place assignments like:

- Install a new process or system (computer system, new policies, new process, new procedures, etc.).
- Integrate diverse systems, processes, or procedures across decentralized and/or dispersed units.
- Manage the renovation of an office, floor, building, meeting room, warehouse, etc.
- Plan a new site for a building (plant, field office, headquarters, etc.).

DRIVE FOR RESULTS

Plan an off-site meeting, conference, convention, trade show, event, etc.

Manage the purchase of a major product, equipment, materials, program, or system.

Visit Malcolm Baldrige National Quality Award or Deming Prize winners and report back on your findings, showing how they would help your organization.

Launch a new product, service, or process.

Relaunch an existing product or service that's not doing well.

Manage an ad hoc, temporary group of balky and resisting people through an unpopular change or project.

Manage an ad hoc, temporary group of low-competence people through a task they couldn't do by themselves.

Manage an ad hoc, temporary group including former peers to accomplish a task.

Manage an ad hoc, temporary group of people who are older and/or more experienced to accomplish a task.

Manage an ad hoc, temporary group of people where the temporary manager is a towering expert and the people in the group are not.

Manage an ad hoc, temporary group of people where the people in the group are towering experts but the temporary manager is not.

Manage an ad hoc, temporary group of people involved in tackling a fix-it or turnaround project.

Assemble an ad hoc team of diverse people to accomplish a difficult task.

Manage liquidation/sale of products, equipment, materials, a business, furniture, overstock, etc.

Manage a dissatisfied internal or external customer; troubleshoot a performance or quality problem with a product or service.

Manage a group through a significant business crisis.

Take on a task you dislike or hate to do.

Audit cost overruns to assess the problem and present your findings to the person or people involved.

Work on a team looking at a reorganization plan where there will be more people than positions.

Work on a crisis management team.

3. Best references to ask about or check:
Direct Boss
Boss' Boss(es)
Past Associates/Constituencies

G. Learning Agility Evaluation:
4. Spectator/Passive vs. Player/Participant
6. Reacting/Responsive vs. Adapting
10. Reactive vs. Initiating
13. Simple Views vs. Complex Views
14. Sameness vs. Broad Ranging
19. External Standards vs. Internal Standards
22. Focus on Accomplishments vs. Focus on Solving Problems

H. The LEADERSHIP ARCHITECT® Sort Card Connections:
1. Good (positive) if combined with high:
High speed 1, 16
Can get through chaos 2, 40
Caring while getting results 3, 7, 10, 21, 23
Gets input 3, 33
Builds a team to help get results 18, 33, 36, 60
Gets a lot out of people 9, 20, 36, 39

DRIVE FOR RESULTS

Can work through tough problems 12, 34, 57
Makes tough calls on poor performers 12, 13, 56
Ingenious way to getting things done 14, 28, 32, 51
Gets it right the first time 17, 51, 63
Very orderly and structured ways of getting things done 20, 35, 39, 47, 52
Can work around the politics 38, 48
Broad strategic perspective 46, 58, 65
Knows what to focus on 50

2. **Bad (negative) if combined with low or high (+):**
   Fire, ready, aim (+1, 16) 32, 41
   Doesn't listen for input 3, 31, 33
   May not care what the people think 7, 10, 21, 23
   Overwhelming (+9, 16, 20, 35, 57)
   Doesn't make the tough calls on people 12, 13
   Can only do it the old fashioned way 14, 28, 46, 61
   Does too much themselves 18, 19, 42, 60
   Just scream and shout 18, 36, 60
   Results at any cost 22, 29
   Very tactical 46, 58, 65
   Doesn't make choices; everything's important 50, 62
   Workaholic (+1, 43) 66

3. **Too much can contribute to the following Stallers and Stoppers:**

   A. **What too much looks like (overused):**

   May go for results at all costs without appropriate concern for people, teams, due process, or possibly norms and ethics; may have high turnover under them due to the pressure for results; may not build team spirit; may not celebrate and share successes; may be very self-centered.

   B. **Too much might lead to these Stallers and Stoppers:**
   Overly Ambitious (103)   Failure to Build a Team (110)
   Blocked Personal Learner (106)   Non-Strategic (114)
   Defensiveness (108)   Overmanaging (117)
   Lack of Ethics and Values (109)   Performance Problems (118)

   C. **Compensators:**
   How to compensate for too much of this competency:
   3, 7, 19, 22, 23, 29, 31, 33, 36, 41, 46, 60, 64

   D. **Things to watch for:**
   Always looking over everyone's shoulder
   Damages others to get to their/the organization's goals
   Doesn't change goals comfortably
   Doesn't listen; doesn't have time for others
   Hard to please
   May damage themselves physically or psychologically
   Only has one speed forward; only uses the high inside fast ball
   Leaves trouble in their wake
   Values are questionable

DRIVE FOR RESULTS

4. Too little can contribute to the following Stallers and Stoppers:

A. What too little looks like (unskilled):

Doesn't deliver results consistently; doesn't get things done on time; wastes time and resources pursuing non-essentials; something always gets in the way–personal disorganization, failure to set priorities, underestimating time frames, overcoming resistance; not bold or committed enough to push it through; procrastinates around whatever gets in their way; doesn't go all out to complete tasks; does the least to get by.

B. Too little might lead to these Stallers and Stoppers:

Overdependence on an Advocate (115)
Performance Problems (118)

C. Compensators:

How to substitute for too little of this competency:
1, 5, 9, 16, 24, 28, 35, 36, 39, 43, 50, 52, 60, 63

I. LEARNING ARCHITECT® Connections:

Look for people who act like and/or show evidence of:

1a. Pure Action	6. Contentious
1b. Trial and Error	13. Focused
1c. Following a Plan	15. Cautious
2a. Problem Solving	17. Selected Sources
2b. Visioning	18. Straightforward
2c. Intuition	19. What
3a. Checking Feelings	20. Events
3b. Self-Talk	25. Personal Change
3c. Personal Experience	29. Essence
4a. Getting Information	30. Mastery
4b. Modeling	31. Rationality
4c. Actively Involve	36. Comfort with Paradox
5. New	

J. CHOICES ARCHITECT® Connections:

Look for people who act like and/or show evidence of:

First Edition (Released 1994)
2. Essence
20. Forging Ahead
21. Taking the Heat
23. Self-Talk

Second Edition (Released 2000)
6. Essence
9. Agile Communicator
22. Taking the Heat
23. Visioning
25. Delivers Results
26. Drive

K. Difficulty to Develop:

19 (of 34)–Easier

54. SELF-DEVELOPMENT

A. Definition:

Is personally committed to and actively works to continuously improve him/herself; understands that different situations and levels may call for different skills and approaches; works to deploy strengths; works on compensating for weakness and limits.

B. Arenas/Domains to Explore:

1. Attending courses
2. Career growth
3. Career management
4. Changing jobs
5. Getting feedback
6. Personal growth
7. Professional growth
8. Self-help reading
9. Taking risky assignments
10. Trying things for the first-time
11. Using mentors

C. Sample Questions:

Dimension 1: Been there, done that–has had direct personal experience(s) involving the competency–candidate was the prime player   Note: * means OK for campus

1. Do you take any courses more for personal than for job development?*
2. Give me an example of when you compensated for one of your weaknesses with other skills you have.*
3. Give me an example of when you worked around one of your personal weaknesses to get something done.*
4. Has anyone ever accused you of messing something up because you didn't work on your own development?
5. Have you ever been through an assessment center process?
6. Have you ever come back from a course excited about what you've learned and then had trouble implementing the change back in the workplace?
7. Have you ever had an occasion where a prior strength actually turned out to be a weakness in another setting?*
8. Have you ever switched jobs to make better use of your strengths?
9. Have you ever volunteered for an evaluation or assessment event or process?
10. How do you get feedback?*
11. How do you go about matching yourself to a new job opportunity?
12. How do you make the time for personal development?
13. How do you react to courses and workshops that have assessment linked to them?
14. How many times did you switch majors in college?*
15. How often do you try things you are not good at?*
16. Is your current job in the same line as your education?
17. Tell me about a time when you finally accepted that you weren't good at something you previously rated yourself high on.*
18. Tell me about a time when you had to work around one of your weaknesses.*
19. Tell me about a time when you took a new job that required a much different set of skills.
20. Tell me about a time when you went into a situation with substantially different norms than you were used to.*
21. Tell me about a time when you were very surprised by a piece of negative feedback about yourself.*

SELF-DEVELOPMENT

22. Tell me about a time when your effort at self-development got you into trouble.
23. Tell me about a time when your effort at self-development worked really well for you.
24. Tell me about the most developmental job you've had.
25. What associations do you belong to?*
26. What do you do to leverage your strengths?*
27. What do you do when you get a piece of critical feedback you think isn't true or is unfair?*
28. What informal groups do you belong to?*
29. What recent self help or improvement books have you read?*
30. What were the best and worst courses you've ever taken?*

Dimension 2: Seen/been around others who were involved with the competency–good and bad; learns from others about self

31. Contrast the most and least skilled people you know in self-development.*
32. Has self-development ever been in any 360° survey done on you? Was your score among your highest, middle, or lowest?
33. Has lack of self-development on someone else's part ever created an obstacle for you or got in the way of something you were trying to accomplish?*
34. Have you ever talked with a coach or mentor about your self-development skills?
35. Have you ever watched someone fail/get fired because they did not develop themselves?*
36. Have you ever watched someone overdo self-development to the point that it backfired?
37. Have you ever watched someone succeed because of developing themselves?*
38. Have you ever worked with a coach on self-development?*
39. Have you ever worked with a person who excelled at self-development?
40. Have you ever worked with a skills coach on self-development?*
41. How do you get feedback about yourself on self-development?
42. How often do you check with multiple sources when you get a piece of critical feedback on your self-development skills?
43. Is there a historical figure you consider a model of self-development?
44. What do others who are not your fans say about your self-development efforts?
45. What do others who like you say about your self-development efforts?
46. Which boss was the best at developing themselves?
47. Which boss was the worst at developing themselves?
48. Which direct report was the best at developing themselves?
49. Which direct report was the worst at developing themselves?
50. Which peer was the best at developing themselves?
51. Which peer was the worst at developing themselves?
52. Who in your field or business is the best at self-development?
53. Who do you consider a role model of self-development?*
54. Who do you go to for advice on self-development?
55. Who have you learned the most from about self-development?*
56. Who is a higher-management role model for you on self-development?
57. Who outside of work is a role model of self-development?

SELF-DEVELOPMENT

Dimension 3: Knows how the competency works in theory; shows understanding

58. Are there situations or settings where someone should develop themselves differently?
59. Do you think self-development skills can be learned; how do you think people develop self-development skills?
60. Do you think there is a way to compensate or work around low self-development skills?
61. Has anyone asked you for your opinions/advice on self-development?*
62. Have you ever attended a course on self-development?
63. Have you ever been in a situation where you and others put self-development on a success profile?
64. Have you ever been part of an effort to create a policy or a mission statement containing reference to self-development efforts?
65. Have you ever been someone's coach or mentor who had problems with self-development?
66. Have you ever created a self-development plan for someone?
67. Have you ever criticized someone for not developing themselves?
68. Have you ever designed a program on self-development?
69. Have you ever given a speech on self-development?
70. Have you ever rewarded or recognized someone for developing themselves?
71. Have you ever taught a course on self-development?
72. Have you ever tried to help someone deal more effectively with self-development?*
73. Have you ever tried to help someone improve their self-development skills?
74. How do you think people develop self-development skills?
75. How much self-development is good to have and how much is too much?
76. How much of success do you think is due to self-development efforts compared with other characteristics?
77. How would you know if someone is bad at developing themselves?
78. How would you know if someone is good at developing themselves?
79. If you had to write a book on self-development, what would the chapter headings be?
80. What are the benefits to someone who is really good at self-development?
81. What are the consequences to someone who is really poor at self-development?
82. What do you think the standard is on self-development skills for someone in your role?
83. What happens when two people try to work together who have very different self-development skills?
84. What wisdom would you pass onto others trying to become better at self-development?
85. When you select others, what do you look for in self-development skills?
86. Why do you think people end up having different self-development skills?

Dimension 4: Shows personal change and sense-making; learned it one place and applied it in another; can compare and contrast experiences; changes viewpoints across time; can explain personal development or evolution related to the competency

87. Compare and contrast examples of being effective and ineffective at developing yourself?
88. Contrast your on- and off-the-job efforts at self-development.
89. Did you ever pass up a job or assignment because you were not confident enough that you could develop yourself once in it?
90. Do you ever use other skills to cover for your lack of skill in developing yourself?
91. Has becoming better at self-development ever helped you in other areas?
92. Has lack of self-development ever figured in a failure, struggle, or setback you have had?
93. Has poor self-development ever been the subject of a development plan for you?

SELF-DEVELOPMENT

94. Has your orientation to developing yourself always been this way?
95. Have you ever delegated or assigned someone a task because you didn't think you could develop yourself to do it?
96. Have you ever made significant strides at becoming better at self-development?
97. Have your self-development skills, good or bad, ever been the subject of your performance review or a career discussion?
98. How different are you across situations in your self-development?
99. How do you decide how much self-development to do?
100. How much of your success is due to your self-development?
101. How transferable are your self-development skills to other situations?
102. If you had to become better at developing yourself in a hurry, what would you do?
103. In your career, have you ever moved a weakness all the way to a strength?
104. Was there a time when you were not as good at self-development?
105. What are some areas you've improved in recently?*
106. What are you lousy at and what do you do about it?*
107. What caused you to work to change your skills at developing yourself?
108. What do you do differently as a friend than you did a year ago? Why?*
109. What do you do differently as a manager than you did a year ago? Why?
110. What do you do differently as a person than you did a year ago? Why?*
111. What do you do differently as a student than you did a year ago? Why?*
112. What event or series of events had the most impact on your self-development?
113. What have you tried the hardest to develop over your career?
114. What used to be a weakness for you?*
115. What's the most varied you can be in your self-development?
116. What was the shortest amount of time in which you increased your level of skill at developing yourself?
117. When did you first realize your level of skill at self-development?
118. When you know ahead of time that your usual ways of developing yourself won't work, what do you do?
119. Why do you think you deal with self-development the way you do?
120. Why do you think your orientation toward self development is the way it is?*

D. Follow-up Probes:

1. Are there times when you work on your own development like that and times when you don't?
2. Could you contrast those two bosses for me?
3. Could you give me a few examples of how you've used or applied that?
4. Do you always work on your own development like that or was that a special situation?
5. Do you think that's teachable?
6. Do you think you're better at developing yourself than most? Why?
7. Do you think you would perform any differently if you could be more effective at developing yourself?
8. Have you always worked on your own development that way or is this a recent change for you?
9. How did the others react when you did that?
10. How did you adjust to that weakness after finding out about it?
11. How did you come up with that approach to working on your development in the first place?
12. How did you feel when you discovered that others thought you had a major weakness you didn't know about?

SELF-DEVELOPMENT

13. How did you know that method of developing yourself would work?
14. How do others you have known approach that?
15. How typical is this for you?
16. How would you approach that same situation today?
17. Is this natural for you, or do you really have to dig for it?
18. Was there a time when you didn't understand this about yourself?
19. What did you do after you got that feedback?
20. What did you do to adapt to that?
21. What did you learn from that?
22. When did you realize you were wrong about yourself?
23. Why did you choose that approach?
24. Why did you decide to take the risk?
25. Why did you do it that way?
26. Why did you time your attempt to develop yourself like that?
27. Why do you think that didn't work?
28. Why do you think that happened that way?
29. Why do you think that worked?
30. Why do you think you have difficulty with that sometimes?
31. Would you have done it that way with looser deadlines?
32. Would you have done it that way with tighter deadlines?

E. Themes/Things to Look for:

Ability to sense differential requirements of jobs and situations

Accepting feedback from people they dislike

Aware of strengths

Complex and varied tactics to get around weaknesses

Enjoyment at conquering a weakness

Focused changes

Follows role models

Has weaknesses that are credible

High personal standards

Informing others so they're not blindsided

Jump shift experiences where prior strengths were weaknesses

Jump shift experiences where prior weaknesses were strengths

Knows how they learns best

Life long commitment to continuous improvement

Not having to give socially acceptable answers (I've improved my patience or I'm less driven–those are strengths disguised as weaknesses–in this case, the person is saying I have high standards, I'm very achievement-oriented, etc.)

Open to multiple ways of growing–experiences, reading, courses, learning from others

Perseverance in the face of a weakness

Resilience in the face of negative data

Sees weaknesses as challenges, not limits

SELF-DEVELOPMENT

Sense of personal limits
Takes action on weaknesses
Takes advice from trusted others
Uses mentors to monitor progress
Acknowledges limits
Knows what they are lousy at
Many sources

F. Most Likely Résumé:

1. Look for jobs like:

Cross-Moves	Significant People Demands
International Assignments	Staff to Line Shifts
Scope (complexity) Assignments	Start-Ups

2. Look for develop-in-place assignments like:

Attend a self-awareness/assessment course that includes feedback.

Attend a course or event which will push you personally beyond your usual limits or outside your comfort zone (e.g., Outward Bound, language immersion training, sensitivity group, public speaking).

Try to learn something frivolous and fun to see how good you can get (e.g., juggling, square dancing, magic).

Teach a course, seminar, or workshop on something you don't know well.

Teach/coach someone how to do something you are not an expert in.

Manage an ad hoc, temporary group of people where the people in the group are towering experts but the temporary manager is not.

Take on a task you dislike or hate to do.

Make peace with an enemy or someone you've disappointed with a product or service or someone you've had some trouble with or don't get along well with.

3. Best references to ask about or check:

Human Resource Professionals	Spouse
Natural Mentors	Yourself

G. Learning Agility Evaluation:

1. What/Describing vs. Why/Explain
3. Ordinary/Socially Acceptable vs. Insightful/Different
4. Spectator/Passive vs. Player/Participant
7. Passive vs. Intrigued/Curious
10. Reactive vs. Initiating
12. Rehearsed/Socially Acceptable vs. Candid
14. Sameness vs. Broad Ranging
17. Avoid Discussion of Weaknesses vs. Comfortably Sharing Shortcomings
19. External Standards vs. Internal Standards
20. Avoids Responsibility for Mistakes vs. Admits and Learns from Mistakes

SELF-DEVELOPMENT

H. The LEADERSHIP ARCHITECT® Sort Card Connections:

1. Good (positive) if combined with high:
Works to get ready for next job 6, 58
Can handle trying new things in a workshop 11, 26, 41
Develops both self and others 19
Doesn't blindside others 27, 44, 55
Gets monitoring feedback easily 32, 33, 45
Persists 43
Focuses changes where they have impact 46, 50, 51, 53
Makes the time 62
Balanced between personal and work development 66

2. Bad (negative) if combined with low or high (+):
Knows but doesn't do anything about it 1, 6, 43, 45, 51
Never finds the time 1, 62
Can't project much into the future 2, 40, 58
Has trouble getting feedback on progress 3, 32, 33
Doesn't integrate personal change 55
Has trouble practicing new skills 11, 12, 44
Doesn't make good choices about what to develop 17, 50, 51, 55
Doesn't pick up on need for different skills 30, 32, 46

3. Too much can contribute to the following Stallers and Stoppers:

A. What too much looks like (overused):
May be a self-help development junkie; may be self-absorbed; may confuse others with constant efforts to improve and change; may be too self-centered; may be susceptible to self-help fads; may spend too much time improving and too little time acting and performing.

B. Too much might lead to these Stallers and Stoppers:
Overly Ambitious (103)

C. Compensators:
How to compensate for too much of this competency:
    1, 24, 43, 46, 50, 51, 53, 55, 57, 63

D. Things to watch for:
Always wants others to join in; becomes a missionary
Applies their own personal solution indiscriminately to others
Away from the job too often
Can't accept themselves as they are
May have too high a need to please others
Susceptible to snake oil salesperson
At the extreme, may not change; may just collect techniques

SELF-DEVELOPMENT

4. Too little can contribute to the following Stallers and Stoppers:

A. What too little looks like (unskilled):

Doesn't put in the effort to grow and change; doesn't do anything to act on constructive feedback; may not know what to work on or how; may know what but doesn't act on it; doesn't adjust approach to different audiences and situations; may be immune to negative feedback–arrogant or defensive; may fear failure and the risk of admitting shortcomings; may not believe people really change therefore it's not worth the effort; may believe current skills will last; may believe in development but is always too busy.

B. Too little might lead to these Stallers and Stoppers:

Arrogance (104)
Blocked Personal Learner (106)
Defensiveness (108)
Key Skill Deficiencies (113)
Performance Problems (118)

C. Compensators:

How to substitute for too little of this competency:
1, 6, 19, 32, 33, 44, 45, 55, 61

I. LEARNING ARCHITECT® Connections:

Look for people who act like and/or show evidence of:

1c. Following a Plan
3b. Self-Talk
3c. Personal Experience
7. Risks
25. Personal Change
30. Mastery

J. CHOICES ARCHITECT® Connections:

Look for people who act like and/or show evidence of:

First Edition (Released 1994)
10. Responds to Feedback

Second Edition (Released 2000)
16. Personal Learner
17. Responds to Feedback

K. Difficulty to Develop:

24 (of 34)–Moderate

55. SELF-KNOWLEDGE

A. Definition:

Knows personal strengths, weaknesses, opportunities, and limits; seeks feedback; gains insights from mistakes; is open to criticism; isn't defensive; is receptive to talking about shortcomings; looks forward to balanced (pluses and minuses) performance reviews and career discussions.

B. Arenas/Domains to Explore:

1. 360° feedback
2. Advice from enemies
3. Advice from friends
4. As a personal contributor
5. Asking for feedback
6. Assessments in courses/workshops
7. Career discussions
8. Debriefs with self and others
9. Discussions with mentors
10. During crises
11. Failures
12. Getting feedback
13. Hot Q & A
14. Losing out on getting a job
15. Losing out on getting a promotion
16. Peer review
17. Performance reviews
18. Personal
19. Personal witnessing
20. Professional
21. Role model for others
22. Self-initiated assessment
23. Self-talk
24. Sharing style workshops
25. Social
26. Successes
27. Watching others fail
28. Watching others succeed
29. Working alone on a tough task
30. Working internationally

C. Sample Questions:

Dimension 1: Been there, done that–has had direct personal experience(s) involving the competency–candidate was the prime player   Note: * means OK for campus

1. Do you admit to shortcomings in speeches or presentations?
2. Do you ever make fun of yourself?*
3. Do you tend to over or under rate yourself compared with others?*
4. Has anyone ever accused you of messing something up because you didn't know yourself well enough?
5. Have you ever been through a comprehensive 360°? How close were your ratings to others who gave you feedback?
6. Have you ever been through an assessment center process?
7. Have you ever managed anything where the people or units reporting to you were in different locations? How did you get feedback from them about yourself?
8. Have you ever volunteered for an evaluation or assessment event, course, or process?
9. How do you feel when you get a piece of negative feedback?*
10. How do you manage your emotions during career discussions?
11. How do you manage your emotions during performance reviews?
12. How do you react to courses and workshops that have assessment linked to them?
13. How do you react when you receive critical feedback you think is untrue or unfair?*
14. Tell me about a time when you went out and pushed someone to give you feedback.*

SELF-KNOWLEDGE

15. Tell me about a time when your understanding of yourself got you into trouble.
16. Tell me about a time when your understanding of yourself worked really well for you.
17. To what extent do the people around you know your true strengths and weaknesses?*
18. What are you lousy at?

Dimension 2: Seen/been around others who were involved with the competency–good and bad; learns from others about self

19. Contrast the people you know who are most and least informed about themselves.*
20. Has lack of self-knowledge on someone else's part ever created an obstacle for you or got in the way of something you were trying to accomplish?*
21. Has self-knowledge ever been in any 360° survey done on you? Was your score among your highest, middle, or lowest?
22. Have you ever talked with a coach or mentor about your self-knowledge?
23. Have you ever watched someone fail/get fired because they did not know themselves very well?*
24. Have you ever watched someone overdo self-knowledge to the point that it backfired?
25. Have you ever watched someone succeed because they knew themselves well?*
26. Have you ever worked with a coach on self-knowledge?*
27. Have you ever worked with a person who excelled at knowing themselves?
28. Have you ever worked with a skills coach on self-knowledge?*
29. How do you get feedback about yourself on how well you know yourself?
30. How often do you check with multiple sources when you get a piece of critical feedback on the extent of your self-knowledge?
31. Is there a historical figure you consider a model of knowing themselves?
32. What do others who are not your fans say about how well you know yourself?
33. What do others who know you the best say about how well you know yourself?
34. What do others who like you say about how well you know yourself?
35. Which boss was the best at knowing themselves?
36. Which boss was the worst at knowing themselves?
37. Which direct report was the best at knowing themselves?
38. Which direct report was the worst at knowing themselves?
39. Which peer was the best at knowing themselves?
40. Which peer was the worst at knowing themselves?
41. Who in your field or business knows themselves the best?
42. Who do you consider a role model of knowing themselves?*
43. Who do you go to for advice on self-knowledge?
44. Who have you learned the most from about self-knowledge?*
45. Who is a higher-management role model for you on self-knowledge?
46. Who is a role model for knowing themselves outside of work?

Dimension 3: Knows how the competency works in theory; shows understanding

47. Do you think there is a way to compensate or work around low self-knowledge?
48. Has anyone asked you for your opinions/advice on knowing oneself?*
49. Have you ever attended a course on knowing yourself?
50. Have you ever been in a situation where you and others put self-knowledge on a success profile?
51. Have you ever been part of an effort to create a policy or a mission statement containing reference to self-knowledge?

SELF-KNOWLEDGE

52. Have you ever been someone's coach or mentor who had problems with knowing themselves?
53. Have you ever created a development plan for someone on self-knowledge?
54. Have you ever criticized someone for lacking self-knowledge?
55. Have you ever designed a program on self-knowledge?
56. Have you ever given a speech on self-knowledge?
57. Have you ever rewarded or recognized someone for knowing themselves?
58. Have you ever taught a course on self-knowledge?
59. Have you ever tried to help someone deal more effectively with knowing themselves?*
60. Have you ever tried to help someone improve their self-knowledge?
61. How do you think people develop self-knowledge skills?
62. How much self-knowledge is good to have and how much is too much?
63. How much of success do you think is due to self-knowledge compared with other characteristics?
64. How would you know if someone is bad at knowing themselves?
65. How would you know if someone is good at knowing themselves?
66. If you had to write a book on self-knowledge, what would the chapter headings be?
67. What are the benefits to someone who is really good at knowing themselves?
68. What are the consequences to someone who is really poor at knowing themselves?
69. What do you think the standard is on self-knowledge for someone in your role?
70. What happens when two people try to work together have very different levels of self-knowledge?
71. What wisdom would you pass on to others trying to develop self-knowledge skills?
72. When you select others, what do you look for in self-knowledge?
73. Why do you think people end up being different in knowing themselves?

Dimension 4: Shows personal change and sense-making; learned it one place and applied it in another; can compare and contrast experiences; changes viewpoints across time; can explain personal development or evolution related to the competency

74. At what point in your life do you think you came to realize your true, long-term strengths and weaknesses?
75. Compare and contrast examples of being effective and ineffective at knowing yourself.
76. Contrast your on- and off-the-job level of self-knowledge.
77. Did you ever pass up a job or assignment because you didn't know yourself well enough yet?
78. Do you ever use other skills to cover for your lack of self-knowledge?
79. Has becoming better at knowing yourself ever helped you in other areas?
80. Has not knowing your strengths and weaknesses ever figured in a failure, struggle, or setback you have had?
81. Has poor self-knowledge ever been the subject of a development plan for you?
82. Has your self-knowledge always been pretty much this way?
83. Has your self-knowledge, good or bad, ever been the subject of your performance review or a career discussion?
84. Have you ever delegated or assigned someone a task because you didn't know if you could handle whatever problems came up?
85. Have you ever made significant strides at becoming better at knowing your strengths and weaknesses?
86. How different are you across situations in your self-knowledge?
87. How do you stay up-to-date about yourself?*
88. How do you work around your weaknesses?*
89. How have your strengths grown over time?*

SELF-KNOWLEDGE

90. How much of your success is due to your knowing your strengths and weaknesses?
91. If you had to become better at knowing your strengths and weaknesses in a hurry, what would you do?
92. Was there a time when you were not as good at knowing your strengths and weaknesses?
93. What caused you to work to improve your ability at knowing yourself?
94. What event or series of events had the most impact on your ability to know your strengths and weaknesses?
95. What have been some personal moments of truth for you, when you learned a few things about yourself you didn't know?*
96. What's the most varied you can be in your self-knowledge?
97. What was the shortest amount of time in which you increased your level of self-knowledge?
98. When did you first realize at what level you knew your strengths and weaknesses?
99. When you know ahead of time that your self-knowledge isn't up to standard, what do you do?
100. Why do you think you deal with your strengths and weaknesses the way you do?
101. Why do you think your self-knowledge is the way it is?*

D. Follow-up Probes:

1. Could you contrast those two bosses for me?
2. Could you give me a few examples of how you've used or applied that?
3. Do you suppose if others would just try a little harder, they could learn to be more accurate about themselves like you?
4. Do you think that's teachable?
5. Do you think you know yourself better than most? Why?
6. Do you think you would perform any differently if you knew yourself better?
7. Have you always understood yourself that well or is this a recent development in you?
8. Have you ever had to take feedback from someone you really disliked?
9. How did the others react when you did that?
10. How did you come up with that approach to getting to know more about yourself in the first place?
11. How did you feel when you got that feedback?
12. How did you know that method of getting feedback about yourself would work?
13. How do others you have known approach that?
14. How hard did you have to work to get the feedback?
15. How typical is this for you?
16. How would you approach that same situation today?
17. Is this natural for you, or do you really have to dig for it?
18. Was there a time when you didn't understand this about yourself?
19. What did you do after you got that feedback?
20. What did you do to adapt to that?
21. What did you do when that feedback contradicted what you thought you knew about yourself?
22. What did you learn from that?
23. Why did you choose that approach?
24. Why did you decide to take the risk?
25. Why did you do it that way?
26. Why did you time your attempt to get information about yourself like that?
27. Why do you think that didn't work?

SELF-KNOWLEDGE

28. Why do you think that happened that way?
29. Why do you think that worked?
30. Why do you think you have difficulty with that sometimes?
31. Would you have done it that way with looser deadlines?
32. Would you have done it that way with tighter deadlines?

E. Themes/Things to Look for:

A good sense of the requirements of a situation/job

Admits mistakes

Answers not just socially acceptable (Saying "I've learned to be more patient or be less driven" are strengths in disguise; saying "My spouse and kids or direct reports keep me straight" sounds good, but spouse and kids know nothing about work behavior, and direct reports are a single source, and often a reluctant one)

Comfortable disclosing

Comfortable with not being perfect

Comfortable with self

Has a sense of priorities about what's important as a strength

Has credible weaknesses

Has made mistakes

Knows strengths, weaknesses and limits in detail

Not overly driven by a need to be liked or to look good to others

Open to feedback

Optimistic about getting around weaknesses

Resilient

Seeks feedback from multiple sources

Tolerant, modest; discusses self matter of factly; neither has to gloat nor overdramatize

Manages emotions; doesn't wallow in them

F. Most Likely Résumé:

1. Look for jobs like:

None Apply

2. Look for develop-in-place assignments like:

Join a self-help or support group.

Try to learn something frivolous and fun to see how good you can get (e.g., juggling, square dancing, magic).

Manage an ad hoc, temporary group of people where the people in the group are towering experts but the temporary manager is not.

Take on a tough and undoable project, one where others who have tried it have failed.

Take on a task you dislike or hate to do.

Make peace with an enemy or someone you've disappointed with a product or service or someone you've had some trouble with or don't get along well with.

3. Best references to ask about or check:

Development Professionals	Natural Mentors
Human Resource Professionals	Spouse

SELF-KNOWLEDGE

G. Learning Agility Evaluation:
1. What/Describing vs. Why/Explain
2. All or Nothing vs. Can See Many Sides
3. Ordinary/Socially Acceptable vs. Insightful/Different
7. Passive vs. Intrigued/Curious
10. Reactive vs. Initiating
12. Rehearsed/Socially Acceptable vs. Candid
13. Simple Views vs. Complex Views
17. Avoid Discussion of Weaknesses vs. Comfortably Sharing Shortcomings
20. Avoids Responsibility for Mistakes vs. Admits and Learns from Mistakes

H. The LEADERSHIP ARCHITECT® Sort Card Connections:

1. Good (positive) if combined with high:
Seeks improvement 1, 54
Can maintain internal stability amidst chaos on the outside 2, 11, 40
Others offer feedback 3, 33, 41
Broad sources 3, 4, 36, 42, 66
Makes an accurate career assessment 6, 17, 51
Nondefensive 11, 33, 44
Has a firm foundation 22, 34, 57
Can make fun of self 26, 44
Aware of their impact on others 33, 45
Deploys themselves well in the maze 38, 48
Works on the right things 45, 54
Balanced; everyone doesn't have to like or agree 57

2. Bad (negative) if combined with low or high (+):
Knowledge leads nowhere (+33) 54
Doesn't use the knowledge for any advantage 1, 6, 12, 16, 37
Doesn't share self knowledge 26, 27, 44
May get out of date 32, 33

3. Too much can contribute to the following Stallers and Stoppers:

A. What too much looks like (overused):
May be too self-critical, too open about self; may not move past knowledge to improvement and action; may spend too much time in self-insight activities; may be too dependent upon waiting for feedback; may overly solicit feedback.

B. Too much might lead to these Stallers and Stoppers:
Failure to Staff Effectively (111)

C. Compensators:
How to compensate for too much of this competency:
1, 4, 11, 22, 27, 29, 33, 42, 44, 46, 48, 52, 54, 64

SELF-KNOWLEDGE

D. Things to watch for:

May avoid doing things not in line with strengths
May be complacent and too accepting of who they are
May decide on too small a sample
May dwell too much on the negatives
Tells you more than you asked for about themselves
Tells you more than you ever wanted to know about them
May have trouble just acting without reflecting first

4. Too little can contribute to the following Stallers and Stoppers:

A. What too little looks like (unskilled):

Doesn't know him/herself well–strengths, weaknesses or limits; doesn't seek feedback–may be defensive or arrogant; doesn't listen to or learn from feedback; may misestimate his/her performance–either too high or too low; may rush in where he/she shouldn't, or not move when he/she should; may be surprised by or not know own impact; may know some shortcomings but will not share with others; avoids discussions about him/herself; may assume he/she already knows when he/she doesn't; may be an excuse-maker and blamer; doesn't learn from mistakes; doesn't get much from personal insight exercises or performance discussions; is surprised by negative personal data.

B. Too little might lead to these Stallers and Stoppers:

Unable to Adapt to Differences (101)	Failure to Build a Team (110)
Arrogant (104)	Failure to Staff Effectively (111)
Blocked Personal Learner (106)	Key Skill Deficiencies (113)
Defensiveness (108)	Political Missteps (119)

C. Compensators:

How to substitute for too little of this competency:
6, 19, 32, 33, 44, 45, 54, 56, 64

I. LEARNING ARCHITECT® Connections:

Look for people who act like and/or show evidence of:

2c. Intuition	15. Cautious
3b. Self-Talk	17. Selected Sources
3c. Personal Experience	24. Discloser
4a. Getting Information	26. Self-Aware
9. Multiple Sources	37. Flexibility
14. Controlled	38. Resilience

J. CHOICES ARCHITECT® Connections:

Look for people who act like and/or show evidence of:

First Edition (Released 1994)

9. Self-Aware
10. Responds to Feedback
22. Self-Talk

Second Edition (Released 2000)

17. Responds to Feedback
19. Self-Aware

SELF-KNOWLEDGE

K. Difficulty to Develop:
25 (of 34)–Moderate

56. SIZING UP PEOPLE

A. Definition:

Is a good judge of talent; after reasonable exposure, can articulate the strengths and limitations of people inside or outside the organization; can accurately project what people are likely to do across a variety of situations.

B. Arenas/Domains to Explore:

1. Assembling teams
2. Assessing candidates for public office
3. Assessing merger partners
4. Assigning people to tasks
5. Back-up charts
6. Career evaluations
7. Coaching
8. Doing means testing before acting with someone
9. Fraternity/sorority pledge management
10. Going into business with someone
11. Handling hot Q & A
12. Hiring people from the outside
13. Joining a small firm
14. Knowing the opposition
15. Making calls on people outside culture/country
16. Managing layoffs
17. Military command experience
18. Need to assess what people are going to do next
19. Nominating people for professional association boards
20. Pairing up assigned mentors
21. Performance evaluations
22. Picking bosses
23. Picking friends
24. Picking professors
25. Picking study partners
26. Picking taskforce members
27. Picking vacation partners
28. Picking vendors/suppliers
29. Selecting consultants
30. Selecting office partners
31. Selecting roommates
32. Selecting spouses
33. Staffing decisions inside
34. Start-ups
35. Succession planning
36. Teaching

C. Sample Questions:

Dimension 1: Been there, done that–has had direct personal experience(s) involving the competency–candidate was the prime player   Note: * means OK for campus

1. Are you a people watcher in airports? What do you look for?*
2. Are you generally a strength or a weakness finder? What are you better at?*
3. Do you usually find yourself in agreement or at odds with others on reading people?*
4. Has anyone ever accused you of messing something up because of poor people-reading skills?
5. Have you ever hired anyone who has passed you up in the organization?
6. Have you ever managed anything where the people or units reporting to you were in different locations? How did you size up those people from afar?
7. Have you ever selected someone for a team, who had some personal trait no one else had, to balance the team?
8. Have you had much occasion to evaluate people from other countries and cultures?*
9. How does your impression of a person change what you might do?*
10. How many people who worked under you have quit in the past five years? Were fired? Promoted? Why?
11. How much time does it take you to get a good read on someone?*

SIZING UP PEOPLE

12. Tell me about a time when you had to communicate something important to someone who did not speak your language very well.
13. Tell me about a time when your first impression was way off and you changed your mind after you got to know the person. What threw you off?*
14. Tell me about a time when your ability to read people got you into trouble.
15. Tell me about a time when your ability to read people worked really well for you.
16. Was there a time when you had the lone negative opinion on someone? What happened?*
17. Was there a time when you had the lone positive opinion on someone? What happened?*
18. What are the little things about people that you tend to note? Why?
19. What has been your success at picking roommates?*
20. What's the worst people call you can remember making?
21. When you joined a new group, club, school, how did you learn about the people–what made them tick, what their strengths and weaknesses were?*

Dimension 2: Seen/been around others who were involved with the competency–good and bad; learns from others about self

22. Contrast the people you know who are most and least skilled at reading people.*
23. Has sizing up or reading people ever been in any 360° survey done on you? Was your score among your highest, middle, or lowest?
24. Has inaccurate people reading on someone else's part ever created an obstacle for you or got in the way of something you were trying to accomplish?*
25. Have you ever talked with a coach or mentor about your people reading skills?
26. Have you ever watched someone fail/get fired because they did not read people accurately?*
27. Have you ever watched someone overdo sizing up or reading people to the point that it backfired?
28. Have you ever watched someone succeed because they read people accurately?*
29. Have you ever worked with a coach on sizing up or reading people?*
30. Have you ever worked with a person who excelled at sizing up or reading people?
31. Have you ever worked with a skills coach on sizing up or reading people?*
32. How do you get feedback about yourself on sizing up or reading people?
33. How often do you check with multiple sources when you get a piece of critical feedback on your people reading skills?
34. Is there a historical figure you consider a model of sizing up or reading people?
35. What do others who are not your fans say about your people reading skills?
36. What do others who like you say about your people reading skills?
37. Which boss was the best at sizing up people
38. Which boss was the worst at sizing up people?
39. Which direct report was the best at sizing up people?
40. Which direct report was the worst at sizing up people?
41. Which peer was the best at sizing up people?
42. Which peer was the worst at sizing up people?
43. Who in your field or business is the best at sizing up people?
44. Who do you consider a role model of sizing up or reading people?*
45. Who do you go to for advice on sizing up people?
46. Who have you learned the most from about sizing up people?*
47. Who is a higher-management role model for you on sizing up people?
48. Who is a role model of sizing up people outside of work?

SIZING UP PEOPLE

Dimension 3: Knows how the competency works in theory; shows understanding

49. Are there situations or settings where someone should read people differently?
50. Can you think of any popular stereotypes of people that are more true than not?*
51. Do you think people reading skills can be learned; how do you think individuals develop people reading skills?
52. Do you think being personally creative and recognizing other people's creativity go together?
53. Do you think intelligence and creativity are related?
54. Do you think leadership and management are the same or different?
55. Do you think people from different countries are more the same or more different?*
56. Do you think there is a way to compensate or work around low people reading skills?
57. Has anyone asked you for your opinions/advice on sizing up or reading people?*
58. Have you ever attended a course on sizing up or reading people?
59. Have you ever been in a situation where you and others put sizing up or reading people on a success profile?
60. Have you ever been part of an effort to create a policy or a mission statement containing reference to people reading skills?
61. Have you ever coached or mentored someone who had problems with sizing up or reading people?
62. Have you ever created a development plan for someone on sizing up or reading people?
63. Have you ever criticized someone for not sizing up or reading people correctly?
64. Have you ever designed a program on sizing up or reading people?
65. Have you ever given a speech on sizing up or reading people?
66. Have you ever rewarded or recognized someone for reading people correctly?
67. Have you ever taught a course on sizing up or reading people?
68. Have you ever tried to help someone deal more effectively with sizing up or reading people?*
69. Have you ever tried to help someone improve their ability to read or size up people?
70. How do you think people develop people-reading skills?
71. How important is body language or non-verbal communication? Do you use it when you try to assess people?*
72. How much ability to read or size up people is good to have and how much is too much?
73. How much of an adult's behavior do you think is nature, and how much is due to upbringing?*
74. How much of success do you think is due to people-reading skills compared with other characteristics?
75. How would you know if someone is bad at sizing up or reading people?
76. How would you know if someone is good at sizing up or reading people?
77. If you had to write a book on sizing up or reading people, what would the chapter headings be?
78. In the work setting, do you think men and women are the same or are there meaningful differences?*
79. What are some of the key indicators of talent for different jobs you know something about?
80. What are the benefits to someone who is really good at sizing up or reading people?
81. What are the consequences to someone who is really poor at sizing up or reading people?
82. What do you think the standard is on people reading skills for someone in your role?
83. What happens if you have or use too much of your skill in sizing up or reading people?
84. What happens when two people try to work together who have very different people reading skills?
85. What wisdom would you pass onto others trying to become better at people reading?
86. What's your hit rate at accurately understanding and predicting what public/political figures will do?
87. When you select others, what do you look for in their ability to read or size up people?
88. Why do you think people end up being different in their ability to read or size up people?

SIZING UP PEOPLE

Dimension 4: Shows personal change and sense-making; learned it one place and applied it in another; can compare and contrast experiences; changes viewpoints across time; can explain personal development or evolution related to the competency

89. Compare and contrast examples of being effective and ineffective at reading people.
90. Contrast your on- and off-the-job accuracy at sizing up people.
91. Did you ever pass up a job or assignment because you were not confident enough in your skills at sizing up people?
92. Do you ever use other skills to cover for your lack of ability to read people well?
93. Has becoming better at reading people ever helped you in other areas?
94. Has poor assessment of people ever been the subject of a development plan for you?
95. Has poor people assessment skills ever figured in a failure, struggle, or setback you have had?
96. Has your skill at assessing people always been this way?
97. Have you ever delegated or assigned someone a task because you didn't read people particularly well?
98. Have you ever made significant strides at becoming better at assessing people?
99. Have your sizing up people skills, good or bad, ever been the subject of your performance review or a career discussion?
100. How accurate are you usually at projecting what someone is going to do?*
101. How different are you across situations in your assessment of people?
102. How do you decide how carefully to read people?
103. How much of your success is due to your skill in reading others?
104. How transferable are your assessment of people skills to other situations?
105. If you had to become better at sizing up people in a hurry, what would you do?
106. Was there a time when you were not as good at reading people?
107. What attributes are harder to find out about from outsiders?*
108. What caused you to work to improve your skills at sizing up people?
109. What characteristics about people are you usually right about?*
110. What characteristics about people are you usually wrong about?*
111. What event or series of events had the most impact on your skill in reading people?
112. What were some of your misses in sizing up people? Why?*
113. What was the shortest amount of time in which you increased your level of skill at assessing people?
114. When did you first realize your level of skill at assessing people?
115. When you are looking outside the organization for talent, do you look for different attributes than you would use inside?
116. When you have made an error in reading someone, what has usually been the cause?*
117. When you know ahead of time that your usual way of assessing people isn't adequate, what do you do?
118. Who are the best people you've ever assembled and why?* What happened to them later?
119. Who is the best person for your boss' job?
120. Who's the best person for your job (either specific or general)?
121. Why do you think you deal with the assessment of people the way you do?
122. Why do you think your reading of people is the way it is?*

D. Follow-up Probes:

1. Are there times when you can read people like that and times when you can't?
2. Could you contrast those two bosses for me?
3. Could you give me a few examples of how you've used or applied that?
4. Do you always make calls on people like that, or was that a special situation?

SIZING UP PEOPLE

5. Do you suppose if others would just try harder, they could learn to be more effective at reading people like you do?
6. Do you think that's teachable?
7. Do you think you're better at sizing up people than most? Why?
8. Do you think you would perform any differently if you could be more effective at sizing up people?
9. Have you always been able to read people that way or is this a recent development in you?
10. How did the others react when you did that?
11. How did you come up with that approach to sizing up people in the first place?
12. How do others you have known approach that?
13. How typical is this for you?
14. How would you approach that same situation today?
15. Is this natural for you, or do you really have to dig for it?
16. Was there a time when you didn't understand this about yourself?
17. What did you do after you got that feedback?
18. What did you do to adapt to that?
19. What did you learn from that?
20. Why did you choose that approach?
21. Why did you decide to take the risk?
22. Why did you do it that way?
23. Why do you think that didn't work?
24. Why do you think that happened that way?
25. Why do you think that worked?
26. Why do you think you have difficulty with that sometimes?
27. Would you have done it that way with looser deadlines?
28. Would you have done it that way with tighter deadlines?

E. **Themes/Things to Look for:**
   Admits mistakes
   Always on the lookout for talent
   Appreciation of differences
   Below the surface–isn't thrown by flash; can spot slow starters/quiet people
   Bone-deep belief that talent always wins
   Can quickly read people
   Can run people scenarios in their head
   Changes view as more data comes in
   Complex models of people
   Criteria vary by job
   Draws parallels between people
   Gives criteria and examples, not adjectives
   Goes beyond the obvious
   Goes deep for evidence
   History of picking good people
   Knows strengths and limits of people–isn't looking for a superhuman
   Knows when to quit
   Large difference between best talent and least talent
   Not hesitant to have some people in the bad bucket

SIZING UP PEOPLE

Not mundane–has more texture than "they were bright and aggressive"
Sees differences
Sees good in bad people and bad in good people
Skills go beyond home culture/country
Understands what skills and attributes go with what traits
Willing to make the tough calls
Picks up on small clues about people
Learns from poor assessments

F. Most Likely Résumé:

1. Look for jobs like:

Cross-Moves
Fix-Its/Turnarounds
International Assignments
Significant People Demands
Staff Leadership (Influencing Without Authority)
Start-Ups

2. Look for develop-in-place assignments like:

Go to a campus as a recruiter.

Construct a success and derailment profile for a unit or the entire organization, and present it to decision makers for adoption.

Do a study of successful executives in your organization, and report the findings to top management.

Do a study of failed executives in your organization, including interviewing people still with the organization who knew or worked with them, and report the findings to top management.

Go on a business trip to a foreign country you've not been to before.

Train and work as an assessor in an assessment center.

Be a change agent; create a symbol for change; lead the rallying cry; champion a significant change and implementation.

Hire/staff a team from outside your unit or organization.

Manage an ad hoc, temporary group of "green," inexperienced people as their coach, teacher, orienter, etc.

Manage an ad hoc, temporary group of balky and resisting people through an unpopular change or project.

Manage an ad hoc, temporary group of low-competence people through a task they couldn't do by themselves.

Manage an ad hoc, temporary group of people involved in tackling a fix-it or turnaround project.

Assemble an ad hoc team of diverse people to accomplish a difficult task.

Handle a tough negotiation with an internal or external client or customer.

Help shut down a plant, regional office, product line, business, operation, etc.

Prepare and present a proposal of some consequence to top management.

Work on a team that's deciding who to keep and who to let go in a layoff, shutdown, delayering, or divestiture.

Manage the outplacement of a group of people.

Resolve an issue in conflict between two people, units, geographies, functions, etc.

Build a multifunctional project team to tackle a common business issue or problem.

Manage a project team of people who are older and more experienced.

3. Best references to ask about or check:

Direct Boss
Human Resource Professionals
Natural Mentors

SIZING UP PEOPLE

G. Learning Agility Evaluation:
1. What/Describing vs. Why/Explain
2. All or Nothing vs. Can See Many Sides
3. Ordinary/Socially Acceptable vs. Insightful/Different
7. Passive vs. Intrigued/Curious
8. Sameness vs. Diversity
9. Vague/General vs. Sharp/Specific
13. Simple Views vs. Complex Views
15. Linear vs. Use Contrasts/Analogies
20. Avoids Responsibility for Mistakes vs. Admits and Learns from Mistakes

H. The LEADERSHIP ARCHITECT® Sort Card Connections:

1. Good (positive) if combined with high:
Makes a quick read 1, 16, 32
Can get through complexity to the essence 2, 40, 41
Gets a lot of people data 3, 31, 33
Reads and builds for the future 5, 19, 58
Reads soft data 7, 10, 21, 23
Willing to make the tough calls 12, 13, 34, 57
Makes good hires 17, 25
Assigns tasks appropriately 18, 20, 35
Selects and develops 19, 25, 41
Gets through surface differences 21, 46
Reads the politics of people 38, 48
Reads teams of people 42, 60, 64
Uses broad criteria 46
Molds a staff 60

2. Bad (negative) if combined with low or high (+):
Doesn't wait to collect enough information (+1, 16) 41
Only reads clear signals 2, 21, 40
Really has to fight to get data 3, 31, 33
Very cold and mechanical reads 7, 10, 21, 23
Won't make the tough calls 12, 13, 34, 57
Reads not-used-for development 18, 19
Only understands their own kind 21, 64
Uses reads for own purposes 22, 29
Doesn't change views often 32, 33
Reads only for tactical outcomes 46, 58, 65

3. Too much can contribute to the following Stallers and Stoppers:

A. What too much looks like (overused):

May be hypercritical of others; may be unwilling to alter an initial judgment about others; may not look for or be open to further evidence; may miss on slow starters and quiet and/or less expressive people.

SIZING UP PEOPLE

B. Too much might lead to these Stallers and Stoppers:
Failure to Staff Effectively (111)

C. Compensators:
How to compensate for too much of this competency:
19, 21, 31, 33, 38, 41, 46, 48, 60, 64

D. Things to watch for:
Allows judgments from one sample to generalize too broadly
Decides on too little data
May not be patient enough to appreciate diversity
Never looks again past initial call
When people disappoint, throws them out

4. Too little can contribute to the following Stallers and Stoppers:

A. What too little looks like (unskilled):
Isn't accurate in his/her appraisals of people; does not evaluate the strengths and weaknesses of others well; biases and stereotyping may play too much in his/her appraisals; may have simplistic models of people; may make instant judgments on almost no data; doesn't change after the initial appraisal; his/her estimates and projections of what people will do in certain circumstances turn out to be wrong; may be such a poor listener and observer of others that he/she really doesn't know what they're like.

B. Too little might lead to these Stallers and Stoppers:
Unable to Adapt to Differences (101)   Political Missteps (119)
Failure to Staff Effectively (111)

C. Compensators:
How to substitute for too little of this competency:
7, 21, 23, 25, 32, 33, 35, 46, 51, 55, 64

I. LEARNING ARCHITECT® Connections:

Look for people who act like and/or show evidence of:

2b. Visioning	15. Cautious
2c. Intuition	21. Changer
3c. Personal Experience	23. Orchestrator
4a. Getting Information	32. Diversity in Others
11. Why/How	34. Sizing Up Others

J. CHOICES ARCHITECT® Connections:

Look for people who act like and/or show evidence of:

First Edition (Released 1994)	Second Edition (Released 2000)
14. Transaction Quality	9. Agile Communicator
23. Communicator	15. People-Smart

K. Difficulty to Develop:
27 (of 34)–Harder

57. STANDING ALONE

A. Definition:

Will stand up and be counted; doesn't shirk from personal responsibility; can be counted on when times are tough; willing to be the only champion for an idea or position; is comfortable working alone on a tough assignment.

B. Arenas/Domains to Explore:

1. Asked for negative comment in a public forum
2. Being the first to speak up on an issue
3. Complaining about poor treatment/service
4. Crises
5. Defending someone against majority opinion
6. Dispatched to solve a problem by boss
7. Doing audits
8. During hard times
9. First into a situation
10. Going against the prevailing culture
11. Going against the prevailing opinion
12. Individual contributor
13. International assignments on own
14. Lonely times
15. Moral/ethical dilemmas
16. Negative feedback across boundaries
17. New person in an established group
18. Pilot a new process/system/technology
19. Problem others have turned away from
20. Proving a point on a shoestring budget
21. Pushing a strongly held belief in the face of resistance
22. Single person taskforce
23. Take over a group as an outsider
24. Takes blame
25. Taking a negative stand on someone against majority opinion
26. Taking point; being a scout, pioneer
27. Taking responsibility for one's work
28. Taking the lead on an issue
29. Unpopular cause
30. Volunteers to do it themselves
31. Whistleblowing
32. Working the issue on personal time

C. Sample Questions:

*Dimension 1: Been there, done that–has had direct personal experience(s) involving the competency–candidate was the prime player   Note: * means OK for campus*

1. Has anyone ever accused you of messing something up because you haven't taken a stand on something?
2. Have you been in a situation where others have grown tired of your frequent, lone stands?*
3. Have you ever had to audit a situation and bring back more negative news than people expected?
4. Have you ever had to make a negative call on a friend?*
5. Have you ever left a job or organization over an issue of principles?
6. Have you ever lost a friend because of your stance on an issue?*
7. Have you ever managed anything where the people or units reporting to you were in different locations? How did you make your views and stands on issues known to them?
8. Have you ever volunteered to take on an issue nobody else was willing to tackle?*
9. Have you ever worked on something on your own time or with your own money because of your beliefs about it?
10. How do you involve others to help you solve issues and problems?*
11. How often do you find yourself with the minority opinion?*
12. Tell me about a project where you had to plow new ground and then sell it to a skeptical audience.*

STANDING ALONE

13. Tell me about a time when you decided to do something against some of your own beliefs.*
14. Tell me about a time when you had to blow the whistle on something or someone.*
15. Tell me about a time when you had to stand up for what was right.*
16. Tell me about a time when you presented an unpopular proposal.*
17. Tell me about a time when you pushed something through that few wanted at first.*
18. Tell me about a time when you took more responsibility for a mistake than was necessary to protect someone else.*
19. Tell me about a time when you took on an orphan project/process and got it accepted.*
20. Tell me about a time when you were asked to do something against your own beliefs.*
21. Tell me about a time when you were the lone, negative voice regarding a person.*
22. Tell me about a time when you were the lone, positive voice regarding a person.*
23. Tell me about a time when taking a stand got you into trouble.
24. Tell me about a time when taking a stand worked really well for you.
25. Was there a time when others in a group slowed you down because you had the answer earlier than they did?*
26. Was there a time when you alone had to carry the burden of a problem or issue until help arrived?*
27. Was there a time when you were the sole blame for something that went wrong, and you had to declare that fact in front of others?*
28. What's the most alone you have ever felt pushing an idea or project?*

Dimension 2: Seen/been around others who were involved with the competency–good and bad; learns from others about self

29. Contrast the people you know who are most and least willing to take a tough stand and be personally responsible.*
30. Has taking personal responsibility ever been in any 360° survey done on you? Was your score among your highest, middle, or lowest?
31. Has being unwilling to take personal responsibility on someone else's part ever created an obstacle for you or got in the way of something you were trying to accomplish?*
32. Have you ever talked with a coach or mentor about your willingness to take a tough stand and being personally responsible?
33. Have you ever watched someone fail/get fired because they did not take a stand or were unwilling to assume personal responsibility?*
34. Have you ever watched someone overdo willingness to take a tough stand and being personally responsible to the point that it backfired?
35. Have you ever watched someone succeed because they took a stand and were willing to assume personal responsibility?*
36. Have you ever worked with a coach on taking personal responsibility?*
37. Have you ever worked with a person who excelled at willingness to take tough stands and assume personal responsibility?
38. Have you ever worked with a skills coach on taking tougher stands and assuming more personal responsibility?*
39. How do you get feedback about yourself on taking personal responsibility?
40. How often do you check with multiple sources when you get a piece of critical feedback on your willingness to take tough stands and assume personal responsibility?
41. Is there a historical figure you consider a model of taking tough stands and assuming personal responsibility?

STANDING ALONE

42. What do others who are not your fans say about your taking tough stands and assuming personal responsibility?
43. What do others who like you say about your taking tough stands and assuming personal responsibility?
44. Which boss was the best at taking tough stands and assuming personal responsibility?
45. Which boss was the worst at taking tough stands and assuming personal responsibility?
46. Which direct report was the best at taking tough stands and assuming personal responsibility?
47. Which direct report was the worst at taking tough stands and assuming personal responsibility?
48. Which peer was the best at taking tough stands and assuming personal responsibility?
49. Which peer was the worst at taking tough stands and assuming personal responsibility?
50. Who in your field or business is best at taking tough stands and assuming personal responsibility?
51. Who do you consider a role model of taking personal responsibility?*
52. Who do you go to for advice on taking tough stands and assuming personal responsibility?
53. Who have you learned the most from about taking tough stands and assuming personal responsibility?*
54. Who is a higher-management role model for you on taking tough stands and assuming personal responsibility?
55. Who is a role model of taking tough stands and assuming personal responsibility outside of work?

Dimension 3: Knows how the competency works in theory; shows understanding

56. Are there situations or settings where someone should act differently in taking tough stands and assuming personal responsibility?
57. Do you think personal responsibility can be learned; how do you think people develop the ability to take tough stands and assume personal responsibility?
58. Do you think there is a way to compensate or work around a low ability to take tough stands and assume personal responsibility?
59. Has anyone asked you for your opinions/advice on taking personal responsibility?*
60. Have you ever attended a course on taking personal responsibility?
61. Have you ever been in a situation where you and others put taking personal responsibility on a success profile?
62. Have you ever been part of an effort to create a policy or a mission statement containing reference to taking personal responsibility?
63. Have you ever been someone's coach or mentor who had problems with taking personal responsibility?
64. Have you ever created a development plan for someone on taking personal responsibility?
65. Have you ever criticized someone for not taking personal responsibility?
66. Have you ever designed a program on taking personal responsibility?
67. Have you ever given a speech on taking personal responsibility?
68. Have you ever rewarded or recognized someone for having taken a stand or having been willing to take personal responsibility?
69. Have you ever taught a course on taking personal responsibility?
70. Have you ever tried to help someone deal more effectively with taking personal responsibility?*
71. Have you ever tried to help someone improve their ability to take personal responsibility?
72. How do you think people develop the ability to take tough stands and assume personal responsibility?
73. How much ability to take tough stands and assume personal responsibility is good to have and how much is too much?
74. How much of success do you think is due to taking personal responsibility compared with other characteristics?

STANDING ALONE

75. How would you know if someone is bad at taking personal responsibility?
76. How would you know if someone is good at taking personal responsibility?
77. If you had to write a book on taking personal responsibility, what would the chapter headings be?
78. What are the benefits to someone who is really good at taking personal responsibility?
79. What are the consequences to someone who is really poor at taking personal responsibility?
80. What do you think the standard is on taking personal responsibility for someone in your role?
81. What happens if you take too much personal responsibility?
82. What happens when two people try to work together who have very different abilities with taking tough stands and assuming personal responsibility?
83. What wisdom would you pass on to others trying to become better at taking personal responsibility?
84. When you select others, what do you look for in willingness to take a tough stand and being personally responsible?
85. Why do you think people end up being different in the ability to take tough stands and assume personal responsibility?

Dimension 4: Shows personal change and sense-making; learned it one place and applied it in another; can compare and contrast experiences; changes viewpoints across time; can explain personal development or evolution related to the competency

86. Compare and contrast examples of being effective and ineffective at taking tough stands and assuming personal responsibility.*
87. Contrast your on- and off-the-job use of tough stands and assuming personal responsibility.
88. Did you ever pass up a job or assignment because you were not confident enough in your ability to take tough stands and assume personal responsibility?
89. Do you ever use other skills to cover for your lack of ability to take tough stands and assume personal responsibility?
90. Do you like working alone on issues and problems, or do you prefer working on a team, in a group, or with one or two others?*
91. Has being unwilling to stand alone ever figured in a failure, struggle, or setback you have had?
92. Has becoming better at taking tough stands and assuming personal responsibility ever helped you in other areas?
93. Has not taking tough stands and assuming personal responsibility ever been the subject of a development plan for you?
94. Has your ability to take a lone stand always been this way?
95. Have you ever delegated or assigned someone a task because you didn't take tough stands and assume personal responsibility well enough?
96. Have you ever made significant strides at becoming better at taking a lone stand?
97. Have your standing-alone skills, good or bad, ever been the subject of your performance review or a career discussion?
98. How different are you across situations in your ability to take a tough stand?
99. How do you decide how much you need to take a tough stand and assume personal responsibility?
100. How do you pick your battles? When is it worth standing alone?*
101. How important is it for you to be right?*
102. How important is it for you to win?*
103. How long will you stick with an issue before you stop pushing?*
104. How much of your success is due to your ability to stand alone?
105. How transferable are your standing alone skills to other situations?

STANDING ALONE

106. If you had to become better at being able to stand alone in a hurry, what would you do?
107. Was there a time when you were not as good at taking a stand?
108. What caused you to work to change your skills at taking tough stands and assuming personal responsibility?
109. What event or series of events had the most impact on your ability to take a strong stand?
110. What's the most varied you can be in your inclination to take a lone stand?
111. What was the shortest amount of time in which you increased your level of skill at taking tough stands and assuming personal responsibility?
112. When did you first realize your level of skill at taking a stand and assuming personal responsibility?
113. When you know ahead of time that your usual approach to taking tough stands and assuming personal responsibility won't work, what do you do?
114. Why do you think you deal with taking a stand the way you do?
115. Why do you think your ability to take a stand is the way it is?*

D. Follow-up Probes:
1. Are there times when you take stands like that and times when you don't?
2. Could you contrast those two bosses for me?
3. Could you give me a few examples of how you've used or applied that?
4. Do you always stand up for what you believe like that, or was that a special situation?
5. Do you enjoy being a contrarian?
6. Do you generally speak out first on an issue?
7. Do you suppose if others would just try harder, they could learn to more often stand up for what they believe like you do?
8. Do you think that's teachable?
9. Do you think you're better at standing up for what you believe and taking responsibility for what you do than most? Why?
10. Do you think you would perform any differently if you would be more willing to stand up for what you believe in and take more responsibility for what you do?
11. How did the others react when you did that?
12. How did you come up with that approach to standing alone in the first place?
13. How did you feel when you had to take the blame?
14. How did you feel when you were the only one pushing that viewpoint?
15. How did you know that method of taking personal responsibility would work?
16. How do others you have known approach that?
17. How do you know when to give up?
18. How often do you find yourself at odds with the rest of the organization?
19. How typical is this for you?
20. How would you approach that same situation today?
21. Is this natural for you, or do you really have to dig for it?
22. Was there a time when you didn't understand this about yourself?
23. What's the most you have ever risked on a lone stand?
24. What's your win/loss record when you take on unpopular causes?
25. What did you do after you got that feedback?
26. What did you do to adapt to that?
27. What did you learn from that?

STANDING ALONE

28. Why did you choose that approach?
29. Why did you decide to take that on yourself?
30. Why did you decide to take the risk?
31. Why did you do it that way?
32. Why did you time your accepting the blame like that?
33. Why do you prefer to work alone like that?
34. Why do you suppose organizations work that way?
35. Why do you think that didn't work?
36. Why do you think that happened that way?
37. Why do you think that worked?
38. Why were you the only one who volunteered to do that?
39. Why do you think you have difficulty with that sometimes?
40. Would you have done it that way with looser deadlines?
41. Would you have done it that way with tighter deadlines?

E. Themes/Things to Look for:

Ability to admit mistakes
Able to take the heat
Anticipates roadblocks/areas of resistance
Attacking problems, not people
Calmness under pressure/stress
Can walk away
Comfortable not having all the answers
Coming up with new arguments, not just repeating old ones
Contention/conflict skills
Courage
Doesn't dodge tough issues
Doesn't personalize rejection
Doesn't stop after the first no
Enjoys working alone
Fights the right issues
Goes after the toughest issues
Keeps discussions on issues
Keeps personal feelings from getting in the way
Knows when and how to push
Knows when to cut bait
Loves a challenge
Loves a good fight
Not afraid to intimidate if necessary
Passionate commitment to what's right
Perseverance
Political sensitivity
Pushes harder when resisted

STANDING ALONE

Resilience
Sense of priorities
Stands alone but not making mountains out of mole hills
Understands the opposition
Willingness to lose a battle to win the war
Willingness to take risks
Willingness to be first
Willingness to take the blame in public
Wins the point but maintains the relationship

F. Most Likely Résumé:

1. Look for jobs like:

Chair of Projects/Task Forces
Fix-Its/Turnarounds
International Assignments
Scope (complexity) Assignments
Staff to Line Shifts
Start-Ups

2. Look for develop-in-place assignments like:

Integrate diverse systems, processes, or procedures across decentralized and/or dispersed units.
Manage the renovation of an office, floor, building, meeting room, warehouse, etc.
Plan a new site for a building (plant, field office, headquarters, etc.).
Plan an off-site meeting, conference, convention, trade show, event, etc.
Coach a children's sports team.
Become a referee for an athletic league or program.
Write a proposal for a new policy, process, mission, charter, product, service, or system, and present and sell it to top management.
Plan for and start up something small (secretarial pool, athletic program, suggestion system, program, etc.).
Launch a new product, service, or process.
Be a change agent; create a symbol for change; lead the rallying cry; champion a significant change and implementation.
Relaunch an existing product or service that's not doing well.
Seek out and use a seed budget to create and pursue a personal idea, product, or service.
Hire/staff a team from outside your unit or organization.
Manage an ad hoc, temporary group of balky and resisting people through an unpopular change or project.
Manage an ad hoc, temporary group including former peers to accomplish a task.
Manage an ad hoc, temporary group of people who are older and/or more experienced to accomplish a task.
Manage an ad hoc, temporary group of people involved in tackling a fix-it or turnaround project.
Handle a tough negotiation with an internal or external client or customer.
Help shut down a plant, regional office, product line, business, operation, etc.
Prepare and present a proposal of some consequence to top management.
Manage a dissatisfied internal or external customer; troubleshoot a performance or quality problem with a product or service.
Manage a group through a significant business crisis.
Take on a tough and undoable project, one where others who have tried it have failed.
Resolve an issue in conflict between two people, units, geographies, functions, etc.

STANDING ALONE

Make peace with an enemy or someone you've disappointed with a product or service or someone you've had some trouble with or don't get along well with.

Do a postmortem on a failed project, and present it to the people involved.

Audit cost overruns to assess the problem, and present your findings to the person or people involved.

Manage a project team of people who are older and more experienced.

3. Best references to ask about or check:

Direct Boss   Human Resource Professionals
Boss' Boss(es)   Past Associates/Constituencies

G. Learning Agility Evaluation:

4. Spectator/Passive vs. Player/Participant
9. Vague/General vs. Sharp/Specific
10. Reactive vs. Initiating
12. Rehearsed/Socially Acceptable vs. Candid
19. External Standards vs. Internal Standards
22. Focus on Accomplishments vs. Focus on Solving Problems

H. The LEADERSHIP ARCHITECT® Sort Card Connections:

1. Good (positive) if combined with high:

Flexible 2, 12, 32, 40, 41
Gets data to make decisions 3, 31, 33
Issues have a firm foundation 5, 22, 24, 46, 61
Gets it done for the customer 9, 15, 16, 37, 63
Takes tough positions on people 13, 25, 56
Ingenious champion 14, 28
Captures meaning; uses it to shift gears 16, 32, 45
Takes on tough development projects 19, 25
Sensitive to others 31, 33, 64
Knows how to couch issues 38, 48
Willing to admit mistakes 44

2. Bad (negative) if combined with low or high (+):

Decides on issues too quickly (+1, 16, 32) 41
Has to work alone 3, 31, 33, 42
Views limited to today's issues 5, 46, 58
Maybe prefers working alone too much 7, 10, 21, 23
Gets in trouble taking stands 8, 38, 48
Pushes on everything too hard (+9, 12, 34)
Folds under pressure; stops after one no 11, 12, 34
Does too much themselves 18, 20
Loner 18, 42, 60
Can't influence others 27, 36, 49, 67
Doesn't get the necessary input 32, 33
May not always pick the right issues 46, 50

STANDING ALONE

3. **Too much can contribute to the following Stallers and Stoppers:**

   A. *What too much looks like (overused):*

   May be a loner and not a good team player or team builder; may not give appropriate credit to others; may be seen as too self-centered; may not wear well over time.

   B. *Too much might lead to these Stallers and Stoppers:*

   Overly Ambitious (103)   Failure to Build a Team (110)
   Blocked Personal Learner (106) Overmanaging (117)

   C. *Compensators:*

   How to compensate for too much of this competency:
   3, 4, 7, 15, 19, 27, 33, 36, 42, 60, 64

   D. *Things to watch for:*

   Doesn't listen   Never asks
   Fights all fights   Rejects others not on the same wavelength
   Fights windmills without Pancho Won't ask for help

4. **Too little can contribute to the following Stallers and Stoppers:**

   A. *What too little looks like (unskilled):*

   Isn't comfortable going it alone; prefers to be in the background; may prefer to be one of many or be part of a team; doesn't take the lead on unpopular stands; doesn't take on controversial issues by themselves; may avoid and shrink from dispute and conflict; may not have a passion, may be burned out.

   B. *Too little might lead to these Stallers and Stoppers:*

   Betrayal of Trust (105)   Failure to Staff Effectively (110)
   Defensiveness (108)   Overdependence on an Advocate (115)
   Lack of Ethics and Values (109)

   C. *Compensators:*

   How to substitute for too little of this competency:
   1, 8, 9, 12, 22, 27, 31, 34, 38, 43, 48, 53

I. **LEARNING ARCHITECT® Connections:**

   Look for people who act like and/or show evidence of:

   1a. Pure Action   7. Risks
   1b. Trial and Error   8. Initiate
   3b. Self-Talk   17. Selected Sources
   3c. Personal Experience   21. Changer
   6. Contentious   38. Resilience

STANDING ALONE

J. CHOICES ARCHITECT® Connections:

Look for people who act like and/or show evidence of:

First Edition (Released 1994)
20. Forging Ahead
21. Taking the Heat

Second Edition (Released 2000)
22. Taking the Heat
23. Visioning
25. Delivers Results
26. Drive
27. Presence

K. Difficulty to Develop:
23 (of 34)–Moderate

58. STRATEGIC AGILITY

A. Definition:

Sees ahead clearly; can anticipate future consequences and trends accurately; has broad knowledge and perspective; is future-oriented; can articulately paint credible pictures and visions of possibilities and likelihoods; can create competitive and breakthrough strategies and plans.

B. Arenas/Domains to Explore:

1. "Future" speeches
2. Academic history
3. Annual plans
4. Anticipating legal consequences
5. Brainstorming possibilities
6. Building alliances
7. Building facilities
8. Building office space
9. Building training curricula
10. Career plans
11. Competitive analysis
12. Conference planning
13. Harvard case studies
14. Investing in new, major equipment
15. Long-term consulting projects
16. Mission/value/vision off-sites
17. Personal financial management
18. Planning mergers/strategic alliances
19. Planning political campaigns
20. Political prognostication
21. Preparing a major legal case
22. Professional association activities
23. Projecting trends
24. Reading habits
25. Reading market trends
26. Running scenarios
27. Setting strategic Intent
28. Starting up a new organization
29. Strategic plans
30. Succession planning
31. Understanding history
32. Working with community organizations

C. Sample Questions:

Dimension 1: Been there, done that–has had direct personal experience(s) involving the competency–candidate was the prime player   Note: * means OK for campus

1. Has anyone ever accused you of messing something up because of poor strategic judgment on your part?
2. Has anyone ever accused you of messing something up because of poor strategic planning?
3. Have you been part of a fix-it or turnaround?
4. Have you been part of a start-up?
5. Have you ever been with an organization where the strategy failed?
6. Have you ever done business in a country with a different political system than your own?
7. Have you ever done business in a foreign country? How was it different?
8. Have you ever done business in Mexico? What was different?
9. Have you ever done work in Canada? How was it different?
10. Have you ever managed anything where the people or units reporting to you were in different locations? How did you design a strategy covering remote locations?
11. Have you ever worked in an international job?
12. Have you served on a strategic taskforce?
13. Have your ideas ever led to a new product or service?
14. How far out do you plan your financial situation?

STRATEGIC AGILITY

15. How many foreign countries have you spent any time in?*
16. How many foreign nationals have you worked with?
17. Tell me about a time when your attempt to be strategic got you into trouble.
18. Tell me about a time when your attempt to be strategic worked really well for you.
19. What was your worst strategic plan that was implemented but didn't work?
20. When you are on a team plotting a new strategy, what role do you usually play?

Dimension 2: Seen/been around others who were involved with the competency–good and bad; learns from others about self

21. Contrast the best and worst strategists you know.*
22. Has strategic planning ever been in any 360° survey done on you? Was your score among your highest, middle, or lowest?
23. Has poor strategic planning on someone else's part ever created an obstacle for you or got in the way of something you were trying to accomplish?*
24. Have you ever talked with a coach or mentor about your strategic planning skills?
25. Have you ever watched someone fail/get fired because they did not have strategic planning skills?*
26. Have you ever watched someone overdo strategic planning to the point that it backfired?
27. Have you ever watched someone succeed because they had strategic planning skills?*
28. Have you ever worked with a coach on strategic planning?*
29. Have you ever worked with a person who excelled at strategic planning?
30. Have you ever worked with a skills coach on strategic planning skills?*
31. How do you get feedback about yourself on strategic skills?
32. How often do you check with multiple sources when you get a piece of critical feedback on your strategic planning skills?
33. Is there a historical figure you consider a model of strategic planning?
34. What do others who are not your fans say about your strategic planning skills?
35. What do others who like you say about your strategic planning skills?
36. Which boss was the best at strategic planning?
37. Which boss was the worst at strategic planning?
38. Which direct report was the best at strategic planning?
39. Which direct report was the worst at strategic planning?
40. Which peer was the best at strategic planning?
41. Which peer was the worst at strategic planning?
42. Who in your field or business is the best strategist?
43. Who do you consider a role model of strategic planning?*
44. Who do you go to for advice on strategic planning?
45. Who have you learned the most from about strategic planning?*
46. Who is a higher-management role model for you on strategic planning?
47. Who is a role model of strategic planning outside of work?

Dimension 3: Knows how the competency works in theory; shows understanding

48. Are there situations or settings where someone should strategize differently?
49. Do you subscribe to *HBR, Fortune, WSJ* or *Business Week?*
50. Do you think strategic planning skills can be learned; how do you think people develop strategic planning skills?
51. Do you think the U.S. government could go bankrupt?*
52. Do you think there is a way to compensate or work around low strategic skills?

STRATEGIC AGILITY

53. Do you think we need a space station?*
54. Early on, computer scientists predicted two to three computers would be able to handle all of the information needs in the U.S.; what didn't they understand?*
55. Has anyone asked you for your opinions/advice on strategic planning?*
56. Have you ever attended a course on strategic planning?
57. Have you ever been in a situation where you and others put strategic planning on a success profile?
58. Have you ever been part of an effort to create a policy or a mission statement containing reference to being strategists?
59. Have you ever been someone's coach or mentor who had problems with strategic skills?
60. Have you ever created a plan for someone on building strategic skills?
61. Have you ever criticized someone for not being strategic?
62. Have you ever designed a program on strategy?
63. Have you ever given a speech on building strategic skills?
64. Have you ever rewarded or recognized someone for having strategic skills?
65. Have you ever taught a course on strategy?
66. Have you ever tried to help someone deal more effectively with building strategic skills?*
67. Have you ever tried to help someone improve their strategic skills?
68. How can one learn about the future?*
69. How do you keep up with consumer trends?
70. How do you think people develop strategic skills?
71. How does doing business around the world differ?
72. How far ahead do you think a typical manager should be able to accurately predict?
73. How much strategic planning ability is good to have and how much is too much?
74. How much of success do you think is due to strategic skills compared with other characteristics?
75. How would you know if someone is bad at strategic planning?
76. How would you know if someone is good at strategic planning?
77. If you had to write a book on strategic planning, what would the chapter headings be?
78. It's five years from now. What will we see geopolitically that impacts your business/field?*
79. Should we spend the money to go to Mars?*
80. Tell me about some interesting facts, trends, anomalies you think have relevance to your field/business/major.*
81. What are one or two things that are going to happen beyond the current year that are going to make a big difference in how we do business?*
82. What are the benefits to someone who is really good at strategic planning?
83. What are the consequences to someone who is really poor at strategic planning?
84. What are three major things that are going to happen in the future that will affect your business?
85. What are your major sources of business information?*
86. What did IBM miss that Dell knew?*
87. What do you think the standard is on strategic planning for someone in your role?
88. What edges do your competitors have long-term?
89. What foreign country will be the strongest in the next three to five years?*
90. What happens if you have or use too much of strategic-planning ability?
91. What happens when two people try to work together who have very different strategic-planning ability?
92. What if all financial transactions were electronic and there was no physical money? What would change?
93. What is it about the future that fascinates you?

STRATEGIC AGILITY

94. What kind of a world will the next generation grow up in?*
95. What wisdom would you pass on to others trying to become better at strategic planning?
96. When you select others, what do you look for in strategic-planning ability?
97. Why do you think people end up being different on strategic-planning ability?
98. Why have GM, Kodak, IBM, Lucent, Sears, and Xerox stumbled?*

Dimension 4: Shows personal change and sense-making; learned it one place and applied it in another; can compare and contrast experiences; changes viewpoints across time; can explain personal development or evolution related to the competency

99. Compare and contrast examples of being effective and ineffective at strategic planning.
100. Contrast your on- and off-the-job use of strategic skills.
101. Did you ever pass up a job or assignment because you were not confident enough in your skills at strategic planning?
102. Do you ever use other skills to cover for your lack of strategic skills?
103. Has becoming better at strategic planning ever helped you in other areas?
104. Has poor strategic planning ever been the subject of a development plan for you?
105. Has your strategic agility always been this way?
106. Have poor strategic-planning skills ever figured in a failure, struggle, or setback you have had?
107. Have you ever attended a speech by a futurist? How did you apply your learning from the speech?
108. Have you ever delegated or assigned someone a task because you didn't do strategic planning particularly well?
109. Have you ever made significant strides at becoming better at strategic planning?
110. Have your strategic skills, good or bad, ever been the subject of your performance review or a career discussion?
111. How can you tell how a trend is going to play out?*
112. How different are you across situations in your strategic skills?
113. How do you decide how strategic to be?
114. How much of your success is due to your strategic skills?
115. How transferable are your strategic skills to other situations?
116. If you had to become better at strategic skills in a hurry, what would you do?
117. Tell me about some strategies that you conceived and implemented. What do they have in common, how are they different, what about them would be repeatable anywhere? How did you think of them? What were your sources?*
118. Was there a time when you were not as good at developing strategy?
119. What caused you to work to improve your skills at strategic planning?
120. What event or series of events had the most impact on your strategic skills?
121. What's the most varied you can be in strategic agility?
122. What was the shortest amount of time in which you increased your level of strategic planning skill?
123. What's your general prediction hit rate out beyond a year or two?
124. When did you first realize your level of skill at strategic planning?
125. When you know ahead of time that your level of strategic skills isn't adequate, what do you do?
126. Why do you think you deal with strategy the way you do?
127. Why do you think your strategic skill is the way it is?*

D. Follow-up Probes:

1. Are there times when you are able to strategize like that and times when you aren't?
2. Could you contrast those two bosses for me?

STRATEGIC AGILITY

3. Could you give me a few examples of how you've used or applied that?
4. Do you always plan strategies like that, or was that a special situation?
5. Do you suppose if others would just try harder, they could learn to be more effective at strategic planning?
6. Do you think that's teachable?
7. Do you think you're better at strategic planning than most? Why?
8. Do you think you would perform any differently if you could be more effective at strategic planning?
9. Have you always done strategic planning that way or is this a recent development in you?
10. How could some very smart people miss the trends?
11. How could someone get better at predicting the future?
12. How did the others react when you did that?
13. How did you come up with that approach to strategic planning in the first place?
14. How did you know that method of getting over that strategic barrier would work?
15. How do others you have known approach that?
16. How likely do you think it is that that will happen?
17. How typical is this for you?
18. How would you approach that same situation today?
19. If that doesn't happen, what else may occur in its place?
20. Is this natural for you, or do you really have to dig for it?
21. Was there a time when you didn't understand this about yourself?
22. What did you do after you got that feedback?
23. What did you do to adapt to that?
24. What did you learn from that?
25. Why did you choose that approach?
26. Why did you decide to take the risk?
27. Why did you do it that way?
28. Why do you think that didn't work?
29. Why do you think that happened that way?
30. Why do you think that worked?
31. Why do you use those sources of information?
32. Why don't you plan further out than that?
33. Why do you think you have difficulty with that sometimes?
34. Would you have done it that way with looser deadlines?
35. Would you have done it that way with tighter deadlines?

E. **Themes/Things to Look for:**
   Ability to realistically project how things are going to play out
   Analyzes successes and failures for clues
   Asks lots of questions
   Can articulate visions
   Can run a trend out to its logical conclusion
   Can run scenarios in their head
   Can run simulations to check downstream consequences
   Capable of creating the big picture
   Change master
   Comfortable doing "what ifs"
   Comfortable estimating/projecting into the future

STRATEGIC AGILITY

Comfortable with complexity
Comfortable with the low hit rate in predicting the future
Deep interest in chosen areas
Drawing parallels from the past
Future sense
Good at doing "if thens"
Has interests outside their home field
Has published views of future
Interest in anomalies/trends/unusual facts
Interest in history of business strategies and their present day outcomes
Interest in world affairs
Likes being a futurist
Likes studying competitors
Loves to explore the new/unique/different/foreign
Makes unusual connections
Many categories and themes
Openness to ways of thinking, unusual opinions
Understands multiple forces
Understands Yin and Yang
Uses multiple sources
Visionary

F. Most Likely Résumé:

1. Look for jobs like:
Heavy Strategic Demands
Line to Staff Switches
Scope (complexity) Assignments

2. Look for develop-in-place assignments like:
Study history and draw parallels for a current business issue or problem, and present your findings to others for comment.
Launch a new product, service, or process.
Relaunch an existing product or service that's not doing well.

3. Best references to ask about or check:

Direct Boss	Natural Mentors
Boss' Boss(es)	Past Associates/Constituencies

G. Learning Agility Evaluation:
1. What/Describing vs. Why/Explain
2. All or Nothing vs. Can See Many Sides
3. Ordinary/Socially Acceptable vs. Insightful/Different
5. Tight/Rigid vs. Loose/Flexible
7. Passive vs. Intrigued/Curious
9. Vague/General vs. Sharp/Specific

STRATEGIC AGILITY

11. Generalizations vs. Specific Learnings
14. Sameness vs. Broad Ranging
15. Linear vs. Use Contrasts/Analogies
16. Few Rules of Thumb vs. Many and Varied Rules of Thumb
18. Stays Close to Home vs. Lots of Curiosity

H. The LEADERSHIP ARCHITECT® Sort Card Connections:

1. Good (positive) if combined with high:
Acts on strategies 1, 9, 16, 28, 57
Can plan out of chaos 2, 40
Practical strategies 5, 15, 24, 46, 50
Takes the politics of the situation into account 8, 38, 48
Fights the tough strategic battles 9, 12, 34, 57
Inventive 14, 28, 30
Good at people strategies 19, 21, 25, 56, 64
Translates strategies into systems 28, 52, 59, 63
Eye on essential detail 35, 39, 47
Can get consensus 36, 42, 60, 65
Can sell strategies 36, 49, 65

2. Bad (negative) if combined with low or high (+):
Strategies not translated into action 1, 16, 53
Uncomfortable with long-term predictions 2, 40, 46
Uses mostly cold sources 3, 31, 33
Strategies limited to functional base 5, 15, 46 (+24, 61)
Strategies may not be realistic for functions to execute (+5, 15, 46) 24, 61
Strategies don't take people into account 7, 10, 21, 23
May avoid tough, strategic battles 12, 13, 34, 37, 57
Has the strategy but can't articulate it 27, 36, 49, 67
Strategies may not take advantage of emerging technologies 30, 32, 61
Strategies not translated into processes 35, 52, 59, 63
Can't get consensus 36, 42, 60
Doesn't take political realities into account 38, 48
Too many strategies; too little focus 47, 50, 52

3. Too much can contribute to the following Stallers and Stoppers:

A. What too much looks like (overused):
May be seen as too theoretical; may not be tolerant of or have patience with day-to-day details; may overcomplicate plans; may not be able to communicate with tactical or less complex people.

B. Too much might lead to these Stallers and Stoppers:
Being a Poor Administrator (102)   Performance Problems (118)

C. Compensators:
How to compensate for too much of this competency:
5, 16, 17, 24, 27, 35, 38, 39, 46, 47, 50, 52, 53, 59, 61, 63

STRATEGIC AGILITY

D. Things to watch for:

Creates anxiety in those with limited view	Not good executing today's tasks
Hard to find people to talk to	Rejects the strategic views of others
Loses others when talking about the future	Spends time planning for things that will never be

4. Too little can contribute to the following Stallers and Stoppers:

A. What too little looks like (unskilled):

Doesn't think or talk strategy; can't put together a compelling strategic plan; more comfortable in the tactical here and now; lacks the perspective to pull together varying elements into a coherent strategic view; can't weave a vision of the future; may reject the usefulness of strategy, considering it pie in the sky; may have narrow experience and not be knowledgeable of business and world events; may try to simplify too much or be very tactical; may lack the disciplined thought processes necessary to construct a strategic view.

B. Too little might lead to these Stallers and Stoppers:

Unable to Adapt to Differences (101)	Failure to Build a Team (110)
Blocked Personal Learner (106)	Non-Strategic (114)
Lack of Composure (107)	Performance Problems (118)
Political Missteps (119)	

C. Compensators:

How to substitute for too little of this competency:
5, 14, 17, 24, 28, 30, 32, 46, 47, 50, 61, 65

I. LEARNING ARCHITECT® Connections:

Look for people who act like and/or show evidence of:

2a. Problem Solving	11. Why/How
2b. Visioning	12. Rules of Thumb
2c. Intuition	27. Conceptualizer
3c. Personal Experience	28. Creator
4a. Getting Information	35. Breadth
9. Multiple Sources	

J. CHOICES ARCHITECT® Connections:

Look for people who act like and/or show evidence of:

First Edition (Released 1994)	Second Edition (Released 2000)
1. Inquisitive	1. Broad Scanner
2. Essence	2. Complexity
4. Complexity	3. Connector
5. Connector	4. Critical Thinker
6. Visionary	6. Essence
16. Cold/Indirect Sources	7. Inquisitive

K. Difficulty to Develop:

28 (of 34)–Harder

59. MANAGING THROUGH SYSTEMS

A. Definition:

Can design practices, processes, and procedures which allow managing from a distance; is comfortable letting things manage themselves without intervening; can make things work through others without being there; can impact people and results remotely.

B. Arenas/Domains to Explore:

1. Arranging an international tour
2. Arranging an international visit
3. Arranging major meeting across organizations
4. Building a facility
5. Building a home
6. Building office space
7. Computerized scheduling systems
8. Creating the rules of the road
9. Customer service monitoring
10. Delegating major tasks with only periodic checking-in
11. Designing monitoring software
12. Designing multiple event series
13. Establishing multiple unit practices/processes
14. Geographically spread units
15. Implementing audit programs
16. Installing a common system across countries
17. Lending your resources to another manager
18. Managing a fund drive
19. Managing a political campaign
20. Managing distributors
21. Managing renovations
22. Managing sales representatives
23. Managing volunteers
24. Preparing legislation
25. Preparing mission/vision/value document
26. Preparing regulations
27. Remote control systems
28. Remote event planning
29. Sending a delegate
30. Working in corporations with strong divisions
31. Working through others
32. Working with vendors/suppliers
33. Working with consultants
34. Writing a speech to be delivered by multiple people

C. Sample Questions:

Dimension 1: Been there, done that–has had direct personal experience(s) involving the competency–candidate was the prime player   Note: * means OK for campus

1. At what point in your career did you start to manage people you have never met personally?
2. At what point in your career did you start to put policies and practices in writing in addition to communicating them yourself?
3. Has anyone ever accused you of messing something up because of a lack of remote management systems?
4. Have you ever designed a software program to remotely monitor anything?
5. Have you ever had to implement a new system somewhere without physically going there?
6. Have you ever implemented a system designed to capture data remotely about how things were going?
7. Have you ever made a videotape that was used to communicate to a broad audience without you ever being there?
8. Have you ever managed anything where the people or units reporting to you were in different locations? How did you manage them from afar?
9. Have you ever managed anything where the people or units reporting to you were in different countries?
10. Have you ever managed anything where the people or units reporting to you were in different cities?

MANAGING THROUGH SYSTEMS

11. Have you ever managed anything where the people or units reporting to you were in different buildings?
12. How do you detect the need to increase or decrease formal policies, practices and procedures?
13. How do you keep yourself from intervening too quickly when something slips?
14. How much do you enjoy doing the hands-on work as opposed to letting others who are under your supervision, do the work?
15. If you were on vacation or out of touch, how would your people know what to do in a crisis?
16. Tell me about a few times when delegating really paid off for you.
17. Tell me about a time when delegating led to some bad outcomes.
18. Tell me about a time when you became too hands-on and had to let go.*
19. Tell me about a time when you had to figure how to get your message across to remote locations without going there.*
20. Tell me about a time when you installed a new system.*
21. Tell me about a time when you moved into a job (took on a project) that was too big for you to get your arms around.*
22. Tell me about a time when you moved into a job where the work processes/ systems/work groups were messed up and had to be fixed.*
23. Tell me about a time when you set up something that was self-managing.*
24. Tell me about a time when you used delegation or stayed away from a problem to help develop a person.
25. Tell me about a time where something you thought was being managed got out of control, and you found out about it too late.
26. What process do you follow to update policies, practices and procedures?
27. What proportion of the people who report to you can safely be delegated to?

Dimension 2: Seen/been around others who were involved with the competency–good and bad; learns from others about self

28. Contrast the best and worst people you know at managing remotely or from a distance.*
29. Has managing remotely or from a distance ever been in any 360º survey done on you? Was your score among your highest, middle, or lowest?
30. Has inability to manage people remotely on someone else's part ever created an obstacle for you or got in the way of something you were trying to accomplish?*
31. Have you ever talked with a coach or mentor about your remote management skills?
32. Have you ever watched someone fail/get fired because they did not manage well from a distance?*
33. Have you ever watched someone overmanage from a distance to the point that it backfired?
34. Have you ever watched someone succeed because they managed well without being there personally?*
35. Have you ever worked with a coach on managing remotely?*
36. Have you ever worked with a person who excelled at managing remotely or from a distance?
37. Have you ever worked with a skills coach on remote management skills?*
38. How do you get feedback about yourself on your ability to manage remotely?
39. How often do you check with multiple sources when you get a piece of critical feedback on your remote management skills?
40. Is there a historical figure you consider a model of managing remotely?
41. What do others who are not your fans say about your ability to manage remotely?
42. What do others who like you say about your ability to manage remotely?
43. Which boss was the best at managing remotely?
44. Which boss was the worst at managing remotely?

MANAGING THROUGH SYSTEMS

45. Which direct report was the best at managing remotely?
46. Which direct report was the worst at managing remotely?
47. Which peer was the best at managing remotely?
48. Which peer was the worst at managing remotely?
49. Who in your field or business is the best at managing remotely or from a distance?
50. Who do you consider a role model of managing remotely?*
51. Who do you go to for advice on managing remotely?
52. Who have you learned the most from about managing remotely?*
53. Who is a higher-management role model for you on managing remotely?
54. Who is a role model of managing remotely outside of work?

Dimension 3: Knows how the competency works in theory; shows understanding

55. Are there situations or settings where someone should be different on managing remotely or from a distance?
56. Do you think remote-management skills can be learned; how do you think people develop remote-management skills?
57. Do you think there is a way to compensate or work around low remote-management skills?
58. Has anyone asked you for your opinions/advice on managing remotely?*
59. Have you ever attended a course on managing remotely?
60. Have you ever been in a situation where you and others put managing remotely or from a distance on a success profile?
61. Have you ever been part of an effort to create a policy or a mission statement containing reference to managing remotely or from a distance?
62. Have you ever been someone's coach or mentor who had problems with managing remotely or from a distance?
63. Have you ever created a development plan for someone on managing remotely or from a distance?
64. Have you ever criticized someone for not managing well remotely or from a distance?
65. Have you ever designed a program on managing well remotely or from a distance?
66. Have you ever given a speech on managing well remotely or from a distance?
67. Have you ever rewarded or recognized someone for managing well remotely or from a distance?
68. Have you ever taught a course on managing well remotely or from a distance?
69. Have you ever tried to help someone deal more effectively managing well remotely or from a distance?*
70. Have you ever tried to help someone improve their skills at managing remotely or from a distance?
71. How do you think people develop the ability to manage remotely or from a distance?
72. How much ability to manage remotely or from a distance is good to have and how much is too much?
73. How much of success do you think is due to managing well remotely or from a distance compared with other characteristics?
74. How would you know if someone is bad at managing remotely or from a distance?
75. How would you know if someone is good at managing from a distance or managing remotely?
76. If you had to write a book on managing well remotely or from a distance, what would the chapter headings be?
77. What are the benefits to someone who is really good at managing remotely or from a distance?
78. What are the consequences to someone who is really poor at managing remotely or from a distance?
79. What do you think the standard is on managing remotely or from a distance for someone in your role?
80. What happens if you have too much ability to manage remotely or from a distance?

MANAGING THROUGH SYSTEMS

81. What happens when two people try to work together who have very different methods of managing remotely or from a distance?
82. What wisdom would you pass onto others trying to become better at managing remotely or from a distance?
83. When you select others, what do you look for in the ability to manage remotely or from a distance?
84. Why do you think people end up being different in their ability to manage remotely or from a distance?

Dimension 4: Shows personal change and sense-making; learned it one place and applied it in another; can compare and contrast experiences; changes viewpoints across time; can explain personal development or evolution related to the competency

85. Compare and contrast examples of being effective and ineffective at managing from a distance or managing remotely.
86. Contrast remote monitoring systems that work with those that don't.
87. Contrast your on- and off-the-job use of managing through systems.
88. Did you ever pass up a job or assignment because you were not confident enough in your skills at managing remotely?
89. Do you ever use other skills to cover for your lack of remote management skills?
90. Has a system for remote management ever figured in a failure, struggle, or setback you have had?
91. Has becoming better at managing from a distance ever helped you in other areas?
92. Has poor remote-management system design ever been the subject of a development plan for you?
93. Has your design of remote-management systems always been this way?
94. Have you ever delegated or assigned someone a task because you didn't manage from a distance particularly well?
95. Have you ever made significant strides at becoming better at remote management system design and use?
96. Have your remote-management skills, good or bad, ever been the subject of your performance review or a career discussion?
97. How different are you across situations in your remote-management system design and use?
98. How do you decide what kinds of remote-management systems are needed?
99. How much of your success is due to your design of systems for remote management?
100. How transferable are your remote-management system skills to other situations?
101. If you had to become better at remote-management in a hurry, what would you do?
102. Was there a time when you were not as good at remote-management system design?
103. What adjustments have you made to more effectively deal with virtual employees/customers/peers, etc.?
104. What caused you to work to improve your skills at managing remotely or from a distance?
105. What event or series of events had the most impact on your remote management system design skills?
106. What's the most varied you can be in managing through remote systems?
107. What was the shortest amount of time in which you increased your level of skill at managing from a distance?
108. When did you first realize your level of skill at remote-management system design?
109. When you know ahead of time that your level of skill in remote-management system design isn't adequate, what do you do?
110. Why do you think you deal with remote-management systems the way you do?
111. Why do you think your remote-management system design skill is the way it is?*

MANAGING THROUGH SYSTEMS

D. Follow-up Probes:

1. Are there times when you were willing to manage remotely like that and times when you were not?
2. Could you contrast those two bosses for me?
3. Could you give me a few examples of how you've used or applied that?
4. Did you have trouble sleeping knowing that somewhere out there people were against executing your processes and systems?
5. Do you always manage remotely like that or was that a special situation?
6. Do you have some general rules for when you do it that way?
7. Do you prefer personally being there to managing remotely?
8. Do you suppose if others would just try harder, they could learn to be more effective at managing remotely like you do?
9. Do you think that's teachable?
10. Do you think you're better at managing remotely than most? Why?
11. Do you think you would perform any differently if you could be more effective at managing through remote systems rather than having to be there personally all the time?
12. Have you always understood how to manage from afar, or is this a recent development in you?
13. How comfortable were you with how things were going even though you weren't there yourself?
14. How did the others react when you did that?
15. How did you come up with that approach to managing through remote systems in the first place?
16. How did you know that method of getting things done through remote management would work?
17. How do others you have known approach that?
18. How typical is this for you?
19. How would you approach that same situation today?
20. If you are not there personally, what's missing?
21. Is this natural for you, or do you really have to dig for it?
22. Was there a time when you didn't understand this about yourself?
23. What did you do after you got that feedback?
24. What did you do to adapt to that?
25. What did you learn from that?
26. Why did you choose that approach?
27. Why did you decide to take the risk?
28. Why did you do it that way?
29. Why did you time your application of remote management like that?
30. Why do you think that's easier to do than most?
31. Why do you think that didn't work?
32. Why do you think that happened that way?
33. Why do you think that worked?
34. Why do you think you have difficulties with that sometimes?
35. Would you have done it that way with looser deadlines?
36. Would you have done it that way with tighter deadlines?

MANAGING THROUGH SYSTEMS

E. Themes/Things to Look for:

Ability to manage simultaneous projects
Able to break complex tasks down into steps
Able to estimate how long things should take
Able to have high impact on short visit
An early-knower
Articulate directions/instructions
Can see multiple connections
Clear areas of responsibility
Committed to incremental improvement
Complex and varied ways to get something done
Detailing what requires their involvement and what doesn't
Good writing skills
Having fail-safes
High involvement on parameters, specified exceptions, outcomes; hands-off on most other matters
Keeping people well informed
Knowing what leads to what; how things really work
Knowing when to personally intervene
Knows systems theory
Letting go
Orderly/logical
Precise use of words
Provides timely feedback to people
Reading signs/trends
Running process simulations in their head
Setting up communications loops
Sharing the bigger picture
Staying informed
Timely decision maker
Trust in others
Willing to define only the outcomes; not methods
Willing to empower
Willing to take risks
Willingness to delegate

F. Most Likely Résumé:

1. Look for jobs like:
Line to Staff Switches   Significant People Demands
Scale (size shift) Assignments   Staff Leadership (Influencing Without Authority)

2. Look for develop-in-place assignments like:
Integrate diverse systems, processes, or procedures across decentralized and/or dispersed units.
Manage something "remote", away from your location.
Assign a project to a group with a tight deadline.

MANAGING THROUGH SYSTEMS

Manage an ad hoc, temporary group of people in a stable and static operation.
Manage an ad hoc, temporary group of people in a rapidly expanding operation.
Help shut down a plant, regional office, product line, business, operation, etc.

3. Best references to ask about or check:
Human Resource Professionals
Direct Reports

G. Learning Agility Evaluation:
5. Tight/Rigid vs. Loose/Flexible
6. Reacting/Responsive vs. Adapting
11. Generalizations vs. Specific Learnings
15. Linear vs. Use Contrasts/Analogies
16. Few Rules of Thumb vs. Many and Varied Rules of Thumb
19. External Standards vs. Internal Standards

H. The LEADERSHIP ARCHITECT® Sort Card Connections:

1. Good (positive) if combined with high:
Gets input into systems 3, 31, 33
Work on the right systems 5, 17, 46, 50
Systems very practical 5, 15, 24, 53
Systems take people into consideration 7, 10, 21, 23
Takes on the tough challenges for systems 12, 13, 34, 57
Continuous improvement 14, 28, 63
Astonishing process manager 18, 20, 35, 39, 47, 52
Can sell in the system 27, 36, 49, 65
Systems take political realities into account 38, 48
Systems designed for the long run 46, 58, 65

2. Bad (negative) if combined with low or high (+):
Too remote 3, 31, 42, 60
System may not be practical 5, 15, 35, 52, 53
Doesn't consider people in the system 7, 10, 21, 23
Can't overcome resistance 12, 34, 57
Systems not very innovative 14, 28
May apply system resources to wrong problem 17, 50, 51
Systems may not take advantage of the latest technology 30, 46, 61
Can't sell in the system 31, 42, 48, 60
System may not take political realities into account 38, 48
System not very efficient 39, 47, 62, 63
System lacks long-term payback 46, 58, 65
Misreads people's capabilities 56, 64

MANAGING THROUGH SYSTEMS

3. **Too much can contribute to the following Stallers and Stoppers:**

    A. *What too much looks like (overused):*

    May be too hard to reach and talk to, out of touch with the details; may get too comfortable having things run on autopilot; may get surprised by negative events; may be slow to change existing systems.

    B. *Too much might lead to these Stallers and Stoppers:*

Arrogant (104)	Failure to Build a Team (110)
Lack of Composure (107)	Non-Strategic (114)

    C. *Compensators:*

    How to compensate for too much of this competency:
    3, 10, 12, 14, 15, 21, 23, 31, 33, 36, 44, 60, 64

    D. *Things to watch for:*

Doesn't check in often enough	Trusts others too much
Goes overboard on delegating	Gets surprised by reactions to systems
Hard to tell what work they do	Blindsided by unanticipated consequences
May not be comfortable with extended contact	

4. **Too little can contribute to the following Stallers and Stoppers:**

    A. *What too little looks like (unskilled):*

    Prefers hands on management; relies on personal intervention; has to physically be there for things to go well; doesn't think or manage in terms of policies, practices, and systems; doesn't delegate much; doesn't really believe people can perform on their own; doesn't set up rules, procedures, and tie breakers so people know what to do in his/her absence; may be very controlling and a micromanager; may not communicate clearly enough for people to know what to do without repeated inquiries of him/her.

    B. *Too little might lead to these Stallers and Stoppers:*

Being a Poor Administrator (102)	Performance Problems (118)
Failure to Build a Team (110)	

    C. *Compensators:*

    How to substitute for too little of this competency:
    18, 20, 27, 35, 39, 47, 52

I. LEARNING ARCHITECT® Connections:

Look for people who act like and/or show evidence of:

1c. Following a Plan	12. Rules of Thumb
2b. Visioning	15. Cautious
4c. Actively Involve	23. Orchestrator

J. CHOICES ARCHITECT® Connections:

Look for people who act like and/or show evidence of:

First Edition (Released 1994)	Second Edition (Released 2000)
4. Complexity	2. Complexity

K. Difficulty to Develop:

28 (of 34)–Harder

60. BUILDING EFFECTIVE TEAMS

A. Definition:

Blends people into teams when needed; creates strong morale and spirit in his/her team; shares wins and successes; fosters open dialogue; lets people finish and be responsible for their work; defines success in terms of the whole team; creates a feeling of belonging in the team.

B. Arenas/Domains to Explore:

1. Any supervisory event
2. Athletic team captains
3. Audit teams
4. Case study breakout groups
5. Club/professional association leadership
6. Coaching sports
7. Committee head
8. Conference chair
9. Consulting team
10. Coordinating across boundaries
11. Cross-unit grant proposal
12. Different team-building settings
13. During crises
14. Fix-its
15. Fraternity/sorority leadership
16. Fund-raising
17. Joint sales/marketing calls
18. Joint product/service promotions
19. Jury foreperson
20. Managing volunteers
21. Meeting facilitation
22. Military command experience
23. Motivating vendors/suppliers
24. Onerous tasks
25. Political campaigns
26. Project teams
27. Start-ups
28. Student government
29. Study groups
30. With direct reports
31. Task with impossible deadlines
32. Task forces
33. Teaching
34. United Way
35. Using resources that aren't your own
36. With peers/colleagues
37. Working with unions

C. Sample Questions:

Dimension 1: Been there, done that–has had direct personal experience(s) involving the competency–candidate was the prime player   Note: * means OK for campus

1. Do you interact with members of your team off-work?
2. Has anyone ever accused you of messing something up because you didn't build a team?
3. Have teams you managed won awards?
4. Have you ever been a member of a team with very low morale? Why was that?*
5. Have you ever been on a team with astonishing morale? Why was that?*
6. Have you ever managed anything where the people or units reporting to you were in different locations? How did you manage morale?
7. Have you ever managed anything where the team reporting to you was in different countries? How did you maintain good morale?
8. How do you celebrate successes with your team?*
9. How do you create the feeling that we are all in this together?*
10. How do you delegate important tasks?*

BUILDING EFFECTIVE TEAMS

11. How do you let people know that you are open to input?*
12. How hard is it to get internal people to join your team?
13. Over time, what percent of your team gets promoted?
14. Over time, what percent of your team turns over?
15. Tell me about a time when you became too hands-on and had to let go and let the team do more.*
16. Tell me about a time when you had to revitalize a stagnant team.*
17. Tell me about a time when you hired many or most of your team yourself.
18. Tell me about a time when you managed a team during a downsizing.
19. Tell me about a time when you managed a team during a fix-it.
20. Tell me about a time when you managed a team during a start-up.
21. Tell me about a time when you managed a team where they were the experts and you knew little.*
22. Tell me about a time when you managed a team where you were the expert and they knew little.*
23. Tell me about a time when you used delegation as a tool to motivate.
24. Tell me about a time when your attempt to team build got you into trouble.
25. Tell me about a time when your attempt to team build worked really well for you.
26. Were you an officer in the military?
27. Were you ever elected captain or head of a group?
28. Were you ever elected captain or head of an athletic team?
29. What do you do when the team doesn't want to do something you want them to do?*
30. What do you do when the team rejects a new member?*
31. What do you do with the one bad apple on the team whose skills you need?*
32. When you are working in a team of peers, what role do you usually play?*

Dimension 2: Seen/been around others who were involved with the competency–good and bad; learns from others about self

33. Contrast the most and least effective team builders you know.*
34. Has team building ever been in any 360° survey done on you? Was your score among your highest, middle, or lowest?
35. Has poor team building on someone else's part ever created an obstacle for you or got in the way of something you were trying to accomplish?*
36. Have you ever talked with a coach or mentor about your team-building skills?
37. Have you ever watched someone fail/get fired because they did not build effective teams?*
38. Have you ever watched someone overdo team building to the point that it backfired?
39. Have you ever watched someone succeed because they built effective teams?*
40. Have you ever worked with a coach on team-building skills?*
41. Have you ever worked with a person who excelled at team building?
42. Have you ever worked with a skills coach on team-building skills?*
43. How do you get feedback about yourself on team-building skills?
44. How often do you check with multiple sources when you get a piece of critical feedback on your team-building skills?
45. Is there a historical figure you consider a model of building effective teams?
46. What do others who are not your fans say about your team-building skills?
47. What do others who like you say about your team-building skills?
48. Which boss was the best at building effective teams?
49. Which boss was the worst at building effective teams?
50. Which direct report was the best at building effective teams?

BUILDING EFFECTIVE TEAMS

51. Which direct report was the worst at building effective teams?
52. Which peer was the best at building effective teams?
53. Which peer was the worst at building effective teams?
54. Who in your field or business is the best at building effective teams?
55. Who do you consider a role model of team-building skills?*
56. Who do you go to for advice on building effective teams?
57. Who have you learned the most from about building effective teams?*
58. Who is a higher-management role model for you on building effective teams?
59. Who is a role model of team-building skills outside of work?

Dimension 3: Knows how the competency works in theory; shows understanding
60. Are most things or tasks better done in teams?*
61. Are there situations or settings where someone should use different team-building skills?
62. Do you think team-building skills can be learned; how do you think people develop team-building skills?
63. Do you think there is a way to compensate or work around low team-building skills?
64. Does high morale correlate with high production?*
65. Has anyone asked you for your opinions/advice on building effective teams?*
66. Have you ever attended a course on building effective teams?
67. Have you ever been in a situation where you and others put team-building skills on a success profile?
68. Have you ever been part of an effort to create a policy or a mission statement containing reference to building effective teams?
69. Have you ever been someone's coach or mentor who had problems with building effective teams?
70. Have you ever created a development plan for someone on building effective teams?
71. Have you ever criticized someone for not building effective teams?
72. Have you ever designed a program on building effective teams?
73. Have you ever given a speech on building effective teams?
74. Have you ever rewarded or recognized someone for building effective teams?
75. Have you ever taught a course on building effective teams?
76. Have you ever tried to help someone deal more effectively with building effective teams?*
77. Have you ever tried to help someone improve their skill at building effective teams?
78. How do you think people develop the skills to build effective teams?
79. How much team building ability is good to have and how much is too much?
80. How much of success do you think is due to building effective teams compared with other characteristics?
81. How would you know if someone is bad at building effective teams?
82. How would you know if someone is good at building effective teams?
83. If you had to write a book on building effective teams, what would the chapter headings be?
84. What are the benefits to someone who is really good at building effective teams?
85. What are the consequences to someone who is really poor at building effective teams?
86. What do you think the standard is on building effective teams for someone in your role?
87. What happens if you have or use too many team-building skills?
88. What happens when two people try to work together who have very different team-building skills?
89. What wisdom would you pass on to others trying to become better at building effective teams?
90. When you have an opening on your team, how do you determine the specifications of who you are looking for?
91. When you select others, what do you look for in team-building skills?
92. Why do you think people end up being different in their ability to build effective teams?

BUILDING EFFECTIVE TEAMS

Dimension 4: Shows personal change and sense-making; learned it one place and applied it in another; can compare and contrast experiences; changes viewpoints across time; can explain personal development or evolution related to the competency

93. Compare and contrast examples of being effective and ineffective at team building.
94. Compare leading a team in a crisis with leading a team during calmer times.
95. Contrast team building techniques that work with those that don't.*
96. Contrast your on- and off-the-job use of team-building skills.
97. Did you ever pass up a job or assignment because you were not confident enough in your skills at team building?
98. Do you ever use other skills to cover for your lack of team-building skills?
99. Do you prefer to work alone or in teams?*
100. Do you tend to be the kind of person who treats all people on your team equally?
101. Has becoming better at team building ever helped you in other areas?
102. Has not building effective teams ever figured in a failure, struggle, or setback you have had?
103. Has poor team building ever been the subject of a development plan for you?
104. Has your ability to build effective teams always been this way?
105. Have you ever delegated or assigned someone a task because you didn't build a team particularly well?
106. Have you ever made significant strides at becoming better at team building?
107. Have your team-building skills, good or bad, ever been the subject of your performance review or a career discussion?
108. How different are you across situations in your ability to build effective teams?
109. How do you balance individual and team needs?*
110. How do you build a team containing very different levels of competence?*
111. How do you build a team containing very different personalities?*
112. How do you decide how much team building to do?
113. How much of your success is due to your ability to build effective teams?
114. How transferable are your team-building skills to other situations?
115. How would you describe the atmosphere in teams you have managed?
116. If you had to become better at building effective teams in a hurry, what would you do?
117. Was there a time when you were not as good at building effective teams?
118. What caused you to work to improve your skills at building effective teams?
119. What event or series of events had the most impact on your ability to build effective teams?
120. What's the most varied you can be in building effective teams?
121. What was the shortest amount of time in which you increased your level of skill at building a team?
122. When did you first realize your level of skill at building effective teams?
123. When you know ahead of time that your usual way of team building won't work, what do you do?
124. Why do you think you deal with building effective teams the way you do?
125. Why do you think your ability to build effective teams is the way it is?*

BUILDING EFFECTIVE TEAMS

D. Follow-up Probes:
1. Are there times when you use your team-building skills like that and times when you don't?
2. Could you contrast those two bosses for me?
3. Could you give me a few examples of how you've used or applied that?
4. Do you always team build in situations like that, or was that a special situation?
5. Do you suppose if others would just try harder, they could learn to be more effective at team building like you?
6. Do you think that's teachable?
7. Do you think you have better team-building skills than most? Why?
8. Do you think you would perform any differently if you could be more effective at building teams?
9. Have you always built teams that way or is this a recent development in you?
10. Have you ever had to build a team out of people you really disliked?
11. How did the others react when you did that?
12. How did you come up with that approach to building teams in the first place?
13. How did you know that method of building the team would work?
14. How do others you have known approach that?
15. How do you feel about a team if they need to be motivated before they will perform well?
16. How do you know when the effort isn't worth it?
17. How typical is this for you?
18. How would you approach that same situation today?
19. Is this natural for you, or do you really have to dig for it?
20. Was there a time when you didn't understand this about yourself?
21. What did you do after you got that feedback?
22. What did you do to adapt to that?
23. What did you learn from that?
24. Why did you choose that approach?
25. Why did you decide to take the risk?
26. Why did you do it that way?
27. Why did you think it was important to build up the team instead of just managing individuals one-on-one?
28. Why did you time your attempt to build the morale of the team like that?
29. Why do you suppose teams work that way?
30. Why do you think that didn't work?
31. Why do you think that happened that way?
32. Why do you think that worked?
33. Why do you think you have difficulty with that sometimes?
34. Would you have done it that way with looser deadlines?
35. Would you have done it that way with tighter deadlines?

BUILDING EFFECTIVE TEAMS

E. Themes/Things to Look for:

A feel about how people are impacted by processes	Finding points of agreement
A range of approaches to use to build the team	Generosity
Ability to motivate others	Giving room for growth
Ability to predict how people are going to react	Good couching skills
Ability to relieve tensions	Good teacher/instructor
Able to find common ground	Lets others save face
Able to take the heat	Listening skills
Appreciation of due process	Lots of specifics
Awareness of impact on others	Open to disagreement
Being approachable	Patience
Belief in equitable treatment	Seeing differences; one size does not fit all
Can keep personal feelings from getting in the way	Sense of purpose
Ceremonies; promoting feelings of belonging	Sensitive to what people are good at
Checking in with people often	Sharing credit
Clear communicator	Straight with others
Communicating the larger picture	Tolerance of diversity of views
Different tactics in different settings; doesn't describe teams as "all the same"	Trusting others
	Willingness to delegate
Empowerment	Willingness to share thoughts
Fairness and candor	Win/win skills

F. Most Likely Résumé:

1. Look for jobs like:

Fix-Its/Turnarounds   Significant People Demands
Scale (size shift) Assignments   Start-Ups

2. Look for develop-in-place assignments like:

Create employee involvement teams.

Manage an ad hoc, temporary group of "green," inexperienced people as their coach, teacher, orienter, etc.

Manage an ad hoc, temporary group of balky and resisting people through an unpopular change or project.

Manage an ad hoc, temporary group including former peers to accomplish a task.

Manage an ad hoc, temporary group of people who are older and/or more experienced to accomplish a task.

Manage an ad hoc, temporary group of people where the temporary manager is a towering expert and the people in the group are not.

Manage an ad hoc, temporary group of people where the people in the group are towering experts but the temporary manager is not.

Manage an ad hoc, temporary group of people involved in tackling a fix-it or turnaround project.

Assemble an ad hoc team of diverse people to accomplish a difficult task.

Manage a project team of people who are older and more experienced.

3. Best references to ask about or check:

Human Resource Professionals

Past Associates/Constituencies

Direct Reports

BUILDING EFFECTIVE TEAMS

G. **Learning Agility Evaluation:**
   4. Spectator/Passive vs. Player/Participant
   5. Tight/Rigid vs. Loose/Flexible
   6. Reacting/Responsive vs. Adapting
   9. Vague/General vs. Sharp/Specific
   10. Reactive vs. Initiating
   11. Generalizations vs. Specific Learnings
   13. Simple Views vs. Complex Views
   15. Linear vs. Use Contrasts/Analogies
   21. View from Self vs. View from Point of View of Others

H. **The LEADERSHIP ARCHITECT® Sort Card Connections:**

   1. **Good (positive) if combined with high:**
      Gets input from the team 3, 31, 33
      Can team build with higher levels 4, 8 , 48
      Only uses teams when appropriate 5, 24, 46, 53
      Caring for all team members 7, 10
      Tough when necessary 9, 13, 34, 57
      Doesn't lose individual focus 18, 19, 20, 36
      Fair across the team 21, 22, 23
      Assembles a diverse team 21, 25
      Selects the right people for the team 25, 56
      Can relieve team tensions 26
      Can sell a vision and build a sense of team 38, 42, 49, 65
      Can team build across boundaries 38, 48
      Uses sound team processes 39, 47, 52
      Can team build with peers 42
      Reads team members accurately 56, 64

   2. **Bad (negative) if combined with low or high (+):**
      Takes too long to get things done through team 1, 16, 50, 62
      Doesn't get enough input from the team 3, 31, 33
      Not really interested in the people 7, 10, 21, 23
      Team building too one way (+9, 12, 13, 20, 35, 36, 53)
      Doesn't handle team tension well 12, 13, 26, 34, 57
      Team may not be very diverse 21
      Selects the wrong mix of people 25, 56, 64
      Doesn't set high enough standards for the team 35, 53
      Doesn't install good process in the team 39, 47, 52

   3. **Too much can contribute to the following Stallers and Stoppers:**

      A. *What too much looks like (overused):*

      May not treat others as unique individuals; may slow down reasonable process by having everything open for debate; may go too far in not hurting people's feelings and not making tough decisions; may not develop individual leaders; might not provide take-charge leadership during tough times.

BUILDING EFFECTIVE TEAMS

B. Too much might lead to these Stallers and Stoppers:
Failure to Staff Effectively (111)

C. Compensators:
How to compensate for too much of this competency:
9, 12, 13, 18, 19, 20, 21, 34, 36, 56, 57, 64

D. Things to watch for:
Always settles on vanilla so no one gets hurt
Holds back the good people waiting for the incompetent to catch up
Takes in too much input; afraid to make a decision
Takes too long to get things done
Too much of a cheerleader
Uses teams for too many tasks
Uses the team to avoid individual responsibility

4. Too little can contribute to the following Stallers and Stoppers:

A. What too little looks like (unskilled):
Doesn't assemble, build or manage in a team fashion; manages people on a one-to-one basis; doesn't create a common mindset or common challenge; rewards and compliments individuals, not the team; may not hold many team meetings; doesn't create any synergies in the team; everyone works on his/her own projects; doesn't manage in a way that builds team morale or energy; doesn't have the skills or interest to build a team; may be very action and control-oriented, and won't trust a team to perform.

B. Too little might lead to these Stallers and Stoppers:
Overly Ambitious (103)	Insensitive to Others (112)
Arrogant (104)	Overmanaging (117)
Failure to Build a Team (110)	Political Missteps (119)

C. Compensators:
How to substitute for too little of this competency:
3, 7, 18, 36, 39, 42, 52, 63

I. LEARNING ARCHITECT® Connections:
Look for people who act like and/or show evidence of:

3b. Self-Talk	16. Collaborate
4a. Getting Information	23. Orchestrator
4c. Actively Involve	

J. CHOICES ARCHITECT® Connections:
Look for people who act like and/or show evidence of:

First Edition (Released 1994)	Second Edition (Released 2000)
14. Transaction Quality	9. Agile Communicator
15. Helps Others Succeed	10. Conflict Manager
	12. Helps Others Succeed
	24. Inspires Others

K. Difficulty to Develop:
29 (of 34)–Harder

61. TECHNICAL LEARNING

A. Definition:

Picks up on technical things quickly; can learn new skills and knowledge; is good at learning new industry, company, product, or technical knowledge developments such as e-commerce; does well in technical courses and seminars.

B. Arenas/Domains to Explore:

1. Academic background
2. Adult toys
3. Can program their VCR
4. Can run audio/visual equipment
5. Computer literacy
6. Conference/trade show attendance
7. Family occupational history
8. Formal technical knowledge/skills
9. Handiness
10. Has a cellular phone
11. Has a laptop
12. Has done video conference
13. Learning new technical systems
14. Magazine/journal subscriptions
15. Mechanical ability
16. Military training
17. Patents/trademarks/copyrights
18. Professional memberships
19. Reading habits
20. Technical hobbies
21. Technical mentors
22. Technical publications
23. Technical speeches
24. The internet
25. TV watching choices
26. Workshops attended

C. Sample Questions:

Dimension 1: Been there, done that–has had direct personal experience(s) involving the competency–candidate was the prime player   Note: * means OK for campus

1. Are you very mechanical?*
2. Do you enjoy figuring out how things work under the hood or inside the box, or do you just like to use it?*
3. Do you fix things yourself?*
4. Has anyone ever accused you of messing something up because you didn't learn a new technology, like using the Internet?
5. Have you ever crashed a computer system by doing something you shouldn't have done?*
6. Have you ever implemented a technical system designed to capture data remotely about how things were going?
7. Have you ever made a videotape teaching a new technology?
8. Have you ever managed anything where the technology people or units reporting to you were using in different locations was different? How did you keep them up to date on various technologies?
9. How proven does a new technology have to be to gain your support for spending?
10. Tell me about a time when learning a new technology got you into trouble.
11. Tell me about a time when learning a new technology worked really well for you.
12. Tell me about a time when you had to figure how to get your message across to remote locations using technology.
13. Tell me about a time when you installed a new technical system.
14. Tell me about a time when you volunteered to be the tester for some new technology.
15. Tell me about a time when you were an early adopter of some new technology.*

TECHNICAL LEARNING

16. What are your best and worst technical skills?*
17. What are your hobbies and interests?*
18. What do you like and not like to do at work (school)?*
19. What do you think is the oldest piece of technology you still use and work to keep running?
20. What do you use the Internet for?
21. What kinds of mechanical and technical "toys" do you buy and use?
22. What kinds of things do you do with your computer?*

Dimension 2: Seen/been around others who were involved with the competency–good and bad; learns from others about self

23. Contrast the best and worst learners of new technical skills you know.*
24. Has new technical learning ever been in any 360° survey done on you? Was your score among your highest, middle, or lowest?
25. Has poor technical learning skills on someone else's part ever created an obstacle for you or got in the way of something you were trying to accomplish?*
26. Have you ever talked with a coach or mentor about your learning of new technical skills?
27. Have you ever watched someone fail/get fired because they did not keep up with technology?*
28. Have you ever watched someone overdo learning new technical skills to the point that it backfired?
29. Have you ever watched someone succeed because they kept up with technology?*
30. Have you ever worked with a person who excelled at learning new technical skills?
31. Have you ever worked with a skills coach on technical learning skills?*
32. How do you get feedback about yourself on technical learning skills?
33. How often do you check with multiple sources when you get critical feedback on your technical learning skills?
34. Is there a historical figure you consider a model of learning new technical skills?
35. What do others who are not your fans say about your technical learning skills?
36. What do others who like you say about your technical learning skills?
37. Which boss was the best at learning new technical skills?
38. Which boss was the worst at learning new technical skills?
39. Which direct report was the best at learning new technical skills?
40. Which direct report was the worst at learning new technical skills?
41. Which peer was the best at learning new technical skills?
42. Which peer was the worst at learning new technical skills?
43. Who in your field or business is the best at learning new technical skills?
44. Who do you consider a role model of learning new technical skills?*
45. Who do you go to for advice on learning new technical skills?
46. Who have you learned the most from about learning new technical skills?*
47. Who is a higher-management role model for you on learning new technical skills?
48. Who is a role model of learning new technology outside of work?

Dimension 3: Knows how the competency works in theory; shows understanding

49. Are there situations or settings where someone should approach technical learning differently?
50. Do you get technical journals?*
51. Do you read technical books?*
52. Do you spend much time going to trade or electronic shows to see what's coming next?

TECHNICAL LEARNING

53. Do you think it's possible to build technical-learning skills; how do you think people develop these skills?
54. Do you think there is a way to compensate or work around low technical-learning skills?
55. Do you watch technical shows on TV?*
56. Has anyone asked you for your opinions/advice on learning new technical skills?*
57. Have you ever attended a course on new technology?
58. Have you ever been in a situation where you and others put technical learning skills on a success profile?
59. Have you ever been part of an effort to create a policy or a mission statement containing reference to technical-learning skills?
60. Have you ever coached or mentored someone who had problems with technical learning?
61. Have you ever created a development plan for someone on technical-learning skills?
62. Have you ever criticized someone for their inability to learn new technical skills?
63. Have you ever designed a program on learning new technical skills?
64. Have you ever designed a software program?
65. Have you ever given a speech on learning new technical skills?
66. Have you ever rewarded or recognized someone for technical learning?
67. Have you ever taken a purely technical course on something new?*
68. Have you ever taught a course on new technology?
69. Have you ever tried to help someone deal with technical learning more effectively?*
70. Have you ever tried to help someone improve their technical learning skills?
71. How do you think people develop technical learning skills?
72. How much technical learning is good to have and how much is too much?
73. How much of success do you think is due to technical learning compared with other characteristics?
74. How would you know if someone is bad at technical learning?
75. How would you know if someone is good at technical learning?
76. If you had to write a book on technical learning, what would the chapter headings be?
77. What are the benefits to someone who is really good at learning new technical skills?
78. What are the consequences to someone who is really poor at keeping up with new technology?
79. What could you write a book on?
80. What courses do you like to attend?
81. What do you think the standard is on technical learning for someone in your role?
82. What happens if you have or use too much new technology?
83. What happens when two people try to work together who have very different technical-learning skills?
84. What wisdom would you pass on to others trying to become better at technical learning?
85. When you select others, what do you look for in current technological skill?
86. Why do you think people end up being different when keeping up with technology?

Dimension 4: Shows personal change and sense-making; learned it one place and applied it in another; can compare and contrast experiences; changes viewpoints across time; can explain personal development or evolution related to the competency

87. Compare and contrast examples of being effective and ineffective at learning new technical skills?
88. Contrast your on- and off-the-job learning of new technical skills.
89. Did you ever pass up a job or assignment because you were not confident enough in your ability to learn new technical skills?
90. Do you ever use other skills to cover for your lack of facility in learning new technical skills?

TECHNICAL LEARNING

91. Has becoming better at learning new technical skills ever helped you in other areas?
92. Has not learning a new technical skill well enough ever figured in a failure, struggle, or setback you have had?
93. Has poor learning of new technical skills ever been the subject of a development plan for you?
94. Has your learning of new technical skills, good or bad, ever been the subject of your performance review or a career discussion?
95. Have your technical learning abilities always been this way?
96. Have you ever delegated or assigned someone a task because you didn't learn new technical skills particularly well?
97. Have you ever made significant strides at becoming better at learning new technical skills?
98. How different are you across situations in your learning of new technical skills?
99. How do you decide what new technical skills to learn?
100. How do you keep up with the state of the art in your field?*
101. How much of your success is due to your learning of new technical skills?
102. How transferable is your learning of new technical skills to other situations?
103. If you had to become better at a technical skill in a hurry, what would you do?
104. Was there a time when you were not as good at learning new technologies?
105. What caused you to work to improve your ability to learn new technical skills?
106. What do you think you've mastered?*
107. What event or series of events had the most impact on your ability to learn new technical skills?
108. What's the most varied you can be in learning new technical skills?
109. What was the shortest amount of time in which you increased your technical skill level?
110. When did you first realize your level of skill at learning new technologies?
111. When you know ahead of time that your ability to learn new technical skills isn't adequate, what do you do?
112. Why do you think you deal with learning technical skills the way you do?
113. Why do you think your level of learning new technical skills is the way it is?*

D. **Follow-up Probes:**

1. Are there times when you learn new technologies and times when you don't?
2. Could you contrast those two bosses for me?
3. Could you give me a few examples of how you've used or applied that?
4. Do people consider you to be very technical?
5. Do you always learn new technologies like that, or was that a special situation?
6. Do you enjoy science fiction?
7. Do you generally adopt new technologies first, last, or in between?
8. Do you generally buy new technologies early, or do you wait until they really work well?
9. Do you like to know how things are made?
10. Do you suppose if others would just try harder, they could learn to be more effective at learning new technologies like you do?
11. Do you think that's teachable?
12. Do you think you have better technical-learning skills than most? Why?
13. Do you think you would perform any differently if you could be more effective at understanding new technologies?
14. Do you tour factories when you can?

TECHNICAL LEARNING

15. Do you visit technical museums?
16. Have you always been able to learn new technologies that way, or is this a recent development in you?
17. Have you always had an interest in technical things?
18. How did the others react when you did that?
19. How did you come up with that approach to learning new technologies in the first place?
20. How did you know that method of learning a new technology would work?
21. How do others you have known approach that?
22. How typical is this for you?
23. How would you approach that same situation today?
24. Is this natural for you, or do you really have to dig for it?
25. Was there a time when you didn't understand this about yourself?
26. What did you do after you got that feedback?
27. What did you do to adapt to that?
28. What did you learn from that?
29. Why are you interested in new technology?
30. Why did you choose that approach?
31. Why did you decide to take the risk?
32. Why did you do it that way?
33. Why do you think that didn't work?
34. Why do you think that happened that way?
35. Why do you think that worked?
36. Why do you think you have difficulties with that sometimes?
37. Would you have done it that way with looser deadlines?
38. Would you have done it that way with tighter deadlines?

E. Themes/Things to Look for:

- Adds technology to get things done easier and faster
- Appreciation for technical skills in others
- Asks lots of questions
- Capacity for complexity
- Comfortable pushing buttons to see what happens
- Deep, technical knowledge and interest
- Excited about doing technical work
- One of the first to try new technologies
- Loves to explore the new/unique/advanced/state of the art
- Makes unique and unusual connections
- Network in technical areas
- Off-work technical interests/hobbies
- Sought after for technical knowledge
- Technical visionary
- Understand how technical things work

F. Most Likely Résumé:

1. Look for jobs like:

- Chair of Projects/Task Forces
- Fix-Its/Turnarounds
- Member of Projects/Task Forces
- Line to Staff Switches
- Scope (complexity) Assignments
- Staff Leadership (Influencing Without Authority)
- Start-Ups

TECHNICAL LEARNING

2. Look for develop-in-place assignments like:

Do a problem-prevention analysis on a product or service, and present it to the people involved.
Plan a new site for a building (plant, field office, headquarters, etc.).
Manage the purchase of a major product, equipment, materials, program, or system.
Manage an ad hoc, temporary group including former peers to accomplish a task.
Manage a cost-cutting project.
Build a multifunctional project team to tackle a common business issue or problem.

3. Best references to ask about or check:

Direct Boss	Peers and Colleagues
Customers	Direct Reports

G. Learning Agility Evaluation:

1. What/Describing vs. Why/Explain
3. Ordinary/Socially Acceptable vs. Insightful/Different
7. Passive vs. Intrigued/Curious
10. Reactive vs. Initiating
11. Generalizations vs. Specific Learnings
18. Stays Close to Home vs. Lots of Curiosity
19. External Standards vs. Internal Standards
22. Focus on Accomplishments vs. Focus on Solving Problems

H. The LEADERSHIP ARCHITECT® Sort Card Connections:

1. Good (positive) if combined with high:

Acts on technical knowledge 1, 16, 50, 57
Open to others input 3, 33
Interest in broader technical issues 5, 15, 46, 58
Patient with the less adept 10, 41
Technical wizard 14, 24, 30, 57
Could be a technical mentor 18, 19
Shares with others 19, 27, 36
Puts technical expertise to use 51, 52, 53

2. Bad (negative) if combined with low or high (+):

Doesn't do much with the knowledge 1, 16, 53
Can't make the technology practical 5, 24, 28
Likes technology more than people 7, 10, 21, 23
Doesn't fight to have new technology implemented 12, 34, 37, 57
Doesn't see connections with the work 14, 32
Spends time on the wrong new technologies 17, 50, 58, 62
Unlikely to teach others 18, 19
Isolated 3, 4, 42

TECHNICAL LEARNING

3. **Too much can contribute to the following Stallers and Stoppers:**

    A. *What too much looks like (overused):*

    May learn but not act; may overdo learning at the expense of using it; may be seen as too academic; may not relate well to those who can't catch on as quickly.

    B. *Too much might lead to these Stallers and Stoppers:*
    Arrogant (104)
    Overdependence on a Single Skill (116)
    Overmanaging (117)

    C. *Compensators:*
    How to compensate for too much of this competency:
    1, 3, 5, 15, 26, 33, 36, 41, 45, 46, 53, 54, 57

    D. *Things to watch for:*

Can't/won't communicate with mere mortals	Misses the soul of the machine
May not be able to apply new technologies	Too far out ahead to make use of the knowledge
May too quickly reject the old	

4. **Too little can contribute to the following Stallers and Stoppers:**

    A. *What too little looks like (unskilled):*

    Doesn't learn new technical skills readily; is among the last to learn or adopt new technology; may be stuck and wed to past technologies and resist switching to new ones; may be intimidated by technology; may lack experience or exposure with new technologies; may not be interested in things technical or areas involving lots of detail; may not know how to or may reject using others to learn new technologies.

    B. *Too little might lead to these Stallers and Stoppers:*

Unable to Adapt to Differences (101)	Non-Strategic (114)
Blocked Personal Learner (106)	Performance Problems (118)
Key Skill Deficiencies (113)	

    C. *Compensators:*
    How to substitute for too little of this competency:
    5, 14, 28, 32, 46, 51, 58

I. **LEARNING ARCHITECT® Connections:**

Look for people who act like and/or show evidence of:

1c. Following a Plan	15. Cautious
2a. Problem Solving	27. Conceptualizer
4a. Getting Information	28. Creator
5. New	30. Mastery
9. Multiple Sources	33. Diversity of Sources
10. Complexity	35. Breadth
13. Focused	

TECHNICAL LEARNING

J. CHOICES ARCHITECT® Connections:

Look for people who act like and/or show evidence of:

First Edition (Released 1994)
11. Open to Diversity
18. Into Everything

Second Edition (Released 2000)
7. Inquisitive

K. Difficulty to Develop:
20 (of 34)–Easier

62. TIME MANAGEMENT

A. Definition:

Uses his/her time effectively and efficiently; values time; concentrates their efforts on the more important priorities; gets more done in less time than others; can attend to a broader range of activities.

B. Arenas/Domains to Explore:

1. Allocating time to different projects
2. Allocating time to team/direct reports
3. Between jobs
4. Competing demands on time
5. Crises
6. Cutting off debate
7. Down time
8. Focus on the few
9. Gets exercise time In
10. Hobby time
11. Holiday management
12. Impossible deadlines
13. Leisure time
14. Many attractive alternatives for time
15. Not locked into someone else's agenda/schedule
16. Others are late
17. Personal time
18. Quality family time
19. Saying good-bye
20. Summers in school
21. Timeliness to meetings/appointments
22. Too much to do at once
23. Tour habits
24. Travel efficiency
25. Two people want their time
26. Using other people's time
27. Using technology to help manage time
28. Vacation time
29. Waiting for others
30. Waiting in airports
31. When things change
32. Work on trains/planes
33. Work time

C. Sample Questions:

*Dimension 1: Been there, done that–has had direct personal experience(s) involving the competency–candidate was the prime player   Note: * means OK for campus*

1. Are you the kind of person who can keep a lot of balls in the air at the same time?*
2. Are you usually early, on time, or a little late for meetings?*
3. Do you generally eat at the same time each day?*
4. Do you get your assignments in before the due date, on time, or a little late?
5. Do you have a method for organizing your day?*
6. Do you tend to get things done just before they are due?*
7. Do you use any technology to manage your time?*
8. Do you work on airplanes?
9. Do you write things-to-do lists?*
10. Has anyone ever accused you of messing something up because you mismanaged your time?
11. Have you ever managed anything where the people or units reporting to you were in different locations? How did you manage your time among them?
12. How do you close out people who you think are wasting your time?*

TIME MANAGEMENT

13. How do you handle interruptions, phone calls, mail, meetings you call, meetings others call, getting time to work on priorities?*
14. How do you manage your time off?*
15. How do you vacation?
16. How good are you at estimating time without a watch?*
17. How important is it to you to finish everything you start?
18. How much of your typical workday goes as you scheduled it the day before?
19. How much time do you like to have between flights?
20. How often do you make agenda-changing and timing suggestions in a meeting that you are not running?
21. If you had two days to tour Paris, how would you manage the time?*
22. Tell me about a time when you had too much to do and had to do less than all of it.*
23. Tell me about a time when you moved into a job (took on a project) that was too big for you to get your arms around.*
24. Tell me about a time when you put your foot down and said no to a request for your time from an important person.
25. What do you do on a layover in an airport?
26. What do you do with windfall time, such as when a meeting is canceled?*
27. What do you tend to do when in the middle of a meeting you come to the conclusion that it is a waste of your time?
28. When two meetings occur at the same time, how do you make the call?
29. When two people want you at the same time, how do you make the call?
30. When you get overwhelmed with things to do, how do you make decisions about what to focus on?*
31. When you go to a conference, concert, or play, how long do you stay?*

Dimension 2: Seen/been around others who were involved with the competency–good and bad; learns from others about self

32. Contrast the people you know who are the best and worst time managers.*
33. Has time management ever been in any 360° survey done on you? Was your score among your highest, middle, or lowest?
34. Has poor time management on someone else's part ever created an obstacle for you or got in the way of something you were trying to accomplish?*
35. Have you ever talked with a coach or mentor about your time-management skills?
36. Have you ever watched someone fail/get fired because they did not manage their time well?*
37. Have you ever watched someone overmanage their time to the point that it backfired?
38. Have you ever watched someone succeed because they managed time well?*
39. Have you ever worked with a coach on time management?*
40. Have you ever worked with a person who excelled at time management?
41. Have you ever worked with a skills coach on time management?*
42. How do you get feedback about yourself on how well you manage your time?
43. How often do you check with multiple sources when you get critical feedback on your time management?
44. Is there a historical figure you consider a model of managing their time well?
45. What do others who are not your fans say about how well you manage your time?
46. What do others who like you say about how well you manage your time?
47. Which boss was the best at managing their time?
48. Which boss was the worst at managing their time?

TIME MANAGEMENT

49. Which direct report was the best at managing their time?
50. Which direct report was the worst at managing their time?
51. Which peer was the best at managing their time?
52. Which peer was the worst at managing their time?
53. Who deals with managing their time the best in your field or business?
54. Who do you consider a current role model of managing their time well?*
55. Who do you go to for advice on time management?
56. Who have you learned the most from about time management?*
57. Who is a higher-management role model for you on time management?
58. Who is a role model of time management skills outside of work?

Dimension 3: Knows how the competency works in theory; shows understanding

59. Are there situations or settings where someone should employ different time management skills?
60. Do you think time management skills can be learned; how do you think people develop time management skills?
61. Do you think there is a way to compensate or work around low time-management skills?
62. Has anyone asked you for your opinions/advice on time management?*
63. Have you ever attended a course on time management?
64. Have you ever been in a situation where you and others put time management on a success profile?
65. Have you ever been part of an effort to create a policy or a mission statement containing reference to time-management skills?
66. Have you ever been someone's coach or mentor who had problems with time management?
67. Have you ever created a development plan for someone on time management?
68. Have you ever criticized someone for not managing their time well?
69. Have you ever designed a program on time management?
70. Have you ever given a speech on time management?
71. Have you ever rewarded or recognized someone for having managed their time well?
72. Have you ever taught a course on time management?
73. Have you ever tried to help someone deal more effectively with managing their time?*
74. Have you ever tried to help someone improve their time management skills?
75. How do you think people develop time management skills?
76. How much time management is good and how much is too much?
77. How much of success do you think is due to time management skills compared with other characteristics?
78. How would you know if someone is bad at managing their time?
79. How would you know if someone is good at managing their time?
80. If you had to write a book on time management, what would the chapter headings be?
81. What are the benefits to someone who is really good at managing their time?
82. What are the consequences to someone who is really poor at managing their time?
83. What do you think the standard is on time management for someone in your role?
84. What happens if you manage your time too closely?
85. What happens when two people try to work together who are very different time managers?
86. What wisdom would you pass on to others trying to become better at managing their time?
87. When you select others, what do you look for in time management skills?
88. Why do you think people end up managing their time differently?

TIME MANAGEMENT

Dimension 4: Shows personal change and sense-making; learned it one place and applied it in another; can compare and contrast experiences; changes viewpoints across time; can explain personal development or evolution related to the competency

89. Compare and contrast examples of being effective and ineffective at managing your time.
90. Contrast your on- and off-the-job use of time management.
91. Did you ever pass up a job or assignment because you were not confident enough in your skills at managing your time?
92. Do you ever use other skills to cover for your lack of time-management skills?
93. Has becoming better at time management ever helped you in other areas?
94. Has not managing your time well ever figured in a failure, struggle, or setback you have had?
95. Has poor time management ever been the subject of a development plan for you?
96. Has your time management always been this way?
97. Have you ever delegated or assigned someone a task because you didn't manage your time particularly well?
98. Have you ever made significant strides at becoming better at time management?
99. Have your time management skills, good or bad, ever been the subject of your performance review or a career discussion?
100. How different are you across situations in your time management?
101. How do you balance time availability with getting your work done?*
102. How do you decide how much in control of your time to be?
103. How much of your success is due to your time management skills?
104. How transferable are your time management skills to other situations?
105. If you had to become better at time management in a hurry, what would you do?
106. If you had total control over how you spend your work day, what changes would you make?*
107. Was there a time when you were not as good at time management?
108. What caused you to work to improve your skills at managing your time?
109. What event or series of events had the most impact on your time management?
110. What's the most varied you can be in time management?
111. What was the shortest amount of time in which you increased your level of skill at time management?
112. When did you first realize your level of skill at time management?
113. When you know ahead of time that your usual way of managing your time won't work, what do you do?
114. Why do you think you deal with time management the way you do?
115. Why do you think your time management is the way it is?*

TIME MANAGEMENT

D. Follow-up Probes:

1. Are there times when you manage your time like that and times when you don't?
2. Could you contrast those two bosses for me?
3. Could you give me a few examples of how you've used or applied that?
4. Do you always manage your time like that, or was that a special situation?
5. Do you feel guilty when you just sit and rest/relax?
6. Do you suppose if others would just try harder, they could learn to be more effective at managing their time like you do?
7. Do you think that's teachable?
8. Do you think you have better time-management skills than most? Why?
9. Do you think you would perform any differently if you could be more effective at managing your time?
10. Have you always managed your time that way, or is this a recent development in you?
11. How did the others react when you did that?
12. How did you come up with that approach to managing your time in the first place?
13. How did you know that method of managing you time would work?
14. How do others you have known approach that?
15. How typical is this for you?
16. How would you approach that same situation today?
17. Is this natural for you, or do you really have to dig for it?
18. Was there a time when you didn't understand this about yourself?
19. What did you do after you got that feedback?
20. What did you do to adapt to that?
21. What did you learn from that?
22. When are you ever down?
23. Why did you choose that activity over the others?
24. Why did you choose that approach?
25. Why did you choose that meeting to go to rather than the other one?
26. Why did you choose that person to attend to over the others?
27. Why did you decide to take the risk?
28. Why did you do it that way?
29. Why do you always have to be doing something?
30. Why do you think that didn't work?
31. Why do you think that happened that way?
32. Why do you think that worked?
33. Why do you think you have difficulties doing that?
34. Would you have done it that way with looser deadlines?
35. Would you have done it that way with tighter deadlines?

TIME MANAGEMENT

E. Themes/Things to Look for:
Ability to create accurate schedules
Ability to estimate how long things should take
Ability to handle simultaneous projects/tracks
Able to run time simulations in their head
Being approachable even when busy
Can shift priorities easily when circumstances change
Clear sense of priorities
Compulsive about time
Essence detector
Guards time
Knows when to cut losses and move on
Multiple techniques to check progress of things
Organizing data quickly
Plans ahead
Preserving blocks of time for different activities
Quality time in whatever they are doing
Respects other people's time
Scheduled crash/rejuvenation time
Systematic, orderly
Timely decision maker
Unafraid to place a value on things, tasks, outcomes, and people
Values-driven priorities
Willingness to delegate when overwhelmed

F. Most Likely Résumé:

1. Look for jobs like:
Chair of Projects/Task forces	Scale (size shift) Assignments
Cross-Moves	Scope (complexity) Assignments
Fix-Its/Turnarounds	Staff to Line Shifts
International Assignments	Start-Ups

2. Look for develop-in-place assignments like:
Plan a new site for a building (plant, field office, headquarters, etc.).
Plan an off-site meeting, conference, convention, trade show, event, etc.
Manage an ad hoc, temporary group of balky and resisting people through an unpopular change or project.
Manage an ad hoc, temporary group of people involved in tackling a fix-it or turnaround project.
Work on a crisis management team.

3. Best references to ask about or check:
Direct Reports

TIME MANAGEMENT

G. Learning Agility Evaluation:

   5. Tight/Rigid vs. Loose/Flexible
   6. Reacting/Responsive vs. Adapting
   10. Reactive vs. Initiating
   11. Generalizations vs. Specific Learnings

H. The LEADERSHIP ARCHITECT® Sort Card Connections:

1. Good (positive) if combined with high:

   Not much wasted time; gets more done than others 1, 16, 50, 53
   Flexible; can change schedule on short notice 2, 12
   Can schedule through a chaos storm 2, 40
   Makes themselves accessible 3, 7, 31, 33, 41
   Makes the tough time decisions 12, 34, 57
   Uses time well to solve problems 14, 17, 50, 51
   Helps others develop 18, 19, 33
   Takes time to share the big picture; what's going on 27, 36, 65
   Balances self with team time needs 36, 60
   Saves themselves some personal development time 44, 45, 54, 55
   Saves time for quality, family life 66

2. Bad (negative) if combined with low or high (+):

   Has trouble getting things done; does things at the last minute 1, 16
   Spins wheels 2, 40
   Doesn't have enough time to help others grow 19, 33, 41
   Doesn't have enough time to tell other what's going on 27
   Helter-skelter 47, 50
   Speaks too long 49
   Doesn't always deliver on time 53
   Low quality family time 66

3. Too much can contribute to the following Stallers and Stoppers:

   #### A. What too much looks like (overused):

   May be impatient with other people's agenda and pace; may not take the time to stop and smell the roses; may not give people enough rapport time with them to get comfortable.

   #### B. Too much might lead to these Stallers and Stoppers:

   Blocked Personal Learner (106)   Insensitive to Others (112)
   Defensiveness (108)   Overmanaging (117)

   #### C. Compensators:

   How to compensate for too much of this competency:
        2, 3, 7, 12, 14, 17, 26, 27, 31, 33, 36, 41, 46, 51, 60

TIME MANAGEMENT

D. Things to watch for:
Makes others uncomfortable about taking their time
Must always be in control of schedule/agenda
Never sits
Obsessive/compulsive about time
Underestimates how long things take
You can see their timer go off

4. Too little can contribute to the following Stallers and Stoppers:

A. What too little looks like (unskilled):
Is disorganized and wastes time and resources; flits from activity to activity with little rhyme or reason; doesn't set priorities; can't say no; can only concentrate on one thing at a time; is very easily distracted; mostly reactive to what's hot at the moment; doesn't have or follow a plan or method for his/her time; can't cut off transactions politely; doesn't have a clock in his/her head; may do all right on important priorities and issues, but not good with the little things.

B. Too little might lead to these Stallers and Stoppers:
Being a Poor Administrator (102)
Performance Problems (118)

C. Compensators:
How to substitute for too little of this competency:
17, 39, 47, 50, 52, 63, 66

I. LEARNING ARCHITECT® Connections:

Look for people who act like and/or show evidence of:

1a. Pure Action	12. Rules of Thumb
1c. Following a Plan	13. Focused
2a. Problem Solving	

J. CHOICES ARCHITECT® Connections:

Look for people who act like and/or show evidence of:

First Edition (Released 1994)
None Apply

Second Edition (Released 2000)
None Apply

K. Difficulty to Develop:
19 (of 34)–Easier

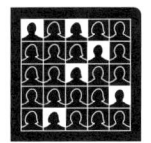

63. TOTAL WORK SYSTEMS (E.G., TQM/ISO/SIX SIGMA)

A. Definition:

Is dedicated to providing organization or enterprise-wide common systems for designing and measuring work processes; seeks to reduce variances in organization processes; delivers the highest quality products and services which meet the needs and requirements of internal and external customers; is committed to continuous improvement through empowerment and management by data; leverages technology to positively impact quality; is willing to re-engineer processes from scratch; is open to suggestions and experimentation; creates a learning environment leading to the most efficient and effective work processes.

B. Arenas/Domains to Explore:

1. Any attempt to redesign work
2. Any cost/benefit analysis of a process
3. Any customer feedback system
4. Any customer service job
5. Any empowerment program
6. Any external customer event
7. Any internal customer event
8. Any supervisory event
9. Any team management event
10. Any workflow
11. Benchmarking studies
12. Competing for the Malcolm Baldrige Award
13. Conference management
14. Cost-cutting projects
15. Customer complaints
16. Customer needs analysis
17. Customer phone interviews
18. Customer surveys
19. Employee suggestion systems
20. ISO 9000 certification
21. Mission/vision/values statements
22. New product/service start-up
23. Product specifications
24. Professional association management
25. Service specifications
26. Student government
27. Time-to-market studies
28. Working with suppliers/vendors
29. Workflow measurement/feedback systems

C. Sample Questions:

Dimension 1: Been there, done that–has had direct personal experience(s) involving the competency–candidate was the prime player   Note: * means OK for campus

1. Has anyone ever accused you of messing something up because of poorly designed workflow systems?
2. Have you ever been part of a Six Sigma quality effort?
3. Have you ever been part of a TQM/Process Re-engineering/ISO implementation?
4. Have you ever done a study of lost customers?
5. Have you ever had to implement a new quality system?
6. Have you ever handled customer complaints in person?*
7. Have you ever handled customer complaints over the phone?*
8. Have you ever made a suggestion to improve a work flow that your boss accepted and implemented?*
9. Have you ever managed an employee suggestion system?
10. Have you ever managed anything where the people or units reporting to you were in different locations? How did you maintain quality?
11. Have you ever surveyed customers by phone? In person?*
12. Have you ever used a fish bone diagram?
13. Have you ever used a run chart?

TOTAL WORK SYSTEMS (e.g., TQM/ISO/Six Sigma)

14. Have you ever written product or service specifications after surveying the potential customers?
15. How do you generally collect employee input into quality improvement efforts?
16. How often do you complain as a customer?
17. How often do you write to a company complaining about poor service?
18. Tell me about a time when customer data or feedback pointed out that you were wrong.
19. Tell me about a time when you installed a new system to improve the quality of a product or a service.
20. Tell me about a time when you moved into a job where the work processes/systems/work groups were delivering poor quality and had to be fixed.*
21. Tell me about a time when you reengineered a process you originally designed.
22. Tell me about a time when your team pushed back against a process idea you had and changed your mind.
23. Tell me about a time when your attempt to improve quality got you into trouble.
24. Tell me about a time when your attempt at improving quality worked really well for you.
25. Tell me about some times when you exceeded customer expectations?
26. What do you do when you became part of a poor work design; waiting in endless lines to get something simple done?*
27. What kind of relationships do you maintain with key customers?
28. What's the most significant improvement you have ever made to a work process?*
29. What's the worst work process you've personally experienced?*
30. When you have worked as part of a quality improvement team, what role do you usually play?

Dimension 2: Seen/been around others who were involved with the competency–good and bad; learns from others about self

31. Contrast the most and least process oriented (TQM/Process Re-engineering/ISO/Six Sigma) people you know.*
32. Has TQM/Process Re-engineering/ISO/Six Sigma ever been in any 360° survey done on you? Was your score among your highest, middle, or lowest?
33. Has lack of formal workflow-design-system skills on someone else's part ever created an obstacle for you or got in the way of something you were trying to accomplish?*
34. Have you ever talked with a coach or mentor about your formal workflow-design-system skills?
35. Have you ever watched someone fail/get fired because they did not have formal workflow-design-system skills?*
36. Have you ever watched someone overdo applying formal workflow-design-system skills to the point that it backfired?
37. Have you ever watched someone succeed because they possessed formal workflow-design-system skills?*
38. Have you ever worked with a coach on your formal workflow-design-system skills?*
39. Have you ever worked with a person who excelled at formal workflow-design-system skills?
40. Have you ever worked with a skills coach on formal workflow-design-system skills?*
41. How do you get feedback about yourself on your formal workflow-design-system skills?
42. How often do you check with multiple sources when you get a piece of critical feedback on your formal workflow-design-system skills?
43. Is there a historical figure you consider a model of formal workflow-design-system skills?
44. What do others who are not your fans say about your formal workflow-design-system skills?
45. What do others who like you say about your formal workflow-design-system skills?
46. Which boss was the best at formal workflow-design-system skills?
47. Which boss was the worst at formal workflow-design-system skills?
48. Which direct report was the best at formal workflow-design-system skills?
49. Which direct report was the worst at formal workflow-design-system skills?
50. Which peer was the best at formal workflow-design-system skills?

TOTAL WORK SYSTEMS (e.g., TQM/ISO/Six Sigma)

51. Which peer was the worst at formal workflow-design-system skills?
52. Who is the best in your field or business at formal workflow-design-system skills?
53. Who do you consider a current role model of applying formal workflow-design-systems?*
54. Who do you go to for advice on formal workflow-design-systems?
55. Who have you learned the most from about formal workflow-design-systems?*
56. Who is a higher-management role model for you on formal workflow-design-systems?
57. Who is a role model of formal workflow-design-systems?

Dimension 3: Knows how the competency works in theory; shows understanding

58. Are there situations or settings where someone should be applying different formal workflow-design-systems?
59. Do you study other workflow-design-systems for process improvement hints?
60. Do you think formal workflow-design-system skills can be learned; how do you think people develop formal workflow-design-systems skills?
61. Do you think there is a way to compensate or work around low formal workflow-design-system skills?
62. Has anyone asked you for your opinions/advice on formal workflow-design-systems?*
63. Have you ever attended a course on workflow design, TQM, or process re-engineering?
64. Have you ever been in a company that had ISO certification?
65. Have you ever been in a situation where you and others put formal workflow-design-system skills on a success profile?
66. Have you ever been part of an effort to create a policy or a mission statement containing reference to having formal workflow-design-systems?
67. Have you ever been someone's coach or mentor who had problems with workflow design, TQM, or process re-engineering?
68. Have you ever created a development plan for someone on workflow design, TQM, or process re-engineering?
69. Have you ever criticized someone for not demonstrating formal workflow-design-system skills?
70. Have you ever designed a program on workflow design, TQM, or process re-engineering?
71. Have you ever designed a software program to monitor quality?
72. Have you ever done a benchmarking study of a product, service, or process?
73. Have you ever given a speech on workflow design, TQM, or process re-engineering?
74. Have you ever made a video training tape on workflow design, TQM, or process re-engineering?
75. Have you ever rewarded or recognized someone for having formal workflow-design-system skills?
76. Have you ever taught a course on workflow design, TQM, or process re-engineering?
77. Have you ever tried to help someone deal more effectively with workflow design, TQM, or process re-engineering?*
78. Have you ever tried to help someone improve their workflow design, TQM, or process re-engineering?
79. Have you studied Deming? Juran? Crosby? Hammer? Champy?
80. Have you studied SPC (Statistical Process Control)?
81. Hotels have made nightly turndown service optional. Why do you suppose they've done that?*
82. How do you think people develop workflow design, TQM, or process re-engineering skills?
83. How many TQM/process re-engineering/ISO/Six Sigma efforts are good to have, and how many are too much?
84. How much of success do you think is due to workflow design, TQM, or process re-engineering compared with other characteristics?
85. How much reading have you done on TQM/process re-engineering/Six Sigma/ISO?
86. How would you know if someone is bad at workflow design, TQM, or process re-engineering?

TOTAL WORK SYSTEMS (e.g., TQM/ISO/Six Sigma)

87. How would you know if someone is good at workflow design, TQM, or process re-engineering?
88. If you had to write a book on workflow design, TQM, or process re-engineering, what would the chapter headings be?
89. What are the benefits to someone who is really good at workflow design, TQM, or process re-engineering?
90. What are the consequences to someone who is really poor at workflow design, TQM, or process re-engineering?
91. What do you think the standard is on workflow design, TQM, or process re-engineering for someone in your role?
92. What happens if you use workflow design, TQM, or process re-engineering skills too often?
93. What happens when two people try to work together who have very different workflow design, TQM, or process re-engineering abilities?
94. What wisdom would you pass onto others trying to become better at workflow design, TQM, or process re-engineering?
95. When you select others, what do you look for in workflow design, TQM, or process re-engineering skills?
96. Why do you think people end up having different workflow design, TQM, or process re-engineering skills?

Dimension 4: Shows personal change and sense-making; learned it one place and applied it in another; can compare and contrast experiences; changes viewpoints across time; can explain personal development or evolution related to the competency

97. Compare and contrast examples of being effective and ineffective at applying formal workflow-design-systems (e.g.;TQM, ISO, Six Sigma.
98. Contrast your on- and off-the-job use of formal workflow-design-systems.
99. Did you ever pass up a job or assignment because you were not confident enough in your skills at applying formal workflow-design-systems?
100. Do you ever use other skills to cover for your lack of formal workflow-design skills?
101. Everyone says quality is a given in their operation. How do you know?
102. Has lack of formal workflow-design-system skills ever figured in a failure, struggle, or setback you have had?
103. Has learning more about formal workflow-design-systems ever helped you in other areas?
104. Has poor workflow-design skills ever been the subject of a development plan for you?
105. Has your workflow-design ability always been this way?
106. Have you ever delegated or assigned someone a task because you didn't apply formal workflow-design systems particularly well?
107. Have you ever made significant strides at becoming better at formal workflow design?
108. Have your formal workflow-design skills, good or bad, ever been the subject of your performance review or a career discussion?
109. How different are you across situations in your workflow-design success?
110. How do you decide how much workflow-design technology to apply?
111. How do you know if a work process is doing what it's supposed to?
112. How much of your success is due to your formal workflow-design skills?
113. How transferable are your formal workflow-design skills to other situations?
114. If you had to become better at formal workflow-design in a hurry, what would you do?
115. Was there a time when you were not as good at workflow-design?
116. What caused you to work to improve your skills at formal workflow-design?
117. What event or series of events had the most impact on your formal workflow-design skills?
118. What's the most varied you can be in workflow design technology?
119. What was the shortest amount of time in which you increased your level of skill at formal workflow design?
120. When you know ahead of time that your level of skill at formal workflow design won't work, what do you do?
121. Why do you think you address workflow design the way you do?

TOTAL WORK SYSTEMS (e.g., TQM/ISO/Six Sigma)

D. Follow-up Probes:

1. Are there times when you use your workflow-design skills like that and times when you don't?
2. Could you contrast those two bosses for me?
3. Could you give me a few examples of how you've used or applied that?
4. Did you lead the effort or were you part of a team?
5. Did you originally resist TQM/Process Re-engineering?
6. Do you always attempt to redesign and improve workflow or was that a special situation?
7. Do you suppose if others would just try harder, they could learn to be more effective at implementing efficient and effective workflows like you do?
8. Do you think that's teachable?
9. Do you think this quality stuff is just a fad?
10. Do you think you have better work flow design, TQM, or process re-engineering skills than most? Why?
11. Do you think you would perform any differently if you could be more effective at work flow design, TQM, or process re-engineering?
12. Have you always understood work flow design, TQM, or process re-engineering that way or is this a recent development in you?
13. Can you do the statistics related to TQM?
14. How did the others react when you did that?
15. How did the people on the team react to working together on that?
16. How did you come up with that approach to work flow design, TQM, or process re-engineering in the first place?
17. How did you feel about empowering your people to design their own workflow?
18. How did you know that method of work flow design, TQM, or process re-engineering would work?
19. How do others you have known approach that?
20. How long did it take you to really learn that?
21. How much does it bother you when you witness a bad work flow or process?
22. How much time or money did you save by redesigning it that way?
23. How typical is this for you?
24. How would you approach that same situation today?
25. Is this natural for you, or do you really have to dig for it?
26. Was it hard to manage more by data?
27. Was there a time when you didn't understand this about yourself?
28. What did you do after you got that feedback?
29. What did you do to adapt to that?
30. What did you learn from that?
31. Why did you choose that approach?
32. Why did you decide to take the risk?
33. Why did you do it that way?
34. Why did you time your attempt to redesign the work flow like that?
35. Why do you think that didn't work?
36. Why do you think that happened that way?
37. Why do you think that worked?
38. Why do you think you have difficulties with that?
39. Would you have done it that way with looser deadlines?
40. Would you have done it that way with tighter deadlines?

TOTAL WORK SYSTEMS (e.g., TQM/ISO/Six Sigma)

E. Themes/Things to Look for:

A feel for how people are impacted by workflow design
A natural feel for sequence; what follows what
Ability to analyze workflow
Able to run different flow scenarios in their head
An eye for process detail
Bone-deep belief in people doing the work designing it
Can describe process
Creating learning environment
Deep commitment to the customer
Efficient user of resources
Empowerment
Experiments/incremental improvements
Gets upset with bad work flow
Going out of one's way customer service
Handling irate customers comfortably
Has high standards for work process
Interest in how things work outside their home territory
Learning from other organizations/fields
Lifelong commitment to continuous improvement
Management by data
Motivated to learn how things work
Sensing mechanisms
Setting up customer feedback loops
Student of Deming, Juran, Crosby, etc.
Student of how work processes flow
Understanding customer needs
Understanding of SPC
Understanding person/machine interface
Understanding product/service features/benefits
Willing to share best practices with others
Willingness to implement best practices from others
Willingness to learn from others

F. Most Likely Résumé:

1. Look for jobs like:

Scale (size shift) Assignments
Significant People Demands

2. Look for develop-in-place assignments like:

Work on a process-simplification team to take steps and costs out of a process.

Do a problem-prevention analysis on a product or service, and present it to the people involved.

Benchmark innovative practices, processes, products, or services of competitors, vendors, suppliers, or customers, and present a report to others to create recommendations for change.

Visit Malcolm Baldrige National Quality Award or Deming Prize winners and report back on your findings, showing how they would help your organization.

Relaunch an existing product or service that's not doing well.

Create employee involvement teams.

Manage a cost-cutting project.

Build a multifunctional project team to tackle a common business issue or problem.

3. Best references to ask about or check:

Direct Reports

G. Learning Agility Evaluation:

1. What/Describing vs. Why/Explain
2. All or Nothing vs. Can See Many Sides
3. Ordinary/Socially Acceptable vs. Insightful/Different
6. Reacting/Responsive vs. Adapting
7. Passive vs. Intrigued/Curious
16. Few Rules of Thumb vs. Many and Varied Rules of Thumb
18. Stays Close to Home vs. Lots of Curiosity
19. External Standards vs. Internal Standards
20. Avoids Responsibility for Mistakes vs. Admits and Learns from Mistakes

TOTAL WORK SYSTEMS (e.g., TQM/ISO/Six Sigma)

H. The LEADERSHIP ARCHITECT® Sort Card Connections:

1. **Good (positive) if combined with high:**

   Quick to adjust work flow design 1, 2, 16, 53
   Flexible 2, 40
   Open to suggestions 3, 33, 60
   Works on the highest priority work flows 5, 15, 50, 53
   Builds best practices work designs 5, 24, 47, 39, 51, 52
   Manages the conflict 11, 12, 37
   Knows what to measure 15, 20, 35, 53
   Attuned to customer needs 15, 32, 33, 51
   Makes sense of information; sets up TQM 15, 35, 52, 59
   Empowers others to work on their own designs 18, 36, 42, 60
   Can set a learning environment 32, 61
   Takes the political realities into account when designing work flows 38, 48
   Work designs last longer than most 46, 58, 65

2. **Bad (negative) if combined with low or high (+):**

   Slow to improve work processes 1, 16, 43
   Not open to suggestions from team 3, 33, 42, 60
   Improves unnecessary processes 5, 15, 50, 53
   Doesn't take people into account in work flow design 7, 10, 21, 23
   Too one sided; mostly top down (+9, 12, 36, 53, 57) 18
   Doesn't take on the sacred cows 11, 12, 34, 57
   Slow to get the message that a process isn't working 15, 16, 32, 33
   Redesign work too short term 15, 46, 58, 65
   Unrealistic about what the function can do 24, 61
   Misreads people's work capabilities 25, 56, 64
   Doesn't take political realities into account 38, 48
   Redesigns are isolated from related work processes 39, 47, 52

3. **Too much can contribute to the following Stallers and Stoppers:**

   A. *What too much looks like (overused):*

   May become a quality or re-engineering missionary to the exclusion of everything else; may make marginal incremental changes which are more disruptive than helpful; may reject other approaches and non-believers; may be overdependent on a single guru or approach.

   B. *Too much might lead to these Stallers and Stoppers:*

   None Apply

   C. *Compensators:*

   How to compensate for too much of this competency:
   2, 32, 33, 40, 46, 57, 58

   D. *Things to watch for:*

"If I were in charge, it would work better"	Has the answer to every workflow problem
Can't communicate with the non-believers	Inveterate tinkerer
Can't leave anything alone for long	Siding with the customer too much

TOTAL WORK SYSTEMS (e.g., TQM/ISO/Six Sigma)

Doesn't apply cost/benefit analysis to efforts to improve "Crosby says... ."
Everybody has to share their beliefs

4. Too little can contribute to the following Stallers and Stoppers:

A. What too little looks like (unskilled):

Doesn't think broadly regarding the impact of work processes; doesn't comply or work to build commonalities in processes; doesn't create effective and efficient work processes; isn't customer focused in how he/she designs and manages the work; isn't dedicated to continuous improvement of work processes; doesn't leverage technology to improve work processes; doesn't know the tools and techniques to improve work processes; sticks to the old and familiar rather than stepping back and seeing the larger pattern; isn't willing to scrap the past in favor of the new and improved; doesn't listen to employees about improving work design; doesn't empower others to design their own work processes; doesn't create an environment where the whole unit learns together how better to serve the customer.

B. Too little might lead to these Stallers and Stoppers:
Failure to Build a Team (110)
Overmanaging (117)
Performance Problems (118)

C. Compensators:
How to substitute for too little of this competency:
5, 15, 16, 20, 28, 32, 33, 35, 39, 47, 52, 53, 65

I. LEARNING ARCHITECT® Connections:

Look for people who act like and/or show evidence of:

1c. Following a Plan	13. Focused
2a. Problem Solving	16. Collaborate
4a. Getting Information	19. What
4c. Actively Involve	31. Rationality
9. Multiple Sources	

J. CHOICES ARCHITECT® Connections:

Look for people who act like and/or show evidence of:

First Edition (Released 1994)	Second Edition (Released 2000)
2. Essence	2. Complexity
4. Complexity	6. Essence
7. Helping Others Think	9. Agile Communicator
19. Tinkerer	20. Experimenter
23. Communicator	

K. Difficulty to Develop:
19 (of 34)–Easier

64. UNDERSTANDING OTHERS

A. Definition:

Understands why groups do what they do; picks up the sense of the group in terms of positions, intentions, and needs; what they value and how to motivate them; can predict what groups will do across different situations.

B. Arenas/Domains to Explore:

1. Adding a person to an existing team
2. Athletic competition
3. Coaching
4. Consolidating offices
5. Cross-boundary taskforce
6. Cross-culture taskforce
7. Dealing with community leaders/groups
8. Dealing with different divisions
9. Dealing with different levels
10. Dealing with government agencies
11. Debates
12. Different ethnic/racial groups
13. Forming cross-boundary teams
14. Fraternity/sorority management
15. Getting financing
16. Military command experience
17. Negotiations
18. Office space management; who's together
19. Picking a course to attend
20. Picking professional organizations to join
21. Picking schools
22. Picking teams for assignments
23. Predicting legal outcomes
24. Predicting political events
25. Professional association management
26. Putting parties together
27. Reading choices
28. Reorganizations
29. Selecting a group to join
30. Selecting consultant teams
31. Selecting law firms
32. Selecting suppliers
33. Selecting vendors
34. Student government
35. Studying competitors
36. Teaching
37. Working on mergers/acquisitions
38. Working with boards

C. Sample Questions:

Dimension 1: Been there, done that–has had direct personal experience(s) involving the competency–candidate was the prime player   Note: * means OK for campus

1. Has anyone ever accused you of messing something up because of poor group-reading skills on your part?
2. Have you even been part of a union negotiation?
3. Have you ever been "expelled" from a group?*
4. Have you ever been a member of a group that was hard to read and predict even though you were part of it?*
5. Have you ever been part of disbanding or shutting down a group?
6. Have you ever been rejected for membership in a group?*
7. Have you ever changed allegiances to an opposing truth; moved to the other side?*
8. Have you ever dealt extensively in or with another culture?
9. Have you ever had to implement a new system somewhere without knowing the group very well?
10. Have you ever managed anything where the people or units reporting to you were in different locations? How did you learn to read the differences among groups?

UNDERSTANDING OTHERS

11. Have you ever played the role of a gatekeeper of a group, determining who got in?*
12. Have you ever quit a group after you found out what they really stood for?*
13. Have you ever served as a mediator between two groups in conflict?
14. Have you ever started a group from scratch? How did it form? Is it still in existence today?*
15. How do you deal with groups/people who come to you with the same problems again and again?*
16. How do you deal with groups/people who come to you with unimportant problems?*
17. How do you deal with groups/people you don't like or don't agree with?*
18. Tell me about a time when you had a good relationship with a single member of a group you didn't get along with.*
19. Tell me about a time when you had to communicate something important to someone who did not speak your language very well.
20. Tell me about a time when you had to figure out what the hidden agendas of a group were.*
21. Tell me about a time when you had to separate liking a group from working with them.*
22. Tell me about a time when you predicted accurately what a group would do.*
23. Tell me about a time when you read how a group was feeling or reacting to something.*
24. Tell me about a time when you read non-verbal behavior (body language) of a group and this paid off for you.*
25. Tell me about a time when you were able to get a group to change its mind.*
26. Tell me about a time when you were involved in a tough negotiation with an outside group.*
27. Tell me about a time when you were not accurate in predicting what a group would do.*
28. Tell me about two groups you know well at work (at school). How well can you anticipate what they will say or do?*
29. What group have you been the most accurate about?*
30. What group have you had the hardest time trying to figure out and predict what it will do?*
31. What was the biggest failure you ever had at trying to influence a group to think or do something it didn't want to do?*
32. What was your best success story of you getting a group excited about something?*
33. What's the worst group you ever had to deal with?

Dimension 2: Seen/been around others who were involved with the competency–good and bad; learns from others about self

34. Contrast the people you know who are the best and worst at reading or understanding groups.*
35. Has reading or understanding groups ever been in any 360° survey done on you? Was your score among your highest, middle, or lowest?
36. Has lack of the ability to read and understand groups on someone else's part ever created an obstacle for you or got in the way of something you were trying to accomplish?*
37. Have you ever talked with a coach or mentor about your ability to read and understand groups?
38. Have you ever watched someone fail/get fired because they did not read or understand groups?*
39. Have you ever watched someone overdo reading or understanding groups to the point that it backfired?
40. Have you ever watched someone succeed because they understood groups?*
41. Have you ever worked with a coach on reading/understanding groups?*
42. Have you ever worked with a person who excelled at reading and understanding groups?
43. Have you ever worked with a skills coach on reading and understanding groups?*
44. How do you get feedback about yourself on reading/understanding groups?
45. How often do you check with multiple sources when you get critical feedback on your ability to read and understand groups?

UNDERSTANDING OTHERS

46. Is there a historical figure you consider a model of reading and understanding groups?
47. What do others who are not your fans say about your ability to read and understand groups?
48. What do others who like you say about your ability to read and understand groups?
49. Which boss was the best at reading and understanding groups?
50. Which boss was the worst at reading and understanding groups?
51. Which direct report was the best at reading and understanding groups?
52. Which direct report was the worst at reading and understanding groups?
53. Which peer was the best at reading and understanding groups?
54. Which peer was the worst at reading and understanding groups?
55. Who is the best at reading and understanding groups in your field or business?
56. Who do you consider a current role model of reading and understanding groups?*
57. Who do you go to for advice on reading and understanding groups?
58. Who have you learned the most from about reading and understanding groups?*
59. Who is a higher-management role model for you on reading and understanding groups?
60. Who is a role model of reading and understanding groups outside of work?

Dimension 3: Knows how the competency works in theory; shows understanding

61. Are there situations or settings where someone should read groups differently?
62. Do you think an ability to read and understand groups can be learned; how do you think people develop this skill?
63. Do you think there is a way to compensate or work around a low ability to read and understand groups?
64. Has anyone asked you for your opinions/advice on reading or understanding groups?*
65. Have you ever attended a course on reading or understanding groups?
66. Have you ever been in a situation where you and others put the ability to read and understand groups on a success profile?
67. Have you ever been part of an effort to create a policy or a mission statement containing reference to having the ability to read and understand groups?
68. Have you ever been someone's coach or mentor who had problems reading or understanding groups?
69. Have you ever created a development plan for someone on reading or understanding groups?
70. Have you ever criticized someone for not reading/understanding groups accurately?
71. Have you ever designed a program on reading/understanding groups?
72. Have you ever given a speech on reading/understanding groups?
73. Have you ever rewarded or recognized someone for the ability to read/understand a group?
74. Have you ever taught a course on reading or understanding groups?
75. Have you ever tried to help someone more effectively read or understand groups?*
76. Have you ever tried to help someone improve their ability to read and understand groups?
77. How do you think people develop skills for reading or understanding groups?
78. How much of success do you think is due to the ability to read and understand groups compared with other characteristics?
79. How would you know if someone is bad at reading or understanding groups?
80. How would you know if someone is good at reading or understanding groups?
81. If you had to write a book on reading/understanding groups, what would the chapter headings be?
82. What are the benefits to someone who is really good at reading or understanding groups?
83. What are the consequences to someone who is really poor at reading or understanding groups?
84. What do you think the standard is on reading or understanding groups for someone in your role?

UNDERSTANDING OTHERS

85. What group stereotypes do you think have just a little bit of truth in them?*
86. What happens if you are too focused on reading or understanding groups?
87. What happens when two people try to work together who have very different abilities in reading and understanding groups?
88. What wisdom would you pass on to others trying to become better at reading or understanding groups?
89. When you select others, what do you look for in their ability to read or understand groups?
90. Why do you think people end up having different abilities to read and understand groups?

Dimension 4: Shows personal change and sense-making; learned it one place and applied it in another; can compare and contrast experiences; changes viewpoints across time; can explain personal development or evolution related to the competency

91. Compare and contrast examples of being effective and ineffective at understanding groups and predicting their behavior.
92. Contrast your on- and off-the-job experience in understanding groups and predicting their behavior.
93. Did you ever pass up a job or assignment because you were not confident enough in your skills at reading and understanding groups?
94. Do you ever use other skills to cover for your lack of ability to understand groups and predict their behavior?
95. Has becoming better at reading and understanding groups ever helped you in other areas?
96. Has lack of understanding groups ever figured in a failure, struggle, or setback you have had?
97. Have poor skills at understanding groups and predicting their behavior ever been the subject of a development plan for you?
98. Has your ability to understand groups and predict their behavior always been this way?
99. Has your ability to understand groups and predict their behavior, good or bad, ever been the subject of your performance review or a career discussion?
100. Have you ever delegated or assigned someone a task because you didn't understand groups and predict their behavior particularly well?
101. Have you ever made significant strides at becoming better at understanding groups and predicting their behavior?
102. How different are you across situations in your ability to understand groups and predict their behavior?
103. How do you decide how much attention to pay to understanding groups and predicting their behavior?
104. How have the events on September 11, 2001 changed your effectiveness in understanding groups and predicting their behavior?
105. How much of your success is due to your understanding groups and predicting their behavior?
106. How transferable is your ability to understand groups and predict their behavior to other situations?
107. If you had to become better at understanding groups and predicting their behavior in a hurry, what would you do?
108. Was there a time when you were not as good at understanding groups and predicting their behavior?
109. What caused you to work to change your skills at understanding groups and predicting their behavior?
110. What cues do you look for to better understand what your employees/ peers/customers/bosses, etc. will do in certain situations?
111. What event or series of events had the most impact on your understanding of groups?
112. What's the most varied you can be in understanding groups and predicting their behavior?
113. What was the shortest amount of time in which you increased your level of skill at understanding groups and predicting their behavior?
114. When did you first realize your level of skill at understanding groups and predicting their behavior?
115. When you know ahead of time that your level of understanding of a group won't be enough, what do you do?

UNDERSTANDING OTHERS

116. Why do you think you deal with understanding groups and predicting their behavior the way you do?
117. Why do you think your understanding of groups is the way it is?*

D. Follow-up Probes:
1. Are there times when you read groups accurately like that and times when you don't?
2. Are you better reading some types of groups than others?
3. Could you contrast those two bosses for me?
4. Could you give me a few examples of how you've used or applied that?
5. Do you always read groups like that, or was that a special situation?
6. Do you suppose if others would just try harder, they could learn to be more effective at reading groups like you do?
7. Do you think that's teachable?
8. Do you think you have better group reading skills than most? Why?
9. Do you think you would perform any differently if you could be more effective at reading and predicting what groups are going to do?
10. Have you always understood groups that way or is this a recent development in you?
11. How did the others react when you said/did that?
12. How did you come up with that approach to analyzing groups in the first place?
13. How did you know that method of analyzing groups would work?
14. How do others you have known approach that?
15. How many individuals in a group does it take to get it to change direction?
16. How typical is this for you?
17. How would you approach that same situation today?
18. Is this natural for you, or do you really have to dig for it?
19. Was there a time when you didn't understand this about yourself?
20. What did you do after you got that feedback?
21. What did you do to adapt to that?
22. What did you learn from that?
23. What do you think made the group go off in another direction?
24. What made you change your read of the group?
25. Why did the group change its mind?
26. Why did the group do that?
27. Why did you choose that approach?
28. Why did you decide to take the risk?
29. Why did you do it that way?
30. Why do you suppose groups work that way?
31. Why do you think that didn't work?
32. Why do you think that happened that way?
33. Why do you think that worked?
34. Why do you think you have difficulty with that?
35. Why do you think your first read of the group was off?
36. Would you have done it that way with looser deadlines?
37. Would you have done it that way with tighter deadlines?

UNDERSTANDING OTHERS

E. Themes/Things to Look for:

Ability to predict how groups will react	Rules of thumb for understanding groups
Ability to predict what groups will do	Seeing things through the eyes of others
Can read groups from different cultures	Sees differences; one size does not fit all
Can run group scenarios in their head	Sees large differences between good and bad groups
Complex and varied tools to analyze groups	Sees some good in poor groups and some bad in good groups
Complex models of group behavior	Student of group process
Describes groups in detail	Studies the history of groups
Draws parallels between groups	Tools to influence groups
Good observer of people and group detail	Understands /accepts differences/points of view
Listens	Understands but not necessarily agrees with groups
Not hesitant to have some groups in the bad bucket	

F. Most Likely Résumé:

1. Look for jobs like:

Cross-Moves	Scale Assignments
International Assignments	Significant People Demands
Line to Staff Switches	Staff Leadership (Influencing Without Authority)
Member of Projects/Task forces	Start-Ups

2. Look for develop-in-place assignments like:

Integrate diverse systems, processes, or procedures across decentralized and/or dispersed units.

Go to a campus as a recruiter.

Do a study of failed executives in your organization, including interviewing people still with the organization who knew or worked with them, and report the findings to top management.

Go on a business trip to a foreign country you've not been to before.

Be a change agent; create a symbol for change; lead the rallying cry; champion a significant change and implementation.

Create employee involvement teams.

Work on a team forming a joint venture or partnership.

Manage an ad hoc, temporary group of "green," inexperienced people as their coach, teacher, orienter, etc.

Manage an ad hoc, temporary group of balky and resisting people through an unpopular change or project.

Manage an ad hoc, temporary group including former peers to accomplish a task.

Manage an ad hoc, temporary group of people who are older and/or more experienced to accomplish a task.

Manage an ad hoc, temporary group of people where the temporary manager is a towering expert and the people in the group are not.

Manage an ad hoc, temporary group of people where the people in the group are towering experts but the temporary manager is not.

Handle a tough negotiation with an internal or external client or customer.

Help shut down a plant, regional office, product line, business, operation, etc.

Prepare and present a proposal of some consequence to top management.

Manage a dissatisfied internal or external customer; troubleshoot a performance or quality problem with a product or service.

Manage the assigning/allocating of office space in a contested situation.

UNDERSTANDING OTHERS

Manage the outplacement of a group of people.

Resolve an issue in conflict between two people, units, geographies, functions, etc.

Make peace with an enemy or someone you've disappointed with a product or service or someone you've had some trouble with or don't get along well with.

Write a speech for someone higher up in the organization.

Be a member of a union-negotiating or grievance-handling team.

Manage a project team of people who are older and more experienced.

3. **Best references to ask about or check:**

   Human Resource Professionals   Peers and Colleagues
   Natural Mentors   Direct Reports
   Past Associates/Constituencies

G. Learning Agility Evaluation:
   1. What/Describing vs. Why/Explain
   2. All or Nothing vs. Can See Many Sides
   3. Ordinary/Socially Acceptable vs. Insightful/Different
   7. Passive vs. Intrigued/Curious
   8. Sameness vs. Diversity
   13. Simple Views vs. Complex Views
   16. Few Rules of Thumb vs. Many and Varied Rules of Thumb
   21. View from Self vs. View from Point of View of Others

H. The LEADERSHIP ARCHITECT® Sort Card Connections:

   1. **Good (positive) if combined with high:**
      Can read groups of people higher up in the organization 4, 8 , 46, 48, 56
      Can read customer groups 5, 15
      Will take on groups on tough issues 12, 13, 34, 57
      Can help develop group's skills 19, 56, 60
      Can read groups from different cultures 21, 46
      Assembles effective teams 25, 56, 60
      Can read groups quickly 32, 33
      Can set standards for group performance 35, 53
      Really understands how groups operate 38, 39, 52, 60
      Can read a group in a highly political environment 38, 48
      Can read groups of peers and colleagues 42, 56
      Understands strengths and limitations of individuals in the group 56

   2. **Bad (negative) if combined with low or high (+):**
      May not read higher-ups as well 4, 8 , 46
      Doesn't use the knowledge to take on groups on the tough issues 12, 13, 34, 57
      Can't read groups outside their culture well 21
      Reads the group but misses on individuals 25, 56
      Doesn't put group reads into a bigger picture 38, 46, 48, 52, 59

UNDERSTANDING OTHERS

Doesn't take the political realities into account 38, 48

May not read like-level groups as well 42, 60

3. **Too much can contribute to the following Stallers and Stoppers:**

   A. *What too much looks like (overused):*

   > May spend too much time trying to analyze what a group might or might not do; may generalize from his/her group appraisal to individuals, letting personal impressions of a group cover individuals as well; may discount variety of opinion; may have trouble dealing with individuals when he/she is in conflict with the group the individual belongs to; may spend too much energy understanding and analyzing group actions.

   B. *Too much might lead to these Stallers and Stoppers:*
   Failure to Staff Effectively (111)

   C. *Compensators:*
   How to compensate for too much of this competency:
   1, 2, 12, 13, 16, 17, 21, 34, 37, 40, 50, 52, 53, 57, 59

   D. *Things to watch for:*
   Group read covers all members of the group–good or bad
   Misreads individuals in the group
   Spends too much time looking at the group level
   Confuses understanding with agreement
   Others read understanding as agreement

4. **Too little can contribute to the following Stallers and Stoppers:**

   A. *What too little looks like (unskilled):*

   > Doesn't read groups well; doesn't understand how groups operate or what purposes groups serve; can't predict what groups will do; stereotypes or pre-judges groups; may only understand groups similar to them in purpose and characteristics; sees people as individuals only; doesn't understand how group membership affects people's views and behavior; prefers working one-on-one; can't reach or motivate groups; may be a loner and not really a member of any voluntary groups.

   B. *Too little might lead to these Stallers and Stoppers:*

Unable to Adapt to Differences (101)	Failure to Staff Effectively (111)
Blocked Personal Learner (106)	Insensitive to Others (112)
Defensiveness (108)	Political Missteps (119)
Failure to Build a Team (110)	

   C. *Compensators:*
   How to substitute for too little of this competency:
   8, 15, 21, 32, 33, 36, 38, 39, 46, 51, 52, 56

UNDERSTANDING OTHERS

I. LEARNING ARCHITECT® Connections:
Look for people who act like and/or show evidence of:

2a. Problem Solving
2b. Visioning
3b. Self-Talk
4a. Getting Information
9. Multiple Sources
11. Why/How
12. Rules of Thumb
15. Cautious
16. Collaborate
21. Changer
23. Orchestrator
32. Diversity in Others
34. Sizing Up Others

J. CHOICES ARCHITECT® Connections:
Look for people who act like and/or show evidence of:

First Edition (Released 1994)
7. Helping Others Think
11. Open to Diversity
14. Transaction Quality
17. Hot/Direct Sources
23. Communicator

Second Edition (Released 2000)
9. Agile Communicator
10. Conflict Manager
14. Open-Minded
15. People-Smart

K. Difficulty to Develop:
34 (of 34)–Hardest

UNDERSTANDING OTHERS

65. *MANAGING* VISION AND PURPOSE

A. Definition:

Communicates a compelling and inspired vision or sense of core purpose; talks beyond today; talks about possibilities; is optimistic; creates mileposts and symbols to rally support behind the vision; makes the vision sharable by everyone; can inspire and motivate entire units or organizations.

B. Arenas/Domains to Explore:

1. Advertising and marketing
2. Chair of United Way
3. Coach
4. Dean
5. Energizing stagnant situations
6. Fraternity/sorority leadership
7. Fund-raising
8. Getting new members for a group
9. Getting people to volunteer
10. Grant proposals
11. Hosting a conference
12. Lobbying
13. Military command experience
14. Mission/vision/values work sessions
15. Political campaigns
16. Professional association leadership
17. Public relations
18. Religious instruction
19. Selling a taskforce finding
20. Selling annual plans
21. Selling consulting projects
22. Selling customers on relationship
23. Selling investors
24. Selling merger partners
25. Selling people on joining company
26. Selling potential acquisition
27. Selling strategic plans
28. Starting a new group
29. Vision presentations to employees
30. Vision presentations to shareholders
31. Vision presentations to strategic partners
32. Vision presentations to the board
33. Vision presentations to Wall Street analysts
34. Volunteer groups

C. Sample Questions:

Dimension 1: Been there, done that–has had direct personal experience(s) involving the competency–candidate was the prime player   Note: * means OK for campus

1. Can you tell me about a time when you created a slogan, logo, or icon that became a symbol for a new vision?
2. Has a vision message you've delivered ever gotten rejected?
3. Has anyone ever accused you of messing something up because you couldn't communicate or implement the vision?
4. Have you ever been around a situation where an impossible vision took the wind out of the sails for everyone?
5. Have you ever been involved in creating a mission or values statement for an organization and then had to communicate it to various audiences?
6. Have you ever been on the side arguing that a vision was too much of a stretch?
7. Have you ever delivered a vision message to motivate people to stay with the organization?
8. Have you ever had to deliver a vision message you didn't agree with?
9. Have you ever made a videotape communicating a vision?
10. Have you ever managed anything where the people or units reporting to you were in different locations? How did you communicate and implement your vision from afar?

MANAGING VISION AND PURPOSE

11. Have you written vision speeches for others to present?
12. How do you create milestones or benchmarks for measuring progress against the vision?
13. How do you involve people around you in creating the vision?
14. How do you share your view of the future with your people?
15. Tell me about a time when you had to figure how to get your vision message across to remote locations without going there.
16. Tell me about a time when you installed a new vision.*
17. Tell me about a time when your attempt to communicate a vision got you into trouble.
18. Tell me about a time when your attempt to communicate a vision worked really well for you.
19. Tell me about a time you communicated a new direction during a reorganization or start-up.
20. Tell me about a time you inherited a dejected/balky or underpowered work group and turned it around with a new vision.*
21. Tell me about a time you managed a group/unit that was heading south and you wanted them to head north.*
22. Tell me about a time you performed a symbolic act or acts in order to make a vision point.*
23. Tell me about a time you sold a new vision.*
24. Were you ever around a situation where a well-communicated vision turned an organization around?
25. When you are part of a team creating a new vision, what role do you usually play?

Dimension 2: Seen/been around others who were involved with the competency—good and bad; learns from others about self

26. Contrast people you know who are the best and worst communicators of a vision.*
27. Has managing vision and purpose ever been in any 360° survey done on you? Was your score among your highest, middle, or lowest?
28. Has poor vision communicating skills on someone else's part ever created an obstacle for you or got in the way of something you were trying to accomplish?*
29. Have you ever talked with a coach or mentor about your managing vision and purpose skills?
30. Have you ever watched someone fail/get fired because they did not have skills in communicating the vision?*
31. Have you ever watched someone overdo communicating the vision to the point that it backfired?
32. Have you ever watched someone succeed because they communicated the vision effectively?*
33. Have you ever worked with a coach on managing vision and purpose skills?*
34. Have you ever worked with a person who excelled at managing and communicating vision and purpose?
35. Have you ever worked with a skills coach on managing vision and purpose?*
36. How do you get feedback about yourself on managing vision and purpose?
37. How often do you check with multiple sources when you get critical feedback on your managing vision and purpose skills?
38. Is there a historical figure you consider a model of managing vision and purpose?
39. What do others who are not your fans say about your managing vision and purpose skills?
40. What do others who like you say about your managing vision and purpose skills?
41. Which boss was the best at managing vision and purpose?
42. Which boss was the worst at managing vision and purpose?
43. Which direct report was the best at managing vision and purpose?
44. Which direct report was the worst at managing vision and purpose?
45. Which peer was the best at managing vision and purpose?
46. Which peer was the worst at managing and communicating vision and purpose?
47. Who in your field or business is the best at managing and communicating vision and purpose?

MANAGING VISION AND PURPOSE

48. Who do you consider a current role model of managing and communicating vision and purpose?*
49. Who do you go to for advice on managing and communicating vision and purpose?
50. Who have you learned the most from about managing and communicating vision and purpose?*
51. Who is a higher-management role model for you on managing and communicating vision and purpose?
52. Who is a role model of managing and communicating vision and purpose outside of work?

Dimension 3: Knows how the competency works in theory; shows understanding

53. Are there situations or settings where someone should communicate and implement a vision differently?
54. Do you think communicating and implementing a vision can be learned; how do you think people develop these skills?
55. Do you think there is a way to compensate or work around a low ability to communicate and implement a vision?
56. Has anyone asked you for your opinions/advice on communicating and implementing a vision?
57. Have you ever attended a course on communicating and implementing a vision?
58. Have you ever been in a situation where you and others put communicating and implementing a vision on a success profile?
59. Have you ever been part of an effort to create a policy or a mission statement containing reference to communicating and implementing a vision?
60. Have you ever been someone's coach or mentor who had problems with communicating and implementing a vision?
61. Have you ever created a development plan for someone on communicating and implementing a vision?
62. Have you ever criticized someone for not communicating and implementing a vision?
63. Have you ever designed a program on communicating and implementing a vision?
64. Have you ever given a speech on communicating and implementing a vision?
65. Have you ever rewarded or recognized someone for communicating and implementing a vision well?
66. Have you ever taught a course on communicating and implementing a vision?
67. Have you ever tried to help someone deal more effectively with communicating and implementing a vision?*
68. Have you ever tried to help someone improve their ability in communicating and implementing a vision?
69. How do you think people develop the ability to communicating and implementing a vision?
70. How much skill in communicating and implementing a vision is good to have and how much is too much?
71. How much of success do you think is due to the ability to communicate and implement a vision compared with other characteristics?
72. How would you know if someone is bad at communicating and implementing a vision?
73. How would you know if someone is good at communicating and implementing a vision?
74. If you had to write a book on communicating and implementing a vision, what would the chapter headings be?
75. What are the benefits to someone who is really good at communicating and implementing a vision?
76. What are the consequences to someone who is really poor at communicating and implementing a vision?
77. What do you think the standard is on communicating and implementing a vision for someone in your role?
78. What happens when two people try to work together who have very different abilities in communicating and implementing a vision?
79. What wisdom would you pass on to others trying to become better at communicating and implementing a vision?
80. When you select others, what do you look for in skills in communicating and implementing a vision?
81. Why do you think people end up being different in their ability to communicate and implement a vision?

MANAGING VISION AND PURPOSE

Dimension 4: Shows personal change and sense-making; learned it one place and applied it in another; can compare and contrast experiences; changes viewpoints across time; can explain personal development or evolution related to the competency

82. Compare and contrast examples of being effective and ineffective at managing and communicating vision and purpose.
83. Contrast your on- and off-the-job use of managing and communicating vision and purpose.
84. Did you ever pass up a job or assignment because you were not confident enough in your skills at communicating and implementing a vision?
85. Do you ever use other skills to cover for your lack of skill at communicating and implementing a vision?
86. Has becoming better at communicating and implementing a vision ever helped you in other areas?
87. Has not communicating and implementing a clear vision ever figured in a failure, struggle, or setback you have had?
88. Has poor communicating and implementing a vision ever been the subject of a development plan for you?
89. Has your skill level at communicating and implementing a vision always been this way?
90. Have you ever delegated or assigned someone a task because you didn't communicate and implement a vision particularly well?
91. Have you ever made significant strides at becoming better at communicating and implementing a vision?
92. Have your communicating and implementing vision skills, good or bad, ever been the subject of your performance review or a career discussion?
93. How different are you across situations in the way you communicate and implement of a vision?
94. How do you adjust your communication style to get messages across to different levels of employees?
95. How do you decide how much of your skill at communicating and implementing a vision to use?
96. How have the demands of your job forced you to communicate beyond the here and now?
97. How much of your success is due to your skills at communicating and implementing a clear vision?
98. How transferable are your communicating and implementing vision skills to other situations?
99. If you had to become better at communicating and implementing vision in a hurry, what would you do?
100. Was there a time when you were not as good at communicating and implementing a vision?
101. What caused you to work to improve your skills at communicating and implementing a vision?
102. What event or series of events had the most impact on your skill level at communicating and implementing a vision?
103. What's the most varied you can be in communicating and implementing a vision?
104. What was the shortest amount of time in which you increased your level of skill at communicating and implementing a vision?
105. When did you first realize your level of skill at communicating and implementing a vision?
106. When you know ahead of time that your usual way of communicating and implementing a vision won't work, what do you do?
107. Why do you think you deal with communicating and implementing a vision the way you do?
108. Why do you think your level of skill at communicating and implementing a vision is the way it is?*

MANAGING VISION AND PURPOSE

D. Follow-up Probes:

1. Are there times when you use your vision management skills like that and times when you don't?
2. Could you contrast those two bosses for me?
3. Could you give me a few examples of how you've used or applied that?
4. Did the vision actually come true?
5. Did you observe someone else give the same vision presentation? What did you think?
6. Do you always try to manage visions like that, or was that a special situation?
7. Do you suppose if others would just try harder, they could learn to be more effective at selling in a vision like you do?
8. Do you think that's teachable?
9. Do you think you have better vision management skills than most? Why?
10. Do you think you would perform any differently if you could be more effective at communicating and managing vision?
11. Have you always communicated and managed visions that way, or is this a recent development in you?
12. Have you ever had to sell a vision to someone you really disliked?
13. How did the others react when you did that?
14. How did you adapt the presentation for different audiences?
15. How did you come up with that approach to communicating and managing vision in the first place?
16. How did you come up with that symbol for the vision?
17. How did you get yourself up for those repeated presentations?
18. How did you know that method of communicating a vision would work?
19. How do others you have known approach that?
20. How much difference in performance was there after the vision was communicated?
21. How typical is this for you?
22. How would you approach that same situation today?
23. Is this natural for you, or do you really have to dig for it?
24. Was that a fair way to sell in a vision?
25. Was there a time when you didn't understand this about yourself?
26. What did you do after you got that feedback?
27. What did you do to adapt to that?
28. What did you learn from that?
29. Why did you choose that approach?
30. Why did you decide to take the risk?
31. Why did you disagree with the vision?
32. Why did you do it that way?
33. Why did you time your attempt to sell the vision like that?
34. Why do you suppose organizations need visions?
35. Why do you think that's so easy for you to do?
36. Why do you think that didn't work?
37. Why do you think that happened that way?
38. Why do you think that worked?
39. Why do you think you have difficulty doing that?
40. Would you have done it that way with looser deadlines?
41. Would you have done it that way with tighter deadlines?

MANAGING VISION AND PURPOSE

E. Themes/Things to Look for:

A way with words; can turn a phrase	Knowing measures of achievement
Ability to project how things are going to turn out	Making unusual connections
Able to predict what people will respond to	Matching pace and complexity to the audience
Appreciation of people who create the vision	Openness to different ways of thinking
Broad perspective	Passion
Can create symbols	Patience with the unconverted
Can pull people into the vision	Perseverance
Can run out a trend to its logical conclusion	Persuasive speaker
Charisma	Seeing the bigger picture
Comfortable speculating	Seeing things from the other person's viewpoint
Drawing parallels	Simple, visual statements
Emotional energy	Staying state of the art
Future sense	Storytelling skills
Global view	Tying things together
Good at Q & A	Understanding multiple forces
Good sales and marketing skills	Varied presentation skills
Influence skills	Willingness to make it bigger than it really is
Inspirational	

F. Most Likely Résumé:

1. Look for jobs like:

Heavy Strategic Demands	Scope (complexity) Assignments
International Assignments	Significant People Demands
Scale (size shift) Assignments	Start-Ups

2. Look for develop-in-place assignments like:

Work on a project that involves travel and study of an issue, acquisition, or joint venture off-shore or overseas, with a report back to management.

Launch a new product, service, or process.

Be a change agent; create a symbol for change; lead the rallying cry; champion a significant change and implementation.

Relaunch an existing product or service that's not doing well.

Manage an ad hoc, temporary group of "green," inexperienced people as their coach, teacher, orienter, etc.

Assemble an ad hoc team of diverse people to accomplish a difficult task.

Prepare and present a proposal of some consequence to top management.

Take on a tough and undoable project, one where others who have tried it have failed.

Build a multifunctional project team to tackle a common business issue or problem.

3. Best references to ask about or check:

Direct Boss	Natural Mentors
Boss' Boss(es)	Past Associates/Constituencies

MANAGING VISION AND PURPOSE

G. Learning Agility Evaluation:
1. What/Describing vs. Why/Explain
2. All or Nothing vs. Can See Many Sides
3. Ordinary/Socially Acceptable vs. Insightful/Different
4. Spectator/Passive vs. Player/Participant
9. Vague/General vs. Sharp/Specific
10. Reactive vs. Initiating
15. Linear vs. Use Contrasts/Analogies
19. External Standards vs. Internal Standards
21. View from Self vs. View from Point of View of Others

H. The LEADERSHIP ARCHITECT® Sort Card Connections:

1. Good (positive) if combined with high:
Is charismatic when delivering the vision 1, 9, 14, 36, 49
Dialogues with people about the vision 3, 31, 33
Open to input on how to present vision 3, 33, 64
Can sell a vision up 4, 8 , 46
Can also create the vision 5, 15, 24, 32, 46, 51, 58, 61
Knows substance backing up vision 5, 24, 58
Can add the bigger picture 20, 35
Loyal; looks after organization's best interests 22, 29
Can write good vision scripts 27, 67
Can blend in technology 32, 61
Follows through on vision 35, 39, 47
Takes political realities into account 38, 48
Patience with the unconverted 41
Can sell a vision sideways 42, 60
Can adjust presentation to the audience 56, 64

2. Bad (negative) if combined with low or high (+):
Doesn't walk the talk 1, 16, 53
Only simple visions 2, 40
Isn't as good in small groups 3, 31, 33, 41
Can't create the vision themselves 5, 24, 46, 51, 58
Doesn't know the detail behind the vision; weak Q & A 5, 24, 58
Freezes when challenged 11, 12, 34, 57
Can't weave the vision into the political tapestry 38, 48

3. Too much can contribute to the following Stallers and Stoppers:

A. What too much looks like (overused):
May leave people behind; may lack patience with those who don't understand or share their vision and sense of purpose; may lack appropriate detail-orientation and concern for administrative routine; may lack follow-through on the day-to-day tasks.

B. Too much might lead to these Stallers and Stoppers:
Being a Poor Administrator (102)   Failure to Build a Team (110)
Arrogant (104)   Overmanaging (117)

MANAGING VISION AND PURPOSE

C. Compensators:
How to compensate for too much of this competency:
3, 5, 24, 27, 33, 35, 41, 52, 64, 67

D. Things to watch for:
Doesn't walk their talk
Impatient with the unconverted
Just knows the message; not the details
Looks down on those who don't get it
Out of contact with the people; too far ahead

4. Too little can contribute to the following Stallers and Stoppers:

A. What too little looks like (unskilled):
Can't communicate or sell a vision; not a good presenter; can't turn a good phrase or create compelling one-liners; uncomfortable speculating on the unknown future; isn't charismatic or passionate enough to excite and energize others; can't simplify enough to help people understand complex strategy; may not understand how change happens; doesn't act like he/she really believes in the vision; more comfortable in the here and now.

B. Too little might lead to these Stallers and Stoppers:
Non-Strategic (114)
Performance Problems (118)

C. Compensators:
How to substitute for too little of this competency:
5, 9, 15, 24, 28, 36, 46, 49, 59, 63

I. LEARNING ARCHITECT® Connections:

Look for people who act like and/or show evidence of:

1c. Following a Plan
2a. Problem Solving
2b. Visioning
2c. Intuition
12. Rules of Thumb
11. Why/How
13. Focused
18. Straightforward
23. Orchestrator
27. Conceptualizer

J. CHOICES ARCHITECT® Connections:

Look for people who act like and/or show evidence of:

First Edition (Released 1994)
6. Visionary
20. Forging Ahead
21. Taking the Heat
23. Communicator

Second Edition (Released 2000)
9. Agile Communicator
21. Innovation Manager
22. Taking the Heat
23. Visioning
24. Inspires Others
27. Presence

K. Difficulty to Develop:
25 (of 34)–Moderate

66. WORK/LIFE BALANCE

A. Definition:

Maintains a conscious balance between work and personal life so that one doesn't dominate the other; is not one-dimensional; knows how to attend to both; gets what he/she wants from both.

B. Arenas/Domains to Explore:

1. Career choices
2. Career goals
3. Career/life goal coordination
4. Downtime activities
5. Elder care time
6. Family/work integrated travel
7. Friends out of work arena
8. Hobbies
9. Holiday rituals
10. Job choices
11. Leisure activities
12. Logical commute planning
13. More to do than there is time
14. Museums/parks/forests/galleries
15. Personal financial management
16. Quality family time
17. Reading habits
18. Recharging methods
19. Religious views
20. Schedule protection
21. Social interests
22. Time management at play
23. Time management at work
24. Time management dilemmas
25. Time management with family
26. Time working/time playing ratio
27. Travel patterns
28. Vacation habits
29. Value placed on time
30. Weekend patterns
31. Working vacations

C. Sample Questions:

Dimension 1: Been there, done that–has had direct personal experience(s) involving the competency–candidate was the prime player   Note: * means OK for campus

1. Do you volunteer for any community service activities?*
2. Has anyone ever accused you of messing something up at work or in your life because of poor balance between the two?
3. Have you ever been part of a commuter pool that had to leave at a specific time?
4. Have you ever had split homes during job transitions? How long did that last?
5. Have you ever left a job or organization because the hours were just unreasonable?
6. Have you ever managed anything where the people or units reporting to you were in different cities and countries? How much travel was involved? Did the job interfere with your personal life?
7. Have you ever stayed away over the weekend instead of coming home and leaving again after just one or two days?
8. Have you ever taken a leave of absence to handle a family or personal matter?
9. Have you ever worked offshore without your family moving to the country?
10. Have you ever worked where they offered sabbaticals? Did you take one?
11. Have you worked with a real workaholic? What happened to them?
12. Have you worked with a work-dedicated person whose personal life fell apart while they were being successful at work?

WORK/LIFE BALANCE

13. How do you adjust after one of those ninety-hour-work-week-with-impossible-deadlines marathons?*
14. How do you make time for your children's school events that happen during work hours?
15. How do you tell when enough work is enough?
16. How late on Fridays do you schedule meetings when you are out of town?
17. On an international trip, do you go early to allow a day or two to adjust to the time change?
18. Tell me about a time when an employee had off-work issues that got in the way of performance.
19. Tell me about a time when you felt the need to rebalance family/personal/ work priorities.*
20. Tell me about a time when you questioned why you were living your life the way you were living it.*
21. Tell me about a time when your employees were feeling overwhelmed at work.
22. Tell me about a time when your work/life balance got you into trouble.
23. Tell me about a time when your work/life balance worked really well for you.
24. What are your hobbies?*
25. What are your interests besides work/school?*
26. What is your version of spending quality time with the people in your life outside of work?
27. What professional memberships do you maintain?
28. What's the longest you've been away from home without your family; traveling for work?
29. When you have a Monday midmorning meeting out of town, when do you go?

Dimension 2: Seen/been around others who were involved with the competency–good and bad; learns from others about self

30. Contrast the most and least work/life balanced people you know.*
31. Has work/life balance ever been in any 360° survey done on you? Was your score among your highest, middle, or lowest?
32. Has poor work/life balance on someone else's part ever created an obstacle for you or got in the way of something you were trying to accomplish?*
33. Have you ever talked with a coach or mentor about your work/life balance?
34. Have you ever watched someone fail/get fired because they did not balance work and personal life?*
35. Have you ever watched someone overdo work/life balance to the point that it backfired?
36. Have you ever watched someone succeed because they balanced work and personal life?*
37. Have you ever worked with a coach on balancing work and personal life?*
38. Have you ever worked with a person who excelled at work/life balance?
39. Have you ever worked with a skills coach on work/life balance?*
40. How do you get feedback about yourself on how well you balance work and personal life?
41. How often do you check with multiple sources when you get a piece of critical feedback on your work/life balance?
42. Is there a historical figure you consider a model of work/life balance?
43. What do others who are not your fans say about your work/life balance?
44. What do others who like you say about your work/life balance?
45. Which boss was the best at balancing work and personal life?
46. Which boss was the worst at balancing work and personal life?
47. Which direct report was the best at balancing work and personal life?
48. Which direct report was the worst at balancing work and personal life?
49. Which peer was the best at balancing work and personal life?
50. Which peer was the worst at balancing work and personal life?
51. Who in your field or business is the best at balancing work and personal life?
52. Who do you consider a role model of balancing work and personal life?*

WORK/LIFE BALANCE

53. Who do you go to for advice on balancing work and personal life?
54. Who have you learned the most from about balancing work and personal life?*
55. Who is a higher-management role model for you on balancing work and personal life?
56. Who is a role model of balancing work and personal life outside of work?

Dimension 3: Knows how the competency works in theory; shows understanding

57. Are there situations or settings where someone should balance their work and personal life differently?
58. Do you think work/life balance skills can be learned; how do you think people develop this skill?
59. Do you think there is a way to compensate or work around a low ability to balance work and personal life?
60. Has anyone asked you for your opinions/advice on work/life balance?*
61. Have you ever attended a course on work/life balance?
62. Have you ever been in a situation where you and others put work/life balance on a success profile?
63. Have you ever been part of an effort to create a policy or a mission statement containing reference to work/life balance
64. Have you ever been someone's coach or mentor who had problems with work/life balance?
65. Have you ever created a development plan for someone on work/life balance?
66. Have you ever criticized someone for not balancing work and personal life well?
67. Have you ever designed a program on work/life balance?
68. Have you ever given a speech on work/life balance?
69. Have you ever rewarded or recognized someone for having a balanced work and personal life?
70. Have you ever taught a course on work/life balance?
71. Have you ever tried to help someone deal with work/life balance more effectively?*
72. Have you ever tried to help someone improve their work/life balance?
73. How do you think people develop work/life balance skills?
74. How much work/life balance is good to have and how much is too much?
75. How much of success do you think is due to work/life balance compared with other characteristics?
76. How would you know if someone is bad at work/life balance?
77. How would you know if someone is good at work/life balance?
78. If you had to write a book on work/life balance, what would the chapter headings be?
79. What are the benefits to someone who is really good at balancing their work and personal life well?
80. What are the consequences to someone who is really poor at balancing their work and personal life?
81. What do you think the standard is on work/life balance for someone in your role?
82. What happens if you have too much work/life balance?
83. What happens when two people try to work together who balance their work/personal lives very differently?
84. What wisdom would you pass on to others trying to become better at work/life balance?
85. When you select others, what do you look for in ability to balance their work and personal lives?
86. Why do you think people end up approaching work/life balance differently?

Dimension 4: Shows personal change and sense-making; learned it one place and applied it in another; can compare and contrast experiences; changes viewpoints across time; can explain personal development or evolution related to the competency

87. Compare and contrast examples of being effective and ineffective at work/life balance.
88. Did you ever pass up a job or assignment because you were not confident enough in your skills at maintaining balance between personal life and work?
89. Do you ever use other skills to cover for your lack of work/life balance?

WORK/LIFE BALANCE

90. Has becoming better at work/life balance ever helped you in other areas?
91. Has lack of work/life balance ever figured in a failure, struggle, or setback you have had?
92. Has poor work/life balance ever been the subject of a development plan for you?
93. Has your work/life balance always been this way?
94. Have you ever delegated or assigned someone a task because you didn't manage the balance between work and personal life particularly well?
95. Have you ever made significant strides at becoming better at work/life balance?
96. Have your work/life balance skills, good or bad, ever been the subject of your performance review or a career discussion?
97. How different are you across situations in your work/life balance?
98. How do you decide how much work/life balance to have?
99. How much of your success is due to your work/life balance?
100. If you had to become better at work/life balance in a hurry, what would you do?
101. If you won a $50 million lottery, what would you do?
102. Was there a time when you were not as good at work/life balance?
103. What caused you to work to improve your work/life balance?
104. What do you do when your life is out of kilter or you're feeling overwhelmed?*
105. What event or series of events had the most impact on your work/life balance?
106. What's the most varied you can be in work/life balance?
107. What was the shortest amount of time in which you increased your level of skill at work/life balance?
108. When did you first realize your level of skill at work/life balance?
109. When you know ahead of time that your usual approach to work/life balance won't work, what do you do?
110. Why do you think you deal with work/life balance the way you do?
111. Why do you think your work/life balance is the way it is?*

D. Follow-up Probes:

1. Are there times when your life is in balance like that and times when it isn't?
2. Could you contrast those two bosses for me?
3. Could you give me a few examples of how you've used or applied that?
4. Do you always try to balance your life like that, or was that a special situation?
5. Do you suppose if others would just try harder, they could learn to be in better personal, family, and work life balance like you?
6. Do you think that's teachable?
7. Do you think that was too high a price to pay?
8. Do you think you have better balance in your life than most? Why?
9. Do you think you would perform any differently if you could be in better life balance?
10. Has that translated into you doing anything different with your life?
11. Have you always balanced your life that way, or is this a recent development in you?
12. How could you have balanced them better?
13. How did that make you feel?
14. How did the others react when you did that?
15. How did you come up with that approach to balancing your life in the first place?
16. How did you know that method of getting your life in better balance would work?

WORK/LIFE BALANCE

17. How do others you have known approach that?
18. How typical is this for you?
19. How would you approach that same situation today?
20. Is this natural for you, or do you really have to dig for it?
21. Was that fair to your family?
22. Was that right for the company to demand of you?
23. Was there a time when you didn't understand this about yourself?
24. What did you do after you got that feedback?
25. What did you do to adapt to that?
26. What did you learn from that?
27. When is the last time you started a new hobby?
28. When is the last time you started a new personal life activity?
29. Why did you choose that approach?
30. Why did you decide to take the risk?
31. Why did you do it that way?
32. Why did you time your attempt to get into better balance like that?
33. Why do you think that didn't work?
34. Why do you think that happened that way?
35. Why do you think that worked?
36. Why do you think you have difficulties with that sometimes?
37. Would you have done it that way with looser deadlines?
38. Would you have done it that way with tighter deadlines?

E. Themes/Things to Look for:

A method of recharging the batteries

Able to monitor personal stress levels

Able to sense family stress levels

Able to sense the needs of children

Adding new and fresh activities (work and non-work)

Conscious balance

Enjoyment from all sectors–personal, family, and work

Having a plan for balance

Knowing the consequences of long-term imbalance

Knowledgeable about and comfortable with whatever the balance is

Shows excitement about both work and personal life

The ability to rest and relax on short notice

Tolerance of temporary imbalance

Variety of interests and obligations

Willingness to adjust to life's realities

Works hard, plays hard

WORK/LIFE BALANCE

F. Most Likely Résumé:

1. Look for jobs like:
Cross-Moves
International Assignments
Staff to Line Shifts

2. Look for develop-in-place assignments like:
Attend a self-awareness/assessment course that includes feedback.
Join a self-help or support group.
Manage the outplacement of a group of people.

3. Best references to ask about or check:
Family Members
Spouse

G. Learning Agility Evaluation:
4. Spectator/Passive vs. Player/Participant
5. Tight/Rigid vs. Loose/Flexible
6. Reacting/Responsive vs. Adapting
10. Reactive vs. Initiating
14. Sameness vs. Broad Ranging
17. Avoid Discussion of Weaknesses vs. Comfortably Sharing Shortcomings
19. External Standards vs. Internal Standards

H. The LEADERSHIP ARCHITECT® Sort Card Connections:

1. Good (positive) if combined with high:
Can make quick switches in balance 1, 16, 53
Doesn't freeze in the face of imbalance/uncertainty 2, 11, 12, 40
Takes time to listen to life and work constituencies 3, 31, 33, 50
Can fairly adjudicate work/life conflicts 6, 12, 17, 23, 50
Spends some of their time helping others 7, 10, 21, 23
Puts aside time for personal growth 32, 45, 54, 55, 62
Broad range of interests 46
Uses time wisely 47, 50, 62

2. Bad (negative) if combined with low or high (+):
Very work dedicated (+1, 6, 9, 16, 24, 34, 39, 43, 53, 57)
May not have the stomach for the tough issues 12, 13, 34, 37, 57
Doesn't leave any time for their own development 45, 54, 55
Narrow interests 46
Doesn't use time wisely 47, 50, 62

WORK/LIFE BALANCE

3. **Too much can contribute to the following Stallers and Stoppers:**

    A. *What too much looks like (overused):*

    > May not be flexible enough when work or personal life demands change dramatically; may not be willing to adjust one at the expense of the other; may value balance over temporary discomfort; may try to force his/her view of balance on others.

    B. *Too much might lead to these Stallers and Stoppers:*

    Overly Ambitious (103)   Lack of Ethics and Values (109)
    Lack of Composure (107)   Performance Problems (118)

    C. *Compensators:*
    How to compensate for too much of this competency:
    2, 6, 11, 12, 17, 22, 23, 32, 40, 45, 46, 50, 54, 55

    D. *Things to watch for:*
    Makes illogical choices that cost more downstream
    Missionary for how they does it
    Unwilling to change
    Win a battle and loses a war
    Can't deal with varying points of view

4. **Too little can contribute to the following Stallers and Stoppers:**

    A. *What too little looks like (unskilled):*

    > Lacks balance between work and personal life; overdoes one at the harmful expense of the other; may be a workaholic; may be bored off-work or can't relax; may be a poor time manager and priority setter; may just react; can't turn off one area of life and fully concentrate on the other; can't keep multiple and mixed priorities going at one time; carries troubles from one area of life into the other; can only seem to manage one or the other.

    B. *Too little might lead to these Stallers and Stoppers:*

    Overly Ambitious (103)
    Lack of Composure (107)

    C. *Compensators:*
    How to substitute for too little of this competency:
    1, 3, 7, 10, 26, 39, 45, 47, 54, 55, 62

I. **LEARNING ARCHITECT® Connections:**

Look for people who act like and/or show evidence of:
1c. Following a Plan
3a. Checking Feelings
3b. Self-Talk

WORK/LIFE BALANCE

J. CHOICES ARCHITECT® Connections:

Look for people who act like and/or show evidence of:

First Edition (Released 1994)
13. Role Flexibility

Second Edition (Released 2000)
18. Role Flexibility

K. Difficulty to Develop:
28 (of 34)–Harder

67. WRITTEN COMMUNICATIONS

A. Definition:

Is able to write clearly and succinctly in a variety of communication settings and styles; can get messages across that have the desired effect.

B. Arenas/Domains to Explore:

1. Activity reports
2. Annual business plans
3. Annual report
4. Answering customer inquiries
5. Audit report
6. Brochures
7. Church sermons
8. Customer instructions
9. Development plans
10. E-mail
11. Legal documents
12. Letters
13. Memos
14. Mission/vision/values statements
15. News release
16. Performance appraisals
17. Proposals
18. Public relations releases
19. Publications
20. Regulatory write-ups
21. Reports
22. Resume
23. Sales and marketing presentations
24. Shareholders meetings
25. Speech scripts
26. Strategic plans
27. Taskforce reports
28. Technical writing
29. Testimony
30. Training courses
31. Trip reports
32. Video scripts
33. White papers

C. Sample Questions:

Dimension 1: Been there, done that–has had direct personal experience(s) involving the competency–candidate was the prime player   Note: * means OK for campus

1. Do other people bring you their writing to critique?
2. Do you enjoy writing? What types of writing do you enjoy most?*
3. Do you look forward to writing tasks?*
4. Do you return documents to your people and ask them to rewrite them?
5. Do you rewrite other people's stuff?*
6. Do you spell well?*
7. Do you use a lot of adjectives?*
8. Do you use humor in your writing?*
9. Has anyone ever accused you of messing something up because of poor writing skills?
10. Have you ever drafted a constitution or bylaws for an organization?*
11. Have you ever drafted a mission/vision/values statement for an organization?*
12. Have you ever drafted a strategic plan?
13. Have you ever had a job doing technical writing?
14. Have you ever had anything published?*

WRITTEN COMMUNICATIONS

15. Have you ever managed anything where the people or units reporting to you were in different locations? How did you communicate in writing?
16. Have you ever written for a school newspaper/yearbook?*
17. Have you had to write narratives for performance appraisals?
18. Have you written press releases?
19. Have you written speeches for others?
20. How do you react when given a poor piece of writing to read?*
21. How long are your average sentences?*
22. How long would it take you on average to write a three-page document?
23. How many different writing styles do you think you use?*
24. How many drafts do you go through when writing for general distribution?
25. Tell me about a time when a boss returned a document to you to rewrite.
26. Tell me about a time when you had to communicate something important in writing to someone who did not speak your language very well.
27. Tell me about a time when you installed a new system and had to write instructions to go with it.*
28. What were some of your notable failures at written communications?*
29. What were some of your notable successes at written communications?*
30. What were your grades in English in high school and college?*
31. When you handed in papers in school, were they generally shorter, as requested, or longer than required?*
32. Where does your writing range on a simple-to-complex scale?*

Dimension 2: Seen/been around others who were involved with the competency–good and bad; learns from others about self

33. Contrast the best and worst business writers you know.*
34. Has writing skills or written communications ever been in any 360° survey done on you? Was your score among your highest, middle, or lowest?
35. Has poor writing skills on someone else's part ever created an obstacle for you or got in the way of something you were trying to accomplish?*
36. Have you ever talked with a coach or mentor about your writing skills?
37. Have you ever watched someone fail/get fired because they did not have adequate writing skills?*
38. Have you ever watched someone overdo writing skills to the point that it backfired?
39. Have you ever watched someone succeed because they had good writing skills?*
40. Have you ever worked with a coach on writing skills?*
41. Have you ever worked with a person who excelled at writing skills?
42. Have you ever worked with a skills coach on writing skills?*
43. How do you get feedback about yourself on writing skills and written communications?
44. How often do you check with multiple sources when you get critical feedback on your writing skills?
45. Is there a historical figure you consider a model of writing skills?
46. What do others who are not your fans say about your writing skills?
47. What do others who like you say about your writing skills?
48. Which boss was the best at writing skills?
49. Which boss was the worst at writing skills?
50. Which direct report was the best at writing skills?
51. Which direct report was the worst at writing skills?
52. Which peer was the best at writing skills?

WRITTEN COMMUNICATIONS

53. Which peer was the worst at writing skills?
54. Who is the best writer in your field or business?
55. Who do you consider a role model of writing skills and written communications?*
56. Who do you go to for advice on writing skills?
57. Who have you learned the most from about communicating well in writing?*
58. Who is a higher-management role model for you on writing skills?
59. Who is a role model of writing skills outside of work?

Dimension 3: Knows how the competency works in theory; shows understanding

60. Are there situations or settings where someone should communicate differently in writing?
61. Do you think writing skills can be learned; how do you think people develop writing skills?
62. Do you think there is a way to compensate or work around low writing skills?
63. Has anyone asked you for your opinions/advice on written communications?*
64. Have you ever attended a writing course?
65. Have you ever been in a situation where you and others put writing skills on a success profile?
66. Have you ever been part of an effort to create a policy or a mission statement containing reference to writing skills?
67. Have you ever been someone's coach or mentor who had problems with written communications?
68. Have you ever created a development plan for someone on written communications?
69. Have you ever criticized someone's writing skills or written communications?
70. Have you ever designed a program on written communications?
71. Have you ever given a speech on written communications?
72. Have you ever rewarded or recognized someone for having writing skills?
73. Have you ever taught a course on written communications?
74. Have you ever tried to help someone deal with written communications more effectively?
75. Have you ever tried to help someone improve their writing skills or written communications?
76. How do you think people develop writing skills?
77. How much of success do you think is due to writing skills compared with other characteristics?
78. How would you know if someone is bad at writing?
79. How would you know if someone is good at writing?
80. If you had to write a book on communicating well in writing, what would the chapter headings be?
81. What are the benefits to someone who is really good at communicating well in writing?
82. What are the consequences to someone who is really poor at written communications?
83. What do you think the standard is on writing skills or written communications for someone in your role?
84. What happens if you use written communications too often?
85. What happens when two people try to work together who have very different writing skills?
86. What wisdom would you pass on to others trying to become better at writing?
87. When you select others, what do you look for in writing skills or written communications?
88. Why do you think people end up having different writing skills?

WRITTEN COMMUNICATIONS

Dimension 4: Shows personal change and sense-making; learned it one place and applied it in another; can compare and contrast experiences; changes viewpoints across time; can explain personal development or evolution related to the competency

89. Compare and contrast examples of being effective and ineffective at written communications.
90. Contrast your on- and off-the-job written communications.
91. Did you ever pass up a job or assignment because you were not confident enough in your writing skills?
92. Do you ever use other skills to cover for your lack of writing skills?
93. Do you write different types of memos/speeches/proposals/papers for different audiences/professors? Why?*
94. Has becoming better at writing skills ever helped you in other areas?
95. Has poor writing skills ever been the subject of a development plan for you?
96. Has poor written communications skills ever figured in a failure, struggle, or setback you have had?
97. Have you ever delegated or assigned someone a writing task because you don't write particularly well?
98. Have you ever made significant strides at becoming better at written communications?
99. Have your written communication skills always been this way?
100. Have your written communication skills, good or bad, ever been the subject of your performance review or a career discussion?
101. How different are you across situations in your written communications?
102. How do you decide how much written communication to use?
103. How much of your success is due to your written communications?
104. How transferable are your written communications skills to other situations?
105. If you had to become better at writing skills in a hurry, what would you do?
106. Was there a time when you were not as good at written communications?
107. What caused you to work to change your skills at written communications?
108. What event or series of events had the most impact on your written communications?
109. What's the most varied you can be in written communications?
110. What was the shortest amount of time in which you increased your level of skill at written communications?
111. When did you first realize your level of skill at written communications?
112. When do you write something, and when do you handle it verbally?*
113. When you know ahead of time that your level of skill at written communications won't work, what do you do?
114. Why do you think you deal with written communications the way you do?
115. Why do you think your written communication is the way it is?*

D. Follow-up Probes:

1. Are there times when you use your writing skills like that and times when you don't?
2. Could you contrast those two bosses for me?
3. Could you give me a few examples of how you've used or applied that?
4. Did you change your writing style after that experience?
5. Do you always write like that, or was that a special situation?
6. Do you suppose if others would just try harder, they could learn to be more effective at communicating in writing like you do?
7. Do you think that's teachable?
8. Do you think you have better writing skills than most? Why?

9. Do you think you would perform any differently if you could be more effective at communicating through writing?
10. Have you always written that way, or is this a recent development in you?
11. How did the others react when you did that?
12. How did you come up with that approach to writing in the first place?
13. How did you know that method of writing would work?
14. How do others you have known approach that?
15. How typical is this for you?
16. How would you approach that same situation today?
17. Is this natural for you, or do you really have to dig for it?
18. Was there a time when you didn't understand this about yourself?
19. What did you do after you got that feedback?
20. What did you do to adapt to that?
21. What did you learn from that?
22. Why did you choose that approach?
23. Why did you decide to take the risk?
24. Why did you do it that way?
25. Why did you time your attempt to put that into writing like that?
26. Why didn't you have someone else look at it first before you turned it in?
27. Why do you think that's difficult for you to do?
28. Why do you think that didn't work?
29. Why do you think that happened that way?
30. Why do you think that worked?
31. Why do you think you have difficulties with that sometimes?
32. Would you have done it that way with looser deadlines?
33. Would you have done it that way with tighter deadlines?

E. **Themes/Things to Look for:**

A sense for sequence
Able to change style to match different audiences
Able to manage the passion content
Admires the beauty of good writing
Anticipates questions the reader will have
Can constructively critique the writings of others
Can write presentations that sound like presentations
Can write quickly
Confidence in writing skills
Different audiences, different strategies
Focuses on impact–key points the reader should remember
Likes to write
Matches reading level to different audiences
Methods of breaking through writers block
Orderly mind

WRITTEN COMMUNICATIONS

Plain words
Tolerance of rewrites
Uses humor where it helps
Uses writing for complex arguments or to emphasize a string of points
Willing to commit in writing to an unpopular position
Willing to use an editor if necessary
Willing to write on tough issues

F. Most Likely Résumé:

1. Look for jobs like:
Heavy Strategic Demands

2. Look for develop-in-place assignments like:
Plan a new site for a building (plant, field office, headquarters, etc.).

Manage the purchase of a major product, equipment, materials, program, or system.

Write public press releases for the organization.

Write a proposal for a new policy, process, mission, charter, product, service, or system, and present and sell it to top management.

Draft a mission statement, policy proposal, charter, or goal statement and get feedback from others.

Seek out and use a seed budget to create and pursue a personal idea, product, or service.

Work on a team writing a proposal to obtain significant government or foundation grants or funding of an activity.

Design a training course in an area you're not an expert in.

Design a training course in an area of expertise for you.

Write a speech for someone higher up in the organization.

3. Best references to ask about or check:
Boss
Customers

G. Learning Agility Evaluation:
1. What/Describing vs. Why/Explain
2. All or Nothing vs. Can See Many Sides
3. Ordinary/Socially Acceptable vs. Insightful/Different
6. Reacting/Responsive vs. Adapting
9. Vague/General vs. Sharp/Specific
11. Generalizations vs. Specific Learnings
19. External Standards vs. Internal Standards
21. View from Self vs. View from Point of View of Others

WRITTEN COMMUNICATIONS

H. The LEADERSHIP ARCHITECT® Sort Card Connections:

1. Good (positive) if combined with high:

Can write quickly 1, 16, 53
Can clarify chaos 2, 40, 51
Will accept help 3, 33, 41
Good content 5, 24, 46, 61
Good couching skills 8, 38, 48
Will commit to writing on tough controversial issues 12, 34, 57
Innovative writing 14, 26, 30
Writes good goal statements 20, 35, 53
Good technical writing 24, 61
Model communicator 27, 36, 49, 65
Orderly writer 39, 47, 51, 52
Can write good mission/vision/values statements 46, 58, 65
Can change writing style to match audience 56, 64

2. Bad (negative) if combined with low or high (+):

Takes a long time to complete 1, 16, 53
Has trouble with unclear situations 2, 40
Won't accept help 3, 33, 41
Weak content 5, 24, 46, 61
Poor couching skills 8, 38, 48
Writes soft/easy goal statements 12, 20, 35, 53
Won't commit to controversy in writing 12, 34, 57
Writing lacks flair 14, 26, 28, 46
Not a good technical writer 24, 61
Not as good drafting strategic or vision statements 46, 58, 65
May not write good presentation scripts 49

3. Too much can contribute to the following Stallers and Stoppers:

A. What too much looks like (overused):

May invest too much time crafting communications; may too often try for perfection when something less would do the job; may be overly critical of the written work of others.

B. Too much might lead to these Stallers and Stoppers:

Political Missteps (119)

C. Compensators:

How to compensate for too much of this competency:
1, 2, 3, 12, 15, 17, 27, 32, 38, 44, 46, 48, 50, 51, 53, 57, 62

WRITTEN COMMUNICATIONS

D. *Things to watch for:*
Does it to avoid having to present live
Endless rewrites to get it perfect
Makes it complete to avoid conflict
Misses those who learn through the spoken word
Too complex to be read
Too long to be read
Uses written word to avoid face-to-face conflict

4. Too little can contribute to the following Stallers and Stoppers:

A. *What too little looks like (unskilled):*
Not a clear communicator in writing; may be hard to tell what the point is; may be too wordy or too terse or have grammar/usage problems; may not construct a logical argument well; may not adjust to different audiences; may have a single style of writing.

B. *Too little might lead to these Stallers and Stoppers:*
Being a Poor Administrator (102)

C. *Compensators:*
How to substitute for too little of this competency:
5, 15, 27, 37, 49, 51, 65

I. LEARNING ARCHITECT® Connections:

Look for people who act like and/or show evidence of:

1c. Following a Plan
2a. Problem Solving

J. CHOICES ARCHITECT® Connections:

Look for people who act like and/or show evidence of:

First Edition (Released 1994)
2. Essence
8. Cool Transactor
23. Communicator

Second Edition (Released 2000)
6. Essence
9. Agile Communicator
11. Cool Transactor

K. Difficulty to Develop:
21 (of 34)–Easier

68. LEARNING FROM EXPERIENCE

A. Definition:

The ability and willingness to learn, change, and gain from life experiences; uses failures, successes, and feedback to form rules of thumb, models, maps, paradigms, or templates; applies learning effectively in other quite different situations.

B. Arenas/Domains to Explore:

1. Acquisition/merger management
2. Better competitors
3. Changing a culture
4. Different cultures
5. Disruptive shifts
6. First-time situations
7. Friends
8. Heavy strategic demands
9. Hobbies
10. Interests
11. New combinations
12. New companies
13. New connections
14. New countries
15. New jobs
16. New people
17. New problems
18. New products
19. New questions
20. New services
21. New strategic partners
22. New tasks
23. Planning for the future
24. Professional activities
25. Reading habits
26. Start-ups
27. Transformations
28. Transitions
29. When plans change abruptly

C. Sample Questions:

Dimension 1: Been there, done that–has had direct personal experience(s) involving the competency–candidate was the prime player   Note: * means OK for campus

1. Has anyone ever accused you of messing something up because you didn't learn from an experience?
2. Have you ever managed anything where the people or units reporting to you were in different locations? How did you learn from each unit or location?
3. How are you different now because of an experience you went through?*
4. Tell me about a change in attitude or behavior you had to make to be successful or to fit in.*
5. Tell me about a mistake you've made.*
6. Tell me about a time when information and an experience caused you to change your mind on a long held position.
7. Tell me about a time when you had to act in two contradictory ways at once (you felt pulled both ways).*
8. Tell me about a time when you helped someone else solve a problem they had.
9. Tell me about a time when you received critical feedback about yourself that you were able to finally come to peace with.
10. Tell me about a time when you taught someone a skill.
11. Tell me about a time when you were surprised by the outcome of something you've tried.*
12. Tell me about a transition you made from one group of people to a very different group of people.*
13. Tell me about a transition you made to a new/different job.

LEARNING FROM EXPERIENCE

14. Tell me about an assignment you had in another country.
15. Tell me about the most surprising successes you've had.*
16. Tell me about the transition you made from high school to college.*
17. Tell me about time where you were challenged beyond what you thought your limits were.*
18. What were some of your notable failures at learning the lessons of experience?*
19. What were some of your notable successes at learning the lessons of experience?*
20. What's the most difficult thing you've ever attempted?*
21. When you are part of a team celebrating a win, what role do you usually play?
22. When you are part of a team debriefing a failure, what role do you usually play?

Dimension 2: Seen/been around others who were involved with the competency–good and bad; learns from others about self

23. Contrast the people you know who learn the most and least from experience.*
24. Has learning from experience ever been in any 360° survey done on you? Was your score among your highest, middle, or lowest?
25. Has not learning from experience on someone else's part ever created an obstacle for you or got in the way of something you were trying to accomplish?*
26. Have you ever talked with a coach or mentor about your ability to learn from experience?
27. Have you ever watched someone fail/get fired because they did not learn from experience?*
28. Have you ever watched someone overdo learning from experience to the point that it backfired?
29. Have you ever watched someone succeed because they learned from experience?*
30. Have you ever worked with a coach on learning from experience?*
31. Have you ever worked with a person who excelled at learning from experience?
32. Have you ever worked with a skills coach on learning from experience?*
33. How do you get feedback about yourself on how well you learn from experience?
34. How often do you check with multiple sources when you get critical feedback on how well you learn from experience?
35. Is there a historical figure you consider a model of learning from experience?
36. What do others who are not your fans say about your ability to learn from experience?
37. What do others who like you say about your ability to learn from experience?
38. Which boss was the best at learning from experience?
39. Which boss was the worst at learning from experience?
40. Which direct report was the best at learning from experience?
41. Which direct report was the worst at learning from experience?
42. Which peer was the best at learning from experience?
43. Which peer was the worst at learning from experience?
44. Who in your field or business is the best at learning from experience?
45. Who do you consider a current role model of learning from experience?*
46. Who do you go to for advice on learning from experience?
47. Who have you learned the most from about learning from experience?*
48. Who is a higher-management role model for you on learning from experience?
49. Who is a role model of learning from experience outside of work?

Dimension 3: Knows how the competency works in theory; shows understanding

50. Are there situations or settings where someone should learn differently from experience?
51. Do you think learning from experience skills can be learned; how do you think people develop these?

LEARNING FROM EXPERIENCE

52. Do you think there is a way to compensate or work around a low ability to learn from experience?
53. Has anyone asked you for your opinions/advice on learning from experience?*
54. Have you ever attended a course on learning from experience?
55. Have you ever been in a situation where you and others put learning from experience on a success profile?
56. Have you ever been part of an effort to create a policy or a mission statement containing reference to learning from experience?
57. Have you ever been someone's coach or mentor who had problems with learning from experience?
58. Have you ever created a development plan for someone on learning from experience?
59. Have you ever criticized someone for not learning from experience?
60. Have you ever designed a program on learning from experience?
61. Have you ever given a speech on learning from experience?
62. Have you ever rewarded or recognized someone for learning from experience?
63. Have you ever taught a course on learning from experience?
64. Have you ever tried to help someone deal more effectively with learning from experience?*
65. Have you ever tried to help someone learn from their experience?
66. How do you think people develop learning-from-experience skills?
67. How much of success do you think is due to learning from experience compared with other characteristics?
68. How would you know if someone is bad at learning from experience?
69. How would you know if someone is good at learning from experience?
70. If you had to write a book on learning from experience, what would the chapter headings be?
71. What are the benefits to someone who is really good at learning from experience?
72. What are the consequences to someone who is really poor at learning from experience?
73. What do you think the standard is on learning from experience for someone in your role?
74. What happens if too much of your learning is from experience?
75. What happens when two people try to work together who are very different in the way they learn from experience?
76. What wisdom would you pass on to others trying to become better at learning from experience?
77. When you select others, what do you look for in their ability to learn from experience?
78. Why do you think people end up being different in the way they learn from experience?

Dimension 4: Shows personal change and sense-making; learned it one place and applied it in another; can compare and contrast experiences; changes viewpoints across time; can explain personal development or evolution related to the competency

79. Compare and contrast examples of being effective and ineffective at learning from experience.
80. Contrast your on- and off-the-job use of learning from experience.
81. Did you ever pass up a job or assignment because you were not confident enough in your skills at learning from experience?
82. Do you enjoy learning from experience? What types of learning do you enjoy most?*
83. Do you ever use other skills to cover for your lack of learning from experience?
84. Do you learn new things easily?*
85. Do you look forward to learning new skills?*
86. Do you use different types of learning techniques to learn different things?*
87. Has becoming better at learning from experience ever helped you in other areas?
88. Has the inability to learn from experience ever been the subject of a development plan for you?
89. Has the inability to learn from experience ever figured in a failure, struggle, or setback you have had?
90. Has your skill in learning from experience always been this way?

LEARNING FROM EXPERIENCE

91. Have you ever delegated or assigned someone a task because you didn't learn from experience particularly well?
92. Have you ever made significant strides at becoming better at learning from experience?
93. Have your learning from experience skills, good or bad, ever been the subject of your performance review or a career discussion?
94. How different across situations are you in your learning from experience?
95. How do you decide which experiences are worth learning from?
96. How much of your success is due to your ability to learn from experience?
97. How transferable are your learning from experience skills to other situations?
98. If you had to become better at learning from experience in a hurry, what would you do?
99. Was there a time when you were not good at learning from experience?
100. What caused you to work to improve your skills in learning from experience?
101. What event or series of events had the most impact on your learning from experience?
102. What's the most varied you can be in learning from experience?
103. What was the shortest amount of time in which you increased your level of skill at learning from experience?
104. When did you first realize your level of skill at learning from experience?
105. When you know ahead of time that your level of learning from experience won't work, what do you do?
106. When you want to learn something new, what do you do?*
107. Why do you think you deal with learning from experience the way you do?
108. Why do you think your learning from experience is the way it is?*

D. Follow-up Probes:

1. Are there times when you use your learning skills like that and times when you don't?
2. Are you now more open to new experiences?
3. Could you contrast those two bosses for me?
4. Did that have a permanent effect on you?
5. Did you change your learning style after that experience?
6. Did you share that insight about yourself with anyone else?
7. Did you think differently or do something different after that experience?
8. Do you always learn like that, or was that a special situation?
9. Do you suppose if others would just try harder, they could learn to be more effective at learning from experience like you do?
10. Do you think that's teachable?
11. Do you think you have better skills at learning new things than most? Why?
12. Do you think you would perform any differently if you could be more effective at learning from experience?
13. Have you always learned that way, or is this a recent development in you?
14. How did the others react when you did that?
15. How did you come up with that approach to learning in the first place?
16. How did you know that method of learning would work?
17. How do others you have known approach that?
18. How typical is this for you?
19. How would you approach that same situation today?
20. Is this natural for you, or do you really have to dig for it?
21. Was there a real change in you after that experience?
22. Was there a time when you didn't understand this about yourself?
23. What did you do after you got that feedback?

LEARNING FROM EXPERIENCE

24. What did you do to adapt to that?
25. What did you learn from that?
26. Why did you choose that approach?
27. Why did you decide to take the risk?
28. Why did you do it that way?
29. Why did you time your attempt to put your learning into action like that?
30. Why do you think that's difficult for you to do?
31. Why do you think that didn't work?
32. Why do you think that happened that way?
33. Why do you think that worked?
34. Would you have done it that way with looser deadlines?
35. Would you have done it that way with tighter deadlines?

E. Themes/Things to Look for:

Adding new learning all the time
Can see the big picture
Capable of dealing with complexity
Comfortable facing paradox
Comfortably going through stark transitions
Comfortably making shifts
Coming to new understandings
Essence detector
Experiments
Gaining new insights
Going through personal transformations
Knowing how things work
Learning hobbies
Learns from mistakes
Looks under rocks

Making contrasts
Making incremental gains
Making new connections
Making new discoveries
Playful with ideas
Seeing consequences
Seeing contrasts
Seeing differences
Seeing parallels
Seeing similarities
Seeing what's missing
Testing limits
Tinkers
Trial and error

F. Most Likely Résumé:

1. Look for jobs like:

Cross-Moves
Fix-Its/Turnarounds
Heavy Strategic Demands
International Assignments
Line to Staff Switches
Scope (complexity) Assignments
Start-Ups

2. Look for develop-in-place assignments like:

Relaunch an existing project or service that's not doing well.
Teach/coach someone how to do something you are not an expert in.
Assemble an ad hoc team of diverse people to accomplish a difficult task.
Take on a tough and undoable project, one where others have tried it and failed.
Take on a task you dislike or hate to do.

LEARNING FROM EXPERIENCE

3. **Best references to ask about or check:**
   Natural Mentor
   Direct Boss
   Human Resource Professionals

G. Learning Agility Evaluation:

1. What/Describing vs. Why/Explain
2. All or Nothing vs. Can See Many Sides
3. Ordinary/Socially Acceptable vs. Insightful/Different
4. Spectator/Passive vs. Player/Participant
5. Tight/Rigid vs. Loose/Flexible
6. Reacting/Responsive vs. Adapting
7. Passive vs. Intrigued/Curious
8. Sameness vs. Diversity
9. Vague/General vs. Sharp/Specific
10. Reactive vs. Initiating
11. Generalizations vs. Specific Learnings
13. Simple Views vs. Complex Views
14. Narrow Interest vs. Broad Interests
15. Linear vs. Branching
16. Few Absolute Rules Vs. Multiple Rules of Thumb
17. Not Self-Aware Vs. Self-Aware
18. Comfort Zone vs. Curious
19. External Standards vs. Internal Standards
21. View from Self vs. View from Point of View of Others
22. Perfect vs. Admits Mistakes

H. The LEADERSHIP ARCHITECT® Sort Card Connections:

1. Good (positive) if combined with high:
Learns quickly 1, 16, 32
Learns from dealing with tough issues head-on 11, 12, 34, 57
Learns from mistakes 11, 12, 41
Can learn from uncertainty 2, 32, 40
Thinks about the future 2, 46, 58
Learns about new cultures/different ways of doing things 21, 46
Can articulate learnings for others 27, 44, 49, 67
Gets lots of input from others 3, 31, 33, 41
Can learn complex things 30, 32, 51
Learns from peers/colleagues 33, 42, 60
Spends time learning useful things 47, 50, 62
Learns new job content easily 5, 24, 61
Learns things about them self well 6, 45, 54, 55
Learns from those above them 8, 38, 48

LEARNING FROM EXPERIENCE

2. **Bad (negative) if combined with low or high (+):**

   Too quick for others to follow (+1, 16) 41
   Self-contained learner 3, 31, 33, 41
   Doesn't learn much from higher-ups 4, 8, 38, 48
   Weak content; impractical applications 5, 24, 61
   Avoids controversial learnings 12, 13, 34, 57
   May prematurely reject the proven (+14, 28, 30)
   Learnings don't extend to people 21, 25, 56, 64
   Can't pass the learnings on to others 27, 49, 67
   Doesn't add to personal portfolio of learnings 45, 54, 55, 66
   May waste time on nonfruitful learnings 50, 62

3. **Too much can contribute to the following Stallers and Stoppers:**

   A. *What too much looks like (overused):*

   May invest disproportionate time looking for the new and unique; may inappropriately reject the tried and true; may not be tolerant of those not learning as fast; may tinker with things beyond value; may put the mission at risk by not paying attention to the daily tasks at hand; may change so much that it leaves others confused and distrustful.

   B. *Too much might lead to these Stallers and Stoppers:*

   Poor Administrator (102)   Insensitive to Others (112)
   Arrogant (104)   Performance Problems (118)
   Betrayal of Trust (105)   Political Missteps (119)

   C. *Compensators:*

   How to compensate for too much of this competency:
   5, 27, 24, 27, 33, 39, 41, 43, 47, 52, 59

   D. *Things to watch for:*

   Nothing old is good enough   Bored easily
   Intolerance of slow learners   This month's flavor
   Can't explain insights to others   Sees something new when there's little or nothing there
   Speaks at too-complex a level

4. **Too little can contribute to the following Stallers and Stoppers:**

   A. *What too little looks like (unskilled):*

   Prefers to repeat whatever has worked in the past; over relies on current strengths and knowledge; likes the familiar; not curious or interested in the new and different; acts nervous or intimidated by those who learn quickly; resists change more than most.

   B. *Too little might lead to these Stallers and Stoppers:*

   Unable to Adapt to Differences (101)   Non-strategic (114)
   Blocked Personal Learner (106)   Overdependence on a Single Skill (116)
   Lack of Composure (107)   Performance Problems (118)
   Defensiveness (108)   Political Missteps (119)
   Key Skill Deficiencies (113)

LEARNING FROM EXPERIENCE

C. Compensators:
How to substitute for too little of this competency:
5, 14, 16, 30, 32, 33, 50, 51, 58, 61

I. LEARNING ARCHITECT® Connections:
Look for people who act like and/or show evidence of:

1a. Pure Action	11. Why/How
1b. Trial and Error	12. Rules of Thumb
2. Problem Solving	19. What
2b. Visioning	21. Changer
3b. Self-Talk	22. Experimenter
3c. Personal Experience	25. Personal Change
4a. Getting Information	26. Self-Aware
4b. Modeling	27. Conceptualizer
4c. Actively Involve	28. Creator
5. New	30. Mastery
6. Contentious	32. Diversity in Others
7. Risks	33. Diversity of Sources
8. Initiate	35. Breadth
9. Multiple Sources	37. Flexibility
10. Complexity	

J. CHOICES ARCHITECT® Connections:
Look for people who act like and/or show evidence of:

First Edition (Released 1994)	Second Edition (Released 2000)
1. Inquisitive	1. Broad Scanner
3. Creator	2. Complexity
4. Complexity	3. Connector
5. Connector	4. Critical Thinker
6. Visionary	5. Easy Shifter
9. Self-Aware	7. Inquisitive
10. Responds to Feedback	8. Solution Finder
11. Open to Diversity	10. Conflict Manager
12. Experimenter	14. Open-Minded
14. Transaction Quality	16. Personal Learner
16. Cold/Indirect Sources	17. Responds to Feedback
17. Hot/Direct Sources	19. Self-Aware
18. Into Everything	20. Experimenter
19. Tinkerer	21. Innovation Manager
20. Forging Ahead	23. Visioning
22. Self-Talk	25. Delivers Results

K. Difficulty to Develop:
30 (of 34)–Hardest

There are no competencies 69-80. Those numbers are reserved for future additions.

THE TEN
PERFORMANCE MANAGEMENT ARCHITECT® DIMENSIONS

81. QUANTITY OF WORK OUTPUT

A. Definition:

The amount of work produced by this person is simply amazing; no matter how high the production or output goals are set, more is produced than expected in all or most areas; almost always number one in productivity; defines hard work for the rest.

B. Arenas/Domains to Explore:

1. Any activity, goal, task, job
2. Athletics
3. Getting resistant people to produce
4. Career goals
5. Charitable drives
6. Church events
7. Club activities
8. Collecting debts
9. Deadlines
10. Delegation practices
11. Evidence of results
12. Goal-setting
13. Hobbies
14. Inspiring others to produce
15. Managing contractors
16. Military activities
17. Producing in hard times
18. Productivity examples
19. Reengineering
20. Sales contests
21. School assignments
22. Scouting achievements
23. Servicing customers
24. Setting up work flows
25. Use of feedback and feedback loops
26. Vacations

C. Sample Questions:

Dimension 1: What the Person Did   Note: * means OK for campus   ** means campus only

1. Have you ever been assigned to a fix-it situation? What did you do to improve performance?
2. Have you ever managed anything where the people reporting to you were in different locations? How did you ensure productivity?
3. Have you ever won a performance or sales contest? What did you do to win that others apparently didn't do as well?*
4. Have you ever worked in direct sales? What were the keys to producing results?*
5. How do you monitor progress toward goals?*
6. How do you usually find out when something goes wrong and will interfere with work getting done? How do you recover from this?*
7. How many people who worked under you have quit in the last five years? How many have been fired or promoted? Why was that?
8. If you have three challenging tasks to complete by roughly the same deadline, how do you get all three done?*
9. Tell me about a time when you designed some problem prevention procedures for a task you were doing.*
10. Tell me about a time when you had to manage a dispirited, low-performing group.
11. Tell me about a time when you produced a lot against the odds.*
12. Tell me about a time when you produced a lot even though some major obstacles were in your path (uncooperative people, lack of resources, for example). What did you do that others in the same situation didn't?*
13. Tell me about a time when you produced a lot in a very short time.*

QUANTITY OF WORK OUTPUT

14. Tell me about a time when you produced a lot when others tried and failed.*
15. Tell me about a time when you produced far beyond expectations.*
16. Tell me about a time when you saved someone who just couldn't get the work out.*
17. Tell me about a time when you watched someone get results at all costs and pay a big price for it.*
18. Tell me about a time you managed a work project (group) of very different people. How did you appeal to each to get the work out?
19. Tell me about three people you have worked with who differed in how much work they could accomplish. If you wanted to help the less productive accomplish more, what would (did) you do?*
20. Tell me how you go about setting goals with people who work for you.
21. What are your general work habits? When do you get to work? When do you leave? Do you do any work at home?
22. What do you do when customers make unreasonable productivity demands ("I need it by yesterday.")?*
23. What do you do when customers truly need something, and it will be a stretch to produce it?
24. What do you do when people will have to work long hours to meet a customer demand?
25. What do you do when someone or a group is blocking your efforts to produce?*
26. What triggers you to intervene and offer advice and corrections?*

Dimension 2: Seeing Others Do This

27. Contrast the most and least productive people you know.*
28. Has productivity or quantity of work you produce ever been in any 360° survey done on you? Was your score among your highest, middle, or lowest?
29. Has poor productivity or quantity of work on someone else's part ever created an obstacle for you or got in the way of something you were trying to accomplish?*
30. Have you ever talked with a coach or mentor about your productivity or the quantity of work you produce?
31. Have you ever watched someone fail/get fired because they did not produce enough work?*
32. Have you ever watched someone overdo productivity or the quantity of work they produced to the point that it backfired?
33. Have you ever watched someone succeed because of their productivity or the quantity of work they produced?*
34. Have you ever worked with a coach on improving your productivity or the quantity of work you produce?*
35. Have you ever worked with a person who excelled at productivity or the quantity of work they produced?
36. Have you ever worked with a skills coach on your productivity or the quantity of work you produce?*
37. How do you get feedback about yourself on your productivity or the quantity of work you produce?
38. How often do you check with multiple sources when you get a piece of critical feedback on your productivity or the quantity of work you produce?
39. Is there a historical figure you consider a model of productivity or the quantity of work produced?
40. What do others who are not your fans say about your productivity or the quantity of work you produce?
41. What do others who like you say about your productivity or the quantity of work you produce?
42. Which boss was the best at productivity or the quantity of work they produced?
43. Which boss was the worst at productivity or the quantity of work they produced?
44. Which direct report was the best at productivity or the quantity of work they produced?
45. Which direct report was the worst at productivity or the quantity of work they produced?
46. Which peer was the best at productivity or the quantity of work they produced?
47. Which peer was the worst at productivity or the quantity of work they produced?
48. Who deals with productivity or the quantity of work they produce the best in your field or business?

QUANTITY OF WORK OUTPUT

49. Who do you consider a current role model of productivity or the quantity of work to produce?*
50. Who do you go to for advice on productivity or quantity of work to produce?
51. Who have you learned the most from about productivity or quantity of work to produce?*
52. Who is a higher-management role model for you on productivity or quantity of work to produce?
53. Who is a role model of productivity or quantity of work to produce outside of work?

Dimension 3: Knowing How This Works

54. Are there situations or settings where someone should be different on getting work out?
55. Do you think personal productivity can be learned? If so, how do you think people develop personal productivity skills?
56. Do you think there is a way to compensate or work around low personal productivity or the quantity of work you produce?
57. Has anyone asked you for your opinions/advice on personal productivity or how to get more work done?*
58. Have you ever attended a course on personal productivity or generating greater quantities of work?
59. Have you ever been in a situation where you and others put personal productivity or how to get more work done on a success profile?
60. Have you ever been part of an effort to create a policy or a mission statement containing reference to being more productive and getting more work out?
61. Have you ever been someone's coach or mentor who had problems with personal productivity skills?
62. Have you ever created a development plan for someone on being more productive and getting more work done?
63. Have you ever criticized someone for not being more productive and getting more work done
64. Have you ever designed a program on being more productive and getting more work done?
65. Have you ever given a speech on being more productive and getting more work done?
66. Have you ever rewarded or recognized someone for being more productive and getting more work done
67. Have you ever taught a course on how to get more work out?
68. Have you ever tried to help someone deal more effectively with personal productivity or how to get more work done?*
69. Have you ever tried to help someone improve their personal productivity skills?
70. How much personal productivity is good to have and how much is too much?
71. How much of success do you think is due to being more productive and getting more work done compared with other characteristics?
72. How would you know if someone is bad at being productive and getting work done?
73. How would you know if someone is good at being productive and getting work done?
74. If you had to write a book on being productive and getting work done, what would the chapter headings be?
75. What are the benefits to someone who is really good at being productive and getting work done?
76. What are the consequences to someone who is really poor at being productive and getting work done?
77. What do you think the standard is on being productive and getting work done for someone in your role?
78. What happens if you have or use too much of your personal productivity skills?
79. What happens when two people try to work together who are very different on being productive and getting work done?
80. What wisdom would you pass onto others trying to become better at being productive and getting work done?
81. Why do you think people end up being different in their productivity levels and the way they get work done?

QUANTITY OF WORK OUTPUT

Dimension 4: Personal Learning

82. Compare and contrast examples of being effective and ineffective at getting work out?
83. Contrast your on- and of-the-job use of personal productivity.
84. Did you ever pass up a job or assignment because you were not confident enough in your skills at getting work out or generating quantities of work?
85. Do you ever use other skills to cover for your lack of productivity?
86. Has personal productivity ever figured in a failure, struggle, or setback you have had?
87. Has becoming better at being productive and getting more work done ever helped you in other areas?
88. Has personal productivity or the quantity of work you produce ever been the subject of a development plan for you?
89. Has your personal productivity or the quantity of work you produce always been this way?
90. Have you ever delegated or assigned someone a task because of your lack of productivity.
91. Have you ever made significant strides at becoming better at being productive and getting work done?
92. Have your personal productivity skills, good or bad, ever been the subject of your performance review or a career discussion?
93. How different are you across situations in your personal productivity or the quantity of work you produce?
94. How do you decide how personally productive to be or how much work to produce?
95. How much of your success is due to your personal productivity skills?
96. How transferable are your personal productivity skills to other situations?
97. If you had to become better at personal productivity in a hurry, what would you do?
98. Was there a time when you were not good at being productive and getting work done?
99. What caused you to work to change your skills at being productive and getting work done?
100. What event or series of events had the most impact on your being productive and getting work done?
101. What's the most varied you can be in being productive and getting work done?
102. What's the shortest amount of time in which you learned to become better at being productive and getting work done?
103. When did you first realize your level of skill at being productive and getting work done?
104. When you know ahead of time that your level of being productive and getting work done won't work, what do you do?
105. Why do you think you deal with being productive and getting work done the way you do?
106. Why do you think your personal productivity skills are the way they are?*
107. Do you have an orderly way to get the work out? How do you do it?*
108. Are there times when you push for quantity and times that you don't?*
109. How do you get things done without burning yourself/others out?*
110. How do you balance the need to produce against the needs of others?*
111. Tell me about what your career discussions and performance reviews have taught you about your success in producing lots of work.
112. Do you have any personal rules of thumb so you can produce more? What are they?*
113. How much monitoring of work is good and how much is too much?
114. What is your goal-setting philosophy with yourself and others?

QUANTITY OF WORK OUTPUT

D. Follow-up Probes:

Dimension 1: What the Person Did

1. Can you give me a few examples of that?
2. How consistently do you do this across situations?
3. How did others react when you did that?
4. How far would you go before you would stop and try another approach?
5. How typical is this for you?
6. How would you have done this differently with looser deadlines?
7. How would you have done this differently with tighter deadlines?
8. Tell me about times when you are not like this or wouldn't do this.
9. Tell me about times when you do this and times when you don't.
10. Was this comfortable for you, or were you forcing yourself?

Dimension 2: Seeing Others Do This

11. Did you later change your assessment of this person?
12. Do you know a good and a bad example of this? Contrast those two people for me.
13. Do you think most people would react that way?
14. Have you worked for a person like that since?
15. How could this person have been more effective?
16. How do others you have known approach that?
17. What do you think this person was trying to do?
18. What was it like to work with someone like that?
19. What was it like to work with someone you seem to have disliked?

Dimension 3: Knowing How This Works

20. How would you teach this to someone else?
21. What do you think the key aspects of it are?
22. Where do people learn this?
23. Why do you suppose organizations work that way?
24. Why do you suppose teams work that way?
25. Why do you think people do that?
26. Why do you think that happened?

Dimension 4: Personal Learning

27. Do you think you can get others to do this better than most people can? If so, how do you know?
28. Do you think you do this better or worse than most people can? How do you know?
29. Do you try to act that way with everyone? What's your thinking on that?
30. How did you come up with that approach?
31. How do you see that as a customer yourself?
32. How would you do this differently next time?
33. What did you do after you got that feedback?
34. What did you learn about dealing with that kind of person?
35. What did you learn about dealing with that kind of situation?
36. What did you learn about how customers are gained?

QUANTITY OF WORK OUTPUT

37. What did you learn about how customers are lost?
38. What did you learn about yourself?
39. What did you learn from that?
40. What do you think you learned that would be repeatable in other situations?
41. What lessons do you think you came away with?
42. What were the negative consequences of this?
43. What were you thinking when you took that approach?
44. What were you thinking when you took that risk?
45. What would you tell your children about that experience?
46. What would you tell your friend about that experience?
47. What would you tell your mentor about that experience?
48. What's your thinking about why that didn't work?
49. What's your thinking about why that worked?
50. What's your view of why things happened that way?
51. Where did you learn to do it that way?
52. Why did you think that method of getting over that barrier would work?
53. Why do you do it that way?

E. Themes/Things to Look for:

A drive to produce efficiently	Pitching in to help
Confronting issues promptly	Response to stretch goals
Consistency across situations	Sheer perseverance
Doing the impossible	Sizing up people accurately
Focus on overcoming obstacles	Streamlining processes
Focus on productivity	Teaching people to get the work out
Focus on removing obstacles	Understanding human motivation
How many different approaches they tried	Using feedback to produce more
Life long focus on producing	Winning awards and contests
Long-term work habits	

F. Most Likely Résumé:

1. Look for jobs like:

Chair of Projects/Task Forces	Scope (complexity) Assignments
Fix-Its/Turnarounds	Staff Leadership (Influencing Without Authority)
Member of Projects/Task Forces	Start-ups
Scale (size shift) Assignments	

2. Look for develop-in-place assignments like:

Install a new process or system (computer system, new policies, new process, new procedures, etc.).
Work on a process-simplification team to take steps and costs out of a process.
Do a problem-prevention analysis on a product or service and present it to the people involved.
Manage something "remote", away from your location.
Go to a campus as a recruiter.
Do a study of lost customers, including interviewing a sample, and report the findings to the people involved.

QUANTITY OF WORK OUTPUT

Coach a children's sports team.

Be a change agent; create a symbol for change; lead the rallying cry; champion a significant change and implementation.

Manage a joint project with another unit, function, geography, etc.

Teach a course, seminar, or workshop on something you know a lot about.

Assign a project to a group with a tight deadline.

Manage an ad hoc, temporary group of low-competence people through a task they couldn't do by themselves.

Manage an ad hoc, temporary group of people where the temporary manager is a towering expert and the people in the group are not.

Manage an ad hoc, temporary group of people involved in tackling a fix-it or turnaround project.

Manage the interface between consultants and the organization on a critical assignment.

Hire and manage a temporary group of people to accomplish a tough or time-tight assignment.

Take on a tough and undoable project, one where others who have tried it have failed.

3. Best references to ask about or check:

Direct Boss

Human Resource Professionals

Internal and External Customers

Natural Mentors

Past Associates/Constituencies

Peers and Colleagues

Spouses

Direct Reports

G. Learning Orientation Evaluation:

2. All or Nothing vs. Can See Many Sides
4. Spectator/Passive vs. Player/Participant
5. Tight/Rigid vs. Loose/Flexible
6. Reactive/Responsive vs. Adapting
8. Sameness vs. Diversity
16. Few Rules of Thumb vs. Many and Varied Rules of Thumb
19. External Standards vs. Internal Standards

H. The LEADERSHIP ARCHITECT® Sort Card Connections:

1. Good (positive) if combined with high:

Timely 1, 16

Produces the right things 17, 47, 50, 53

Efficient 39, 47, 52

Flexible 2, 40

Uses feedback well 20, 35

2. Bad (negative) if combined with low or high (+):

Produces on the wrong things 50

Drives too hard (+1, 16, 53) 41, 66

Cold and impersonal 3, 31, 33, 41 (+53)

Too confronting (+9, 13, 34, 57)

Can't get productivity through others 18, 20, 39

Poor quality (35, 52, 63)

QUANTITY OF WORK OUTPUT

3. **Too much can contribute to the following Stallers and Stoppers:**

    A. *What too much looks like (overused):*

    The amount of work coming from this person or his or her group is so high that sometimes quality and morale suffer because things are so intense and the pace is so fast. Can be so single-mindedly focused on getting the most work out that all other matters including concern for self and others suffer.

    B. *Too much might lead to these Stallers and Stoppers:*

    Arrogant (104)
    Insensitive to Others (112)
    Overmanaging (117)
    Performance Problems (118)

    C. *Compensators:*

    How to compensate for too much of this PERFORMANCE MANAGEMENT ARCHITECT® dimension:
    3, 7, 17, 18, 20, 23, 33, 36, 41, 50, 52, 60

    D. *Things to watch for:*

    Drives self and others
    Little concern for others
    Little concern for work/life balance
    Expects miracles
    Unrealistic

4. **Too little can contribute to the following Stallers and Stoppers:**

    A. *What too little looks like (unskilled):*

    Low amount of work produced; lags behind most other people or groups; significant goals are missed; productivity is lower than most others; makes a few goals but misses others.

    B. *Too little can contribute to the following Stallers and Stoppers:*

    Overdependence on a Single Skill (116)   Performance Problems (118)

    C. *Compensators:*

    How to substitute for too little of this PERFORMANCE MANAGEMENT ARCHITECT® dimension:
    1, 14, 16, 18, 19, 20, 24, 36, 42, 43, 52, 59, 61, 63

I. LEARNING ARCHITECT® Connections:

Look for people who act like and/or show evidence of:

1a. Pure Action	12. Rules of Thumb
1b. Trial and Error	13. Focused
1c. Following a Plan	16. Collaborate
2a. Problem Solving	22. Experimenter
3c. Personal Experience	23. Orchestrator
4a. Getting Information	25. Personal Change
4b. Modeling	28. Creator
4c. Actively Involve	31. Rationality
6. Contentious	32. Diversity in Others
7. Risks	33. Diversity of Sources
8. Initiate	34. Sizing Up Others
10. Complexity	37. Flexibility
11. Why/How	38. Resilience

QUANTITY OF WORK OUTPUT

J. CHOICES ARCHITECT® Connections:

Look for people who act like and/or show evidence of:

First Edition (Released 1994)
1. Inquisitive
3. Creator
7. Helping Others Think
8. Cool Transactor
10. Responds to Feedback
11. Open to Diversity
12. Experimenter
13. Role Flexibility
15. Helps Others Succeed
17. Hot/Direct Sources
18. Into Everything
19. Tinkerer
20. Forging Ahead

Second Edition (Released 2000)
4. Critical Thinker
7. Inquisitive
8. Solution Finder
12. Helps Others Succeed
14. Open-Minded
16. Personal Learner
17. Responds to Feedback
18. Role Flexibility
20. Experimenter
24. Inspires Others
25. Delivers Results
26. Drive

QUANTITY OF WORK OUTPUT

82. TIMELINESS OF DELIVERY OF OUTPUT

A. Definition:

Always the first or among the first to finish; even unreasonable or difficult time targets and goals are met and some are actually exceeded; sets the speed standard for the rest.

B. Arenas/Domains to Explore:

1. Ambiguous situations
2. Athletic performance
3. Career decisions
4. Conflict situations
5. Day to day choices
6. Emergencies
7. Layoffs
8. Legal proceedings
9. Making decisions when the call is close
10. Managing deadlines
11. Managing marginal performers
12. Medical emergencies
13. Submitting applications
14. Preparing speeches/reports
15. School assignments
16. Sudden changes
17. Task forces
18. Tax filing
19. Timed events
20. Under conflicting priorities

C. Sample Questions:

Dimension 1: What the Person Did Note: * means OK for campus ** means campus only

1. Give me some examples of how you have made decisions quickly.*
2. Has anyone ever labeled you a perfectionist?
3. Have you ever managed anything where the people reporting to you were in different locations? How did you ensure timeliness of delivery of work?
4. Have you or any group you've managed come in first and won an award or gotten special recognition?
5. How do you monitor the progress of others?
6. How do your monitor your progress?*
7. How do you react when given what you think is an unreasonable deadline?
8. Tell me about a time when a marginal performer got in the way of getting things done on time.*
9. Tell me about a time when a person tried to purposefully block you from getting something done on time.*
10. Tell me about a time when you balanced timeliness with efficient use of resources.*
11. Tell me about a time when you balanced timeliness with quality concerns.*
12. Tell me about a time when you delivered work on time because you had designed some problem prevention or corrective measures into the process.
13. Tell me about a time when you finished some work on time but thought it wasn't worth the cost to you.*
14. Tell me about a time when you finished some work on time but thought it wasn't worth the cost to others.*
15. Tell me about a time when you had multiple important priorities, all demanding work completion around the same time.*
16. Tell me about a time when you had to essentially run over or through others to get things done on time.*
17. Tell me about a time when you had to get something done in less time than you thought was right.*
18. Tell me about a time when you had to resolve a conflict in order to get things done on time.*
19. Tell me about a time when you irritated people with your push to get things done on time.*
20. Tell me about a time when you just couldn't get finished on time.*

TIMELINESS OF DELIVERY OF OUTPUT

21. Tell me about a time when you made quick decisions in an orderly manner.*
22. Tell me about a time when you met an "impossible" deadline.*
23. Tell me about a time when you missed a deadline because you didn't anticipate problems.*
24. Tell me about a time when you overcame obstacles in order to get something done on time.*
25. Tell me how you estimate the time it will take to complete a major piece of work.*
26. Tell me how you have responded to unreasonable demands from customers.

Dimension 2: Seeing Others Do This

27. Contrast the most and least deadline-oriented people you know.*
28. Has getting things done on time ever been in any 360° survey done on you? Was your score among your highest, middle, or lowest?
29. Has poor ability to deliver work on time on someone else's part ever created an obstacle for you or got in the way of something you were trying to accomplish?*
30. Have you ever talked with a coach or mentor about your ability to deliver work on time?
31. Have you ever watched someone fail/get fired because they did not get things done on time?*
32. Have you ever watched someone overdo pushing to get something done on time to the point that it backfired?
33. Have you ever watched someone succeed because they did push to get something done on time?*
34. Have you ever worked with a coach on improving your ability to get things done on time?*
35. Have you ever worked with a person who excelled at getting things done on time?
36. Have you ever worked with a skills coach on improving your ability to get things done on time?*
37. How do you get feedback about yourself on your ability to get things done on time?
38. How often do you check with multiple sources when you get a piece of critical feedback on your ability to get things done on time?
39. Is there a historical figure you consider a model of ability to deliver work on time?
40. What do others who are not your fans say about your ability to deliver work on time?
41. What do others who like you say about your ability to deliver work on time?
42. Which boss was the best at getting things done on time?
43. Which boss was the worst at getting things done on time?
44. Which direct report was the best at getting things done on time?
45. Which direct report was the worst at getting things done on time?
46. Which peer was the best at getting things done on time?
47. Which peer was the worst at getting things done on time?
48. Who in your field or business deals best with getting things done on time?
49. Who do you consider a current role model of getting things done on time?*
50. Who do you go to for advice on getting things done on time?
51. Who have you learned the most from about getting things done on time?*
52. Who is a higher-management role model for you on getting things done on time?
53. Who is a role model of getting things done on time outside of work?

Dimension 3: Knowing How This Works

54. Are there situations or settings where someone should be different in their ability to deliver work on time?
55. Do you think the ability to deliver work on time can be learned; how do you think people develop this skill?
56. Do you think there is a way to compensate or work around a low ability to deliver work on time?
57. Has anyone asked you for your opinions/advice on getting things done on time?*

TIMELINESS OF DELIVERY OF OUTPUT

58. Have you ever attended a course on getting things done on time?
59. Have you ever been in a situation where you and others put getting things done on time on a success profile?
60. Have you ever been part of an effort to create a policy or a mission statement containing reference to the ability to deliver work on time?
61. Have you ever been someone's coach or mentor who had problems with getting things done on time?
62. Have you ever created a development plan for someone on getting things done on time?
63. Have you ever criticized someone for not getting things done on time
64. Have you ever designed a program on getting things done on time?
65. Have you ever given a speech on getting things done on time?
66. Have you ever rewarded or recognized someone for getting things done on time?
67. Have you ever taught a course on getting things done on time?
68. Have you ever tried to help someone deal more effectively with getting things done on time?*
69. Have you ever tried to help someone improve their ability to deliver work on time?
70. How much deadline-orientation is good to have and how much is too much?
71. How much of success do you think is due to the ability to deliver work on time compared with other characteristics?
72. How would you know if someone is bad at getting things done on time?
73. How would you know if someone is good at getting things done on time?
74. If you had to write a book on getting things done on time, what would the chapter headings be?
75. What are the benefits to someone who is really good at getting things done on time?
76. What are the consequences to someone who is really poor at getting things done on time?
77. What do you think the standard is on the ability to deliver work on time for someone in your role?
78. What happens if you have or use too much of your ability to get things done on time?
79. What happens when two people try to work together who are very different in ability to deliver work on time?
80. What wisdom would you pass onto others trying to become better at getting things done on time?
81. Why do you think people end up being different in ability to deliver work on time?

Dimension 4: Personal Learning

82. Compare and contrast examples of being effective and ineffective at getting things done on time?
83. Contrast your on- and off-the-job use of the ability to deliver work on time.
84. Did you ever pass up a job or assignment because you were not confident enough in your ability to deliver work on time?
85. Do you ever use other skills to cover for your lack of ability to deliver work on time?
86. Has getting things done on time ever figured in a failure, struggle, or setback you have had?
87. Has becoming better at getting things done on time ever helped you in other areas?
88. Has poor ability to deliver work on time ever been the subject of a development plan for you?
89. Has your ability to deliver work on time always been this way?
90. Have you ever delegated or assigned someone a task because you lack the ability to deliver work on time.
91. Have you ever made significant strides at becoming better at getting things done on time?
92. Has your ability to deliver work on time ever been the subject of your performance review or a career discussion?
93. How different are you across situations in your ability to deliver work on time?
94. How do you decide how deadline-oriented to be?
95. How much of your success is due to your ability to deliver work on time?
96. How transferable are skills at getting things done on time to other situations?

TIMELINESS OF DELIVERY OF OUTPUT

97. If you had to become better at your ability to deliver work on time in a hurry, what would you do?
98. Was there a time when you were not good at getting things done on time?
99. What caused you to work to change your skills at ….?
100. What event or series of events had the most impact on your ability to deliver work on time?
101. What's the most varied you can be in getting things done on time?
102. What's the shortest amount of time in which you learned to become better at getting things done on time?
103. When did you first realize your level of skill at getting things done on time?
104. When you know ahead of time that your level of ability to deliver work on time won't work, what do you do?
105. Why do you think you deal with getting things done on time the way you do?
106. Why do you think your ability to deliver work on time is the way it is?*
107. Tell me how you go about making big or critical decisions.*
108. What factors slow you down the most and what do you do about them?*

D. **Follow-up Probes:**

Dimension 1: What the Person Did
1. Can you give me a few examples of that?
2. How far would you go before you would stop and try another approach?
3. Tell me about times when you do this and times when you don't.
4. Tell me about times when you are not like this or wouldn't do this.
5. Was this comfortable for you, or were you forcing yourself?
6. How typical is this for you?
7. How consistently do you do this across situations?
8. How would you have done this differently with tighter deadlines?
9. How would you have done this differently with looser deadlines?
10. How did others react when you did that?

Dimension 2: Seeing Others Do This
11. How do others you have known approach that?
12. Do you know a good and a bad example of this? Contrast those two people for me.
13. What do you think this person was trying to do?
14. Have you worked for a person like that since?
15. How could this person have been more effective?
16. Did you later change your assessment of this person?
17. What was it like to work with someone like that?
18. What was it like to work with someone you seem to have disliked?
19. Do you think most people would react that way?

Dimension 3: Knowing How This Works
20. Why do you think people do that?
21. Where do people learn this?
22. What do you think the key aspects of it are?
23. How would you teach this to someone else?
24. Why do you suppose teams work that way?
25. Why do you suppose organizations work that way?
26. Why do you think that happened?

TIMELINESS OF DELIVERY OF OUTPUT

Dimension 4: Personal Learning

27. Where did you learn to do it that way?
28. What did you learn from that?
29. What do you think you learned that would be repeatable in other situations?
30. Do you try to act that way with everyone? What's your thinking on that?
31. Do you think you do this better or worse than most people can? How do you know?
32. Do you think you can get others to do this better than most people can? If so, how do you know?
33. Why do you do it that way?
34. How did you come up with that approach?
35. Why did you think that method of getting over that barrier would work?
36. What were the negative consequences of this?
37. How would you do this differently next time?
38. What did you learn about how customers are gained?
39. What did you learn about how customers are lost?
40. How do you see that as a customer yourself?
41. What did you learn about yourself?
42. What did you learn about dealing with that kind of person?
43. What did you learn about dealing with that kind of situation?
44. What did you do after you got that feedback?
45. What were you thinking when you took that risk?
46. What were you thinking when you took that approach?
47. What's your view of why things happened that way?
48. What's your thinking about why that worked?
49. What's your thinking about why that didn't work?
50. What lessons do you think you came away with?
51. What would you tell your children about that experience?
52. What would you tell your mentor about that experience?
53. What would you tell your friend about that experience?

E. **Themes/Things to Look for:**

Admitting mistakes and learning from them
Comfort with loose ends
Cool in a crisis
Doesn't expect everything to be fair
Doesn't just do things; has a plan of action
Driven to get things done on time
Establishing feedback loops so they don't stumble into disaster
Goes into detail only if needed
Quality
Balance between being orderly and timely
Timeliness
Tries to meet unfair requests; doesn't get angry; just does their best to get it done
Resourcefulness/scavenger

TIMELINESS OF DELIVERY OF OUTPUT

Spending extra to speed things up
Outsourcing where possible
Tries to get deadline relief
Works more than usual
Laser like focus
Doesn't accept excuses
Sets high standards
Multiple tracked

F. Most Likely Résumé:

1. Look for jobs like:

Chair of Projects/Task Forces
Fix-Its/Turnarounds
Scope (complexity) Assignments
Staff to Line Shifts
Start-ups

2. Look for develop-in-place assignments like:

Manage the renovation of an office, floor, building, meeting room, warehouse, etc.
Plan a new site for a building (plant, field office, headquarters, etc.).
Plan an off-site meeting, conference, convention, trade show, event, etc.
Become a referee for an athletic league or program.
Plan for and start up something small (secretarial pool, athletic program, suggestion system, program, etc.).
Launch a new product, service, or process.
Re-launch an existing product or service that's not doing well.
Assign a project to a group with a tight deadline.
Manage an ad hoc, temporary group of people involved in tackling a fix-it or turnaround project.
Help shut down a plant, regional office, product line, business, operation, etc.
Manage liquidation/sale of products, equipment, materials, a business, furniture, overstock, etc.
Manage a group through a significant business crisis.
Work on a crisis management team.

3. Best references to ask about or check:

Direct Boss
Human Resource Professionals
Internal and External Customers
Past Associates/Constituencies
Peers and Colleagues
Direct Reports

G. Learning Orientation Evaluation:

4. Spectator/Passive vs. Player/Participant
5. Tight/Rigid vs. Loose/Flexible
6. Reactive/Responsive vs. Adapting
8. Sameness vs. Diversity
10. Reactive vs. Initiating
11. Generalizations vs. Specific Learnings
20. Defensiveness vs. Admits Weaknesses
22. Focus on Accomplishments vs. Focusing on Solving Problems

TIMELINESS OF DELIVERY OF OUTPUT

H. The LEADERSHIP ARCHITECT® Sort Card Connections:

1. Good (positive) if combined with high:
Works through conflicts quickly (1, 12, 16, 57)
Gets the right things done first (15, 50)
Timely and thoughtful (17, 30, 32, 51, 61)
Has a plan for work (47, 52)
Calm under pressure (2, 11, 41)
Learns, doesn't just do (32, 45)
Anticipates obstacles (38, 39, 47, 48)
Can get a lot done at once (1, 2, 16, 39, 50)
Can change priorities on the run (1, 2, 11, 16, 32, 39, 50)

2. Bad (negative) if combined with low or high (+):
Too impulsive; can be a loose cannon (+1) 41, 47
Drives people relentlessly (+1, 9) 7, 50
Aloof 3, 33
Leaves bodies everywhere 3, 7, 31
Work is substandard 17, 47, 52, 63
Wastes resources 35, 39, 47
Doesn't include others 31, 36, 60
Doesn't learn 32, 35, 51
Can't build a team of timely performers 18, 19, 20
Makes quick decisions that leave other behind (+1, 2, 9, 16, 57) 18, 60

3. Too much can contribute to the following Stallers and Stoppers:

A. *What too much looks like (overused):*
So committed to meeting deadlines and getting things done on time that things get too intense; as the delivery target comes closer things like quality, costs, or morale suffer at the last minute; getting it done on time becomes too important.

B. *Too much might lead to these Stallers and Stoppers:*
Unable to Adapt to Differences (101)   Insensitive to Others (112)
Poor Administrator (103)   Overmanaging (117)
Lack of Ethics and Values (109)   Performance Problems (118)
Failure to Build a Team (110)

C. *Compensators:*
How to compensate for too much of this PERFORMANCE MANAGEMENT ARCHITECT® dimension:
3, 11, 17, 33, 39, 41, 46, 47, 50, 51, 52, 58, 59, 63, 65

D. *Things to watch for:*
Cost overruns   Poor use of resources
Doesn't think things through   Quality slippage
Drives others too hard   Rework
Impulsiveness   Runs over others

TIMELINESS OF DELIVERY OF OUTPUT

4. Too little can contribute to the following Stallers and Stoppers:

   A. What too little looks like (unskilled):

      Always among the last to finish; misses important deadlines by a significant amount and barely meets standard for others; among the slowest people or groups around.

   B. Too little can contribute to the following Stallers and Stoppers:

      Poor Administrator (102)   Failure to Build a Team (110)
      Betrayal of Trust (105)   Performance Problems (118)
      Defensiveness (108)

   C. Compensators:

      How to substitute for too little of this PERFORMANCE MANAGEMENT ARCHITECT® dimension:
      1, 2, 12, 17, 18, 32, 37, 40, 43, 50, 51, 52, 53, 62

I. LEARNING ARCHITECT® Connections:

Look for people who act like and/or show evidence of:

1a. Pure Action	9. Multiple Sources
1b. Trial and Error	13. Focused
1c. Following a Plan	22. Experimenter
2a. Problem Solving	23. Orchestrator
2c. Intuition	28. Creator
4a. Getting Information	33. Diversity of Sources
4c. Actively Involve	36. Comfort with Paradox
7. Risks	37. Flexibility
8. Initiate	

J. CHOICES ARCHITECT® Connections:

Look for people who act like and/or show evidence of:

First Edition (Released 1994)	Second Edition (Released 2000)
12. Experimenter	5. Easy Shifter
13. Role Flexibility	18. Role Flexibility
20. Forging Ahead	20. Experimenter
	23. Visioning

83. QUALITY OF WORK OUTPUT

A. Definition:
The quality of the work from this person is always among the best; produces work that is mostly error free the first time with little waste or redone work.

B. Arenas/Domains to Explore:
1. Academic history
2. Analytical tasks
3. Art projects
4. Awards
5. Benchmarking studies
6. Complex tasks
7. Computer literacy
8. Cost/benefit analysis
9. Crafts
10. Crossword puzzles
11. Customer feedback systems
12. Customer service jobs
13. Debate team
14. Detail wood working
15. Drafting
16. Electrical work
17. Helping other solve problems
18. Intricate/precision hobbies
19. Mechanical repair/restoration
20. Military occupations
21. Paramedic training
22. Product specifications
23. Service specifications
24. Work Redesign

C. Sample Questions:

Dimension 1: What the Person Did   Note: * means OK for campus   ** means campus only

1. Tell me about a time when you missed a deadline on some work.*
2. Tell me about a time when you missed a deadline on some work for a customer.
3. Do you rewrite things your people draft or write?
4. Give me some examples of what you do to decrease the number of errors in your work.*
5. Give me some examples of what you do to efficiently use resources in your work.*
6. Have you ever given up on something or just refused to do it because you believed a job not done well is a job not worth doing?
7. Have you ever managed anything where the people reporting to you were in different locations? How did you ensure quality of work?
8. Have you ever written product or service specifications after surveying the eventual customers? If so, how did you go about this work?
9. How often do you complain as a customer? Have you ever written to a company complaining about a product or service?*
10. Tell me about a time when you delivered quality work, but it was overkill because it took too long and used too many resources.*
11. Tell me about a time when you designed in some corrective steps so quality didn't suffer.
12. Tell me about a time when you designed in some problem prevention checkpoints to alert you to a quality problem.*
13. Tell me about a time when you failed to meet a high quality standard for customers.*
14. Tell me about a time when you had to do some work twice because you didn't think it through properly.*
15. Tell me about a time when you handled customer complaints.*

QUALITY OF WORK OUTPUT

16. Tell me about a time when you improved a workflow or process.*
17. Tell me about a time when you installed a new system to improve the quality of a product or service.
18. Tell me about a time when you met a high quality standard for customers.
19. Tell me about a time when you missed a deadline because you weren't satisfied with the quality.*
20. Tell me about a time when you moved into a job where the work processes/systems/work groups were delivering poor quality and had to be fixed.
21. Tell me about a time when you solved a problem that others couldn't.*
22. Tell me about a time when you streamlined a process.*
23. Tell me about a time when you surveyed customers by phone.
24. Tell me about a time when you surveyed customers in person.
25. Tell me about a time when you tried to stop a group from implementing its first solution.*
26. Tell me about a time when you went outside your group to get help on a quality problem.
27. Tell me about a time when your mistakes caught up with you.*
28. Were you ever part of the implementation of TQM, Process Re-engineering, ISO or Six Sigma?
29. What do you do to check the quality of work along the way?*
30. What's the most significant improvement you have ever made to a work process?
31. What's the worst work process you have personally experienced?*

Dimension 2: Seeing Others Do This

32. Contrast the most and least quality-oriented people you know.*
33. Has the quality of your work ever been in any 360° survey done on you? Was your score among your highest, middle, or lowest?
34. Has poor quality work on someone else's part ever created an obstacle for you or got in the way of something you were trying to accomplish?*
35. Have you ever talked with a coach or mentor about the quality of your work
36. Have you ever watched someone fail/get fired because they did not do quality work?*
37. Have you ever watched someone overdo the quality of the work they produced to the point that it backfired?
38. Have you ever watched someone succeed because they did quality work?*
39. Have you ever worked with a coach on improving the quality of your work?*
40. Have you ever worked with a person who excelled at delivering quality work?
41. Have you ever worked with a skills coach on improving the quality of your work?*
42. How do you get feedback about yourself on the quality of your work?
43. How often do you check with multiple sources when you get a piece of critical feedback on the quality of your work?
44. Is there a historical figure you consider a model of delivering quality work?
45. What do others who are not your fans say about the quality of your work?
46. What do others who like you say about the quality of your work?
47. Which boss was the best at delivering quality work?
48. Which boss was the worst at delivering quality work?
49. Which direct report was the best at delivering quality work?
50. Which direct report was the worst at delivering quality work?
51. Which peer was the best at delivering quality work?
52. Which peer was the worst at delivering quality work?
53. Who in your field or business deals best with delivering quality work?
54. Who do you consider a current role model of delivering quality work?*
55. Who do you go to for advice on delivering quality work?

QUALITY OF WORK OUTPUT

56. Who have you learned the most from about delivering quality work?*
57. Who is a higher-management role model for you on delivering quality work?
58. Who is a role model of delivering quality work outside of work?

Dimension 3: Knowing How This Works

59. Are there situations or settings where someone should be different in the quality of their work?
60. Do you think a quality orientation can be learned; how do you think people develop this orientation?
61. Do you think there is a way to compensate or work around a low ability to deliver quality work?
62. Has anyone asked you for your opinions/advice on delivering quality work?*
3. Have you ever attended a course on delivering quality work?
64. Have you ever been in a situation where you and others put delivering quality work on a success profile?
65. Have you ever been part of an effort to create a policy or a mission statement containing reference to the ability to deliver quality work?
66. Have you ever been someone's coach or mentor who had problems with delivering quality work?
67. Have you ever created a development plan for someone on improving the ability to deliver quality work?
68. Have you ever criticized someone for not delivering quality work
69. Have you ever designed a program on delivering quality work?
70. Have you ever given a speech on delivering quality work?
71. Have you ever rewarded or recognized someone for delivering quality work?
72. Have you ever taught a course on delivering quality work?
73. Have you ever tried to help someone deal more effectively with their ability to deliver quality work?*
74. Have you ever tried to help someone improve their ability to deliver quality work?
75. How much quality orientation is good to have and how much is too much?
76. How much of success do you think is due to the ability to deliver quality work compared with other characteristics?
77. How would you know if someone is bad at delivering quality work?
78. How would you know if someone is good at delivering quality work?
79. If you had to write a book on delivering quality work, what would the chapter headings be?
80. What are the benefits to someone who is really good at delivering quality work?
81. What are the consequences to someone who is really poor at delivering quality work?
82. What do you think the standard is on delivering quality work for someone in your role?
83. What happens if you have or use too much of a quality orientation?
84. What happens when two people try to work together who are very different in their the ability to deliver quality work?
85. What wisdom would you pass onto others trying to become better at delivering quality work?
86. Why do you think people end up being different in the ability to deliver quality work?
87. Many say that completing the last ten percent of work can take too much time; that getting something ninety percent right and later fixing it is a more productive strategy. What's your view on that?*

Dimension 4: Personal Learning

88. Compare and contrast examples of being effective and ineffective at delivering quality work?
89. Contrast your on- and off-the-job use of your ability to deliver quality work
90. Did you ever pass up a job or assignment because you were not confident enough in your ability to deliver quality work?
91. Do you ever use other skills to cover for your lack of ability to deliver quality work?
92. Has the ability to deliver quality work ever figured in a failure, struggle, or setback you have had?
93. Has becoming better at delivering quality work ever helped you in other areas?

QUALITY OF WORK OUTPUT

94. Has poor ability to deliver quality work ever been the subject of a development plan for you?
95. Has your ability to deliver quality work always been this way?
96. Have you ever delegated or assigned someone a task because of your inability to produce quality work?
97. Have you ever made significant strides at becoming better at delivering quality work?
98. Has your ability to deliver quality work ever been the subject of your performance review or a career discussion?
99. How different are you across situations in your ability to deliver quality work?
100. How do you decide how quality-oriented to be?
101. How much of your success is due to your ability to deliver quality work?
102. How transferable is your ability to deliver quality work to other situations?
103. If you had to become better at delivering quality work in a hurry, what would you do?
104. Was there a time when you were not good at delivering quality work?
105. What caused you to work to change your skills at delivering quality work?
106. What event or series of events had the most impact on your ability to deliver quality work?
107. What's the most varied you can be in delivering quality work?
108. What's the shortest amount of time in which you learned to become better at delivering quality work?
109. When did you first realize your level of ability to deliver quality work?
110. When you know ahead of time that your level of ability to deliver quality work won't work, what do you do?
111. Why do you think you deal with delivering quality work the way you do?
112. Why do you think your ability to deliver quality work is the way it is?*
113. How do you balance quality with timeliness?*
114. How do you balance quality with not using too many resources?*
115. How do you decide what to delegate and what not to?

D. Follow-up Probes:

Dimension 1: What the Person Did

1. Can you give me a few examples of that?
2. How consistently do you do this across situations?
3. How did others react when you did that?
4. How far would you go before you would stop and try another approach?
5. How typical is this for you?
6. How would you have done this differently with looser deadlines?
7. How would you have done this differently with tighter deadlines?
8. Tell me about times when you are not like this or wouldn't do this.
9. Tell me about times when you do this and times when you don't.
10. Was this comfortable for you, or were you forcing yourself?

Dimension 2: Seeing Others Do This

11. Did you later change your assessment of this person?
12. Do you know a good and a bad example of this? Contrast those two people for me.
13. Do you think most people would react that way?
14. Have you worked for a person like that since?
15. How could this person have been more effective?

QUALITY OF WORK OUTPUT

16. How do others you have known approach that?
17. What do you think this person was trying to do?
18. What was it like to work with someone like that?
19. What was it like to work with someone you seem to have disliked?

Dimension 3: Knowing How This Works
20. How would you teach this to someone else?
21. What do you think the key aspects of it are?
22. Where do people learn this?
23. Why do you suppose organizations work that way?
24. Why do you suppose teams work that way?
25. Why do you think people do that?
26. Why do you think that happened?

Dimension 4: Personal Learning
27. Do you think you can get others to do this better than most people can? If so, how do you know?
28. Do you think you do this better or worse than most people can? How do you know?
29. Do you try to act that way with everyone? What's your thinking on that?
30. How did you come up with that approach?
31. How do you see that as a customer yourself?
32. How would you do this differently next time?
33. What did you do after you got that feedback?
34. What did you learn about dealing with that kind of person?
35. What did you learn about dealing with that kind of situation?
36. What did you learn about how customers are gained?
37. What did you learn about how customers are lost?
38. What did you learn about yourself?
39. What did you learn from that?
40. What do you think you learned that would be repeatable in other situations?
41. What lessons do you think you came away with?
42. What were the negative consequences of this?
43. What were you thinking when you took that approach?
44. What were you thinking when you took that risk?
45. What would you tell your children about that experience?
46. What would you tell your friend about that experience?
47. What would you tell your mentor about that experience?
48. What's your thinking about why that didn't work?
49. What's your thinking about why that worked?
50. What's your view of why things happened that way?
51. Where did you learn to do it that way?
52. Why did you think that method of getting over that barrier would work?
53. Why do you do it that way?

QUALITY OF WORK OUTPUT

E. Themes/Things to Look for:

A feel for how work is supposed to flow
A picky customer
A sense of balance between quality and timeliness
A sense of balance between quality and use of resources
Can describe the process of producing quality
Challenges the solutions of others
Challenges the way things have always been done
Complains about poor work designs when they are a customer
Incremental improvements
Involvement with TQM/ISO/Six Sigma
Learning from mistakes
Learning from other models, organizations
Mechanical intricate hobbies
Not satisfied with the first solution
Seeing problems as a chance to improve something
Sense of what is likely to go wrong
Sense of what is likely to hurt quality
Setting up customer feedback loops
Thinks and talks continuous improvement
Upset about poor work designs
Wants to know how things work
Will look anywhere for ideas

F. Most Likely Résumé:

1. Look for jobs like:

Fix-Its/Turnarounds   Scope (complexity) Assignments
Scale (size shift) Assignments

2. Look for develop-in-place assignments like:

Interview or work with a "tutor" or mentor on a skill you need to develop.
Integrate diverse systems, processes, or procedures across decentralized and/or dispersed units.
Work on a process-simplification team to take steps and costs out of a process.
Do a problem-prevention analysis on a product or service and present it to the people involved.
Do a customer-satisfaction survey in person or by phone and present it to the people involved.
Benchmark innovative practices, processes, products, or services of competitors, vendors, suppliers, or customers and present a report to others to create recommendations for change.
Visit Malcolm Baldrige National Quality Award or Deming Prize winners and report back on your findings, showing how they would help your organization.
Relaunch an existing product or service that's not doing well.
Create employee involvement teams.
Manage an ad hoc, temporary group of people involved in tackling a fix-it or turnaround project.
Handle a tough negotiation with an internal or external client or customer.

QUALITY OF WORK OUTPUT

Manage a cost-cutting project.

Take on a task you dislike or hate to do.

Build a multifunctional project team to tackle a common business issue or problem.

3. Best references to ask about or check:

Internal and External Customers

Peers and Colleagues

Direct Reports

G. Learning Orientation Evaluation:

1. What/Describing vs. Why/Explain
2. All or Nothing vs. Can See Many Sides
6. Reactive/Responsive vs. Adapting
7. Passive vs. Intrigued/Curious
8. Sameness vs. Diversity
9. Vague/General vs. Sharp/Specific
13. Simple Views vs. Complex Views
16. Few Rules of Thumb vs. Many and Varied Rules of Thumb
18. Comfort Zone vs. Curious
19. External Standards vs. Internal Standards
20. Defensiveness vs. Admits Weaknesses
22. Focus on Accomplishments vs. Focusing on Solving Problems

H. The LEADERSHIP ARCHITECT® Sort Card Connections:

1. Good (positive) if combined with high:

Knows what's important (5, 24, 50, 58)

Comes up with clever methods (14, 28, 51, 52, 63)

Inspires a team (18, 35, 36, 65)

Learns from feedback (32, 33, 45, 61, 63)

Adaptable (2, 40, 52, 63)

Fast (1, 16, 53)

Good troubleshooter (35, 47, 51)

Uses resources efficiently (38, 39)

2. Bad (negative) if combined with low or high (+):

Perfectionist; too slow 1, 16 (47+)

Wastes resources 38, 39

Does too much her/himself 18, 60 (+24, 57, 61)

Puts too much effort into low payoff work 5, 50, 58

Not attuned to others 3, 31

Slows down everyone else (+57) 50

QUALITY OF WORK OUTPUT

3. **Too much can contribute to the following Stallers and Stoppers:**

   A. *What too much looks like (overused):*

   > Produces high quality work but perfectionism leads to lower productivity, some missed deadlines, using too many resources to finish or taking too long to get there; quality standards exceed what's reasonable.

   B. *Too much might lead to these Stallers and Stoppers:*

Unable to Adapt to Differences (101)	Insensitive to Others (112)
Defensiveness (108)	Overmanaging (117)
Failure to Build a Team (110)	Performance Problems (118)

   C. *Compensators:*

   How to compensate for too much of this PERFORMANCE MANAGEMENT ARCHITECT® dimension:
   2, 5, 16, 32, 33, 35, 40, 45, 50, 58

   D. *Things to watch for:*

A lot of rework by their people	Missed deadlines
All or nothing quality standards	Quality, quality, quality; nothing else matters
Cost overruns	Tinkers too much
Know it all	

4. **Too little can contribute to the following Stallers and Stoppers:**

   A. *What too little looks like (unskilled):*

   > Produces work that's below the quality standard; contains notable and sloppy errors; usually requires rework before it can be used and then barely meets average minimum quality standards or specifications.

   B. *Too little can contribute to the following Stallers and Stoppers:*

Poor Administrator (102)	Key Skill Deficiencies (113)
Betrayal of Trust (105)	Performance Problems (118)

   C. *Compensators:*

   How to substitute for too little of this PERFORMANCE MANAGEMENT ARCHITECT® dimension:
   5, 15, 16, 18, 20, 28, 32, 33, 35, 39, 47, 50, 52, 53, 65

I. **LEARNING ARCHITECT® Connections:**

Look for people who act like and/or show evidence of:

1b. Trial and Error	16. Collaborate
1c. Following a Plan	19. What
2a. Problem Solving	22. Experimenter
2b. Visioning	23. Orchestrator
4a. Getting Information	29. Essence
4c. Actively Involve	30. Mastery
9. Multiple Sources	31. Rationality
10. Complexity	33. Diversity of Sources
11. Why/How	35. Breadth
13. Focused	37. Flexibility

QUALITY OF WORK OUTPUT

J. CHOICES ARCHITECT® Connections:

Look for people who act like and/or show evidence of:

First Edition (Released 1994)	Second Edition (Released 2000)
1. Inquisitive	1. Broad Scanner
2. Essence	3. Connector
5. Connector	4. Critical Thinker
10. Responds to Feedback	5. Easy Shifter
11. Open to Diversity	6. Essence
12. Experimenter	7. Inquisitive
16. Cold/Indirect Sources	8. Solution Finder
17. Hot/Direct Sources	14. Open-Minded
19. Tinkerer	16. Personal Learner
	17. Responds to Feedback
	20. Experimenter
	22. Taking the Heat
	26. Drive

QUALITY OF WORK OUTPUT

84. USE OF RESOURCES

A. Definition:

Uses fewer resources in terms of time, material, money and people than almost any other group; gets more things done with less; a model of resourcefulness; always or almost always comes in under budget in all areas.

B. Arenas/Domains to Explore:

1. Allocating time to different projects/tasks
2. Building facilities
3. Charity work
4. Church work
5. Competing demands on time
6. Complex processes
7. Coordinating large projects
8. Cost management
9. Club/association management
10. Deploying resources across different geographic areas
11. Event/conference management
12. Family asset/financial management
13. Family business
14. Grant Proposals
15. Group/Team leader
16. Home renovation
17. Managing consultants
18. Managing outside contractors
19. Managing direct reports
20. Managing suppliers/vendors
21. Managing volunteers
22. Military supply management
23. Process re-engineering projects
24. Project/task force leader
25. Renovating office space
26. Responsible for workflow
27. Starting up a product or service
28. Starting up an organization

C. Sample Questions:

Dimension 1: What the Person Did   Note: * means OK for campus   ** means campus only

1. Give me some examples of what you do to decrease the number of errors in your work.*
2. Have you ever written product or service specifications after surveying the eventual customers? If so, how did you go about this work?*
3. Give me some examples of what you do to efficiently use resources in your work.*
4. Have you ever managed anything where the people reporting to you were in different locations? How did you insure efficient use of resources?
5. Have you ever turned budget money back in?
6. How do you generally work against a budget?
7. How do you go about getting the most from your outside resources?
8. How do you handle multiple demands on your time?*
9. How do you usually handle work interruptions to keep them as brief as possible?*
10. How much of a reserve do you tend to build into your budget requests?
11. Tell me about a time when you delegated or divided work among your direct reports or people on a project.*
12. Tell me about a time when you delivered good work, but it was overkill because it took too long and used too many resources.*
13. Tell me about a time when you designed in some corrective steps so you didn't run out of resources.
14. Tell me about a time when you designed in some problem prevention checkpoints to alert you to a resource problem.

USE OF RESOURCES

15. Tell me about a time when you got the work done, but the people working for you felt overburdened.*
16. Tell me about a time when you improved a work flow or process.*
17. Tell me about a time when you managed office renovations.
18. Tell me about a time when you missed a deadline on some work.*
19. Tell me about a time when you moved into a job where the work processes/systems/work groups were delivering poor quality and had to be fixed.
20. Tell me about a time when you organized consultants to get something done within budget.
21. Tell me about a time when you organized volunteers to get something done within budget.*
22. Tell me about a time when you streamlined a process.*
23. Tell me about a time you managed a conference or large meeting.*
24. Tell me about a time you managed building a facility.
25. Tell me about a time you were faced with a broken-down process that had to be fixed.*
26. What do you do to check the use of resources along the way?
27. What have you done when half of the project is complete but you have less than half the budget left?
28. What have you done when you have taken over something with what you consider a less than adequate budget?
29. What's the most significant improvement you have ever made to a work process?*
30. What's the worst work process you have personally experienced?*
31. When you design a work process, how do you estimate the resources it will take?

Dimension 2: Seeing Others Do This

32. Contrast the most and least resourceful people you know.*
33. Has resourcefulness ever been in any 360° survey done on you? Was your score among your highest, middle, or lowest?
34. Has poor use of resources on someone else's part ever created an obstacle for you or got in the way of something you were trying to accomplish?*
35. Have you ever talked with a coach or mentor about your inefficient use of resources?
36. Have you ever watched someone fail/get fired because of an inefficient use of resources?*
37. Have you ever watched someone overdo resourcefulness to the point that it backfired?
38. Have you ever watched someone succeed because of an efficient use of resources?*
39. Have you ever worked with a coach on using resources more efficiently?*
40. Have you ever worked with a person who excelled at using resources efficiently?
41. Have you ever worked with a skills coach on using resources efficiently?*
42. How do you get feedback about yourself on your ability to use resources?
43. How often do you check with multiple sources when you get a piece of critical feedback on your use of resources?
44. Is there a historical figure you consider a model of resourcefulness?
45. What do others who are not your fans say about your efficient use of resources?
46. What do others who like you say about your efficient use of resources?
47. Which boss was the best at using resources efficiently?
48. Which boss was the worst at using resources efficiently?
49. Which direct report was the best at using resources efficiently?
50. Which direct report was the worst at using resources efficiently?
51. Which peer was the best at using resources efficiently?
52. Which peer was the worst at using resources efficiently?

USE OF RESOURCES

53. Who is the best in your field or business at using resources efficiently?
54. Who do you consider a current role model of using resources efficiently?*
55. Who do you go to for advice on using resources efficiently?
56. Who have you learned the most from about using resources efficiently?*
57. Who is a higher-management role model for you on using resources efficiently?
58. Who is a role model of efficient use of resources outside of work?

Dimension 3: Knowing How This Works

59. Are there situations or settings where someone should be different in the way they uses resources?
60. Do you think using resources efficiently can be learned; how do you think people develop this skill?
61. Do you think there is a way to compensate or work around a low ability to use resources efficiently?
62. Has anyone asked you for your opinions/advice on using resources efficiently?*
63. Have you ever attended a course on using resources efficiently?
64. Have you ever been in a situation where you and others put using resources efficiently on a success profile?
65. Have you ever been part of an effort to create a policy or a mission statement containing reference to being resourceful?
66. Have you ever been someone's coach or mentor who had problems with using resources efficiently?
67. Have you ever created a development plan for someone on using resources efficiently?
68. Have you ever criticized someone for not using resources efficiently
69. Have you ever designed a program on using resources efficiently?
70. Have you ever given a speech on using resources efficiently?
71. Have you ever rewarded or recognized someone for having efficiently used resources?
72. Have you ever taught a course on using resources efficiently?
73. Have you ever tried to help someone deal more effectively with their use of resources?*
74. Have you ever tried to help someone improve their use of resources?
75. How much resourcefulness is good to have and how much is too much?
76. How much of success do you think is due to resourcefulness compared with other characteristics?
77. How would you know if someone is bad at using resources efficiently?
78. How would you know if someone is good at using resources efficiently?
79. If you had to write a book on using resources efficiently, what would the chapter headings be?
80. What are the benefits to someone who is really good at using resources efficiently?
81. What are the consequences to someone who is really poor at using resources efficiently?
82. What do you think the standard is on efficiently use resources for someone in your role?
83. What happens if you have or use too much resourcefulness?
84. What happens when two people try to work together who are very different in their ability to use resources efficiently?
85. What wisdom would you pass onto others trying to become better at using resources efficiently?
86. Why do you think people end up being different in their ability to use resources efficiently?

Dimension 4: Personal Learning

87. Compare and contrast examples of being effective and ineffective at using resources efficiently?
88. Contrast your on- and off-the-job use of resources.
89. Did you ever pass up a job or assignment because you were not confident enough in your skills at using resources efficiently?
90. Do you ever use other skills to cover for your lack of resourcefulness?

USE OF RESOURCES

91. Has inefficient use of resources ever figured in a failure, struggle, or setback you have had?
92. Has becoming better at using resources efficiently ever helped you in other areas?
93. Has poor use of resources ever been the subject of a development plan for you?
94. Has your ability to use resources efficiently always been this way?
95. Have you ever delegated or assigned someone a task because of your inability to use resources efficiently?
96. Have you ever made significant strides at becoming better at using resources efficiently?
97. Have your skills at using resources efficiently, good or bad, ever been the subject of your performance review or a career discussion?
98. How different are you across situations in your use of resources?
99. How do you decide how resourceful to be?
100. How much of your success is due to your resourcefulness?
101. How transferable is your ability to use resources efficiently to other situations?
102. If you had to become better at using resources efficiently in a hurry, what would you do?
103. Was there a time when you were not good at using resources efficiently?
104. What caused you to work to change your skills at using resources efficiently?
105. What event or series of events had the most impact on your ability to use resources efficiently?
106. What's the most varied you can be in ability to use resources efficiently?
107. What's the shortest amount of time in which you learned to become better at efficiently using resources?
108. When did you first realize your level of skill at using resources efficiently?
109. When you know ahead of time that your level of ability to use resources efficiently won't work, what do you do?
110. Why do you think you deal with your use of resources the way you do?
111. Why do you think your ability to use resources efficiently is the way it is?*
112. What do you think are wise and unwise ways to organize resources?*
113. How do you go about getting resources that are not under your direct control?*
114. How do you balance quality with not using too many resources?

D. Follow-up Probes:

Dimension 1: What the Person Did

1. Can you give me a few examples of that?
2. How consistently do you do this across situations?
3. How did others react when you did that?
4. How far would you go before you would stop and try another approach?
5. How typical is this for you?
6. How would you have done this differently with looser deadlines?
7. How would you have done this differently with tighter deadlines?
8. Tell me about times when you are not like this or wouldn't do this.
9. Tell me about times when you do this and times when you don't.
10. Was this comfortable for you, or were you forcing yourself?

USE OF RESOURCES

Dimension 2: Seeing Others Do This

11. Did you later change your assessment of this person?
12. Do you know a good and a bad example of this? Contrast those two people for me.
13. Do you think most people would react that way?
14. Have you worked for a person like that since?
15. How could this person have been more effective?
16. How do others you have known approach that?
17. What do you think this person was trying to do?
18. What was it like to work with someone like that?
19. What was it like to work with someone you seem to have disliked?

Dimension 3: Knowing How This Works

20. How would you teach this to someone else?
21. What do you think the key aspects of it are?
22. Where do people learn this?
23. Why do you suppose organizations work that way?
24. Why do you suppose teams work that way?
25. Why do you think people do that?
26. Why do you think that happened?

Dimension 4: Personal Learning

27. Do you think you can get others to do this better than most people can? If so, how do you know?
28. Do you think you do this better or worse than most people can? How do you know?
29. Do you try to act that way with everyone? What's your thinking on that?
30. How did you come up with that approach?
31. How do you see that as a customer yourself?
32. How would you do this differently next time?
33. What did you do after you got that feedback?
34. What did you learn about dealing with that kind of person?
35. What did you learn about dealing with that kind of situation?
36. What did you learn about how customers are gained?
37. What did you learn about how customers are lost?
38. What did you learn about yourself?
39. What did you learn from that?
40. What do you think you learned that would be repeatable in other situations?
41. What lessons do you think you came away with?
42. What were the negative consequences of this?
43. What were you thinking when you took that approach?
44. What were you thinking when you took that risk?
45. What would you tell your children about that experience?
46. What would you tell your friend about that experience?
47. What would you tell your mentor about that experience?
48. What's your thinking about why that didn't work?
49. What's your thinking about why that worked?

USE OF RESOURCES

50. What's your view of why things happened that way?
51. Where did you learn to do it that way?
52. Why did you think that method of getting over that barrier would work?
53. Why do you do it that way?

E. Themes/Things to Look for:

A broad view of resources–materials, money, people, time
A sense of how processes play out
Agility with numbers
An eye for detail
Anticipating consequences and problems
Budget or plan for each step
Checking in with people often
Clear sense of priorities
Contingency planning
Cool head under delivery pressure
Estimating time and costs well
Good negotiator
Making comparisons to similar work to help in estimating
Proud of efficiency
Scavenger of resources
Sensitive to how much people can do
Sensitive to what people are good at
Tracking carefully
Trading to get resources
Values personal time

F. Most Likely Résumé:

1. Look for jobs like:

Chair of Projects/Task Forces
Fix-Its/Turnarounds
Scale (size shift) Assignments
Scope (complexity) Assignments
Staff Leadership (Influencing Without Authority)
Start-ups

2. Look for develop-in-place assignments like:

Install a new process or system (computer system, new policies, new process, new procedures, etc.).
Integrate diverse systems, processes, or procedures across decentralized and/or dispersed units.
Manage the renovation of an office, floor, building, meeting room, warehouse, etc.
Plan a new site for a building (plant, field office, headquarters, etc.).
Plan an off-site meeting, conference, convention, trade show, event, etc.
Manage the purchase of a major product, equipment, materials, program, or system.
Monitor and follow a new product or service through the entire idea, design, test market, and launch cycle.
Visit Malcolm Baldrige National Quality Award or Deming Prize winners and report back on your findings, showing how they would help your organization.

USE OF RESOURCES

Launch a new product, service, or process.

Relaunch an existing product or service that's not doing well.

Work on a team writing a proposal to obtain significant government or foundation grants or funding of an activity.

Manage the interface between consultants and the organization on a critical assignment.

Manage the assigning/allocating of office space in a contested situation.

Work on a team that's deciding who to keep and who to let go in a layoff, shutdown, delayering, or divestiture.

Manage a cost-cutting project.

Build a multifunctional project team to tackle a common business issue or problem.

3. **Best references to ask about or check:**

   Boss' Boss(es)
   Direct Boss
   Internal and External Customers
   Past Associates/Constituencies
   Peers and Colleagues
   Direct Reports

G. Learning Orientation Evaluation:

1. What/Describing vs. Why/Explain
2. All or Nothing vs. Can See Many Sides
4. Spectator/Passive vs. Player/Participant
5. Tight/Rigid vs. Loose/Flexible
6. Reactive/Responsive vs. Adapting
8. Sameness vs. Diversity
20. Defensiveness vs. Admits Weaknesses
22. Focus on Accomplishments vs. Focusing on Solving Problems

H. The LEADERSHIP ARCHITECT® Sort Card Connections:

1. **Good (positive) if combined with high:**

   Gets it done 15, 43, 53
   Helps others 3, 18, 31, 33, 42
   Spreads work out 18, 20, 23
   Good at workflows 20, 47, 50, 52
   Good project manager 35, 39, 47, 52
   Strikes deals with others 37, 38, 42
   Gets the right things done 15, 50, 53, 65

2. **Bad (negative) if combined with low or high (+):**

   Doesn't empower 3, 18, 33, 36, 60
   Distributes the load unevenly 18, 21, 23, 56
   Uses too many resources on less critical work 15, 50
   Quality suffers 52, 63
   Doesn't use time well; just does a lot of work 50, 62

USE OF RESOURCES

3. **Too much can contribute to the following Stallers and Stoppers:**

    A. *What too much looks like (overused):*

    > Although this person comes in on or even below budget, sometimes this is at the price of lower quantity or quality; so concerned with making or beating the budget plan that other things suffer; may cut corners on costs so tight that there are problems later in the work flow.

    B. *Too much might lead to these Stallers and Stoppers:*

Overly Ambitious (103)	Overmanaging (117)
Insensitive to Others (112)	Performance Problems (118)
Key Skill Deficiencies (113)	

    C. *Compensators:*

    How to compensate for too much of this PERFORMANCE MANAGEMENT ARCHITECT® dimension:
    3, 10, 15, 26, 31, 33, 46, 47, 50, 52, 58, 60, 64

    D. *Things to watch for:*

Causes problems down the line	Overwhelmed staff or coworkers
Doesn't distinguish the more from the less important	Rework
High output, poor quality	Too focused on numbers and use of materials
High turnover	Too much into detail

4. **Too little can contribute to the following Stallers and Stoppers:**

    A. *What too little looks like (unskilled):*

    > Uses resources inefficiently and even with the additional resources, just meets minimum standards; usually over budget on everything or significantly over on some and on budget on others; wastes time, money, material and people's productivity.

    B. *Too little can contribute to the following Stallers and Stoppers:*

Unable to Adapt to Differences (101)	Non-strategic (114)
Poor Administrator (102)	Performance Problems (118)

    C. *Compensators:*

    How to substitute for too little of this PERFORMANCE MANAGEMENT ARCHITECT® dimension:
    5, 15, 17, 18, 20, 24, 32, 33, 35, 39, 47, 50, 51, 58, 59

I. LEARNING ARCHITECT® Connections:

Look for people who act like and/or show evidence of:

1a. Pure Action	14. Controlled
1b. Trial and Error	16. Collaborate
1c. Following a Plan	19. What
2a. Problem Solving	23. Orchestrator
4a. Getting Information	29. Essence
4c. Actively Involve	31. Rationality
12. Rules of Thumb	37. Flexibility
13. Focused	

USE OF RESOURCES

J. CHOICES ARCHITECT® Connections:

Look for people who act like and/or show evidence of:

First Edition (Released 1994)
- 2. Essence
- 4. Complexity
- 7. Helping Others Think
- 13. Role Flexibility
- 15. Helps Others Succeed
- 20. Forging Ahead

Second Edition (Released 2000)
- 2. Complexity
- 6. Essence
- 8. Solution Finder
- 12. Helps Others Succeed
- 18. Role Flexibility
- 24. Inspires Others

USE OF RESOURCES

85. CUSTOMER IMPACT/VALUE ADDED

A. Definition:

Produces goods and services that consistently meets and sometimes exceed the standards and expectations of internal and external customers; always up to date about customer needs and expectations; the feedback from customers is almost always positive.

B. Arenas/Domains to Explore:

1. Across-boundary projects
2. Associations
3. Bargaining with peers
4. Clubs
5. Concierge jobs
6. Conference management
7. Current or past external customers
8. Current or past internal customers
9. Customer service jobs
10. Customer survey projects
11. Desk clerk jobs
12. Event planning
13. Market research projects
14. Meeting planning
15. Personal customer experiences
16. Sales jobs
17. Service jobs
18. Teaching
19. Technical service jobs
20. TQM/ISO/Six Sigma/process re-engineering projects
21. Volunteer work

C. Sample Questions:

Dimension 1: What the Person Did   Note: * means OK for campus   ** means campus only

1. Give me some examples of what you do to decrease the number of errors in your work for customers.
2. Give me some examples of what you do to efficiently use resources in your work for customers.*
3. Have you ever managed anything where the people reporting to you were in different locations? How did you ensure excellent customer service?
4. How do you get and keep up-to-date information from customers and what do you do with it?
5. Tell me about a time when an internal customer said you weren't delivering quality work.*
6. Tell me about a time when an internal customer said you weren't delivering work soon enough.*
7. Tell me about a time when you almost lost some customers and had to turn it around.
8. Tell me about a time when you and a peer argued over what should be done for a customer.*
9. Tell me about a time when you designed in checkpoints to alert you to a potential problem before customers would be affected.*
10. Tell me about a time when you designed in some corrective steps so quality to your customers didn't suffer.
11. Tell me about a time when you had to confront a co-worker in order to get something for a customer.*
12. Tell me about a time when you had to confront a customer.*
13. Tell me about a time when you had to deal with unreasonable requests from customers.*
14. Tell me about a time when you handled customer complaints.*
15. Tell me about a time when you lost a customer.*
16. Tell me about a time when you met a high quality standard for customers.*
17. Tell me about a time when you overdid customer service; you gave too much away.*
18. Tell me about a time when you persuaded a customer to see your point of view.*
19. Tell me about a time when you surveyed customers by phone.*
20. Tell me about a time when you surveyed customers in person.*

CUSTOMER IMPACT/VALUE ADDED

21. Tell me about a time when you talked a customer out of buying something from you.*
22. Tell me about a time when you used your interpersonal skills to get something done for a customer.*
23. Tell me about a time when you violated policy to get something for a customer.
24. Tell me about a time when you were able to get something done for a customer because of a relationship you have.*
25. Tell me about a time when you were at odds with peers over getting something done for a customer.*
26. Tell me about a time when you were treated badly as a customer.*
27. Tell me about a time when you were treated exceptionally well as a customer.*
28. Tell me about a time you had a job in direct sales.*
29. Tell me about a time you had to sell something as a school project/job.*
30. Tell me five pieces of feedback you've received from customers*.
31. What do customers do that irritates you? How do you react?*
32. What do you do when you feel the sale slipping away from you?*
33. Who are your best and worst customers?

Dimension 2: Seeing Others Do This

34. Contrast the most and least customer-focused people you know.*
35. Has having a customer service mentality ever been in any 360° survey done on you? Was your score among your highest, middle, or lowest?
36. Has poor customer service on someone else's part ever created an obstacle for you or got in the way of something you were trying to accomplish?*
37. Have you ever talked with a coach or mentor about your customer service skills?
38. Have you ever watched someone fail/get fired because they did not service the customer well?*
39. Have you ever watched someone overdo customer service to the point that it backfired?
40. Have you ever watched someone succeed because of customer service skills ?*
41. Have you ever worked with a coach on improving your customer service skills?*
42. Have you ever worked with a person who excelled at customer service?
43. Have you ever worked with a skills coach on improving your customer service skills?*
44. How do you get feedback about yourself on your customer service skills?
45. How often do you check with multiple sources when you get a piece of critical feedback on your customer service skills?
46. Is there a historical figure you consider a model of customer service mentality?
47. What do others who are not your fans say about your customer service skills?
48. What do others who like you say about your customer service skills?
49. Which boss was the best at serving customers?
50. Which boss was the worst at serving customers?
51. Which direct report was the best at serving customers?
52. Which direct report was the worst at serving customers?
53. Which peer was the best at serving customers?
54. Which peer was the worst at serving customers?
55. Who deals with serving customers the best in your field or business?
56. Who do you consider a current role model of customer service?*
57. Who do you go to for advice on customer service?
58. Who have you learned the most from about customer service?*
59. Who is a higher-management role model for you on serving customers?
60. Who is a role model of serving customers outside of work?

CUSTOMER IMPACT/VALUE ADDED

Dimension 3: Knowing How This Works

61. Are there situations or settings where someone should be different in the way they serves customers?
62. Do you think customer service skills can be learned; how do you think people develop these skills?
63. Do you think there is a way to compensate or work around low customer service skills?
64. Has anyone asked you for your opinions/advice on customer service?*
65. Have you ever attended a course on customer service?
66. Have you ever been in a situation where you and others put customer service on a success profile?
67. Have you ever been part of an effort to create a policy or a mission statement containing reference to having a customer service mentality?
68. Have you ever been someone's coach or mentor who had problems with customer service?
69. Have you ever created a development plan for someone on building customer service skills?
70. Have you ever criticized someone for not having a customer service mentality?
71. Have you ever designed a program on customer service?
72. Have you ever given a speech on customer service?
73. Have you ever rewarded or recognized someone for having a customer service mentality?
74. Have you ever taught a course on customer service?
75. Have you ever tried to help someone deal more effectively with serving customers?*
76. Have you ever tried to help someone improve their customer service skills?
77. How much of a customer service mentality is good to have and how much is too much?
78. How much of success do you think is due to customer service skills compared with other characteristics?
79. How would you know if someone is bad at customer service skills?
80. How would you know if someone is good at customer service skills?
81. If you had to write a book on serving customers, what would the chapter headings be?
82. What are the benefits to someone who is really good at serving customers?
83. What are the consequences to someone who is really poor at serving customers?
84. What do you think the standard is on serving customers for someone in your role?
85. What happens if you have or use too much of a customer service mentality?
86. What happens when two people try to work together who are very different in their ability to serve customers?
87. What wisdom would you pass onto others trying to become better at serving customers?
88. Why do you think people end up being different in their ability to serve customers?
89. Which companies do badly in customer service? Why is that?*
90. When you think of companies that serve customers well, which ones come to mind? Why is that?*
91. What does your organization do that results in losing its customers? What do you think can be done about it?*

Dimension 4: Personal Learning

92. Compare and contrast examples of being effective and ineffective at serving customers?
93. Contrast your on- and off-the-job use of customer service skills.
94. Did you ever pass up a job or assignment because you were not confident enough in your skills at serving customers?
95. Do you ever use other skills to cover for your lack of customer service skills?
96. Have a lack of customer service skills ever figured in a failure, struggle, or setback you have had?
97. Has becoming better at serving customers ever helped you in other areas?
98. Have poor customer service skills ever been the subject of a development plan for you?
99. Have your customer service skills always been this way?

CUSTOMER IMPACT/VALUE ADDED

100. Have you ever delegated or assigned someone a task because you didn't serve customers particularly well.
101. Have you ever made significant strides at becoming better at serving customers?
102. Have your customer service skills, good or bad, ever been the subject of your performance review or a career discussion?
103. How different are you across situations in your customer service skills?
104. How do you decide how customer-focused to be?
105. How much of your success is due to your customer service skills?
106. How transferable are your customer service skills to other situations?
107. If you had to become better at serving customers in a hurry, what would you do?
108. Was there a time when you were not good at serving customers?
109. What caused you to work to change your skills at serving customers?
110. What event or series of events had the most impact on your customer service skills?
111. What's the most varied you can be in serving customers?
112. What was the shortest amount of time in which you learned to become better at serving customers?
113. When did you first realize your level of skill at serving customers?
114. When you know ahead of time that your level of ability to serve customers won't work, what do you do?
115. Why do you think you deal with serving customers the way you do?
116. Why do you think your ability to serve customers is the way it is?*
117. What's your view of the balance point between serving customers well and hurting the organization by using too many resources?
118. When are exceptions to customers warranted and not warranted?
119. What's different about dealing with internal versus external customers?

D. Follow-up Probes:

Dimension 1: What the Person Did
1. Can you give me a few examples of that?
2. How consistently do you do this across situations?
3. How did others react when you did that?
4. How far would you go before you would stop and try another approach?
5. How typical is this for you?
6. How would you have done this differently with looser deadlines?
7. How would you have done this differently with tighter deadlines?
8. Tell me about times when you are not like this or wouldn't do this.
9. Tell me about times when you do this and times when you don't.
10. Was this comfortable for you, or were you forcing yourself?

Dimension 2: Seeing Others Do This
11. Did you later change your assessment of this person?
12. Do you know a good and a bad example of this? Contrast those two people for me.
13. Do you think most people would react that way?
14. Have you worked for a person like that since?
15. How could this person have been more effective?
16. How do others you have known approach that?
17. What do you think this person was trying to do?
18. What was it like to work with someone like that?
19. What was it like to work with someone you seem to have disliked?

CUSTOMER IMPACT/VALUE ADDED

Dimension 3: Knowing How This Works
20. How would you teach this to someone else?
21. What do you think the key aspects of it are?
22. Where do people learn this?
23. Why do you suppose organizations work that way?
24. Why do you suppose teams work that way?
25. Why do you think people do that?
26. Why do you think that happened?

Dimension 4: Personal Learning
27. Do you think you can get others to do this better than most people can? If so, how do you know?
28. Do you think you do this better or worse than most people can? How do you know?
29. Do you try to act that way with everyone? What's your thinking on that?
30. How did you come up with that approach?
31. How do you see that as a customer yourself?
32. How would you do this differently next time?
33. What did you do after you got that feedback?
34. What did you learn about dealing with that kind of person?
35. What did you learn about dealing with that kind of situation?
36. What did you learn about how customers are gained?
37. What did you learn about how customers are lost?
38. What did you learn about yourself?
39. What did you learn from that?
40. What do you think you learned that would be repeatable in other situations?
41. What lessons do you think you came away with?
42. What were the negative consequences of this?
43. What were you thinking when you took that approach?
44. What were you thinking when you took that risk?
45. What would you tell your children about that experience?
46. What would you tell your friend about that experience?
47. What would you tell your mentor about that experience?
48. What's your thinking about why that didn't work?
49. What's your thinking about why that worked?
50. What's your view of why things happened that way?
51. Where did you learn to do it that way?
52. Why did you think that method of getting over that barrier would work?
53. Why do you do it that way?

CUSTOMER IMPACT/VALUE ADDED

E. Themes/Things to Look for:

Admits mistakes and goofs
Builds in process checkpoints
Clarifies expectations well
Conflict skills
Considers customer feedback as a chance to learn
Customer satisfaction measurement
Differentiates one kind of customer from another
Enjoys meeting customers
Excited about happy customers
Finds common ground
Finds the essence of a complaint or suggestion
History of customer loyalty
Is a straight talker
Is planful
Keeps the end in mind
Knows when to stop; can stand up for the organization's needs as well
Listens to customer complaints without getting upset
Personal sacrifice to keep a customer
Positive view of customers; not customers as adversaries
Practices problem prevention
Specific about deliverables
Takes a problem-solving approach
Takes time to define the problem
Treats internal customers about the same as those external
Will lose a battle for long-term gain
Willing to take the heat inside to please a customer outside
Willingness to "fire" customers

F. Most Likely Résumé:

1. Look for jobs like:

Chair of Projects/Task Forces
Fix-Its/Turnarounds
Heavy Strategic Demands
International Assignments
Scale (size shift) Assignments
Scope (complexity) Assignments
Staff Leadership (Influencing Without Authority)
Start-ups

2. Look for develop-in-place assignments like:

Plan an off-site meeting, conference, convention, trade show, event, etc.
Manage the purchase of a major product, equipment, materials, program, or system.
Study and establish internal or external customer needs, requirements, specifications, and expectations and present it to the people involved.
Do a customer-satisfaction survey in person or by phone and present it to the people involved.
Help someone outside your unit or the organization solve a business problem.

CUSTOMER IMPACT/VALUE ADDED

Do a feasibility study on an important opportunity and make recommendations to those who will decide.

Visit Malcolm Baldrige National Quality Award or Deming Prize winners and report back on your findings, showing how they would help your organization.

Work a few shifts in the telemarketing or customer service department, handling complaints and inquiries from customers.

Make speeches/be a spokesperson for the organization on the outside.

Represent the organization at a trade show, convention, exposition, etc.

Spend time with internal or external customers, write a report on your observations, and present it to the people involved with the customers in the organization.

Launch a new product, service, or process.

Relaunch an existing product or service that's not doing well.

Train customers in the use of the organization's products or services.

Manage an ad hoc, temporary group of balky and resisting people through an unpopular change or project.

Manage an ad hoc, temporary group of people involved in tackling a fix-it or turnaround project.

Manage the interface between consultants and the organization on a critical assignment.

Handle a tough negotiation with an internal or external client or customer.

Manage liquidation/sale of products, equipment, materials, a business, furniture, overstock, etc.

Prepare and present a proposal of some consequence to top management

Manage a dissatisfied internal or external customer; troubleshoot a performance or quality problem with a product or service.

Manage the assigning/allocating of office space in a contested situation.

Manage a cost-cutting project.

Resolve an issue in conflict between two people, units, geographies, functions, etc

Write a speech for someone higher up in the organization.

Do a postmortem on a failed project and present it to the people involved.

Work on a crisis management team.

3. Best references to ask about or check:

Direct Boss
Internal and External Customers
Past Associates/Constituencies
Peers and Colleagues

G. Learning Orientation Evaluation:

2. All or Nothing vs. Can See Many Sides
4. Spectator/Passive vs. Player/Participant
5. Tight/Rigid vs. Loose/Flexible
6. Reactive/Responsive vs. Adapting
11. Generalizations vs. Specific Learnings
12. Rehearsed/Socially Acceptable vs. Candid
13. Simple Views vs. Complex Views
20. Defensiveness vs. Admits Weaknesses
21. Focus on Self vs. Focus on Others
22. Focus on Accomplishments vs. Focusing on Solving Problems

CUSTOMER IMPACT/VALUE ADDED

H. The LEADERSHIP ARCHITECT® Sort Card Connections:

1. Good (positive) if combined with high:
Satisfies customers 1, 15, 16, 50, 53, 63
Knows the content 5, 24, 61
Good listener 3, 31, 33
Can hear a complaint 32, 33, 41
Treats internal people as customers 4, 8, 15, 42, 60, 64
Can stand up when need be 34, 40, 50, 57
Candid 29
Efficiently serves customers 15, 35, 52, 63
Spots problems early 35, 39, 47, 50, 51
Really understands customers 15, 33, 56, 64

2. Bad (negative) if combined with low or high (+):
Doesn't treat internal people as customers 4, 8, 15, 42, 48, 60
Won't stand up 9, 34, 57
Can't handle conflicts 11, 12
Doesn't understand customer needs well 15, 33, 56, 64
Too many exceptions 35, 39, 47, 52, 59
Doesn't improve products/services 33, 53, 63

3. Too much can contribute to the following Stallers and Stoppers:

A. What too much looks like (overused):
Gives customers too much for what the organization receives in return; overly committed to produce goods and services that consistently meet and exceed the standards and expectations of internal and external customers; uses too many resources; loses sight of other important goals and objectives and becomes an unreasonable advocate for customers at the expense of other organizational values and policies.

B. Too much might lead to these Stallers and Stoppers:
Unable to Adapt to Differences (101)   Performance Problems (118)
Poor Administrator (102)   Political Problems (119)
Betrayal of Trust (105)

C. Compensators:
How to compensate for too much of this PERFORMANCE MANAGEMENT ARCHITECT® dimension:
5, 9, 12, 34, 35, 38, 39, 47, 50, 51, 52, 53, 57, 58, 59, 63, 65

D. Things to watch for:
Causes problems for others in the organization by giving away too much
Changes things almost anytime there is a complaint
Cost overruns
Criticizes own organization
Everything is an exception
Gets in debates inside the organization

CUSTOMER IMPACT/VALUE ADDED

Lack of proper documentation
Loses credibility
Panics when customers complain
Provides products and services customers don't need
Sides with the customer
Wins one customer; loses others

4. Too little can contribute to the following Stallers and Stoppers:

A. What too little looks like (unskilled):

Produces goods and services that don't meet the minimum standards and expectations of internal and external customers; there are steady complaints and extensive rework is necessary to keep customers minimally happy.

B. Too little can contribute to the following Stallers and Stoppers:

Betrayal of Trust (105)	Performance Problems (118)
Defensiveness (108)	Political Problems (119)
Insensitive to Others (112)	

C. Compensators:

How to substitute for too little of this PERFORMANCE MANAGEMENT ARCHITECT® dimension:
1, 3, 9, 16, 24, 27, 31, 32, 33, 38, 39, 43, 47, 48, 50, 51, 52, 53, 61, 63

I. LEARNING ARCHITECT® Connections:

Look for people who act like and/or show evidence of:

1a. Pure Action	16. Collaborate
1c. Following a Plan	20. Events
2a. Problem Solving	23. Orchestrator
3c. Personal Experience	24. Discloser
4a. Getting Information	30. Mastery
4c. Actively Involve	32. Diversity in Others
9. Multiple Sources	33. Diversity of Sources
12. Rules of Thumb	34. Sizing Up Others
13. Focused	37. Flexibility

CUSTOMER IMPACT/VALUE ADDED

J. CHOICES ARCHITECT® Connections:

Look for people who act like and/or show evidence of:

First Edition (Released 1994)
1. Inquisitive
7. Helping Others Think
8. Cool Transactor
10. Responds to Feedback
11. Open to Diversity
13. Role Flexibility
14. Transaction Quality
23. Communicator

Second Edition (Released 2000)
7. Inquisitive
8. Solution Finder
9. Agile Communicator
10. Conflict Manager
11. Cool Transactor
13. Light Touch
14. Open-Minded
15. People-Smart
17. Responds to Feedback
18. Role Flexibility
25. Delivers Results

86. FREEDOM FROM UNPLANNED SUPPORT

A. Definition:

Performs up to standard independently; takes minimal support from bosses and other sources and needs little unplanned guidance or help; independent, self starting; requires much less support than most other people or groups

B. Arenas/Domains to Explore:

1. Accident recovery
2. Acting
3. Activities
4. Adventure travel
5. Art education/training
6. Athletic skills
7. Causes
8. College
9. Crises
10. Delegating
11. First time away from home
12. First to speak up
13. Hobbies
14. Independent studies in college
15. Independent travel
16. Investment decisions
17. Major life decisions
18. Music education/training
19. Performing
20. Project work
21. Remote locations
22. Scouting/4H projects
23. Self-study activities
24. Start-ups
25. Tasks

C. Sample Questions:

*Dimension 1: What the Person Did   Note: * means OK for campus   ** means campus only*

1. Do you prefer making errors of omission or commission when it comes to bosses?
2. Give me some examples of what you have done to encourage the independence of your staff.
3. Has a boss ever said they don't see or talk to you enough?
4. Have you ever been part of a leaderless or self managed team?
5. Have you ever managed anything where the people reporting to you were in different locations? How did you help them work independently from you?
6. How do you decide when it is time to take something to your boss?
7. How do you view asking a boss or someone else for assistance?*
8. How much of your boss' advice and council do you follow?
9. Tell me about a time when you avoided getting your boss involved in something you were doing.
10. Tell me about a time when you pushed something through that few people wanted at first.*
11. Tell me about a time when you seized an opportunity and ran with it yourself.*
12. Tell me about a time when you took on a project nobody else was willing to tackle.*
13. Tell me about a time when you were the lone negative voice regarding a person.*
14. Tell me about a time when you were the lone positive voice regarding a person.*
15. Tell me about a time when you worked with someone who was very dependent on you.*
16. Tell me about some of your favorite work tasks and projects.*
17. What are your hobbies?*
18. What conditions lead you to not delegate something?

FREEDOM FROM UNPLANNED SUPPORT

19. What off-work (extracurricular) activities are you involved with?*
20. When you and your teammates or colleagues decide to take something to the boss for a decision, are you the first to suggest or the last to agree that that's a correct course?
21. Would others describe you as more a loner or a team player?*

Dimension 2: Seeing Others Do This

22. Contrast the most and least independent people you know.*
23. Has being independent or a self-starter ever been in any 360° survey done on you? Was your score among your highest, middle, or lowest?
24. Has the inability to act independently on someone else's part ever created an obstacle for you or got in the way of something you were trying to accomplish?*
25. Have you ever talked with a coach or mentor about your ability to act independently?
26. Have you ever watched someone fail/get fired because of their inability to act independently?*
27. Have you ever watched someone overdo acting independently to the point that it backfired?
28. Have you ever watched someone succeed because they acted independently?*
29. Have you ever worked with a coach on improving your ability to act independently?*
30. Have you ever worked with a person who excelled at acting independently?
31. Have you ever worked with a skills coach on improving your ability to act independently?*
32. How do you get feedback about yourself on your ability to act independently?
33. How often do you check with multiple sources when you get a piece of critical feedback on your ability to act independently?
34. Is there a historical figure you consider a model of being independent or a self-starter?
35. What do others who are not your fans say about your ability to act independently?
36. What do others who like you say about your ability to act independently?
37. Which boss was the best at acting independently?
38. Which boss was the worst at acting independently?
39. Which direct report was the best at acting independently?
40. Which direct report was the worst at acting independently?
41. Which peer was the best at acting independently?
42. Which peer was the worst at acting independently?
43. Who in your field or business deals best with acting independently?
44. Who do you consider a current role model of acting independently?*
45. Who do you go to for advice on acting independently?
46. Who have you learned the most from about acting independently?*
47. Who is a higher-management role model for you on acting independently?
48. Who is a role model of acting independently outside of work?

Dimension 3: Knowing How This Works

49. Are there situations or settings where someone should be different in being independent or a self-starter?
50. Do you think acting independently can be learned; how do you think people develop this skill?
51. Do you think there is a way to compensate or work around low ability to act independently?
52. Has anyone asked you for your opinions/advice on acting independently?*
53. Have you ever attended a course on being independent or a self-starter?
54. Have you ever been in a situation where you and others put being independent or a self-starter on a success profile?
55. Have you ever been part of an effort to create a policy or a mission statement containing reference to being independent or a self-starter?

FREEDOM FROM UNPLANNED SUPPORT

56. Have you ever been someone's coach or mentor who had problems with being independent or a self-starter?
57. Have you ever created a development plan for acting independently?
58. Have you ever criticized someone for not acting independently.
59. Have you ever designed a program on acting independently?
60. Have you ever given a speech on being independent or a self-starter?
61. Have you ever rewarded or recognized someone for acting independently?
62. Have you ever taught a course on acting independently?
63. Have you ever tried to help someone deal more effectively with acting independently?*
64. Have you ever tried to help someone improve their ability to act independently?
65. How much independence is good to have and how much is too much?
66. How much of success do you think is due to acting independently compared with other characteristics?
67. How would you know if someone is bad at being independent or a self-starter?
68. How would you know if someone is good at being independent or a self-starter?
69. If you had to write a book on being independent or a self-starter, what would the chapter headings be?
70. What are the benefits to someone who is really good at acting independently?
71. What are the consequences to someone who is really poor at acting independently?
72. What do you think the standard is on acting independently for someone in your role?
73. What happens if you act too independently?
74. What happens when two people try to work together who are very different in their ability to act independently?
75. What wisdom would you pass onto others trying to become better at acting independently?
76. Why do you think people end up being different in their ability to act independently?
77. What do you think of the saying "If you want something done well, do it yourself?"*

Dimension 4: Personal Learning

78. Compare and contrast examples of being effective and ineffective at acting independently?
79. Contrast your on- and off-the-job use of acting independently.
80. Did you ever pass up a job or assignment because you were not confident enough in your ability to act independently?
81. Do you ever use other skills to cover for your lack of ability to act independently?
82. Has the inability to act independently ever figured in a failure, struggle, or setback you have had?
83. Has becoming better at acting independently ever helped you in other areas?
84. Has the inability to act independently ever been the subject of a development plan for you?
85. Has your ability to act independently always been this way?
86. Have you ever delegated or assigned someone a task because of your inability to act independently.
87. Have you ever made significant strides at becoming better at acting independently?
88. Has your ability to act independently ever been the subject of your performance review or a career discussion?
89. How different are you across situations in your ability to act independently?
90. How do you decide how independent to be?
91. How much of your success is due to your ability to act independently?
92. How transferable is your ability to act independently to other situations?
93. If you had to become better at acting independently in a hurry, what would you do?
94. Was there a time when you were not good at acting independently?
95. What caused you to work to change your skills at acting independently?
96. What event or series of events had the most impact on your ability to act independently?

FREEDOM FROM UNPLANNED SUPPORT

97. What's the most varied you can be in acting independently?
98. What was the shortest amount of time in which you learned to act independently?
99. When did you first realize your level of skill at acting independently?
100. When you know ahead of time that your level of ability to act independently won't work, what do you do?
101. Why do you think you deal with acting independently the way you do?
102. Why do you think your ability to act independently is the way it is?*
103. Do you prefer working alone, on a team, a group, or with one or two others? Please explain your preference(s).*
104. Do you enjoy delegating or doing the work yourself? Please explain.

D. Follow-up Probes:

Dimension 1: What the Person Did

1. Can you give me a few examples of that?
2. How consistently do you do this across situations?
3. How did others react when you did that?
4. How far would you go before you would stop and try another approach?
5. How typical is this for you?
6. How would you have done this differently with looser deadlines?
7. How would you have done this differently with tighter deadlines?
8. Tell me about times when you are not like this or wouldn't do this.
9. Tell me about times when you do this and times when you don't.
10. Was this comfortable for you, or were you forcing yourself?

Dimension 2: Seeing Others Do This

11. Did you later change your assessment of this person?
12. Do you know a good and a bad example of this? Contrast those two people for me.
13. Do you think most people would react that way?
14. Have you worked for a person like that since?
15. How could this person have been more effective?
16. How do others you have known approach that?
17. What do you think this person was trying to do?
18. What was it like to work with someone like that?
19. What was it like to work with someone you seem to have disliked?

Dimension 3: Knowing How This Works

20. How would you teach this to someone else?
21. What do you think the key aspects of it are?
22. Where do people learn this?
23. Why do you suppose organizations work that way?
24. Why do you suppose teams work that way?
25. Why do you think people do that?
26. Why do you think that happened?

Dimension 4: Personal Learning

27. Do you think you can get others to do this better than most people can? If so, how do you know?
28. Do you think you do this better or worse than most people can? How do you know?

FREEDOM FROM UNPLANNED SUPPORT

29. Do you try to act that way with everyone? What's your thinking on that?
30. How did you come up with that approach?
31. How do you see that as a customer yourself?
32. How would you do this differently next time?
33. What did you do after you got that feedback?
34. What did you learn about dealing with that kind of person?
35. What did you learn about dealing with that kind of situation?
36. What did you learn about how customers are gained?
37. What did you learn about how customers are lost?
38. What did you learn about yourself?
39. What did you learn from that?
40. What do you think you learned that would be repeatable in other situations?
41. What lessons do you think you came away with?
42. What were the negative consequences of this?
43. What were you thinking when you took that approach?
44. What were you thinking when you took that risk?
45. What would you tell your children about that experience?
46. What would you tell your friend about that experience?
47. What would you tell your mentor about that experience?
48. What's your thinking about why that didn't work?
49. What's your thinking about why that worked?
50. What's your view of why things happened that way?
51. Where did you learn to do it that way?
52. Why did you think that method of getting over that barrier would work?
53. Why do you do it that way?

E. **Themes/Things to Look for:**

Anticipates problems and roadblocks
Avoids bosses
Calm
Comfortable being the lone voice
Comfortable with taking risks
Comfortable making mistakes
Enjoys solitary activities
Enjoys working alone
International travel to tough locations
Not afraid to make decisions

Only does exception reporting to bosses
Persevering
Pride of workmanship
Sensitive to boss' time constraints
Takes all of the leeway bosses will allow
Takes personal responsibility
Thinks through how to get from start to finish
Volunteering for remote locations
Willing to be first
Working on unpopular missions

FREEDOM FROM UNPLANNED SUPPORT

F. Most Likely Résumé:

1. Look for jobs like:
International Assignments
Line to Staff Switches
Start-ups

2. Look for develop-in-place assignments like:
Complete a self-study course or project in an important area for you.
Attend a course or event which will push you personally beyond your usual limits or outside your comfort zone (e.g., Outward Bound, language immersion training, sensitivity group, public speaking).
Teach a child a new skill (e.g., reading, running a computer, a sport).
Become a referee for an athletic league or program.
Plan for and start up something small (secretarial pool, athletic program, suggestion system, program, etc.).
Launch a new product, service, or process.
Be a change agent; create a symbol for change; lead the rallying cry; champion a significant change and implementation.
Relaunch an existing product or service that's not doing well.
Seek out and use a seed budget to create and pursue a personal idea, product, or service.
Handle a tough negotiation with an internal or external client or customer.
Prepare and present a proposal of some consequence to top management.
Manage a dissatisfied internal or external customer; troubleshoot a performance or quality problem with a product or service.
Take on a tough and undoable project, one where others who have tried it have failed.
Make peace with an enemy or someone you've disappointed with a product or service or someone you've had some trouble with or don't get along well with.
Do a postmortem on a failed project and present it to the people involved.
Audit cost overruns to assess the problem and present your findings to the person or people involved.

3. Best references to ask about or check:

Direct Boss	Past Associates/Constituencies
Development Professionals	Peers and Colleagues
Family Members	Direct Reports
Human Resource Professionals	

G. Learning Orientation Evaluation:
3. Ordinary/Socially Acceptable vs. Insightful/Different
4. Spectator/Passive vs. Player/Participant
9. Vague/General vs. Sharp/Specific
10. Reactive vs. Initiating
12. Rehearsed/Socially Acceptable vs. Candid
19. External Standards vs. Internal Standards
20. Defensiveness vs. Admits Weaknesses
22. Focus on Accomplishments vs. Focusing on Solving Problems

FREEDOM FROM UNPLANNED SUPPORT

H. The LEADERSHIP ARCHITECT® Sort Card Connections:

1. **Good (positive) if combined with high:**
   Flexible 2, 12, 32, 40
   Gets data 31, 33, 38
   Firm foundation 5, 24, 46, 61
   Candid with others 13, 34, 56
   A champion 14, 28, 58
   Takes responsibility 9, 34, 57
   Delivers results 11, 43, 53
   Can delegate as well 18, 56, 59

2. **Bad (negative) if combined with low or high (+):**
   Prefers to work alone 3, 4, 31, 33, 42, 60
   Performs only for today 5, 46, 58
   Too quick to decide to do it all alone (+1, 16) 41
   Won't delegate (+1, 57) 18, 20
   Pushes too hard (+12, 34, 57)
   Problems with pressure 11
   Loner 4, 8, 18, 42, 60
   Doesn't get enough data 32, 33
   Not a team player 38, 48, 60 (+57)

3. **Too much can contribute to the following Stallers and Stoppers:**

    ### A. What too much looks like (overused):
    So driven to work independently that they are an unreasonable loner; doesn't want any help, goes own way and works on own objectives; may waste time and resources working on the wrong thing or in the wrong way.

    ### B. Too much might lead to these Stallers and Stoppers:
    Overly Ambitious (103)   Overmanaging (117)
    Arrogant (104)   Political Missteps (119)
    Failure to Build a Team (110)

    ### C. Compensators:
    How to compensate for too much of this PERFORMANCE MANAGEMENT ARCHITECT® dimension:
       3, 4, 7, 8, 15, 18, 19, 20, 27, 33, 36, 42, 60, 64

    ### D. Things to watch for:
    Can't build a team   Know it all
    Doesn't listen   Makes unnecessary mistakes
    Doesn't make efficient use of resources; has to do it their way Not invented here mentality
    Has own agenda   Poor manager of others
    Has to do rework   Won't ask for help
    Just trying to get ahead   Works on pet projects

FREEDOM FROM UNPLANNED SUPPORT

4. Too little can contribute to the following Stallers and Stoppers:

A. *What too little looks like (unskilled):*

> Needs significantly more than average support and time from bosses and others to meet minimum standards; takes more maintenance and support than most people or groups to be able to contribute up to standard; not enough time left for bosses to support other people or groups

B. *Too little can contribute to the following Stallers and Stoppers:*

Betrayal of Trust (105) Overdependence on an Advocate (115)
Defensiveness (108) Performance Problems (118)

C. *Compensators:*

How to substitute for too little of this PERFORMANCE MANAGEMENT ARCHITECT® dimension:
1, 9, 12, 16, 27, 31, 34, 38, 39, 43, 47, 48, 50, 53

I. LEARNING ARCHITECT® Connections:

Look for people who act like and/or show evidence of:

1a. Pure Action	8. Initiate
1b. Trial and Error	13. Focused
1c. Following a Plan	17. Selected Sources
2a. Problem Solving	21. Changer
2c. Intuition	22. Experimenter
3b. Self-Talk	23. Orchestrator
3c. Personal Experience	28. Creator
4a. Getting Information	30. Mastery
6. Contentious	38. Resilience
7. Risks	

J. CHOICES ARCHITECT® Connections:

Look for people who act like and/or show evidence of:

First Edition (Released 1994)	Second Edition (Released 2000)
1. Inquisitive	7. Inquisitive
3. Creator	8. Solution Finder
6. Visionary	20. Experimenter
12. Experimenter	22. Taking the Heat
16. Cold/Indirect Sources	23. Visioning
18. Into Everything	26. Drive
20. Forging Ahead	27. Presence
21. Taking the Heat	

87. TEAM/UNIT CONTRIBUTION

A. Definition:

Always helpful to the rest of the team or other units in getting work done; among the first to help others succeed; will share anything if it's for the team or organization; a model of sharing, caring and cooperation.

B. Arenas/Domains to Explore:

1. Across boundaries
2. Athletic team sports
3. Charitable work
4. Church work
5. Clubs
6. College project teams
7. Customers
8. Different groups
9. Disclosing to coworkers
10. Informing
11. Internal negotiations
12. Meeting people for the first time
13. Military operations
14. Office space allocation
15. Orienting new people
16. Scouting/4H
17. Shared Goals
18. Sharing resources
19. Shared facilities
20. Social settings
21. Team sales calls
22. Volunteer work
23. With people they don't like

C. Sample Questions:

*Dimension 1: What the Person Did   Note: * means OK for campus   ** means campus only*

1. Have you ever had to bargain with a peer over resources when the result was win/lose? How did it come out?*
2. Have you ever had to resolve a conflict with another unit? What did you do?*
3. Have you ever had to resolve a conflict within your work group? What did you do?*
4. Have you ever had to work with people you didn't like or didn't trust? What did you do?*
5. Have you ever managed anything where the people reporting to you were in different locations? How did you ensure cooperative and helpful behavior without your being there?
6. Have you ever stumbled because you didn't know how to get something done in your work unit?*
7. Have you ever stumbled because you didn't know how to get something done with another work unit?*
8. Have you ever worked with someone who was too dependent on you? What did you do to help this person?*
9. Tell me about a time when you had to choose between watching out for your own interests or sacrificing your own agenda to help someone else out.
10. Tell me about a time when you helped another unit get something done.*
11. Tell me about a time when you helped someone get some resources they needed.*
12. Tell me about a time when you helped someone with a work problem.*
13. Tell me about a time when you helped with office space allocation.
14. Tell me about a time when you sacrificed your own personal time to help someone else out of a jam.
15. Tell me about a time when you were able to get something done because you had a good relationship with someone.*

TEAM/UNIT CONTRIBUTION

16. Tell me about some times when you have resisted helping out a coworker.*
17. Tell me about some times when you have resisted helping out another unit.*
18. Tell me about some times when you shared resources with another unit.*
19. Tell me about times you made a personal sacrifice for the good of the work unit, another unit or the organization.*
20. What do you do to welcome new people to the work group?*
21. What do you find are good ways to keep people informed about what's going on in the unit?*
22. What do you find are good ways to keep people informed about what's going on across units?*
23. When you are part of a team made up of members from across units, what role do you usually play?

Dimension 2: Seeing Others Do This

24. Contrast the most and least team-oriented people you know.*
25. Has the ability to be a team player ever been in any 360° survey done on you? Was your score among your highest, middle, or lowest?
26. Has poor ability to be a team player on someone else's part ever created an obstacle for you or got in the way of something you were trying to accomplish?*
27. Have you ever talked with a coach or mentor about your ability to be a team player?
28. Have you ever watched someone fail/get fired because of an inability to be a team player?*
29. Have you ever watched someone overdo being team focused to the point that it backfired?
30. Have you ever watched someone succeed because of an ability to be a team player ?*
31. Have you ever worked with a coach on improving your ability to be a team player?*
32. Have you ever worked with a person who excelled at being a team player?
33. Have you ever worked with a skills coach on improving your ability to be a team player?*
34. How do you get feedback about yourself on being a team player?
35. How often do you check with multiple sources when you get a piece of critical feedback on your inability to act as a team player?
36. Is there a historical figure you consider a model of being a team player?
37. What do others who are not your fans say about your ability to be a team player?
38. What do others who like you say about your ability to be a team player?
39. Which boss was the best at being a team player?
40. Which boss was the worst at being a team player?
41. Which direct report was the best at being a team player?
42. Which direct report was the worst at being a team player?
43. Which peer was the best at being a team player?
44. Which peer was the worst at being a team player?
45. Who in your field or business deals best with being a team player?
46. Who do you consider a current role model of being a team player?*
47. Who do you go to for advice on being a team player?
48. Who have you learned the most from about being a team player?*
49. Who is a higher-management role model for you on being a team player?
50. Who is a role model of being a team player outside of work?

Dimension 3: Knowing How This Works

51. Are there situations or settings where someone should be different in being a team player?
52. Do you think being a team player can be learned; how do you think people develop these skills?

TEAM/UNIT CONTRIBUTION

53. Do you think there is a way to compensate or work around a low ability to be a team player?
54. Has anyone asked you for your opinions/advice on being a team player?*
55. Have you ever attended a course on working as a team?
56. Have you ever been in a situation where you and others put being a team player on a success profile?
57. Have you ever been part of an effort to create a policy or a mission statement containing reference to being a team player?
58. Have you ever been someone's coach or mentor who had problems with being a team player?
59. Have you ever created a development plan for someone on being a team player?
60. Have you ever criticized someone for not being a team player?
61. Have you ever designed a program on being a team player?
62. Have you ever given a speech on being a team player?
63. Have you ever rewarded or recognized someone for their ability to be a team player?
64. Have you ever taught a course on being a team player?
65. Have you ever tried to help someone deal more effectively with a team?*
66. Have you ever tried to help someone improve their ability to be a team player?
67. How much team focus is good to have and how much is too much?
68. How much of success do you think is due to being a team player compared with other characteristics?
69. How would you know if someone is bad at being a team player?
70. How would you know if someone is good at being a team player?
71. If you had to write a book on being a team player, what would the chapter headings be?
72. What are the benefits to someone who is really good at being a team player?
73. What are the consequences to someone who is really poor at being a team player?
74. What do you think the standard is on being a team player for someone in your role?
75. What happens if you have or use too much of a team orientation?
76. What happens when two people try to work together who are very different in their ability to be team players?
77. What wisdom would you pass onto others trying to become better at being a team player?
78. Why do you think people end up being different in their ability to be team players?

Dimension 4: Personal Learning

79. Compare and contrast examples of being effective and ineffective at being a team player?
80. Contrast your on- and off-the-job use of team focus.
81. Did you ever pass up a job or assignment because you were not confident enough in your skills at being a team player?
82. Do you ever use other skills to cover for your inability to be a team player?
83. Has inability to be a team player ever figured in a failure, struggle, or setback you have had?
84. Has becoming better at being a team player ever helped you in other areas?
85. Has the inability to be a team player ever been the subject of a development plan for you?
86. Has your ability to be a team player always been this way?
87. Have you ever delegated or assigned someone a task because of inability to be a team player?
88. Have you ever made significant strides at becoming better at being a team player?
89. Has your ability to be a team player ever been the subject of your performance review or a career discussion?
90. How different are you across situations in your ability to be a team player?

TEAM/UNIT CONTRIBUTION

91. How do you decide how team-focused to be?
92. How much of your success is due to your ability to be a team player?
93. How transferable is your ability to be a team player to other situations?
94. If you had to become better at being a team player in a hurry, what would you do?
95. Was there a time when you were not good at being a team player?
96. What caused you to work to change your skills at being a team player?
97. What event or series of events had the most impact on your ability to be a team player?
98. What's the most varied you can be in your ability to be a team player?
99. What was the shortest amount of time in which you learned to become better at being a team player?
100. When did you first realize your level of skill at being a team player?
101. When you know ahead of time that your level of ability to be a team player won't work, what do you do?
102. Why do you think you deal with being a team player the way you do?
103. Why do you think your ability to be a team player is the way it is?*
104. How do you form close working relationships with coworkers?*

D. Follow-up Probes:

Dimension 1: What the Person Did

1. Can you give me a few examples of that?
2. How consistently do you do this across situations?
3. How did others react when you did that?
4. How far would you go before you would stop and try another approach?
5. How typical is this for you?
6. How would you have done this differently with looser deadlines?
7. How would you have done this differently with tighter deadlines?
8. Tell me about times when you are not like this or wouldn't do this.
9. Tell me about times when you do this and times when you don't.
10. Was this comfortable for you, or were you forcing yourself?

Dimension 2: Seeing Others Do This

11. Did you later change your assessment of this person?
12. Do you know a good and a bad example of this? Contrast those two people for me.
13. Do you think most people would react that way?
14. Have you worked for a person like that since?
15. How could this person have been more effective?
16. How do others you have known approach that?
17. What do you think this person was trying to do?
18. What was it like to work with someone like that?
19. What was it like to work with someone you seem to have disliked?

Dimension 3: Knowing How This Works

20. How would you teach this to someone else?
21. What do you think the key aspects of it are?
22. Where do people learn this?
23. Why do you suppose organizations work that way?
24. Why do you suppose teams work that way?

TEAM/UNIT CONTRIBUTION

25. Why do you think people do that?
26. Why do you think that happened?

Dimension 4: Personal Learning

27. Do you think you can get others to do this better than most people can? If so, how do you know?
28. Do you think you do this better or worse than most people can? How do you know?
29. Do you try to act that way with everyone? What's your thinking on that?
30. How did you come up with that approach?
31. How do you see that as a customer yourself?
32. How would you do this differently next time?
33. What did you do after you got that feedback?
34. What did you learn about dealing with that kind of person?
35. What did you learn about dealing with that kind of situation?
36. What did you learn about how customers are gained?
37. What did you learn about how customers are lost?
38. What did you learn about yourself?
39. What did you learn from that?
40. What do you think you learned that would be repeatable in other situations?
41. What lessons do you think you came away with?
42. What were the negative consequences of this?
43. What were you thinking when you took that approach?
44. What were you thinking when you took that risk?
45. What would you tell your children about that experience?
46. What would you tell your friend about that experience?
47. What would you tell your mentor about that experience?
48. What's your thinking about why that didn't work?
49. What's your thinking about why that worked?
50. What's your view of why things happened that way?
51. Where did you learn to do it that way?
52. Why did you think that method of getting over that barrier would work?
53. Why do you do it that way?

E. Themes/Things to Look for:

Can delay personal gratification	Personal sacrifices to help others
Congratulates others	Practices give and take
Delegates and defers to others	Seeks others out
Doesn't have to win them all	Sets up criteria and priorities for helping
Equitable	Takes the broader view of performance–what's good for all
Fair to all, regardless of personal opinion	Welcoming
Listens	Will pitch in
Offers first	Works comfortably across boundaries
Orients and informs	

TEAM/UNIT CONTRIBUTION

F. Most Likely Résumé:

1. Look for jobs like:

Chair of Projects/Task Forces
Cross-Moves
Line to Staff Switches
Significant People Demands
Staff Leadership (Influencing Without Authority)

2. Look for develop-in-place assignments like:

Integrate diverse systems, processes, or procedures across decentralized and/or dispersed units.

Manage the renovation of an office, floor, building, meeting room, warehouse, etc.

Help someone outside your unit or the organization solve a business problem.

Become a volunteer for a year or more for an outside organization.

Work for a year or more with a charitable organization.

Lobby for your organization on a contested issue in local, regional, state, or federal government.

Create employee involvement teams.

Join a community board.

Teach a course, seminar, or workshop on something you know a lot about.

Teach/coach someone how to do something you're an expert in.

Become someone's assigned mentor, coach, sponsor, champion, or orienteer.

Manage an ad hoc, temporary group of "green," inexperienced people as their coach, teacher, orienteer, etc.

Take over for someone on vacation or a long trip.

Manage a dissatisfied internal or external customer; troubleshoot a performance or quality problem with a product or service.

Manage the assigning/allocating of office space in a contested situation.

Manage a cost-cutting project.

Resolve an issue in conflict between two people, units, geographies, functions, etc.

3. Best references to ask about or check:

Internal and External Customers
Family Members
Human Resource Professionals
Past Associates/Constituencies
Peers and Colleagues
Direct Reports

G. Learning Orientation Evaluation:

2. All or Nothing vs. Can See Many Sides
4. Spectator/Passive vs. Player/Participant
5. Tight/Rigid vs. Loose/Flexible
6. Reactive/Responsive vs. Adapting
7. Passive vs. Intrigued/Curious
8. Sameness vs. Diversity
21. Focus on Self vs. Focus on Others

TEAM/UNIT CONTRIBUTION

H. The LEADERSHIP ARCHITECT® Sort Card Connections:

1. **Good (positive) if combined with high:**
   Can resolve tough issues 12, 33, 37
   Can trade 37, 39, 42, 56
   Cooperates on the right projects 50, 53, 65
   Flexible 2, 40, 45
   Good at customer service 15, 31, 51
   Good with many people 21, 23, 64
   Keeps people up to date 3, 27, 33
   Knows how to get things done 38, 42, 48
   Organization comes first 22, 29
   Team leader 9, 36, 60

2. **Bad (negative) if combined with low or high (+):**
   Can't say no 12, 50, 53, 62
   Folds under pressure from others 11, 12, 37
   High need to be liked (+3, 7, 10, 23)
   Just goes along 9, 12, 34, 57
   Too involved in everyone else's business (+3, 31, 48, 60)
   Works on less important projects 5, 50, 53, 58, 62

3. **Too much can contribute to the following Stallers and Stoppers:**

   A. *What too much looks like (overused):*

   Such a team player that own performance sometimes suffers; takes too much time and energy helping others succeed; sometimes runs out of time and resources for own work.

   B. *Too much might lead to these Stallers and Stoppers:*
   Performance Problems (118)

   C. *Compensators:*
   How to compensate for too much of this PERFORMANCE MANAGEMENT ARCHITECT® dimension:
   9, 12, 13, 20, 29, 34, 37, 50, 53, 57, 62, 65

   D. *Things to watch for:*

A patsy	No sense of own priorities
Agrees just to avoid argument or conflict	Won't take a stand
Becomes the organization's counselor of choice	Not a good time manager
Involved in everyone else's problems	

4. **Too little can contribute to the following Stallers and Stoppers:**

   A. *What too little looks like (unskilled):*

   Rarely helpful to the rest of the team, unit or organization in getting work done or in cooperating with anyone; may chill the efforts of the larger group by hesitating to get involved or even refusing to help; withholds resources and information from the others.

TEAM/UNIT CONTRIBUTION

B. Too little can contribute to the following Stallers and Stoppers:

Unable to Adapt to Others (101)
Arrogant (104)
Defensiveness (108)
Failure to Build a Team (110)
Failure to Staff Effectively (111)
Insensitive to Others (112)
Political Missteps (119)

C. Compensators:

How to substitute for too little of this PERFORMANCE MANAGEMENT ARCHITECT® dimension:
3, 12, 21, 27, 31, 33, 36, 38, 48, 60, 64

I. LEARNING ARCHITECT® Connections:

Look for people who act like and/or show evidence of:

2a. Problem Solving
3a. Checking Feelings
4a. Getting Information
4c. Actively Involve
9. Multiple Sources
16. Collaborate
20. Events
23. Orchestrator
24. Discloser
32. Diversity in Others

J. CHOICES ARCHITECT® Connections:

Look for people who act like and/or show evidence of:

First Edition (Released 1994)

7. Helping Others Think
11. Open to Diversity
14. Transaction Quality
15. Helps Others Succeed
17. Hot/Direct Sources
22. Self-Talk
23. Communicator

Second Edition (Released 2000)

9. Agile Communicator
10. Conflict Manager
12. Helps Others Succeed

88. PRODUCTIVE WORK HABITS

A. Definition:

Very productive and efficient in planning and executing work; accurately scopes out the work, creates efficient workflows and processes, and assigns resources properly; consistently outperforms most other people or groups because of excellence at planning, priority setting and execution.

B. Arenas/Domains to Explore:

1. Allocating resources across projects
2. Allocating office space
3. Building a facility
4. Building office space
5. Career management
6. Club/association management
7. Coaching
8. Competing demands on time and resources
9. Deploying resources across geographic areas
10. Elected leadership positions
11. Event/conference management
12. Fund drives
13. Giving out assignments
14. Group/team leader
15. Hobbies
16. Implementing new programs
17. Installing feedback loops
18. Installing new systems
19. Introducing new policies
20. Managing consultants
21. Managing outside contractors
22. Managing suppliers/vendors
23. Managing volunteers
24. Meeting facilitation
25. Military background
26. Personal financial management and investments
27. Planning for obstacles
28. Preparing grant proposals
29. Project/task force leader
30. Renovations
31. Reorganizations
32. Selecting colleges and schools
33. Selecting projects
34. Selecting neighborhoods
35. Student government positions
36. Tight deadlines
37. Too many things to do at once
38. Vacation management
39. Workflows

C. Sample Questions:

Dimension 1: What the Person Did   Note: * means OK for campus   ** means campus only

1. Give me some examples of what you do to decrease the number of errors in your work.
2. Give me some examples of what you do to efficiently use resources in your work.*
3. Have you ever built a new home or managed a major renovation project?
4. Have you ever managed anything where the people reporting to you were in different locations? How did you ensure productivity?
5. How do you go about getting resources that are not under your direct control?*
6. How do you handle multiple demands on your time?*
7. How do you keep things on track when everyone is busy facing a tight deadline where everything has to be perfect?
8. How do you plan your vacations?
9. How do you usually handle work interruptions to keep them as brief as possible?*
10. How do you make time for your hobbies?

PRODUCTIVE WORK HABITS

11. Tell me about a time when you delegated or divided work among your direct reports or people on a project.*
12. Tell me about a time when you delivered quality work, but it was overkill because it took too long and used too many resources.*
13. Tell me about a time when you designed in some corrective steps so quality didn't suffer.*
14. Tell me about a time when you designed in some problem prevention checkpoints to alert you to a quality problem.
15. Tell me about a time when you had to do some work twice because you didn't think it through properly.*
16. Tell me about a time when you improved a workflow or process.*
17. Tell me about a time when you installed a new system to improve the quality of a product or service.
18. Tell me about a time when you managed office renovations.
19. Tell me about a time when you missed a deadline because you weren't satisfied with the quality.*
20. Tell me about a time when you moved into a job where the work processes/systems/work groups were delivering poor quality and had to be fixed.
21. Tell me about a time when you organized and managed others on a complex task from start to finish.*
22. Tell me about a time when you organized consultants to get something done within budget.
23. Tell me about a time when you organized volunteers to get something done within budget.*
24. Tell me about a time when you solved a problem that others couldn't.*
25. Tell me about a time when you streamlined a process.*
26. Tell me about a time when your mistakes caught up with you.*
27. Tell me about a time you managed a conference or large meeting.*
28. Tell me about a time you managed building a facility.
29. What do you do to check the quality of work along the way?*
30. What do you do to check the use of resources along the way?
31. What kind of a financial plan do you have for your estate?
32. What's the most significant improvement you have ever made to a work process?
33. What's the worst work process you have personally experienced?*
34. When you design a work process, how do you estimate the resources it will take?
35. Tell me about a time you were involved with a benchmarking study of a product, service or process.

Dimension 2: Seeing Others Do This

36. Contrast the most and least productive and efficient people you know.*
37. Has productivity and efficiency ever been in any 360º survey done on you? Was your score among your highest, middle, or lowest?
38. Has poor efficiency on someone else's part ever created an obstacle for you or got in the way of something you were trying to accomplish?*
39. Have you ever talked with a coach or mentor about your productivity and efficiency?
40. Have you ever watched someone fail/get fired because they were not efficient and did not plan well?*
41. Have you ever watched someone overplan to the point that it backfired?
42. Have you ever watched someone succeed because they were productive and efficient?*
43. Have you ever worked with a coach on productivity and efficiency?*
44. Have you ever worked with a person who excelled at productivity and efficiency?
45. Have you ever worked with a skills coach on productivity and efficiency skills?*
46. How do you get feedback about yourself on productivity and efficiency?
47. How often do you check with multiple sources when you get a piece of critical feedback on your productivity and efficiency?

PRODUCTIVE WORK HABITS

48. Is there a historical figure you consider a model of productivity and efficiency?
49. What do others who are not your fans say about your productivity and efficiency?
50. What do others who like you say about your productivity and efficiency?
51. Which boss was the best at being productive and efficient?
52. Which boss was the worst at being productive and efficient?
53. Which direct report was the best at being productive and efficient?
54. Which direct report was the worst at being productive and efficient?
55. Which peer was the best at being productive and efficient?
56. Which peer was the worst at being productive and efficient?
57. Who in your field or business deals best with productivity and efficiency?
58. Who do you consider a current role model of productivity and efficiency?*
59. Who do you go to for advice on productivity and efficiency?
60. Who have you learned the most from about productivity and efficiency?*
61. Who is a higher-management role model for you on productivity and efficiency?
62. Who is a role model of productivity and efficiency outside of work?

Dimension 3: Knowing How This Works
63. Are there situations or settings where someone should be different in the way they plan or set priorities?
64. Do you think productivity and efficiency can be learned; how do you think people develop these skills?
65. Do you think there is a way to compensate or work around a low ability to be productive and efficient?
66. Has anyone asked you for your opinions/advice on productivity and efficiency?*
67. Have you ever attended a course on productivity and efficiency?
68. Have you ever been in a situation where you and others put productivity and efficiency on a success profile?
69. Have you ever been part of an effort to create a policy or a mission statement containing reference to being productive and efficient?
70. Have you ever been someone's coach or mentor who had problems with productivity and efficiency?
71. Have you ever created a development plan for someone on improving their ability to be productive and efficient?
72. Have you ever criticized someone for not being productive and efficient?
73. Have you ever designed a program on productivity and efficiency?
74. Have you ever given a speech on productivity and efficiency?
75. Have you ever rewarded or recognized someone for their ability to be productive and efficient?
76. Have you ever taught a course on productivity and efficiency?
77. Have you ever tried to help someone deal more effectively productivity and efficiency?*
78. Have you ever tried to help someone improve their productivity and efficiency?
79. How much productivity and efficiency is good to have and how much is too much?
80. How much of success do you think is due to productivity and efficiency compared with other characteristics?
81. How would you know if someone is bad at being productive and efficient?
82. How would you know if someone is good at being productive and efficient?
83. If you had to write a book on productivity and efficiency, what would the chapter headings be?
84. What are the consequences to someone who is really good at being productive and efficient?
85. What are the consequences to someone who is really poor at being productive and efficient?
86. What do you think the standard is on productivity and efficiency for someone in your role?

PRODUCTIVE WORK HABITS

87. What happens if you rely on productivity and efficiency too much?
88. What happens when two people try to work together who are very different in their ability to be productive and efficient?
89. What wisdom would you pass onto others trying to become better at being productive and efficient?
90. Why do you think people end up being different in ability to be productive and efficient?
91. Many say that completing the last ten percent of work can take too much time; that getting something ninety percent right and later fixing it is a more productive strategy. What's your view on that?*

Dimension 4: Personal Learning

92. Compare and contrast examples of being effective and ineffective at being productive and efficient?
93. Contrast your on- and off-the-job use of productivity and efficiency.
94. Did you ever pass up a job or assignment because you were not confident enough in your ability to be productive and efficient?
95. Do you ever use other skills to cover for your lack of productivity and efficiency skills?
96. Has being productive and efficient ever figured in a failure, struggle, or setback you have had?
97. Has becoming better at productivity and efficiency ever helped you in other areas?
98. Has poor productivity and efficiency ever been the subject of a development plan for you?
99. Has your ability to be productive and efficient always been this way?
100. Have you ever delegated or assigned someone a task because you aren't particularly productive and efficient?
101. Have you ever made significant strides at becoming better at being productive and efficient?
102. Have your productivity and efficiency skills, good or bad, ever been the subject of your performance review or a career discussion?
103. How different are you across situations in your ability to be productive and efficient?
104. How do you decide how productive to be?
105. How much of your success is due to your ability to be productive and efficient?
106. How transferable are your productivity and efficiency skills to other situations?
107. If you had to become better at being productive and efficient in a hurry, what would you do?
108. Was there a time when you were not good at being productive and efficient?
109. What caused you to work to change your skills at being productive and efficient?
110. What event or series of events had the most impact on your ability to be productive and efficient?
111. What's the most varied you can be in being productive and efficient?
112. What was the shortest amount of time in which you learned to be more productive and efficient?
113. When did you first realize your level of skill at being productive and efficient?
114. When you know ahead of time that your level of ability to be productive and efficient won't work, what do you do?
115. Why do you think you deal with productivity and efficiency the way you do?
116. Why do you think your ability to be productive and efficient is the way it is?*
117. What do you think are smart and dumb ways to organize day to day work?*
118. How do you balance quality with timeliness?*
119. How do you balance quality with resourcefulness?

PRODUCTIVE WORK HABITS

D. Follow-up Probes:

Dimension 1: What the Person Did
1. Can you give me a few examples of that?
2. How consistently do you do this across situations?
3. How did others react when you did that?
4. How far would you go before you would stop and try another approach?
5. How typical is this for you?
6. How would you have done this differently with looser deadlines?
7. How would you have done this differently with tighter deadlines?
8. Tell me about times when you are not like this or wouldn't do this.
9. Tell me about times when you do this and times when you don't.
10. Was this comfortable for you, or were you forcing yourself?

Dimension 2: Seeing Others Do This
11. Did you later change your assessment of this person?
12. Do you know a good and a bad example of this? Contrast those two people for me.
13. Do you think most people would react that way?
14. Have you worked for a person like that since?
15. How could this person have been more effective?
16. How do others you have known approach that?
17. What do you think this person was trying to do?
18. What was it like to work with someone like that?
19. What was it like to work with someone you seem to have disliked?

Dimension 3: Knowing How This Works
20. How would you teach this to someone else?
21. What do you think the key aspects of it are?
22. Where do people learn this?
23. Why do you suppose organizations work that way?
24. Why do you suppose teams work that way?
25. Why do you think people do that?
26. Why do you think that happened?

Dimension 4: Personal Learning
27. Do you think you can get others to do this better than most people can? If so, how do you know?
28. Do you think you do this better or worse than most people can? How do you know?
29. Do you try to act that way with everyone? What's your thinking on that?
30. How did you come up with that approach?
31. How do you see that as a customer yourself?
32. How would you do this differently next time?
33. What did you do after you got that feedback?
34. What did you learn about dealing with that kind of person?
35. What did you learn about dealing with that kind of situation?
36. What did you learn about how customers are gained?

PRODUCTIVE WORK HABITS

37. What did you learn about how customers are lost?
38. What did you learn about yourself?
39. What did you learn from that?
40. What do you think you learned that would be repeatable in other situations?
41. What lessons do you think you came away with?
42. What were the negative consequences of this?
43. What were you thinking when you took that approach?
44. What were you thinking when you took that risk?
45. What would you tell your children about that experience?
46. What would you tell your friend about that experience?
47. What would you tell your mentor about that experience?
48. What's your thinking about why that didn't work?
49. What's your thinking about why that worked?
50. What's your view of why things happened that way?
51. Where did you learn to do it that way?
52. Why did you think that method of getting over that barrier would work?
53. Why do you do it that way?

E. Themes/Things to Look for:

A sense of how things work
Breaking things down into steps
Broad view on what's important
Builds in feedback loops
Can run scenarios
Change priorities when context changes
Checking on progress
Clarity of communications
Estimating costs carefully
Goal and purpose driven
Good teacher
Good time estimation
Little rework

Managing resources tightly
Measures results
Not afraid to outsource
Political savvy
Problem prevention
Running internal simulations to see how things will turn out
Seeing consequences
Takes time to plan
Uses planning software
Values time
Willing to delegate
Written plans

F. Most Likely Résumé:

1. Look for jobs like:

Chair of Projects/Task Forces
Fix-Its/Turnarounds
International Assignments

Scale (size shift) Assignments
Scope (complexity) Assignments
Start-ups

PRODUCTIVE WORK HABITS

2. **Look for develop-in-place assignments like:**

    Install a new process or system (computer system, new policies, new process, new procedures, etc.).

    Integrate diverse systems, processes, or procedures across decentralized and/or dispersed units.

    Manage the renovation of an office, floor, building, meeting room, warehouse, etc.

    Plan a new site for a building (plant, field office, headquarters, etc.).

    Plan an off-site meeting, conference, convention, trade show, event, etc.

    Manage the purchase of a major product, equipment, materials, program, or system.

    Manage the visit of a VIP (member of top management, government official, outside customer, foreign visitor, etc.).

    Launch a new product, service, or process.

    Seek out and use a seed budget to create and pursue a personal idea, product, or service.

    Work on a team writing a proposal to obtain significant government or foundation grants or funding of an activity.

    Manage an ad hoc, temporary group of low-competence people through a task they couldn't do by themselves.

    Assemble an ad hoc team of diverse people to accomplish a difficult task.

    Help shut down a plant, regional office, product line, business, operation, etc.

    Manage liquidation/sale of products, equipment, materials, a business, furniture, overstock, etc.

    Work on a team that's deciding who to keep and who to let go in a layoff, shutdown, delayering, or divestiture.

    Manage a cost-cutting project.

    Build a multifunctional project team to tackle a common business issue or problem.

    Work on a team looking at a reorganization plan where there will be more people than positions.

3. **Best references to ask about or check:**

Direct Boss	Past Associates/Constituencies
Direct Reports	Peers and Colleagues
Internal and External Customers	Spouses

G. Learning Orientation Evaluation:

   4. Spectator/Passive vs. Player/Participant
   6. Reactive/Responsive vs. Adapting
   9. Vague/General vs. Sharp/Specific
   16. Few Rules of Thumb vs. Many and Varied Rules of Thumb
   19. External Standards vs. Internal Standards
   22. Focus on Accomplishments vs. Focusing on Solving Problems

H. The LEADERSHIP ARCHITECT® Sort Card Connections:

1. **Good (positive) if combined with high:**

    Manages work flows well 20, 39, 47, 50, 52

    Sizes work well 35, 39, 47, 52

    Gets a lot done 1, 50, 53, 62

    Spreads the work out 18, 23, 59, 63

    Flexible work planner 2, 5, 46

    Takes on obstacles 9, 12, 34, 57

    Makes changes on the run 2, 32

PRODUCTIVE WORK HABITS

2. **Bad (negative) if combined with low or high (+):**

   Controlling (+1, 9, 57)
   Impatient (+1) 41, 47
   Pressures others (+1, 16, 43, 53)
   Doesn't empower 3, 18, 33, 36, 60
   Plays favorites 18, 19, 21, 23
   Slow 1, 16
   Not adaptable 2, 40

3. **Too much can contribute to the following Stallers and Stoppers:**

   A. What too much looks like (overused):

   So obsessed with doing things in a planned and orderly manner that work is sometimes late or exceeds even reasonable quality standards; easily thrown off-balance by the unexpected and doesn't adjust well to change.

   B. Too much might lead to these Stallers and Stoppers:

   Unable to Adapt to Differences (101)   Overmanaging (117)
   Overly Ambitious (103)   Performance Problems (118)
   Defensiveness (108)

   C. Compensators:

   How to compensate for too much of this PERFORMANCE MANAGEMENT ARCHITECT® dimension:
   1, 2, 3, 14, 15, 16, 32, 33, 40, 46, 50, 58

   D. Things to watch for:

   Slow   Perfectionist
   Not flexible   Too mired in detail
   Obsessive

4. **Too little can contribute to the following Stallers and Stoppers:**

   A. What too little looks like (unskilled):

   Not orderly in approach to work; works on whatever comes up, gets easily diverted into less productive tasks; follow-through is spotty; wastes a lot of time and energy due to being disorganized.

   B. Too little can contribute to the following Stallers and Stoppers:

   Poor Administrator (102)   Key Skill Deficiencies (113)
   Betrayal of Trust (105)   Performance Problems (118)
   Blocked Personal Learner (106)

   C. Compensators:

   How to substitute for too little of this PERFORMANCE MANAGEMENT ARCHITECT® dimension:
   1, 18, 20, 35, 36, 39, 50, 52, 53, 60, 62

PRODUCTIVE WORK HABITS

I. LEARNING ARCHITECT® Connections:

Look for people who act like and/or show evidence of:

1c. Following a Plan	18. Straightforward
2a. Problem Solving	19. What
3c. Personal Experience	20. Events
4a. Getting Information	23. Orchestrator
11. Why/How	30. Mastery
13. Focused	31. Rationality
14. Controlled	38. Resilience

J. CHOICES ARCHITECT® Connections:

Look for people who act like and/or show evidence of:

First Edition (Released 1994)
- 5. Connector
- 8. Cool Transactor
- 20. Forging Ahead

Second Edition (Released 2000)
- 3. Connector
- 8. Solution Finder
- 11. Cool Transactor
- 23. Visioning
- 25. Delivers Results
- 26. Drive

PRODUCTIVE WORK HABITS

89. ADDING SKILLS AND CAPABILITIES

A. Definition:

Eagerly learns new skills and capabilities to improve for the future; makes learning new skills and capabilities a high priority; more and better skilled at the end of the year than at the beginning

B. Arenas/Domains to Explore:

1. Actual advancement
2. Always picks something different or new when faced with a job choice
3. Analyzing failures
4. Analyzing successes
5. Asking for feedback
6. Aspirations
7. Being fired
8. Changing jobs
9. Coaching others
10. Courses attended
11. Definite career plan and execution
12. Developing others
13. Development travel
14. Following a developmental boss
15. Getting others jobs
16. Getting others promoted
17. Giving advice
18. Giving tough feedback
19. Hobbies
20. Interest in the future
21. Monitoring the reactions of others to themselves
22. Changing companies for more challenge
23. Reading habits
24. Self development activities
25. Sought out for advice
26. Takes the toughest assignments
27. Teaching others
28. Trying new activities
29. Variety of background
30. Volunteering for extra duty to learn something
31. Willingness to delegate

C. Sample Questions:

Dimension 1: What the Person Did   Note: * means OK for campus ** means campus only

1. Do you set personal development goals for yourself in the beginning of a new job?
2. Have you ever been in a start-up situation? What did you do to develop your people's skills?
3. Have you ever been in a start-up situation? What did you do to develop your skills?*
4. Have you ever coached or worked with a community group where you had to help people younger or less able than you? What did you do to help this group?*
5. Have you ever had to deal with a problem performer? Describe this person and tell me what you did.
6. Have you ever had a strength that turned out to be a weakness in another setting? How did you respond?*
7. Have you ever managed anything where the people reporting to you were in different locations? How did you insure that people developed their skills?
8. Have you ever taken a job just to get started in a field? What was your eventual goal?
9. Have you ever taken the job with less money because the job was more challenging?
10. How did you select electives outside your major in college?*
11. How do you know which new skills you will need to further your career?*
12. Tell me about a big challenge you provided for someone else.*
13. Tell me about a time when you had to work around one of your weaknesses.*
14. Tell me about a time when you took a new job or assignment that required a much different set of skills.
15. Tell me about a time when you were surprised by a piece of negative feedback about yourself.*

ADDING SKILLS AND CAPABILITIES

16. Tell me about a time you grabbed an opportunity to do something different.*
17. Tell me about a time you worked with a dejected or balky group and convinced them to do something different.*
18. Tell me about a time you worked with an underpowered group and turned it around.*
19. Tell me about people you helped do something they didn't know if they could do.*
20. What are you not so good at and what do you do about it?*
21. What different functions/businesses/type of organization have you worked in?
22. What do you do to leverage your strengths?*
23. What do you like to do at work and dislike to do? What's the difference between the two?*
24. When you are in a self-development course with group exercises, what role do you generally play?*
25. Would you rather use a strength or develop a new skill? Why is one more interesting to you than the other?*

Dimension 2: Seeing Others Do This

26. Contrast the most and least eager-to-learn people you know.*
27. Has an interest in learning new skills ever been in any 360° survey done on you? Was your score among your highest, middle, or lowest?
28. Has the inability to learn a new skill on someone else's part ever created an obstacle for you or got in the way of something you were trying to accomplish?*
29. Have you ever talked with a coach or mentor about your ability and interest in learning new things?
30. Have you ever watched someone fail/get fired because they lacked the ability or interest in learning new skills?*
31. Have you ever watched someone overdo learning new skills to the point that it backfired?
32. Have you ever watched someone succeed because of an ability or interest in learning new skills?*
33. Have you ever worked with a coach on learning new skills?*
34. Have you ever worked with a person who excelled at learning new skills?
35. Have you ever worked with a skills coach on improving your ability to learn new skills?*
36. How do you get feedback about yourself on your ability and interest in learning new things?
37. How often do you check with multiple sources when you get a piece of critical feedback on your ability or interest in learning new skills?
38. Is there a historical figure you consider a model of ability or interest in learning new skills?
39. What do others who are not your fans say about your ability or interest in learning new skills?
40. What do others who like you say about your ability or interest in learning new skills?
41. Which boss was the best at learning new skills?
42. Which boss was the worst at learning new skills?
43. Which direct report was the best at learning new skills?
44. Which direct report was the worst at learning new skills?
45. Which peer was the best at learning new skills?
46. Which peer was the worst at learning new skills?
47. Who in your field or business deals best with learning new skills?
48. Who do you consider a current role model of ability and interest in learning new things?*
49. Who do you go to for advice on learning new skills?
50. Who have you learned the most from about learning new skills?*
51. Who is a higher-management role model for you on learning new skills?
52. Who is a role model of learning new skills outside of work?

ADDING SKILLS AND CAPABILITIES

53. Have you ever worked for someone who really put in the effort to develop you? Tell me how you responded.*
54. Which boss was the best at developing people? What did you learn from this person?
55. Which boss was the worst at developing people? What did you learn from this person?
56. Who do you consider a model of developing others? How do they do it?*

Dimension 3: Knowing How This Works

57. Are there situations or settings where someone should be different in their ability or interest in learning new skills?
58. Do you think the ability or interest in learning new skills can be learned; how do you think people develop these skills?
59. Do you think there is a way to compensate or work around a low ability or interest in learning new skills?
60. Has anyone asked you for your opinions/advice on learning new skills?*
61. Have you ever attended a course on learning new skills?
62. Have you ever been in a situation where you and others put learning new skills on a success profile?
63. Have you ever been part of an effort to create a policy or a mission statement containing reference to the ability or interest in learning new skills?
64. Have you ever been someone's coach or mentor who had problems with learning new skills?
65. Have you ever created a development plan for someone on learning new skills?
66. Have you ever criticized someone for not learning new skills?
67. Have you ever designed a program on learning new skills?
68. Have you ever given a speech on learning new skills?
69. Have you ever rewarded or recognized someone for having the ability or interest in learning new skills?
70. Have you ever taught a course on learning new skills?
71. Have you ever tried to help someone deal more effectively with learning new skills?*
72. Have you ever tried to help someone improve their ability or interest in learning new skills?
73. How much interest in learning new skills is good to have and how much is too much?
74. How much of success do you think is due to the ability and interest in learning new things compared with other characteristics?
75. How would you know if someone is bad at learning new skills?
76. How would you know if someone is good at learning new skills?
77. If you had to write a book on learning new skills, what would the chapter headings be?
78. What are the benefits to someone who is really good at learning new skills?
79. What are the consequences to someone who is really poor at learning new skills?
80. What do you think the standard is on having the ability or interest in learning new skills for someone in your role?
81. What happens if you are too interested in learning new skills?
82. What happens when two people try to work together who are very different in their ability and interest in learning new things?
83. What wisdom would you pass onto others trying to become better at learning new skills?
84. Why do you think people end up being different on learning new skills?
85. Do you do any self-development reading?* Tell me about your reading preferences.*

ADDING SKILLS AND CAPABILITIES

Dimension 4: Personal Learning

86. Compare and contrast examples of being effective and ineffective at learning new skills?
87. Contrast your on- and off-the-job use of ability and interest in learning new things.
88. Did you ever pass up a job or assignment because you were not confident enough in your ability to learn new things?
89. Do you ever use other skills to cover for your lack of ability or interest in learning new skills?
90. Has ability or interest in learning new skills ever figured in a failure, struggle, or setback you have had?
91. Has becoming better at learning new skills ever helped you in other areas?
92. Has poor ability or lack of interest in learning new skills ever been the subject of a development plan for you?
93. Has your ability or interest in learning new skills always been this way?
94. Have you ever delegated or assigned someone a task because you didn't learn new skills easily?
95. Have you ever made significant strides at becoming better at learning new skills?
96. Has your ability to learn new skills ever been the subject of your performance review or a career discussion?
97. How different are you across situations in your ability or interest in learning new skills?
98. How do you decide how much to improve specific skills?
99. How much of your success is due to your ability or interest in learning new skills?
100. How transferable is your ability or interest in learning new skills to other situations?
101. If you had to become better at learning new skills in a hurry, what would you do?
102. Was there a time when you were not good at learning new skills?
103. What caused you to work to change your ability or interest in learning new skills?
104. What event or series of events had the most impact on your ability or interest in learning new skills?
105. What's the most varied you can be in learning new skills?
106. What was the shortest amount of time in which you learned a new skill?
107. When did you first realize your level of ability or interest in learning new skills?
108. When you know ahead of time that your level of ability or interest in learning new skills won't work, what do you do?
109. Why do you think you deal with learning new skills the way you do?
110. Why do you think your ability or interest in learning new skills is the way it is?*
111. Have you ever changed careers? What was your thinking in doing this?
112. Did you ever have a career setback? How did you respond?
113. How do you work with or work around your weaknesses?*
114. Have you ever moved a weakness all the way to a strength?
115. What are some areas you have improved in recently?*
116. What do you do differently than you did a year ago? How did you change or develop this?*

D. Follow-up Probes:

Dimension 1: What the Person Did

1. Can you give me a few examples of that?
2. How consistently do you do this across situations?
3. How did others react when you did that?
4. How far would you go before you would stop and try another approach?
5. How typical is this for you?

ADDING SKILLS AND CAPABILITIES

6. How would you have done this differently with looser deadlines?
7. How would you have done this differently with tighter deadlines?
8. Tell me about times when you are not like this or wouldn't do this.
9. Tell me about times when you do this and times when you don't.
10. Was this comfortable for you, or were you forcing yourself?

Dimension 2: Seeing Others Do This

11. Did you later change your assessment of this person?
12. Do you know a good and a bad example of this? Contrast those two people for me.
13. Do you think most people would react that way?
14. Have you worked for a person like that since?
15. How could this person have been more effective?
16. How do others you have known approach that?
17. What do you think this person was trying to do?
18. What was it like to work with someone like that?
19. What was it like to work with someone you seem to have disliked?

Dimension 3: Knowing How This Works

20. How would you teach this to someone else?
21. What do you think the key aspects of it are?
22. Where do people learn this?
23. Why do you suppose organizations work that way?
24. Why do you suppose teams work that way?
25. Why do you think people do that?
26. Why do you think that happened?

Dimension 4: Personal Learning

27. Do you think you can get others to do this better than most people can? If so, how do you know?
28. Do you think you do this better or worse than most people can? How do you know?
29. Do you try to act that way with everyone? What's your thinking on that?
30. How did you come up with that approach?
31. How do you see that as a customer yourself?
32. How would you do this differently next time?
33. What did you do after you got that feedback?
34. What did you learn about dealing with that kind of person?
35. What did you learn about dealing with that kind of situation?
36. What did you learn about how customers are gained?
37. What did you learn about how customers are lost?
38. What did you learn about yourself?
39. What did you learn from that?
40. What do you think you learned that would be repeatable in other situations?
41. What lessons do you think you came away with?
42. What were the negative consequences of this?
43. What were you thinking when you took that approach?
44. What were you thinking when you took that risk?

ADDING SKILLS AND CAPABILITIES

45. What would you tell your children about that experience?
46. What would you tell your friend about that experience?
47. What would you tell your mentor about that experience?
48. What's your thinking about why that didn't work?
49. What's your thinking about why that worked?
50. What's your view of why things happened that way?
51. Where did you learn to do it that way?
52. Why did you think that method of getting over that barrier would work?
53. Why do you do it that way?

E. Themes/Things to Look for:

Admits mistakes	Reads for personal growth
Asks for feedback	Sees life as continuous striving to get better
Broad interests	Senses what skills are needed
Excited about learning new skills	Sought out for advice
Has a plan for personal growth	Switches jobs for variety
Interested in skill development	Takes career risks
Leads learning activities for teammates	Takes classes on own
Likes challenge	Takes less money in exchange for a new challenge
Likes newness	Technology comfortable
Likes to develop others	Travels for broadening
Likes to do things differently	Varied background
Likes to help others	Volunteers for developmental assignments

F. Most Likely Résumé:

1. Look for jobs like:

Cross-Moves	Significant People Demands
International Assignments	Staff to Line Shifts
Line to Staff Switches	Start-ups
Scope (complexity) Assignments	

2. Look for develop-in-place assignments like:

Complete a self-study course or project in an important area for you.

Attend a self-awareness/assessment course that includes feedback.

Study some aspect of your job or a new technical area you haven't studied before that you need to be more effective.

Attend a course or event which will push you personally beyond your usual limits or outside your comfort zone (e.g., Outward Bound, language immersion training, sensitivity group, public speaking).

Try to learn something frivolous and fun to see how good you can get (e.g., juggling, square dancing, magic).

Teach a course, seminar, or workshop on something you know a lot about.

Teach a course, seminar, or workshop on something you don't know well.

Teach/coach someone how to do something you are not an expert in.

Become someone's assigned mentor, coach, sponsor, champion, or orienteer.

ADDING SKILLS AND CAPABILITIES

Manage an ad hoc, temporary group of people where the people in the group are towering experts but the temporary manager is not.

Take on a task you dislike or hate to do.

Make peace with an enemy or someone you've disappointed with a product or service or someone you've had some trouble with or don't get along well with.

3. Best references to ask about or check:

Direct Boss
Development Professionals
Human Resource Professionals
Natural Mentors
Off-work Friends/Associates
Past Associates/Constituencies
Spouses
Self

G. Learning Orientation Evaluation:

4. Spectator/Passive vs. Player/Participant
5. Tight/Rigid vs. Loose/Flexible
6. Reactive/Responsive vs. Adapting
7. Passive vs. Intrigued/Curious
8. Sameness vs. Diversity
10. Reactive vs. Initiating
14. Sameness vs. Broad Ranging Interests
17. Avoids Weaknesses vs. Comfortably Shares
18. Comfort Zone vs. Curious
20. Defensiveness vs. Admits Weaknesses
22. Focus on Accomplishments vs. Focusing on Solving Problems

H. The LEADERSHIP ARCHITECT® Sort Card Connections:

1. Good (positive) if combined with high:

Likes to lead 9, 20, 36, 60
Gets results 16, 17, 50, 53
Invites feedback 3, 33, 45, 55
Develops others 18, 19
Knows personal limits 55
Develops the right skills 5, 46, 50, 58
Invests the time 6, 47, 62

2. Bad (negative) if combined with low or high (+):

Too self-focused (+43, 54, 57) 4, 42, 60
Works on the wrong things 5, 46, 50, 58
Always changing things (+2, 45, 52)
Not interested in developing others (+57) 18, 19
Arrogant 3, 7, 31

ADDING SKILLS AND CAPABILITIES

3. Too much can contribute to the following Stallers and Stoppers:

   A. *What too much looks like (overused):*

   Spends so much time skill building that doesn't focus enough on the day to day work; sometimes work on skills that turn out to be only marginally helpful later.

   B. *Too much might lead to these Stallers and Stoppers:*
   Poor Administrator (102)
   Overly Ambitious (103)
   Performance Problems (118)

   C. *Compensators:*
   How to compensate for too much of this PERFORMANCE MANAGEMENT ARCHITECT® dimension:
   19, 24, 43, 45, 46, 50, 51, 53, 55, 57, 63

   D. *Things to watch for:*

Changes for change sake	Not focused on day to day work
Develops skills that are not useful or are marginal	Self-focused
Goes to frequent conferences	Self-help junkie/expert
Insecure; can't accept limitations	Wants everyone else to join in

4. Too little can contribute to the following Stallers and Stoppers:

   A. *What too little looks like (unskilled):*

   Shows little interest in learning and building new skills and knowledge; stuck in a comfort zone–getting out-of-date; appears content with skills as they are.

   B. *Too little can contribute to the following Stallers and Stoppers:*

Arrogant (104)	Key Skill Deficiencies (113)
Blocked Personal Learner (106)	Non-Strategic (114)
Defensiveness (108)	Performance Problems (118)

   C. *Compensators:*
   How to substitute for too little of this PERFORMANCE MANAGEMENT ARCHITECT® dimension:
   1, 6, 18, 19, 32, 33, 44, 45, 54, 55, 61

I. **LEARNING ARCHITECT® Connections:**

   Look for people who act like and/or show evidence of:

1b. Trial and Error	22. Experimenter
3a. Checking Feelings	24. Discloser
3b. Self-Talk	25. Personal Change
3c. Personal Experience	26. Self-Aware
4a. Getting Information	30. Mastery
4b. Modeling	35. Breadth
5. New	36. Comfort with Paradox
7. Risks	
8. Initiate	

ADDING SKILLS AND CAPABILITIES

J. **CHOICES ARCHITECT® Connections:**

Look for people who act like and/or show evidence of:

First Edition (Released 1994)
1. Inquisitive
6. Visionary
9. Self-Aware
10. Responds to Feedback
12. Experimenter
15. Helps Others Succeed
16. Cold/Indirect Sources
17. Hot/Direct Sources
18. Into Everything

Second Edition (Released 2000)
1. Broad Scanner
7. Inquisitive
12. Helps Others Succeed
16. Personal Learner
17. Responds to Feedback
19. Self-Aware
20. Experimenter
23. Visioning
26. Drive

ADDING SKILLS AND CAPABILITIES

90. ALIGNMENT AND COMPLIANCE: WALKING THE TALK

A. Definition:

Willingly does things the organization's way; follows the values, culture and mission of the organization with zeal; aligns behaviors with the organization's expressed or preferred way to act; encourages others to do the same.

B. Arenas/Domains to Explore:

1. Acquisitions
2. Adjusting to new leaders
3. Athletic teams
4. Boards
5. Causes
6. Certified or licensed professional
7. Changing college majors
8. Changing colleges
9. Changing political affiliations
10. Charities
11. Club memberships
12. Diverse neighbors
13. Diverse workforce
14. Joining a new organization
15. Joining a new team
16. Mergers
17. Military training
18. Out of home country experiences
19. Professional memberships
20. PTA
21. Religious affiliations
22. Rituals and ceremonies
23. Scouting/4H
24. Stepfamilies
25. Strategic alliances
26. Taking over an established group
27. Turnarounds, fix-its
28. Volunteer work
29. Working in a political campaign
30. Working with customers

C. Sample Questions:

Dimension 1: What the Person Did   Note: * means OK for campus ** means campus only

1. Are there times when you hold in expressing your beliefs because you know the people around you will not agree?*
2. Have you ever acted in a public play where the character you were playing was substantially different in beliefs and behaviors from you?*
3. Have you ever been an official spokesperson for an organization and had to give out information, some of which was contrary to your own thinking?
4. Have you ever been in a licensed profession with a set of rules and obligations?
5. Have you ever been in a situation where a significant number of people entered the picture who had a very different set of values and beliefs?*
6. Have you ever been in a situation where you and others hammered out the values or mission of a new organization?
7. Have you ever been in a teaching or coaching situation where you had to teach something that inside you didn't agree with?*
8. Have you ever been part of a merger when you were with the smaller or less powerful organization?
9. Have you ever been part of an effort to change the culture or values of an organization?
10. Have you ever been part of an organization or club where there was an oath to conform to a set of principles?*
11. Have you ever been with an organization that was acquired?

ALIGNMENT AND COMPLIANCE: WALKING THE TALK

12. Have you ever faked agreeing with others around you to fit in or to accomplish something of importance to you?*
13. Have you ever had to service a customer whose values and beliefs were quite different than yours and your organization's?
14. Have you ever joined a club or association to be with people who were more like you?*
15. Have you ever left an organization because you couldn't live with their values or culture?*
16. Have you ever lived in another country quite different from your own?
17. Have you ever lived with someone or had a roommate with substantially different beliefs and values than yours?*
18. Have you ever quit a club or organization because you could not abide by their rules and regulations?*
19. Have you ever worked on a political campaign where the candidate's matched only some of your beliefs?
20. How different are you off work?
21. Tell me about a time when you changed your beliefs or values because of a long-term association with a person or group of people.
22. Tell me about a time when you changed your beliefs or values because of a long-term association with an organization.
23. Tell me about a time when you had to compromise what you believed in to fit in.*
24. Tell me about a time when you had to defend the culture and preferred behaviors of an organization you belonged to a critic.
25. Tell me about a time when you took over an established group with beliefs and values quite different than your own.
26. Tell me about a time when you were considered by others to be a rebel or a boat rocker.*
27. Were you ever a docent for a museum or historic place where the story you told was contrary to your own beliefs and values?*
28. What's the biggest belief or value shift you can remember making?*
29. What are the two most different organizations or groups you have belonged to at the same time?*
30. When you are on a team examining culture and values, what role do you usually play?

Dimension 2: Seeing Others Do This

31. Contrast the most and least organizationally compliant and aligned people you know.*
32. Has organizational compliance or alignment ever been in any 360° survey done on you? Was your score among your highest, middle, or lowest?
33. Has poor organizational compliance or alignment on someone else's part ever created an obstacle for you or got in the way of something you were trying to accomplish?*
34. Have you ever talked with a coach or mentor about your ability to align yourself to the organization?
35. Have you ever watched someone fail/get fired because they did not align themselves with the organization?*
36. Have you ever watched someone overdo organizational compliance or alignment to the point that it backfired?
37. Have you ever watched someone succeed because they aligned themselves with the organization ?*
38. Have you ever worked with a coach on your ability to align yourself to the organization?*
39. Have you ever worked with a person who excelled at being organizationally aligned and compliant?
40. Have you ever worked with a skills coach on improving your ability to align yourself to the organization?*
41. How do you get feedback about yourself on becoming organizationally aligned and compliant?
42. How often do you check with multiple sources when you get a piece of critical feedback on your ability to align yourself to the organization?
43. Is there a historical figure you consider a model of walking the talk?

ALIGNMENT AND COMPLIANCE: WALKING THE TALK

44. What do others who are not your fans say about your ability to walk the talk?
45. What do others who like you say about your ability to walk the talk?
46. Which boss was the best at walking the talk?
47. Which boss was the worst at walking the talk?
48. Which direct report was the best at walking the talk?
49. Which direct report was the worst at walking the talk?
50. Which peer was the best at walking the talk?
51. Which peer was the worst at walking the talk?
52. Who deals with walking the talk the best in your field or business?
53. Who do you consider a current role model of walking the talk?*
54. Who do you go to for advice on walking the talk?
55. Who have you learned the most from about organizational compliance or alignment?*
56. Who is a higher-management role model for you on organizational compliance or alignment?
57. Who is a role model of organizational compliance or alignment outside of work?

Dimension 3: Knowing How This Works

58. Are there situations or settings where someone should be different in the way they walk the talk?
59. Do you think walking the talk can be learned; how do you think people develop these skills?
60. Do you think there is a way to compensate or work around a low ability to align yourself to the organization?
61. Has anyone asked you for your opinions/advice on organizational compliance or alignment?*
62. Have you ever attended a course on walking the talk?
63. Have you ever been in a situation where you and others put walking the talk on a success profile?
64. Have you ever been part of an effort to create a policy or a mission statement containing reference to organizational compliance or alignment?
65. Have you ever been someone's coach or mentor who had problems with organizational compliance or alignment?
66. Have you ever created a development plan for someone on organizational compliance or alignment?
67. Have you ever criticized someone for not walking the talk?
68. Have you ever designed a program on organizational compliance or alignment?
69. Have you ever given a speech on organizational compliance or alignment?
70. Have you ever rewarded or recognized someone for walking the talk?
71. Have you ever taught a course on organizational compliance or alignment?
72. Have you ever tried to help someone deal more effectively with walking the talk?*
73. Have you ever tried to help someone improve their ability to walk the talk?
74. How much organizational compliance or alignment is good to have and how much is too much?
75. How much of success do you think is due to organizational compliance or alignment compared with other characteristics?
76. How would you know if someone is bad at walking the talk?
77. How would you know if someone is good at walking the talk?
78. If you had to write a book on organizational compliance or alignment, what would the chapter headings be?
79. What are the consequences to someone who is really good at walking the talk?
80. What are the consequences to someone who is really poor at walking the talk?
81. What do you think the standard is on organizational compliance or alignment for someone in your role?

ALIGNMENT AND COMPLIANCE: WALKING THE TALK

82. What happens if you are too aligned with the organization?
83. What happens when two people try to work together who are very different in their ability to walk the talk?
84. What wisdom would you pass onto others trying to become better at walking the talk?
85. Why do you think people end up being different in ability to align themselves with the organization?

Dimension 4: Personal Learning

86. Compare and contrast examples of being effective and ineffective at walking the talk?
87. Contrast your on- and off-the-job use of organizational compliance or alignment.
88. Did you ever pass up a job or assignment because you were not confident enough in your skills at walking the talk?
89. Do you ever use other skills to cover for your lack of ability to align yourself to the organization?
90. Has ability to walk the talk ever figured in a failure, struggle, or setback you have had?
91. Has becoming better at walking the talk ever helped you in other areas?
92. Has poor ability to align yourself to the organization ever been the subject of a development plan for you?
93. Has your ability to align yourself to the organization always been this way?
94. Have you ever delegated or assigned someone a task because you didn't walk the talk particularly well.
95. Have you ever made significant strides at becoming better at walking the talk?
96. Has your ability to align yourself to the organization ever been the subject of your performance review or a career discussion?
97. How different are you across situations in your ability to align yourself to the organization?
98. How do you decide how closely to align yourself to the organization?
99. How much of your success is due to your ability to align yourself to the organization?
100. How transferable is your ability to align yourself to the organization to other situations?
101. If you had to become better at walking the talk in a hurry, what would you do?
102. Was there a time when you were not good at walking the talk?
103. What caused you to work to change your ability to align yourself to the organization?
104. What event or series of events had the most impact on your ability to align yourself to the organization?
105. What's the most varied you can be in the ability to align yourself to the organization?
106. What was the shortest amount of in which you learned to become better at walking the talk?
107. When did you first realize your level of ability to align yourself to the organization?
108. When you know ahead of time that your level of ability to align yourself to the organization won't work, what do you do?
109. Why do you think you deal with walking the talk the way you do?
110. Why do you think your ability to align yourself to the organization is the way it is?*

D. Follow-up Probes:

Dimension 1: What the Person Did

1. Can you give me a few examples of that?
2. How consistently do you do this across situations?
3. How did others react when you did that?
4. How far would you go before you would stop and try another approach?
5. How typical is this for you?
6. How would you have done this differently with looser deadlines?
7. How would you have done this differently with tighter deadlines?

ALIGNMENT AND COMPLIANCE: WALKING THE TALK

8. Tell me about times when you are not like this or wouldn't do this.
9. Tell me about times when you do this and times when you don't.
10. Was this comfortable for you, or were you forcing yourself?

Dimension 2: Seeing Others Do This

11. Did you later change your assessment of this person?
12. Do you know a good and a bad example of this? Contrast those two people for me.
13. Do you think most people would react that way?
14. Have you worked for a person like that since?
15. How could this person have been more effective?
16. How do others you have known approach that?
17. What do you think this person was trying to do?
18. What was it like to work with someone like that?
19. What was it like to work with someone you seem to have disliked?

Dimension 3: Knowing How This Works

20. How would you teach this to someone else?
21. What do you think the key aspects of it are?
22. Where do people learn this?
23. Why do you suppose organizations work that way?
24. Why do you suppose teams work that way?
25. Why do you think people do that?
26. Why do you think that happened?

Dimension 4: Personal Learning

27. Do you think you can get others to do this better than most people can? If so, how do you know?
28. Do you think you do this better or worse than most people can? How do you know?
29. Do you try to act that way with everyone? What's your thinking on that?
30. How did you come up with that approach?
31. How do you see that as a customer yourself?
32. How would you do this differently next time?
33. What did you do after you got that feedback?
34. What did you learn about dealing with that kind of person?
35. What did you learn about dealing with that kind of situation?
36. What did you learn about how customers are gained?
37. What did you learn about how customers are lost?
38. What did you learn about yourself?
39. What did you learn from that?
40. What do you think you learned that would be repeatable in other situations?
41. What lessons do you think you came away with?
42. What were the negative consequences of this?
43. What were you thinking when you took that approach?
44. What were you thinking when you took that risk?
45. What would you tell your children about that experience?
46. What would you tell your friend about that experience?

ALIGNMENT AND COMPLIANCE: WALKING THE TALK

47. What would you tell your mentor about that experience?
48. What's your thinking about why that didn't work?
49. What's your thinking about why that worked?
50. What's your view of why things happened that way?
51. Where did you learn to do it that way?
52. Why did you think that method of getting over that barrier would work?
53. Why do you do it that way?

E. Themes/Things to Look for:

Adjusts behavior to achieve something
Changes to fit in
Conforms over time
Defers to the norms of others
Does the right things
Goes against own true self and beliefs
Holds in true views
Joins similar organizations
Learns new ways easily
Learns new ways quickly
Reads cultures accurately
Seeks out like colleagues
Shows a broad band width of possible styles
Urges others to get with the program
Good observer of norms and values
Open to personal change

F. Most Likely Résumé:

1. Look for jobs like:
Cross-Moves
Line to Staff Switches
International Assignments
Staff to Line Shifts
Turnarounds/Fix-its

2. Look for develop-in-place assignments like:

Attend a self-awareness/assessment course that includes feedback.

Find and spend time with an expert to learn something new to you.

Study some aspect of your job or a new technical area you haven't studied before that you need to be more effective.

Work closely with a higher-level manager who is very good at something you need to learn.

Attend a course or event which will push you personally beyond your usual limits or outside your comfort zone (e.g., Outward Bound, language immersion training, sensitivity group, public speaking).

Interview or work with a "tutor" or mentor on a skill you need to develop.

Study an admired person who has a skill you need.

Volunteer to do a special project for and with a person you admire and who has a skill you need to develop.

Go to a campus as a recruiter.

Write public press (PR) releases for the organization.

Manage the visit of a VIP (member of top management, government official, outside customer, foreign visitor, etc.).

Construct a success and derailment profile for a unit or the entire organization and present it to decision makers for adoption.

Do a study of successful executives in your organization and report the findings to top management.

Do a study of failed executives in your organization, including interviewing people still with the organization who knew or worked with them, and report the findings to top management.

Become a volunteer for a year or more for an outside organization.

ALIGNMENT AND COMPLIANCE: WALKING THE TALK

Go on a business trip to a foreign country you've not been to before.

Lobby for your organization on a contested issue in local, regional, state, or federal government.

Interview outsiders on their view of your organization and present your findings to management.

Work on a project that involves travel and study of an issue, acquisition, or joint venture off-shore or overseas, with a report back to management.

Manage a project team made up of nationals from a number of countries.

Become an officer in a professional association.

Make speeches/be a spokesperson for the organization on the outside.

Represent the organization at a trade show, convention, exposition, etc.

Draft a mission statement, policy proposal, charter, or goal statement and get feedback from others.

Join a community board.

Become someone's assigned mentor, coach, sponsor, champion, or orienteer.

Write a speech for someone higher up in the organization.

3. **Best references to ask about or check:**

All Other Superiors
Assigned Mentors
Boss' Boss(es)
Direct Boss
Human Resource Professionals

Natural Mentors
Past Associates/Constituencies
Peers and Colleagues
Direct Reports

G. Learning Orientation Evaluation:

2. All of Nothing vs. Can See Many Sides
6. Reactive/Responsive vs. Adapting
21. Focus on Self vs. Focus on Others

H. The LEADERSHIP ARCHITECT® Sort Card Connections:

1. Good (positive) if combined with high:

Can couch values in context 5, 38, 46, 48
Flexible 2, 40, 45
Gets things done the preferred way 1, 15, 16, 22, 52, 53
Improves upon 14, 28, 34, 37, 46, 58, 65
Makes allowances 2, 21, 46, 56, 64
Picks the right ones 5, 15, 50, 58, 65
Still has the courage to question 28, 34, 57
Can build a committed team 36, 60, 65
Expands on values 32, 45

ALIGNMENT AND COMPLIANCE: WALKING THE TALK

2. **Bad (negative) if combined with low or high (+):**

   Zealot 41, (+22, 29)
   Values never change 2, 32, 40, 46, 48
   Too compliant (+6, 8, 48) 57
   Pushes values too much 48 (+9, 13, 34, 44, 57)
   Values out of date 5, 15, 21, 23, 46, 64
   Selects for values 25, 56, 58, 64
   Doesn't adjust for nuances 2, 21, 40, 46, 64
   Politically incorrect (+21, 46, 48, 56, 64)
   Rejects anyone different 21, 64)

3. **Too much can contribute to the following Stallers and Stoppers:**

   A. **What too much looks like (overused):**

   This person is so dedicated to doing it the organization's way that judgment sometimes gets clouded; only sees things one way and sometimes misses important exceptions that should be made; may be so compliant with organizational values and culture that effective decision-making, innovation and risk-taking are stalled.

   B. **Too much might lead to these Stallers and Stoppers:**

   Unable to Adapt to Differences (101)   Key Skills Deficiencies (113)
   Blocked Personal Learner (106)   Overmanaging (117)
   Failure to Staff Effectively (111)

   C. **Compensators:**

   How to compensate for too much of this PERFORMANCE MANAGEMENT ARCHITECT® dimension:
   2, 5, 10, 14, 21, 26, 28, 32, 33, 40, 41, 45, 48, 64

   D. **Things to watch for:**

   Arrogant   Rejects others not in line
   Doesn't question anything   Resists change
   Looks for jobs and organizations that closely fits self Too binary–either is or isn't
   Pontificates   Uses litmus tests for others

4. **Too little can contribute to the following Stallers and Stoppers:**

   A. **What too little looks like (unskilled):**

   Always out of line with the organization's culture, values and mission; insists on doing things differently from others; rocks the values boat; a real maverick, always doing things their own way regardless of the norms and preferences of the organization.

   B. **Too little can contribute to the following Stallers and Stoppers:**

   Unable to Adapt to Differences (101)   Blocked Personal Learner (106)
   Arrogant (104)   Political Missteps (119)

   C. **Compensators:**

   How to substitute for too little of this PERFORMANCE MANAGEMENT ARCHITECT® dimension:
   2, 3, 4, 17, 22, 24, 26, 29, 30, 31, 40, 48, 53, 57, 61

ALIGNMENT AND COMPLIANCE: WALKING THE TALK

I. LEARNING ARCHITECT® Connections:

Look for people who act like and/or show evidence of:

1c. Following a Plan	15. Cautious
3b. Self-Talk	17. Selected Sources
3c. Personal Experience	18. Straightforward
4a. Getting Information	19. What
13. Focused	30. Mastery
14. Controlled	36. Comfort with Paradox

J. CHOICES ARCHITECT® Connections:

Look for people who act like and/or show evidence of:

First Edition (Released 1994)	Second Edition (Released 2000)
13. Role Flexibility	12. Helps Others Succeed
15. Helps Others Succeed	17. Responds to Feedback
22. Self-Talk	18. Role Flexibility
23. Communicator	24. Inspires Others
	27. Presence

ALIGNMENT AND COMPLIANCE: WALKING THE TALK

APPENDIX A. Generic questions that can be used with any competency A-1

APPENDIX B. Generic probes that can be used with any competency B-1

APPENDIX C. Quick reference guide C-1

Supplemental Forms Available Online

Additional Forms are available for download that can assist you with preparing for and conducting an INTERVIEW ARCHITECT® Professional interview. To access these forms free of charge go to the following site: www.lominger.com/pdf/IAPSF.pdf

APPENDIX A

GENERIC QUESTIONS THAT CAN BE USED WITH ANY COMPETENCY

*Dimension 1: What the Person Did   Note: * means OK for campus*

☐ 1. Tell me about a time when you had an experience where _____ played an important part.

☐ 2. Tell me about a time when your _____ got you into trouble.

☐ 3. Tell me about a time when your _____ worked really well for you.

☐ 4. Tell me about a time where you used too much _____.

☐ 5. Tell me about a time when _____ got you out of trouble.

Dimension 2: Seeing Others Do This

☐ 6. Contrast the most and least _____ people you know.*

☐ 7. Has poor _____ on someone else's part ever created an obstacle for you or got in the way of something you were trying to accomplish?*

☐ 8. Which boss/direct report/peer/person was the best at _____?

☐ 9. Which boss/direct report/peer/person was the worst at _____?

☐ 10. Who have you learned the most from about _____?*

* OK for campus

APPENDIX A

Dimension 3: Knowing How This Works

☐ 11. Has anyone asked you for your opinions/advice on _____; what wisdom would you pass onto others trying to get better at _____?*

☐ 12. Have you ever attended a course/designed a program/written an article/given a speech/taught a course/created a policy or a mission statement/put _____ on a success profile on _____?

☐ 13. Have you ever been someone's coach or mentor who had problems with _____?

☐ 14. Have you ever criticized someone for not _____ and/or created a development plan for someone on _____?

☐ 15. Have you ever rewarded or recognized someone for having _____.

Dimension 4: Personal Learning

☐ 16. Compare and contrast examples of being effective and ineffective at _____?

☐ 17. Contrast your on and off the job use of _____.

☐ 18. Do you ever use other skills to cover for your lack of _____?

☐ 19. Has the lack of _____ ever figured in a failure or struggle or setback you have had?

☐ 20. Has your _____ always been this way?

* OK for campus

APPENDIX B

GENERIC PROBES THAT CAN BE USED WITH ANY COMPETENCY

Dimension 1: What the Person Did

☐ 1. Can you give me a few examples of that?

☐ 2. How consistently do you do this across situations?

☐ 3. How did others react when you did that?

☐ 4. How far would you go before you would stop and try another approach?

☐ 5. How typical is this for you?

Dimension 2: Seeing Others Do This

☐ 6. Did you later change your assessment of this person?

☐ 7. Do you know a good and a bad example of this? Contrast those two people for me.

☐ 8. Do you think most people would react that way?

☐ 9. How could this person have been more effective?

☐ 10. What do you think this person was trying to do?

APPENDIX B

Dimension 3: Knowing How This Works

☐ 11. How would you teach this to someone else?

☐ 12. What do you think the key aspects of it are?

☐ 13. Where do people learn this?

☐ 14. Why do you think people do that?

☐ 15. Why do you think that happened?

Dimension 4: Personal Learning

☐ 16. Do you think you can get others to do this better than most people can? If so, how do you know?

☐ 17. Do you think you do this better or worse than most people can? How do you know?

☐ 18. Do you try to act that way with everyone? What's your thinking on that?

☐ 19. How did you come up with that approach?

☐ 20. How would you do this differently next time?

APPENDIX C

F. MOST LIKELY RÉSUMÉ F.1 LOOK FOR JOBS LIKE:

Chair of Projects/Task Forces
Cross-Moves
Heavy Strategic Demands
Fix-Its/Turnarounds
International Assignments
Line to Staff Switches
Member of Projects/Task Forces
Scale (size shift) Assignments
Scope (complexity) Assignments
Significant People Demands
Staff Leadership (Influencing Without Authority)
Staff to Line Shifts
Start-ups

F. MOST LIKELY RÉSUMÉ F.2 LOOK FOR DEVELOP-IN-PLACE ASSIGNMENTS LIKE:

BEING A STUDENT

Complete a self-study course or project
Attend self-awareness course
Spend time with an expert
Study new area
Work with a higher-level manager
Attend personally stretching course
Work with tutor/mentor
Study admired person
Work with admired person
Work with negative role model

CREATING COMPLEX SYSTEMS

Install a new system
Integrate diverse systems across decentralized units
Manage a renovation
Simplify a work process
Complete a prevention analysis
Create a crisis contingency plan
Create a security plan
Manage something remote

INDIVIDUAL PROJECTS

Create site plan for new facility
Plan/run off-site meeting
Manage major purchase
Recruit on campus
Plan/run picnic/outing
Manage furnishing/re-furnishing offices
Write press release
Manage VIP visit
Complete competitive analysis
Study a customer/needs
Complete customer survey personally
Do a postmortem on successful project
Study training impact
Construct success/derailment profile
Create affirmative action plan
Help outside person solve problem
Study lost customers
Study successful executives
Study failed executives
Conduct tour
Do feasibility study
Study humor in business

APPENDIX C

F. MOST LIKELY RÉSUMÉ F.2 LOOK FOR DEVELOP-IN-PLACE ASSIGNMENTS LIKE: *(continued)*

OFF-WORK ASSIGNMENTS
Serve with community agency
Be a volunteer in community
Coach sports team
Work with charity
Join self-help group
Teach child new skill
Try to learn something frivolous
Referee a sports event

PERSPECTIVE BUILDING
Visit foreign country on business
Lobby for your organization
Be a loaned executive
Work short periods in other units
Study new product cycle
Study new trend
Benchmark competitors
Visit Baldrige winner
Interview outsiders
Work in assessment center
Study history of issue
Be active in professional group
Work short periods in customer service
Work on off-shore project
Manage multi-national team
Negotiate international contract
Be an officer in a professional group

SPOKESPERSON / ADVOCATE
Be a spokesperson for organization
Work a trade show
Represent nonexempts' concerns
Write and present a proposal
Spend time with customers
Draft mission statement

START-UP
Something small
Launch a new product
Act as a change agent
Relaunch something
Get seed funding
Staff a new team
Create employee involvement teams

TASK FORCE / PROJECT
Chair a task force
Be on a task force
Manage study team
Serve on product review team
Manage joint effort with other units
Serve on board
Join a community board
Form joint venture
Write a grant proposal
Study an acquisition
Serve on credit union board
Chair credit union board

TEACHING OTHERS
Teach something you know well
Teach something new to you
Coach something new to you
Coach something you know well
Design course in new area
Design course in an area you know well
Be a mentor
Train customers
Present unit strategy

F. MOST LIKELY RÉSUMÉ F.2 LOOK FOR DEVELOP-IN-PLACE ASSIGNMENTS LIKE: *(continued)*

TEMPORARY MANAGER

Assign tight schedule to group
Manage green or novice team
Manage difficult team
Manage low competence team
Manage former peers
Temporarily manage older or more experienced team
Manage in area of expertise
Manage out of area of expertise
Manage fix-it
Manage stable team
Manage in expanding operation
Manage diverse team
Manage consultants
Substitute for vacationer
Underfill higher level job
Manage a temporary team against tight schedule

TOUGH CHALLENGE

Handle tough negotiation
Shut down something
Liquidate something
Prepare and present critical proposal
Manage dissatisfied customer
Manage office space allocation
Decide who to let go
Manage a crisis
Take on an undoable project
Manage outplacement
Manage cost-cutting project
Do something you dislike
Mediate conflict
Make peace with an enemy
Write speech for someone
Do postmortem on failed project
Build multifunctional team
Negotiate with union
Study cost overruns
Work on reorganization and layoff
Manage older or more experienced team
Work on crisis team

F. MOST LIKELY RÉSUMÉ F.3 BEST REFERENCES TO ASK ABOUT OR CHECK

Direct Boss
Boss' Boss(es)
Internal and External Customers
Development Professionals
Family Members
Human Resource Professionals
Assigned Mentors/Sponsors
Natural Mentors

Off-work Friends/Associates
Past Associates/Constituencies
Peers and Colleagues
All Other Superiors
Spouse
Direct Reports
Yourself

APPENDIX C

G. LEARNING AGILITY EVALUATION

1. What/describing– Events and accomplishments vs. Why/explain– Why and how something happened

2. All or nothing– Simple, straightforward views vs. Can see many sides/grays– Lets things be as complex as they are

3. Ordinary/socially acceptable– Won't ruffle feathers vs. Insightful/different, candid, even controversial

4. Spectator/passive vs. Player/participant/active

5. Tight/rigid/problems with change vs. Flexible

6. Reacting/responding to circumstances vs. Adapting–Changes self to meet new circumstances

7. Passive–Closed to fresh views vs. Intrigued/curious/open

8. Sameness in sources, ideas, methods, people vs. Diversity of sources, ideas, methods, people

9. Vague/general learning vs. Sharp/specific learnings

10. Reactive to change vs. Initiating change

11. Generalizations–Hard to summarize what the person said was learned vs. Specific learnings–Why and how he/she did it

12. Always has answer– May sound socially acceptable vs. Candid (perhaps to a fault)

13. Simpler view of people/jobs, fewer nuances vs. Complex views–Gives more elements and reasons

14. A high degree of sameness– Function in comfort zone vs. Broad range of different interests which may not be similar to each other

15. Often linear, point by point– Rarely describe thought processes vs. Uses contrasts, comparisons, analogies to make points

16. Few rules of thumb–Tends to return to what worked not why it worked vs. Has many different rules of thumb – Can explain where they came from

17. Weaknesses are often socially acceptable– Trouble describing real limitations vs. Can discuss strengths, weaknesses, limits (things he/she is lousy at)

18. Stays close to what they know vs. Lots of curiosity

19. Looks for external standards (organizational, boss, money) vs. Focuses mostly on internal standards, measures of success and failure–Committed to lifelong continuous improvement

20. Doesn't add new behavior as readily; learning from mistakes is often reactive – Talks about how to avoid this in the future vs. Admits mistakes–talks about how he/she changed behavior

21. More likely to talk about what did to others not the point of view of others vs. More attuned to the impact of actions on others

22. Focuses on accomplishment vs. Focuses on solving problems and learning from them

APPENDIX C

H3B & H4. INDEX OF CAREER STALLERS AND STOPPERS

Unable to Adapt to Differences
Poor Administrator
Overly Ambitious
Arrogant
Betrayal of Trust
Blocked Personal Learner
Lack of Composure
Defensiveness
Lack of Ethics and Values
Failure to Build a Team
Failure to Staff Effectively
Insensitive to Others
Key Skill Deficiencies
Non-Strategic
Overdependence on an Advocate
Overdependence on a Single Skill
Overmanaging
Performance Problems
Political Missteps

APPENDIX C

I. LEARNING ARCHITECT® CONNECTIONS

1A PURE ACTION
Quick diagnosis, then making a selection among ready alternatives

1B TRIAL AND ERROR
Learn from small successes and failures

1C FOLLOWING A PLAN
A step-by-step plan of action and adjusting along the way

2A PROBLEM SOLVING
Formal intentional methods of thinking through problems

2B VISIONING
Envisioning a desirable end state and creating a plan to get there

2C INTUITION
Use of instinct, hunches, the odd, or unusual in problem solving

3A CHECKING FEELINGS
How we feel about our thinking and the actions we may take

3B SELF-TALK
Monitoring ourselves in real time; questioning and editing our actions as we go

3C PERSONAL EXPERIENCE
The examination of one's past to better understand the meaning of the present

4A GETTING INFORMATION
Gathering information from people indirectly through books, role models, courses and consultants

4B MODELING
Observing or studying someone else for guidance and direction

4C ACTIVELY INVOLVE
Fully involving others in the problem and its solution

1A-4C	LEARNING TACTICS™	
5-20	LEARNING PROFILE™	
21-38	LEARNING AGILITY™	

5 NEW
Preference for the new, untried, and first time

6 CONTENTIOUS
Preference for getting at conflicts and agendas directly

7 RISKS
Preference for the bold; tolerance for making mistakes

8 INITIATE
Preference for using one's own ideas and solutions

9 MULTIPLE SOURCES
Wide knowledge and contacts

10 COMPLEXITY
Preference for multiple methods, multiple things at the same time

11 WHY/HOW
Figuring out how and why things happen; focus on principles and processes

12 RULES OF THUMB
Drawing upon general rules from the past to parallels in the present

13 FOCUSED
Preference for a focused, proven, or tried set of activities

14 CONTROLLED
Measured consideration of problems, contexts, and people

15 CAUTIOUS
Reliable; planful, careful, safe

16 COLLABORATE
Working jointly with others to reach the same objectives

17 SELECTED SOURCES
Few sources of input

18 STRAIGHTFORWARD
Uses common sense, simple/direct paths

19 WHAT
Observer of events, facts, and what steps lead to what outcomes

20 EVENTS
Focus on present facts and events

21 CHANGER
Takes the lead on change efforts

22 EXPERIMENTER
Sets up laboratories to test out ideas

23 ORCHESTRATOR
Brings people and resources together

24 DISCLOSER
Lets others know where she/he is coming from

25 PERSONAL CHANGE
Is a continuous improver

26 SELF-AWARE
Continually edits her/his autobiography

27 CONCEPTUALIZER
Wrests meaning from areas where none is apparent

28 CREATOR
Relishes the new; does the unique

29 ESSENCE
Incisive, can usually state positions/ideas in a sentence or two

30 MASTERY
Watches, admires, and seeks excellence

31 RATIONALITY
Objectively deals with life

32 DIVERSITY IN OTHERS
Openness to many types of people

33 DIVERSITY OF SOURCES
Will look anywhere for ideas

34 SIZING UP OTHERS
Reads people accurately; sees people as they are

35 BREADTH
interested in the world around him/her

36 COMFORT WITH PARADOX
Able to balance off opposites in her/his behavior

37 FLEXIBILITY
Easily shifts gears

38 RESILIENCE
Can keep on even when negative personal consequences loom ahead

APPENDIX C

J. CHOICES ARCHITECT® CONNECTIONS: FIRST EDITION

FACTOR I
MENTAL AGILITY

1 INQUISITIVE
Curious, oriented toward the new, enjoys a challenge. Interested in the future.

2 ESSENCE
Looks for root causes; interested in why; good at boiling things down.

3 CREATOR
Comes up with the new, different, unique and breakthrough.

4 COMPLEXITY
Comfortable with things that don't initially fit; has many conceptual buckets and creates more.

5 CONNECTOR
Can put together seemingly unrelated events, streams of thought, or facts to clarify a current issue.

6 VISIONARY
Can project into the future, fill in the gaps, see consequences.

7 HELPING OTHERS THINK
Can help others think things through without having to define them in his/her terms.

8 COOL TRANSACTOR
Accurate, fair, others will listen to what this person says.

FACTOR II
PERSONAL AGILITY

9 SELF-AWARE
Candid, knows what he/she is good and lousy at.

10 RESPONDS TO FEEDBACK
A continuous improver; makes personal changes when called for.

11 OPEN TO DIVERSITY
Open to the ideas and opinions of others.

12 EXPERIMENTER
Will try almost anything once; incremental.

13 ROLE FLEXIBILITY
Can move in many directions, play different roles.

14 TRANSACTION QUALITY
Constructive with others; gets more out of every transaction with others.

15 HELPS OTHERS SUCCEED
Likes to see others do well.

FACTOR III
SOURCE AGILITY

16 COLD/INDIRECT SOURCES
Has a variety of hobbies; reads anything that might be relevant; collects and stores all kinds of information.

17 HOT/DIRECT SOURCES
Learns widely from other people; seeks out role models.

FACTOR IV
CHANGE AGILITY

18 INTO EVERYTHING
Searches for the new; can work on many things at once.

19 TINKERER
Likes testing things–ideas, products, services.

20 FORGING AHEAD
Energetic, passionate, persevering, pushing, unsinkable.

21 TAKING THE HEAT
Knows that people will be upset by change; knows negative consequences are possible.

FACTOR V
COMMUNICATION AGILITY

22 SELF-TALK
Self-monitoring, watches for subtle cues from others, adjusts quickly.

23 COMMUNICATOR
Considers the audience in choosing communication techniques, level, and pace.

APPENDIX C

J. CHOICES ARCHITECT® CONNECTIONS: SECOND EDITION

FACTOR I
MENTAL AGILITY

1. **BROAD SCANNER**
   Very knowledgeable on a host of work and non-work topics.

2. **COMPLEXITY**
   Comfortable with things that don't initially fit; has many conceptual buckets and creates more.

3. **CONNECTOR**
   Can put together seemingly unrelated events, streams of thought, or facts to clarify a current issue.

4. **CRITICAL THINKER**
   Takes the time to look at conventional wisdom; doesn't accept much as a given.

5. **EASY SHIFTER**
   Comfortable when things are up in the air; shifts gears easily.

6. **ESSENCE**
   Looks for root causes; interested in why; good at boiling things down.

7. **INQUISITIVE**
   Curious, oriented toward the new, enjoys a challenge. Interested in the future.

8. **SOLUTION FINDER**
   Ingenious problem solver; can combine parts of ideas, come up with missing pieces.

FACTOR II
PEOPLE AGILITY

9. **AGILE COMMUNICATOR**
   Considers the audience; is articulate, can make the complex understandable.

10. **CONFLICT MANAGER**
    Constructive with others; knows how to work through conflicts and disagreements; watches others closely and adjusts to accommodate.

11. **COOL TRANSACTOR**
    Accurate, fair, others will listen to what this person says.

12. **HELPS OTHERS SUCCEED**
    Likes to see others do well.

13. **LIGHT TOUCH**
    Uses humor well; knows how to lighten things up.

14. **OPEN-MINDED**
    Open to others, new ideas, solutions.

15. **PEOPLE-SMART**
    Interested in what people have to say; pays attention; good at sizing up people.

16. **PERSONAL LEARNER**
    A continuous improver; actively seeks personal learning and skill building.

17. **RESPONDS TO FEEDBACK**
    A continuous improver; makes personal changes when called for.

18. **ROLE FLEXIBILITY**
    Can move in many directions, play different roles.

19. **SELF AWARE**
    Candid, knows what he/she is good and lousy at.

FACTOR III
CHANGE AGILITY

20. **EXPERIMENTER**
    Will try almost anything once; incremental.

21. **INNOVATION MANAGER**
    Can manage ideas so they become practice; team and organizationally savvy.

22. **TAKING THE HEAT**
    Knows that people will be upset by change; knows negative consequences are possible.

23. **VISIONING**
    Can project into the future, fill in the gaps, see consequences.

FACTOR IV
RESULTS AGILITY

24. **INSPIRES OTHERS**
    Can build a team through motivation.

25. **DELIVERS RESULTS**
    Performs well under first-time, changing or tough conditions.

26. **DRIVE**
    Works hard on many fronts; high standards of excellence.

27. **PRESENCE**
    Self-assured, can be passionate about beliefs.

APPENDIX C

K. DIFFICULTY TO DEVELOP:
DEVELOPMENTAL DIFFICULTY OF THE 67 LEADERSHIP ARCHITECT® COMPETENCIES AND CHARACTERISTICS

#	Competencies	Difficulty to Develop
1	Action Oriented	17
2	*Dealing with Ambiguity*	28
3	Approachability	24
4	Boss Relationships	25
5	Business Acumen	23
6	Career Ambition	24
7	Caring About Direct Reports	24
8	Comfort Around Higher Management	26
9	Command Skills	24
10	Compassion	28
11	Composure	27
12	Conflict Management	32
13	Confronting Direct Reports	27
14	Creativity	25
15	Customer Focus	18
16	*Timely* Decision Making	18
17	Decision Quality	20
18	Delegation	21
19	Developing Direct Reports and Others	27
20	Directing Others	21
21	Managing Diversity	28
22	Ethics and Values	26
23	Fairness to Direct Reports	22
24	Functional/Technical Skills	13
25	Hiring and Staffing	24
26	Humor	24
27	Informing	17
28	Innovation Management	29
29	Integrity and Trust	20
30	Intellectual Horsepower	22
31	Interpersonal Savvy	28
32	Learning on the Fly	24
33	Listening	20

#	Competencies	Difficulty to Develop
34	Managerial Courage	29
35	Managing and Measuring Work	20
36	Motivating Others	26
37	Negotiating	27
38	Organizational Agility	28
39	Organizing	20
40	*Dealing with Paradox*	28
41	Patience	23
42	Peer Relationships	22
43	Perseverance	18
44	Personal Disclosure	27
45	Personal Learning	30
46	Perspective	25
47	Planning	18
48	Political Savvy	32
49	Presentation Skills	24
50	Priority Setting	20
51	Problem Solving	24
52	Process Management	24
53	*Drive for* Results	19
54	Self-Development	24
55	Self-Knowledge	25
56	Sizing Up People	27
57	Standing Alone	23
58	Strategic Agility	27
59	*Managing Through* Systems	28
60	*Building Effective* Teams	28
61	Technical Learning	20
62	Time Management	19
63	Total Work Systems	19
64	Understanding Others	34
65	*Managing* Vision and Purpose	25
66	Work/Life Balance	28
67	Written Communications	21
68	Learning from Experience	30

K. DEGREE OF DIFFICULTY SCALE
13-18	Easiest		27-28	Harder
19-22	Easier		29-34	Hardest
23-26	Moderate			

Supplemental Forms Available Online

Additional forms are available for download that can assist you with preparing for and conducting an INTERVIEW ARCHITECT® Professional interview.
To access these forms free-of-charge, go to the following site:

www.lominger.com/pdf/IAPSF.pdf